THE
GUITAR
HANDBOOK

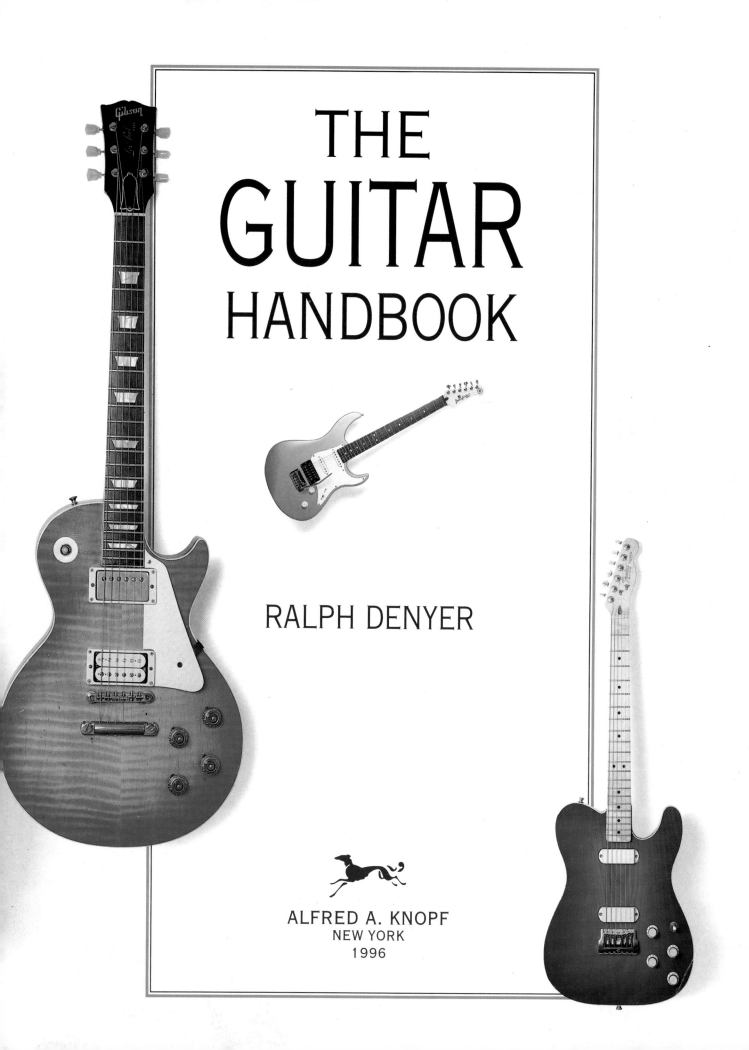

THE GUITAR HANDBOOK

RALPH DENYER

ALFRED A. KNOPF
NEW YORK
1996

A DORLING KINDERSLEY BOOK

This edition is a Borzoi Book published in 1992
by Alfred A. Knopf, Inc. by arrangement with
Dorling Kindersley.

Special Contributors
Isaac Guillory, Alastair M. Crawford

Published December 4, 1992
Reprinted Three Times
Fifth Printing, January 1996
Editor **Alan Buckingham**
Assistant editor **Tim Shackleton**
Designer **Ron Pickless**
Assistant designer **Nick Harris**
Art director **Stuart Jackman**

Revised edition

Project editor **Terry Burrows**
Art editor **Claire Legemah**
Editorial assistant **Laurence Henderson**
Design assistant **Dawn Terrey**
Editorial director **Jane Laing**
Art director **Nick Harris**

Copyright ©1982 and 1992
Dorling Kindersley Ltd, London
Text copyright © 1982 and 1992
by Ralph Denyer

All rights reserved under International and Pan-
American Copyright Conventions. Published in
the United States by Alfred A. Knopf, Inc, New
York, and simultaneously in Canada by Random
House of Canada Limited, Toronto. Distributed
by Random House, Inc., New York.

ISBN 0-679-74275-1
Library of Congress 92-53164

Typeset by Rowland Phototypesetting Limited
and Point Five Studios Limited
Reproduction by F. E. Burman Limited and Dot
Gradations Limited
Printed in Spain by Artes Gráficas Toledo, S.A.
D.L.TO:1383-1995

CONTENTS

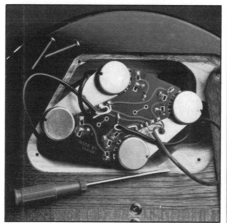

FOREWORD

When I was given my first guitar – a battered old Spanish thing – it had only five strings. The much-needed sixth string did not arrive until half a year later, at which point the possibilities of tuning the thing were slowly dawning on me. My first E, B and A seventh were learned by desperately trying to memorize the funny shapes I had seen older, sophisticated youths playing in the yard at school.

Despite the anxiety and desperation which dogged my first untutored steps on the guitar, I was nevertheless utterly seduced. Within eighteen months or so I was, maybe naively, attempting to copy Django Reinhardt's solo on "Nuages". As time passed, I met more and more guitar-mad kids with whom I was able to trade tricky chord shapes and the inevitable Hank Marvin lick. Naturally, I used these to my advantage with the girls and also as a means of one-upmanship with rival guitar players.

The point I'm trying to make is that, had a book like this existed then, I would have saved myself a great deal of time and trouble. Now it is here. This book will provide you with a solid foundation for the basics of playing and the workings of the guitar. It took me many years to acquire the information presented here, and I envy those of you who can start with this wonderful advantage. I suggest that you take it step by step and have fun on the way: what we are climbing here is a mountain and it never ends!

It is important to realize that the goal we are seeking is one which eventually transcends all considerations of plectrums and strings, etc. It is the realm of pure music. It is my belief that this book will provide the foundation and doorway into a world where wonders never cease. Bon voyage!

Andy Summers 1982

Since the first edition of this book, guitar technology and practice has changed hugely. In 1982 there was still a widespread prejudice against technical competence and knowledge. Today we assume the guitarist is familiar with a variety of "exotic" scales and rhythms: finger-tapping and picked semi-quavers at 152 bpm are reasonable requests. Multi-effects units, small and relatively affordable, become smaller and more affordable. The emphasis has changed from guitar-as-synthesizer to the modification of guitar sound. Amplifier simulation is available as a direct signal, and amplification now combines tube, solid-state, and digital effects.

We expect an electric guitarist to plug in, play like Paganini and sound like the universe crying - or laughing, or singing - in stereo, with tap delay, pitch shifting and chorus.

The beginning guitarist may be overwhelmed by these standards and expectations. This is my advice to us:

• *We begin with the possible and gradually move towards the impossible. This implies knowing where we are, knowing where we are going (that is, being clear of our aim), knowing what we have to do to get there, and knowing what resources we may draw upon.*

• *Do one small thing superbly, then move to the next. In a relatively short time, all of these small things will become the body of our playing.*

• *Find a teacher, or instructor. This will save time. A good player is self-taught, with the help of a teacher. The real value of a qualified instructor is a personal and direct connection to a school or tradition.*

• *Our practice may usefully be divided into four:*

  1. Calisthenics. This is the efficiency and sense of grace within effortless physical movement.
  2. Fingerboard knowledge.
  3. Musical knowledge and repertoire.
  4. Play. Abandon personal judgement and have fun.

• *Learn to trust the inexpressible benevolence of the creative impulse.*

• *This is the tuning which I use, from low to high strings: C - G - D - A - E - G.*

Musicians deal with music, professional musicians deal with business. If our aim is to be a musician then probably better not become a professional musician. If our aim is to serve music, then this is part of the price we pay for that privilege.

Robert Fripp 1992

The Guitar Handbook is invaluable for players of any standard because there is always something to learn. It is invaluable in every department. I've taken the book on Eric Clapton's world tours about three times. My copy has been to Australia, Hong Kong, New Zealand, Singapore, Argentina, Japan, Chile, Brazil: pretty much everywhere on the touring circuit. It's always in my flightcase. Once you start reading it, it's very hard to put down. I can't really sing its praises much higher than that.

Lee Dickson 1992
Guitar technician to Eric Clapton

THE GUITAR INNOVATORS

The musicians appearing here have all, in some way, made an original contribution to guitar playing. The range of their personalities, attitudes and backgrounds just goes to show that there is no single "ideal" way to play the guitar. The important thing to realize is that, glorious though the guitar's past may be, all the major innovators have simply used the guitar as a vehicle for their own individual musical self-expression. This is the common factor that links Frank Zappa with Django Reinhardt, and Robert Fripp with Charlie Christian. The twenty-four profiles contained in this chapter act as an introduction to the art of guitar playing. Listening to their recordings will give you a taste of what is possible on the acoustic or electric guitar, and will perhaps inspire you to make new advances in your own playing. During the eighties and nineties superb musicians like Steve Vai and Eddie Van Halen took the instrument to new heights and inspired a whole new generation of guitarists. Also, after helping lay down the foundations of popular music, half a century on, master bluesman John Lee Hooker has found public acclaim around the globe. The guitar remains a vibrant and expressive force in popular music.

Django Reinhardt

Since coming to prominence in the 1930s, the acoustic jazz guitarist Django Reinhardt has provided inspiration for generations of guitarists, as well as exhausting many a writer's stock of superlatives.

Jean Baptiste "Django" Reinhardt was born into a nomadic, caravan-dwelling gypsy family on 23rd January 1919. They travelled through Belgium and France during Django's early life, though Paris later became the center of most of his musical activities. Django displayed an early interest in music: by the age of thirteen he was playing banjo or banjo guitar at the Bal-Musette, a notorious hangout of Parisian low-life. At the age of fifteen he heard American jazz for the first time. He was converted instantly.

The now-legendary tragedy struck when Django was just eighteen: he was severely burned when he accidentally started a fire in his caravan. After months of treatment, the 3rd and 4th fingers of his left hand were left permanently deformed and paralyzed.

However, he not only fought to overcome the disability but developed a unique range of techniques and a new style of playing.

In 1933, while Django and the violinist Stephane Grappelli were playing together in the same band at the Hotel Claridge in Paris, they decided to form their own band. It featured Django on guitar, Grappelli on violin, Django's brother Joseph and Roger Chaput on rhythm guitars, and Louis Vola on double bass. They were to become internationally famous as the Quintet du Hot Club de France. At their first concert, they created such a strong impression that the newly formed Ultraphone recording company offered to record them on a trial basis. Their first recording session was so successful that the company gave them a firm contract. The quintet continued to work together until the outbreak of the Second World War.

In 1946, Django made his debut in the United States, touring the country with Duke Ellington. His records and his reputation had preceded him and he was received enthusiastically.

Django's name is synonymous with the Maccaferri guitar. The distinctive acoustic guitars which Django was frequently seen playing were made by the Henry Selmer company of France to engineer Mario Maccaferri's individual designs (see p. 47).

They were produced to give the maximum power, and were therefore ideally suited to Django's requirements, playing as he did in noisy clubs without the aid of amplification.

It is hard to list the qualities that went to make up Django's ability. The emotional content of his music was just as impressive as the technical skills he had at his disposal. His strong vibrato, individual octave playing (see p. 149) and rhythm work have now inspired several generations of guitarists. His compositions rank among the best ever written for the acoustic guitar.

He didn't read music, and it is widely thought that he couldn't even read or write. Yet, at a private party, he was able to astound Segovia with his playing. When the father of the modern classical guitar asked him where he could buy music for the piece, Django laughed and said that he had just been improvising.

Django died in May 1953 at the age of 43. To this day there is a strong interest in his guitar playing, and recordings on which he is featured have sold steadily for the past fifty-five years. He left a rich heritage of guitar music that continues to delight, confuse, confound, and stimulate guitarists the whole world over.

The Quintet du Hot Club de France (*below*)
The unique jazz "string quintet" formed in 1934 by Django Reinhardt and Stephane Grappelli.

1932 Selmer Maccaferri (*below*)
Used by Reinhardt during the 1930s, Maccaferri's design for the French Selmer company featured an internal sound chamber to increase volume.

Electric (*above*)
In the 1950s, Django began using electric guitars like the Gibson L5SEC.

Charlie Christian

Although there were guitarists who had played amplified guitars before him, it was jazz musician Charlie Christian who established the electric guitar as a serious proposition. He developed the style of single-note, melodic electric guitar playing that placed the instrument on a par with the saxophone, trumpet, clarinet and other solo voices in jazz. He also combined a rhythmic percussive style with diminished and augmented chord structures in an original way that gave birth to what he and his co-innovators called "modern" jazz, though the form has since become widely known as "bop" or "bebop."

It is widely thought that Charles Christian was born in Dallas, Texas, in 1919, although some jazz historians place his year of birth earlier, in 1916. His father was a singer-guitarist and his four brothers are all thought to have played musical instruments. The Christian family moved to Oklahoma when Charlie was just two years old.

His interest in music began by playing the trumpet at the age of twelve, but he also learned to play acoustic guitar, double bass, and piano, though not necessarily in that order. It was as a double-bass player that Christian got his first professional gig with Alphonso Trent's band in 1934. He played in several other bands before coming into contact with Eddie Durham in 1937. Durham was an arranger, trombonist and pioneering electric guitarist with Count Basie. Christian had been impressed with Durham's electric guitar work, and also by that of Floyd Smith who had been playing an amplified Hawaiian guitar. When he met Durham, he quizzed him on his playing technique. At the time Christian did not own a guitar, and when Durham told him to get one of his own, he turned up with an extremely rough instrument for which he had paid five dollars. Durham was amused by the instrument but impressed with Christian's desire to learn and his instant ability to assimilate all he was shown.

By 1938, Christian had acquired an "Electric Spanish" Gibson ES-150 guitar (see p. 54) which he most likely used in conjunction with a Gibson amplifier. The guitar was the first model sold complete with a fitted magnetic pick-up. Suitably equipped, he rejoined Al Trent's band, but this time as a guitar player. The response to his playing, from both audiences and other musicians, combined astonishment with admiration. Although other guitarists,

Pioneer of the electric guitar solo (right)
A rare photograph of Charlie Christian – seen here playing a Gibson ES-150. In a tragically short career, Christian single-handedly revolutionized the role of the electric guitar in jazz and influenced a generation of guitarists that followed.

not least Django Reinhardt, had mastered the *acoustic* guitar as a solo voice, this was the first time an *electric* guitar had taken on such a role.

By the time he was discovered by the jazz entrepreneur John Hammond, Christian had become something of a local hero in Oklahoma. Hammond thought that Christian would be a perfect addition to Benny Goodman's small jazz group, and flew him to California for an audition. Goodman, however, showed no interest in hearing Christian play. Hammond's style of persuasion was to set up Christian's guitar amplifier on stage prior to a Goodman concert. When the band was ready to start playing, Christian also took to the stage. Goodman was enraged but felt forced to let the guitarist play for at least one number. Forty-five minutes later, the band finished the number to be greeted by the greatest ovation that Hammond had ever seen a Goodman group receive. That night the Benny Goodman quintet became a sextet.

Christian stayed with Goodman until his death less than two years later. However, after playing with Goodman in the evening, he would frequently head for Minton's Playhouse, a jazz club in Harlem. There he would play for hours with such influential jazz musicians as Dizzy Gillespie, Thelonius Monk, and Charlie "Bird" Parker. Along

with Christian himself, they are considered to be among the founders of "bebop" jazz.

In July of 1941, following two years of intensive activity – the period in which the majority of his best-known recordings were made – Christian collapsed and was admitted to Bellevue Hospital, New York. He was suffering from tuberculosis. During early 1942, while convalescing at Seaview Hospital, Staten Island, he contracted pneumonia. He died on 2nd March 1942.

On record (*below*)
Christian's best-known recordings were made between 1939 and 1941, shortly before his death.

Chuck Berry

Charles Edward Berry was born in St Louis, Missouri, on 18th October 1931, or alternatively in San Jose, California, on 15th January 1926. Interviewers who have tried to ascertain which date is correct have always been told by Berry, "that's personal and nobody's business."

He is a witty, sharp and suspicious man who makes a policy of avoiding interviews. He appears to loathe the media: no doubt his continual clashes with the law – starting as a teenager, with two years at reform school for armed robbery – have a great deal to do with this attitude.

Chuck Berry is the single most important founder-figure in the story of rock'n'roll guitar playing. His instantly recognizable guitar riffs, solos, and rhythm playing complement perfectly the witty scenarios of teenage life in America during the fifties and sixties contained within his lyrics.

Berry grew up in Elleardsville, St Louis. Of his earliest influences, he says:

"I was singing at the age of six in church. Then the feeling to harmonize began to be a desire of mine. To get away from the normal melody and add my own melody and harmony was imperial, and I guess that grew into the appreciation for music. Rock'n'roll. Actually I don't think. . . matter of fact I know it wasn't called that then."

His most important early guitar influences were T-Bone Walker, Carl Hogan and B. B. King. He also listened to jazz and mentions a liking for Charlie Christian's work with the Benny Goodman band.

Berry had "played around" on guitar while at High School but had not taken the instrument seriously until a local R&B performer by the name of Joe Sherman made him a present of a Kay electric. In the early fifties, Berry had a trio which played at small local functions. He had studied and, at that time, was working as a hair dresser in case his guitar playing could not always pay the rent. In fact, he hung on to his hairdressing booth right up until the time he was paid an advance on his first recording contract. He used to perform a wide range of material in his efforts to get work, playing ballads and country music alongside his first love, the blues. His repertoire included compositions by Nat King Cole and Hank Williams.

One night during 1955, Muddy Waters let Berry sit in to play one song with his band. Waters was impressed by Berry's guitar

playing and told him that he should visit Leonard Chess at the Chicago-based Chess label and "get him to record you." Berry went to Chess courtesy of the Waters introduction and took with him a demo tape of six songs that he had written and recorded on a cheap mono tape recorder. Chess was impressed and immediately offered Berry his first recording contract. Though Berry was apparently keen to promote himself as a blues singer and guitarist, Chess saw greater sales potential in the up-tempo song "Maybellene" which brought elements of country music and the

blues together in a new and accessible way. Chess released "Maybellene" as an A-side, and it became a top-ten hit immediately.

The importance of "Maybellene" cannot be over-estimated. Its success was obviously good for Berry, but it was also good for Chess Records. The sales of their previous records had been limited to a mostly black audience. "Maybellene" became one of the very first rock'n'roll songs to break through to white audiences on a large scale. It was not until the following year – 1956 – that Elvis Presley had his first major national hit with "Heartbreak Hotel."

The original rock'n'roller
Chuck Berry's "Maybellene" – released in 1955 – is considered by many to be the birth of rock'n'roll. It combined elements from both country music and blues in a completely new way.

Bo Diddley

Berry followed his success by going on to write, perform and record a series of songs which collectively make up the greatest contribution any individual has made to rock'n'roll. The succession of gems include "Johnny B. Goode," "Sweet Little Sixteen," and "Roll Over Beethoven."

At the height of his powers, at the end of the fifties, Berry had a further run-in with the law. He was charged with transporting a minor across a state line for immoral purposes. The racist attitudes displayed at his first trial were so flagrant that a re-trial was granted. But two years later the verdict went against him, and he found himself unable to avoid a two-year prison sentence.

However, he had not been idle during the time he had been waiting for the re-trial. He had added to a stockpile of recorded masters that Chess continued to release during his incarceration. The titles included "Bye Bye, Johnny," "Route 66," "Talkin' 'Bout You," "Go, Go, Go," "Come On," "Too Much Monkey Business," "Memphis Tennessee," and "Reelin' and Rockin'."

Throughout most of his playing career Berry has chosen to travel alone with his guitar, making the promoter responsible for arranging for his amplification and backing band. As a consequence, performances have sometimes been marred by the quality of the musicians provided.

Berry's principal aim has always been to "entertain." His famous "duck walk" has been a high-point of his shows since it first appeared in 1956:

"I had to outfit my trio, the three of us, and I always remember that the suits cost me 66 dollars – 22 dollars apiece. We had to buy shoes and everything. So, anyway, when we got to New York, the suits – they were rayon – but looked like seersucker by the time we got there . . . so we had one suit, we didn't know we were supposed to change. I did that duck walk to hide the wrinkles in the suit. I got an ovation, so I figured I pleased the audience. So I did it again, and again, and I'll probably do it again tonight."

He seems to show little preference where amplification is concerned: his only requirement being that it works. He has nearly always played Gibson semi-acoustic guitars, frequently an ES-335 stereo model.

While Berry still makes the occasional live appearance, his frequent problems with the law now gain him more attention. The scope of his eventful life is documented in his revealing 1988 autobiography.

Chuck Berry has always seen himself as an entertainer. He is also one of the most important rock musicians of all time, a fact of which he seems surprisingly unaware.

Bo Diddley was born Otha Ellas Bates in McComb, Missisippi, on 28th December 1928 but he grew up in Chicago where he was exposed to post-war blues. As a boy he played violin before switching to guitar.

Diddley was a contemporary and stablemate of Chuck Berry, both recording for the Chicago-based Chess label. His music was heavily influenced by post-war Chicago blues, but what separated him from other blues performers were his unique "jungle rhythms," as he called them. Diddley rarely played twelve-bar blues, choosing instead to make the verses of his songs long and based around one chord, changing only for the chorus or hook lines. His distinctive rhythmic style largely relied on the line-up of his band. It featured Diddley on guitar and vocals, Jerome Green on maracas, Otis Span on piano, Billy Boy Arnold on harmonica, and Norma Jean Wofford (the "Duchess") on guitar and backing vocals. Jerome's maracas, the bass, drums and piano fused together with Diddley's rhythm guitar to create the rhythms. Diddley was a major influence on a number of his contemporaries. His first record release, "Bo Diddley" has been recorded and performed by a wide spectrum of artists. The Rolling Stones, among others, have featured note-for-note arrangements of many of his songs on stage and on record. Diddley's influence is further underlined by the fact that David Bowie used the basic structure of Diddley's "Cops and Robbers" when he recorded his own song, "Jean Genie" in 1972.

In the best tradition of the early rock'n'roll performers, Bo Diddley had a visual gimmick: Gretsch built his guitars for him in an wide assortment of shapes and finishes, including oblong and fur-covered

Vintage Bo Diddley
One of the "gutsiest" of the early rock'n'roll guitarists, Diddley's classic records were heavily blues-based and featured his distinctive, syncopated "jungle rhythms". His style found its way into the sound of many of the most successful sixties rock bands in America and Britain.

B. B. King

B. B. King was born Riley King on 16th September 1925 in Itta Bena, Mississippi. From the age of eight, he worked on a plantation, walking miles to a schoolhouse on the days when it rained. He was paid 35 cents for every hundred pounds of cotton he picked. King first got hooked on the blues through hearing records by Blind Lemon Jefferson, T-Bone Walker, and Lonnie Johnson, which a teenage aunt brought home. He was also strongly influenced by gospel music.

By the time he was fourteen he got his first guitar – a three-quarter-sized Stella costing fifteen dollars. As that was his monthly salary at the time, he paid a deposit of seven dollars and fifty cents and the balance the following month. His next guitar was a Gibson acoustic which he bought with some help from a country cousin – the legendary blues bottle-neck player, Bukka White – and to which he fitted a DeArmond pick-up. He also had an early Fender Telecaster but has been using Gibson ES-335 guitars since around 1958. King currently plays a custom-built Gibson. It is based on a 335 but with a closed body to reduce the amount of uncontrolled feedback. Previously, King had stuffed the insides of his 335s with towels in order to overcome this problem. The tailpiece is a Gibson TP-6, which he claims doesn't snag his cuffs and hands the way the old ones used to. His first choice for amplification and strings has tended to be Gibson.

He acquired the initials "B. B." early in his career when Sonny Boy Williamson II (Rice Boy), hosting the American King Biscuit, gave him a ten-minute, unpaid DJ spot on the show. They nicknamed him "The Blues Boy from Beale Street" which was eventually abbreviated to the initials B. B. Between shows, he played guitar with visiting jazz and blues musicians.

B. B. King was a great fan of Charlie Christian and Django Reinhardt, and their influence can be heard in his playing. He combined some of the raw elements of the blues with the cleaner, more concise, melodic approach of the jazz players. King still claims that he can only play single-note lead guitar, though he knows a few chords. He says he has never played rhythm and is not very good at it. He also claims that it's impossible for him to play the guitar and sing at the same time.

B. B. King is thought to be the originator of the vibrato technique of moving the finger in small movements across the string rather than along its length. He was also one of the pioneers of note-bending techniques – developed to simulate the bottleneck style of guitarists like Elmore James – which have become an integral

part of blues and rock guitar playing.

B. B. King's first record release was "Miss Martha King" on the Bullet label in 1949. After recording for a number of small labels, he had his first national hit on the R&B charts in 1950 with a song called "Three O'Clock Blues." Successes that followed included "Woke Up This Morning," "Sweet Little Angel," and "Eyesight To The Blind." In the early sixties, he recorded the "Live At The Regal" album, followed by the highly rated "Alive And Well" and "Completely Well" albums. In 1970, he hit the American top thirty with the "Indianola Mississippi Seeds" album, recorded with star names that included Leon Russell, Joe Walsh and Carol King.

Making Lucille sing
Since 1949, B. B. King has always named his current guitar Lucille. When a critic said that King would sing and then make Lucille sing, he took it as the greatest of all compliments: his aim has always been to play with maximum feeling.

During the 1980s King received numerous music business accolades, but his playing was also discovered by a new generation when in 1989 he featured on U2's "When Love Comes To Town", taken from the film *Rattle and Hum*.

B. B. King is proficient in a number of other instruments. He has also been described as a "musicologist", owning a collection of over 30,000 records, some of which date back to his disc jockey days.

Freddie King

Freddie King was born in Gilmer, Texas, in 1934. His mother and his uncles played guitar, which exposed Freddie to blues and gospel music when he was just a small child. He started to play the guitar at the age of six, and his first instrument was a Silvertone acoustic. His influences included many of the major blues players. He mentions having listened to, among others, Lightnin' Hopkins, Robert Johnson, T-Bone Walker, Muddy Waters, Jimmy Rogers (who also played in Waters' band), and B. B. King.

In his early teens he moved on to electric guitar. Before long, he was making trips to Chicago to seek out the guitar players he had heard on record. In 1975, he told me:

"Well, that was a Blues Town. It was the bluesiest town I ever knew! Every youngster you'd see there was playing the blues. There were a lot of players but they were from all over the country. From Mississippi, Louisiana, yeah...Alabama, Arkansas. All those guys livin' and playin' there but they were from the South."

King says that he played on a number of sessions with some of the major players before recording under his own name. He mentions Howlin' Wolf, Muddy Waters, and the harmonica player Little Walter in this context. He had a great deal of respect for Howlin' Wolf:

"Well, Wolf, he played some rockin' stuff, man. He's just not a laid-back cat all the time. He'd get up and move, you know?... So I put my style right between T-Bone, Muddy Waters, Lightnin' Hopkins, and B.

B. King. Now T-Bone, he's the first cat that started this style on electric, and he was followed by B. B. King."

Although he made recordings under his own name as early as 1956 (on the El-Bee label), it was not until 1961 that he had his first major success on record. At the time, he had been making a living by driving a bulldozer during the day and playing the blues at night.

"Yeah, that was "Hideaway". Well, the first release was "Have You Ever Loved A Woman" and "You've Got To Have Love With A Feelin'". Then came "Hideaway". Then just some pickin' on things like "San José." At that time I made a whole album of instrumentals. People think it was my first album, but it wasn't. My first album was "Freddie King Sings" and it was all vocals. Then the all-instrumental one was second."

As he points out, his first album release was "Freddie King Sings" on which all the tracks were vocal. The instrumental "Let's Hide Away And Dance Away With Freddie King" album followed. Incredibly, it was also subsequently re-packaged and marketed as "Freddie King Goes Surfin'." After making a number of recordings for Leon Russell's Shelter label he finally signed a deal with RSO Records, who released the last two albums he was to record. They were "Burglar" (which featured a special guest appearance by Eric Clapton) and "Larger Than Life." Both albums were produced by Mike Vernon.

While he was playing a gig in Dallas on Christmas Day 1976, Freddie King suffered a fatal heart attack.

King played a number of Gibson guitars throughout his professional life. For "Hideaway" and most of his influential instrumental recordings, he used a vintage Gibson Les Paul. On stage he also used a Gibson ES-335, an ES-345, and an ES-355. His string configuration was slightly unusual: the top three strings were light gauge and unwound, and the three bass strings were Gibson medium gauge. Since his early days in Chicago, he wore a plastic thumbpick and a steel fingerpick on his first finger, using the thumb to pick out bass lines and the fingerpick for treble lead lines. A widespread misapprehension was that Freddie King and B. B. King were brothers.

Classic blues innovator
Freddie King, seen here shortly before his death in 1976, was one of the most imaginative and consistent of the great blues players. One way or another his blues licks have found their way into almost every rock guitarist's style.

Eddie Cochran

Although Eddie Cochran frequently referred to himself as "just a guitar picker from Okie," Elvis Presley considered him to be the one man who could take his crown as the King of rock'n'roll. The lead guitar playing on most of Presley's records was supplied by session players like the legendary Scotty Moore. On stage Elvis virtually used the guitar as a visual prop. He was apparently a little unnerved at the way Cochran was able to accompany his raw and forceful vocals with such formidable lead and rhythm guitar playing, frequently overdubbing all the other instruments on his recordings.

Edward Ray Cochran was born in Oklahoma City on 13th October 1938. By the time of his death on 17th April 1960 at the age of 21 – he was killed in a car crash while on tour in the UK with Gene Vincent – he had been called "the James Dean of rock'n'roll," having recorded a number of musically influential all-time classics including "Summertime Blues," "Somethin' Else," "Twenty Flight Rock," "Three Steps To Heaven," and "C'mon Everybody."

Eddie had started out playing country music, but after a tour date supporting Presley on the Big D Jamboree in Dallas he embraced rock'n'roll and his music took an entirely different course. While at school he had wanted to play trombone but later opted for guitar. His main early country music influences included guitarist Chet Atkins and singer/songwriter Hank Williams. In his early days, Eddie played along endlessly with records on the radio, the

music ranging from bland and lifeless pop, to the raw jazz and rhythm and blues being broadcast from Chicago and Detroit. Around the age of sixteen he carefully studied jazz records by Joe Pass and Johnny Smith, whose triad and two-note melodic runs influenced him in particular.

Eddie experimented with just about every style of American fifties music. It's worth noting that as a result he produced a number of very middle-of-the-road tracks that are most definitely only for the most dedicated collectors and historians. However, the numerous available compilation albums and CDs comprise mainly his classic hits.

On several of his records Eddie played acoustic rhythm guitar with a rhythm section, adding electric lead guitar and vocals later. He recorded on two-and three-track tape machines, employing sound-on-sound overdubbing techniques. He was very much in control in the studio, devising all of the famous bass riffs himself and giving his musicians exact instructions as to what he required them to play. He would often record a number of different versions of the same song, relentlessly seeking the sounds he wanted, and experimenting with

microphone and recording techniques. While others were still restricted by the concept of simulating the sound of a band live on stage, Eddie was fusing the sounds of instruments together and altering their relative recording levels. Listen to the intensely powerful combination of bass guitar and drums with semi-open hi-hat on "Somethin' Else," or the way he altered the relative perspective of the acoustic rhythm guitar on "Summertime Blues," creating an effect that was unheard of at the time.

The electric guitar Eddie used from his mid-teens until his death was a Gretsch Chet Atkins model No 6120 orange F-hole semi-acoustic, to which at some point he fitted a Gibson single-coil six-pole black cover pick-up (not a twin-coil humbucker) and a Bigsby tremelo arm. He's quoted as saying that he fitted the Gibson pick-up to give him more of a mellow sound, and also to enable him to produce more volume on stage.

He played his guitar through a Fender Bassman amplifier. Eddie used to mix various gauge sets of V.C. Squier strings, partly because at times he used non-standard tunings. In the studio his relentlessly driving acoustic rhythm guitar parts were all played on a Martin D-18.

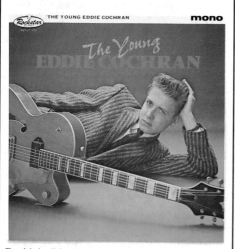

Rock'n'roll legend (above)
Even 30 years after his death, record labels like Rockstar regularly issue unreleased material to an ever-increasing audience.

Recording artist (right)
As well as being one of rock's first guitar heroes, Cochran was one of the first major artists to discover the creative possibilities of the recording studio. Many of his best-known recordings saw him overdubbing all of the instruments himself.

Duane Eddy

The fact that dazzling technique is not necessarily an integral feature of good rock'n'roll guitar playing is exemplified by the remarkably successful career of Duane Eddy during the late fifties and early sixties. Around this time, village halls, ballrooms, and clubs everywhere reverberated with the sound of guitarists imitating Duane Eddy. His popularity was such that in 1960, New Musical Express readers voted him "The World's Top Musical Personality."

Duane Eddy was born in Corning, New York, on 26th April 1938 but did most of his growing up in Arizona. He took up guitar at the age of five, learning first on an old Martin acoustic. For his thirteenth birthday, he was given a Gibson Les Paul, which he had traded in for a Gretsch Chet Atkins by the time he was fifteen, when he was sitting in at local roadhouses with Al Casey's band. He was influenced by jazz, country, and blues guitarists like Chet Atkins, Les Paul, Howard Roberts, Charlie Christian, B. B. King, and Barney Kessel, whom he particularly admired.

Much of the music he recorded was a genuine development of what many of these guitarists had been playing, but it appeared only on later albums and B-sides of singles. His "Three-Thirty Blues," for example, was a test piece for aspiring guitarists that was also a unique example of placing blues guitar in a rock setting. In Britain, during the 1950s, the influence he exerted on young guitar players was enormous.

However, for his initial success, he limited his playing to fit in with record producer Lee Hazlewood's concept of a simple, saleable format. Duane Eddy's commercial success was all about sound, feel and basic melody. He reaped considerable benefit from this enforced discipline, becoming the biggest-selling instrumentalist of his day.

At the time, many people thought that he tuned his guitar down. In fact, Eddy would write and play most of the tunes in A and E, allowing open-string root notes to ring on. The problem was that these were not good keys for Plas Johnson who played the fiery sax solos that were an important part of the records. Therefore, Eddy would tune his guitar down a semi-tone so that his fingerings would be the same but he could play in A flat and E flat, or he would tune up a semi-tone to play in F and B flat. Later, he experimented further.

Eddy was nineteen years old when, in 1957, he cut his first hit with Hazlewood at Audio Recorders Studio, Arizona. According to the guitarist, the sound and concept should be jointly accredited to Hazlewood, Casey, and himself. The simple melody lines played on the bass strings were greatly enhanced by Hazlewood's pioneering studio techniques. A grain silo (an airproof chamber used for storing grain) was used to create the reverberating "big sound," Eddy's use of the tremelo arm to create vibrato and sliding notes was integral to the sound, as was the use of a fairly slow electronic vibrato, probably built into the amp.

Eddy stuck to playing his original Gretsch Chet Atkins for most of his career, in spite of the fact that he worked with Guild on the development of a "Duane Eddy" model. He only used this guitar briefly himself: he was unhappy with the pick-ups that Guild used on the early models and lost interest in the endorsement deal.

In the early days, he used a souped-up Magnaton amplifier. Later, Tom Macormack of Phoenix built him a custom-made 100-watt model which he used throughout the most influential period of his recording career. By the mid-seventies, for the purposes of touring, he found it more convenient to use a solid-state amplifier.

Duane Eddy has made a number of come-backs. The strangest, and most successful, was his 1986 hit, "Peter Gunn" – with the English synthesizer group, The Art of Noise. It was originally a hit for Eddy twenty-seven years earlier.

The "Guitar Man" (*above*) Best known for his Gretsch Chet Atkins, Eddy also used a classical guitar.

The instrumental era (*below*) Duane Eddy's "twangy" bass-string style influenced a tide of instrumental bands.

Eric Clapton

Eric Clapton was born in Ripley, Surrey, on 30th March 1945. In his early teens, after hearing blues tunes on the radio, he developed an interest in the music. He sought out records by American musicians like Muddy Waters and Big Bill Broonzy, and was soon playing guitar along with the records. Like many other musicians of his day, he also cites Chuck Berry and Buddy Holly as major influences along with the older blues players.

1963 was a hectic year for the British R&B scene. The Rolling Stones became the focus of attention when their single of Chuck Berry's "Come On" made the national charts. Halfway through the year, the Yardbirds emerged, and Clapton accepted an offer to join them. At the famous Crawdaddy Club in Richmond, the Yardbirds took over the Stones' previous Sunday-night residency. Although rock historians paint a picture of the Yardbirds as being blues purists, their debut single, much against Clapton's wishes, was a mainstream pop song, Graham Gouldman's, "For Your Love." As a result he left the group.

Clapton soon came to the attention of British blues crusader John Mayall, who invited him to join his Bluesbreakers band. Though there were several good English blues guitarists, Clapton was outstanding. He had perfected a feedback-assisted sustain and an overdriven valve sound with Marshall amplifiers. With the American blues players as his main inspiration, he developed a superior blend of technique and control, producing guitar solos which had an unequalled power and emotion.

In 1966, Clapton left the Bluesbreakers, to form Cream with respected bass guitarist Jack Bruce and drummer Ginger Baker. The group was to do far more than play straight blues. Jack Bruce had a classical background and Ginger Baker was essentially a jazz drummer. Heavy guitar riffs, played in unison with the bass guitar, became one of Cream's most recognizable, and most imitated, trademarks.

Cream's enormous success began in America, where they were the first band to take rock music to the huge venues like Madison Square Gardens. Their "Fresh Cream" and "Disraeli Gears" albums, both released in 1967, are fine examples of commercial blues-based rock of the period.

Following Cream's acrimonious split in 1968, a false start with the "super-group" Blind Faith, and a brief spell as a backing guitarist with Delaney & Bonnie and Friends, in 1970, Clapton finally formed his own band, Derek and the Dominoes. The band, assisted by Duane Allman, recorded the double album "Layla and Other Assorted Love Songs" in less than 10 days. However, the recording of the album was punctuated by heavy drug-taking and by the time he returned to England he was supporting a £1,000-per-week heroin habit.

It was not until the mid-seventies that Clapton beat his addiction. He went back to work, recording his highly rated "461 Ocean Boulevard" album and returning to the stage. The live album "E. C. Was Here," recorded during 1975, saw Clapton demonstrating that his guitar playing was, once again, in fine shape.

By the end of the 1980s Clapton had reached unique legendary status. He had also developed into an accomplished vocalist and songwriter. His annual concert series at The Royal Albert Hall has featured guest blues guitarists of the highest order and his musical collaborator Michael Kamen leading a full symphony orchestra for a memorable performance of "Layla."

In his early days, Clapton developed the style of American electric blues guitar which used valve amplifiers as an extension of the instrument: as well as being used for amplification, it contributed to the actual sound. Up until he left the Bluesbreakers, he used a combo amp. Playing with Cream, he moved on to stacks consisting of separate 4x12 speaker cabinets that were used in conjunction with individual amplifiers.

Living legend
After a long period where he seemed reluctant to accept his former status as a guitarist, the eighties saw Clapton taking an increasingly high profile, to the point where he has, once again, become one of rock's major attractions.

John Lee Hooker

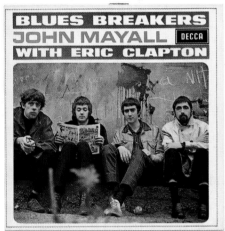

Bluesbreaker
Clapton (second from left) was 21 when he played on John Mayall's first studio album. Clapton left the band while the album was in the UK top ten.

Initially, Clapton most frequently used Gibson guitars. He was one of the first British guitarists to discover how ideally suited the vintage Les Paul guitars, with their distinctive humbucking sound, were for blues-based guitar playing.

In 1968, Clapton became influenced by the guitar playing of Robbie Robertson after hearing the Band's "Music From The Big Pink" album. Robertson used the characteristically cleaner sounding Fender Stratocaster and Telecaster guitars. Clapton was soon playing Stratocasters more than any other models. By the 1980s, Clapton was using vintage Stratocasters for stage work. His favorite, a black 1956 instrument, he dubbed "Blackie."

For his major 1992 tour Eric was using black Fender "Eric Clapton Signature" Stratocasters based on "Blackie" but with active electronics that allowed him, for some numbers, to switch in a mid-range boost to create a thick humbucking Les Paul type of sound. On Stratocasters, Clapton uses Ernie Ball Super Slinky .10, .13, .17, .26, .36 and .46 gauge strings.

On stage, Clapton now uses Samson wireless transmitters, a Soldano 100-watt Superlead Overdrive amplifier through a Marshall 4x12 cabinet fitted with Electrovoice speakers. An identical second set-up is on stage as a spare and for guest guitarists to jam through. The only effects he uses are chorus and a standard Jim Dunlop Cry Baby wah-wah pedal.

For the 1992 tour Eric played an acoustic guitar spot for the first time. He used a nylon-string Alvarez miked through the PA, as did second guitarist Andy Fairweather-Low. Nathan East played a Guild acoustic four-string bass directly injected into the PA.

"When Adam and Eve first saw each other, that's when the blues started. No matter what anybody says, it comes down to the same thing: a man and a woman and a broken heart, and a broken home - you know what I mean?"

These are the thoughts of 69-year-old John Lee Hooker on the cover of his 1989 Grammy Award winning and best-seller album "The Healer." By then he'd recorded over 100 albums and could not have anticipated such a huge success. The album featured a host of top musicians like Carlos Santana, Bonnie Raitt, Canned Heat and Los Lobos. His follow up, "Mr Lucky" also featured top musicians like Ry Cooder and Albert Collins. All of these musicians considered appearing on John Lee's albums to be a great honor as his guitar playing has influenced them all.

"The Hook" is one of the original delta blues musicians who has been rediscovered by successive new waves of musicians. He was one of the prime influences on the British sixties blues and beat group booms and their American counterparts – bands like Canned Heat. The tension, intensity and rawness first heard on John Lee's first records can be heard on every album he's made right up to "Mr Lucky."

John Lee was born on 22nd August 1920 in Clarksdale, in the Missispi Delta region. In 1941 he settled in Detroit, worked with local bands and got his first electric guitar from T-Bone Walker, which he used to record his first USA hit "Boogie Chillun" in 1948. John Lee's almost ominous vocals, unique boogie rhythm and lead guitar playing can be heard on any number of tracks, some of the best known and most influential being "Boom Boom," "Dimples," "I'm In The Mood," and "Tupelo."

A long wait
In an influential 40-year recording career, John Lee Hooker had to wait until the late eighties to achieve widespread public acclaim.

Jimi Hendrix

James Marshall Hendricks was born on 27th November 1942. From the beginning, he was exposed to blues and R&B music through his father's record collection. He was given a harmonica at the age of four, and an acoustic guitar at ten. He went "electric" a year later when his father bought him his second guitar. Initially, blues guitarists Elmore James, B.B. King, and Muddy Waters were his major influences.

While still in his teens, Hendrix was already gaining a considerable word-of-mouth reputation as an outstanding guitarist playing back-up for touring acts like Ike and Tina Turner, Little Richard, The Isley Brothers and B.B. King.

In 1965, Hendrix formed his own band, adopting the name Jimmy James and the Blue Flames. By now, Bob Dylan, who had seen him play in Greenwich Village, had taken over as his main inspiration. At the same time, the guitar playing of Pete Townshend and Eric Clapton also made a big impression. When the Animals' bass guitarist, Chas Chandler, heard Hendrix play he offered to bring him to London.

With the release of his first single on the Polydor label, Hendrix reverted from Jimmy James to his own name, although with the modified spelling. Chas Chandler had hastily put Hendrix together with guitarist Noel Redding – who played bass just to get the gig – and a drummer named Mitch Mitchell. They became the Jimi Hendrix Experience. The single "Hey Joe" (written by Tim Rose), released at the end of 1966, was a number four hit. In 1967, in the space of nine months, he followed up with three more hit singles that stand out as all-time classics: "Purple Haze," "And the Wind Cries Mary" and "The Burning of the Midnight Lamp."

In 1967, on the recommendation of Paul McCartney, Hendrix returned to America with the Experience to play at the Monterey Pop Festival. Hendrix played to unanimous acclaim, ending his spot by setting fire to and smashing his guitar. While his English co-manager Mike Jeffreys is reported to have complained bitterly about the damage to equipment, top promoter Bill Graham eagerly booked the band to play at his prestigious Fillmore West venue. They were booked for several nights with Jefferson Airplane. On the first night Hendrix was unstoppable. The Airplane dropped out of the following shows.

In may 1967, the first Jimi Hendrix album – "Are You Experienced" – was released. It is now widely regarded as one of the all-time classic rock albums. In 1968 he followed it up with "Axis: Bold as Love" and then the celebrated double album "Electric Ladyland."

By 1969, Hendrix was dissatisfied with his music. Eventually, in order to do justice to himself, he disbanded the Experience and recorded a live album called "Band of Gypsies" featuring Billy Cox on bass and Buddy Miles on drums. It was not very successful. He then falteringly reformed the Experience. He seemed to dither between doing what he should in order for his music to progress, and maintaining personal loyalties to Mitchell, Redding, and the many people who wanted him to keep the Experience together. He began to shy away from live performances because it was on stage that his dilemma was greatest. He had his own "Electric Ladyland" studios constructed in New York and was thinking far more in terms of recording than playing live. The month before he died, he said:

"I've turned full circle. I'm right back where I started. I've given this era of music everything, but I still sound the same. My music's the same and I can't think of anything to add to it in its present state. When the last American tour finished I just wanted to go away and forget everything. I just wanted to record and see if I could write something. Then I started thinking. Thinking about the future. Thinking that this era of music, sparked off by The Beatles, had come to an end. Something new has to come and Jimi Hendrix will be there.

The main thing that used to bug me was that people wanted too many visual things of me. When I didn't do it, people thought I was being moody, but I can only freak when I feel like doing so. I wanted the music to get across so that the people could just sit back and close their eyes, and know exactly what was going on, without caring a damn about what we were doing on stage.

I think I'm a better guitarist than I was. I've learned a lot."

Within days of his death – 18thSeptember 1970 – he was to have started work with orchestrator and arranger Gil Evans, who had collaborated on the Miles Davis album, "Sketches of Spain."

For the majority of his playing career, Hendrix played right-handed Fender Stratocasters upside down with the strings reversed. He also variously used a Gibson Les Paul, Fender Jaguar, and, later on, a left-handed Gibson Flying V which he called his "Flying angel."

His amplification usually consisted of six Marshall 4x12 cabinets, one 4x12 monitor and four customized Marshall amp heads. Road crews were at times hard-pressed to keep his equipment going during a performance as he constantly drove his amplification well past the limit.

During his lifetime, Jimi Hendrix made only five albums. However, since his death, over 300 recordings (*not* including the bootlegs) have found their way on to the market: many of them contain jam sessions that were never originally intended for release. 1990, the twentieth anniversary of Hendrix's death, saw the successful repackaging of his work on compact disc.

The influence that Jimi Hendrix has had on the development of electric guitar playing remains inestimable.

Hendrix's guitars (*left*)
Despite being left-handed, Hendrix preferred right-handed guitars. This meant that he was able to use the controls and the tremelo arm – then at the top – in his own unique way. Here, he is playing a Fender Jaguar turned upside down.

Live on stage (*right*)
As a showman, Hendrix was matchless – playing the guitar with his teeth, setting fire to it, smashing it up while still extracting sound from it. At the same time he re-defined the possibilites of the electric guitar. There was no precedent: the style and the effects that he created were totally new. His work is constantly being re-evaluated while his reputation as *the* master of the electric guitar continues to grow.

Frank Zappa

Frank Zappa is unique. He has survived rock music's most turbulent years, while still remaining at odds with the music business. He is one of rock music's most prolific writers and performers, with, to date, well over fifty albums to his credit.

Zappa's music brings together a huge kaleidoscope of influences from American black music to the European classical composers like Edgar Varese and Pierre Boulez. His poignant musical parodies of life in America – particularly those made during the sixties – are bitingly satirical.

Born 21st December 1940 in Baltimore, Maryland, Zappa started playing drums at the age of twelve. In an interview in 1979, I asked him what music had first inspired him to play.

"When I was twelve. I didn't listen to any music...my parents couldn't afford a record player. There was nothing good on the radio, I just wanted to play the drums, I liked the way they sounded."

He then moved on to the guitar. When asked if he had listened to players like Scotty Moore or James Burton on the early Elvis records, his reply was unequivocal:

"You mean session guitarists? That's not what I would call a guitar solo. A guitar solo is like "Three Hours Past Midnight" by Johnny Guitar Watson or "The Story Of My Life" by Guitar Slim. That's a guitar solo, nothing freeze-dried. Something really stinkin', that's what I was looking for."

In the early days, Zappa also listened to Clarence "Gatemouth" Brown and Matt Murphy. Later, he rated quite highly the playing of Jeff Beck, John McLaughlin, and Brian May of Queen.

After a brief period working in the advertizing industry, he wrote the music for several less-than-celebrated movies. His soundtrack to *Run Home Slow* earned him the money to buy a small recording studio where he recorded a band called the Omens – whose members went on to form both the Mothers of Invention and Captain Beefheart's Magic Band.

Zappa has strong ideas about the way an electric guitar should sound:

"From the very beginning when I used to hear those solos on those old records I used to say: now here is an instrument that is capable of spewing forth true obscenity, you know? If ever there's an obscene noise to be made on an instrument, it's going to come out of a guitar. . . Let's be realistic about this, the guitar can be the single most blasphemous device on the face of

the earth. That's why I like it . . . The disgusting stink of a too-loud electric guitar: now that's my idea of a good time."

Zappa's break came in 1966 when Tom Wilson, Bob Dylan's producer, heard Zappa's band playing at the Whiskey A Go-Go club in Los Angeles and wanted to record them. The result was the Mothers of Invention's ground-breaking debut album, "Freak Out!" A second album, "Absolutely Free," followed in 1967.

The Mothers of Invention moved to New York in 1968 and, during November of that year, started a six-month season playing fourteen shows a week at the Garrick Theatre. Both the overt theatricality and outrageous nature of their shows have since become a part of rock legend, influencing many in the process.

The guitarist as composer/performer/producer
Frank Zappa considers himself to be a primarily a composer "who happens to operate an instrument called a guitar." In the studio he assumes the additional role of being his own producer.

After the first two Mothers albums, Zappa released his first solo record: "Lumpy Gravy." The album that followed, "Hot Rats," was the first to feature the extended guitar soloing that has since become a trademark. It also contains some of his most highly rated guitar playing.

Throughout the seventies, Zappa's live concerts gradually began to feature more intricate music and fewer theatrics. A typical performance consisted of two hours of tightly arranged music with one song segued into the next. As ever, he continued to drill his bands to perfection. Always insistent on the highest standards, his

Steve Cropper

Freaking out
Pop music met the avant garde in 1966 when the Mothers of Invention released the controversial double album, "Freak Out!"

backing bands spawned players of the caliber of Adrian Belew and Steve Vai.

Zappa has a heavy right-hand technique and favors heavy Fender plectrums. In the past he has employed a wah wah pedal like a tone or distortion control, leaving it set in one position rather than rocking it back and forth. On stage he generally plays clean extended lead lines, using valve amps and the wah-wah pedal to give a regular, slightly distorted rock sound. In the recording studio, he has always experimented with different sounds and musical ideas.

For the first three albums, Zappa used a Gibson ES-5 Switchmaster guitar. After a spell with a Gibson Les Paul, he has played Gibson SGs on stage more often than any other instrument. He also uses a Fender Stratocaster which has a Barcus Berry contact transducer imbedded in the neck. This allows finger and plectrum noises to be mixed in with the signal from the pick-ups.

Over the years, Zappa has played with a variety of amplifiers. Originally, he used a Fender Deluxe, but he has often recorded with Pignose and Boogie amps. On stage he generally prefers Marshall 100-watt tops used in conjunction with 4x12 cabinets that have been fitted with JBL speakers.

The eighties saw a divergence in Zappa's activities. He conducted modern classical works by Varese and Webern, and developed an interest in the compositional possibilities proffered by the massive digital "work stations" like the NED Synclavier. It was an interest that apparently lead him to abandon the guitar for a while. His efforts can be heard on the Grammy award winning 1988 album "Jazz From Hell."

Whether as a guitarist, composer, producer, philosopher, or even would-be politician, Frank Zappa's movements are always worthy of careful scrutiny.

In a lull during a Memphis recording session in 1962 the musicians – all session players for the Stax label – began jamming. The line-up was Booker T. Jones on Hammond organ, Steve Cropper on guitar, Al Jackson, Jr. on drums and Steinberg Lewis on bass. The session was recorded and one of the resulting tracks, "Green Onions," by Booker T. & the MGs, became a US million seller. The record featured Booker T's Hammond organ playing and Steve Cropper's sparse, rhythmic, and atmospheric guitar chops, played on a Fender Telecaster, both of which became an important ingredient in the evolution of black soul music.

Steve Cropper was to become a songwriter, guitar player, arranger, and record producer for many great soul artists like Wilson Pickett, Eddie Floyd and, most notably, Otis Redding.

Born on 21st October 1944, Steve Cropper had a rural white upbringing. He moved to Memphis in 1951 where, exposed to black R&B music, he soon adopted the music of the Memphis area. After years of associating his guitar style with the core black culture of the Stax sound, many are amazed to find that he is caucasian. Of his work in the sixties, Steve says:

"If there was anything about the Stax sound it was really music with licks in it. We liked to call them money licks."

Making something simple sound identifiable on record was one of Cropper's specialities. And it wasn't only the guitar licks. He wrote the Memphis Horns introduction on Wilson Pickett's "In The Midnight Hour" on guitar using his characteristic parallel chord approach. As he himself says, referring to the fretboard markers on the fingerboard of his Telecaster:

"Just follow the dots and you can't get into trouble."

When arranged for horns the part is instantly identifiable. When he was sitting with Eddie Floyd, writing "Knock On Wood," Cropper came up with the idea of simply playing the introduction he had written for "In The Midnight Hour" in reverse. He did, it worked, and another million-seller was born.

Steve Cropper executed simple ideas with consummate good taste, originality, and feel. Jimi Hendrix, Syd Barrett and countless other important players have quoted Cropper as a major influence. He can be heard on any good Otis Redding compilation playing classics – co-written with Redding – like "(Sittin' On) The Dock Of The Bay" or "Fa-fa-fa-fa-fa (Sad Song)." If the term "getting your chops together" was not coined in reference to Steve Cropper then it should have been.

The ultimate craftsman
Happy to leave the pursuit of stardom to others, Steve Cropper's major strength was always as a collaborator. As well as co-writing and co-producing some of the Stax label's greatest hits, he also "wrote the book" on soul guitar licks.

Pete Townshend

Pete Townshend was born in Chiswick, London, on 19th May 1945. Although his father was an accomplished saxophone and clarinet player and worked as a band leader and session musician, Townshend reacted in the traditional way – with teenage rebellion. Right from the start he was more interested in sound, songwriting and self-expression than in music theory.

He did, however, learn the banjo joining a traditional jazz band playing revivalist New Orleans jazz. The trumpet player in the band was John Entwistle, who later formed a number of groups with Townshend before becoming the Who's bass guitarist.

Townshend's first electric guitar was a single pick-up Harmony Stratocruiser. When he joined a group called the Detours, the lead guitarist – Roger Daltrey – sold him an Epiphone solid on "easy payments". By the time the group was calling itself the High Numbers they were, in all but name, the Who. Their one and only single as the High Numbers was "Zoot Suit/I'm A Face" – the latter written around the basic format of Slim Harpo's "Got Love If You Want It." The single was unsuccessful and is now a rare collector's item, but it also established the group as a "mod" band. They accepted the mod image to a degree – combining it with flamboyant "op art" fashion. The result was a flashy image with which young mod audiences could identify. Their raw, high-energy music, strongly influenced by American R&B, reflected the youthful frustration of their generation. By the time they changed their name to the Who, the band had become synonymous with the mod movement.

Townshend was to channel his self-expression through the group's overall sound, the songs he wrote for them, his rhythm guitar, and his on-stage image. This separated him from most of his peers: Jeff Beck and Eric Clapton, for example, were very much lead guitarists. Townshend was not. Frustrated because he was unable to get the kind of sounds that Clapton and Beck could, he discovered his own solution.

One night, while he was on stage at the Ealing Club in West London, he accidentally put the head of his guitar – a Rickenbacker – through the false ceiling above him, snapping off the neck. When the audience started to laugh, Townshend smashed the rest of the guitar to pieces, picked up a twelve-string guitar, and continued to play for the rest of the show as if nothing had happened. On the following night, the club was packed out. Subsequently, ritualistic equipment-smashing became the climax of many of the Who's stage and television appearances over the next few years.

By this time, Townshend, the inventor of the "rock power chord" and a pioneer user of controlled feedback, had developed a unique playing style. Laced with on-stage acrobatics and his trademark, windmilling arm motions, it provided a solid, powerful foundation for the rest of the band. The basic format of guitar, bass, and drums, uncluttered by excessive soloing, allowed John Entwistle and Keith Moon much more freedom than they would have had within the tight constraints of a conventional rhythm section. Their early hit singles – "My Generation," "Anyway, Anyhow, Anytime," "I Can't Explain," and "Substitute" – all displayed a raw and uncompromising style that contrasted sharply with other bands of the day. One of the first bands that successfully spanned the divide between pop and rock, the Who became one of the most emulated of the sixties rock bands.

Managers Chris Stamp and Kit Lambert played an important role in the initial development of the Who. It was Lambert who suggested to Townshend that he try writing an extended piece to "pad out the playing time" when they ended up about ten minutes short of material for their second album. Still convinced that the three-minute format was the standard framework for pop records, Townshend was sceptical. Lambert then suggested that he link together several short songs with an overall concept. The result was "A Quick One" which appeared on "The Who Sell Out" album. When, in 1968, the Pretty Things extended the idea to a whole album with "S. F. Sorrow," Townshend was impressed, and began work on "Tommy."

The framework provided him with a stimulus for new ideas. Townshend had developed considerably as a guitarist, and was by this time playing keyboards and writing songs at the piano. The music on "Tommy" is ambitious and features some of his strongest material.

In the seventies, the Who consolidated their status as a rock band with a series of classic LPs like "Live at Leeds" (considered by many to be the best live album ever made), "Who's Next" and, another concept album, "Quadrophenia."

The Who (*below*)
John Entwistle, Keith Moon, Roger Daltrey and Pete Townshend, seen miming on an American television show in the late sixties.

Syd Barrett

The Townshend power chord (*above*)
The windmill arm motion became Townshend's trademark. An impressive stage gimmick, it underlined the energy of his playing.

During the early days of the band, John Entwistle obtained one of the first 4x12 speaker cabinets made by Marshall for use with the bass guitar. Townshend noticed that he was getting twice the volume and projection as before, and promptly obtained one for himself. He soon followed it with a second cabinet, placing one on top of the other. Because the top cabinet was at ear level, he could hear himself more clearly, and because the speakers were in line with his guitar pick-ups, it was easier to employ controlled feedback. He initially used the Marshall cabinets in conjunction with Fender or Marshall amplifiers. He subsequently settled down with a similar set-up using Hi-watt amplifiers and cabinets. For recording, he has used combo amplifiers, like the MESA Boogie.

The strong individual personalities of the Who members meant that the band's history was punctuated with regular – often public – arguments. Yet somehow the Who managed to stay together. They survived Keith Moon's death in 1978, continuing with Kenny Jones on drums and "Rabbit" Bundrick on keyboards. While they officially split in 1983, the Who have periodically reformed, most notably for the "Live Aid" concert in 1985.

Over the past 25 years, Pete Townshend's influence as both player and performer has been enormous. He has always been regarded as one of the key guitarists in rock music.

Pink Floyd's first album "Piper At The Gates Of Dawn" was released in the UK during 1967 just a short time before the Beatles released "Sgt Pepper's Lonely Hearts Club Band". This was during the original psychedelic "Summer of Love". The hallucinogenic drug LSD had a great influence on many musicians including Pink Floyd's prime creative force, guitarist, singer, and songwriter, Syd Barrett. Their album, "The Piper At The Gates Of Dawn" defined a whole genre of music and must be regarded as historically important.

Born on 6th January 1946 in Cambridge, Barrett's first musical instrument was a banjo. For a while he played bass guitar in a college blues band until he was taught guitar by Dave Gilmour. Barrett moved to London to study art during 1965. Roger Waters, Rick Wright, and Nick Mason were all friends and students studying at Regent Street Polytechnic, in London. They were introduced to Barrett by Dave Mason, and he was asked to join their band. Mainly through Barrett's influence they moved away from American blues standards and launched into avant-garde experimentation.

The Beatles and many other people who took LSD did not suffer lasting negative effects. However for Barrett the drug proved to be extremely dangerous. Fueled on LSD, Barrett had, in a welter of creativity, been the driving force behind the first two Pink Floyd singles "Arnold Lane" and "See Emily Play," and their album "The Piper At The Gates Of Dawn."

Just as Pink Floyd's initial success placed him in the spotlight he began to suffer a serious decline in mental health. He seemed to be plagued by an increasing inability to communicate or express himself. Sadly, many of his problems were seen more as bold anti-establishment actions, and, a source of great amusement.

Things deteriorated during their first American tour. Barrett refused to mime on "Dick Clark's Bandstand" TV show and he stared blankly in silent response to questions on the Pat Boone show. Within days the tour was curtailed and the band returned to London. Yet Barrett showed no sign of creative decline. Despite efforts by the band to cling on to some kind of viable working relationship, it proved impossible. He was replaced by Dave Gilmour.

Whereas for Beck and Clapton, blues music was their main inspiration, Barrett, though not as technically adept, took rock guitar in a totally new direction. His freeform excursions into banks of textural sound, playing his Telecaster through a bank of echo devices, opened the door for a whole new school of rock guitar playing.

After leaving Pink Floyd he was to record the poignant solo albums "The Madcap Laughs" and "Barrett," but otherwise was reclusive and suffered a continuing history of mental ill health.

Pink Floyd (*below*)
From left to right, Roger Waters, Syd Barrett, Nick Mason and Rick Wright perform Barrett's "See Emily Play" on television in 1967.

Stanley Clarke

Stanley Clarke was born in Philadelphia in 1951. He began violin lessons at the age of twelve, but being very tall and having long fingers caused problems; after trying cello he decided a double bass was the right-sized instrument for him. He wasn't too keen on the "rough sound" but decided he could work around that.

By the time Clarke was sixteen, he had started playing bass guitar. His musical interests encompassed Wagner, Bach, James Brown, Sly Stone, Jimi Hendrix, and the Beatles, as well as jazz greats like Miles Davis. While continuing his classical music studies, he was also playing all kinds of popular music with local groups. After leaving school he went to the Philadelphia Musical Academy, taking a course covering symphonic double bass playing.

Two years later, after moving to New York, he successfully auditioned for jazz pianist Horace Silver's group and stayed for a year. He worked with several jazz and improvisational groups before meeting keyboard player Chick Corea. In 1971 they led the first line-up of Return To Forever, and recorded the album of the same name.

Finger technique
(*above*) Clarke utilizes aspects of double bass technique on the bass guitar – for example, resting the thumb of his right hand on the edge of the fingerboard to give an anchor point and to enable him to play pizzicato (Italian for "pinched"). This means that he is pulling and then releasing – as opposed to striking or plucking – the strings. The effect of their slapping back against the frets and the fingerboard creates a unique percussive sound that has been widely copied.

Distinctive sound (*left*)
The combination of the Alembic bass (with active electronics built-in) and solid-state amplification has helped to Stanley Clarke to create his own distinctive sound.

After a gig at the Boarding House in Los Angeles with Chick Corea, a man named Rick Turner told Clarke he thought his playing was great but his sound was lousy. The following night, Turner arrived at the club with one of his early two-octave Alembic bass guitars. The instrument, with its long scale, active electronics, long sustain and rich sound convinced Clarke, and Turner made him a custom instrument, thus initiating the combination that resulted in his distinctive sound.

By 1976, Clarke had become something of a legend, his "Stanley Clarke" solo album an accepted masterpiece. He went on to form his own group, as well as work with artists like Jeff Beck, George Duke, and Keith Richards. In 1988, Clarke moved well away from jazz-rock territory when he teamed up with former Police drummer Stewart Copeland and Deborah Holland to form Animal Logic.

Stanley Clarke's playing is a synthesis of classical, jazz, soul, and rock music. He believes that the bass guitar can be played as both a rhythm and solo instrument at the same time. He never uses a plectrum, preferring to use two or three fingers.

During the 1980s, the influence of Stanley Clarke's melodic, rhythmic and percussive playing could be found everywhere: no self-respecting dance band could be heard without a "slap" bass player. Equally influential has been his pioneering approach to instruments with active-circuitry and his use of solid-state amplification.

Jeff Beck

Jeff Beck, born in Surrey, England, in June 1944, first gained attention as a guitarist when he joined the Yardbirds in 1965 as Eric Clapton's replacement. At that time, the band was going through a transitional phase – Beck has since described them as "the first psychedelic band" – and Beck's style was well suited to their increasingly experimental approach. However, the following year, during a tour of the United States, the same personality problems that have since seemed to dog his career resulted in his being sacked from the band. Beck then embarked on a solo career. Initial success came in 1967 with the Micky Most production "Hi Ho Silver Lining," a totally unrepresentative pop song – featuring one of Beck's extremely rare vocal performances – that established him as a mixture of pop star and cult-figure.

He went on to form the Jeff Beck Group, the best-known line-up of which featured Rod Stewart, Ron Wood and Aynsley Dunbar. The albums "Truth" and "Beckola," along with the band's live appearances, enhanced his reputation as one of rock's major performers. In 1969, after a variety of personality problems, Stewart and Wood left to form the Faces.

In 1972, Beck teamed up with Tim Bogert and Carmine Appice, both formerly of American band Vanilla Fudge. Their relationship dated back to Beck's days as a Yardbird: he stood in one night when Vanilla Fudge's lead guitarist failed to show up for a gig. They had planned to form a band as early as 1969; however, Beck was hospitalized following a serious car crash, and Bogart and Appice went off to form Cactus. Three years on, they were finally free to form their trio. Unfortunately, by this time, the concept of the powerhouse trio had become somewhat outdated. The band recorded two albums, only one of which was released. Beck withdrew from the rock scene altogether and began a period of self-examination and experimentation.

The Jeff Beck that re-emerged on the 1975 album "Blow By Blow" – produced by George Martin, famous for his work with the Beatles – was a very different guitarist indeed. The intervening period had seen the emergence of bands capable of combining a high level of musicianship with popular appeal. Beck was especially impressed by John McLaughlin's Mahavishnu Orchestra, in particular the keyboard and synthesizer skills of Jan Hammer. A combination of jazz-rock, funk, and soul made the "Blow By Blow" album a massive commercial success. He followed it up with, "Wired," featuring the Jan Hammer Group, which moved even further into jazz-rock territory.

The eighties saw Beck produce three acclaimed albums. "There and Back," released in 1981 saw Beck, once again, helped out by Jan Hammer. The 1985 album "Flash" even spawned a rare hit single when Beck reunited with Rod Stewart to cover Curtis Mayfield's "People Get Ready." In 1989 he emerged with "Jeff Beck's Guitar Shop With Terry Bozzio And Tony Hymas" for which he received a Grammy award.

Beck's appearances on other people's records can be seen as an indication of the level of respect he enjoys among his fellow musicians. Outstanding examples of his session work can be found on "Lookin' For Another Pure Love" on Stevie Wonder's "Talking Book," "Hello Jeff" on Stanley Clarke's "Journey To Love," and on Mick Jagger's "She's The Boss" album.

Over the years, Beck has used a variety of guitars and amplifiers. In 1975, at the time of "Blow by Blow," he played a vintage 1954 Gibson Les Paul Standard fitted with two humbuckers and, on occasions, a Fender Stratocaster.

He generally played through 100-watt Marshall amplifiers with Fender speaker cabinets. He used a pre-amp to get an overdriven valve sound and a wah-wah pedal. He also used a "voice box" on the track "She's A Woman." By 1980, he was favouring a standard Stratocaster and a Telecaster fitted with Gibson humbuckers.

New territory (*above*)
The album "Blow By Blow," produced by George Martin, famous for his work with the Beatles, marked a transitional point in Beck's career. It was his first highly successful excursion into jazz-rock.

The Yardbirds (*below*)
Seen here performing on the British television series "Ready Steady Go," the Yardbirds were one of the most interesting groups of the mid-sixties. Beck is on the right playing the sun-burst Gibson Les Paul. In his early days, the Yardbirds made a cameo appearance in Antonioni's classic movie *Blow up*. Beck can be seen rather unconvincingly smashing a guitar in the manner of Pete Townshend.

Brian May

Brian May was born 19th July 1947, in Twickenham, London. He studied infra-red astronomy at Imperial College, London, but was sidetracked into music before the completion of his PhD. May played in various groups as a teenager, but it was as a member of the band Smile that he met drummer Roger Taylor, who, along with vocalist Freddie Mercury and bassist John Deacon would form Queen.

They were all intelligent young men who felt that they should be able to avoid many of the pitfalls that most bands encounter when they start out, namely getting seriously ripped off by their management. Throughout the late seventies and the whole of the eighties, Queen became one of the most successful rock bands of all time.

From Queen's earliest days, Brian May's guitar playing won him universal acclaim and the admiration of thousands of aspiring guitarists. Queen spent many years developing and refining their music. A big surprise for many people who were not particular fans of the band was the quality of their performance at the 1985 Live Aid concert. The culmination of ten years playing huge stadium venues seemed to come together and Queen played a short but classic set that many people regarded as the highlight of the day. Their set provided an object lesson in just how musical and harmonically rich a sound can be created by a vocals, guitar, bass, and drums line-up.

May was initially inspired to play guitar by listening to the Everly Brothers, Buddy Holly, and the Shadows; but later, through hearing the Yardbirds and the Rolling Stones, he became more interested in Chuck Berry and Bo Diddley, the people who had given birth to rock'n'roll music. Jimi Hendrix and The Beatles were to have a profound influence on Queen as a group. It was George Martin's production techniques that provided inspiration for the way Queen would utilize recording studio technology to the full.

One of the most striking features of Brian May's playing is his use of multi-layered guitar harmonies:

"It was something that I was always interested in and I wanted to do it best and first. I always liked the effect since I heard Jeff Beck on "Hi Ho Silver Lining", where he double-tracked his guitar and there's this one little spot where he went into harmony. I just thought that if you could get that sound under control then it would be such an amazing sound. And that was always in my head right from the very beginning. With Queen we just pressed on and were able to get it done. From that we just went on to more complex arrangements and you can actually build up whole orchestras that way and why not?"

May has always used the same home-built guitar. The instrument, constructed using the most basic of materials, was designed to respond specifically to feedback. To achieve this he set the coils of the Burns pick-ups in Araldite adhesive, made the instrument out of very solid timber, and cut acoustic pockets in the body, causing it to resonate at frequencies around the middle of the guitar's frequency range. Setting the pick-up coils in adhesive prevents them from being microphonic so that the strings feedback but the pick-ups don't whistle. Interestingly, instead of playing with a standard plectrum, he favours an old English sixpenny piece.

In the spotlight
After years of happily letting the late Freddie Mercury take center-stage, 1991 saw a higher-profile Brian May. Not only was he featured prominently at the Seville "Guitar Legends" concert series, but he also enjoyed his first solo top ten single, "Driven By You".

Jaco Pastorius

There are many parallels between the early careers of bass guitarists Jaco Pastorius and Stanley Clarke, yet their musical styles are so clearly defined that there can be no mistaking their playing or influence.

Jaco Pastorius was born in Norristown, Pennsylvania on 12th January 1951. When he was seven years old his family moved to Florida where he was raised. He talked of a lack of musical prejudice in Florida during the fifties and sixties and he consequently listened to a wide variety of music from Miles Davis to the Beatles. Although it would seem that drugs and alchohol took their toll on the musician later on in his life, throughout his early days Pastorius was not an obsessional type of musician: he also enjoyed playing sports, painting, and being a family man.

Jaco did not start out playing bass guitar. He worked his way through saxophone, piano, guitar, and drums before centering attention on the bass, and this would seem to have been a purely pragmatic choice. At the age of thirteen Jaco had been seriously hurt playing football. His left hand was almost severed. At this time he was playing drums in a local band, but a couple of years later gave up, lacking in left hand strength and unable to lay down a strong enough back beat. A week later the group's bass guitarist left and they asked Jaco if he thought he could handle playing the instrument. He had four hundred dollars in the bank and a job delivering newspapers. The next day he bought a Fender Jazz bass.

Like Jimi Hendrix, Pastorius was to gain an enormous amount of extremely varied live experience before beginning his recording career. He played in many soul bands and claims to have played just about every soul tune written during the sixties. Playing popular music came easily to him. The turning point came when he also began to play jazz standards. To begin with, according to Pastorius, encompassing jazz was just a way of making more money, but this first exposure was merely an overture to a rapid move towards jazz music.

He began to develop a reputation through playing one-nighters with Wayne Cochran and the C. C. Riders, but he left during 1971 and spent a year in what he saw as his first serious study of music and the bass guitar. Pastorius had already met jazz musician and composer Ira Sullivan who had moved from Chicago to Florida

Fretless pioneer
Jaco Pastorius was almost single-handedly responsible for the popularity of the fretless bass. He originally used a Fender Jazz with the frets removed. His revolutionary use of harmonics in melody can be heard to great effect on the solo pieces on his 1976 debut album "Jaco Pastorius."

to teach. Soon he was writing and arranging for Ira Sullivan's Baker's Dozen and The Peter Graves' Big Band.

His breakthrough came in 1976 when he joined Weather Report, a band formed by ex-Miles Davis players, Joe Zawinul and Wayne Shorter. He contributed significantly to the "Black Market" album. That same year, supported by musicians of the stature of Herbie Hancock, Don Alias, and Mike Gibbs, he also recorded an eponymously titled solo album.

Playing a Fender Jazz Bass with the frets removed, Pastorius was immediately hailed as a musician of great importance and originality. Weather Report enjoyed enormous commercial success, in particular

with the 1977 "Heavy Weather" album, which featured two Pastorius compositions.

He is also widely respected for his work with Pat Metheny and, in particular, his entrancing playing on Joni Mitchell's "Don Juan's Reckless Daughter" and "Mingus" recordings. His second solo album, "Twins," was released to great acclaim during 1982.

Jaco said he was most influenced by vocalists, especially in the way they were able to put so much expression into their music. His use of melody, harmonics, and chords on fretless bass were all really secondary to his personal musical expressiveness. Tragically, he died as a result of a violent incident outside a Miami nightclub on 21st December 1987.

Andy Summers

"A guitarist for all seasons" would be rather an apt title for Andy Summers. Over a period of three decades he has worked in numerous bands and played in many different styles.

He first came to notice playing slick, soulful licks in Zoot Money's Big Roll Band in the sixties and stayed with them during their subsequent foray into psychedelia as Dantalion's Chariot. In 1968, he moved on to the more aggressive Animals (by then known as Eric Burden and the New Animals), to the free-improvisational Soft Machine, to backing bands for eccentric English singer-songwriters Kevin Ayers and Kevin Coyne.

During 1977, Summers met former Curved Air drummer Stewart Copeland and singer/bass player Gordon Matthew "Sting" Sumner when all three were booked for the same recording session. Impressed by what they told him about their group, the Police, Summers sat in with them at the Marquee Club in London. As Sting tells it, "he demanded to be in the group, so he was in."

Summers has said that he saw the Police as a challenge to try and do something new with a three-piece band. Instead of turning the amps on full, thrashing hell out of the drums and squeezing as many notes per second out of the lead guitar as possible, he told me during 1980:

"We approached it the other way, much more of a minimal thing, trying to use a lot more space – and that's where reggae really helped us a lot . . . we fused reggae with rock".

While their initial success was on the back of the "New Wave" bandwagon, the Police rapidly became superstars. A succession of number one hit singles like "Message In A Bottle," "Don't Stand So Close," "Every Breath You Take", and "Every Little Thing She Does Is Magic," and the multi-platinum selling "Synchronicity" album, made them one of the biggest selling acts world-wide. They brilliantly combined success as "pop stars" with musical credibility in a way that no band since the Beatles had managed.

At the heart of this success was Andy Summers' tasteful and disciplined guitar work. His playing has helped to re-define the role of the guitarist in a rock band. Consciously drawing on as many different musical styles and influences as possible, he explained that the Police aimed to do away with the conventional concept of a rhythm section as simply providing a backing for a soloist:

"It's a linear rather than a horizontal thing. I think we would regard it – in broad terms – as three soloists going along three parallel lines, creating a fabric rather than a straight line upwards . . . I can change the way I play the guitar all along that line, in terms of playing fragmented chords, whole chords, changing the progression, and playing solos, depending on what is happening with the bass and drums in the space available.

I can also color all my sounds with contemporary modifying devices."

Examples of Summers' eclectic approach can be found in the two instrumental albums he cut with King Crimson's Robert Fripp – "I Advance Masked" and "Bewitched," both of which charted in the U.S.A. In 1987, Summers released "XYZ", his first album to feature his own vocals.

Summers has been quick to embrace new technology. He successfully experimented with the early Roland guitar synthesizers, and was one of the first major guitarists to be seen on stage with MIDI rack effects.

Anyone who has listened to his playing will be familiar with the formidable range of sounds and textures that Andy Summers is capable of creating with a skillful blend of technique and sophisticated electronics.

At work (*left*)
In the early eighties, with their ability to recreate the sparce sound of their hits, the Police were one of the major live attractions in the rock world.

At play (*below*)
Andy Summers was one of the first major guitarists to fully embrace the proliferation of new technology.

Robert Fripp

The 1960s saw the emergence of many great rock guitarists. Most followed a more-or-less parallel development, based heavily on the music of American blues players. However, Robert Fripp – born in Wimborne, Dorset, in 1946 – took rock guitar playing in a totally different direction from that of the mainstream. Although he uses both acoustic and electric guitars to produce a wide variety of musical textures, it is through his forceful solo electric playing that he has had the greatest impact as a guitarist. His frequently distorted and overdriven guitar sound is combined with a flowing, unrestricted playing style gained from years of study into the scales, chordal structures, and harmony of musical cultures from all over the world. His chosen and well-thought-out path has enabled him continually to break new ground.

It was as a founder member of the group King Crimson that Fripp first gained attention, although he had previously recorded an album with the trio Giles, Giles and Fripp. The impact of King Crimson was immediate and substantial. In the vanguard of "progressive rock" bands, they combined classical and symphonic concepts with elements of rock. Fripp's experimental guitar work, accentuated by the insistency of his raw, distorted, lead sound, was one of the highlights.

Fripp was the one constant member of King Crimson from its origin in 1969 to its initial demise in 1974. Plagued by frequent personnel changes and by problems associated with Fripp's uncompromising and somewhat dictatorial stance, King Crimson nevertheless made some excellent recordings: "In the Court Of The Crimson King," "Larks' Tongues In Aspic," "Red," and "Starless and Bible Black".

In 1973, Fripp teamed up with synthesist Brian Eno to produce the influential "No Pussyfooting," an album of Fripp's solo guitar processed through a tape delay line. Fripp developed this approach into what he later referred to as "Frippertronics."

After King Crimson broke up in 1974, Fripp was responsible for putting together the compilation album "A Young Person's Guide to King Crimson."

In the mid-seventies, Fripp began to withdraw from the music scene "to pursue alternative education". He did, however, take time out to record a second collaboration with Brian Eno, "Evening Star," and, in 1976, his first solo album, "Exposure." He also worked with Eno again the following year, the pair of them making major contributions to David Bowie's "Heroes" album: Fripp's distinctive guitar playing dominates the hit single of the same name.

Guest guitarist (*left*) Throughout his career, Fripp has made many guest appearances on other people's records. David Bowie, Peter Gabriel, Blondie and Talking Heads, to name a few, have all gained from his contributions.

No Pussyfooting (*below*) "Frippertronics" was born when two Revox A77 tape decks were set up, allowing Fripp to record layer after layer of repeated sound for use as a backdrop to soloing.

When Fripp returned, he began the execution of a carefully planned strategy. In a series of articles written for *Musician, Player and Listener* in America, and *Sound International* in Britain, he expressed his highly individual views on music and the state of the music industry. He also announced his future intention to operate as a "small mobile intelligence unit".

At the beginning of the eighties, after briefly forming the all-instrumental, new wave-influenced band, the League Of Gentlemen, a new Fripp band was created. They were originally to be called Discipline, with a line-up consisting of Fripp, former Yes drummer Bill Bruford, bassist Tony Levin (playing the fascinating Chapman Stick), and Adrian Belew, who had previously worked with Frank Zappa and Talking Heads. They changed their name to King Crimson and recorded a superb album entitled "Discipline".

The new-look King Crimson seemed to be as popular as before and toured extensively throughout Europe. Two more albums, "Beat" and "Three Of A Perfect Pair", were recorded, before personality problems once again caused a split.

Fripp feels that his most important work as a guitarist has happened since the early eighties. In addition to his periodic collaborations with Andy Summers (see p. 28), his main activity has been with the now well-established "Guitar Craft" project, a series of practical seminars that attempt a radical approach to guitar tuition.

Never a man to be dictated to by the market place, Robert Fripp continues to go his own way, whether as a producer, "guest" guitarist, solo performer, or bandleader. His well-placed guitar work and provocative views on music have provided inspiration for a new generation of guitarists and other musicians.

His "Frippertronics" technique – to which several albums have now been dedicated – and the album "Exposure" have made Robert Fripp one of the most influential guitarists of the past 20 years.

Eddie Van Halen

Towards the end of the 1970s, mainstream rock guitar playing fell into the doldrums. Then, in 1978, Warner Brothers Records released "Van Halen," an album that has since become one of the most influential on guitarists since Jimi Hendrix's "Are You Experienced?" (see p. 18). Eddie Van Halen's guitar playing on the album was to inspire and stimulate a whole new generation of rock guitarists.

Eddie Van Halen combines musicality with a stunningly effective range of techniques. Whilst others had previously employed right hand fret-tapping, Van Halen was to develop variations on this technique to bring a wider means of expression to rock guitar playing.

With a brand of music that hovered between heavy rock and heavy metal, Van Halen was a band perfectly suited to the stadium rock circuit. A ready-made audience was waiting for them to happen. Eddie Van Halen was soon hailed a major talent by just about every notable guitarist.

Brothers Eddie and Alex Van Halen were born in Nijmegen in Holland, Eddie on 26th January 1957 and Alex on 8th May 1955. They both studied the piano at the instigation of their father. In 1968 the family moved to California.

In the USA, Eddie was exposed to rock music and, after hearing Cream and Jimi Hendrix, decided he wanted to play drums. Alex took up the guitar. While Eddie delivered papers to keep up the payments on the drums,

Signature model
In 1991, the Ernie Ball Music Man Edward Van Halen guitar made a big impression at the top end of the guitar market.

Alex would play the kit. When Eddie heard Alex play the drum solo for the instrumental hit "Wipe Out" he realized he'd better hand the kit over to his brother. He took up the guitar instead. His first instrument was an inexpensive four pick-up Teisco Del Ray.

During 1973, the Van Halens formed a band called the Broken Combs but they went on to form a new band with their singing acquaintance from school, David Lee Roth. They recruited a bass guitarist – Michael Anthony – and began working under the name Mammoth.

Up to 1976, Van Halen built a growing reputation in and around Los Angeles, supporting headliners like Santana. Eddie's outstanding and exciting guitar playing combined with David Lee Roth's over-the-top performances made the band increasingly successful.

Roth's extrovert personality was custom-made for the life of a rock star and was undoubtedly responsible for much of the media attention and the eventual popularity of the band. Some of their own songs were quite accessible to a wide, young audience and their cover versions of songs like the Kinks' "You Really Got Me" helped to propel the Van Halen machine along with ever increasing momentum.

The incredible sounds that Eddie managed to achieve on the first album were made with the most basic guitar that he assembled from spare parts: a 50

Stadium stars
Van Halen are well established as a major stadium attraction. In 1986, veteran rocker Sammy Hagar *(right)* replaced the wild vocalist David Lee Roth.

dollar Charvel body, an 80 dollar neck, and a Gibson P.A.F. pick-up rewound to his own specification, which was controlled via a single volume control. He played his guitar through a Marshall amplifier via a pedalboard on which the controls for an Echoplex and an MXR phaser and flanger were mounted.

Van Halen recorded a series of albums with Roth until 1985, increasing their popularity and record sales with each one. Then, not long after the single "Jump" had elevated the group to superstar status, Roth went solo and Van Halen replaced him with Sammy Hagar, already a successful and well-respected solo artist.

Through the eighties, Eddie Van Halen redefined what could be achieved with an electric guitar. He became the hero of guitar magazines, winning polls and yet retaining the common touch that made his music appealing to rock fans as well as guitarists.

When Eddie Van Halen recorded his encyclopedic solo "Eruption" on the first Van Halen album, he made one of the strongest musical statements in the history of the guitar. He learned from listening to the records of Eric Clapton, Jimmy Page, and Jimi Hendrix, but always strived to create something original in his own music. Although thousands of guitarists have now imitated him, his own work, with his explosive use of sound, rhythm, right hand

Pat Metheny

Born in Lee's Summit, Kansas City, Missouri on 12th August 1954, Pat Metheny initially took up the French horn, which he continued to play throughout his school years. He first played guitar at the age of thirteen, predominantly under the influence of Wes Montgomery. Metheny's musical development was staggering: by the end of his teens, he was teaching at both the University of Miami and the prestigious Berklee School of Music – training ground to many great contemporary jazz musicians.

He first attracted public attention at the age of nineteen, when vibraphone virtuoso Gary Burton asked him to join his band. In 1977, after recording three LPs, he left to form the Pat Metheny Group with keyboard player and co-composer Lyle Mays.

By 1980, the Pat Metheny Group had recorded superb albums like "Brighter Size Life," "Watercolors," and "American Garage" for Manfred Eicher's ECM label.

Strong features of all the recordings were the accessibilty of the compositions, Metheny's intensely melodic and fluid improvised playing and his trademark clean, "choroused" guitar sound.

During the eighties, Metheny and Mays began developing a parallel career writing film scores like John Schlesinger's *The Falcon and The Snowman*. He also realized an ambition when he recorded the album "Song X" with Ornette Coleman, one of his idols. At this time, Metheny began to experiment with the NED Synclavier, which he played via a MIDI link to his guitar.

Pat Metheny has become one of an elite group of jazz musicians who have managed to achieve world-wide commercial success while at the the same time enjoying the respect and admiration of their peers. In fact, the list of musicians with whom Metheny has now worked reads like an A to Z of contemporary jazz.

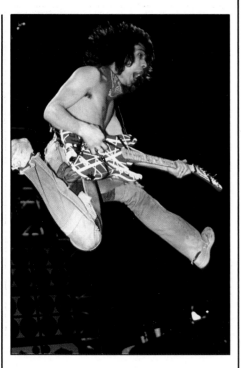

"Jump"
In the mid-eighties, Van Halen reached a new height of popularity. Their single "Jump" spent five weeks at the top of the U.S. charts.

fret tapping (see p. 157), harmonics and feedback all combine in a musical statement that is difficult to over-estimate.

Following a brief sponsorship deal with Kramer, for the 1991 album "For Unlawful Carnal Knowledge", he used an Ernie Ball Music Man Edward Van Halen guitar. This is an uncompromisingly designed instrument. The body consists of basswood with a figured maple front. The neck is similar to a Stratocaster. Dudley Gimpel of Music Man computerized Eddie's own body design which was then refined using computer-aided design and manufacturing systems. The two pick-ups were made by Larry Dimarzio to Eddie's own specification.

Eddie's prime set-up for the "For Unlawful Carnal Knowledge" album was his Music Man guitar played through a Marshall 4x12 cabinet miked up with two Shure SM58 microphones both positioned close to the cone of one of the speakers, one mike central and one slightly set off to one side of the axis. In addition to his vintage Marshall Super 100 amplifier, he has also used a Soldano head.

By the time Van Halen toured in 1992, he was using a new Peavey 5150 model amplifier and 4x12 cabinets specially created by designer James Brown.

A rare example of Eddie Van Halen's guitar playing outside of the band is his classic solo on Michael Jackson's "Beat It."

Jazz superstar
Pat Metheny enjoys a level of commercial success usually open only to rock musicians. His concerts pull huge crowds and his records sell well in excess of 100,000 copies – a rare feat for a jazz player. Metheny has achieved all of this without having to compromise his work.

Steve Vai

On Saturday 19th October 1991, the last of the Expo 92 Festival "Guitar Legends" concerts took place. On stage with Joe Satriani, the evening's musical director, Brian May announced: "The genius – the master of the space age guitar – Mr Steve Vai." Playing unison harmony parts, Vai and May launched into "Liberty" from Vai's second solo album "Passion And Warfare." It was the first time Vai had performed any of the material from this seminal album.

"Passion And Warfare" is an uncompromising guitarist's album that, during 1990, was a surprising chart success in both the U.S.A. and the U.K. Steve Vai has been a frequent winner of polls in musicians' magazines, most spectacularly in 1991 when he won *Guitar Player* magazine's annual readers' polls in no less than four different categories.

Steve Vai is an interesting man, to say the least. He has gone from the extremes of playing guitar with Frank Zappa to David Lee Roth. He follows Zappa's hard working didactic approach to composition and performance yet embraces the theatrics and dress fashion of heavy rock. His music is powerful, fast, and dynamic. Yet Vai also has a humanistic, philosophical, and at times spiritual approach to his music and his way of life.

Steve Vai was born on 6th June 1960. He grew up in Brooklyn, New York, taking up the guitar at the age of fourteen. As a teenager he would write endlessly, keeping diaries, documenting dreams, and studying music and orchestration.

He seems to have studied just about every important group and guitarist in rock, including John Lee Hooker, Led Zeppelin, The Jimi Hendrix Experience, Roy Buchanan and Carlos Santana.

He was a student at Berklee School of Music and also studied with guitar teacher/performer Joe Satriani, fondly recalling long jam sessions with Satriani as among his most enjoyable experiences.

Vai played second guitar to Frank Zappa during the 1970s when Zappa would introduce him as the band's "little Italian virtuoso." He went on to work with Alcatrazz, replacing Yngwie Malmsteem, moving on to ex-Van Halen vocalist Dave Lee Roth's band, playing on the "Eat 'em And Smile" and "Skyscraper" albums. He then recorded "Flex-able," his first solo album, before briefly joining Whitesnake.

His first two solo albums may be a little inaccessible to those neither into heavy metal/rock or the guitar, but if you're into both, you owe it to yourself to check out Steve Vai's music. Transcriptions of both albums are also available in book form.

Not a collector of vintage instruments, Vai uses Ibanez six-string Jem and seven-string Universe guitars, designed and endorsed by the guitarist himself. He prefers the sound of Marshall amplifiers though in the early 1990s for touring he used Soldano equipment, finding it more reliable. He uses various sound processing effects, including an Eventide H3000 harmonizer.

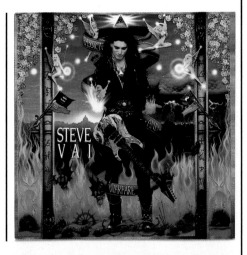

Rock classic (*right*)
The award-winning "Passion And Warfare," a showcase for Steve Vai's stunning technical virtuosity, is already thought of by many as one of the greatest guitar albums.

Design for the future (*right*)
Steve Vai collaborated with Ibanez in the design process of his own signature model. Note the distinctive "hand-grip" above the pick-ups.

ACOUSTIC GUITARS

Modern acoustic guitars come in two forms – those with steel strings and those with nylon strings. Although nylon-string guitars are always used for classical and flamenco music, and steel-string guitars are more common in folk, blues and even jazz and rock, there are no real rules. It is impossible to say that one kind of guitar must be used only for a certain type of music. From model to model there are, of course, countless variations in design, shape, construction, sound characteristics and usage. Yet the basic idea of the acoustic guitar has remained more or less the same for over a century. The steel-string guitar is the direct descendant of the "Spanish" or "classical" guitar – a masterpiece of design in terms of both physics and craftsmanship. All modern guitar-makers owe an incalculable debt to Antonio de Torres Jurado, the man whose nineteenth-century guitar designs are still closely followed for classical instruments. The major part of the development of the steel-string acoustic as we know it today was carried out by American guitar-makers – most notably by the Gibson and Martin companies. In recent years, the Japanese have applied their manufacturing skills to the acoustic guitar, with the result that excellent instruments are now well within reach of most people. This chapter deals with all the different types of acoustic guitar available, detailing the important stages in their development and describing how they are designed and constructed.

The anatomy of the acoustic guitar

The principle by which all acoustic guitars produce musical sounds is generally agreed to be the same. When you strike a guitar string, you apply energy to it and make it vibrate. However, this string vibration alone is not sufficient to create sound waves in the surrounding air that can be clearly heard.

In this respect, a guitar string can be thought of as being similar to a tuning fork. A tuning fork also vibrates when struck, but it is virtually inaudible until you bring it into contact with a mass of lower density which can transmit the vibrations to the air more efficiently.

It is for this reason that acoustic guitars have a hollow body. The body is a carefully designed "soundbox". The energy of the vibrating strings is transferred to the soundbox via the saddle and the bridge over which the strings pass. The soundbox then vibrates in sympathy with the guitar strings to create "amplified" – and therefore audible – airborne sound waves that can be heard up to a reasonable distance from the guitar. In other words, it is the soundbox that is responsible for the guitar's projection and volume.

A simple way of illustrating this point is to play an acoustic guitar alongside a solid-body electric guitar which you have not plugged into an amplifier. The un-amplified electric guitar is much quieter. Its solid body is mainly just a mounting block for the bridge, pick-ups and controls. Because it has no soundbox, the sound waves it generates are much weaker.

To sum up then, an acoustic guitar amplifies the sound of the vibrating strings *acoustically* – through the design of the body or the soundbox. But the sound of a solid-body electric guitar must be amplified *electronically* – through an amplifier and loudspeaker.

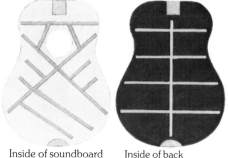

Inside of soundboard   Inside of back

The soundboard and back
Shown above are typical patterns of "strutting" or "bracing" for the soundboard and back of a flat-top acoustic guitar. The design of the struts must strike a compromise between strengthening the wood to prevent it from distorting and allowing it to vibrate in such a way as to give the best tone.

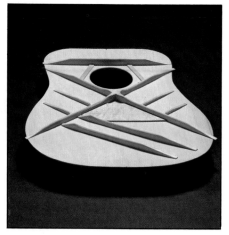

"X-bracing" inside an Ibanez soundboard.

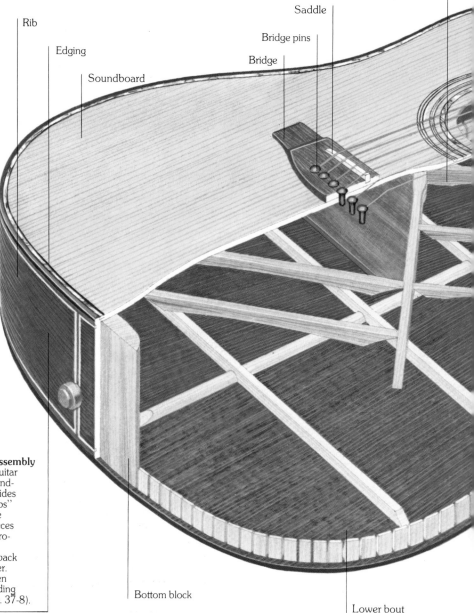

Rib
Edging
Soundboard
Saddle
Bridge pins
Bridge
Bottom block
Lower bout

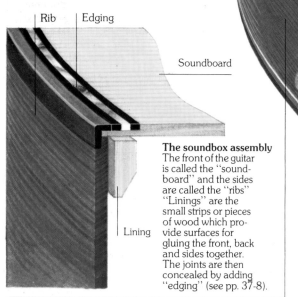

Rib   Edging
Soundboard
Lining

The soundbox assembly
The front of the guitar is called the "soundboard" and the sides are called the "ribs". "Linings" are the small strips or pieces of wood which provide surfaces for gluing the front, back and sides together. The joints are then concealed by adding "edging" (see pp. 37-8).

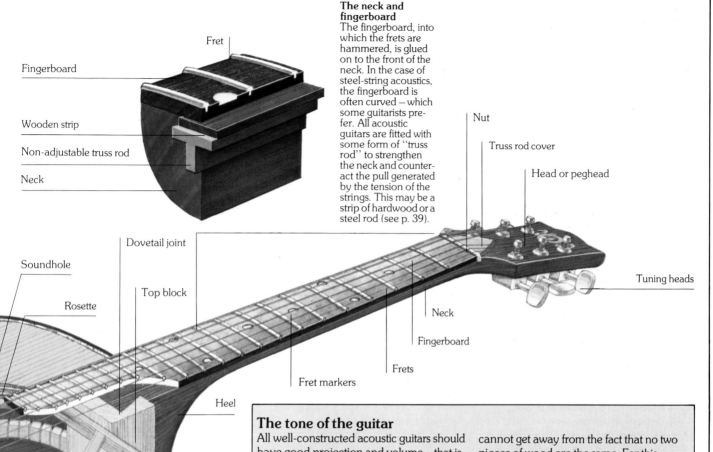

Fret

Fingerboard

Wooden strip

Non-adjustable truss rod

Neck

The neck and fingerboard
The fingerboard, into which the frets are hammered, is glued on to the front of the neck. In the case of steel-string acoustics, the fingerboard is often curved – which some guitarists prefer. All acoustic guitars are fitted with some form of "truss rod" to strengthen the neck and counter-act the pull generated by the tension of the strings. This may be a strip of hardwood or a steel rod (see p. 39).

Nut

Truss rod cover

Head or peghead

Tuning heads

Dovetail joint

Soundhole

Top block

Rosette

Neck

Fingerboard

Frets

Fret markers

Heel

Upper bout

Struts or braces

Back

Waist

Lining

The tone of the guitar

All well-constructed acoustic guitars should have good projection and volume – that is, they should make efficient use of the initial energy applied by the guitarist striking the strings. However, if you listen to two well-made guitars, they will almost certainly sound different. This quality is referred to as the *tone*.

Guitar-makers (known as "luthiers") constantly contradict one another with their varying theories as to why an acoustic guitar has a good or bad tone. The tonal characteristic is determined by a number of interacting factors which are hard – if not impossible – to isolate. However, the "soundboard" (the top or front of the soundbox) is the most important part of the guitar with regard to tone. In fact, legend has it that, to prove this, the nineteenth-century Spanish luthier Torres (see *Classical and flamenco guitars*, p. 42) once made a guitar with a body that consisted entirely of papier-mâché except for the wooden soundboard. Guitarists who played his experimental instrument were apparently amazed by its fine tone.

Theoretically, you might think it would be possible to build a series of different guitars with slightly varying construction details in order to establish one way or another what determines the tone quality. In practice, many top guitar-makers do exactly this – by changing their design slightly to produce an instrument with the sound characteristics requested by a particular customer. But you cannot get away from the fact that no two pieces of wood are the same. For this reason, no two guitars have quite the same tone; every guitar is unique to some degree.

As a general rule, all acoustic guitars should have an even gradation of tone, from the lowest bass note right up to the high treble notes on the top strings. There should be no "dead spots" where the tone or volume changes uncharacteristically, nor should there be any over-accentuated harmonic features.

Slight differences in the construction of "flat-top" acoustic guitars can result in tonal variations which make certain instruments better suited to particular playing styles and types of music. Martin flat-tops are very popular with fingerstyle guitarists because they suit that style of playing especially well. They have a clarity which gives a clearly defined bass pattern when a melody is played simultaneously on the top strings. Gibson flat-tops, on the other hand, are frequently used by country-music guitarists since they give a chunky, rhythmic sound when chords are strummed on them. Gibsons are also highly suited to flatpicking guitar styles.

Both Gibson and Martin are makers of high quality guitars and, although both makes of instrument have their own tonal characteristics which give them an edge when played in particular ways, both will also sound excellent when played in any number of styles.

How acoustic guitars are constructed

As soon as you start to look at the enormous variety of acoustic guitars which are available you will see that different types are constructed in different ways. As far as "flat-top" acoustic guitars are concerned, the differences – which are quite often subtle – are beyond quantification. There are, however, basic limits of practical design which make certain features common to them all.

We will begin by examining the choice of materials used in the construction of guitars and then move on to look in detail at the individual parts of the instrument.

The choice of wood

A guitar made from properly "seasoned" or "kiln-dried" wood will stand up to remarkable changes in temperature as well as humidity and – with just a reasonable amount of care and attention – will have a quite surprising life-span. The use of poor materials in guitar construction usually results in a poor sounding instrument and one that may soon become distorted from its original shape.

A guitar made of "green" timber straight from the tree and not seasoned or kiln-dried at all would be a complete disaster. In fact, the timber would probably shrink and distort so much while still in the hands of the guitar-maker that even the most modest standards would be impossible to attain.

So why use wood at all if it tends to be so problematic? The fact is that wood really has quite a lot going for it. For a start, no other material has been found to give anywhere

near as good a tone. But wood also has a warm feel, and when well finished is very attractive.

What are the criteria for choosing woods best suited to guitar-making? First, the wood – in particular that used for the soundboard – must have the required tonal quality. Second, it must have the required strength and stability. Third, the wood must lend itself to being finished or varnished for protective and decorative purposes.

Why does wood have to be seasoned or kiln-dried? The answer is simple. A tree and a guitar make totally different demands on their basic material. A tree is a complex living entity which must remain subtle enough to stand up to over two hundred years of changing seasons. The tree has a complex hydraulic system which pumps water around to where it is needed to cope with dramatic changes in weather conditions.

As soon as a tree is felled it starts to dry out. The way in which a tree is sawn and shaped into planks and pieces of timber, as well as the way in which it is stored, will affect the qualities of the wood finally used in the making of a guitar.

Seasoned wood is timber that has been carefully stored in controlled conditions with good ventilation for the period during which it gradually loses most – but not all – of the moisture it contains. After being exposed to the varying temperature and humidity changes of several seasons of spring, summer, autumn and winter, the wood becomes

relatively stable. Thus the term "seasoned". However, the process is long and expensive, and traditional seasoning of timber has become increasingly rare.

It is *kiln-dried* wood that meets most of the demands for timber in the twentieth century. Kiln-drying is a process by which the moisture is removed from new timber far more quickly than by seasoning. The wood is placed in a kiln which acts virtually like a slow oven. The time involved is therefore closer to weeks than to the months or years required for traditional seasoning.

Most guitars are now manufactured from kiln-dried wood. Nevertheless, individual guitar-makers may allow the wood to season for a further period – depending on their standards – and it is not at all rare to hear of a maker keeping kiln-dried wood for several years before using it for a guitar.

Some of the very best guitar-builders flatly refuse to accept kiln-dried timber for their instruments – in particular for the soundboards. Yet good timber is in very short supply generally – regardless of whether it is kiln-dried or seasoned. As a result, the last ten years or so have seen some of the best European makers traveling to Switzerland and Germany to seek out what they consider to be the ideal spruce or pine tree. The Spanish-born master guitar-maker Romanillos has been known to have a Swiss pine felled and sawn to his own requirements before seasoning the wood for a further five or more years.

The shape and size of the guitar

The majority of acoustic guitars all have the same basic shape: the characteristic figure-eight comprising the *upper bout*, the thin *waist* and the *lower bout*. However, the relative dimensions of the upper bout, waist and lower bout often vary. The smaller upper bout enhances the treble frequencies while the larger lower bout enhances the bass frequencies. Dropping a plectrum

through the soundhole into the soundbox of the guitar and shaking the instrument so that the plectrum rattles as it moves around from bout to bout demonstrates this quite clearly. The overall size of acoustic guitars also varies from one type of instrument to another. Flat-top steel-string acoustic guitars range from a "standard" size up to the larger "jumbo" and "Dreadnought"

sizes. The standard instrument is very similar to a classical guitar in both shape and size. It is a common practice with major guitar manufacturers to use a standard "scale length" (see p. 40) for a complete range of different-sized instruments.

"Three-quarter-sized" guitars are intended for children or adults with small hands and are not considered here.

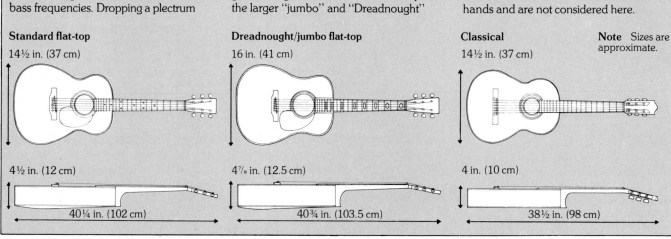

Standard flat-top
14½ in. (37 cm)

4½ in. (12 cm)

40¼ in. (102 cm)

Dreadnought/jumbo flat-top
16 in. (41 cm)

4⅞ in. (12.5 cm)

40¾ in. (103.5 cm)

Classical
14½ in. (37 cm)

4 in. (10 cm)

38½ in. (98 cm)

Note Sizes are approximate.

The soundbox

The body of an acoustic guitar is called the *soundbox*. It is made up of the *soundboard* at the front, the *ribs* (its sides) and the *back*. These pieces of wood are joined together with *linings* and the joints are then finished with decorative *edging*.

The soundboard

The most important part of the soundbox as regards the tone of the guitar is the *soundboard* – also known as the "table".

The very best soundboard would theoretically be made from best-quality, unblemished, "quarter-sawn", "book-matched", well-seasoned, straight-grained pine or spruce.

The term *quarter-sawn* refers to the way in which the timber is cut when the tree is initially sawn into planks.

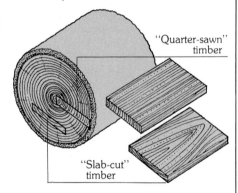

"Quarter-sawn" timber

"Slab-cut" timber

As far as soundboards and backs are concerned, the term *book-matched* describes two pieces of wood which have been sawn from one piece so that the grain of the two pieces matches.

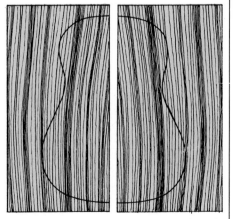

Two pieces of "book-matched" timber.

In practice, you will rarely see a soundboard of this quality. In fact, any pine or spruce which is unblemished and fairly straight-grained will make a fine soundboard for a flat-top steel-string guitar. Other woods also used include cedar and redwood. Redwood is popular with American guitar-makers as it is easily available in the United States.

In some cases, guitar soundboards are made from "plywood" or "laminated" tim-

bers. *Plywood* consists of thin layers of wood which are glued together so that the grain of each alternate layer runs at right angles. Such a piece of wood is likely to be extremely strong – much stronger than a solid piece of pine or spruce – but it will be much more rigid, will not vibrate in the same way and will therefore not produce as good a tone.

The term *laminated* is used for a type of plywood sheeting made with better quality veneers. It also differs in that the grain of each layer sometimes runs in the same direction. Parallel-grained laminated soundboards are used mainly by manufacturers of lower-priced instruments.

Contrary to expectation, not all "flat-top" steel-string acoustic guitars actually have flat tops. The soundboard is in fact often given a slight curve or "arch". The reasons for this are as follows. From a structural point of view, giving the soundboard and the back of the guitar body a slight curve will make it stronger and help prevent cracking and distortion of shape. Such soundboards are also less likely to be affected by extreme changes of humidity and temperature. Some guitar-makers also claim that a curved soundboard gives the instrument a better tone; this is, of course, a subjective judgment.

All guitar soundboards are strengthened by a pattern of struts and braces on the inside of the soundbox (see p. 34). However, the designs for internal strutting and bracing vary considerably. Ideally, a soundboard should vibrate in a uniform way, with the strutting giving only structural support and strength. The strutting pattern can radically affect the sound of a guitar.

To give extra strength to the bridge area of the soundboard, a piece of wood is usually fitted to the underside directly beneath the bridge. Some makers also glue a thin veneer of timber to the underside of the soundboard around the soundhole/rosette area to add some extra strength.

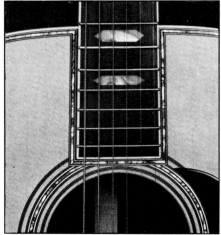

Soundboard decoration
The soundboards of Martin's top guitars are made from best-quality, solid spruce. The D-45 shown here has abalone inlaid by hand around the soundhole, fingerboard and linings.

The *rosette* is the decorative inlay around the soundhole. Traditionally, it is made in a similar way to the edgings, with a series of wood veneers which may be in natural colors or dyed to provide contrasting colors. However, synthetic materials are being used more and more frequently. The rosette is generally regarded as purely decorative, but it in fact strengthens the area of the soundboard weakened by the soundhole. Design themes featured in the edgings and other parts of the instrument are frequently continued with the rosette.

The ribs, back and body construction

The *ribs* of an acoustic guitar are the shaped sides which follow the curved outline of the soundbox. Whereas the soundboards of quality instruments tend to be made only from spruce, the less crucial ribs and back can be made in various timbers with good results. The ribs and back are usually made in a matching hardwood. At the top end of the market, Brazilian rosewood remains the first choice – in both classical and steel-string guitar construction. However, many makers settle for Indian rosewood as a close second since the Brazilian variety is in increasingly short supply. Other hardwoods frequently and successfully used include African walnut, mahogany, maple and sycamore.

In ideal terms, the guitar back should be made using two pieces of book-matched timber. However, designs do vary – even to the extent of making the back from three pieces of wood.

The standard two-piece back is made by butting the two pieces of timber together with a glued joint. This joint is usually strengthened on the inside surface with a fairly flat-section strip of hardwood which should have its grain set at right angles to that of the back. The back is then strutted or braced in a similar way to the soundboard, and it is quite often curved in the same way by making the struts to a slightly convex shape. Sometimes a decorative inlay is set along the joint in the center of the back.

The ribs are made up of two pieces of hardwood which meet at the point where the neck will be fitted onto the soundbox (the *top block*) and again at the opposite point at the tail end of the soundbox (the *bottom block*). The join at the top block will eventually be covered by the neck and its heel. The join at the bottom block is dealt with in a variety of ways. Some makers set a wedge-shaped piece of wood at this point. Others decorate or disguise the join using inlays. Some lower-priced instruments simply have a butt joint.

The top block is usually far more substantial than the bottom block as it has to accommodate the female slot of the dovetail joint by which the neck is attached to the body. Honduras mahogany is a popular choice for both blocks but the choice of wood varies. The top block is traditionally made from one solid piece of timber, but many makers prefer to use a laminated block which will give far more strength.

The most common method of forming and assembling the body of an acoustic guitar involves the use of a *mold* or *former*.

When the ribs have been cut to shape and prepared, they have to be formed or shaped into the curves that follow the shape of the body. To achieve this, the wood is first soaked in water until it becomes pliable. The ribs are then bent into shape around a metal *bending pipe* which is heated so that, as the ribs are placed against it, the water turns to steam and the dried-out wood retains the shape it is given. After shaping, it is common practice to clamp the ribs in the mold overnight or at least for a few hours to prevent them from losing the shape they have been given.

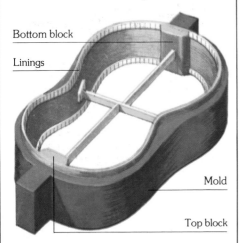

Bottom block

Linings

Mold

Top block

Construction molds

Guitar-makers usually have a number of different molds which will give them a variety of body shapes and dimensions. Molds are traditionally made in one piece, using hardwood for maximum stability, but in recent years metal molds (as here) and two-piece molds have become more common.

This is the point at which the guitar soundbox really starts to take shape. With the ribs in position in the mold, the top and bottom blocks are glued and clamped into place – thus joining the two ribs and forming the outline shape of the guitar soundbox. The "linings" are then glued and clamped to the ribs so that finally the soundboard and back can also be glued and clamped in place.

The linings

Linings are continuous strips of wood employed solely for the purpose of making good joints inside the soundbox – between the soundboard, ribs and back. Without them, the thickness of the soundboard, ribs and back is not sufficient to allow reasonable joints to be made. To aid the bending of the linings and so that they match the shape formed by the ribs, they are "kerfed". This means that a saw cut is made through the bulk of the lining every ¼ in. (6 mm) or ½ in. (12.5 mm) along its length.

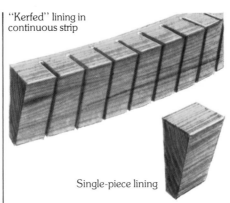

"Kerfed" lining in continuous strip

Single-piece lining

Small wedge-shaped pieces of wood are an alternative to continuous linings. They are fixed in exactly the same way – by gluing and then clamping. Whichever method is used, the wood is tapered or rounded to do away with superfluous timber. By doing this the maker can keep the weight of the linings down and also ensure that their shape will have a minimal effect on the internal dimensions of the soundbox.

Top-class hand-made instruments might be made with pine linings joining the soundboard and the ribs and hardwood linings joining the ribs and back. Some American makers prefer to use basswood for linings. Mass-produced guitars are sometimes made with linings which are in fact laminations of two or three strips of wood.

The edging

Edging, *edge binding* and *purfling* are names given to the protective strip fitted along the outside edges of the soundbox of the guitar, where the soundboard and back join the ribs. It should be made of a durable material so that it can withstand the bangs and knocks that any guitar is bound to receive. Edging also acts as an effective moisture seal for the vulnerable end grain and forms an attractive finish to conceal the joints that would otherwise be visible.

Edging is traditionally made from thin veneers or strips of hardwood laminated together. First-class instrument-makers still employ rosewood, maple and other hardwoods for the edging on the guitars they

A selection of decorative edgings.

make, but plastic edging is by far the most widely used material on the majority of guitars being made today.

The edging pattern is sometimes repeated at the bottom of the instrument to camouflage the joint there between the ribs. The same pattern used in the edging – or a variation of it – is sometimes repeated along the edges of the neck and on the head of the instrument.

Some makers choose to elaborate on edgings by using such materials as mother-of-pearl; they may actually put more effort into edging and decoration than others put into making an entire instrument. This is, of course, all a matter of personal taste. Other makers feel that decoration should be kept to a minimum for aesthetic and tonal reasons.

Fingerplates

Also known as "scratch plates" or "pickguards", *fingerplates* have no function other than to protect the soundboard from the scratching and wear caused by the guitarist's plectrums and fingerpicks. Classical guitars do not have fingerplates, but they are almost always added to steel-string guitars.

The traditional material used for fingerplates has always been tortoiseshell but more than adequate man-made imitations are readily available nowadays. Fingerplates are sometimes decorated with engraving and inlays.

The fingerplate is really a compromise. Ideally the soundboard should be as flexible as possible and should be allowed to vibrate freely. This is why fingerplates should be moderately thin and made from a material that will not inhibit the sound of the instrument. Of course, some famous guitars have very large, very thick fingerplates (Gibson "Everly Brothers", for example); the amount by which this affects the tone is open to debate.

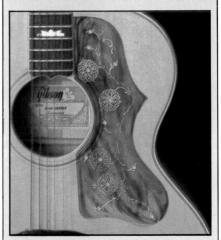

Decorative fingerplates

This large, elaborately embellished tortoiseshell fingerplate is one of the most distinctive features of the Gibson J-200 Artist.

The neck and truss rod

The construction of necks for acoustic guitars varies considerably. The simplest type is shaped from a single piece of wood – usually a hardwood such as mahogany, maple, rosewood or African walnut. But this method is expensive, and a far more popular alternative is to make the neck up in its rough, unshaped form by using three pieces of wood. A further variation involves building up the section from which the *heel* will be formed by means of laminated layers of wood. Laminated

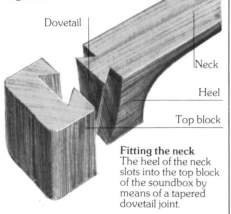

Neck construction
When carving a one-piece neck, some sixty per cent or more of the wood is cut away. The process is hardly cost-effective. One-piece necks are often preferred by traditionalists but they are rarely seen these days.

necks are highly regarded because of their strength and stability.

A dovetail joint is the most common method used for fitting the neck of a flat-top steel-string guitar to the body of the instrument. The end of the neck and heel are shaped into the male part of the dovetail joint. The recess or female slot is cut out of the top block. The neck is then inserted and the joint is glued.

Fitting the neck
The heel of the neck slots into the top block of the soundbox by means of a tapered dovetail joint.

Some classical guitar-makers choose to fit an additional hardwood strip set into a groove in the neck underneath the fingerboard. This is to provide more strength against the pull of the strings. Steel-string guitars, however, have a far greater string tension so something stronger is needed. In the early days of flat-top guitar construction it became common

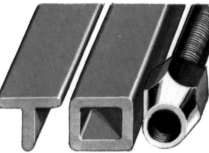

Adjustable truss rod set inside guitar neck beneath fingerboard.

Truss rods
Most modern steel-string guitars (with the noticeable exception of Martin) are now fitted with adjustable truss rods. Increasing or reducing the amount of tension on the rod can help to keep the neck straight when switching to different gauge strings.

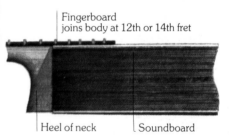

Martin T-bar Martin hollow bar Gibson adjustable truss rod

practice to fit a metal strip, tube or "T" section into a similar groove running along the length of the neck just below the fingerboard. This metal strengthening piece is called the *truss rod* or *neck rod*.

During the 1920s the Gibson company came up with an *adjustable* truss rod which they fitted to their arch-top f-hole guitars with great success. Gibson-type adjustable truss rods – and subsequent developments of them – are fitted to the vast majority of steel-string guitars being made today.

The rod is situated in a central groove or channel running along the length of the neck in more or less the same position as the hardwood strip or steel section fitted in non-adjustable guitar necks. A further strip of wood is often fitted to close the top of the channel before the fingerboard is added (see p. 35). The truss rod is usually fixed securely in the heel. Because the head of the guitar is tilted back at an angle to the neck, the truss rod can be made to finish below the surface of the head and yet still be accessible for adjustment. With most guitars, a small cover-plate which butts up to the nut is all that has to be removed to reveal the adjusting nut of the truss rod. The end of the truss rod is threaded to accept the adjusting nut and washer. (Some guitars have a slightly different arrangement which may mean they are adjusted with a screwdriver, Allen key or a special tool provided by the guitar-maker.) See p. 168 for how the adjustment is made.

The fingerboard

The *fingerboard* or *fretboard* is the piece of wood fitted to the front of the neck. The frets are set into it. Traditionally, ebony is the first choice of material, but rosewood and other dark hardwoods are more common today.

When the neck is jointed onto the guitar soundbox, its front surface is finished flush with the soundboard. The fingerboard is then glued on so that it runs along the front of the neck and the front of the soundboard. On steel-string guitars, the 12th or 14th fret is usually in line with the join between the neck and body, and there are usually a further six frets on the part of the fingerboard that fits onto the soundboard. On classical guitars, the neck is shorter and joins the body at the 12th fret. This fret is called the *body fret*.

A series of saw cuts is made in the fingerboard to accept the frets. The frets are "T" shaped in section. The top of the fret is rounded so there are no sharp edges to damage the fingers or strings. The upright stem of the "T" is serrated which means it has a roughened edge that grips the sides of the slot in the fingerboard when it has been gently hammered into place. Most steel-string guitars also have *fret markers* inlaid into the fingerboard. They are simply a visual aid to help the guitarist identify fingering positions.

Classical and flamenco guitars usually have flat fingerboards, but many steel-string guitars

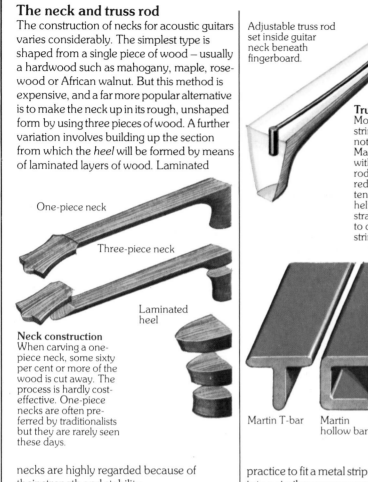

Fingerboard joins body at 12th or 14th fret

Heel of neck   Soundboard

have fingerboards with a slightly convex curve to the fretted playing surface.

All fingerboards are narrower at the nut (where the strings are closer together) than they are at the other end. But the actual width varies quite a bit from guitar to guitar.

In my experience, I have found that a preference for different widths and shapes is very much a matter of personal choice. Some guitarists are very adaptable and feel totally at home playing different instruments with varying widths of fingerboard. Others go into a state of depression if they lose their number-one guitar and claim that they feel uncomfortable even with an exact replacement model. Beginners tend to become used to the instrument on which they learn to play and usually feel awkward when forced to change to a different guitar. The only advice I can give is to learn on different types – for instance, an electric guitar with a relatively narrow neck and a classical guitar with a fairly wide neck. You should then find it easy to pick up virtually any guitar and play without difficulty.

The bridge

The vibrations or energy from the guitar strings are transmitted to the soundboard through the saddle and bridge. The bridge must be efficient in the transmission of this energy and strong in both its construction and the way it is attached to the soundboard. There are two basic types of bridge. One is the *floating bridge* (usually used on f-hole guitars) and the other is the *fixed bridge* (generally the type fitted to flat-tops).

A floating bridge is so-called because it is not actually fixed to the soundboard but is held in place simply by the tension of the strings which pass over it. The strings are secured to a fixed *tailpiece*. Floating bridges can therefore be moved backwards and forwards to correct the intonation if necessary.

Fixed bridges are glued to the top of the soundboard and cannot be moved. There is usually no separate tailpiece; instead, the strings are anchored directly to the bridge. The joint between the bridge and the soundboard must be first class. Both surfaces are usually "toothed" or "keyed", meaning that the surfaces of the wood are roughened in order to make the joint stronger.

The traditional and by far the best material for fixed bridges is ebony. It has a high density which aids sustain and the transference of vibration. Substitute woods used to good effect include rosewood, masonia, mahogany and walnut.

On flat-top guitars, the strings are usually secured to a fixed bridge by *bridge pins*.

These hold the ends of the strings in place in the *bridge pin holes*. They are tapered so that when they are inserted in the holes in the bridge a snug fit is achieved without the pins becoming too tight. There should be a small groove in the bridge at the point where each string comes out of the bridge pin hole and turns at a sharp angle towards the saddle.

The *slotted bridge* is a fairly recent innovation and differs from a standard fixed bridge only in the way the strings are attached. The bridge pins and holes are replaced by slots through which the strings are passed. The slots are large enough to allow the strings to pass through them but small enough to catch the metal "barrels" or "end-pieces" attached to the ends of the strings.

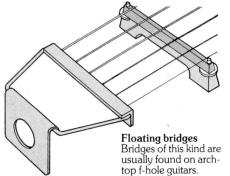

Floating bridges
Bridges of this kind are usually found on arch-top f-hole guitars.

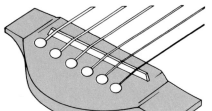

Fixed bridges
Standard on most flat-tops, the bridge is fixed to the soundboard and cannot be moved.

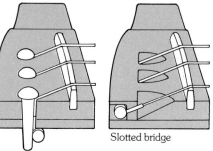

Bridge pins

Slotted bridge

The scale length and string-tension allowances

Scale length is the term used for the total length of the vibrating open string and it is measured from the inside edge of the nut to the point at which the top E string comes into contact with the saddle.

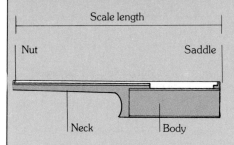

Scale lengths of most flat-top steel-string acoustic guitars range between 24 in. (61 cm) and 26 in. (66 cm). String tension increases with scale length. This is not very noticeable on six-string guitars but it is on twelve-string and bass guitars. It is generally considerably easier to fret notes on a short-scale bass than on one with a standard scale length.

Fret positions can be arrived at by a mathematical formula called the "rule of eighteen" – though it should really be known as the "rule of 17.835". The application of the formula is as follows. First, decide on the overall scale length. To find the distance between the nut and the first fret, divide the scale length by 17.835. To find the distance between the first fret and the second fret, divide the remaining distance by 17.835. This procedure is followed until the position of the final top fret is determined. Problems sometimes arise because the calculations have to be rounded to the nearest measurable fraction. With a figure like 17.835 some compromise must be reached. But there are checks which can prevent accumulative errors: the twelfth fret should be precisely in the center of the scale length; the seventh fret should be precisely two-thirds of the way between the nut and the twelfth fret.

When a fretted note is played – as opposed to a note played on an open string – the action of pushing the string down onto the fret increases the string tension. This is because the string is being stretched slightly. If no correction is made, the increase in tension will make each note played on a higher fret progressively sharper. The "intonation" of the guitar, as it is called, will then be inaccurate. Makers generally overcome this problem by moving the bridge/saddle slightly further away from the soundhole – thus increasing the length of vibrating string. The actual distance varies between makers and will vary with different scale lengths and with the height of the guitar's "action". The lighter the action, the more the string is stretched when fretted (see *Setting the intonation*, p. 171).

On most flat-top steel-string guitars, the saddle is set at an angle so that the bottom E string is between $3/16$ in. (4.8 mm) and $1/4$ in. (6.4 mm) longer than the top E string. This also relates to string tension and intonation. With any given set of six guitar strings, the top E string increases in tension the least when fretted. The B string increases slightly more because it is a slightly heavier gauge. In other words, the heavier the gauge of the string the longer it must be to avoid its pitch going up higher than the required interval when it is pushed down onto the frets. The saddle is therefore sloped as a standard procedure with flat-tops to compensate for this increase in string tension towards the heavier and thicker bass strings.

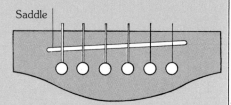

The slanted saddle
The "sloping" saddle is designed to make the thicker bass strings slightly longer than the treble strings and therefore to maintain correct intonation when their pitch rises as they are pushed down onto the frets.

The saddle

The *saddle* slots into a groove in the bridge. The strings pass over it and it provides the point at which the vibrating section of each string begins. The saddle also transmits the vibrations from the strings through the bridge to the soundboard. Though it may look rather insignificant, the saddle can have a definite effect on the tone, volume and tuning of the guitar. In the past, the best and traditionally used material has been ivory. Bone is also regarded as a good material, though it does have a tendency to yellow with age. Plastic and synthetic materials are being used more and more by the bulk of manufacturers – although they are still avoided by the makers of top-quality hand-built instruments. This is because plastics do not transfer the energy or vibration as efficiently and because a bridge made of bone or ivory will give more volume than one made from most alternative materials.

Saddles usually have a set of six (or twelve) small notches or semi-circular grooves along their top edge. The strings sit in these so that they do not slide about over the saddle when played fairly hard.

Guitars with flat fingerboards must have flat saddles; guitars with curved fingerboards should have saddles with a matching convex shape. The saddles on better-made guitars

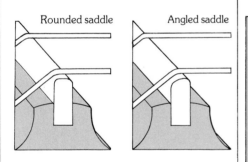

Rounded saddle   Angled saddle

also tend to be shaped or "angled" at the top (instead of rounded) so that the highest point – where the saddle comes into contact with the strings – is toward the fingerboard.

Some steel-string guitars have adjustable saddles which can be raised or lowered to alter the "action" (see *Setting the action*, p. 166). Others are supplied with a number of small spacing pieces. One or any number of these can be inserted in the slot in the bridge underneath the saddle to increase the height of the strings in relation to the fingerboard.

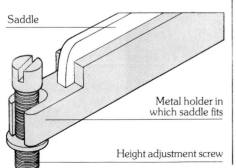

Saddle

Metal holder in which saddle fits

Height adjustment screw

The nut

The *nut* is situated on the head of the guitar at the end of the fingerboard. With the majority of flat-top steel-string acoustic guitars the nut is the point at which the scale length and the vibrating part of the string ends. As with the saddle, the traditional materials used for the nut are bone and ivory, but, as a result of cost and lack of availability, plastic and other synthetic materials are more commonplace now.

Usually, the nut is simply a piece of material with slots or grooves in which the guitar strings sit. As with the saddle, the grooves may have to be set on a curve to match that of the fingerboard. The depth of the grooves is crucial. Ideally, they should be such that fretting notes on the first fret is no harder than fretting notes on the second fret if a capo is placed on the first fret. However, if the grooves are too shallow, the strings may rattle and cause "fret buzz" and the open strings may not even sound at all. Needless to say, altering the height of the nut or the depth of the grooves will affect the "action".

On some other guitars, an extra "zero fret" is employed in conjunction with the nut. In this case, it is the extra fret – not the nut – that sets the string height and scale length. The grooves in the nut are deeper so that a downward pull is created which makes the strings sit firmly on the extra fret.

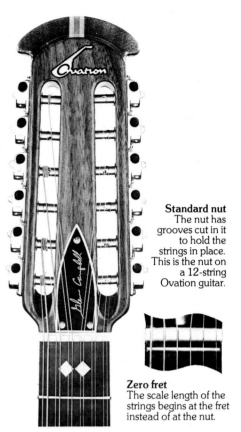

Standard nut
The nut has grooves cut in it to hold the strings in place. This is the nut on a 12-string Ovation guitar.

Zero fret
The scale length of the strings begins at the fret instead of at the nut.

The tuning heads

The *tuning heads* or *machine heads* increase or reduce the tension exerted on each string, thus raising or lowering its pitch and allowing the guitar to be correctly tuned. The tuning heads generally fitted to flat-top steel-string acoustic guitars consist of a capstan, a worm gear and a tuning button on a metal shaft, all mounted on a metal fixing plate. Some tuning heads have individual fixing plates – which means that you can replace a single tuning head should one develop a fault. Others consist of two pairs of three tuning heads which are mounted on a pair of fixing plates so that each group of three tuning heads is at a set distance apart.

Any quality tuning head should have a metal bush inserted into the hole in the headstock through which the capstan passes. This prevents undue wear and stops the capstan from binding against the wood of the head. Some kind of gearing is necessary to facilitate fine tuning, to allow the tuning button to be turned with relative ease and to prevent the string tension from turning the capstan. Gear-ratios can differ considerably, but anything in the region of 10:1 will make re-stringing and tuning relatively easy. Top-line manufacturers of tuning heads (such as Grover, for instance) have the gearing section totally enclosed to allow permanent lubrication.

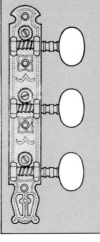

Tuning head design
On the left are three tuning heads set on a single fixing plate. This plate is attached to the side of the headstock. Most often used on classical guitars, they are of the "open" type, which means that the cogs are exposed. On the right is an exploded view of a single Ibanez tuning head. It is enclosed in a sealed housing.

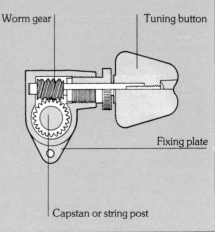

Worm gear   Tuning button

Fixing plate

Capstan or string post

Classical and flamenco guitars

Although volumes have been written on the history and origins of the "classical" or "Spanish" guitar, no precise documentation of the instrument's early development exists. Fragmented information from ancient times clearly indicates the existence of plucked and bowed stringed instruments, but the point at which the guitar as we know it first appeared is not recorded. The indications are that a form of guitar has been made and played since at least the twelfth century. Whether or not the *rebec*, lute, Moorish guitar, North African *aud* (or *al'ud*) or any of the many other stringed instruments to be found in medieval Europe were the direct antecedents of the modern classical guitar remains unproven.

What is certain is the fact that Spain was at the center of its development. Of the handful of great men who truly shaped the history of the classical guitar, most were from Spain. The influence of one of the greatest – guitarist, composer and teacher José Ferdinand Sor (1778-1839), better known as Fernando Sor – is still felt to this day. Born in Barcelona, he took up the guitar after studying violin, cello, harmony and composition. By the age of sixteen he was able to play his own compositions on the guitar with a virtuosity that set new standards. He went on to compose over 400 pieces, many of which are considered essential to the contemporary classical guitarist's repertoire. Sor was also known as a teacher and as the author of his famous "Method", an extensive work which documented his style and technique in great detail.

Sor traveled extensively in Europe. In Paris he met the French guitar-maker, René-Francois Lacôte, and in London he met another well-known luthier, Louis Panormo. Both were impressed by the superior tone and quality of the Spanish-made guitars that he played, and both began to employ Spanish methods of construction and design in their own workshops. In fact, Panormo's instruments were subsequently given labels stating "The only maker of guitars in the Spanish style – Louis Panormo".

Nevertheless, Panormo and Lacôte were exceptional in their adoption of Spanish methods. In general, guitars made in other European countries had their own regional characteristics. The English, French, Italians and others were making finely crafted and beautifully decorated instruments, but when it came to tone, projection and sustain Spanish guitars were far superior.

The instruments played by Sor and his most famous contemporaries – Dionisio Aguado (1784-1849) and Matteo Carcassi (1792-1853), for instance – were, however, far inferior to the guitars at the disposal of today's players. All that changed – with a quantum jump in the development of classi-

cal guitar construction – at the hands of a carpenter from San Sebastian de Almería, Antonio de Torres Jurado (1817-1892). Better known simply as Torres, he was without a doubt the most important figure in the history of guitar design and construction. Musicians who played his guitars immediately discarded those of other makers. Throughout Spain luthiers adopted Torres's designs. In fact, to this day, classical guitar-makers still construct their instruments almost exactly in the manner of Torres.

Torres first learned the principles of guitar-making in the Grenada workshops of José Pernas. His friend and guitarist, Julian Arcas, suggested that he work on ways of improving the tone of the guitar. This he did. By the middle of the nineteenth century he was making guitars bearing his own name, and over a period of years he gradually refined his ideas, building experimental instruments of varying

The classical guitar
Classical guitars now have nylon strings (though they were originally gut) as these give a more appropriate tone. The system of internal bracing still owes a great deal to Torres. In spite of slight variations and modifications (for example, the famous classical guitar made in 1956 by the Frenchman Robert Bouchet), his basic fan-shaped pattern is still widely used.

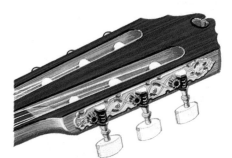

Tuning heads   Worm-gear tuning heads with ivory, bone or plastic capstans on which strings are wound.

Fingerboard   African ebony or dark rosewood.

Neck   Usually mahogany or cedar. Classical necks are shorter and wider than those on steel-string guitars; they have only 19 frets and join the body at the 12th fret.

Soundboard   European spruce or pine.

Ribs and back   Rosewood – although maple, walnut, birch and other hardwoods are often used successfully.

Bridge   Nylon strings threaded through holes and then knotted.

Guitar made in 1854

Guitar made in 1888

The development of Torres's guitar designs
Two of Torres's guitars illustrate how he evolved the basic design of the modern classical guitar.

sizes and shapes and trying constructional methods which were quite revolutionary.

He increased the area of the soundboard and the size of the soundbox, making his guitars "deeper" (the soundboard-to-back measurement of the guitar had previously been 2 in. [5 cm] or less). He rounded the bouts and changed their relative proportions. He reduced the thickness of the timbers used for the soundboard, ribs and back, and used lighter and more flexible woods. He evolved a system of "fan" strutting that allowed the soundboard to vibrate far more efficiently, he arrived at the 65 cm (approx. 25½ in.) scale length, and he improved guitar varnishes.

By completely re-defining the science of guitar construction, Torres improved the instrument to such a degree that major musical advances were almost inevitable. It was another Spaniard who was to utilize these advantages. His name was Francisco Eixea Tárrega (1852-1909). Tárrega is universally considered to be the father of all modern classical guitar technique.

He evolved the posture, hand positions and use of the foot-stool to raise the left foot that are taught to every student of the classical guitar today. He also transcribed the works of such great composers as Bach, Beethoven and Mozart for the guitar, and, although he was not the first to adapt music written for other instruments, he was the first to challenge the long-held opinion that the guitar was an inferior instrument incapable of doing justice to such music.

It is of course impossible to talk about the development of the classical guitar without acknowledging Andrés Torres Segovia (b. 1893). Having made his concert debut in Paris in 1924, by the 1930s Segovia's name was known around the world. Perhaps more than any other single player, he has been responsible for the acceptance of the guitar as a valid concert instrument for the performance of classical music.

Andrés Segovia
Segovia is an avid student of every aspect of the guitar and its most knowledgeable historian.

Flamenco guitars

Flamenco is the music of the gypsy people of Andalucia, the region of Spain bounded by Córdoba in the north, Cadiz in the south, Almeria in the east and Huelva in the west. The origins of flamenco are obscure, although it is generally accepted to have North African (Moorish) influences. It emerged towards the end of the eighteenth century when it was always played as a combination of dance, song and guitar accompaniment. Later, the original form gave rise to two subsequent developments: *cante flamenco* (based on different song forms) and solo flamenco guitar. The man credited for the birth of the solo guitar form is Ramón Montoya (1880-1949).

Flamenco has traditionally been passed from generation to generation without the aid of musical notation. The music is frequently regarded as a loose, undisciplined form. In fact, this is not so. It is a combination of improvisation and strict rhythmic structures, of which there are many. Flamenco is no simple man's music. The *soleares*, for example, one of the four most important structures, has a rhythm based on a twelve-beat form, with accents on the third, sixth, eighth and tenth beats, and is played in ¾ time. Several of the other song forms have rhythmic patterns that are considerably more complex, and a guitarist often specializes in only one of them.

The flamenco guitar
Flamenco guitar construction is based on the design of the Spanish classical guitar, with modifications to suit the requirements of flamenco. Once again, Torres is the key figure: he evolved the basic design to which today's makers still adhere. The flamenco guitar is usually slightly smaller than the classical guitar. Its back and ribs are made from Spanish cyprus tooled very thinly to produce a more brilliant, more penetrating sound and to give the instrument greater volume. This does, however, result in a loss of mellowness and tone which explains why some solo flamenco guitarists play classical guitars.

Tuning heads Traditionally, wooden pegs are considered to give a better tone than geared.

Fingerboard Usually African ebony.

Neck Various hardwoods – often mahogany.

Strings Set closer to the body to give a faster "action". Flamenco guitars are often strung with higher tension strings.

Soundboard European spruce or pine.

Ribs and back Spanish cyprus.

Golpe Special "tap" plates to protect the face of the guitar – since "golpe strokes" (striking and tapping with the fingers) are an integral part of the rhythm and sound of flamenco music.

Bridge Most flamenco guitars have the same style of bridge as those fitted to classical guitars. For details on how to fit and tie the knots on the strings, see p. 165.

Steel-string acoustic guitars

The steel-string guitar as we know it today evolved in America, though the majority of the instrument makers who contributed to its development were European or of European descent. During the latter half of the nineteenth and the early part of the twentieth century, America had become a huge cultural melting pot. For a number of reasons – including racial, religious and political persecution – thousands of European, Russian and other emigrants were crossing the Atlantic and seeking a new life in America. Among them were highly skilled musical instrument makers who were to dominate the construction and production of the steel-string acoustic guitar.

Two distinctly different methods of construction evolved. The first led to what is known as the *flat-top* guitar and, basically, adapted European classical guitar-making techniques. The second method produced the *arch-top* (or *f-hole*) guitar, with a contoured or arched soundboard and back carved from a solid piece of wood. Its design and construction were derived from European violin-making techniques.

Any history of steel-string acoustic guitars must begin with the names Martin and Gibson, the most influential of all the manufacturers. Over the next few pages we will take a look at the Martin organization and its guitars, at the Gibson company, and at a few of the other manufacturers who have made, and still make, excellent and lasting guitars.

Martin guitars
In 1833, Christian Frederick Martin (1796-1873) emigrated from his native Germany to America and opened a combined workshop and music store in New York. He was already an accomplished instrument maker, having worked as foreman for the highly regarded luthier, Johann Stauffer, in Vienna. The first guitars Christian Frederick made in New York were heavily influenced by Stauffer's gut-string classical instruments. They featured a floating fingerboard, an adjustable neck and all six machine heads on one side of the headstock. They were also quite narrow, as was typical before the influence of Torres (see p. 42). Before long, however, Martin evolved more personal and more original designs and

How to identify Martin guitars

The system Martin uses for cataloguing its guitars is quite complex and has been further complicated by a long history during which models have been refined, altered, discontinued and re-introduced. However, in simple terms, this is how it works.

Each guitar has a two-part "code". The first part (either a letter or a number) indicates the *size* of the guitar, and the second part (a number) indicates the *style*. A Martin OO-18, for example, is therefore a "OO" size guitar made and decorated in the "18" style. A D-28 is a "Dreadnought" size, "28" style guitar. It follows that "45" style guitars

– those with spruce tops, rosewood backs and sides, ebony fingerboards and the famous abalone pearl inlays – can be found in various different sizes. They can – the OO-45, OOO-45, OM-45 and D-45.

There are, of course, exceptions to the rule. There are also further complications such as the addition of a "12" to indicate a 12-string guitar, a "K" to distinguish one with a koa wood body, or a "C" which can mean either "classical", "carved-top" or "cutaway". Many early Martins had a number as the first half of their code, and some still do (e.g., the 7-28 or the 5-18).

What the letters mean	
O	Concert size
OO	Grand concert size
OOO	Auditorium size
D	Dreadnought size
DS	Dreadnought with a slotted headstock and 12 frets to the body not 14
M	Grand auditorium size
MC	Grand auditorium with cutaway
OM	Orchestra model
C	Classical or carved-top model
N	"European-style" classical model
F	F-hole model
T	Tenor or "Terz" 4-string banjo guitar
K	Koa wood soundbox instead of the customary spruce plus rosewood or mahogany

O-16NY
First introduced 1971 as new, authentic version of original pre-1929 "New York Martin". Small "O" size and "16" style. Spruce top, quartersawn mahogany back and sides, slotted headstock, wide rosewood fingerboard, no fret markers or fingerplate.

OO-18
"OO" size guitars date back to mid-1800s and "18" style first appeared 1857. Current "18" style features 14-fret neck, solid headstock, white dot fret markers, "belly" bridge, dark edgings and fingerplate.

OOO-28
"OOO" size guitars also go back to mid-19th century. The famous "28" style emerged sometime before 1874 and remains almost unchanged. Rosewood back and sides, spruce top, white edging.

OM-45
When first introduced between 1929 and 1933, "OM" series were first Martin guitars to have 14-fret necks. Size is same as current "OOO" 14-fret guitars. "45" styling dates from 1904 and includes inlays of pearl abalone all around soundbox, rosette, fingerboard and headstock.

M-38
First appeared in 1977 as updated version of vintage 1930s Martin f-hole guitars (the F-7 and F-9) – but with flat top and round soundhole instead of original carved top.

MC-28
Same size as "Grand Auditorium" M-38 and M-28, but with a body cutaway allowing easier access to the high frets. Also features an oval soundhole. This is Martin's newest guitar.

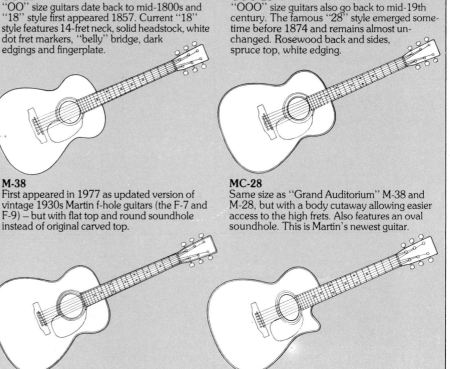

One of Martin's earliest guitars
This gut-string instrument was built by C.F. Martin in about 1834 and its distinctive shape owes a lot to his former boss, Johann Stauffer. The angle of the neck can be adjusted by means of a clock key inserted in the back of the heel.

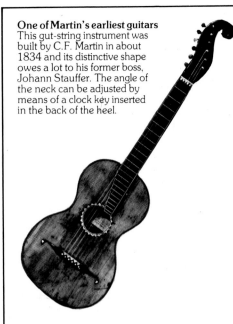

gained himself a reputation as a fine maker of classical guitars in his own right.

Christian Frederick did not enjoy New York city life and so, in 1839, he moved to Nazareth, Pennsylvania, which has remained the home of the Martin factory to this day. Initially, an agency called C.A. Zoebisch & Sons acted as sole New York distributor for Martin after the move. Christian Frederick, his son, Christian Frederick II, and a nephew, Christian Frederick Hartman, all worked together in the company until Christian Frederick Senior died in 1873. When, in 1888, Christian Frederick II also died, his son Frank Henry Martin took over the company. He terminated the unsatisfactory distribution agreement with C.A. Zoebisch and from that time sold instruments directly from Nazareth.

Under Frank Henry Martin, the company continued to grow – modifying and improving designs and introducing new models and new instruments (mandolins, ukuleles, mando-cellos and "tenor" guitars). In fact, the 1920s and 1930s were a time of considerable innovation.

It was at the beginning of the 1920s that the company started making steel-string guitars in earnest. To some extent, this was in response to the increasing demand for steel-string guitars fueled by the popularity of folk and country and western music. At first, Martin simply strengthened their highly regarded classical guitars in order to make the switch from gut strings to steel strings. Later, other changes were made – the "belly" bridge and truss rod were introduced to give additional support against the increased string tension, the saddle was slanted, and the dimensions of the bracing were re-designed.

Like Gibson, Martin made a variety of stringed instruments at different times to meet changing popular demands. But it was their flat-top steel string acoustics which set the standards of excellence and which became probably the most copied guitars of their type.

Martin "Dreadnoughts"

These are perhaps the most legendary of all Martin guitars. Named after the British battleship *Dreadnaught*, they were first introduced by Martin in 1931. In fact, however, they date back to 1916 when the company made a range of guitars for the Ditson company of Boston. The design of these "Ditson Spanish Models" was agreed between Harry Hunt of Ditson's New York showroom and Frank Henry Martin. They all had the now-famous wide waists and narrow, sloping shoulders. When the Ditson company folded in the late 1920s, Martin realized that there was nevertheless a considerable demand for the largest of the Ditson guitars. They therefore began making prototype instruments using designs closer to their own guitars. They changed the "fan bracing" – which was a feature of the Ditsons – to the "X-bracing" used on most Martin soundboards.

The first true Martin Dreadnoughts were the D-18 and D-28. They were based on the existing "18" and "28" styles but were built to the enlarged "D" (for Dreadnought) size. The original models had necks which joined the body at the 12th fret, but by about 1934 customer demand had made 14-fret necks the standard feature (partly because a lot of banjo players, changing over to the guitar at the time, were used to slightly longer-necked instruments).

Dreadnoughts have had an enormous influence on acoustic guitar design. Their somewhat "bassier" tone has made them popular in folk, country and bluegrass music, as well as rock. They have been copied in some form or another by just about every other guitar manufacturer. Vintage D-45s (with their beautiful abalone inlay) and HD-28s are highly coveted, very rare and very expensive.

Close-up of herringbone inlay

Martin HD-28
The first prototype for the HD-28 was made in 1931 for a country singer called "Arkie". It was a 12-fret model and was called the D-2. Over the next few years, the guitar went into production as the HD-28 – the "H" standing for the famous herringbone pattern edging – and it became one of Martin's most highly regarded instruments.

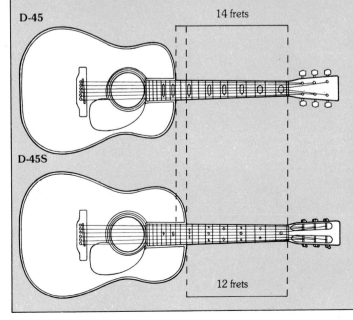

D-45

D-45S

14 frets

12 frets

Neck lengths
When, in 1934, Martin introduced their new 14-fret Dreadnoughts, the term "DS" was used to designate the superseded, original 12-fret models. These drawings illustrate the difference.

However, Martin themselves – as well as most discerning guitar players – were in fact aware that the 12-fret guitars, with their longer sound-boxes, actually had a superior tone.

Finally, in 1967, the original style was re-introduced as an alternative in the form of the D-18S, D-28S, D-35S and, later, the legendary D-45S.

Arch-top guitars

These instruments (also known as "cello", "plectrum", "orchestra" or "f-hole" guitars) came into their own during the 1920s when jazz was a vibrant, evolving musical force and the "Big Band Era" was in full swing. As the guitar began to overtake the banjo in popularity, guitarists were looking for an instrument that produced enough volume to be heard clearly – not only as part of a relatively small group playing "loud syncopated jazz music" but also in big bands such as the Duke Ellington Orchestra. Since regular flat-top or gut-string classical guitars did not project sufficiently, they turned to the new arch-top steel-strings like Gibson's Master Tone L-5.

The fundamental difference between an arch-top and a flat-top acoustic guitar lies in the construction of the soundbox or body. Traditionally, the soundboard and back of an arch-top are carved from fairly thick, solid pieces of wood – a technique which allows for much greater "arching" or "contouring" than on flat-top guitars.

In fact, as arch-top guitars gained in popularity, the Gretsch company started using a different process. Instead of carving the soundboard and back, they laminated them. The soundboard and back each consisted of several thin layers of flat wood which were held in a former or mold while being glued together. When the glue had set and the wood was removed from the mold, it retained its required arched shape.

Gibson's arch-top guitars also saw the introduction of the "adjustable two-footed floating bridge" – a design adapted from the violin family. The strings are fixed to a "tailpiece" and merely pass over the bridge instead of being anchored to it. Moreover, the floating bridge itself is not glued to the face of the soundboard but is held in place simply by the tension of the strings.

In the very early days, some arch-top guitars were made with round or oval soundholes. But, following the example of Gibson's L-5, most makers switched to the now-standard "f-hole" design – another feature borrowed from the violin.

All arch-tops have a much simpler system of internal bracing than flat-top guitars. Essentially, this is because they require fewer struts. Firstly, the arched shape of the soundboard makes it intrinsically stronger. Secondly, the strings are anchored via the tailpiece to the bottom block, not via the bridge to the soundboard.

Arch-top acoustic guitars are no longer as dominant as they were in the twenties and thirties – partly due to a decline of interest in the music for which they were made, but mostly due to the subsequent emergence of the electric guitar. However, some of the most famous models (including early instruments produced by Gibson, Martin, Epiphone, D'Angelico and Vega) are highly regarded and keenly sought by collectors.

Gibson guitars

If Martin is the first name in the history of flat-top acoustics, then Gibson is the most important when it comes to arch-tops.

Orville Gibson was born in Chataugay, New York, in 1856. Keen on wood-carving as well as being an accomplished mandolin and guitar player, he made experimental mandolins that utilized violin construction methods. In the 1890s, he applied the same principles to guitars – producing some fine arch-top, oval-soundhole instruments and pioneering the use of steel instead of gut strings. He carved their arched soundboards and backs from relatively thick pieces of wood, matching the tone of front and back by tapping them and carving the wood until he felt they were compatible.

In 1902, a group of businessmen from the township of Kalamazoo entered into an agreement with Orville Gibson, and the "Gibson Mandolin-Guitar Manufacturing Co. Ltd" was formed. In 1903, the first catalogue appeared and by the time Gibson died in 1918 his company had a solid and formidable reputation.

The death of the founder did not put a stop to the company. In 1920, Lloyd Loar joined Gibson. During the four years he worked there – and before he left to form the unsuccessful Vivi-Tone company – he was responsible for the invention of the famous Gibson L-5, introduced in 1924.

Gibson Harp-Guitar
Built sometime during the 1920s, this very rare instrument was based on an original made by Orville Gibson. It has 12 extra bass strings (one for each key) as well as the standard 6 guitar strings.

Gibson L-5
Invented by Lloyd Loar, the L-5 was the first ever f-hole guitar. This later model (about 1946) has been fitted with a "Charlie Christian" pick-up (see p. 54).

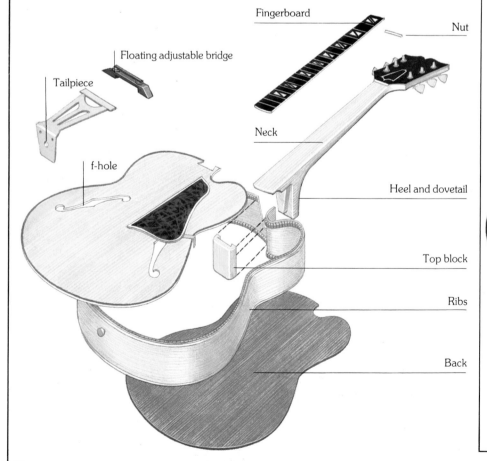

Fingerboard

Nut

Floating adjustable bridge

Tailpiece

Neck

f-hole

Heel and dovetail

Top block

Ribs

Back

The L-5 replaced the single oval soundhole with two "f-holes". It had an adjustable floating bridge which could be raised or lowered, an improved neck design which made it easier to play, and a raised finger-plate. It was also one of the first guitars to be fitted with Ted McHugh's adjustable truss rod. The L-5 was a huge success. It virtually replaced the banjo as a rhythm instrument, but it also had sufficient volume to trigger a new musical era in which the guitar was used for playing single-note solos.

Further innovations were to follow. In 1934, Gibson introduced their Super 400 – so-called because at that time 400 dollars was what it cost. In 1939, in reponse to the growing use of the guitar for lead playing, both the L-5 and Super 400 were brought out with a single "Venetian" cutaway.

Gibson entered the flat-top acoustic guitar market during the mid-1930s with their "jumbo" size guitars, designed to compete with Martin's Dreadnoughts. The successful SJ-200 went into production in 1936-7. In following years it was joined by the J-45 and J-50, and later (in 1962) by the Dove, Hummingbird and Everly Brothers guitars.

Spurred on by strong competition from Guild, Ovation and many smaller companies, Gibson produced a new series of "Mark" flat-tops in 1977. Unfortunately, the guitars have not been a success.

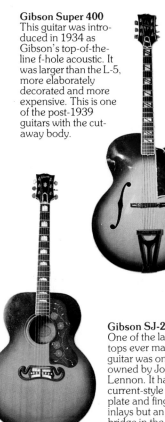

Gibson Super 400
This guitar was introduced in 1934 as Gibson's top-of-the-line f-hole acoustic. It was larger than the L-5, more elaborately decorated and more expensive. This is one of the post-1939 guitars with the cutaway body.

Gibson SJ-200
One of the largest flat-tops ever made, this guitar was once owned by John Lennon. It has the current-style finger-plate and fingerboard inlays but an original bridge in the shape of buffalo horns.

Other American guitar-makers

Martin and Gibson have not been allowed to dominate completely the manufacture of acoustic guitars. Back in the 1890s, the Washburn company was a strong competitor to Martin, and Washburn guitars are still made today. At around the same time, the Vega and Harmony companies were also started. Vega made small numbers of excellent arch-tops; Harmony, in contrast, concentrated on mass production. They claimed to have built 10 million guitars since 1945.

Following the success of Gibson's L-5, Epiphone built a reputation as makers of fine arch-top guitars – with the mid-1930s

D'Angelico New Yorker (left)
Hand-built by John D'Angelico in the 1930s, only about 300 of these superb guitars were ever made.

Guild F-212 (right)
Guild's 12-strings are among the best-known flat-top acoustics.

Japanese guitar-makers

During the 1960s, an influx of well-made, considerably cheaper guitars from Japan posed a grave threat to American manufacturers. Although Martin, Gibson and Guild have all survived the competition – either by

Emperor and Triumph, in particular. On a smaller scale, the now-legendary guitars made by John D'Angelico also appeared.

As the flat-top guitar gained in popularity – reaching a peak in the 1960s – Epiphone and Guild (a company formed in 1952) began producing in very large numbers.

Maccaferri guitars

Mario Maccaferri deserves a special mention. His most famous guitars – those which he designed for the French Selmer company between 1932 and 1933 – are identified in most people's minds with Django Reinhardt. The early models had the distinctive body cutaway, a D-shaped soundhole, and an extra sound chamber *inside* the soundbox.

A very rare 1932 Maccaferri/Selmer guitar.

concentrating on the higher price range or by getting their cheaper models manufactured under license in Japan – Japanese guitars now make up a large percentage of the market in both Europe and the United States.

Yamaha FG-375
One of the first Japanese manufacturers, Yamaha makes a wide selection of flat-top acoustics. More expensive now than they once were, they are nevertheless all excellent guitars.

Ovation guitars

In recent years, Ovation has been responsible for by far the most significant new development in the design and construction of acoustic guitars. The Ovation company, a division of the Kaman aerospace organization, was founded by Charles Kaman in the 1960s. Kaman believed that guitar design could be radically improved if he and his engineers could apply to it some of the principles of vibration and acoustics that they had learned from their work with helicopters and other aircraft. Aware of the fact that in a conventional guitar much of the sound is either "trapped" in the corners of the soundbox or absorbed by the wood, he began building instruments whose back and sides were replaced by a one-piece, rounded bowl made of a fiberglass material called "Lyrachord". This shell-like, molded back has no corners, requires no struts and reflects more of the natural sound. Ovation guitars have wooden soundboards made of sitka spruce tapered from the neck to the bridge. The bracing pattern varies from one model to another and is specially designed to give the sound best

suited to the style of music for which the guitar is intended. The neck is built up from separate pieces of mahogany and maple integrated with a steel tension rod set inside an aluminum channel.

Since its first model, the Balladeer, was introduced in 1966, Ovation has produced from polyurethane and aluminum). well as a complete range of different 6-string instruments. All of these are also available in "acoustic-electric" versions with Ovation's own built-in piezo-electric pickups and battery-operated pre-amp.

The company's newest models are the highly expensive "Adamas" (with a special soundboad made from a laminate of birch veneer and carbon fibre) and a cheaper line of "Matrix" guitars (which have necks made from polyurethane and aluminum).

Ovation guitars have been very successful. Their distinctive tone – together with their strength and the versatility of the acoustic-electric models – appeals to many guitar players and more and more performers are using them both on-stage and in the studio.

Ovation Custom Legend 12-string
The photograph below shows clearly the round-back shape of the fiberglass bowl which has become Ovation's trademark. Because of the strong, five-piece neck construction Ovation employs, the necks on its 12-string guitars are built to the same, easy-to-play dimensions as those on its 6–strings.

Lyrachord bowl

The Adamas
This guitar is Ovation's most expensive model. The soundboard is made from a sheet of birch veneer sandwiched between two layers of "carbon pre-preg" (carbon fibers embedded in epoxy resin). The conventional soundhole is replaced by 22 smaller holes set on either side of the upper bout. This design is intended to minimize feedback when the guitar is amplified. There is also an acoustic-electric version of the Adamas.

Resonator guitars

Metal resonator or resophonic guitars are a variation on the theme of the acoustic guitar. Also known as "National" or "Dobro" guitars, they were first developed in the 1920s when the Dopera brothers founded their "National Guitar Company" and, later, their "Dobro Company". Resonator guitars have a distinctive, metallic, "jangly" sound and effectively project a lot more volume than conventional acoustic instruments. This is because the vibrations of the strings are transferred through the bridge to a round metal dish or cone which acts as a resonator within the guitar and which "amplifies" the sound. Early National guitars had all-metal bodies and a single resonator that was cone-shaped. Early Dobro guitars were wooden-bodied and had a bowl-shaped resonator. Eventually, in 1934, the two companies merged.

Resonator guitars have always been considered ideal for bottleneck slide playing styles. In fact, they were built with both square-section necks as well as conventional round-section necks. They were at their most popular in the 1920s and 1930s during the boom in Hawaiian and country music, but they were also used by many famous old blues players.

National "Duolian"
Made in the early 1930s, this well-used, metal-bodied National now belongs to Rory Gallagher. It is an original 12-fret model.

ELECTRIC GUITARS

The history and development of the electric guitar, like that of the steel-string acoustic, began in America. The feature that unifies all electric guitars is the *pick-up*. It is the pick-up that converts the sound of the instrument or the vibration of the strings into an electrical signal. This signal is then fed to an amplifier and converted back into sound by a loudspeaker. Key names in the evolution of the modern solid-body electric guitar are Lloyd Loar, Adolph Rickenbacker, Leo Fender and Les Paul. Much of the experimental work was centered around the Fender and Gibson companies – still among the market leaders today. In recent years, Japanese and Far Eastern manufacturers have established reputations for inexpensive guitars that represent excellent value for money. Their top-line electrics offer a combination of quality and low cost that keeps the whole industry on its toes. The huge variety of instruments, ranging from vintage American models to the most up-to-date Roland guitar synthesizers, can make choosing an electric guitar something of a nightmare to the uninitiated. For this reason, this chapter sets out the history of the instrument and describes in detail the most important of the many different types and models – explaining how they work, how they are built, and how they differ.

The anatomy of the electric guitar

The solid-body electric guitar developed from early, amplified acoustic guitars. These were simply acoustic instruments with pick-ups attached to them. Like so many innovations in the history of the guitar, it came about as a result of the quest for greater volume.

The heart of the solid-body electric guitar is the magnetic pick-up. It responds directly to the vibration of the strings and transforms this energy into electrical impulses which are then amplified and fed to a loudspeaker (see p. 52). To do this efficiently, the pick-up should be as stable as possible and should not be disturbed by vibrations from the body.

When a pick-up is fitted to the soundboard of an acoustic guitar, two problems can arise. First, the pick-up may move as the sound-board vibrates. Second, speaker "feedback" may be generated. With electric guitars, the solution is to increase the *mass* of the guitar body so that its ability to receive and transmit vibrations is reduced. If this idea were taken to its logical conclusion, the body might be made from concrete or perhaps even lead. In practice, a compromise is reached. Through experiments with various prototype instruments, pioneer makers of electric guitars found that a solid body made of high-density hardwood reduced the problems to a manageable level.

The solid body

There is far more scope for solid-body guitar design than there is for acoustic guitar design. This is because an acoustic guitar has to be constructed within certain design parameters if it is to produce sufficient volume and an acceptable tone. As long as the solid body of an electric guitar keeps the pick-ups fairly stable and provides a mounting for the necessary components, its shape is limited only by practicability and the designer's imagination. Gibson's Flying V and Explorer (see p. 59), the Vox Phantom and the Ovation Bread-winner illustrate some of the endless possibilities that are available.

Well-seasoned or kiln-dried hardwoods such as mahogany, walnut, ash, alder and maple are frequently used in solid-body construction. However, laminated timbers are also common. The original Les Paul guitars actually had a mahogany body with a maple "cap" or front (see p. 58). Several other materials have also been successfully employed – Dan Armstrong's plexiglass guitars, for example.

The material used in the construction of a solid body can in fact affect the sound of the guitar. The denser the material, the longer the natural (not feedback-assisted) sustain the instrument will have. The tone can be altered by changing the wood used for both the body and the neck.

The bridge/saddle
Many different types of bridge are fitted to electric guitars. This one is based on the Gibson "Tune-O-Matic". The height of the whole bridge can be raised or lowered, but each string also sits on its own individually adjustable saddle.

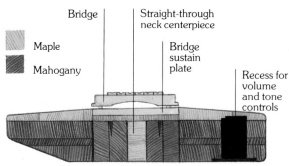

Bridge — Straight-through neck centerpiece

Maple

Mahogany — Bridge sustain plate

Recess for volume and tone controls

Pick-up selector or "toggle" switch

The body
This guitar, the Yamaha SG 2000, features a sandwich construction body and a laminated, straight-through neck. The backbone of the guitar is a laminated block made from a strip of maple in between two pieces of mahogany. This runs from the end of the headstock to the bottom of the body so that there is no join between body and neck. The bulk of the body is then made up of mahogany with a carved maple top on the face of the guitar. A solid piece of brass is set directly beneath the bridge to increase sustain.

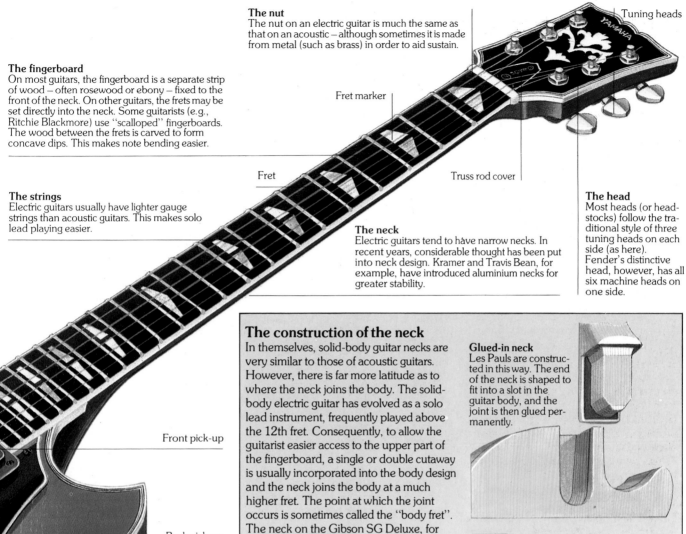

The nut
The nut on an electric guitar is much the same as that on an acoustic – although sometimes it is made from metal (such as brass) in order to aid sustain.

Tuning heads

The fingerboard
On most guitars, the fingerboard is a separate strip of wood – often rosewood or ebony – fixed to the front of the neck. On other guitars, the frets may be set directly into the neck. Some guitarists (e.g., Ritchie Blackmore) use "scalloped" fingerboards. The wood between the frets is carved to form concave dips. This makes note bending easier.

Fret marker

The strings
Electric guitars usually have lighter gauge strings than acoustic guitars. This makes solo lead playing easier.

Fret

Truss rod cover

The neck
Electric guitars tend to have narrow necks. In recent years, considerable thought has been put into neck design. Kramer and Travis Bean, for example, have introduced aluminium necks for greater stability.

The head
Most heads (or headstocks) follow the traditional style of three tuning heads on each side (as here). Fender's distinctive head, however, has all six machine heads on one side.

Front pick-up

Back pick-up

Fingerplate

Tailpiece

Volume control for back pick-up

Volume control for front pick-up

Tone control for back pick-up

Tone control for front pick-up

Output socket
Usually a standard jack plug socket.

The construction of the neck

In themselves, solid-body guitar necks are very similar to those of acoustic guitars. However, there is far more latitude as to where the neck joins the body. The solid-body electric guitar has evolved as a solo lead instrument, frequently played above the 12th fret. Consequently, to allow the guitarist easier access to the upper part of the fingerboard, a single or double cutaway is usually incorporated into the body design and the neck joins the body at a much higher fret. The point at which the joint occurs is sometimes called the "body fret". The neck on the Gibson SG Deluxe, for example, effectively joins the body at the 20th fret.

There is a great deal of controversy concerning the best method of attaching the neck to the body. Most of the arguments revolve around *sustain* – the length of time that a note continues to sound after the string has been struck. Of the three different construction methods, a glued-in neck (similar to the traditional dovetail of acoustic guitars) is felt to give a better joint and therefore more sustain than a bolt-on neck. And a neck constructed from a single piece (or laminated sections) of wood which goes straight through the body is, in turn, considered to give more sustain than a bolt-on neck. The arguments are not conclusive. Sustain also depends on the mass or density of the wood, the material used for the nut and saddle, and the output of the pick-ups.

With fewer design constraints than acoustic guitars, a number of different adjustable truss rods have evolved. Fender guitars have the adjustment screw at the body end of the neck instead of at the headstock end. Rickenbacker developed a double adjustment truss rod to allow the correction of a twisted neck.

Glued-in neck
Les Pauls are constructed in this way. The end of the neck is shaped to fit into a slot in the guitar body, and the joint is then glued permanently.

Bolt-on neck
Fender was responsible for introducing the detachable neck, bolted or screwed to the body. On the Stratocaster, a "neck-tilt" system allows changes to be made to the neck angle.

Straight-through neck
The point of this design (used by Yamaha, Aria and Alembic, among others) is that both ends of the strings are attached to one piece of wood.

Pick-ups and controls

"Transducer" is the name given to any electronic or electro-magnetic device used to convert forms of physical energy into electrical energy. *All* guitar pick-ups are transducers of one kind or another. They convert the energy produced by the vibrating guitar strings into AC (alternating current) electrical pulses which are fed to an amplifier. The amp magnifies these pulses many times before the loudspeaker transforms them back into sound waves.

Electric guitars are generally fitted with *magnetic* pick-ups, although acoustic guitars are often amplified by means of a so-called *contact transducer*. Since magnetic pick-ups only function if they are close to the guitar strings, they are mounted on the body directly beneath the strings. Electric guitars may have one, two or three pick-ups. This means that, by means of the selector switch or volume controls, an individual pick-up or a combination of pick-ups can be used to get different sounds. The rhythm pick-up (which is nearer the center of the strings) has a more mellow sound than the cutting treble of the lead pick-up (which is close to the bridge).

Pick-up positions

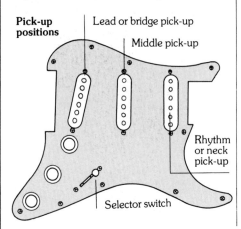

Lead or bridge pick-up
Middle pick-up
Rhythm or neck pick-up
Selector switch

The Fender Stratocaster pick-up
Fender Telecasters and Stratocasters are the guitars most often identified with the single-coil pick-up "sound" – clear and punchy but with a penetrating treble. Instead of using a single bar magnet, Leo Fender employed six individual, magnetic pole-pieces, each slightly staggered in height to help equalize the amplified volume of the six strings. The coil is actually wrapped around the pole-pieces. Originally, it was made with 8,350 turns of copper wire, although modern Strat pick-ups now use only 7,600 turns.

How the single-coil pick-up works
The simplest form of magnetic pick-up consists of a permanent bar magnet with a continuous length of insulated copper wire wrapped around it several thousand times. This winding is an electrical *coil*. The wire is extremely fine – about the same thickness as

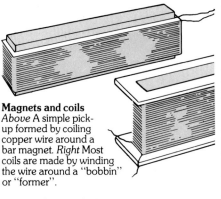

Magnets and coils
Above A simple pick-up formed by coiling copper wire around a bar magnet. *Right* Most coils are made by winding the wire around a "bobbin" or "former".

one single strand of human hair.

The magnet generates a magnetic field around itself, and the pick-up is mounted on the guitar body so that the guitar strings actually pass through the magnetic field – and, because the strings are made of steel, they interact with the magnetic field. While the strings are at rest, the field maintains a regular shape and nothing happens in the coil. But, as soon as a string is struck, its movement alters the shape of the field.

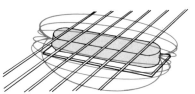

The pick-up's magnetic field
The sole purpose of the magnet is to provide a magnetic field through which the strings pass.

Some of the "lines of force" which make up the magnetic field intersect the coil and, when the vibrating string causes the lines of force to move, small pulses of electrical energy are generated in the coil itself. If the coil is connected to an amplifier, these pulses will travel to the amp in the form of AC.

The precise pattern in which the string vibrates depends on the construction of the guitar and the way the note is sounded. Let's say the pattern is a figure-eight as shown below. If the string is an open A tuned to concert pitch, it will vibrate at 440 cycles per second. In other words, it will complete the figure-eight 440 times every second. This means that the magnetic field surrounding the pick-up will also be "altered" 440 times.

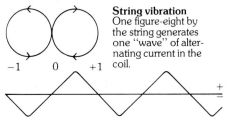

String vibration
One figure-eight by the string generates one "wave" of alternating current in the coil.

As the volume of the note dies away, the distance between the points +1, −1 and 0 becomes shorter until the string is at rest again. Nevertheless, throughout the duration of the note, the actual number of cycles per second remains the same. This tells the amplifier the *pitch* of the note – whether it is an A or a B, for example. The size of the vibrating figure-eight pattern tells the amplifier the *volume* (or "amplitude") of the note. The detailed shape of the figure-eight tells the amplifier the *tone* of the note.

Magnets in pick-ups
Most pick-up magnets are made of Alnico, an alloy of aluminum, nickel and cobalt. However, some manufacturers – such as Alembic – employ alternative "ceramic" or "piezo" magnets. The shape of the magnet varies according to the design of the pick-up. The basic bar magnet may have a "fin" which extends one pole of the magnetic field, taking it closer to the strings; it may have six individual pole-piece extensions – one for each string – and it may be possible to alter the height of each one separately; or it may contain six individual magnets.

In simple terms, the stronger the magnet (and the more windings there are in the coil) the louder the amplified sound will be. However, past a certain point, a strong magnet will "choke" the strings – that is, it will actually restrict the vibratory patterns and create a loss of sustain or a tonal distortion.

For more information on magnets and coils – and on how they can affect the tone and output of the guitar – see pp. 186-96.

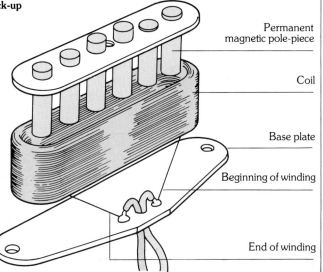

Permanent magnetic pole-piece
Coil
Base plate
Beginning of winding
End of winding

How the twin-coil pick-up works

All pick-up coils are vulnerable to interference from "electro-magnetic radiation". This means they tend to pick up a noise or "hum" when amplifiers or other electrical appliances are nearby. The hum-neutralizing or *humbucking* pick-up first invented by a Gibson engineer called Seth Lover in 1955 was designed to eliminate this problem.

Humbucking pick-ups have two coils instead of one. They are wired in series (so that the current flows first through one, then the next) but out of phase with each other. This means that any rogue interference is sent by one coil as a positive signal and by the other as a negative signal. The two opposite currents, flowing in different directions, therefore cancel each other out, and the "hum" is not passed on to the amplifier.

To guarantee that the two coils do not cancel out the currents generated by the vibrating strings as well, the sets of pole-pieces within each coil have opposite magnetic polarities. The result is that when the

secondary coil inverts the signal from the disturbed magnetic field it *duplicates* – instead of canceling — the electrical pulse. When the two signals are the same, they are said to be "in phase". When the two signals are opposing each other, they are said to be "out of phase" (see p. 192).

Since the mid-1950s, Gibson has been fitting twin-coil humbucking pick-ups to most of their electric guitars. As well as reducing rogue, unwanted interference, the "humbucker" has a sound which is distinctly different from that of the single-coil pick-up. The humbucker's twin-coil design results in less overall sound definition and a decreased response to high frequencies. The fact that Gibson uses humbucking pick-ups on their guitars whereas Fender uses single-coil pick-ups is one of the major reasons why the clear sound and biting top-end of a standard single-coil Fender is quite different from the "fatter" sound of a standard Gibson fitted with twin-coil humbuckers.

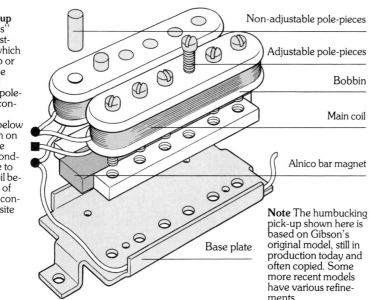

The Gibson pick-up
The "humbucker's" main coil has adjustable pole-pieces which can be screwed up or down. Those in the secondary coil are fixed. Both sets of pole-pieces come into contact with the same magnet, situated below and between them on the base plate. The polarity of the secondary coil is opposite to that of the main coil because the two sets of pole-pieces are in contact with the opposite poles of the bar magnet.

Non-adjustable pole-pieces
Adjustable pole-pieces
Bobbin
Main coil
Alnico bar magnet
Base plate

Note The humbucking pick-up shown here is based on Gibson's original model, still in production today and often copied. Some more recent models have various refinements.

The volume and tone controls

The signal generated in the pick-up coil can be controlled before it reaches the amplifier in two ways: by the volume control and by the tone control. Both are wired in between the pick-up and the guitar's output socket.

The volume control can modify the output by means of a *variable resistor*, commonly known as a *potentiometer* (or "pot"). The volume knob on the face of the guitar is attached to the spindle of the pot. The pot contains a resistive track, usually in the shape of a horseshoe, and a wiper contact is connected to the end of the spindle so that as the control knob is turned the wiper contact moves around the resistive track.

The two wires from the pick-up are connected to each end of the resistive track. At the earthed end of the track the voltage is zero; at the other end it is at maximum. Mov-

ing the sliding wiper contact along the track therefore increases or reduces the voltage fed to the amplifier.

Most guitar tone controls are a combination of a potentiometer and a *capacitor*. They operate by effectively tapping off the high, treble frequencies and sending them to earth. The capacitor acts as a kind of "filter". High frequencies (treble) pass through it, while low frequencies (bass) do not.

The pot (with its sliding wiper contact connected to the tone control knob) determines the amount of high frequencies earthed.

When the tone control is turned full on for maximum treble, the complete signal generated by the pick-up is sent to the amplifier. As the tone control is turned down, an increasing number of the treble frequencies filtered off by the capacitor are earthed by the pot.

Tremelo Units

"Tremelo arms" are mechanical devices that allow guitarists to reduce tension on all six guitar strings at once. As the tremelo arm is pushed towards the body of the guitar the tension on the strings decreases and the pitch of the note drops. When the arm is released, springs return the arm to the normal position. Until the 1980s the best known tremelo arms were made by Fender and Bigsby.

Guitarist Floyd Rose was frustrated with the limitations of Fender tremelo arms: when they were used, they would often put the guitar out of tune. Consequently, he designed the locking nut principle, wherby strings are locked into place at both ends. Fine tuning is made by adjusters behind the bridge.

The Floyd Rose system is so effective that some guitarists can play throughout an entire concert without putting strings out of tune. The only drawback with the system is speed: it is difficult to change a broken string very quickly.

The Floyd Rose system was so successful that by the beginning of the 1990s every major guitar manufacturer fitted it to their guitars or manufactured a version under license from Floyd Rose.

Locking nut *(above)* Strings are tuned approximately and locked using an allen key.

Bridge tuning *(above)* Strings are clamped and finely tuned behind the bridge.

Hollow-body electric guitars

The story of "electric-acoustic" guitars is thought to have begun with a man called Lloyd Loar. Between 1920 and 1924, when he worked for Gibson, Loar experimented with various prototype pick-ups designed to amplify the sound of an acoustic guitar. Unfortunately, he left Gibson to form his own Vivi-Tone company and his idea disappeared until the 1930s.

It was then that the Rowe-DeArmond company began manufacturing the first commercially available magnetic pick-up simply designed to clip onto the soundhole of a flat-top acoustic guitar and therefore to amplify its natural sound.

It was the Gibson company who, in 1935, took things a stage further by introducing their ES-150 "Electric Spanish" model. This was essentially an f-hole, arch-top guitar fitted with a massive pick-up. Two strong magnets housed inside the guitar body were in contact with a single-fin pole-piece which was set beneath the strings. The fin, not the magnets, passed through the coil.

Gibson ES-150
Jazz guitarist, Charlie Christian, used this guitar to such effect that the pick-up became named after him.

"Charlie Christian pick-up"

Other Gibson ES models followed during the 1940s – the single pick-up ES-125 and the twin pick-up ES-300 and ES-350. In 1949, they introduced their three pick-up ES-5, hailed as the "supreme electronic

version" of the original L-5 (see p. 46), and in 1952 it was joined by the Super 400-CES, an electric version of the Super 400 acoustic guitar. During the 1950s and 1960s, many famous guitarists endorsed Gibson electric-acoustics, and the company produced several "named" guitars – the "Johnny Smith" and "Howard Roberts", for example.

From the end of the Second World War onwards, other companies competed with Gibson for the hollow-body electric guitar market. The most successful were Epiphone (until they were bought by Gibson in 1957), Gretsch and Guild.

Gretsch "Country Gentleman"
Designed with the help of Chet Atkins, this 1960 Gretsch has fake f-holes painted on the body.

Gibson Byrdland
This guitar was first developed in 1955 and gets its name from the two guitarists who designed it – Billy Byrd and Hank Garland. Shown above is a 1968 model; the original instrument had "bar magnet" pick-ups instead of modern humbuckers.

Gibson "Johnny Smith" (1961)

Gibson "Howard Roberts" (1974)

"Semi-solid" electric guitars

Feedback has always been a problem with hollow-body electrics. In the late 1950s, Gibson brought out a range of guitars which were designed to minimize this. They were called thin-bodied or "semi-solid" guitars to distinguish them from the ordinary deep-bodied "electric-acoustic" guitars. The first to appear (in August 1958) was the ES-335T, although others in what became known as the "300" series – the ES-355, 345 and 325 – soon followed. They all had double cutaways and thin bodies with arched soundboards and backs made from laminated maple. They were true "acoustic" guitars in that they were hollow and had f-shaped soundholes, but they each had a

solid block of wood set down the center of the body. This was intended to increase sustain and prevent unwanted soundboard vibration from causing feedback. The aim of the guitars was to blend the sustain qualities of a solid-body electric with the warmer, more mellow sound produced by an acoustic instrument.

Semi-solid guitars were very successful. The modified ES-355 TD SV, first introduced in about 1959, had stereo wiring (which meant that the rhythm and lead pick-ups could be played through different amplifiers) and "varitone" circuitry (which allowed the treble cut-off on the tone control to be varied).

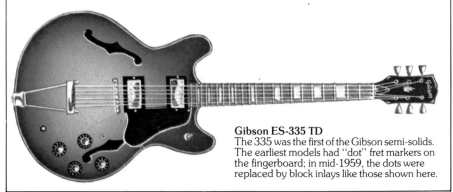

Gibson ES-335 TD
The 335 was the first of the Gibson semi-solids. The earliest models had "dot" fret markers on the fingerboard; in mid-1959, the dots were replaced by block inlays like those shown here.

The first solid-body electric guitars

The development of the truly "electric" guitar – one with a solid body and no soundbox – owes a great deal to the popularity of Hawaiian music in America during the 1920s and 1930s. Hawaiian guitars are solo instruments, played with a metal slide used in the same way as a "bottleneck". Electric Hawaiian guitars were the first commercially available instruments that depended almost entirely on their sound being amplified electrically, not just acoustically.

One of the key figures in their design was Adolph Rickenbacker. He was originally approached to make metal components for the Dopera Brothers' National resonator guitars (see p. 48). At National, he met George Beauchamp and Paul Barth who had been working on the principle of the magnetic pick-up. Together, they formed the Electro String Company and, in 1931, they went into production of their first electric Hawaiian guitars – the A-22 and A-25. The figures 22 and 25 referred to the scale length in inches. The pick-up, with its strong magnets and six individual iron pole-pieces, was rudimentary but effective, and the guitars' success prompted other makers – such as Gibson and National/Dobro – to start producing equivalent instruments.

The Rickenbacker "Frying Pan" The A-22 electric Hawaiian guitar, which became popularly known as the "frying pan" or "pancake", was cast in a single piece of solid aluminum. The pick-up was a high-impedance device with two tungsten-steel chrome-plated horseshoe magnets of considerable power.

By about the 1940s, Gibson's new electric-acoustic models were firmly established, and it is hardly surprising that a number of people were working on ways of applying the solid body of Hawaiian and steel guitars to regular instruments.

In 1944, Leo Fender – who ran a radio repair shop – teamed up with "Doc" Kauffman, an ex-employee of Rickenbacker, and formed the K & F Company. They produced a series of steel guitars and amplifiers. Leo Fender felt – quite rightly – that the massive pick-up magnets in use at the time need not be so large. He had a new pick-up which he wanted to try out and so he built it into a solid-body guitar which was based on the shape of a Hawaiian but which had a regular, properly fretted guitar fingerboard. Though only intended to demonstrate the pick-up, the guitar was soon in demand with local country musicians. In fact, it became so popular that there was a waiting list of people wanting to hire it. When Leo and "Doc" Kauffman parted in 1946, he went on to form his own Fender Electric Instrument Company, and within two years he introduced the now-legendary Broadcaster (see p. 56).

In the meantime, Les Paul was working in the same direction. Although he had experimented with his own pick-ups throughout the 1930s, he was still experiencing the same feedback and resonance problems with amplified f-hole guitars as everyone else. But hearing about a solid-body violin made by the American inventor, Thomas Edison, set him thinking about making a solid-body guitar. He was convinced that the only way to avoid body feedback was to reduce pick-up movement – and the only way to do that was to mount it on a solid piece of wood.

In 1941, he persuaded Epiphone to let him use their workshop on Sundays. There, he built his historic "log" guitar, about which he later said: "You could go out and eat and come back and the note would still be sounding. It didn't sound like a banjo or a mandolin, but like a guitar, an electric guitar. That was the sound I was after." The story of his later role with Gibson is taken up on p. 58.

In 1947, Paul Bigsby (inventor of the Bigsby tremelo arm, p. 53) built a solid-body electric guitar designed in consultation with the renowned guitarist, Merle Travis. It shares certain design features with the Broadcaster that Leo Fender introduced in 1948 – for example, the way the strings pass through the body, and the design of the headstock, with all six tuning heads on one side. In fact, Bigsby and Travis worked on their guitar in

The Les Paul "log" Despite its looks, this guitar was the first real solid-body electric guitar. Les Paul simply cut an Epiphone f-hole acoustic guitar down the middle and inserted a 4 in. by 4 in. (10 cm by 10 cm) block of solid maple on which he mounted two single-coil pick-ups and a Gibson neck.

Bigsby-Travis guitar Built in 1947, this guitar has a single bar-magnet pick-up mounted quite close to the bridge and operated by means of three "pot" controls plus a three-way selector switch. The body and neck are made of bird's eye maple. Employing a construction method years ahead of its time, the neck continues straight through the body in one piece.

California, not far from Fender's center of operations in Fullerton. Controversy has raged over the question of who might have been looking over whose shoulder. Certainly, Leo Fender was not secretive; during the 1940s, Les Paul and others visited his works.

Fender guitars

Following the success of his experimental solid-body steel guitar in the mid-1940s (see p. 55), Leo Fender split with his partner "Doc" Kauffman, set up on his own, and got to work immediately on the design of a new instrument. Fender was concerned with utility and practicality, not aesthetics. He wanted to make a regular guitar with a clear sound similar to that of the electric Hawaiian but without the feedback problems associated with a vibrating soundboard. The result of his labors was the "Broadcaster", which he started manufacturing in 1948.

The Broadcaster had a detachable neck – similar to the banjos of the time. This was simply a question of convenience; Fender felt that the neck was the part of the guitar most likely to cause problems, and his "modular" design meant that it could be replaced in the space of just a few minutes. The choice of maple as the wood from which it was built was apparently due to the popularity of blonde-finish instruments at the time. Natural-wood bodies were made from ash, painted ones from alder. The headstock was designed with all six tuning heads on one side. This made tuning easier and avoided having to fan out the strings.

Fender Broadcaster (1948)
This guitar, one of the first solid-body electrics, belongs to Dave Gilmour of Pink Floyd.

The Broadcaster was fitted with two single-coil pick-ups. These were wired through a three-position selector switch which could be set to either the bridge pick-up, the neck pick-up, or the neck pick-up plus a special capacitor that gave a very bassy sound.

The original guitar featured the same adjustable bridge design still fitted to Telecasters today: three bolts adjust the height and the scale length of the strings in pairs. The Broadcaster also had a clip-on cover-plate

that snapped into place over the bridge and bridge pick-up. This, too, is still fitted to Telecasters, but it is rarely seen on working guitars since most players find that it hinders their technique.

In 1954, Fender went into production with the "Stratocaster". Together with the Telecaster – and with the instruments Les Paul was then making for Gibson – these two guitars must be regarded as having set the standards for solid-body guitar design.

During 1955, Leo Fender contracted an infection that troubled him for the next ten years. By the mid-sixties, convinced that he had only a short time to live, he decided to wind up his business affairs. In 1965 he sold the entire Fender company to CBS for thirteen million dollars. Shortly afterwards he changed doctors and was cured. Within a few months he was working again – this time as a design consultant for CBS Fender, operating from his own research laboratory. This arrangement continued for the next five years. Through his own CLF Research Company, he proceeded to work on Music Man, and G & L guitars. Leo Fender died on 21st March 1991.

Telecasters

Soon after its introduction, the Broadcaster's name was changed to the "Telecaster" – in order to avoid confusion with the Broadcaster drum kits made by Gretsch. The only major differences between the first Broadcaster and modern Telecasters are that a neck truss rod is now fitted, the original black celluloid fingerplate has been replaced by laminated plastic, and the tuning heads now have "slotted" string posts. Necks are still made from maple, with either a rosewood or maple fingerboard.
A number of variations on the basic Telecaster have been introduced during the last thirty years.

Standard Fender Telecaster

Bridge cover-plate conceals single-coil bridge pick-up

Detachable bolt-on neck

Single-coil neck pick-up

Three-way selector switch

Esquire
Introduced 1954: single-coil bridge pick-up only.

Telecaster Thinline
Introduced 1969: semi-acoustic ash body. 1973: 2 humbuckers fitted.

Telecaster Deluxe
Introduced 1972-3: 2 humbuckers, strat-style bridge and headstock.

Telecaster Custom
Introduced 1972-3: 1 single-coil and 1 humbucking pick-up, adjustable neck.

The Stratocaster

Three features immediately distinguished the Fender Stratocaster as being a revolutionary new guitar when it was introduced in 1954. First, it had a contoured, double-cutaway body designed to make it more comfortable to play. The corners were beveled and the back had a dished recess. Second, it featured the brilliantly engineered Fender vibrato or "tremelo" unit built into the special "floating" bridge design (see p. 53). Third, it was the first solid-body electric to be fitted with three pick-ups. These were all single-coils and they were wired to a three-way switch which selected one at a time. However, as guitarists soon discovered, the switch could be balanced between two positions to give a unique "out-of-phase" sound. Realizing the attraction of this, Fender changed the three-way switch to a five-way switch.

Like the Telecaster, the "Strat" has remained virtually unchanged – although in 1972 the Fender "micro-tilt" neck and "bullet" truss-rod adjustments were added. Stratocasters are available in various different finishes and colors, and with or without a rosewood fingerboard. In 1981, the "Strat" appeared in Lake Placid Blue and Candy-Apple Red.

Standard Fender Stratocaster

String guides

Neck pick-up

Middle pick-up

Bridge pick-up

"Bullet" truss rod

Volume control

Selector switch

Paisley Stratocaster
This paisley Strat was Fender's response to the psychedelia of the late sixties. It belongs to the Who and is thought to be the only one in existence.

Other Fender guitars

With the success of the Telecaster and Stratocaster, Fender continued to experiment with new models – the Musicmaster, Jazzmaster, Jaguar and Mustang, for example. These have fluctuated in popularity, as did their less successful excursions into the field of semi-acoustics (the Coronado, Antigua, Montego and, more recently, the Starcaster). When CBS initially bought out Fender in 1965, many guitarists felt that quality standards were allowed to slip, and what became known as "pre-CBS" guitars were more and more prized. Early problems were soon overcome, however, and standards were regained.

Musicmaster
Introduced 1956: 1 single-coil pick-up only.

Jazzmaster
Introduced 1957: 2 single-coil pick-ups with separate tone and volume controls, "floating tremelo".

Jaguar
Introduced 1961: shorter scale length than Jazzmaster, toggle selector replaced by slide switches.

Electric 12-string
Introduced 1965 until 1969: based on Jazzmaster/Jaguar, 2 split pick-ups, "hockey-stick" head.

Mustang
Introduced 1966 to replace "Duo-Sonic": 2 single-coil pick-ups, 2 three-position pick-up and tone slide switches, tremelo arm.

Starcaster
Introduced 1975: semi-solid body with center block, bolt-on neck, 2 humbucking pick-ups.

Lead I
Introduced 1979: 1 humbucking pick-up, coil-tap and series/parallel switches.

Gibson guitars

The story of Gibson guitars stretches right back into the nineteenth century. Gibson pioneered the arch-top acoustic guitar (the L-5 in 1924, see p. 46) and also the hollow-body electric guitar (the ES-150 in 1935, see p. 54). However, their involvement with solid-body electrics came slightly later – *after* Fender's introduction of the Broadcaster – and owes a lot to the renowned Les Paul.

Following his successful weekend experiments with the "log" at the Epiphone factory (see p. 55), Les Paul took his ideas to Gibson. Unfortunately, they were not interested; they called his prototype "the broomstick with a pick-up on it" and turned him down. But, in 1950, they sought him out again and signed him up, agreeing that he would be paid a royalty on *every* electric guitar with his name on it that the company made.

At Gibson, Les Paul went on to develop his ideas, eventually working through fifty to sixty prototype guitars before he felt happy with his final design. In 1952, the "Gibson Les Paul" guitar went into production. At first, Maurice Berlin, the company president, thought that they should be called simply "Les Paul" guitars and that they should not bear the "Gibson" name in case the company's reputation suffered. Before long, he changed his mind, saying, "Maybe we should put the Gibson name on it, just in case it goes anywhere". Time proved him right.

Les Paul wanted the guitars to have a natural twenty-second sustain – which is why they are relatively heavy. The body was made from solid mahogany with a ½ in. (12 mm) maple "cap" or facing on top. The profile of the carved top was, in fact, a Gibson suggestion intended to make it hard to copy.

In 1962, Les Paul's contract with Gibson ended. Occupied by his divorce from Mary Ford at the time, he decided he did not want to be involved with guitars for a while, and the association ended. Les Paul talks with some bitterness about the "Les Paul" guitars Gibson went on to make without his name on them. Nevertheless, in 1967, when rock musicians were paying thousands of dollars for vintage 1957-60 Les Pauls, he contacted Maurice Berlin again and once more became actively involved in Gibson guitars.

In recent years, Gibson has introduced several new guitar lines – the RD series and the man-made "Resonwood" Sonex series, for example – as well as reissuing old favorites, both in their original and in new forms. One of their most recent new guitars is called the 335-S. Somewhat confusingly, it is a solid-body electric guitar loosely based on the shape of the ES-335 semi-solid (see p. 54).

Gibson Les Pauls

The original 1952 Gibson Les Paul had two high-impedance single-coil pick-ups with cream cover-plates (see below). It was fitted with a three-way pick-up selector switch and separate volume and tone controls. At first, Les Paul used his own distinctive "trapeze" tailpiece and bridge. But this caused problems, and in 1955 it was replaced by the new, adjustable "Tune-O-Matic" bridge and tailpiece.

In 1957, the single-coil pick-ups were replaced by the new humbuckers developed by Gibson's Seth Lover and Ted McCarty (see p. 53). Until 1960, the humbucking pick-ups were referred to by the initials "PAF" (Patent Applied For). These 1957-60 Les Pauls are now among the most highly regarded electric guitars ever made.

Les Paul Standard
In 1960, when this guitar was made, Gibson introduced the term "Standard" to distinguish ordinary Les Pauls from Customs, Juniors and Specials. This Standard has a "tigerstripe" sunburst finish.

"Gold-top" Les Paul
The first Les Pauls had a gold luster finish with ivory edging. This is a 1952 model with a trapeze tailpiece.

A short guide to the Les Paul range
Over the thirty years since 1952, the basic Les Paul guitar had been modified, added-to, re-modeled, re-named, withdrawn and reissued countless times. This information is a simplified breakdown of the differences.

Les Paul Standard   Introduced 1952; 1954 stop tailpiece instead of trapeze; 1955 Tune-O-Matic bridge; 1957 two humbuckers replace single-coils; 1958 "sunburst" finish; 1960 discontinued; 1974 reissued.
Les Paul Custom   Introduced 1954, nick-named "Fretless Wonder"/"Black Beauty", flat body, two single-coil pick-ups, Tune-O-Matic bridge; 1957 three humbuckers; 1960 discontinued; 1966 reissued with two humbuckers; 1977 three humbuckers optional.

An unusual "silverburst" Les Paul Custom

Les Paul Junior   Introduced 1954, flat body, one single-coil pick-up; 1959 double cutaway; 1960 discontinued.
Les Paul Special   Introduced 1955, same as Junior but two single-coil pick-ups; 1959 double cutaway; 1960 discontinued; 1966 reissued with carved top.
Les Paul TV   Introduced 1957, same as Junior but slightly different finish; 1960 discontinued.
Les Paul Deluxe   Introduced 1969, two-humbucker version of 1966 Special, carved top.
Les Paul Personal   Introduced 1969, low-impedance pick-ups, gold-plated.
Les Paul Professional   Introduced 1969, low-impedance pick-ups, nickel-plated.
Les Paul Recording   Introduced 1971, re-placed Personal and Professional.
The Les Paul   Introduced 1976, solid maple reissue of Les Paul Custom.
Les Paul Pro Deluxe   Introduced 1977, reissue of early Standard, two 1952-style single-coil pick-ups.

The development of the Gibson SG

Incredible as it may seem now, Gibson found that their Les Paul guitars were not selling well during the late 1950s. They decided that a completely new design was needed. Their first move was to re-model the Les Paul Specials and Juniors, giving them rounded, double-cutaway bodies that many people associate now with the Melody Maker shape. A limited number of these "prototype SG" guitars were made during 1959. Then, in late 1960, they went further. They discontinued the old Les Paul range altogether, and introduced completely new Standards, Customs, Specials and Juniors with the sharp, horn-like double cutaways of the true SG style.

Much of the confusion that arises over these guitars stems from the terminology. Though Les Paul worked on the early design of the double-cutaway models, he never liked them as much as the original Les Paul shape, but it was not until 1961 that Gibson finally removed his name and officially designated them the "SG" (solid guitar) series.

Les Paul shape
The original Les Pauls were all built to this single-cutaway shape.

Les Paul SG shape
The rounded double-cutaway shape of 1959 which marked the transition. Les Paul's name still appeared on these guitars.

Gibson SG
In 1960, the Standard, Custom, Junior and Special were all issued with two re-designed, sharp body cutaways. This shape has been used for all Gibson SGs ever since then.

The Gibson "exotics"

The SG was not Gibson's only response to the problem of flagging sales in the 1950s. Ted McCarty, then company president, and his designers sat down with the following objective: "We wanted to do something really different, something radical to knock everyone out and show them that Gibson was more modern than all the rest". The results of their work appeared in 1958 – the Flying V, the Explorer and the Moderne. Of these three guitars, the Flying V was the most successful; it is still made today. The

Moderne disappeared almost immediately. At the time, the Explorer fared almost as badly; it is estimated that only about 100 were ever made and these are now extremely rare (although Gibson reissued them as a limited edition in 1976).

In 1963, Gibson came out with the Firebird, a "toned-down" version of the unsuccessful Explorer. Unfortunately, there was a legal problem with Fender over the design of the offset body, and in 1965 Gibson changed the shape of their guitars.

This has led to the 1963-65 guitars being known as "reverse-body" Firebirds to distinguish them from the 1965-67 "non-reverse-body" Firebirds. Original reverse-body guitars are highly sought after.

A series of new guitars, first introduced in 1977, harks back to the Explorer and non-reverse Firebirds. Gibson calls them the "RD" series. The RD Artist is the top-of-the-line model, and it features two humbucking pick-ups, "active" electronics (see pp. 194-6) and a fine-tuning tailpiece.

The Gibson Flying V
This is one of the earliest Flying Vs and was made in 1958. It can be distinguished from later models by the shape of the fingerplate and by the way the strings pass right through to the back of the body.

The Gibson Explorer
Production of the Explorer stopped sometime in 1959. It was considered too "futuristic" by most guitarists of the time. However, this guitar is one of the reissue models that Gibson made available during the 1970s.

The Gibson Firebird
This is a 1972 Gibson reissue of the original "reverse-body" Firebird with a Maestro vibrola unit. It has the original "backward-facing" headstock fitted with six banjo-style tuning pegs.

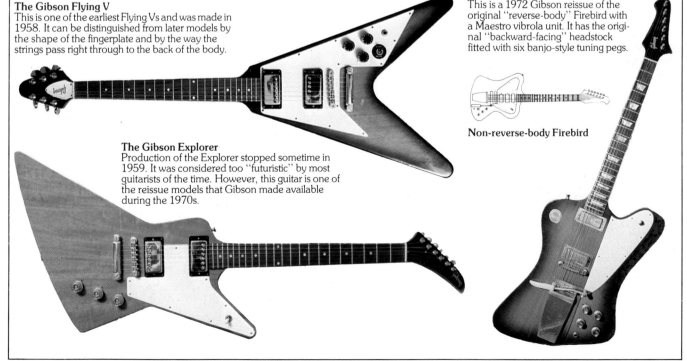

Non-reverse-body Firebird

Bass guitars

By the end of the 1940s, amplification was playing a dominant role in popular music. Amplifiers, PAs, pick-ups and the Fender Telecaster guitar were the main elements of a trend towards louder music.

Some bass players – limited to their huge acoustic double basses – fitted pick-ups to their instruments and put them through adapted amplifiers. Others followed Les Paul's example, playing the bottom strings of electric guitars.

Leo Fender first came up with the idea of a solid-body bass guitar. In 1950, realizing the problems that bass players were facing, and feeling certain that they would prefer a less cumbersome instrument, he went to work on the prototype bass guitar. By changing from the "stand-up" design of the double bass to the idea of a bass guitar supported by the shoulder strap, he thought that guitarists would be better able to "double" on bass when necessary.

The bass is tuned to E, A, D and G – like the bottom four strings of a guitar, but one octave lower. This means that all basses need longer "scale length" and consequently extra strengthening.

Fender basses

Leo Fender's first solid-body electric bass guitar – the Fender Precision – went into production in 1951, and within a couple of years he had a runaway success on his hands. The name was chosen because his bass had frets on the fingerboard – unlike the fretless double bass – and therefore allowed guitarists to play notes with "precision." The earliest Precisions were fitted with one single-coil pick-up with a volume and tone control. In 1957, the pick-up was split into two staggered halves, each with four separate pole-pieces. This was designed to prevent the signal of a vibrating string from fading and to reduce its "attack" – thus cutting down on loudspeaker casualties.

Although other bass guitars have been produced by Fender and other manufacturers, the Precision continues to provide the pulse for much rock music.

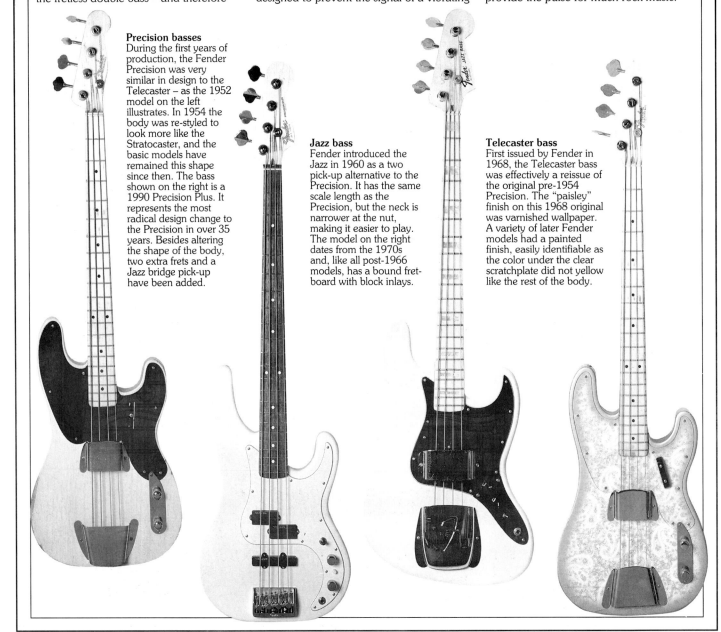

Precision basses
During the first years of production, the Fender Precision was very similar in design to the Telecaster – as the 1952 model on the left illustrates. In 1954 the body was re-styled to look more like the Stratocaster, and the basic models have remained this shape since then. The bass shown on the right is a 1990 Precision Plus. It represents the most radical design change to the Precision in over 35 years. Besides altering the shape of the body, two extra frets and a Jazz bridge pick-up have been added.

Jazz bass
Fender introduced the Jazz in 1960 as a two pick-up alternative to the Precision. It has the same scale length as the Precision, but the neck is narrower at the nut, making it easier to play. The model on the right dates from the 1970s and, like all post-1966 models, has a bound fretboard with block inlays.

Telecaster bass
First issued by Fender in 1968, the Telecaster bass was effectively a reissue of the original pre-1954 Precision. The "paisley" finish on this 1968 original was varnished wallpaper. A variety of later Fender models had a painted finish, easily identifiable as the color under the clear scratchplate did not yellow like the rest of the body.

Gibson basses

Gibson's answer to the Fender Precision appeared in 1953. It was designated the EB-1, but Hofner's copy, used by Paul McCartney, made it known as the "violin bass." Gibson followed it in 1958 with the EB-2, a bass version of their successful ES-335 (see p. 54).

In 1960, the EB-0 and the EB-3 basses appeared with new Gibson "SG" body – the sharp horn-like double cutaway. The EB-0 had one humbucking pick-up and the EB-3 had two. When Gibson introduced the Firebird guitars in 1963, it also launched a bass equivalent – the Thunderbird.

Other Gibson basses have included the Melody Maker (1968), the Grabber (1974) with its single sliding pick-up, the Ripper (1974) and the RD series (1977).

EB-1
The famous violin-shaped body was made from solid mahogany. The body is not, in fact, hollow: the f-holes are simply painted on.

Thunderbird
This 1964 model IV twin-humbucker belongs to John Entwistle, who used it extensively with the Who between 1972 and 1976.

Other important basses

Among the other manufacturers that pioneered the development of the bass guitar, Rickenbacker stands out as being almost as important as Fender. Their first bass guitar, the 4000, was introduced in the late 1950s. Several years later, it was joined by the twin pick-up 4001, which has since become one of the most popular (and most recognizable) of all basses.

During the 1970s, the American Alembic company established itself as one of the leading makers of bass guitars. Alembic was responsible for developing active onboard electronics, now widely adopted by other manufacturers. Their guitars have remained expensive – due to the fact that they are hand-crafted to the highest specifications, using the best possible materials and components. Their advanced designs incorporating exotic laminated woods influenced many guitar makers. Now more affordable instruments inspired by Alembic designs are widely used. Stanley Clarke is probably the most prominent user of Alembic basses.

The story of Japanese manufacturers is as true for bass guitars as it is for their standard electrics. No longer written off as producers of cheap copies based on Fender and Gibson designs, Aria, Ibanez, and Yamaha have all made bass guitars that are excellent instruments in their own right.

In 1979, in the U.S.A., Ned Steinberger started manufacturing his radical L Series headless and composite construction bass guitars. The synthetic body gave the instrument a sustained tone and the composite neck was not susceptible to the warping problems experienced with traditional wooden necks. The on-body tuning heads took guitar design in a new direction, and the L2 has been as imitated as the original Alembic instruments. Other American manufacturers such as Guild, Kramer and Ernie Ball Music Man have all produced excellent basses.

Rickenbacker 4001
All of the Rickenbacker 4000 series basses have a distinctive shape and sound. The 4001, 4002, and 4003 are fitted with stereo outputs allowing signals from the pick-ups to be separated.

Alembic Mark King signature
Started in California in the mid-sixties by Ron Wickersham, Alembic pioneered the concept of the specialist bass guitar maker. The Mark King signature model was launched in 1989.

Japanese and Far Eastern guitars

Yamaha was the first Japanese company to make a significant impact on the international guitar market-place. In the 1960s, they produced a range of flat-top acoustics based on Martin designs. To begin with, their range consisted mostly of inexpensive guitars that cost only a fraction of the price of the American originals. The sound was surprisingly good, especially considering that most of the guitars had laminated soundboards. Their value for money was exceptional. Before long, Yamaha was also making some top-line, hand-built instruments which measured up favorably alongside American Martin, Gibson and Guild guitars.

As the demand for acoustic guitars decreased towards the end of the 1960s, the Japanese were quick to turn their attention to electric instruments. Again, they began with replicas of the successful American makes: the Gibson Les Paul, Fender Stratocaster and Precision bass guitars being especially popular. Often these copies cost a fraction of the price of the genuine article, bringing them within the reach of thousands of amateur and semi-professional players.

During the 1970s, a few of the Japanese manufacturers began to gain a high reputation for their original guitars. These are still generally less expensive than top American instruments, but they stand up very well in comparison.

Several American manufacturers, like Washburn and the Gibson-owned Epiphone company, now cater to the lower end of the market by having their guitars built in Japan and then marketing them throughout the world.

By bringing mass production methods to guitar-making, the Japanese brought prices down and gained a significant foothold in the world market. Once this had been achieved, they proceeded to increase their prices and also moved into the expensive price range of instruments. However, with many non-Japanese makers now offering their own and

Japanese-made instruments, or models made in other newly-developing countries, a wide choice of reasonably priced instruments is now available.

Lower costs have resulted in many guitar makers switching their manufacture to other developing nations. Some instruments with Japanese brand names are made in Korea, Taiwan, and India. During the early nineties, Fender Japan switched the production of some of their cheaper instruments to Mexico.

Tokai TST50 (left)
The first unashamed Japanese copy based on a vintage Stratocaster design, this 1985 guitar represented incredible value for money.

Westone Thunder (left)
Having made guitars for Aria, the Matsumoku company started making instruments under their own Westone brand name. They always offer good value budget guitars for the beginner.

Aria TA60 (above)
Though solid body instruments have dominated the electric guitar scene, Far Eastern makers produce a wide range of models such as the electric-acoustic Aria Titan Arist series.

Ibanez Maxxas (above)
Originally specializing in budget instruments, Ibanez are now among the more expensive guitar makers, producing models like the six-string Jem and seven-string Universe models used by Steve Vai.

Charvel Jackson

The American Charvel Jackson company (see p. 64), like many other well-known American companies, produce a range of outstanding instruments – the "Jackson Professional" range – that are produced in Japan. By taking advantage of the lower manufacturing costs, Charvel Jackson is able to compete in the wider market for lower priced instruments, while separately maintaining their highly-rated, American-made, Jackson and Jackson U.S.A. models.

The Jackson Professional Warrior, launched in 1990, is a good example of how Jackson managed to maintain the distinctive and original styling of their American models by taking advantage of lower manufacturing costs of Japan.

The Jackson Professional 1991 Limited Edition (right) is a fine example of the kind of instrument now being manufactured in Japan. Once again, it features the typical Jackson "dropped headstock" styling, as well as incorporating some of the highest quality components available, such as their JT-90 Floyd Rose licensed double locking tremelo arm.

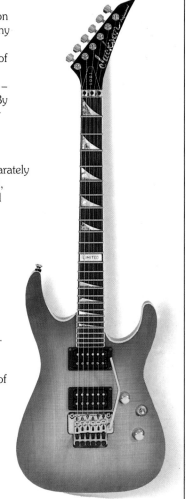

Jackson Professional 1991 Ltd Edition
A superb "rock" guitar that features typical Jackson styling and a Floyd Rose double locking tremelo.

Yamaha Pacifica (left)
Yamaha consistently produce high-quality, affordable instruments like this 1989 Pacifica. During the early nineties, Yamaha began to employ different styling, DiMarzio pick-ups and a Floyd Rose licensed locking tremelo arm.

Hohner G3T (above)
Based on a Steinberger design, though featuring a wooden rather than carbon graphite neck, this guitar represents first class value.

Fender Squier

During the early 1980s, Fender decided to develop a separate range of high-quality Japanese instruments that would allow them to compete with other budget Japanese-made instruments. The most successful have been the Squier Telecaster and the Squier Stratocaster (right).

The magic of the Fender name, the illustrious history of the Stratocaster and the fact that outstanding value for money made the instrument ideal for the first-time buyer gave Fender an outright winner. By the early 1990s Fender claimed that the Squier Stratocaster was the world's biggest selling guitar. The Squier Precision and Jazz models have been equally successful in their domination of the bass guitar market. Squiers are manufactured with a laminated body to keep costs down,

instead of using a single piece of wood, which, in fact, makes for a more consistent quality. An added advantage of buying a Squier over other budget instruments is that the Fender name will ensure a better resale value. The early Japanese Squiers are highly rated and the later Korean-made models also represent very good value.

In recent years, Fender has responded to the increased knowledge of vintage guitars by launching a series of classic re-issues of Stratocasters, Telecasters, and Precisions from the 1950s and 1960s. These instruments are made in Japan but to better specifications than the Squier range, which is reflected in their higher price.

Other American guitars

For almost all the established guitar makers, the 1950s were a time of change and experiment – as they worked on new semi-acoustic and solid-body designs, trying to keep pace with the popularity of jazz and the emergence of rock'n'roll.

Gretsch, Guild and Harmony were all making hollow-body electric guitars during the fifties. In 1955, Gretsch introduced their first solids (the single-cutaway Jet guitars), but their reputation was strongest among country players who were great fans of their semi-acoustics like the Chet Atkins and the White Falcon.

When Epiphone was bought by Gibson in 1957, much of their machinery was sold to Guild – and a lot of their staff went with it. But from 1959, Gibson began making Epiphone guitars at their Kalamazoo factory. They produced electric versions of their well-established acoustic guitars and, in the early 1960s, a series of solid electrics.

Rickenbacker and Danelectro are two other interesting makers. Rickenbacker made its name during the 1960s with a range of distinctively designed instruments. Their classic electric twelve-string sound is best known by Roger McGuinn on the Byrds' "Mr Tambourine Man." Between 1956 and 1968, Danelectro made a limited number of instruments. Use of materials such as masonite gave them a sound that even now finds its way onto records.

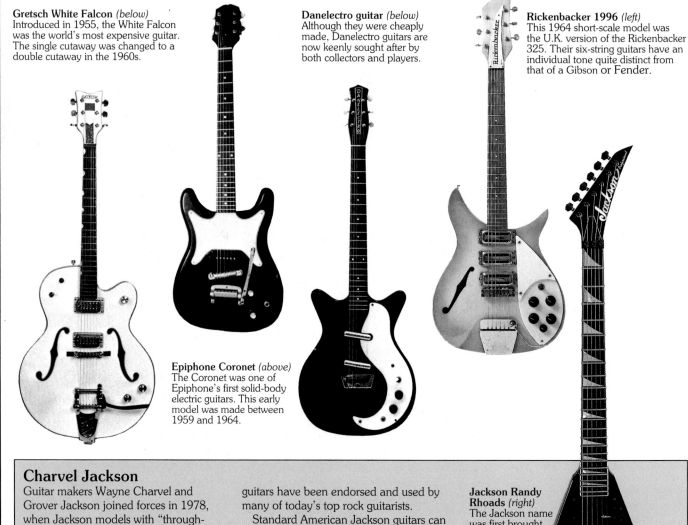

Gretsch White Falcon (below)
Introduced in 1955, the White Falcon was the world's most expensive guitar. The single cutaway was changed to a double cutaway in the 1960s.

Danelectro guitar (below)
Although they were cheaply made, Danelectro guitars are now keenly sought after by both collectors and players.

Rickenbacker 1996 (left)
This 1964 short-scale model was the U.K. version of the Rickenbacker 325. Their six-string guitars have an individual tone quite distinct from that of a Gibson or Fender.

Epiphone Coronet (above)
The Coronet was one of Epiphone's first solid-body electric guitars. This early model was made between 1959 and 1964.

Charvel Jackson

Guitar makers Wayne Charvel and Grover Jackson joined forces in 1978, when Jackson models with "through-necks" were manufactured alongside the Charvel instruments with bolt-on necks. They came to prominence in the early eighties, when they built a custom-designed guitar for Randy Rhoads.

Their distinctive styling, typified by the "drooping" headstock, has, in recent years, become closely identified with heavy rock guitar. Consequently, they have been widely imitated. However, through their use of high-quality materials and superb craftsmanship, Jackson guitars have been endorsed and used by many of today's top rock guitarists.

Standard American Jackson guitars can be ordered from their California workshop; however, the company also operates a custom service and will make instruments according to specialized requirements.

In the eighties, the company also began to manufacture a range of lower priced instruments in Japan. To avoid confusion, American-made Jackson guitars are either described simply as "Jackson" or "Jackson U.S.A." models, whereas the instruments made in Japan are referred to as the "Professional" range.

Jackson Randy Rhoads (right)
The Jackson name was first brought to the attention of the rock guitarist by the late Randy Rhoads.

PLAYING THE GUITAR

The guitar is one of the easiest instruments for the beginner to learn but one of the most difficult to master. For millions of people, a handful of simple chords is all that is needed to work out how to play many of the popular songs we hear every day. But, at the same time, the guitar also offers limitless scope for musical expression to those willing to devote the time and practice to it. The great guitarists will all tell you that the guitar constantly presents you with new challenges and rewards as long as you are willing to seek them out. Learning to play the guitar cannot be done overnight. Our aim in this book has been to set out as clearly as possible – often in easily accessible chart form – a structured system of reference information ranging from the basic to the advanced. This chapter can therefore be used either as an introductory guide to the first steps of learning to play the guitar or as the basis for a more serious study of music theory, music notation and more advanced techniques. Either way, it contains a wealth of information which can be referred to time and time again. No matter at what level you play, use this book for reference and as a source for new ideas. Pick up your guitar and let your hands and ears lead the way.

THE BEGINNER

One of the things that makes the guitar unusual as an instrument is that most people who play it are self-taught. Classical guitarists are an exception, since they usually work with a teacher and follow a set course of training and development. But most rock and folk guitar players simply pick up things as they go along – copying songs from records and trading chords and licks with friends. In fact, some of the world's most influential and innovative guitarists were self-taught. Many of them therefore employ unconventional – but nonetheless effective – techniques.

A complete beginner can pick up a guitar and, within a very short while, produce something that sounds musical. This, together with the guitar's adaptability to so many different styles, is what makes it such a remarkably popular instrument.

All that's needed to get started is enthusiasm. What you play, and where you learn it from, is entirely up to you. The important thing is simply to begin playing.

"I'd play whenever I could get my hands on an electric guitar; I was trying to pick up rock'n'roll riffs and electric blues – the latest Muddy Waters. I'd spend hours and hours on the same track, back again, and back again."

Keith Richards

Where to start

The first thing to do is to get yourself a decent guitar. Initially, it doesn't matter whether it has steel strings or nylon strings, or whether it is electric or acoustic. What does matter is that it is playable. Cheap guitars are often a false economy. If they are badly set up – if the action is too high or too hard (see p. 166), if the neck is out of alignment (see p. 168), if the frets are uneven or poorly finished (see p. 170) and if the intonation is inaccurate (see p. 171) – then even an experienced guitarist will have trouble. Probably more beginners are discouraged by trying to learn on a bad guitar than by any other single factor. So, buy the best guitar you can afford, and check that it has been properly set up.

The next most important thing is *tuning*. Guitars go out of tune all the time – especially if the strings are new, if the temperature changes suddenly, if they get knocked or dropped, and if you play them hard. You must learn to tune the guitar yourself. It is not as difficult as it first appears (see p. 70).

Begin with simple open chords. On p. 74, you will find a *Beginner's chord vocabulary* containing fifteen basic chords. Concentrate on learning these shapes until you can get to them without having to think about it. Make sure that you finger them correctly – so that each separate note sounds clearly – and then go on to develop speed and accuracy.

By this time you should already be starting to explore what happens when you put these chords together in different orders. On p. 76, we explain how *chord sequences* work and show how certain progressions form the basis of hundreds of popular songs. At the heart of this lies the "Roman numeral system". It provides you with a way of analyzing chord progressions and also allows you to "code" them so that they are easier to understand, memorize and transpose to another key. It will help enormously if you learn from the outset to think about what key you are in and what the role is of each chord you play.

Experiment with different right-hand techniques. Try playing with and without a plectrum. Let the strings ring when you play chords, then see what happens when you deaden them – either with your left hand or your right. When you strum, notice the different effects produced by upstrokes and downstrokes. Finally, try *flatpicking* (see p. 79) and *fingerpicking* (see p. 80).

Barre chords are the next step on from simple open chords (see p. 82). Their importance cannot be over-stated. Mastering barre techniques is a major breakthrough point, instantly placing many more chords at your disposal. And, once you understand how they work, they will open up the whole fingerboard to you.

The importance of practicing

Learning to play the guitar is largely a process of committing skills to instinct, of developing the necessary motor skills or what is sometimes known as "finger memory". And the only way to achieve this is by practicing – repeating the same thing over and over until it becomes automatic. As Howard Roberts, one of the great jazz guitarists and a respected teacher, has said:

"Learning to play the guitar is a combination of mental and motor skill acquisition. And to develop motor skills, repetition is essential . . . Whenever musicians have trouble executing a passage, they generally tend to blame themselves for not having enough talent. Actually, all that's wrong is they don't know where their fingers are supposed to go . . . You should learn the piece in your head before you play it. And when you do play it, play it so slow that there's no possibility of making a mistake."

Howard Roberts

However, this tends to make practice sound like unrelenting hard work. It needn't be. There are as many different approaches to practicing as there are guitarists. Some practice regularly, at certain times of the day; others pick up the guitar only when they feel like it. The only real advice is to play as often as you can, either on your own or with other musicians. Think about what you're doing while you are playing, and listen to what it sounds like. Stop and take a break when you become bored or when playing turns into too much of a chore. Any extra work you want to put in on studying scales, chords and harmony will always pay off; it can only help you to improve as a guitarist.

"Practice, practice, practice. Practice until you get a guitar welt on your chest . . . if it makes you feel good, don't stop until you see the blood from your fingers. Then you'll know you're on to something!"

Ted Nugent

Ted Nugent

The basics of music notation

Conventional music notation is a complete, self-contained language. It allows music to be written down on the page and thereby recorded or communicated without its having to be heard. Many rock and folk guitarists never learn to read music. Indeed, many of the best-known and most respected players have got by without it. This is unfortunate not because their music would have been any better if they had learned to read, but because it tends to make beginners think it is not worth the effort. In fact, there are four major reasons why being able to use music notation is a good idea: first, it means you can go into any music shop, take any piece of sheet music, and work out how to play it without ever having heard it before; second, it means you can keep an accurate and permanent record of any of your compositions; third, it means you can convey musical ideas to other musicians without having to play them; and, lastly, the very way in which music is written often helps to explain the theory and principles of how scales, chords, melody, harmony and rhythm are constructed.

In this book, we have not made the ability to read music a prerequisite. We do, however, encourage you to learn. Where possible, we have used music notation alongside other methods of conveying the same information – chord diagrams, fingering patterns, photographs, charts, etc. This leaves the choice up to you.

Basic music notation is not difficult to understand. But, like any language, it takes time and practice to become fluent. Sight-reading is not something you can pick up overnight. However, simply learning what the symbols mean is relatively easy.

The system is essentially very simple. Music notation is plotted on a five-line grid called the *staff* or *stave*. Extra lines (called *leger lines*) can be added as the range of the piece of music dictates. The vertical placement of a note tells you its pitch: the higher the note, the higher its symbol will be placed on the staff. The horizontal placement of the symbol tells you when the note is to be played, simply by reading the notes across the page from left to right.

A *clef* at the start of each line of music indicates the pitch of each line in the staff. A *key signature* tells you what key you are playing in. And a *time signature*, together with the *bar lines* that divide up the staff into smaller units of time, tells you what you need to know about the rhythm.

All these elements, plus those that have not been mentioned, are explained in detail later in this chapter, under the relevant topic. The illustration below, which identifies the most important symbols, can be used as a visual key or summary.

How music notation works The diagram here shows the basic "grid" on which all music notation is written – the five-line staff, divided into bars, and "labeled" with a clef, a key signature and a time signature.

Example This shows the scale of G major written out in standard music notation. The key signature indicates that an F♯ is to be played.

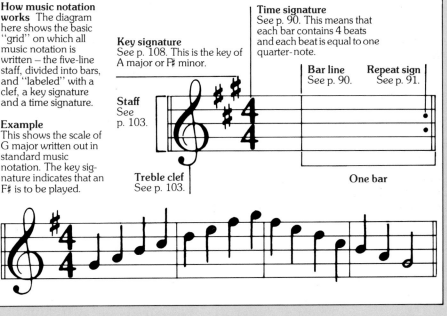

Key signature See p. 108. This is the key of A major or F♯ minor.

Staff See p. 103.

Treble clef See p. 103.

Time signature See p. 90. This means that each bar contains 4 beats and each beat is equal to one quarter-note.

Bar line See p. 90. **Repeat sign** See p. 91.

One bar

Guitar tablature

Tablature is a system of writing down music for the guitar as well as for other fretted instruments. It has existed in various forms through the centuries and has been used for flamenco, folk and lute music. It simply sets out the fingerings for a piece of music in a sort of shorthand. The system relies on you being able to hear the piece of music so that you are familiar with the rhythmic structure of the piece and the timing of the individual notes. In other words, it is used in conjunction with memory. Compared with music notation, it is easy to understand.

However, tablature cannot convey precise information about timing and the duration of notes. Nor does it help you to understand the harmonic structure of a piece in the way that notation can. Don't fall into the trap of thinking you can do everything with tablature that you can do with notation. Treat it for what it is – a form of shorthand.

Tablature is based on a six-line grid (as opposed to the five-line grid of music notation), but the major difference is that each line represents one of the guitar strings. The top line is the 1st (top E) string, and the bottom line is the 6th (bottom E) string. The numbers that appear on the lines are fret numbers. So, a number 3 on the 2nd line from the top, for example, tells you to play D on the 3rd fret of the 2nd string. An O on the same line indicates that you play the open 2nd string.

How tablature works This diagram shows the basic tablature "grid" – six lines, each representing one of the guitar strings. The numbers indicate at which fret the note is to be played.

Example As above, this shows the scale of G major. It starts on the G at the 5th fret on the 4th string.

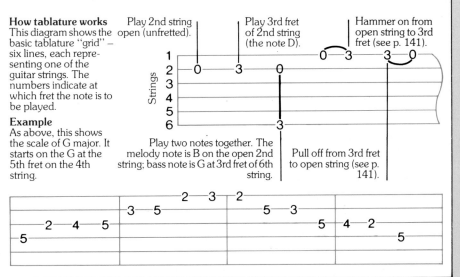

Play 2nd string open (unfretted).

Play 3rd fret of 2nd string (the note D).

Hammer on from open string to 3rd fret (see p. 141).

Play two notes together. The melody note is B on the open 2nd string; bass note is G at 3rd fret of 6th string.

Pull off from 3rd fret to open string (see p. 141).

How the guitar is tuned

If you strike a guitar string, the "pitch" of the note it produces depends on three things – its length, its thickness and the tension it is under. Since all the open strings on a guitar are the same length (although see *Setting the intonation*, p. 171), one variable is removed and only two are left – thickness and tension.

On a six-string guitar, each string is of a different thickness or "gauge" (see p. 162). The thickest, heaviest string gives the lowest note of the six, and the thinnest, lightest string gives the highest.

It is by adjusting the tension of each of these six strings that you can control exactly what the pitch of the notes will be. The tuning heads increase or reduce the tension on the strings. Tightening a string will raise the pitch of the note, and loosening it will lower the pitch.

What we now call "tempered tuning" was established around the time that Bach wrote his *Well-Tempered Clavier* (1722-44). Before then, music was approached differently: each key was considered in terms of its own tonality and for its own distinctive atmosphere. In tempered tuning, all semi-tones are at equal intervals; in the pre-Bach "mean tone temperament", they were not. Since the design of the Spanish guitar pre-dates *The Well-Tempered Clavier*, the instrument has inherited the legacy of being difficult to play in tune. In contrast with the piano, the guitar does have a different atmosphere in each key. This occurs most notably when the guitar is tuned in only one key, and is largely due to the different basic constructions of popular chord shapes and to the response of the strings at different parts of the fingerboard. However, a modern guitar, of good quality and in good condition, can play in tune with any other instrument tuned or calibrated to standard or "concert" pitch.

There is a reference standard for concert pitch, used by most orchestras and recording studios (see opposite). It is also used as a standard by guitar and string manufacturers to judge the intonation and accuracy of their products. It is therefore essential, if your guitar is to play in tune in any key and in any position on the fingerboard, that you begin by tuning to concert pitch.

Standard open-string tunings

Over the years, a standard has evolved for how the six open strings of the guitar are tuned in relation to one another. The thickest or 6th string is tuned to E, the 5th to A, the 4th to D, the 3rd to G, the 2nd to B, and the thinnest or 1st to E. The two Es are the same note but they have a different pitch; the top E is two octaves higher than the bottom E. In other words, this convention establishes the difference or "interval" that there is between each string – E to A to D to G to B to E.

Twelve-string guitars are tuned to the same standard pattern. However, they are sometimes set a tone lower, and the tuning of each pair of strings varies. The 1st and 2nd strings are tuned in "unison", giving identical notes of the same pitch; the other four pairs are each tuned to give the same notes but an octave apart.

Of course, this standard tuning is not the only way a guitar can be tuned. There are many variations and alternatives which might be better suited to a particular tune or style, or which might be used to create a specific sort of "sound". Some of these are covered on p. 158.

1st string = E	
2nd string = B	
3rd string = G	
4th string = D	
5th string = A	
6th string = E	

Six-string tuning
(*left*) With top and bottom strings both tuned to E, there are 2 octaves between high and low open strings.

Twelve-string tuning
(*right*) Although the tuning is the same, a twelve-string guitar produces a much fuller, richer sound.

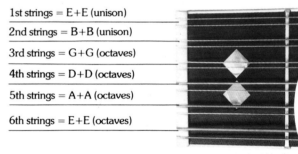

1st strings = E+E (unison)	
2nd strings = B+B (unison)	
3rd strings = G+G (octaves)	
4th strings = D+D (octaves)	
5th strings = A+A (octaves)	
6th strings = E+E (octaves)	

Fretted notes

Horizontal *frets* are set into the fingerboard throughout its length and at right angles to the strings. When you press a string down onto a fret you are effectively shortening it. As we have seen above, the length of the string is one of the variables which determines the pitch of the note it produces. The shorter it is the higher the note, and the longer it is the lower the note. So, "fretting" a string will give a note with a pitch higher than that of the open string.

Frets are spaced out according to a particular mathematical series (see p. 40) which means that each fret produces a note a "semi-tone" (or "half-step") higher than

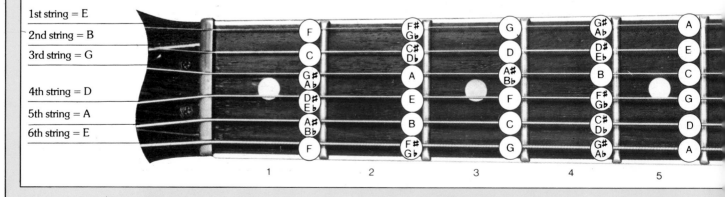

Tuning a guitar to concert pitch

The pitch of a note is determined by the *frequency* of the sound waves generated in the air. Frequency is measured in cycles per second or "Hertz" (Hz). A vibrating string producing a note with a frequency of 220 Hz, for example, will be completing 220 cycles of its particular vibration pattern *every second*.

Concert pitch has been standardized by establishing that the note of A (above middle C on the piano, and on the 5th fret of the 1st string on the guitar) should have a frequency of 440 Hz. The frequency is doubled for a note one octave higher, and halved for a note an octave lower. So, A on the 17th fret of the 1st string vibrates at 880 Hz, A on the 2nd fret of the 3rd string vibrates at 220 Hz, and A on the open 5th string vibrates at 110 Hz.

It is possible for a guitar to be in tune with itself and yet still be above or below concert pitch. But it is a good idea to get into the habit of keeping your guitar at concert pitch; it is better for the accuracy of the instrument and vital when you play in a band with other instruments.

Tuning a guitar to concert pitch can be done by taking reference notes from a well-tuned piano and tuning up or down to them. The open E (1st) string should sound the same as the E that can be found two notes above middle C on the keyboard.

Bear in mind, however, that guitar music is written an octave higher than written keyboard music. Therefore, a middle C played on the guitar (3rd fret of the 5th string) is actually an octave lower in sound than middle C on the piano.

Concert pitch can also be taken from a set of "pitch pipes" (probably easier for beginners, since they produce all six different notes) or a "tuning fork". Most tuning forks give an A of 440 Hz. Tune the 1st string (5th fret), 2nd string (10th fret) and 3rd string (14th fret) to this note, and then tune the other strings in relation to these. The A from the tuning fork also corresponds to the 5th fret harmonic on the open 5th string – that is, the harmonic A two octaves above the open A (see p. 71).

The recent introduction of electronic guitar tuners is a godsend not only to guitarists who wish to play in tune but to any musician who realizes that tuning is an art in itself and to any player who wishes to bring out the best sounds that the guitar can possibly produce.

Pitch pipes
Specifically designed for tuning a guitar, pitch pipes produce six different notes, each corresponding to one of the six open strings.

Tuning fork
When struck and placed on the bridge of the guitar, a tuning fork will emit an A note with a frequency of 440 Hz. This is two octaves above the open A (5th) string and corresponds to A on the 5th fret of the 1st string.

Electronic tuners
Most have a mike for acoustics plus a plug-in socket for electrics. Readouts are by meter needle, liquid crystal or stroboscope. Some emit reference tones.

Notes on the keyboard

Middle C as played on guitar   Middle C on keyboard

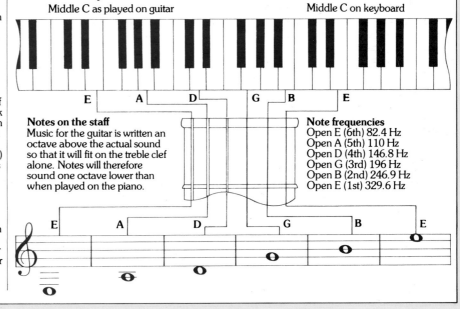

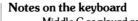

E   A   D   G   B   E

Notes on the staff
Music for the guitar is written an octave above the actual sound so that it will fit on the treble clef alone. Notes will therefore sound one octave lower than when played on the piano.

Note frequencies
Open E (6th) 82.4 Hz
Open A (5th) 110 Hz
Open D (4th) 146.8 Hz
Open G (3rd) 196 Hz
Open B (2nd) 246.9 Hz
Open E (1st) 329.6 Hz

E   A   D   G   B   E

---

the fret below it. If you hold down the open E (1st) string on the 1st fret you get an F, if you hold it down on the 2nd fret you get an F♯, and so on. Similarly, the first fret on the open G (3rd) string gives you a G♯, the 2nd

fret an A, and so on.

The 12th fret is situated about midway between the nut and the saddle of the guitar – that is, it divides the length of the vibrating string in half. This means that the note on

the 12th fret has the same pitch as that of the open string but is an octave higher. The fact that there are twelve frets representing twelve notes in an octave is fundamental to the formation of scales and chords.

Enharmonic notes
Certain notes (the black keys on a piano) are known by more than one name and are therefore called "enharmonic". The note between F and G, for example, may be referred to as either F♯ or G♭ (see p. 103).

The 12th fret and beyond
Notes on the 12th fret have the same names as notes on the open strings, but they are exactly one octave higher in pitch. Fretted notes above the 12th fret simply repeat the pattern shown here. On the open E (1st) string, the 13th fret gives an F, the 14th fret an F♯, etc.

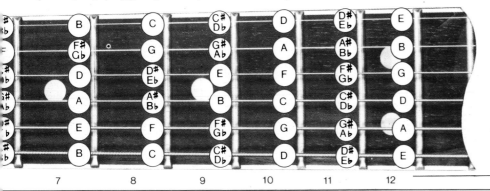

Tuning methods

Many beginners find tuning difficult. The technique depends on the ability of your ears to perceive slight differences in pitch between two separate notes, and also to recognize good intonation when you hear it and the difference when you do not. Although the immediate visual reference provided by electronic tuners is a great help, there is no substitute for the traditional skill of tuning a guitar using just a single reference tone and your ears. Some people find the ability to judge pitch easier than others. If you are one of those who find it difficult, take consolation in the fact that your sense of pitch will develop and improve, along with your technique, the more you play. A good musical "ear" *can* be learned and is a skill which develops with experience.

One of the secrets of good tuning is to take it slowly and calmly. If you are tense or in a hurry, you will not be able to relax, concen-trate and listen objectively, and you will find it hard to recognize whether a particular string is sharp or flat.

You should always use the tuning heads to bring the string you are tuning *up* to pitch. Never try to tune *down* to pitch. Instead, slacken the string so that it goes slightly flat and then tighten it to bring it up into tune. This will help to keep it stable at the right pitch. String slippage is a major problem for all guitarists. It can be more-or-less prevented, however, by fitting the strings properly in the first place (see p. 164) and by "stretching" them – hitting them fairly hard, bending them or pulling them away from the guitar so that you give them a chance to settle down – before you begin playing.

The problem of strings going out of tune is often worse for a lead guitarist who uses light-gauge strings and plays a lot of solos with bent notes than it is for an acoustic guitarist with heavier strings and a lighter fingerstyle technique. Strings also tend to go out of tune if the guitar is suddenly taken from a cold room to a warm room, or vice-versa.

The tuning methods described here will all allow you to tune the guitar to itself. This is called "relative tuning". However, if you want the guitar to be tuned to standard concert pitch – and it ought to be – then you must start by tuning at least one string to an accurate reference note.

Most guitarists use a combination of some or all of these methods. Generally, it is a good idea to start by going through all six strings and getting them approximately to the correct pitch. You can then go back and make slight adjustments where necessary to ensure that each string plays in tune with the others. One should consider tuning in two stages: first, a rough "general tuning" and then a much more precise "fine tuning".

Method 1

1 Beginning with the open E (1st) string at the right pitch, tune the open E (6th) string to the same note but two octaves lower.
2 Play an A on the 5th fret of the 6th string and tune the open A (5th) string to it.
3 Play a D on the 5th fret of the 5th string and tune the open D (4th) string to it.
4 Play a G on the 5th fret of the 4th string and tune the open G (3rd) string to it.
5 Play a B on the 4th fret of the 3rd string and tune the open B (2nd) string to it.
6 Finally, play an E on the 5th fret of the 2nd string and check the open E (1st) string against it. Do not move on to the next string until you are certain that the one you are tuning is correct.

Method 2

1 Beginning with the open E (1st) string at the right pitch, play a B on the 7th fret and tune the open B (2nd) string to it.
2 Play a G on the 3rd fret of the 1st string and tune the open G (3rd) string to it.
3 Play a D on the 3rd fret of the 2nd string and tune the open D (4th) string to it.
4 Play an A on the 2nd fret of the 3rd string and tune the open A (5th) string to it.
5 Play an E on the 2nd fret of the 4th string and tune the open E (6th) string to it.
6 Finally, check the open 1st and 6th strings.

Method 3

1 If you have a tuning fork, begin by tuning the open A (5th) string to it.
2 Play an E on the 7th fret of the 5th string and tune both open E (1st and 6th) strings to it.
3 Play a B on the 7th fret of the 1st string and tune the open B (2nd) string to it.
4 Play a G on the 8th fret of the 2nd string and tune the open G (3rd) string to it.
5 Play a D on the 7th fret of the 3rd string and tune the open D (4th) string to it.
6 Finally, play an A on the 7th fret of the 4th string and check the original open A (5th) string.

Tuning to chords

All guitars tend to sound perfectly in tune in one chord and to be slightly out of tune in all the others. It is in the nature of their construction. Unlike the violin or double bass (which are fretless), the intervals between the notes are fixed by the frets.

In an attempt to minimize the effect of this, the precise positioning of the frets is designed to spread out across the fingerboard any inaccuracies in the intervals between one note and the next, whatever key you are playing in. This means that, to all intents and purposes, the guitar will sound correctly in tune in every key. It is called "tempered tuning".

Tuning to chords is a good way of checking and, if necessary, adjusting this compromise in the tuning. Once the open strings are in tune with one another, play a chord – sounding each individual note and listening carefully to the intervals between them. If you are going to play in the key of C, for

example, begin by playing an open C chord and check that it sounds right. Then play some of the other chords in the same key – F and G, for instance – to see whether they are also in tune. It is also a good idea to play each chord in different shapes up and down the fingerboard to check the tuning in different positions. (Details of how to play these chords, and how they are related to one another, appear on pp. 74-7 and 82-3.)

Fine tuning chords as they are being sounded is a useful technique for checking your tuning while actually performing – although it calls for good judgment in recognizing which string is the offender and the ability to tell how far out it is. With your left hand in position holding down the chord, and while the strings are still ringing, reach across with your right hand and adjust the tuning head. This is a little easier on guitars with all six tuning heads on the top of the headstock.

Tuning to a chord while playing

Tuning with harmonics

"Harmonic" notes are described on p. 116, together with instructions on how to play them. They are often used to check tuning and intonation due to the fact that they have a purer sound than open strings or fretted notes and because of the phenomenon of *beat tones*. Beat tones are generated when two pitches are close but not quite the same. If one note is an A vibrating at 440 Hz and the other is just a little flat, vibrating at, say, 436 Hz, you will be able to hear 4 beat tones or pulses per second when you play the two notes together. As you bring the second note up to the pitch of the first, the beats will slow down – and will eventually disappear when the two notes are in tune with one another. Recognizing the beat tones may be slightly difficult at first, but, with practice, you will quickly develop an "ear" for them. The method is as follows.

Checking 5th and 7th fret harmonics

● Play a 5th fret harmonic E on the 6th string quickly followed by a 7th fret harmonic E on the 5th string so that both notes are ringing together. Tune the strings by bringing the beats together.

● Play a 5th fret harmonic A on the 5th string and a 7th fret harmonic A on the 4th string. Tune these two together.

● Play a 5th fret harmonic D on the 4th string and a 7th fret harmonic D on the 3rd string. Tune these two together.

● Finally, play a 5th fret harmonic B on the 2nd string and 7th fret harmonic B on the 1st string. Tune these two together.

Checking 7th and 12th fret harmonics

● Play a 12th fret harmonic E on the 6th string and a 7th fret harmonic E on the 5th string. Tune these two together.

● Play a 12th fret harmonic A on the 5th string and a 7th fret harmonic A on the 4th string. Tune these two together.

● Play a 12th fret harmonic D on the 4th string and a 7th fret harmonic D on the 3rd string. Tune these two together.

● Finally, play a 12th fret harmonic B on the 2nd string and a 7th fret harmonic B on the 1st string. Tune these two together.

Double checking

To prevent a gradual accumulation of error when tuning, here is an excellent check for ensuring that the two top strings (1st and 2nd) are in tune with the bass string (6th). First, play the 5th fret harmonic E on the 6th string against the 12th fret harmonic E on the 1st string. Next, play the 7th fret harmonic B on the 6th string against the 12th fret harmonic B on the 2nd string.

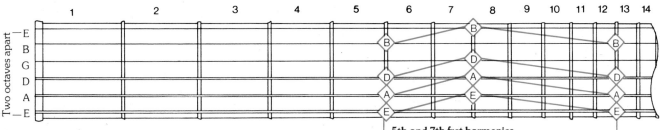

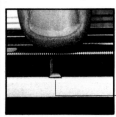

How to play a harmonic note
Place the tip of your finger lightly on the open string exactly over the top of the fret in question. Pluck the string and then remove your finger immediately to let the harmonic note ring (see p. 116).

String is not actually pushed down to fret.

5th and 7th fret harmonics
The harmonic note on the 5th fret of a string is always identical to the harmonic note on the 7th fret of the next string up – except in the case of the 2nd and 3rd strings.

7th and 12th fret harmonics
The harmonic note on the 12th fret of a string is always identical to the harmonic note on the 7th fret of the next string up – except in the case of the 2nd and 3rd strings.

Left-hand technique

The function of your left hand is to press the strings down onto the frets in order to sound the required notes. Before your right hand strikes the strings, your left hand must be in position, creating a specific selection of fretted notes for your right hand to play.

Many of the lead guitarist's left-hand techniques – for example, hammering-on, string-bending, slides and vibratos – are part of the arsenal of tricks associated primarily with the sound of the modern guitar. In contrast, the rhythm guitarist's left hand tends to be more concerned with fingering chord shapes. However, modern rhythm guitarists also use many syncopation and "chop" techniques that rely on the left hand for damping effects. It is, after all, left-hand damping that creates specific time values by releasing the string when it has sounded for the required duration, and that cancels unwanted notes when several strings are played at once.

There are various rules and conventions about how the left hand should be positioned and how the fingers should fret the strings. Classical guitarists are taught to use a specific left-hand technique which allows them to play without altering their basic hand position or posture. Some rock guitarists, however, will use any trick in the book.

Thumb position

The classical approach is that your thumb should always be in the middle of the back of the neck. This means that there should be a clear space between the neck and the palm of your hand, and that your wrist will be slightly bent so that your fingers will rest comfortably on the strings. Your thumb then acts as a fulcrum, allowing you to deliver just the right amount of pressure to your fingertips in order to fret the notes clearly. Many chord positions

are difficult unless your thumb is providing pressure from the back of the neck. This position will give you maximum precision, flexibility and speed.

Many guitarists place their thumb too high on the back of the neck, and end up cradling the neck in their palm. It is an easy habit to slip

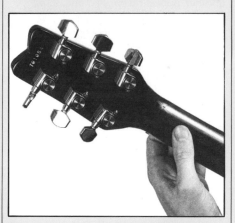

Thumb centered on the back of the guitar neck.

into, since it provides extra support for rock and country techniques. However, regardless of technique, if you sit your guitar on your lap or wear it from a strap, the neck should always be balanced so that it stays in the same position when you take your left hand away.

In some modern styles, the thumb is hooked over the top of the neck to fret notes on the bottom E (6th) string. This may be done either when extending a "barre chord" (see p. 82) or when playing separate melody and bass lines. Although condemned by classical guitarists, the technique does open up other fingering possibilities. It is also useful for getting extra "leverage" when bending strings (see p. 142).

Finger positions

To play a single clear note without touching any other strings, your fingers should be arched so that the tips come down onto the fretboard more or less at right angles to it. This obviously means that your fingernails should not protrude beyond the ends of your fingertips. If they are too long, you will probably find that you cannot fret the strings firmly or that, when you do, you accidentally deaden other strings.

When you fret a string, you should hold it down between two frets, but just *behind* the one you want. The vibrating length of the string will then be the distance from the higher of the frets to the saddle.

Use only as much finger pressure as is necessary to make the note sound clearly. Pressing too hard will tire your fingers and may well hurt. Beginners often experience this immediately – especially with steel strings – since it takes a little while to toughen the fingertips and learn how to apply just the right amount of pressure to the strings.

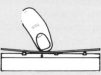

Correct
Fingering the string just behind the fret will produce a clean, ringing note.

Incorrect
Placing your finger too far back may allow the string to rattle or buzz against the fret.

Incorrect
Putting your finger actually on top of the fret will almost certainly muffle the string and dampen the sound.

The "one-fret-per-finger" rule

Classical guitarists approach the fingerboard with the concept that each finger on the left hand should have a fret space to itself and that it should be responsible for all six strings (and therefore all six notes) on that fret. In this way, one hand position will cover four frets; and, theoretically, three hand positions could cover all twelve frets up to the octave.

As a beginner you will find it difficult to use your 4th finger. Nevertheless, it is important to persevere. It will become easier with practice, and strength and independence in your 4th finger is invaluable for advanced chords and fast lead patterns.

Because the guitar is one of the few instruments on which it is possible to play many notes in more than one place, deter-

mining the best position to use is the first consideration of most guitarists learning a new piece of music (see p. 102). However, whatever the position on the fingerboard, playing a melody line is usually easier if you follow the one-fret-per-finger rule. When

you have to change your hand position, each finger moves to cover a new fret.

Sometimes, classical guitarists keep each finger down on the last note it played until it is needed to play a new note. This can produce a "ringing-on" harmonic effect.

Covering twelve frets in three fingering positions

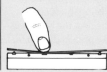

1st fret position
The four fingers cover the four frets from 1st to 4th.

5th fret position
The four fingers cover the four frets from 5th to 8th.

9th fret position
The four fingers cover the four frets from 9th to 12th.

Right-hand technique

Right-hand control is a combination of timing and accuracy. The more you practice, the sooner your right hand will become an extension of your sense of rhythm, and the easier it will be to concentrate on accuracy.

At first you may find it helpful to provide support for your right hand. Your forearm should rest lightly across the upper face of the guitar, leaving your hand free to move and in the right position to play. For even more stability, you can rest your palm on the bridge behind the strings.

The golden rule for all right-hand technique is "minimum movement for maximum effect". Speed, versatility and the energy required for striking the string come from rotating the forearm and wrist. The hand should move only to select the strings and to control the plectrum or fingers.

Generally, the playing area is considered to be the space between the bridge and the body end of the fingerboard. The sound varies according to the exact point of contact: it is sharp and trebly close to the bridge, and becomes progressively more mellow as you move towards the middle of the string.

Whether you choose to play with your fingers or with a plectrum is a personal decision based on the style of the music and the sound you want to produce. With notable exceptions, most blues, rock and jazz guitarists use plectrums. On steel-string guitars, plectrums produce more volume and a clearer tone (due to their sharper attack). In contrast, classical, flamenco, Latin-American and many folk guitarists generally play only with their fingers. It requires considerable fingerstyle technique to match the speed of a plectrum when playing melody lines, but considerable plectrum technique to match the rhythmic versatility of the fingers.

Plectrums

The choice of plectrum is a matter of personal "feel". Thin plectrums, which offer less resistance to the strings, produce a small "click" that emphasizes the treble content of the attack, and they make fast strumming or "mandolin" picking easier. Hard picks produce more volume and a firmer tone. They also offer better control at high speed because they make a more definite contact with the strings.

The plectrum is held between the tip of the thumb and the side of the 1st finger – with the thumb and finger at right angles to one another. There are three ways in which the plectrum can be used to strike the string: as a *downstroke*, as an *upstroke*, or in the form of *alternate strokes*. Each produces its own sound. The basic goal of all plectrum technique should be the ability to use each with equal ease and control.

Plectrum exercises

These exercises are all designed to develop fast and accurate alternate plectrum strokes. Begin by establishing a steady count of 1–2–3–4. On the count, play each open string four times – first with downstrokes, then with upstrokes.

Now, at the same tempo, say the word "and" between each count. Play a downstroke on the count and an upstroke on the "and" – hitting each string eight times over each count of four.

Slow down the tempo and, this time, play a downstroke and an upstroke on each count as well as on each "and". You should now be play-

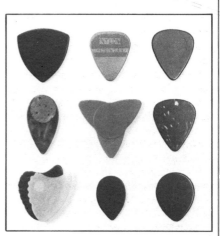

A selection of plectrums
Also called "picks" or "flatpicks", plectrums are made in a variety of materials – plastic, nylon, tortoiseshell, rubber, felt, and even stone. They come in various shapes, sizes and thicknesses.

ing sixteen alternate strokes over each count of four. Try changing chords after each sixteen.

In addition to simple time divisions of four, you should also learn to play alternate strokes in threes. These are called "triplets" (see p. 94). Establish a count of four, as above, but say 2–3 between each count and play the string once for each number spoken.

Maintain a strict down-up movement so that the plectrum never plays two downstrokes or two upstrokes in succession. Finally, try playing different strings for each count or "beat".

Fingerstyles

Most popular fingerstyles are a product of traditional folk styles, and they employ every conceivable application of the four fingers and the thumb. There are few rules and only some similarities between styles since most techniques have developed through tradition, imitation and instinct.

All fingerstyles rely on the thumb to play the bass strings and the fingers to play the top strings. With the thumb playing the downstrokes and the fingers playing the upstrokes, four or five notes can be sounded simultaneously or one after another, as an "arpeggio".

As regards the position of the right hand in relation to the strings, the "classical" technique gives the most freedom and the best response from the guitar.

"Classical" hand position   "Anchor" hand position   "Muting" hand position

Thumbpicks and fingerpicks
Many fingerstyle guitarists keep the nails on their right hand fairly long and use them to strike the strings. Others use metal or plastic fingerpicks which fit over the ends of the fingers and thumb.

Open chords

The first goal of any guitarist wanting to play popular music is to build up a chord vocabulary. This is largely a question of teaching the left hand to remember the various shapes. It does take time, but the more often you use a particular chord, the quicker you will be able to find it and the smoother your playing will sound.

The fifteen simple chords shown here comprise the beginner's chord vocabulary. Using these fifteen, in various combinations, it is possible to play a simplified arrangement of many popular songs.

Begin by looking carefully at each chord and try to memorize its shape or pattern. Get your fingers into position one at a time, then play each string separately to check that all the notes are sounding. If a fretted note does not ring properly, it will be due to imprecise fingering or insufficient pressure. If an open string does not sound, one of your fingers will be getting in the way and damping it.

Simple chord construction

It takes a minimum of three notes to make a chord, and *any* combination of three or more notes – however "discordant" they may sound together – can be considered as a chord of some sort. On the guitar, it is possible to play chords with as many as six different notes in them (one for each string), but all the chords shown here are made up of just three

or four notes – some of which are repeated or "doubled" (see p. 123).

Simple three-note chords are called *triads*; two notes are known as an *interval*. All chords convey to the ear two important musical statements. The first is the "key" or "tone center"; this is the principal note of the chord and it is the one on which it is built. For this reason, it is called the *root* note. The second is the "harmony"; this is the effect produced by sounding the other notes in the chord *in relation to* the root note. It is the particular sound of the chord, and it is determined by the intervals between the root note and the other notes.

Take the three E chords – E major, E seventh and E minor – as an example. All three have E as their root note, but each has a different sound and therefore a different use. E major is a simple three-note triad comprising E, G and B. But, when you play E seventh, you are introducing another note into the chord, a D. This is what makes it sound different from E major. Now play E minor; consider how it differs from E major. Both are three-note triads, but the major chord has a strong, stable sound, whereas the minor chord is slightly sadder, more melancholy. In each case, it is the interval between the root note and the third note in the scale of the chord that determines whether it is a major or a minor (see pp. 104-7).

The beginner's chord vocabulary

Learning these fifteen chords should be your first job. The three E chords are probably the easiest with which to start: first, all six strings are played; second, once you can play E major, you need to remove only one finger to play E seventh or E minor. The C chords and the B seventh call for slightly more precise fingering if all the notes are to sound clearly. And to play the F chord, you must use your 1st finger to hold down two strings at once. This is a simple "barre" (see p. 82). Your thumb should be behind your 1st finger, providing pressure directly opposite the barre.

E major

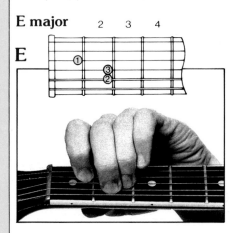

E seventh
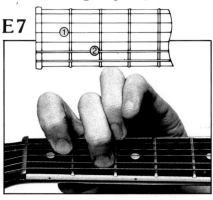

E minor
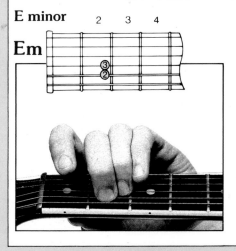

How to read chord diagrams

To learn these fifteen basic chords, you must understand how to read chord diagrams. These are simply box grids representing the strings and the frets on the fingerboard. The six horizontal lines are the strings, with the top E (1st) at the top and the bottom E (6th) at the bottom. The vertical lines are the fret wires, and the spaces in between are numbered to indicate which

part of the fingerboard is being shown. Finger positions are indicated by circles on the strings. The numbers in the circles tell you which finger to use. A circle without a number in it indicates an optional note. If there is no circle on the string, it should be played open (unfretted). If there is an "X" on the string, it forms no part of the chord and should not be sounded at all.

Example: C major

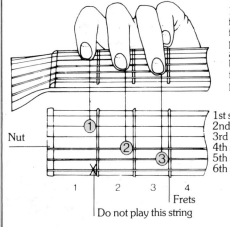

Chord diagram

The circles indicate that the 1st finger plays the 1st fret on the 2nd string, the 2nd finger the 2nd fret on the 4th string, and the 3rd finger the 3rd fret on the 5th string. The 1st and 3rd strings are played open, and the 6th string is not played at all. The thumb should be in the middle of the back of the neck, somewhere level with the 1st fret, so that there is a clear space between the palm and the guitar neck.

1st string
2nd string
3rd string
4th string
5th string
6th string

Nut

1 2 3 4 Frets

Do not play this string

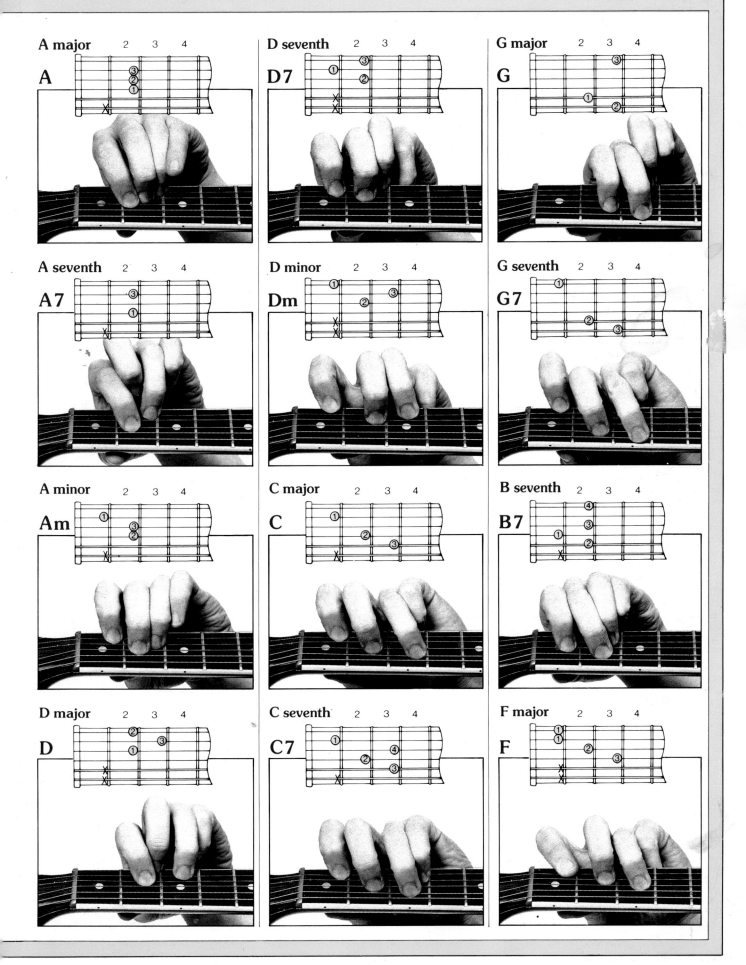

The three-chord theory

As soon as you are able to play the fifteen beginner's chords, it will become obvious that some sound better together than others. In any key, there are three chords which appear in virtually every basic progression. They will always sound good together, whatever order you put them in and whatever key you play them in. They are called the *primary chords*, and they represent the building blocks of all composition.

You can find these three chords in any key by looking at the major scale. Take C as an example. The key of C major has no sharps or flats in it. So, in one octave, the notes are:

C D E F G A B C.

The note of C itself is the root note, and the chord built on this note is C major, called the *tonic* chord. The other two primary chords are the 4th and the 5th in the scale. Counting up four notes, including C itself as the first, brings you to F, and counting up five notes brings you to G. The 4th chord (built on the note of F) is called the *sub-dominant*, and the 5th chord (built on the note of G) is called the *dominant*. F is therefore the sub-dominant chord and G is the dominant chord in the key of C. (For more details on scales, see p. 104, and on chord construction, see p. 121.)

In any key, these three chords have the same relationship to one another. Together, they comprise the "three-chord theory".

Finding the I, IV and V chords

Example: key of C major

I	II	III	IV	V	VI	VII	I
C	D	E	F	G	A	B	C

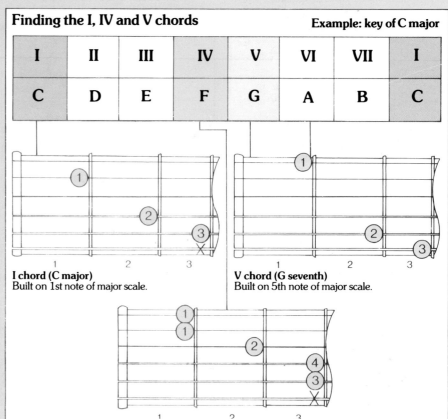

I chord (C major)
Built on 1st note of major scale.

V chord (G seventh)
Built on 5th note of major scale.

IV chord (F major) Built on 4th note of major scale.

The Roman numeral system

There is a system in music theory which can identify each chord in a key by a Roman numeral. The 1st chord, the one built on the root note, is I, the 2nd chord is II, the 3rd is III, and so on up to VII. Chord number VIII is the same as chord number I but an octave higher.

Each chord also has a name according to its position in the scale and its Roman numeral – whatever key you are in. We have already seen that the I chord is the *tonic*, the IV chord is the *sub-dominant*, and the V chord is the *dominant*. The other names are given below, and their function in chord progressions is explained in the following pages.

I	Tonic (root)
II	Supertonic
III	Mediant
IV	Sub-dominant
V	Dominant
VI	Sub-mediant or relative minor
VII	Seventh or leading note
I	Tonic (octave)

Chords built on the major scale in five common keys

	Key of C major		Key of D major		Key of E major		Key of G major		Key of A major
	No sharps		2 sharps		4 sharps		1 sharp		3 sharps
I	C	I	D	I	E	I	G	I	A
II	D	II	E	II	F♯	II	A	II	B
III	E	III	F♯	III	G♯	III	B	III	C♯
IV	F	IV	G	IV	A	IV	C	IV	D
V	G	V	A	V	B	V	D	V	E
VI	A	VI	B	VI	C♯	VI	E	VI	F♯
VII	B	VII	C♯	VII	D♯	VII	F♯	VII	G♯
I	C	I	D	I	E	I	G	I	A

Chord progressions based on the three-chord theory

The best way of taking in this information and of understanding how the three-chord theory works is to familiarize yourself with the *sounds* behind the rules. And the only way to do this is to play the chords one after another, in various combinations, while listening to the effects they create.

On the right is a chart which sets out many of the most common I–IV–V chord progressions using the fifteen beginner's chords from p. 75. The tonic (I) and sub-dominant (IV) chords may be major, minor or seventh forms, but the dominant (V) chord in these examples is always major and is usually played as a seventh.

You will soon discover that many of these chord combinations are familiar and that most of them form the basis of popular songs. What makes one different from another – apart from the order in which the chords are arranged – is the length of time you stay on each chord and the rhythm you give to the sequence.

Try playing them. Give each chord an equal count of anything from one to four, and try all the permutations shown within one key so that you can hear how major, minor and seventh chords will sound in combination.

	I	IV	V	I
Key of E	E	A	B7	E
	Em	A7	B7	Em
	Em	Am	B7	Em
Key of A	A	D	E7	A
	Am	D7	E7	Am
	Am	Dm	E7	Am
Key of D	D	G	A7	D
	Dm	G	A	Dm
	Dm	G7	A7	Dm
Key of G	G	C	D7	G
	G7	C	D7	G
Key of C	C	F	G7	C
	C7	F	G7	C

Blues chord progressions

The blues is a musical form based almost entirely on the three-chord theory. Although the blues was certainly not analyzed by its creators, its formula has survived to become the structure of popular music, the accepted roots of jazz, and the heart of rock.

The most common blues pattern is probably the one known as the *twelve-bar blues*. It gets its name from the fact that it takes twelve "bars" to complete each cycle of the chord progression. "Bars" are explained fully on pp. 89–90, but for now we can say that one bar equals a count of 1-2-3-4.

The blues is difficult to categorize, however. There are many variations on the theme and many different ways of arranging the three chords. Sometimes the chords are majors and sometimes they are sevenths; sometimes the progression is not even twelve bars long, but may be just eight. The blues is characterized just as much by its rhythms (see p. 97) and its vocal and lead solo styles (see p. 144) as by the construction of its chord progressions.

Below are four typical blues chord sequences in the key of E. The first represents what is usually considered to be the basic twelve-bar pattern. The second shows the same progression but with sevenths introduced. The third is a common variation. And the fourth is an eight-bar rather than a twelve-bar sequence.

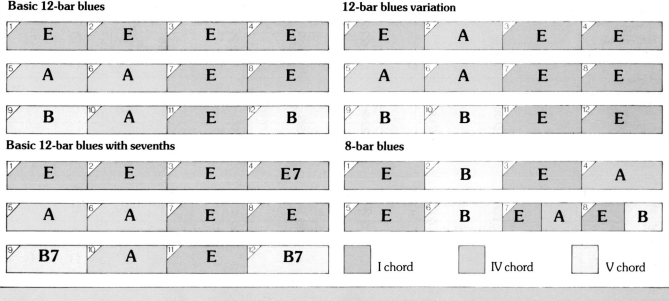

Basic 12-bar blues

1 E	2 E	3 E	4 E
5 A	6 A	7 E	8 E
9 B	10 A	11 E	12 B

12-bar blues variation

1 E	2 A	3 E	4 E
5 A	6 A	7 E	8 E
9 B	10 B	11 E	12 E

Basic 12-bar blues with sevenths

1 E	2 E	3 E	4 E7
5 A	6 A	7 E	8 E
9 B7	10 A	11 E	12 B7

8-bar blues

| 1 E | 2 B | 3 E | 4 A |
| 5 E | 6 B | 7 E A | 8 E B |

I chord   IV chord   V chord

Further chord progressions

On p. 76, we showed how to find the I, IV and V chords built on the 1st, 4th and 5th notes of a "harmonized" major scale. We now move on to introduce the chords built on the 2nd, 3rd and 6th notes. These are called the *secondary chords*. Roman numerals are used to indicate on which note of the scale each chord is based.

The VI chord is built on the 6th note of the major scale in any key, and is called the *relative minor*. Its natural form is as a minor chord, but it can also be played as a major or a seventh. (For more details on its special relation to the tonic or I chord, see p. 106.)

The II chord is built on the 2nd note of the major scale, and is called the *supertonic*. It, too, is usually minor but can be played as a major or a seventh.

The III chord is built on the 3rd note of the major scale, and is called the *mediant* – so-called because it lies midway between the tonic (I) and the dominant (V) chords. It is generally played as a minor but can be a major chord as well.

Because it has no sharps or flats, take the key of C major as an example again. As you can see from the chart on the right, the II chord is a D, the III chord an E, and the VI chord an A. These chords can be worked out in other keys using the same method of counting up the notes in the appropriate major scale. The chart on p. 76 shows them in the five most common keys.

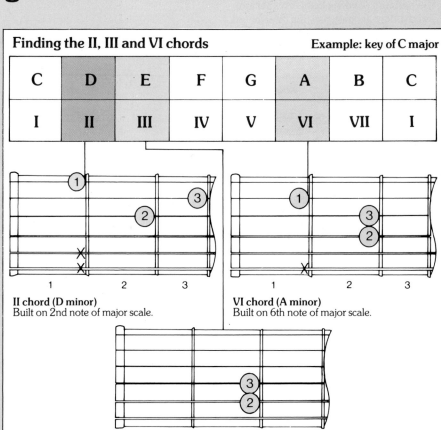

Finding the II, III and VI chords

Example: key of C major

C	D	E	F	G	A	B	C
I	II	III	IV	V	VI	VII	I

II chord (D minor)
Built on 2nd note of major scale.

VI chord (A minor)
Built on 6th note of major scale.

III chord (E minor)
Built on 3rd note of major scale.

Common progressions using the six scale chords

You now have six "scale" chords from which to create chord sequences. The progressions shown here represent most of the variations used in simple popular songs.

Note The last two progressions in the key of G contain a B minor chord. This is usually played as a "barre" (see p. 83 and the *Chord Dictionary*, p. 230).

	I	VI	IV	V	I
Key of C	C	Am	F	G	C
Key of G	G	Em	C	D	G

	I	VI	II	V	I
Key of C	C	Am	Dm	G	C
Key of G	G	E7	A7	D	G

	I	II	IV	V	I
Key of C	C	Dm	F	G	C
Key of G	G	A7	C	D	G

	I	II	VI	V	I
Key of C	C	Dm	Am	G	C
Key of G	G	Am	Em	D	G

	I	III	II	V	I
Key of C	C	E7	Dm	G	C
Key of G	G	B7	Em	D	G

	I	III	VI	V	I
Key of C	C	Em	Am	G	C
Key of G	G	Bm	Em	D	G

	I	III	IV	V	I
Key of C	C	E7	F	G	C
Key of G	G	Bm	C	D	G

Strumming and flatpicking

Basically, strumming is an instinctive action which either comes easily or it doesn't. Most guitarists strum with plectrums, since these give a crisper sound with a clearer "attack", but it is not unknown for players to strum with their fingers, with their thumb or with a thumbpick. As with all right-hand technique, it is important for the overall feel of your playing that you are able to maintain a steady, fluid strum, alternating between downstrokes and upstrokes. Upstrokes produce a sharper sound because they emphasize the top strings; downstrokes produce a fuller sound because the bass strings receive most of the impact of the stroke.

At the same time, you should be aiming to emphasize accents on various beats. Until you can do this, it will be impossible to establish either downbeats or backbeats. As we explained on p. 73, you can use your right-hand palm to mute or deaden the strings by resting it on top of the saddle. You can also use your left hand to dampen strings. This not only provides "space" where required but is also useful for establishing accented beats.

At this point, it should come as no surprise that only practice makes perfect. And the best way to practice smooth strumming is to play with other musicians, with recordings, and with metronomes or rhythm machines.

Flatpicking

A style used chiefly in acoustic folk and country styles, *flatpicking* is a plectrum technique in which you combine open-chord strums and single-string bass notes.

In its simplest form, this consists of alternating the bass notes of any open chord. These are almost always the root note and the "5th" (see p. 121), and the chord diagrams below show you which they are in six of the most commonly used open chords. First, play the bass note of the chord, then the chord itself, then the alternate bass note (the 5th), then the chord again. Over the count of four, this produces a bass note on one and three, and a chord on two and four. The technique evolved partially because it gives the left-hand fingers time to form the rest of the chord when you are playing at fast tempos and making quick chord changes.

When you have mastered these alternate bass notes, the next step is to introduce simple bass lines and fills to connect open chords in a progression. A selection of different connecting patterns is given below. They are written out in tablature, instructions for reading which appear on p. 67.

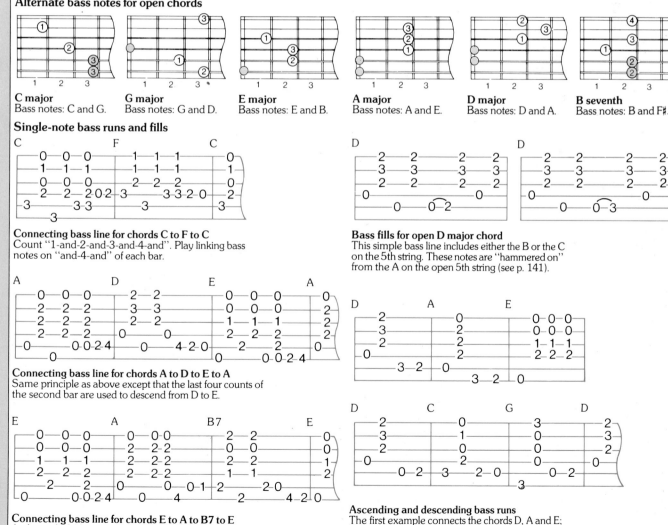

Alternate bass notes for open chords

C major
Bass notes: C and G.

G major
Bass notes: G and D.

E major
Bass notes: E and B.

A major
Bass notes: A and E.

D major
Bass notes: D and A.

B seventh
Bass notes: B and F♯.

Single-note bass runs and fills

Connecting bass line for chords C to F to C
Count "1-and-2-and-3-and-4-and". Play linking bass notes on "and-4-and" of each bar.

Connecting bass line for chords A to D to E to A
Same principle as above except that the last four counts of the second bar are used to descend from D to E.

Connecting bass line for chords E to A to B7 to E
At the end of the second bar a B♭ is used in the ascending run that links A and B seventh.

Bass fills for open D major chord
This simple bass line includes either the B or the C on the 5th string. These notes are "hammered on" from the A on the open 5th string (see p. 141).

Ascending and descending bass runs
The first example connects the chords D, A and E; the second connects D, C and G. Both have four counts to the bar: the bass notes are on 1, 3 and 4.

Fingerpicking and fingerstyles

The basis of most fingerpicking or fingerstyle guitar playing is the development of independent movement in your right-hand thumb and fingers, so that you can play a rhythmic bass line on the bottom strings at the same time as a melody line on the top strings.

There are countless subtleties and variations in more complicated fingerstyle playing, but, initially, it is better to stick to basic pieces in which your thumb plays the bass line and your fingers play the melody.

Much of the music that features American fingerstyles is written with four beats to the bar. These beats are often played as alternating bass notes, so there are two groups of two in each bar (see *Folk and country rhythms*, p. 96). Though something of a trademark in American folk, country and ragtime music, such alternating bass lines are never a feature of classical music nor, necessarily, of advanced fingerstyles.

For fingerpicking, you can use the basic classical right-hand position or adopt any of the others developed through American folk, blues, country, ragtime and rock styles (see p. 73). It is generally accepted that the correct right-hand position is essential to achieve a good tone and technique for classical playing. But the steel-string guitar will produce an acceptable tone with the right hand in various positions. The most common is to rest the edge of the palm on top of the bridge. The palm then acts as a steady anchor point, and it can be used to dampen the bass strings in order to create more of a contrast between the rhythmic bass line and the melody. This works chiefly because muting the bass strings prevents them from ringing on as long as the melody notes.

American fingerpicking styles

The *clawhammer* is just one of many American fingerstyles, but it forms the foundation of much of the technique. It gets its name from the fact that the right-hand position looks something like a curved claw hammer used for pulling nails out of wood. The thumb plays the rhythmic bass notes with downstrokes, while the 1st and 2nd fingers play the melody with upstrokes. The clawhammer was a characteristic of Reverend Gary Davis's style — as it was of many other early blues players. Some guitarists use a three-finger, rather than a two-finger, style. In this case, one finger plays each of the top three strings.

Infinite variations are possible, including playing several strings at once instead of separately (in order to sound chords), and using the thumb to play upstrokes and the fingers to play downstrokes.

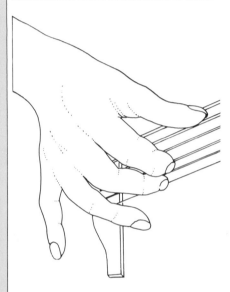

The two-finger clawhammer
The thumb plays the bass line, usually with downstrokes on the bottom three strings (the 6th, 5th and 4th). The 1st and 2nd fingers play melody notes, usually with upstrokes, on the top three strings (the 3rd, 2nd and 1st).

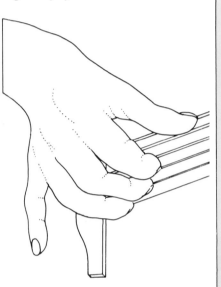

The three-finger technique
Again, the thumb picks the three bass strings, but the 3rd finger is also used so that the 1st finger picks the 3rd string, the 2nd finger picks the 2nd string, and the 3rd finger picks the 1st string — that is, one finger for each of the top strings.

Fingerpicking patterns

The examples shown on the right will give you an idea of how fingerpicking works, will help you to develop independent finger control, and will provide you with a starting point for discovering your own patterns. They are all written in "tablature" form (instructions on how to read this appear on p. 67) and use simple open chords. Although the bass string may vary, the patterns remain basically the same whichever chord you choose.

The first three examples have a very simple bass line, against which the notes on the top strings tend to give a sort of "ripple" or "arpeggio" effect. In the other three examples, the thumb plays an alternating bass, rocking from the 6th string to the 4th string. Begin by playing the exercises slowly and gradually increase the tempo when your right hand has learned the pattern.

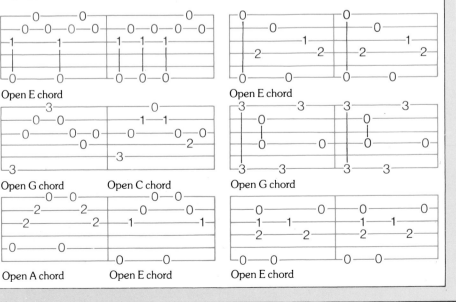

Arpeggio-like patterns

Open E chord

Open G chord   Open C chord

Open A chord   Open E chord

Alternating bass patterns

Open E chord

Open G chord

Open E chord

Changing chords while fingerpicking

Once you have mastered a few of the basic fingerpicking patterns, the next step is to combine them with some of the basic chord progressions you have worked out from pp. 76-8. As with strumming, the most important thing is to keep the rhythm steady while you make each chord change. Playing along with a metronome or a rhythm machine may help you with your timing.

The example below is one of the most common of all chord progressions, a descending sequence of Am, G, F and E. The fingerpicking pattern has a solid alternating bass and is played to a rhythm of 1-and-2-and-3-and-4-and. You stay on each chord for two bars and play the pattern once for each bar. When you change chord, your thumb should change to a new bass string, so that it plays the root note of each chord – the 5th string for A minor, the 6th string for G, the 4th string for F and the 6th string again for E. When you get to the end of the sequence, you can change from E to A minor and start again.

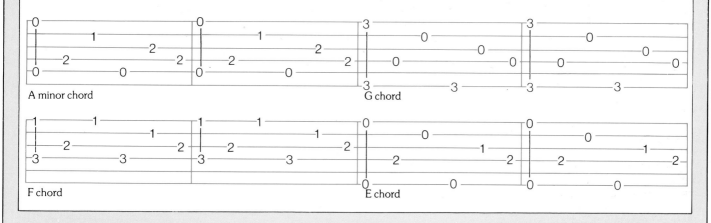

A minor chord   G chord

F chord   E chord

Combining melody and bass line

As well as providing a style for simple chord accompaniments, fingerpicking also gives you the possibility of combining complete bass and melody lines at the same time, so that you can play a two-part arrangement on your own. This sort of style – of which ragtime tunes are a good example – represents steel-string fingerpicking at its most sophisticated. The example given here – a simple arrangement of "When the Saints Go Marching In" – has a regular, unfaltering alternating bass of four beats to the bar. The melody is played on the 1st, 2nd and 3rd strings, and the bass on the bottom three.

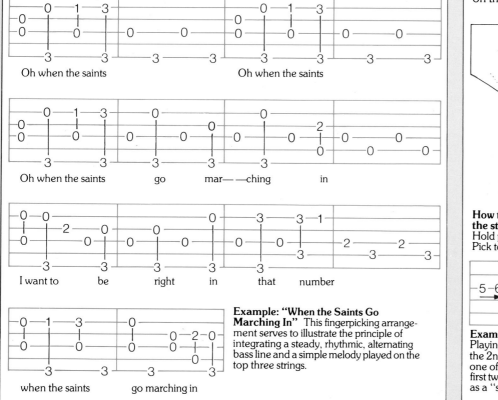

Oh when the saints   Oh when the saints

Oh when the saints   go   mar——ching   in

I want to   be   right   in   that   number

when the saints   go marching in

Example: "When the Saints Go Marching In" This fingerpicking arrangement serves to illustrate the principle of integrating a steady, rhythmic, alternating bass line and a simple melody played on the top three strings.

Plectrum-style fingerpicking

This slightly more tricky but versatile style evolved among country and rock guitarists. It is used by countless top players and means flatpicking and fingerpicking can be combined. You hold your plectrum between your thumb and 1st finger (as for normal plectrum styles), but at the same time use your other fingers to play notes on the higher strings.

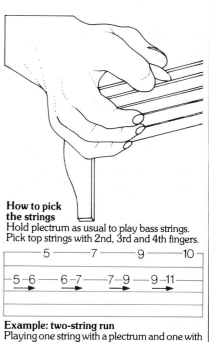

How to pick the strings
Hold plectrum as usual to play bass strings. Pick top strings with 2nd, 3rd and 4th fingers.

Example: two-string run
Playing one string with a plectrum and one with the 2nd finger is ideal for this two-string run, one of the best-known country rock licks. The first two notes in each group of three are played as a "slide" (see p. 142).

Barre chords

On p. 75, we showed you how to play fifteen basic beginner's chords. Over the next four pages, we introduce what are called *barre* chord shapes. Learning the simplest of these will increase your chord vocabulary from fifteen to over 150 chord fingerings.

Barre chords take their name from the role of the 1st finger. It acts as a "bar" across all six strings, replacing the nut, and thereby enabling you to adapt open-string chord shapes to any position on the fingerboard.

The key to understanding barre chords is to realize that they are *movable* forms. The same shape can be moved up and down the fingerboard, from one fret position to another, without altering the fingering at all, to give you any one of twelve different chords. The note at the fret on which the shape is built determines the name of the chord.

As soon as you start to work through the examples that follow, you will also see that, by using the various barre shapes, you can play one chord in several different places on the fingerboard. This demonstrates an important characteristic of the guitar. Being able to choose where you place a chord means that you can play any progression in a variety of ways, each producing a different sound.

There are four basic barre shapes, each derived from an open chord. The "E shape" is based on an open E major, the "A shape" on A major, the "C shape" on C major and the "G shape" on G major. The E shape and A shape can easily be adapted to give minor, seventh, minor seventh and major seventh barre forms.

The 1st finger "barre"
The essence of E and A shape barre chords is that the 1st finger replaces the nut of the guitar – thus creating chord shapes which can be played anywhere on the fingerboard.

E shape barre chords

The principle of all barre chords is to take an open-chord fingering and transform it into a shape that can be moved up the fingerboard. Begin by playing a simple E major chord, the way you were shown on p. 75. Now, in order to release your 1st finger so that it can play the barre, you must change the fingering of the open chord. The second step is therefore to hold down the notes of the chord with your 2nd, 3rd and 4th fingers. The third step is to move this whole shape up one fret, bringing your 1st finger down behind the others and laying it right across the 1st fret so that it covers all six strings. This is the barre. The shape you are now holding is a chord of F major, the chord one fret up from an open E major. The F on the 6th string tells you its name.

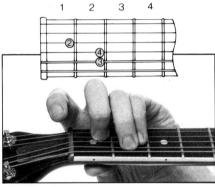

Re-fingered open E major
In order to play a barre, the 1st finger must be free, so the chord is re-fingered: 2nd finger on the 1st fret of 3rd string; 4th finger on 2nd fret of 4th string; 3rd finger on 2nd fret of 5th string.

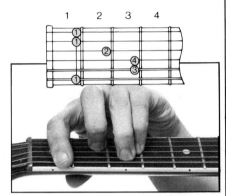

Barre F major
The basic E shape is moved up one fret and the 1st finger holds down a barre behind the other fingers: 1st finger plays barre on 1st fret of 1st, 2nd and 6th strings; 2nd finger on 2nd fret of 3rd string; 4th finger on 3rd fret of 4th string; 3rd finger on 3rd fret of 5th string.

How the E shape moves up the fingerboard

The root note of all E shape barre chords is on the 6th (E) string. When you play a simple open E major, the 6th string is played open – and the bottom E is the root note of the chord. When you play a barre F major, the 6th string is held down on the 1st fret. This gives the note F – and F is the root note of the F major chord.

On the guitar fingerboard, *every* fret represents a "semi-tone" (see p. 68). This means that, *every* time you move a barre shape up one fret, the name of the chord rises by a semi-tone. Moving the F barre shape up one fret gives you F♯ major; moving it up two frets gives you G major, and so on. At the 12th fret, you are playing E again.

Alternative fingering

Many modern guitarists choose to use their thumb to fret the 6th string and play just a two-string barre on the top strings with their 1st finger. The thumb moves from its standard position in the middle of the back of the neck and is hooked over the top of the fingerboard as shown below. This allows the bass note to be damped or altered as well.

The position of root notes for E shape barre chords

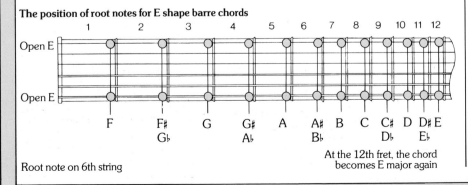

Root note on 6th string

At the 12th fret, the chord becomes E major again

A shape barre chords

The simple open-string form of the A major chord is also a movable form which, when played with a barre, can be positioned anywhere on the fingerboard to produce any one of twelve different chords.

As with the E shape, the A also has to be re-fingered slightly in order to free the 1st finger so that it can play the barre (see right). Start with the re-fingered form, and then slide the whole shape up one fret so that your 1st finger plays a barre across the 1st fret. This will now have transformed the chord from an A major to a B♭ major.

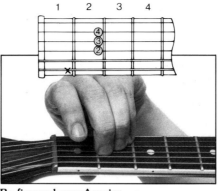

Re-fingered open A major

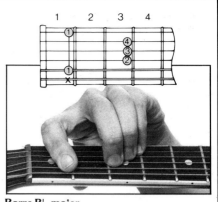

Barre B♭ major

How the A shape moves up the fingerboard

The root note of all A shape barre chords is on the 5th string. When you move up from an open A major to a barre B♭ major, the 5th string is held down by your 1st finger on the 1st fret. This gives the note B♭ – and B♭ is the root note of the B♭ major chord. Moving the B♭ chord up one more fret will give you a chord of B major, and so on up the fingerboard. In short, the note you are holding down on the 5th string will always tell you the name of the chord. At the 12th fret, you will be playing A again.

Alternative fingering

The A shape barre chord is often played with a 3rd finger barre. The three notes on the 4th, 3rd and 2nd strings are held down by flattening the 3rd finger into a smaller "half" barre as shown below.

The position of root notes for A shape barre chords

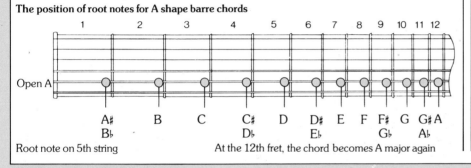

Open A

A♯	B	C	C♯	D	D♯	E	F	F♯	G	G♯	A
B♭			D♭		E♭			G♭		A♭	

Root note on 5th string   At the 12th fret, the chord becomes A major again

Barre minors and sevenths

Movable barre shapes of minor and seventh chords are possible in exactly the same way as they are for the major chords. In some cases, they are even easier to play.

The simple E minor and E seventh chords shown in the beginner's chord dictionary on p. 75 are, in essence, slightly altered forms of the open-string E major chord. By re-fingering them slightly and using a 1st finger barre to take the place of the nut, they can be played anywhere on the fingerboard. The same holds for the A minor and A seventh chords; they, too, can be played as adapted forms of the A shape barre chord.

If you learn to play each bar chord variation in each position – and also memorize the notes on the 5th and 6th strings – you will find your chord vocabulary easily expanded to include twelve major chords, twelve minors and twelve sevenths based on the barre E shape, and twelve majors, twelve minors and twelve sevenths based on the barre A shape. Together, this gives you a total of 72 chord shapes – for 36 different chords. The *Chord Dictionary* (pp. 225-49) shows these chords in their correct positions, using all the barre shapes.

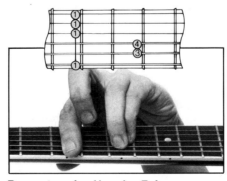

Barre minor chord based on E shape

Barre seventh chord based on E shape

Barre minor chord based on A shape

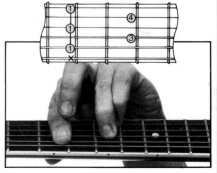

Barre seventh chord based on A shape

C shape barre chords

The third movable barre form is derived from the simple open C chord (see p. 75). The technique is the same as when building other barre chords. You simply re-finger the basic shape so that your 1st finger can play the barre behind your other fingers. The root note of all barre chords based on this shape is on the 5th string and it is played by the 4th finger, not the 1st finger. C shape barre chords are more difficult to play than those derived from the E shape or A shape. The relatively weak 4th finger has to hold down the bass string – involving a considerable stretch, especially at the lower end of the fingerboard where the frets are noticeably further apart.

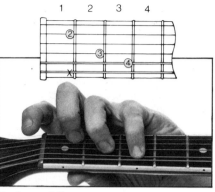

Re-fingered C major
This form frees 1st finger so that it can play barre. As with standard form of open C major, 6th string is not included in chord.

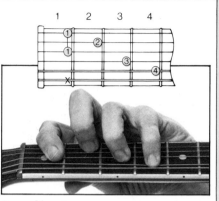

Barre C♯ major
Moved one fret up, with two-finger barre on 1st and 3rd strings. Root note on 5th string is played by 4th finger.

G shape barre chords

The fourth, and last, of the different movable barre forms comes from the simple open G chord (see p. 75). However, the 1st string is not used. All G shape barre chords have their root note on the 6th string – played by the 4th finger, not the 1st finger. Instead, the 1st finger holds down a barre only on the 2nd, 3rd and 4th strings.

Of the four movable barre chords, the G shape is probably the least used, but it is worth learning, if only to understand how it works. It can be handy when used with the C shape, it is a useful shape from which to move to other chords nearby, and it is a good basic position on which to build various "extended" chords.

Re-fingered G major
1st finger is freed to play barre, but 1st string is deadened.

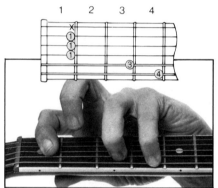

Barre G♯ major
Moved one fret up, with three-finger barre on 2nd, 3rd and 4th strings. Root note on 6th string is played by 4th finger.

The four barre chord shapes summarized

By now it should be apparent that, by using the four barre chord shapes, any major chord can be played in four different places on the fingerboard – more if you go beyond the 12th fret and repeat the fingerings an octave higher. All you have to do is locate the root note and build the right barre chord shape around it.

By way of an example, the illustration below plots out on the fingerboard the positions in which you can play the chord of D major. Its simplest open form is shown at the bottom of the fingerboard. At the 5th fret on the 5th string, the D note can be used as the root note for an A shape barre, and, at the 10th fret on the 6th string, another D forms the root note for a G shape barre and an E shape barre. The C shape barre is rooted on the D at the 17th fret of the 5th string. This gives a chord one octave above the simple open form. Compare these two shapes and you will see how the open D chord fingering is, in fact, a part of the fingering based on the C shape barre form.

Example: five ways to play D major

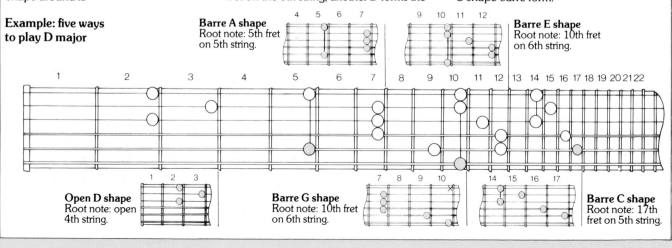

Barre A shape
Root note: 5th fret on 5th string.

Barre E shape
Root note: 10th fret on 6th string.

Open D shape
Root note: open 4th string.

Barre G shape
Root note: 10th fret on 6th string.

Barre C shape
Root note: 17th fret on 5th string.

Barre chord relationships

The best way to incorporate barre chords into your playing is to start using them immediately in chord progressions. And the best way to do this is to go back to the "three-chord theory" (see p. 76). As soon as you apply the I-IV-V rule to barre chords, you will come up against a surprising – and useful – fact: the root notes are always within three frets of each other, whatever key you are in and whether you build the I chord on the 5th string or the 6th string. The diagram below illustrates this principle with the I-IV-V chords in the key of C major.

The second diagram shows where all the other chords built on a major scale can be found in relation to the tonic (I) chord – again in C major, since it has no sharps or flats. It is worth remembering that the VI chord, the "relative minor" can always be found three frets below the I chord on the same string. So, as an example, A minor is played with its root note on the 5th fret of the 6th string – three frets below its tonic (I) chord, C major, played on the 8th fret.

It should now be obvious that you *must* learn the names of the notes on each fret of the 5th and 6th strings. Once you have memorized these, you should have no problem putting together sequences of barre chords in any key.

The position of root notes for I-IV-V barre chords
Using C major as an example, this diagram illustrates how the three most important chords in any key – the I, IV and V – can all be found within the space of three frets. This applies whether the I chord has its root note on the 5th or on the 6th string.

IV (sub-dominant) chord
F major: root note on the 6th string, two frets below I chord.

I (tonic) chord
C major: root note on the 5th string.

IV (sub-dominant) chord F major: root note on the 5th string, same fret as I chord but one string higher.

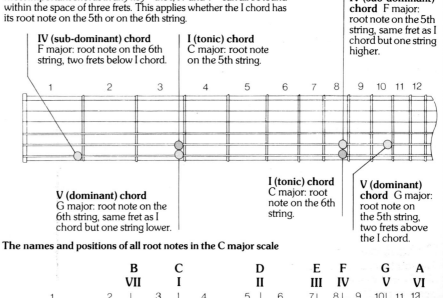

V (dominant) chord
G major: root note on the 6th string, same fret as I chord but one string lower.

I (tonic) chord
C major: root note on the 6th string.

V (dominant) chord G major: root note on the 5th string, two frets above the I chord.

The names and positions of all root notes in the C major scale

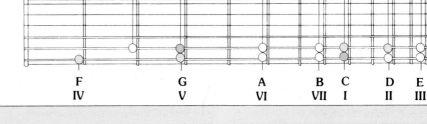

Barre minor sevenths and major sevenths

So far we have only dealt with three types of chords – the major, the minor and the seventh. But, if you look at any page in the *Chord Dictionary* (see pp. 225-49), you will see that there are five different chords in the first column of each key. Generally, these are the five most commonly used chords.

The two we have not yet covered are the *minor seventh* and the *major seventh*. They can both be played as movable barre forms, with their root note on either the 5th string or the 6th string.

The minor seventh chord is derived from the minor chord by introducing an extra note. It therefore becomes a four-note chord instead of a three-note "triad". You can see from the illustrations here that this can be done simply by making a slight alteration to the fingering of the standard barre minor shapes.

The major seventh chord is also a four-note chord. It is derived from the major triad, but differs from the ordinary seventh chord in that the "interval" between the root note and the extra fourth note is not quite the same. It, too, can be played by slightly altering the barre major shapes.

More details on the construction of these and other new chords appear later on pp. 126-9.

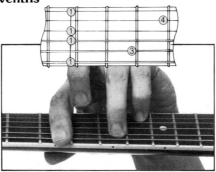

Barre minor seventh chord based on E shape
Movable form with root note on 6th string.

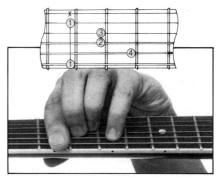

Barre major seventh chord based on E shape
Movable form with root note on 6th string.

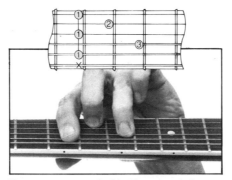

Barre minor seventh chord based on A shape
Movable form with root note on 5th string.

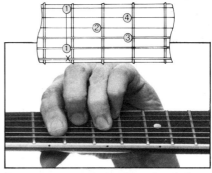

Barre major seventh chord based on A shape
Movable form with root note on 5th string.

Analyzing and transposing songs

Once you master barre positions, you will be able to play major, minor, seventh, minor seventh and major seventh chords. From here it is a simple matter to analyze and "transpose" any simple song. *Transposing* a piece of music (a chord progression, say, or a melody) means playing it in any key that is different from the one in which it is written or the one in which you originally learned it.

There are two reasons why you might want to transpose a chord sequence. First, you may want to sing along with it but find that it is too low or too high for your voice. Second, you may want to use chord shapes or add melody notes which are difficult to play if the music remains in its original key. Transposing the chord progression to an appropriate new key can help to solve both these problems.

Assuming you can play the chord progression you want to transpose, and that you have written down the chord names in

sequence, the first step is to convert — or "code" — it into Roman numerals (see p. 76). Music theory and analysis use these numbers to describe the position of a chord (or note) in the context of its particular key. The numbers are free of any specific note or "pitch" value; they simply convey in theoretical terms a sequence of sounds. The secret to understanding the Roman numeral system is realizing that the sequence of sounds is the same, whatever key it is played in. The relationships between the individual chords described by the sequence of numbers remain intact and will sound the same in all twelve keys — only the actual pitches change.

As we have seen, the Roman numerals are derived from counting the number of steps up the major scale — from the tonic or root note of the key (which is always I) to the root note of the chord in question. The Roman numerals then identify the same "distance"

or number of steps from the tonic or root note in any key. Transposing requires you to find the specific notes or chords in the key to which you are moving. This is done by "decoding" the Roman numerals — translating them back into real notes or chords — using the same kind of scale in the new key. When the new tones or chords are played in the same rhythm and with the same "feel" as the original, the music will have been transposed, with its characteristics completely unchanged, to another key.

Two examples are given below to illustrate exactly how this works. More details of keys — how they are constructed and how "key signatures" are used to label them — are given on pp. 108-9. Transposition should never be confused with "modulation". Modulation involves deliberately moving into a new key in the course of a single chord progression or melody, and it is explained on p. 138.

How to transpose chord progressions

Transposing from, say, C to D is easy — you simply raise the pitch of each chord by one whole-tone. But larger "steps" are more complex. The first thing to do is therefore to "code" the chords by changing them to a series of Roman numerals. This can be done using the chart at the top of the opposite page. You simply look along the top row until you find the key in which the original

chord progression is written. The column beneath it will give you the notes in the major scale and their Roman numerals. Now write out the chord progression using numbers instead of chord names.

To find the names of the chords in the new key, the procedure is simply reversed. You find the vertical column which represents the new key and "de-code" the

Roman numerals by reading off against them the names of the notes in the new major scale.

If you use a major scale to make the original conversion to Roman numerals, you must use the major scale of the new key to de-code them in order to arrive at the correct equivalent notes. Similarly, you must work from minor scale to minor scale.

Transposing a major chord progression

Original chord progression in C major

C	Am	Dm	G	F	Dm	G7	C

How to "code" the chord progression
Give each chord in the progression a Roman numeral using the scale of C major.

Scale of C major

C	D	E	F	G	A	B
I	II	III	IV	V	VI	VII

Original chord progression in Roman numerals

I	VIm	IIm	V	IV	IIm	V7	I

Transposing to G
You now need to know the scale of G major to turn the numerals into chords again.

Scale of G major

G	A	B	C	D	E	F♯
I	II	III	IV	V	VI	VII

Original chord progression transposed to the key of G major

G	Em	Am	D	C	Am	D7	G
I	VIm	IIm	V	IV	IIm	V7	I

Transposing a minor chord progression

Original chord progression in A minor

Am	Dm	E7	Am	F	Dm	E7	Am

How to "code" the chord progression
Give each chord in the progression a Roman numeral using the scale of A minor.

Scale of A minor

A	B	C	D	E	F	G
I	II	III	IV	V	VI	VII

Original chord progression in Roman numerals

Im	IVm	V7	Im	VI	IVm	V7	Im

Transposing to E
You need to know the scale of E minor to turn the numerals into chords again.

Scale of E minor

E	F♯	G	A	B	C	D
I	II	III	IV	V	VI	VII

Original chord progression transposed to the key of E minor

Em	Am	B7	Em	C	Am	B7	Em
Im	IVm	V7	Im	VI	IVm	V7	Im

Major scale transposition chart

Note For details of how to use this chart, see opposite.

Roman numerals for each note of major scale / Twelve keys

I	A	A♯/B♭	B	C	C♯/D♭	D	D♯/E♭	E	F	F♯/G♭	G	G♯/A♭	I
II	B	C	C♯	D	D♯/E♭	E	F	F♯	G	G♯/A♭	A	A♯/B♭	II
III	C♯	D	D♯	E	F	F♯	G	G♯	A	A♯/B♭	B	C	III
IV	D	D♯/E♭	E	F	F♯/G♭	G	G♯/A♭	A	B♭	B	C	C♯/D♭	IV
V	E	F	F♯	G	G♯/A♭	A	A♯/B♭	B	C	C♯/D♭	D	D♯/E♭	V
VI	F♯	G	G♯	A	A♯/B♭	B	C	C♯	D	D♯/E♭	E	F	VI
VII	G♯	A	A♯	B	C	C♯	D	D♯	E	F	F♯	G	VII
I	A	A♯/B♭	B	C	C♯/D♭	D	D♯/E♭	E	F	F♯/G♭	G	G♯/A♭	I

Using a capo

The capo is a clever little device which allows you to play a chord progression in different keys while still retaining the same chord shapes. It works because it acts like a sort of artificial "barre" (see pp. 82-5). The capo fits around the neck of the guitar and raises the pitch of all six strings. The amount by which it raises them is determined by the fret on which it is placed. Putting a capo on the 1st fret will raise the open strings by one semi-tone; putting it on the 2nd fret will raise them by two semi-tones; and so on. This means that an open chord of C major played with a capo on the 1st fret becomes C♯ major, and the same shape played with a capo on the 2nd fret becomes D major. In other words, the fingering remains the same, but the notes are different.

Let's take an example to show how the capo works. Suppose you want to sing a melody to go with the fingerpicking accompaniment shown at the top of p. 81 – the chord progression of Am – G – F – E – but you find that the key in which it is written is too low for your voice. You would feel more comfortable if it were raised a semi-tone to the key of B♭ minor. If you transpose the chord progression using the chart above the sequence becomes B♭m – A♭ – G♭ – F. Now, these four chords can *only* be played as barre forms, which makes an easy chord progression suddenly more difficult – especially if you are fingerpicking. The capo provides the solution. By fitting it to the 1st fret, you can raise the pitch of the whole sequence to the key of B♭ but still use exactly the same chord shapes as in the original key of A minor. This will make the fingering much easier.

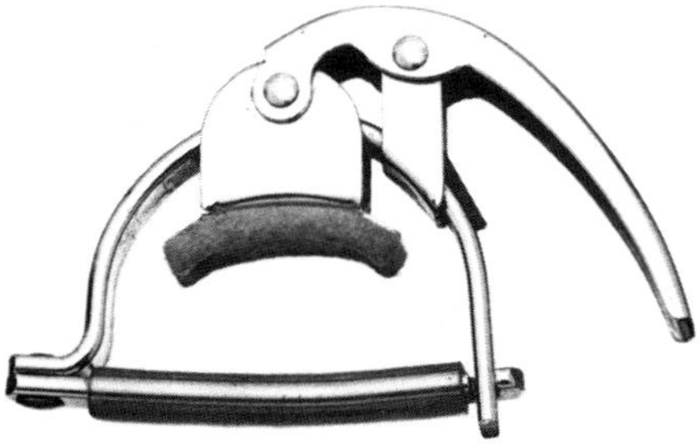

Capo with spring attachment

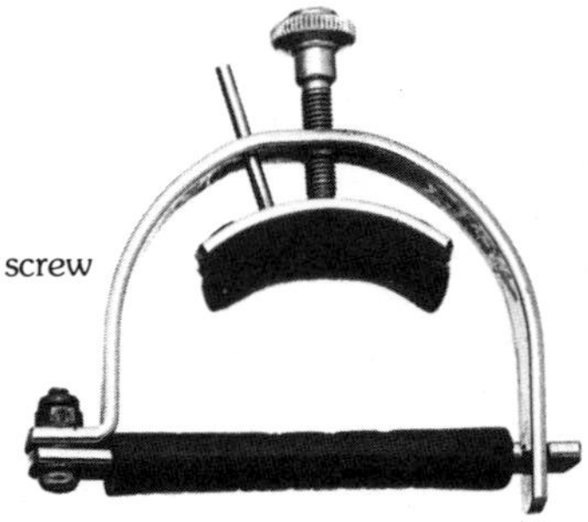

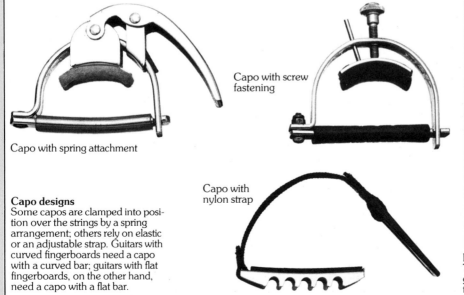

Capo with screw fastening

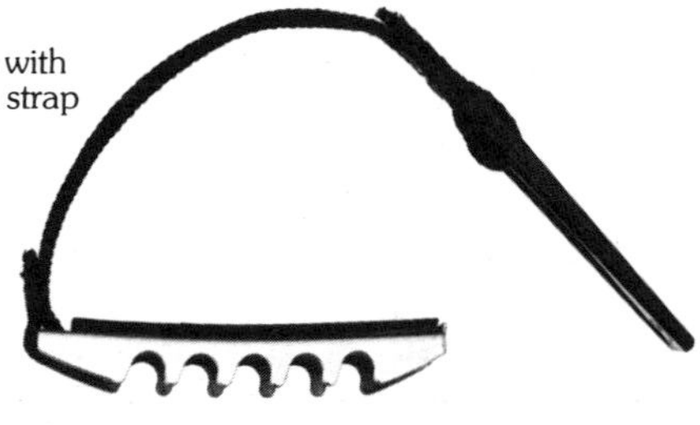

Capo with nylon strap

Capo designs
Some capos are clamped into position over the strings by a spring arrangement; others rely on elastic or an adjustable strap. Guitars with curved fingerboards need a capo with a curved bar; guitars with flat fingerboards, on the other hand, need a capo with a flat bar.

How to fit capos
The capo is clamped over the fingerboard of the guitar just behind the chosen fret so that it raises the pitch of any chord you play.

THE RHYTHM GUITARIST

In the context of most modern music, the drummer and the bassist are considered to be the rhythm section. Both the guitarist and the keyboard players are therefore free to choose between playing *with* the rhythm section or playing *on top of* it.

"What interested me about Chuck Berry was the way he could step out of the rhythm part with such ease, throwing in a nice, simple riff, and then drop straight into the feel of it again. We used to play a lot more rhythm stuff. We'd do away with the differences between lead and rhythm guitar. You can't go into a shop and ask for a "lead guitar". You're a guitar player, and you play a guitar."

Keith Richards

This attitude has its roots in the days of the big bands, when the guitarist and pianist were always thought of as part of the rhythm section. It was the brass and woodwinds that played the melodies and harmonies, while the rhythm section concentrated on providing the pulse and timing for the rest of the band. Playing this kind of rhythm guitar was best summed up by Freddie Green, Count Basie's guitarist for nearly forty years.

"You shouldn't hear the guitar by itself. It should be part of the drums so it sounds like the drummer is playing chords — like the snare is in A or the hi-hat in D minor. You only notice the guitar when it's not there."

Freddie Green

Most modern music still depends heavily on a rhythm guitarist who understands the traditional responsibility of the instrument.

Keith Richards on the Rolling Stones 1973 European tour.

Pete Townshend on stage with the Who.

"I don't think I even approach being a lead player; I think I'm very much part of a band and a riff-maker. I enjoy backing people up and letting people ride on top… I'm musically happiest when I feel I'm driving everyone else to do good things, when I'm not being the pin man."

Pete Townshend

Most guitarists play by ear, relying more on their sense of rhythm than their knowledge of scale and chord theory. This means that when they play they concentrate primarily on their left hand — switching their right hand onto "auto-pilot" and strumming instinctively.

It is the left hand that chooses the notes and chords, and therefore dictates the general direction of the right hand. When playing rhythm, another important contribution of the left hand is *damping*. By holding down or releasing fretted notes, the left hand acts as the sustain control, and may also allow certain notes to ring while damping others.

Its two functions of selecting the notes and controlling their sustain make the left hand comparable to a piano. If this is the case, then the right hand is like the drummer. Playing fingerstyle or with a plectrum, the four right-hand techniques — downstrokes, upstrokes, alternate strokes, and right-hand damping — give the guitarist control over timing, volume and dynamics. Combining the effects possible with both hands produces the wide variety of rhythm styles for which the guitar is so well known.

The musical identity of each rhythm style results from a combination of six basic factors: the choice of plectrum or fingerstyle; the choice of chords — their complexity and application; the degree of sustain or damping; the sub-division of the bar into a rhythmic pattern; the beats that are accented or emphasized; and the tone of the guitar.

In this section of the book, we begin with an analysis of what rhythm is and explain how it is made up of four components — the tempo, the time signature, the note or rest values, and the accented beats. This will give you a solid understanding of how rhythm works, and will allow you to both write and play from written chord charts or rhythm charts.

The section ends with an examination of various rhythm styles — divided into five general sources or categories: folk and country; blues and rock; Spanish and Latin; soul, funk and reggae; and jazz. Listen to as many of these styles as you can, and try to isolate how the rhythm is constructed and what the role of each musician is. You will find that, in rhythm guitar playing, the spaces between chords are as important as the chords themselves.

Tempo, rhythm and timing

Timing is the ability to play a piece right through without speeding it up or slowing it down. It also involves the ability to keep up a rhythm and to emphasize certain notes (or rests) at precisely the same moment as other musicians in the band.

Timing can be difficult, especially in the early stages of learning to play the guitar, when you are concerned primarily with getting your fingers into the right positions and with sounding the notes or chords that you want. But timing is a skill that grows the more you play; it is directly related to confidence and experience. And, like tuning (see pp. 68-71), it is a basic discipline which will spoil the effect of your music if it is not up to standard. If your timing is out and your playing speeds up and slows down, your audience will certainly notice it, even if you do not. In fact, it will probably be more obvious than the odd "bum" note.

Although timing is an "instinctive" thing, it can be analyzed and communicated in terms of written musical notation. Over the next few pages, we devote quite a lot of space to the ways in which timing can be written down. Since most guitarists learn to play by ear, this may seem unnecessary, but there is no doubt

that understanding the components of rhythm will help you learn more quickly, be more aware of what you are doing, and play better. Moreover, a knowledge of rhythmic notation is vital if you want to work out how to play a piece from sheet music or lyric sheets, or if you want to write down songs, chord progressions or arrangements that you have made up yourself.

Timing breaks down into two components – tempo and rhythm. *Tempo* is the speed (or rate) of a piece of music. Any specific tempo is measured as a number of beats per minute – and, generally, one beat is represented by one "quarter-note" (see *Time values*, p. 92). This means that music can be speeded up or slowed down by changing the tempo – that is, by playing more or less beats to the minute. Musical instructions that tell you what tempo to establish are explained on the right. For machines that measure tempo, see below.

Rhythm is the way in which a tempo is played. Whereas the tempo states how long it will take to play a set group of notes, the rhythm dictates which of the notes are emphasized (or "accented") and which are not. The rhythm is, therefore, what produces the "feel" of the music.

Tempo instructions

If the tempo has not been specified as a number of beats per minute – such that it can be set on a metronome – it is the responsibility of the conductor or the drummer to establish the correct tempo. In classical music, Italian phrases are used to describe various tempos.

Italian	English	Beats per minute
Presto	Very fast	168-208
Allegro	Fast	120-168
Moderato	Moderate speed	108-120
Andante	Moderate walking speed	76-108
Adagio	Slow (literally "at ease")	66-76
Largo	Slow and solemn	40-66

♩ = 90

Tempo instruction
This sign means that the music has a tempo of 90 beats per minute.

Developing a sense of timing

The most common error made by the novice guitarist is to attempt to play too fast, too soon. The problem is that you may actually be unaware that your playing speed has increased before you are completely comfortable with an exercise or riff.

Steve Vai is a good example to any budding guitarist. He acquired his brilliant technical skills partly by a well-organized 10-hours-a-day practice regime. One of his recommendations is always to practise with a metronome, and always be able to play an exercise comfortably, before slightly increasing the metronome speed. By gradually increasing speed over a

period of time, as Vai puts it, "soon you're just wailing." Without an approach of this kind, many guitarists may find their playing can be erratic.

One of the best time-honored ways to develop a good general sense of timing is to play along with records. Also, there are many backing tapes available, often with the guitar part left off. Drum machines, sequencers and synthesizers can be used to create simple practice backing tracks that can greatly help musicians to acquire a good sense of timing. By working with such devices a guitarist can set a tempo or basic rhythm and start off fairly slow and gradually increase playing speed and feel.

As with the metronome, the student knows exactly what speed he is working at. Most frequently this is described in "beats per minute" (BPM).

Musicians never play mechanically. In fact, a group will always push and pull with and against a tempo, creating *feel*. When a group practices together, one or two musicians – usually the drummer or the bass player – provide the regular pulse of the music which the other group members follow. So practising with a drum machine can help a guitarist avoid the frustration of getting used to playing to someone else's pulse or rhythm. Feel is a quality that separates great musicians from the rest.

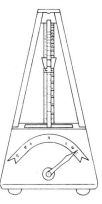

Metronome
This simple clock-work device emits a sharp click on every beat. Its tempo can be adjusted by moving a small counter-balancing weight up or down the arm that swings from side to side. Sometimes metronomes also include a bell that will ring on the off beat.

Alesis SR-16 drum machine (*right*)
The Alesis name has yet to appear on a poor product. The company's drum machines – the budget SR-16 contains over 200 digital samples and dynamic "real-time" programming – offer outstanding value.

Most rock music is based on four beats to the bar with an accent on the downbeat. To make up a simple rhythm track set a hi-hat to play 8 even beats to the bar and a snare drum to play 4 beats to the bar. Give the 2nd and 4th snare drum beats an accent to make them louder.

Time signatures

In written music, any tempo (a succession of regular beats played at a fixed speed) can be divided into small, manageable "chunks". Each chunk contains a certain number of beats or pulses and is called a *bar* (see p. 67). Grouping beats into bars in this way allows you to measure and count a tempo much more easily than if your only information was how many beats there were to every minute.

A *time signature* or *meter* is used to tell you how the bars are organized – that is, how many beats are grouped into each bar, and how long each beat lasts. Each piece of music begins with a time signature. It is always written as two numbers, one on top of the other, in the form of a fraction. The top number determines how many beats there are in one bar, and the bottom number determines the time value of each beat.

In the following explanation of different sorts of time signatures, it is important to remember that the numbers refer to *beats* not to note or time values. Any combination of notes or rests can be played in a bar as long as their total time value adds up to the total time value of the number of beats in the bar. This is explained in detail on p. 92.

Simple time signatures

Take the simplest time signature as an example – 4/4. This is called "four-four time", and is often abbreviated to "C", meaning "common time". In this time signature, there are four beats to the bar, and each beat has the time value of a quarter-note – since it lasts for one quarter of a bar. Music in 2/4 time has beats of the same time value (quarter-notes) but has only two of them in each bar. It is therefore essentially the same as 4/4 but with twice as many bars. The only difference is in the "feel" produced by the way the music is counted and played.

Besides 4/4 time, the most common time signature is 3/4. In 3/4 time (also called "triple time" or "waltz time"), there are three beats to the bar, and each beat has the time value of a quarter-note.

All time signatures based on "duple", "triple" or "quadruple" time are called *simple time signatures*. Compound time signatures are multiples of these.

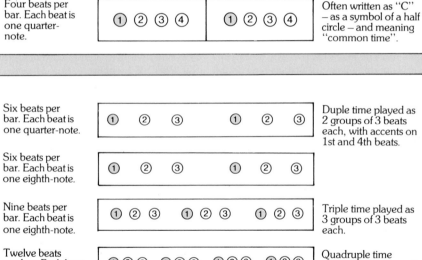

○ = Accented or emphasized beat

2/4 Two beats per bar. Each beat is one quarter-note.
2/4 has same tempo and rhythm as 4/4 but twice as many bars.

3/4 Three beats per bar. Each beat is one quarter-note.
Two bars of 3/4 can be counted and heard as one bar of 6/8.

4/4 Four beats per bar. Each beat is one quarter-note.
Often written as "C" – as a symbol of a half circle – and meaning "common time".

Compound time signatures

If the pulse of a piece of music is not felt as single beats but as groups of three beats, it is said to be in *compound time*. Take, as an example, 2/4 time played in groups of threes: each of the two beats in a bar of 2/4 is divided into three beats. This now produces six beats to a bar, and the time signatures that describe this are 6/4 and 6/8. In the same way, 3/4 time played in three groups of threes becomes 9/4 or 9/8, and 4/4 time played in four groups of threes becomes 12/4 or 12/8. These groups of three beats are called "triplets" (see p. 94).

When music has five, seven or eleven beats in each bar, it is said to be in *asymmetric time* – since these numbers are not divisible by two or by three. However, "accents" still tend to be placed on the beats to form them into groups of two, three or four which then add up to the required five, seven or eleven. This means that 7/4 time, for example, can be played as a group of three plus a group of four, as a group of four plus a group of three, or as a group of two plus a group of three plus another group of two. The way the beats are subdivided should follow the musical phrase and the "accents" on individual notes (see p. 94). An 11/8 bar can be counted as three groups of three beats followed by a group of two, with a pulse or emphasized beat felt at the start of each group.

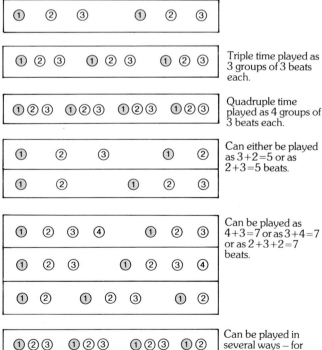

6/4 Six beats per bar. Each beat is one quarter-note.
Duple time played as 2 groups of 3 beats each, with accents on 1st and 4th beats.

6/8 Six beats per bar. Each beat is one eighth-note.

9/8 Nine beats per bar. Each beat is one eighth-note.
Triple time played as 3 groups of 3 beats each.

12/8 Twelve beats per bar. Each beat is one eighth-note.
Quadruple time played as 4 groups of 3 beats each.

5/4 Five beats per bar. Each beat is one quarter-note.
Can either be played as 3+2=5 or as 2+3=5 beats.

7/8 Seven beats per bar. Each beat is one eighth-note.
Can be played as 4+3=7 or as 3+4=7 or as 2+3+2=7 beats.

11/8 Eleven beats per bar. Each beat is one eighth-note.
Can be played in several ways – for example, as 3+3+3+2=11 or as 6+5=11 beats.

Using chord charts

Now that you know what a "bar" is and how to count it, you are ready to read charts that plot out the complete chord progression for any song. A *chord chart* is a sequence of chord symbols written to indicate their relative time values. A lyric sheet with the chord symbols written above the appropriate word or syllable can convey this information – if you know the melody and rhythm – but a chord chart will give it to you, usually in much less space, using bars instead of lyrics to indicate time.

The first thing to do if you want to write a chord chart is to decide on the tempo and the time signature. This establishes the speed at which each bar is to be read. All chord charts should be written with a time signature.

The next thing is simply to decide how long each chord lasts and on which beat of which bar there is a change to a new chord. Vertical strokes indicate beats instead of notes.

Chord charts in this form represent the standard means of communicating information to a guitarist. They leave it up to each player to select an appropriate chord inversion and to choose a rhythmic pattern that gives the right sort of "feel".

How to read chord charts

Chord charts always begin with a time signature to establish how many beats there are in each bar. Chord symbols are then used in the bars, along with other standard forms of musical notation such as rests (*see* p. 92) and repeat signs (*see* below).

One chord per bar
If there is just one chord written in each bar, the chord is played for the duration of the bar. As an initial aid, the "count" for the beats is shown in circles above the bars.

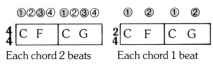

Each chord played for 4 beats

More than one chord per bar
Two, three or four chords in the same bar may be given an equal number of beats – unless vertical strokes indicate otherwise. Each stroke represents one beat of the chord that it follows.

Each chord 2 beats   Each chord 1 beat

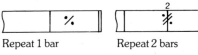

C gets 2 beats   G gets 2 beats

Rests
Conventional rest symbols indicate silence – no chord is played (*see* p. 92).

4 beats res'   2 beats rest

1 beat rest in each bar

Repeats
Chord chart repeat symbols tell you to play the previous bar again. A figure 2 or 4 above the symbol indicates that the previous 2 or 4 bars are to be repeated.

Repeat 1 bar   Repeat 2 bars

Playing directions

We have seen that the time signature is used to define the bar, and that the bar is the basic counting unit of music. However, if you wanted to write down a four-minute song, played at a tempo of 120 beats per minute, you would have to write out 120 bars of music. In fact, most music involves a fair amount of repetition, and conventional notation has a number of symbols that will tell you which parts of the basic theme are to be repeated and in what order. These symbols are the *repeat signs*, *first and second endings*, *capos* and *codas*. They act as the "signposts" or "traffic signals" of all written music.

What the symbols mean

Repeat signs When you come to the second sign, you go back to the first and repeat the section in between the two double bar signs.

First and second endings The first time through, you play the section marked 1. Then go back to the beginning and, on the second time through, play the section marked 2 (omitting section 1).

Da capo Often abbreviated to D.C., *da capo* means "from the head". When you see this sign, you must go back to the beginning of the piece of music.

Dal segno Instead of going right back to the beginning, go back only as far as the sign. *Dal segno* means "from the sign" and is abbreviated to D.S.

Al coda Meaning "to the tail", this tells you that you must go the the end section, which starts with a coda sign.

Example: repeat signs and endings

How to play
Play bars 1 to 4. Go back to the beginning and play bars 1 to 11. Go back to the start of bar 5 and play bars 5 to 10, omit bar 11, and finish with bar 12.

Example: segnos and codas

How to play
Begin by playing bars 1 to 12. When you reach the *dal segno al coda*, go back to the sign at the beginning and play bars 1 to 8. When you reach the *al coda*, go to the start of bar 13 and play bars 13 to 16, repeating them but gradually fading them out (R + F).

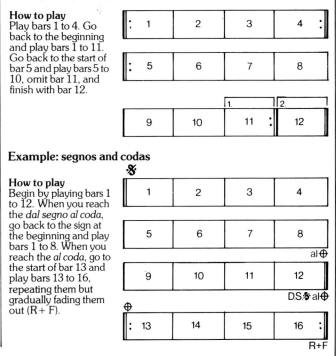

Time values

To play any note, you have to know three things about it – what pitch it has, when you should start playing it, and how long it should last. The question of its pitch is considered on p. 103. The question of its duration is determined by its *time value*.

Basically, there are seven different time values in musical notation – from the "whole-note" (which lasts the longest) to the "sixty-fourth-note" (which is the shortest). However, like the bar, time values are strictly related to the tempo and time signature of a particular piece of music. We have already seen that the bar is the basic unit of time in all music. And we know that the time signature divides it into a certain number of beats, and the tempo determines the speed of these beats. You can therefore give a time value or duration to a note only when you know the tempo and the time signature of the music in which it is to be featured.

Rests

A rest is a direction *not* to play. It is designed to create silence in between separate chords or notes. In all rhythm playing, where what you do not play is always as important as what you do, rests are crucial.

For *every* note symbol, there is a rest symbol with an equal time value. So, like a note, a rest will tell you when to stop playing and for how long. In a bar of 4/4 time, a whole-note rest will mean that you stop playing for four beats, and a sixty-fourth-note rest will mean that you stop playing for just a sixteenth of a beat. Clearly, the value of a rest symbol depends entirely on the time signature.

The rest symbols are shown below. Note that the last four have the same number of "flags" on their stems as their equivalent note symbols.

Rest symbols		
Rest	Time value	Note
▬	Whole-note rest	𝅝
▬	Half-note rest	𝅗𝅥
𝄽	Quarter-note rest	𝅘𝅥
𝄾	Eighth-note rest	𝅘𝅥𝅮
𝄿	Sixteenth-note rest	𝅘𝅥𝅯
𝅀	Thirty-second-note rest	𝅘𝅥𝅰
𝅁	Sixty-fourth-note rest	𝅘𝅥𝅱

Notes

Of the seven different notes in conventional music notation, each has its own relative time value and its own name. However, the terminology differs. The English system calls the longest note a "semi-breve" and the shortest note a "hemi-demi-semi-quaver", whereas the American system has a "whole-note" and a "sixty-fourth-note" as the two extremes. Since the American terminology is becoming increasingly common in Europe, it is the one used here.

The only note not included here is the "breve". It lasts twice as long as the semi-breve (that is, for the length of two whole-notes) but it is now used only rarely.

Note symbols, shown in the chart below, are based on an open circle for a whole-note. As the time value decreases, the circle acquires a "stem", then becomes solid, and then has one, two, three or four "flags" attached to its stem. In most time signatures, either a "quarter-note" or an "eighth-note" represents one beat. It is probably easier to understand time values if you consider one beat as equaling one quarter-note. Notes that last for longer than one beat are then *multiples* of a quarter-note (for example, half-notes and whole-notes), and notes that

do not last as long as one beat are then *sub-divisions* of a quarter-note (for example, eighth-notes, sixteenth-notes, and so on). This means that in one bar of 4/4 time (where there are four beats to every bar) a whole-note will last for the whole bar, and a sixty-fourth-note will last for a mere sixteenth of the bar.

Equivalent values

All notes are simple multiples of one another. Two half-notes last as long as a whole-note, two quarter-notes add up to a half-note, two eighth-notes are the same as a quarter-note, and so on. It is vital that you understand how these values work if you are to learn how they are counted.

Take one bar of 4/4 time as an example. It can comprise one whole-note, or two half-notes, or four quarter-notes, or any combination of notes and rests that adds up to exactly four beats. In one bar of 3/4 time, the same would apply as long as the total number of notes and rests added up to exactly three beats. In one bar of 5/8 time, the notes and rests should add up to exactly five beats – but each eighth-note (not each quarter-note) would represent one beat.

Note symbols							
Note	𝅝	𝅗𝅥	𝅘𝅥	𝅘𝅥𝅮	𝅘𝅥𝅯	𝅘𝅥𝅰	𝅘𝅥𝅱
American name	Whole-note	Half-note	Quarter-note	Eighth-note	Sixteenth-note	Thirty-second-note	Sixty-fourth-note
English name	Semi-breve	Minim	Crotchet	Quaver	Semi-quaver	Demi-semi-quaver	Hemi-demi-semi-quaver

How notes are related
This "family tree" of note values shows clearly that one sixty-fourth-note lasts only for a sixty-fourth of the time that a whole-note lasts. However, notes have no actual time value in themselves; their duration must be taken from the tempo and time signature.

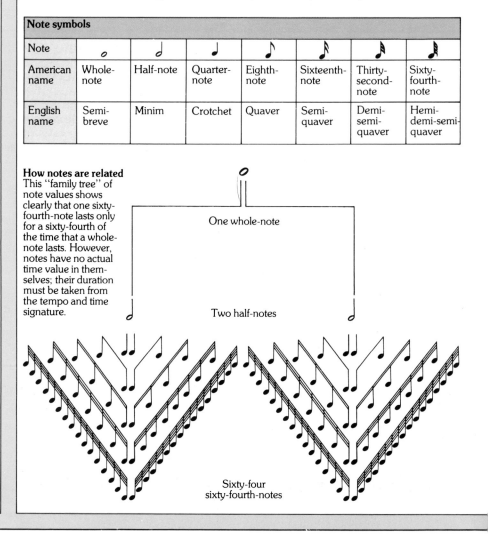

One whole-note

Two half-notes

Sixty-four sixty-fourth-notes

Note divisions

If we take one quarter-note as being equivalent to one beat, then the chart below shows that a whole-note lasts for four beats, an eighth-note for half a beat, and a sixty-fourth-note for a sixteenth of a beat.

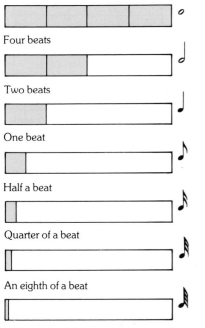

Four beats

Two beats

One beat

Half a beat

Quarter of a beat

An eighth of a beat

A sixteenth of a beat

Note One quarter-note is equivalent to one beat. Each line represents one bar in 4/4 time.

Bars in 4/4 time

All the notes in each bar, whatever their individual time values, must add up to a total of four beats of one quarter-note each.

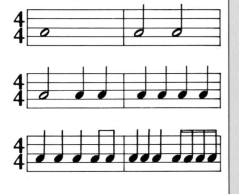

Bars in 3/4 time

All the notes in each bar, whatever their individual time values, must add up to a total of three beats of one quarter-note each.

Dots

If a note is followed by a *dot*, its time value is increased by half again. A half-note normally worth two beats (in 4/4 time), when written with a dot, becomes worth three beats. A whole-note written with a dot would be worth six beats and could therefore only be used in a bar of 6/4 time. In the same way, a "dotted" quarter-note would have the combined value of a quarter-note plus an eighth-note, and a dotted eighth-note would have the value of an eighth-note plus a sixteenth-note.

Dots can also be added to rests. The principle is exactly the same: the dot increases the time value of the rest by half. Examples are given below.

Examples of dotted note and rest values

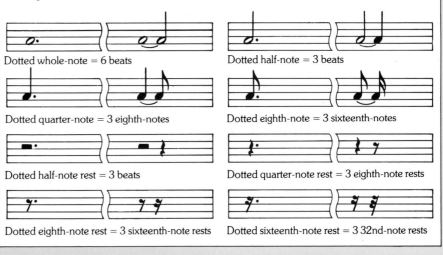

Dotted whole-note = 6 beats

Dotted half-note = 3 beats

Dotted quarter-note = 3 eighth-notes

Dotted eighth-note = 3 sixteenth-notes

Dotted half-note rest = 3 beats

Dotted quarter-note rest = 3 eighth-note rests

Dotted eighth-note rest = 3 sixteenth-note rests

Dotted sixteenth-note rest = 3 32nd-note rests

Ties

So far, all the timing directions have worked within the confines of a bar. To extend an uninterrupted note across a bar line – that is, to play a note which lasts for longer than the time represented by one bar – requires the use of a *tie*. A tie is indicated by a small curved line connecting two notes of the same pitch. It means that the note should be held for the duration of *both* note values. A tie can be used with any pair of notes, either across a bar line or within a bar, but ties are not used with rests. Besides combining two note values into a longer one, ties are used to clarify a complicated phrase so that you can see how it is constructed and where the main beats fall.

Examples of ties

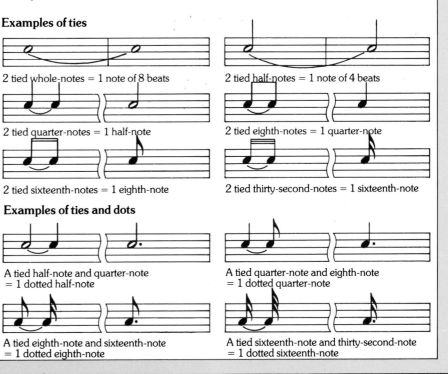

2 tied whole-notes = 1 note of 8 beats

2 tied half-notes = 1 note of 4 beats

2 tied quarter-notes = 1 half-note

2 tied eighth-notes = 1 quarter-note

2 tied sixteenth-notes = 1 eighth-note

2 tied thirty-second-notes = 1 sixteenth-note

Examples of ties and dots

A tied half-note and quarter-note = 1 dotted half-note

A tied quarter-note and eighth-note = 1 dotted quarter-note

A tied eighth-note and sixteenth-note = 1 dotted eighth-note

A tied sixteenth-note and thirty-second-note = 1 dotted sixteenth-note

Triplets

Any group of three notes, in which each note is played with the same time value and the same "stress" or "accent", is called a *triplet*. The three notes are linked with a curved line called a "slur" (similar to a tie) and the number 3 is written over the top or at the bottom.

Triplets are usually used to describe the effect of three notes being played in the space of two. They are a necessary device because there is no other way to indicate dividing a time value into thirds. There are no such note values as a third-note, a sixth-note, a ninth-note, and so on – yet these time values do obviously exist.

In 4/4 time, where one beat equals one quarter-note, a triplet of quarter-notes represents three notes played in the space of two beats, and a triplet of eighth-notes represents three notes played in the space of one beat. The best way to play four triplets of eighth-notes (which make up four beats) is to count *one*-two-three, *two*-two-three, *three*-two-three, *four*-two-three.

In 6/8 or 9/8 time, triplets of eighth-notes can be written without having to add the slur and the number 3. This will produce the same musical effect and "feel".

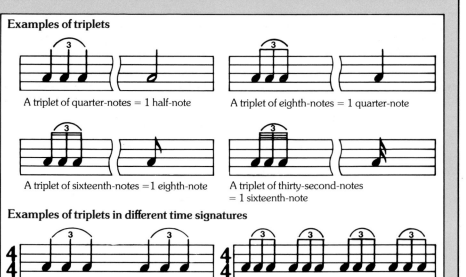

Examples of triplets

A triplet of quarter-notes = 1 half-note

A triplet of eighth-notes = 1 quarter-note

A triplet of sixteenth-notes =1 eighth-note

A triplet of thirty-second-notes = 1 sixteenth-note

Examples of triplets in different time signatures

2 triplets of quarter-notes per bar

4 triplets of eighth-notes per bar

2 triplets of eighth-notes per bar in each case

3 triplets of eighth-notes per bar in each case

Additional symbols

There are three further symbols used to give precise instructions on the execution of specific notes or phrases – the *staccato*, the *portato* and the *accent*.

The *staccato* is a dot either above or below a note. It should not be confused with the dot which increases a note's time value (see p. 93). *Staccato* means "short and sharp", and it tells you to play the note for only half as long as it is written – while still keeping to the rhythm specified. A series of *staccato* notes should be clearly separated from one another. In other words, the symbols create an effect which, otherwise,

could be achieved only by inserting short rests in between each of the notes.

Portato symbols have exactly the opposite effect. They comprise short horizontal dashes written above the note, and they tell you to stress its full value – leaving only as short a gap as possible between it and the note that follows.

Accents mark out notes that are to be emphasized more strongly than they would otherwise be. You should therefore hit the string or strings harder so that the accented note or chord stands out from surrounding un-accented ones.

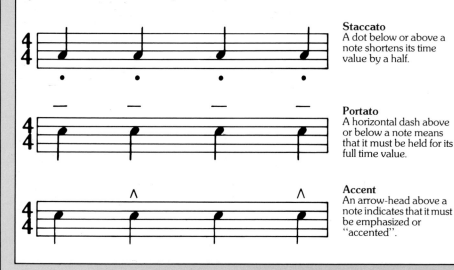

Staccato
A dot below or above a note shortens its time value by a half.

Portato
A horizontal dash above or below a note means that it must be held for its full time value.

Accent
An arrow-head above a note indicates that it must be emphasized or "accented".

Dynamic directions

Although not strictly a part of rhythm playing, musical notation includes a system of "dynamic" instructions. These concern the volume at which you are to play a sequence of chords or a phrase of notes, and they affect the overall "sound".

Most of the directions are in the form of abbreviations of Italian words – as shown below – but there are also symbols to indicate a *crescendo* (meaning that the music should get gradually louder) and a *diminuendo* or *decrescendo* (meaning that it gets gradually softer).

Symbol	Italian word	Direction
ff	*Fortissimo*	Very loud
f	*Forte*	Loud
mf	*Mezzo forte*	Moderately loud
mp	*Mezzo piano*	Moderately soft
p	*Piano*	Soft, quiet
pp	*Pianissimo*	Very soft

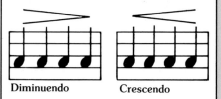

Diminuendo　　　**Crescendo**

Rhythm charts

There is a standard "shorthand" method for writing down the *rhythm* of a series of chords or notes without referring to their pitch. It is most often used with chord progressions and forms a compromise between a simple "chord chart" (see p. 91), which conveys only limited information about rhythm, and full musical notation, which conveys all the information you need but which takes much longer to write out.

Rhythm charts do vary somewhat – as do all shorthand styles – and you may come across slightly different symbols, but the basic principle remains the same. All rhythm charts use bars and time signatures in the standard way. Chord names are written either in, above or below the staff. The precise rhythm in which they are played is indicated by just the "stems" and "flags" of the ordinary note symbols.

The only two notes that cannot be represented by rhythmic shorthand are the whole-note and half-note – since the note symbol itself is needed to indicate the time value. The way around this is to use the vertical strokes representing quarter-notes and "tie" together as many of them as necessary.

Counting out rhythms

Complex rhythm patterns can be very difficult to count – especially if they contain short notes and rests. To help you analyze them and so that you can clearly see and understand what is going on, it is a good idea if you slow down the tempo and divide the number of beats in the bar so that the shortest note has a value of one count. A bar of 4/4 time is shown below written out so that there are eight counts – one for each of the eighth-notes. If the bar had contained sixteenth-notes, it could have been counted out in sixteen separate counts to the bar.

Original notation
This bar is in 4/4, which means that it contains four beats. But, because the eighth-notes and rests have only half a beat each, it is easier to count if written out in eights.

Re-written rhythm chart
The structure of the rhythm becomes more obvious when seen in terms of eight counts to the bar. The green circles indicate the beats to play, and the white circles are rests.

How to read rhythm charts

Rhythm charts observe the basic rule of all music notation: each bar should total the correct number of beats specified by the time signature. These beats can be made up from any combination of notes and rests.

The examples below show various rhythms in different time signatures. On the top line is the conventional notation, and on the bottom line is the equivalent rhythm chart. Play them through using any chords.

95

Folk and country rhythms

The acoustic guitar dominates folk and country music – largely as a result of its musical versatility and its portability. In the absence of a bass player or drummer, the guitarist frequently assumes the role of the rhythm section. The guitar then becomes a primary source of time and harmony.

The "ballad" is the most common form of this music. By definition, it is played at a slow-to-moderate tempo – with any combination of plectrum, thumbpicks, fingerpicks and fingerstyle (see p. 73). Time signatures are usually 3/4 or 4/4, and the songs use simple chords and basic progressions such as those shown on pp. 76-8. The chords are almost always played with full left-hand sustain – which means that they are allowed to ring without being damped. The most common right-hand styles are either full, open strumming, alternate bass notes with strumming, or alternate bass notes with arpeggios. The strums may be either upstrokes or downstrokes, but since an uninterrupted flow of the hand is the most important element in playing a smooth, steady rhythm, the most common pattern is a downstroke on the 1st beat, an upstroke on the 2nd, down on the 3rd, and up on the 4th.

Folk and country styles played at faster tempos are often related to some kind of dance. American bluegrass and mountain music, country and western, western swing, and Irish jigs and reels all share common elements, so the rhythm guitar roles have many similarities. They are based on simple chords and progressions played with full sustain. One of the most important differences lies in which beats are accented – the "downbeat" or the "backbeat". For example, in a bar of 4/4, the 1st and 3rd beats are the downbeats, and the 2nd and 4th beats are the backbeats. The Americanization of Irish music can be heard as a process of evolution in which different beats are emphasized. So, in 4/4 time, with two bass notes per bar, one pattern might be: 1 bass, 2 chord, 3 bass, 4 chord. Each beat is played with a downstroke, and because the chords sound louder than the bass notes, the effect is of a natural backbeat.

In fact, Irish and American bluegrass tunes are usually played at a fast tempo, and the rhythm is in either eighths or sixteenths. As the examples show, the principle of the accented beats remains the same. Bars in eighths are best counted as 1–and–2–and–3–and–4–and; bars in sixteenths become easier to follow if you count four groups of four – **1**–2–3–4, **2**–2–3–4, etc.

Patterns like this are almost always played with an alternating bass. For a C major chord, for example, the 3rd finger would move from the note C (3rd fret, 5th string) to the note G

(3rd fret, 6th string). This technique is explained under *Flatpicking* (see p. 79).

Traditional ballads and Irish jigs and reels arranged for solo guitar represent a highly sophisticated folk guitar style. The bass lines, chords and melodies are interwoven in the same way as they are in much of classical guitar music, and the tunes are always played fingerstyle (see pp. 80-1). Based on modal harmony, alternative tunings (see p. 158), or using as few as two chords, the bass is often sounded to resemble the pipes from which the music originated. The left-hand techniques of hammering-on and pulling-off (see p. 141) are a strong rhythmic feature.

How to read the rhythms

All the rhythm styles set out in the following pages are written in the form of standard rhythm charts (see p. 95). Circled numbers appear above each bar and indicate how the bar should be counted.

② Standard count

⊕ Plus sign indicates a count of "and" (as in 1–and–2–and)

③ Green circles indicate the beats that should be accented or emphasized.

Examples of folk and country rhythms

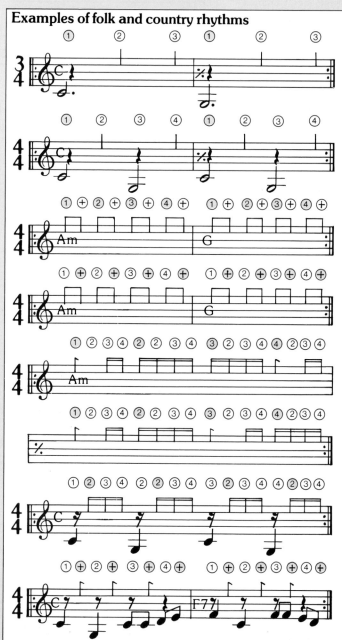

3/4 ballad rhythm with alternating bass Bass note is played on 1st beat, chord on 2nd and 3rd. Bass note changes from C to G.

4/4 ballad rhythm with alternating bass Bass is played either on 1st beat or on the 1st and 3rd, as here.

Downbeat An emphasis on 1st and 3rd beats is characteristic of Irish rhythm guitar styles.

Backbeat An emphasis on 2nd and 4th beats tends to identify American country styles.

Fast Irish fiddle tune rhythm In this example, each bar is divided into sixteenths – best counted as **1**–2–3–4, **2**–2–3–4–, etc. The accent is played on the downbeat – that is, the 1st of each 4 sixteenths.

Fast American country rhythm The bar is divided into sixteenths. The chords emphasize the backbeat.

Country rhythm with moving bass This style often includes a simple bass line as a lead-up to each change of chord (see p. 79).

Blues and rock rhythms

Most forms of modern music have their roots in the blues. In fact, the evolution from blues to rock is the story of the modern guitar. Broadly speaking, any music in 4/4 time based around simple I–IV–V chord progressions (see p. 77) can be considered to have evolved from the blues. Any discussion of where blues stops and country, folk, rock or jazz begin must acknowledge the fact that the styles overlap and divisions have long been blurred.

In its simplest form, a slow blues is played by sounding the chord on the first beat of the bar, leaving it to ring, then playing it again on the second beat and either damping it or cutting it off so that an accent is created. The third and fourth beats repeat the first and second so that a backbeat results. The pattern can also be reversed to produce a sustained chord on the backbeat.

One of the most common of blues rhythms is based on a simple alternating "riff" played on the damped bass strings (see below right). Whatever the tempo, this pattern forms the basis of the "shuffle" feel. It produces the pick-up effect of the bass line striking just before and on each beat, with a slight hesitation (the rest) immediately after each beat.

The basic pattern or riff can be varied in countless ways, and it often is – for example, by varying the number of beats on each pair of notes, by playing the strings individually, by including the note on the 5th fret of the higher string, and so on.

In a small blues band containing a drummer and a bass player, the simplest rhythm guitar patterns are based on one or two chords per bar, or on a steady repetition of a bass-string riff. The riff is usually played with downstrokes, heavily damped, in time with the bass and the bass drum. Chord patterns are usually played as upstrokes, cut off by left-hand damping, in time with the snare.

Rock and roll emerged when musicians increased the tempo of blues patterns, incorporated elements of country and popular music, and changed the lyric content of the songs. Musically, there is not much difference between fast blues and early rock and roll or rhythm and blues. A Chuck Berry guitar solo is a classic example of blues triplets, and the accentuated backbeat is a fixture of all rock and roll. However, what differences there are, though subtle, are important to the guitarist. Many changes of style occurred in the transition from blues to rock. Of these, the most noticeable were perhaps the replacement of the triplet feel by even eighths or sixteenths when playing at a fast tempo, and the use of more sustained chords, often accented on beats other than the downbeat or backbeat.

Examples of blues and rock rhythms

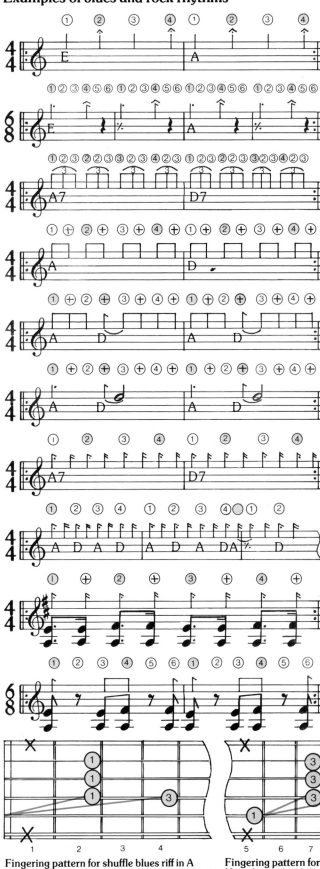

Solo blues rhythm
The 2nd and 4th beats of each bar are accented *staccato* quarter-notes. It is easier to understand this if you see two bars of 4/4 as being four bars of 6/8. In each bar, the rhythm then goes (1–2–3) (4) (5–6).

Triplets
At a slow tempo, this rhythm is typical of Fats Domino. Played faster, it is more like Chuck Berry.

Straight eights
This rhythm, which tended to replace triplets, can be heard from Buddy Holly onwards.

Accented eights
This adaptation of the straight eights rhythm, in which the accent falls on different beats, is characteristic of the transition from blues to rock. It is recognizable as typical of the Rolling Stones, for example.

Shuffle rhythms
These are found throughout rhythm and blues, and rock and roll. The second example, with its syncopated accent on the last beat of the second bar, is a boogie rhythm.

Basic shuffle blues riff The shuffle rhythm is commonly played on two bass strings. It is shown here in A. As with the solo rhythm above, it is easier to count if you transpose the pattern from two bars of 4/4 (which is how it is, in fact, played) to two bars of 6/8.

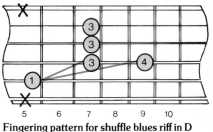

Fingering pattern for shuffle blues riff in A
Play the open 5th string (A) together with the 2nd fret on the 4th string (E). Then the open 5th string (A) with the 4th fret on the 4th string (F♯).

Fingering pattern for shuffle blues riff in D
Using barre chord shapes, the riff can be played anywhere on the fingerboard. The root note for this shape is on the 5th string – in this case D.

Soul, funk and reggae rhythms

Soul and funk are fusions of various roots, and are both recent styles by comparison. Soul gained popularity in the sixties, and funk in the seventies, both as dance music.

The term "rhythm and blues" accurately describes the two key ingredients in early rock and early soul music. Like rock, soul music was born with a rhythm section. Following the tradition of big-band guitarists, the role of the guitarist playing soul music is pre-determined by what the rhythm section plays. The two strongest characteristics of the style are the "chop" and the "stab".

The *chord chop* is played on the backbeat in time with the snare drum. It is usually an upstroke (played with a plectrum) and requires quick left-hand damping if the sound is to have the same "attack" as the snare.

Accented *chord stabs* can be used to imitate a horn section. They are short, sharp patterns, often played while sliding the whole chord up and down over one fret. Try them with any ninth chord (see p. 142).

The crossover from soul to funk has a lot to do with the rhythm section – in particular the bass player – creating a different kind of "space" for faster tempos. There are no traditions in funk other than welding all the instruments into a precise rhythm that is as steady as a rock.

The rhythm guitar part usually involves playing a repetitive pattern in a mid-to-high chord inversion. There is a classic pattern that can be considered a crossover "lick" common to soul, rock and funk styles. A bar of 4/4 is divided into sixteenths – so that there are four groups of four, each group lasting for one beat. In its simplest form, the chord is played only four times in the bar, but on different sixteenths of each beat (see right). This rhythm can be played either as individual upstroke chops punctuated by rests or as fast, continuous, alternate strokes, all deadened except for the accented sixteenths. The latter is particularly characteristic of funk. It demands skillful left-hand damping and a steady right-hand motion. But once you get the hang of "squeezing" the chord with your left hand so that it sounds on just the right accent, you will produce a "busy", highly syncopated rhythm.

The chords used in funk represent an evolution of the harmony found in soul music. Ninths and elevenths (see pp. 132-5) are commonly used where the chord remains basically the same for many bars. And, when the chords do change more often, they are often structured around the I-IV-V formula.

The key to funk is that the rhythm guitar style should be *sparse*. At its simplest, this may mean no more than quick backbeat chord stabs, but it can also involve single-string patterns damped with the right hand.

Reggae, which began as a combination of early American rhythm and blues, calypsos, and a Jamaican rhythm called "blue beat", is also a style that depends heavily on the bass line. As far as the rhythm guitarist is concerned, the backbeat is even more important. The difference is that the drummer need not play the backbeat at all; often, the job falls solely on the rhythm guitarist, who may end up not playing a single downbeat.

The technique is a "chop" again – usually played as a hard downstroke on the second and fourth beats of every bar. The aim is always to create a steady, hypnotic pattern that changes as little as possible. However, damped single-string patterns may also be included, usually in the form of short bursts of triplets to complement the bass pattern.

Examples of soul, funk and reggae rhythms

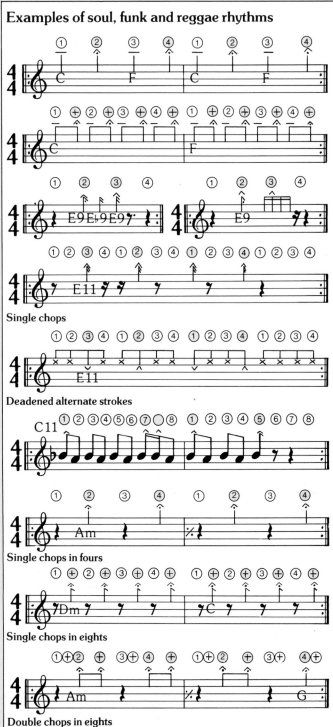

Single chops

Deadened alternate strokes

Single chops in fours

Single chops in eights

Double chops in eights

Chord chops
Emphasizing the backbeat with a sharp upstroke or "chop" is characteristic of all soul music. The first rhythm is in fours and is similar to a blues feel; the second is in eights, at a faster tempo.

Chord stabs
These horn-section riffs for rhythm guitar are ideal for sliding ninth chords.

Soul/funk crossover riffs The pattern is based on dividing a bar of 4/4 into sixteenths and accenting only the 3rd, 6th, 9th and 12th of these. It can either be played as single chops or as continuous, alternate strokes deadened except for the accented beats.

Single-string funk riff Over a C eleventh chord, play a heavily damped, single-string riff, alternating from B♭ to A.

Reggae chops
Regular chops on the backbeat are the foundation of all reggae and ska rhythms. These examples, all in 4/4, show the variations produced by counting in fours and eights and by playing single or double chops. Harmonically, reggae is one of the simpler forms of music – primarily based on the familiar I–IV–V–VIm chord progressions (see p. 78).

Spanish and Latin rhythms

Until fifty years ago, the Spanish guitar (see p. 42) was still the instrument played by the vast majority of guitarists around the world. It is rarely played with a plectrum, since it is generally accepted that the fingers produce a better sound in the styles of music for which the guitar is used. The stylistic range of the Spanish guitar is still wider than that of steel-string guitars, and it is still the only type accepted as a legitimate classical instrument.

The original Spanish flamenco, as well as the songs and ballads related to it, uses mostly simple open chords and is based on a I–V–I structure. An important feature of flamenco is the right-hand technique called *rascuedo*. Starting with the hand clenched, the fingers are "thrown out" so that the fingernails play three or four downstrokes across the strings in quick succession. The palm comes down to provide an immediate damping effect. The thumb alternates with the fingers and plays bass notes independently.

Many former Spanish colonies in Central and South America feature ethnic styles strongly based on the techniques of Spanish music. Simple open chords and open-hand strumming and damping, for example, are the primary techniques of Spanish, Portuguese and Latin American guitar styles.

African and Caribbean musicians playing essentially Spanish-influenced music transferred the accent of the rhythm from the downbeat to the backbeat. The backbeat is an established structure in ethnic African rhythms, and in the earliest examples of American blues and Caribbean music you can hear it clearly.

"Syncopation" is used to describe accents that do not fall on the beat, and it is the chief characteristic of various Caribbean and Latin American rhythms. The patterns are played with a backbeat, which is created by damping the chord with the palm on the third and seventh beats (if you count each bar in eights). This damped backbeat provides a contrast to the syncopated accents so that they have a stronger effect.

Bossa nova (meaning "new style"), the term used for Brazilian jazz, is the most sophisticated of the Latin styles. The thumb almost always plays syncopated bass notes, and the fingers play chords. The chords either fill the spaces between the bass notes with a pattern of their own or play *with* the bass notes, creating a rich harmonic and rhythmic texture equaled by few other styles.

Latin American rhythms such as the *bossa nova*, *samba* and *montuno*, and Caribbean rhythms such as the *rumba*, *mambo* and *cha-cha*, are all part of the repertoire of modern music. To help you learn to identify and use these rhythms, some of the better-known patterns are written out here.

Examples of Spanish and Latin rhythms

Flamenco
This chord progression is standard in flamenco music, and is used with minor scales (see p. 106).

Afro-Cuban
This rhythm is best known as the dance called the "conga".

Caribbean
The accents fall on the middle beat of each group of three chord strokes.

Caribbean/Latin
Count each bar in eights and stress the 1st, 4th and (in the 2nd bar) the 7th beats.

Latin/soul crossover
When played with a backbeat, you should recognize this as a soul rhythm.

Beguine
French West Indian in origin, this dance has a strongly Spanish-influenced rhythm.

Tango
From Argentina, this dance combines South American and West Indian rhythms.

Cha-cha
A fast West Indian/Latin American rhythm derived from earlier "mambos".

Merengue
This rhythm comes from a Dominican and Haitian dance.

Montuno
Count the bar in sixteens and emphasize the green circled beats only.

Sambas
Brazilian dance rhythms with a strong African and West Indian feel. Count the second example in sixteens to each bar if you find it difficult to follow.

Jazz guitar styles

Of the many descendants of the blues, jazz is the form that represents the state of the art in terms of the evolution of popular music. Musically, it is the most sophisticated, the most demanding and, some would say, the most rewarding of popular styles. During the last fifteen years or so, the increasing amount of crossover between mainstream jazz and electric rock has produced the variety of fusion forms that include jazz-rock and jazz-funk. As a result, the distinction – if there ever really was one – between a rock guitarist and a jazz guitarist has become more and more blurred and increasingly meaningless.

In the history of jazz, the guitar has come from nowhere to being accepted as one of the front-line instruments. Its career can be seen in terms of two phases: first, its gradual replacement of the banjo in the rhythm section, and, second, its emergence as a solo instrument. The key factors in this development – chiefly the introduction of amplification and the playing of guitarists like Django Reinhardt and Charlie Christian – are plotted below. The guitar is now established as a major rhythm and solo instrument.

At the heart of jazz lies the concept of *improvisation*. Countless influential guitarists have proved that the guitar is an instrument that allows improvisation rhythmically, melodically and harmonically: *rhythmically* in the choice of accents, emphases and syncopations; *melodically* in the choice of notes for a solo; and *harmonically* in the choice of chords, chord voicings and substitutions.

The role of the guitar in jazz

In the earliest forms of jazz, the guitar played virtually no part at all. The music coming out of New Orleans around the turn of the century featured collective improvisation based on the interplay of three instruments – the trumpet (or cornet), the clarinet and the trombone. These "melodic" instruments were supported by a rhythm section consisting of banjo, drums and bass or tuba. Although the steel-string guitar was around by this time, the banjo tended to be used instead because it had a sufficiently loud "attack" to cut through the volume of the rest of the band.

This was, essentially, the line-up of the Original Dixieland Jazz Band, who in 1917 became the first group in history to make a commercial jazz recording. Their "Dixieland" style, with its roots in gospel, ragtime and the New Orleans sound, featured a strong, alternating bass line on the downbeat (the 1st and 3rd beats of each bar) and accentuated, damped chords on the backbeat (the 2nd and 4th beats of each bar).

The first evidence of a change came in the mid-twenties in Chicago. The King Oliver Band, which included Louis Armstrong, made a series of recordings containing the earliest examples of written jazz. The King Oliver line-up had grown to three reed instruments (clarinets and saxophone), four brass instruments (two trumpets or cornets, trombone and tuba), banjo, drums and piano. There was still no place for the guitar.

It was the introduction of the arch-top acoustic guitar (see p.46) that gave guitarists their first opportunity to challenge the role of the banjo in the rhythm section. Though still not quite as loud, it had a smoother tone and greater harmonic potential. Slowly the guitar started to replace the banjo. By the early 1930s, Duke Ellington, Count Basie and Benny Goodman had established a big band line-up with three trumpets, three trombones, four reeds, and a rhythm section of piano, bass, guitar and drums.

Eddie Lang is often credited as being the first jazz guitarist. Playing with Benny Goodman, Lang inspired musicians everywhere to regard the guitar as a serious jazz instrument rather than one associated mainly with blues, folk and country music. His duet work with another key guitarist, Lonnie Johnson, also demonstrated the potential of the guitar in a small setting.

By this time, the acoustic rhythm guitarist needed a high-quality guitar and considerable technique and musicianship. The chord vocabulary was further expanded, and the guitarist played a continually moving melodic chord pattern, observing the effect of the harmonic progression and often changing the voicing of the chord on every beat.

In smaller groups, where the acoustic guitar could be heard more clearly, several prominent guitarists were beginning to establish their reputations as soloists. This was a major advance for the guitar. But it was the introduction of pick-ups and amplifiers that really gave the guitarist a new status. With the new sound, a new role emerged. The guitarist was confined less to time-keeping and began to move out of the rhythm section into the front line, playing improvised solos or sustained melodic and harmonic phrases.

Nowhere was this more apparent than in the playing of Charlie Christian (see p.9). In 1939, John Hammond brought the young guitarist to the attention of Benny Goodman, and during the three years until his death, Christian eclipsed every other guitarist and opened the door to a new musical era. Considered the first jazz soloist on electric guitar, his melodic ability and his new sound proved that the guitar was the equal of any sax or trumpet in the art of the improvised jazz solo. What he played is widely regarded as the first sign of the new direction in jazz – "bebop" – and as the beginning of the end for the "swing" era.

Something of an anachronism at around this time was Django Reinhardt (see p.8). A

Django Reinhardt with Maccaferri acoustic

self-taught gypsy guitarist, he was more or less the only influential guitar player to come out of Europe until years later. Playing his distinctive Maccaferri/Selmer guitars (see p.47), he demonstrated a complete mastery of melody and the new sophisticated harmony. In the mid-1930s his music established milestones that endure to this day.

By 1940, it was clear that the guitar was equally adept at providing a rhythmic chord backing and at soloing. Playing guitar in the Count Basie Band, Freddie Green epitomized the guitar's harmonic development through the swing era. His superb timing and the flowing sense of harmony he created helped to establish the role of the rhythm guitar as an important part of every rhythm section.

Just before the war, Charlie Christian's solos served as an inspiration to musicians who were growing frustrated at having exploited the diatonic system to its fullest. The music of Duke Ellington was conclusive proof that the essential spirit of improvisation could be orchestrated and directed to new heights. Soloists from Louis Armstrong and Coleman Hawkins to Lester Young and Johnny Hodges, and composers from

Developing an approach to jazz guitar playing

It's difficult to give advice on playing jazz guitar – as it is on any form of improvisation. One thing that *can* be said, however, is that, of all the forms of modern music, jazz is the one that demands the highest level of musicianship in terms of both theory and technique. By the end of the bop era and the beginning of "modern jazz", the role of the guitarist required the following skills.

• A quick "ear", trained to monitor what each member of the band is playing.

• A solid understanding of scales, chords, harmony and fingerboard theory.

• An ability to play any combination of rhythmic accents or syncopations.

• A single-string picking technique capable of handling sixteenth-notes and triplets.

• A good instinct and an imaginative feel for improvisation.

Any guitarist wanting to follow in the jazz tradition should certainly start with the music itself. Get hold of the recordings and, if possible, the sheet music to as many classics as possible. In a small jazz band consisting of, say, sax, keyboards, guitar, bass and drums, the guitarist must be con-

stantly aware of the other musicians. The interplay between the bass and the drummer will suggest certain rhythmic accents, the bass and the keyboards will suggest different approaches to the harmony, the sax and the keyboards will suggest voicings of the harmony, and the combined rhythmic patterns of the other four players will establish the general "feel". Just how the guitar fits in is virtually limitless. The only real way of deciding what to play and when to play it is to use your ears. There are no rules: just listen, then play.

Fletcher Henderson and Jelly Roll Morton to Count Basie and Duke Ellington, had thoroughly explored the possibilities of the eighteenth-century system. Pianists like Earl Hines, Teddy Wilson and Art Tatum had led the way for further variation – largely within the system – and big bands were on the road playing dance music to a new generation of jazz audiences. But the beginning of the war saw the demise of the big-band era, and the end of the war heralded the true arrival of bebop. The diatonic system exploded into a new concept of chromatic harmony, and melodic and rhythmic theories were completely re-evaluated. Small groups appeared everywhere with a new look and a new sound.

The new generation, now able to work from the complete tonal palette, and represented by Charlie Parker, Dizzy Gillespie and Thelonius Monk, arrived at a form which served as a vehicle for exploration. A recognized chord sequence – usually from a pre-war standard – could be given a new melody or top line, and could be played as fast as possible, with liberal extension and alteration of the original chords. The first chorus was played in unison, a chorus was then reserved for each soloist, and the final chorus was the theme in unison again.

Although the guitar did not have a regular role in a bop line-up, developments in theory and technique over the next few years established a new standard for the instrument. Players such as Johnny Smith, Jimmy Raney, Barney Kessel, Tal Farlow, Jim Hall, Herb Ellis, Kenny Burrell, Wes Montgomery, Joe Pass and Howard Roberts have all contributed to the evolution of modern jazz guitar playing.

The "cool jazz", which followed on the heels of bop, demonstrated the speed with which the new chromatic concepts were accepted by musicians. Miles Davis gave jazz a new mood by improvising over a modal instead of a harmonic system. However, the absence of identifiable diatonic

key-centers meant that audiences found it difficult to follow the harmony. The new style became largely musician's music. Ornette Coleman made the break into "modern jazz". In his search for soloist's freedom, he said that musicians must be free to produce any given sound at any given time.

The jazz world was now split into three different "schools": first, the traditionalists who preferred the pre-war diatonic music; second, the "hard bop" era of Parker, Monk and Mingus; and, third, the many variations producing new forms of modern jazz. John Lewis, founder of the Modern Jazz Quartet, combined elements of classical music and jazz, Dizzy Gillespie introduced Afro-Cuban rhythms, and Dave

Brubeck popularized a more commercial stream with the hit "Take Five".

The next major influence on the course of jazz came with Miles Davis's album "Bitches Brew", released in 1970. It introduced jazz to the power of the modern electric rhythm section, and it introduced audiences to the guitar playing of John McLaughlin. Like many great soloists before him, he came blazing in with a new sound and a new style that showed a mastery of past concepts and a vision of a new one. When, in 1971, McLaughlin formed the Mahavishnu Orchestra, and two other members of the Miles Davis group, Joe Zawinul and Wayne Shorter, formed Weather Report, there was no doubt that the fusion of jazz and rock was here to stay.

John McLaughlin playing a Gibson 6/12 twin neck

THE MELODIC GUITARIST

This is the part of the book that explains scales. Scales are the basis of all melody and, to some extent, of all improvisation. Many guitarists – especially those that are self-taught – are suspicious of scales and regard them as an unattractive and unnecessary discipline. This is untrue. While some guitarists often get by without really knowing what they are playing, there are four reasons why it is worth learning scales: first, they teach you the fingerboard, so that you know where all the notes are on each string; second, they will give you the best kind of "ear training" you can have; third, they will – more than almost anything else – increase your speed, fluency and accuracy; and, fourth, they will provide you with a basis for understanding chords – both how they are built and how they relate to one another. In an interview, the guitarist Al DiMeola confirmed the truth of this:

Frank Zappa

"One thing I learned a long time ago was my fretboard, in terms of all the scales in all the positions . . . You have to learn it – there are no two ways about it. I shift between positions so easily now that I really don't have to think about them much . . . I would suggest starting your scale education with the major and minor scales, and after that, diminished, augmented and whole-tone. Then depending on what kind of music you want to play, the modes should be learned. My theory about this kind of thing is that you should learn it all. Once you've learned it you can play whatever you want to play, and I think that your playing will be more advanced, and you'll have a better understanding of the instrument."

Al DiMeola

All scales are essentially just different ways of dividing up the octave. In this section of the book, we begin by looking at the major and minor scales, and explain how they form the basis of the Western diatonic system and how key signatures are used to identify them. We then move on to look at the "modes" and at the "synthetic" scales such as the whole-tone, diminished and pentatonic – all of which can be used simply as alternatives to the familiar diatonic structure.

When learning or practicing scales, you should aim to play them in as many positions and with as many different fingerings as you can. Start slowly, and increase your speed only when you can sound every note clearly. Familiarity with different scales in different fingerings and fingerboard positions is one of

the biggest assets a solo guitarist can have. Their importance goes beyond the question of pure technique. They will improve your ability to "hear" chords, and will help you identify the correct choice of scale intervals. These are the elements from which the ability to create melodies and to improvise your own solo lines is derived.

"My solos are speech-influenced rhythmically; and harmonically, they're either pentatonic, or poly-scale oriented. And there's the mixolydian mode that I also use a lot . . . But I'm more interested in melodic things. I think the biggest challenge when you go to play a solo is trying to invent a melody on the spot."

Frank Zappa

The range of the guitar

Modern flat-top steel-string acoustic guitars normally have clear access to the 14th fret, whereas the fingerboard of a traditional Spanish or classical guitar joins the body at the 12th fret. Electric guitars have cutaways that usually allow you to reach to at least the 19th fret fairly easily; some have as many as 24 clear frets – giving a two-octave range on one string, twice that of a classical guitar.

However, on any guitar, the note on the 13th fret is identical to the 1st fret but one octave higher. For this reason, the overall range of the guitar is considered to be from the open E on the 6th string to the high E on the 12th fret of the 1st string. This gives a span of three octaves, comprising 22 natural notes (not counting sharps and flats).

Unlike the keyboard, the fingerboard does not display the difference between the

natural notes and the sharps and flats, nor does it show the two places where there is only a semi-tone interval instead of a whole-tone (from E to F and from B to C). The big difference lies in the fact that many notes can be found on more than one string. This means that, in the great majority of cases, there is more than one place where you can play the same note.

Of the 22 natural notes contained within the 12-fret range, the three lowest and the three highest are the only notes that have just one position. Six notes can be played in two positions. The remaining ten notes, those in the center of the range, are playable in three different positions. Including both natural notes and sharps and flats, the guitar has an overall 12-fret range of 36 different notes (three octaves at twelve semi-tones

per octave) which can be played in a total of 72 positions (six strings with twelve frets each). The guitar is one of the few instruments that can play so many notes in so many different places.

There are both advantages and disadvantages to this. Learning to play a piece of music on the guitar involves the extra step of deciding which position on the fingerboard is the most appropriate. With different fingerings, it is possible to play almost anything in at least two different ways. The same idea can therefore produce slightly different sounds, even though the actual notes are identical. This unique property of the fingerboard gives guitarists a great advantage over other musicians. The creative possibilities it allows far outweigh the extra difficulties.

Pitch

The first seven letters of the alphabet are used to represent the pitch of the notes that comprise the Western world's musical system. These are C–D–E–F–G–A–B. There are historical reasons why the musical alphabet starts at C instead of A.

There is also a system – used in many non-English-speaking countries – which replaces the letters with names. These are do–re–mi–fa–sol–la–ti (or si). The notes are the same in both systems; only the terminology differs.

In order to name the pitch of every note, from the very lowest to the very highest, the system of seven letters repeats itself. So the note that follows G is A. The distance or "interval" between one note and the next with the same name, either up or down, is described as an octave. Two notes an octave apart will sound the same but will have different pitches; one will be in a higher range or "register" than the other. This is a natural phenomenon based on a 2:1 ratio between the frequencies of the two notes.

The keyboard is the most immediate visual reference to the Western musical system. You will see that the seven "alphabetical" notes we have been describing are represented by the white keys. Starting from C, playing the eight white keys that make up an octave demonstrates the diatonic scale of C major.

However, in the space of this octave, there are also five black keys. How do we identify these "extra" notes – called accidentals – since there are no alphabet letters left to label them? Each black note is named in relation to its closest white notes. The black note between the C and D, for example, is therefore known as C♯ (meaning a "sharpened" or "raised" C) or as D♭ (meaning a "flattened" or "lowered" D). A note referred to by two names is called enharmonic, and the context in which it is used will determine which name is appropriate. Unless the key signature (see p. 108) specifies otherwise, the general rule is to use a sharp when ascending to the note and a flat when descending to it.

The interval between a white note and a black note is called a semi-tone. Two semi-tones equal one tone. If you look at the keyboard, however, you will see that between the C and D and between the E and F, there is no black note. This is because the seven-note octave is not actually divided into equal intervals. C to D and E to F are semi-tones, not whole-tones.

Starting from C, and counting the interval to C♯ as the first semi-tone, there is a total of twelve equal semi-tones in one octave. Playing an octave in semi-tones (that is, playing all the white notes and all the black notes) demonstrates the chromatic scale. This system forms the basis of Western music.

The musical alphabet

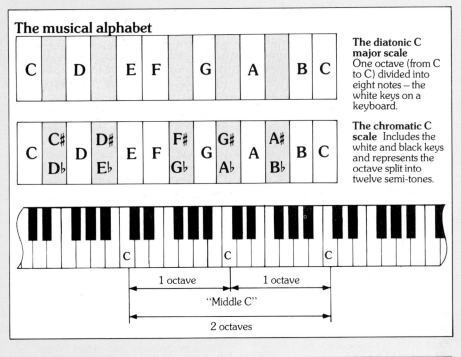

The diatonic C major scale One octave (from C to C) divided into eight notes – the white keys on a keyboard.

The chromatic C scale Includes the white and black keys and represents the octave split into twelve semi-tones.

Pitch notation

Pitch is conveyed in musical notation by placing note symbols on or between the parallel horizontal lines called the staff or stave (see p. 67). A clef at the start of each line of music determines what pitch value each line on the staff has. There are three different clefs – a G (or treble) clef, an F (or bass) clef, and a C clef which is only rarely used. Notes that will not fit on the staff are put on individual leger lines above or below.

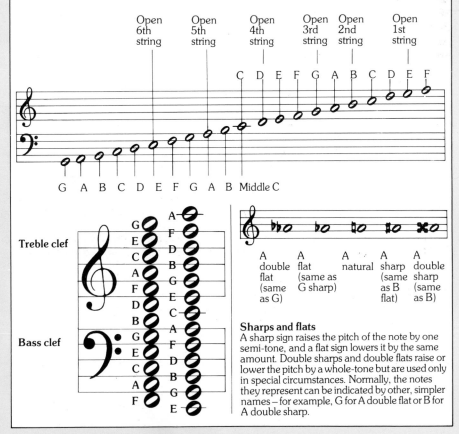

Sharps and flats
A sharp sign raises the pitch of the note by one semi-tone, and a flat sign lowers it by the same amount. Double sharps and double flats raise or lower the pitch by a whole-tone but are used only in special circumstances. Normally, the notes they represent can be indicated by other, simpler names – for example, G for A double flat or B for A double sharp.

The major scale

A *scale* is any consecutive series of notes that forms a progression between one note and its octave. The scale can go either up by an octave or down by an octave. The word comes from the Latin *scala*, meaning "ladder", and this is exactly what a scale is – a way of ascending or descending an octave, with each rung representing one of the notes in between.

There are many different scales, and the history of their development is complex. Any one scale can be distinguished from the others by its step-pattern – that is, by the way its notes divide up the distance represented by an octave. The most important scales in Western music are the diatonic major scale and the three relative minor scales.

The characteristic sound of any scale is determined by its number of steps, by the order in which they occur, and by their "size" – in other words, whether each step is a tone or a semi-tone. If this pattern remains consistent, the scale will have the same sound characteristics whatever note it starts from.

If we go back to the idea of the scale being like a ladder, we can see that the major scale has eight rungs (notes) and that it requires seven steps (intervals) to climb from the first rung to the eighth rung (the octave). In the major scale, the size of each step is as follows: tone (1st to 2nd), tone (2nd to 3rd), semi-tone (3rd to 4th), tone (4th to 5th), tone (5th to 6th), tone (6th to 7th), semi-tone (7th to 8th). The sound of the major scale is therefore

due to the fact that semi-tone steps occur between the 3rd and 4th notes, and between the 7th and 8th notes. Its "major" characteristic is the two-tone interval between the 1st and 3rd notes – this is called a *major third*.

The major scale, derived from the "Ionian mode" (see p. 110), was in use centuries before being accepted by serious composers. In medieval times, the Church strongly disapproved of it – condemning it as *Modus Lascivus* (meaning the "lustful mode") – and it was found primarily in folk songs and dances. However, since about the sixteenth century, when the laws of harmony were established, the major scale has come to represent the basic building material of contemporary music.

How to work out major scales

As we saw on p. 103, Western music divides the octave into twelve steps, each one being equal to a semi-tone. On the keyboard, this is reflected in the twelve different notes (seven white keys and five black keys) within an octave. On the guitar fingerboard, it is even simpler: one octave is divided into twelve frets – one for each note. So a semi-tone is one fret and a tone is two frets.

All major scales have a semi-tone interval between the 3rd and 4th and the 7th and

8th notes, so the pattern is easy to work out along one string: two frets, two frets, one fret, two frets, two frets, two frets, one fret. In the scale of C major, this step-pattern produces no sharps or flats. In fact, on the keyboard, C major is the diatonic scale which employs only the white keys. The scale of G major, however, has one sharp (see below), and the scale of F major has one flat. The scale of C# major, for example, actually has five sharps. This information is

contained in the "key signature" (see p. 108). The presence of the sharpened and flattened notes is essential if the step-pattern of the major scale is to be preserved whatever note it starts on. The notes of all twelve major scales are given in the chart opposite.

The individual notes that make up a major scale are often identified using the Roman numeral system. The way the notes are numbered (and named) is exactly the same as that described on p. 76.

The scale of C major
As an exercise in "hearing" the intervals of the major scale, try playing it up the length of a single string. Start from C on the 1st fret of the 2nd string, as shown below, and remember that one fret represents one semi-tone.

The scale of G major
To play a scale of G major, you must start from a G. Stick to the same step-pattern of tone (2 frets), tone (2 frets), semi-tone (1 fret), and so on. This time you will see that the tone (2 frets) step between the 6th and 7th notes in the scale brings you to F#. The note F is not included in the scale of G major.

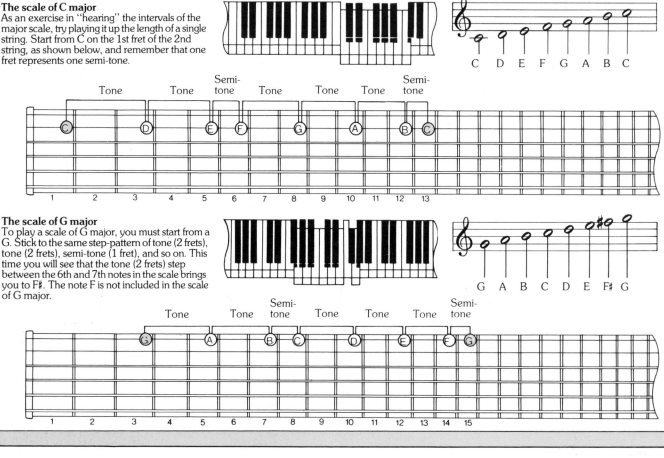

Major scale fingering patterns

It is impractical to play scales up and down the length of a single string. The examples on the opposite page are designed as exercises only, not as real fingerings. Instead, you must learn to play scales *across* the fingerboard, moving from string to string.

All three patterns shown below are within the span of four frets. This enables you to choose one hand position and make each of your four fingers responsible for one fret (see *The one-fret-per-finger rule*, p. 72). In

other words, you should play the complete scale (or scales) moving only your fingers, not your hand.

These are all *movable* fingering patterns that can begin at any note on the lowest string of the pattern. They can then be moved up and down the fingerboard without altering the pattern in order to play scales that start on different notes. The first note of the scale (the tonic or root note) is the first note of the fingering pattern. So, if

you begin on a C, the pattern will give you the scale of C major; if you begin on an A, it will give you the scale of A major. In the diagrams below, the numbers in the circles tell you which finger to use to play each note. The root notes are shaded green.

It is worth practicing these patterns until they feel comfortable. They are not only useful for developing melodic speed, but they also form the foundations of understanding harmony.

Root note on 5th string
This is a one-octave pattern, with the root (I) notes on the 5th and 3rd strings. If you wanted to play a scale of C major, you would begin with your 2nd finger at the C on the 3rd fret of the 5th string.

Root note on 6th string
This is a two-octave pattern. The root (I) notes are on the 6th, 4th and 1st strings. The pattern begins with the 1st note of the scale you want to play. If this were C major, you would start with your 2nd finger at the C on the 7th fret of the 6th string.

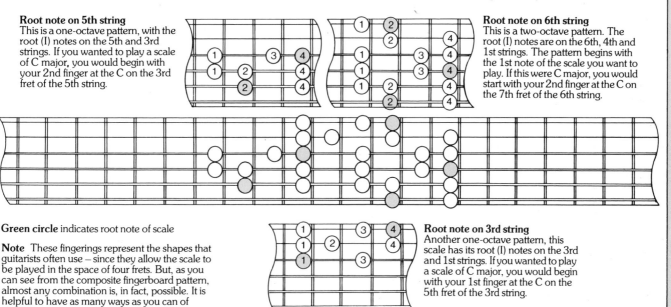

Green circle indicates root note of scale

Note These fingerings represent the shapes that guitarists often use – since they allow the scale to be played in the space of four frets. But, as you can see from the composite fingerboard pattern, almost any combination is, in fact, possible. It is helpful to have as many ways as you can of changing from one basic pattern to another.

Root note on 3rd string
Another one-octave pattern, this scale has its root (I) notes on the 3rd and 1st strings. If you wanted to play a scale of C major, you would begin with your 1st finger at the C on the 5th fret of the 3rd string.

The major scale in all twelve keys

Note Read the scales from left to right.

	I		II		III		IV		V		VI		VII		I
	A		B		C#		D		E		F#		G#		A
	Bb		C		D		Eb		F		G		A		Bb
	B		C#		D#		E		F#		G#		A#		B
Name of key (tonic or root note)	C	**Tone/2 frets**	D	**Tone/2 frets**	E	**Semi-tone/1 fret**	F	**Tone/2 frets**	G	**Tone/2 frets**	A	**Tone/2 frets**	B	**Semi-tone/1 fret**	C
	C#		D#		F		F#		G#		A#		C		C#
	D		E		F#		G		A		B		C#		D
	Eb		F		G		Ab		Bb		C		D		Eb
	E		F#		G#		A		B		C#		D#		E
	F		G		A		Bb		C		D		E		F
	F#		G#		A#		B		C#		D#		F		F#
	G		A		B		C		D		E		F#		G
	Ab		Bb		C		Db		Eb		F		G		Ab

The minor scales

There are three different minor scales – the *natural* or *relative minor* scale, the *harmonic minor* scale and the *melodic minor* scale.

Each has its own individual step-pattern, but they all share one feature that differentiates them from the major scale. The interval between the 1st and 3rd notes in the scale is always a tone and a half (one whole-tone plus one semi-tone). This interval is called a *minor third*, and it contrasts with the *major third* interval (two tones) characteristic of the major scale. The minor scales differ from each other in terms of whether the 6th and 7th steps of the scale are raised (sharpened) or whether they are not.

The principle and formation of minor scales are easier to understand if we start by looking at how the natural minor scale is *related* to the major scale, and then go on to see how it is *altered* to produce the harmonic and melodic minor scales.

How to work out natural minor scales

Just as the "Ionian Mode" was the predecessor of the major scale, the natural minor scale is derived from what was called the "Aeolian Mode" (see p. 110). Both these modes were diatonic scales – played only on the white notes of the keyboard. But, whereas the Ionian started on C, the Aeolian started on A.

This means that the notes of the two scales are the same. However, because the natural minor scale has a different starting point, it has its own step-pattern: tone (1st note to 2nd), semi-tone (2nd to 3rd), tone (3rd to 4th), tone (4th to 5th), semi-tone (5th to 6th), tone (6th to 7th), tone (7th to 8th). The 8th note is the octave.

Compare the C major and the A minor scales. You will see that the 3rd note of the minor scale is the 1st note of the major scale (it is a C), and that the 6th note of the major scale is the 1st note of the minor scale (it is an A). This relationship is the key to understanding the connection between major and minor scales. Each major scale has a *relative* natural minor scale, and each minor scale has a relative major scale.

Working out the relative scales is easy. It is three semi-tones *down* from the major to the minor, and three semi-tones *up* from the minor to the major.

The major scale and its relative natural minor scale share the same "key signature" (see p. 108). They therefore share the same notes. However, because they start at different places, they have a different step-pattern and a different sound.

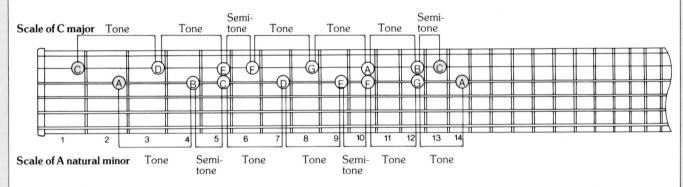

The C major and natural A minor scales
The natural minor scale in A is the relative minor of C major. It contains the same notes as the scale of C major but starts from A. It is plotted here on the 3rd string of the guitar, starting from A three semi-tones below C (2nd string, 1st fret). You will see how the step-pattern therefore differs.

Natural minor scale fingering pattern

Root note on 6th string

C major scale

C D E F G A B C

A natural minor scale

How the C natural minor scale differs from the C major scale

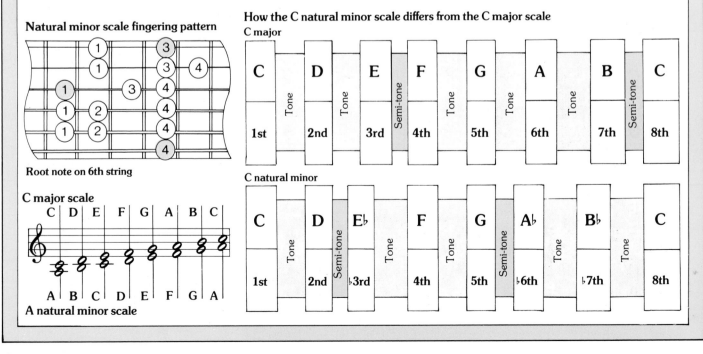

C major

C		D		E		F		G		A		B		C
	Tone		Tone		Semi-tone		Tone		Tone		Tone		Semi-tone	
1st		2nd		3rd		4th		5th		6th		7th		8th

C natural minor

C		D		E♭		F		G		A♭		B♭		C
	Tone		Semi-tone		Tone		Tone		Semi-tone		Tone		Tone	
1st		2nd		♭3rd		4th		5th		♭6th		♭7th		8th

How to work out harmonic minor scales

The harmonic minor scale developed as a result of the principles of harmony applied to the construction of chords (see p. 124).

We have already seen (see pp. 76-8) that a chord can be built on each note of the scale. and that the most important are those built on the 1st note (the "tonic" or I chord) and on the 5th note (the "dominant" or V chord). Now, one of the three notes that goes to make up the dominant chord is the 7th note of the scale. In the major scale, the 7th note is one semi-tone below the tonic. But, in the natural minor scale, the 7th note is a whole-tone below the tonic. This means that dominant chords built on the 5th notes of major and natural minor scales do not have the same effect. In order to overcome this problem the 7th note of the natural minor scale is raised (or "sharpened") by a semi-tone. The new scale is called the *harmonic minor*.

Harmonic minor scale fingering pattern

Root note on 6th string

C major scale

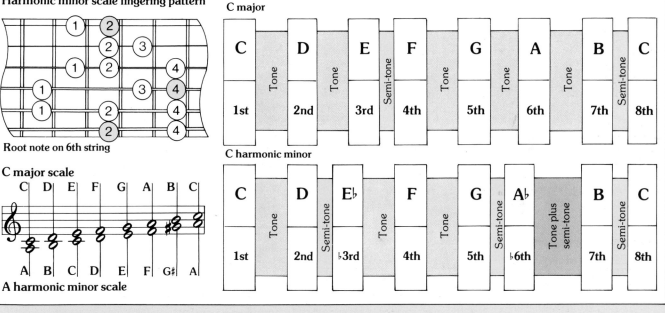

A harmonic minor scale

How the C harmonic minor scale differs from the C major scale

C major

C		D		E		F		G		A		B		C
	Tone		Tone		Semi-tone		Tone		Tone		Tone		Semi-tone	
1st		2nd		3rd		4th		5th		6th		7th		8th

C harmonic minor

C		D		E♭		F		G		A♭		B		C
	Tone		Semi-tone		Tone		Tone		Semi-tone		Tone plus semi-tone		Semi-tone	
1st		2nd		♭3rd		4th		5th		♭6th		7th		8th

How to work out melodic minor scales

The only problem with the harmonic minor scale is that, by reducing the interval between the 7th and 8th notes to a semi-tone, the interval between the 6th and 7th is increased to *three* semi-tones (a minor third). When writing melody lines, this is an unacceptably big jump. The solution to this is to raise the 6th note of the scale by a semi-tone. In A minor, this means raising the F to an F♯, and it reduces the interval between the 6th and 7th notes to a tone. The result is a smoother melodic "flow". This method is used when ascending – going up in pitch – and the scale it produces is called the *melodic minor* for its improved melodic potential. When playing a descending melody, it is not important to have the semi-tone interval between the 7th and 8th notes, because the melodic flow is naturally smooth. Therefore, the ordinary natural minor scale is used.

Melodic minor scale fingering pattern

Root note on 6th string

C major scale

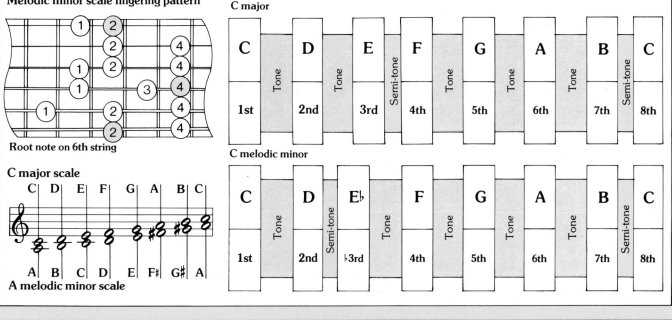

A melodic minor scale

How the C melodic minor scale differs from the C major scale

C major

C		D		E		F		G		A		B		C
	Tone		Tone		Semi-tone		Tone		Tone		Tone		Semi-tone	
1st		2nd		3rd		4th		5th		6th		7th		8th

C melodic minor

C		D		E♭		F		G		A		B		C
	Tone		Semi-tone		Tone		Tone		Tone		Tone		Semi-tone	
1st		2nd		♭3rd		4th		5th		6th		7th		8th

Key signatures

If we say that a scale or a piece of music is in a certain *key*, this defines what is called its "tonality". It tells us what tonic note all the other notes are related to. For example, a melody made up of notes from the scale of C major is said to be in the key of C major. The tonic note (the 1st note of the scale) is the *key-note*, and C major is the *key-center*. Similarly, a melody made up of notes from the scale of E minor is said to be in the key of E minor. All the other notes in the melody will be heard in relation to E, the key-note.

As we saw on p. 86, it is possible to transpose a piece of music from one key to another without altering its sound characteristics. This is because, although the overall *pitch* of the music changes, the *intervals* between the notes or chords do not.

Key signatures are used to label keys and to indicate what notes must be raised or lowered in order to maintain the same intervals for the major and minor scales. If you want to transpose a melody in the key of C major to the key of G major, the new key signature will tell you that you must play an F♯ (instead of an F).

The key signature is indicated by putting the sharps or flats it contains on the staff between the clef and the time signature. So, an F♯ here will tell you that, unless there is a contrary instruction later, the music is in the key of G major (or E minor).

The key of C major is the simplest. It contains no sharps or flats at all. The next simplest are the key of G (which contains one sharp) and the key of F (which contains one flat).

How does the key of G major relate to the key of C major? G is the 5th note (the "dominant") in the scale of C major – it becomes the 1st note of the scale of G major. But, in order to maintain the standard step-pattern of the major scale, the 7th ("leading") note of the new scale must be raised by a semi-tone. This note is F – the 4th ("sub-dominant") note in the scale of C major – and

it must be raised to F♯. The rule is therefore this: the 5th (dominant) note of any scale can be used to start a new scale in which only one note need be raised – this is always the 4th note of the old scale, the one that becomes the 7th note of the new scale. As the chart below illustrates, this rule holds for all keys.

How does the key of F major relate to the key of C major? This time, F is the 4th note (the "sub-dominant") in the scale of C major, and the only note that differs is the 7th ("leading") note – B. It becomes the 4th note of the new scale, and, in order to maintain the step-pattern of the major scale, it must be lowered by a semi-tone – to B♭. This time the rule is different: the 4th (sub-dominant) note of any scale can be used to start a new scale in which only one note need be flattened – this is always the 7th note of the old scale, the one that becomes the 4th note of the new scale. As the chart below illustrates, this rule, too, holds for all keys.

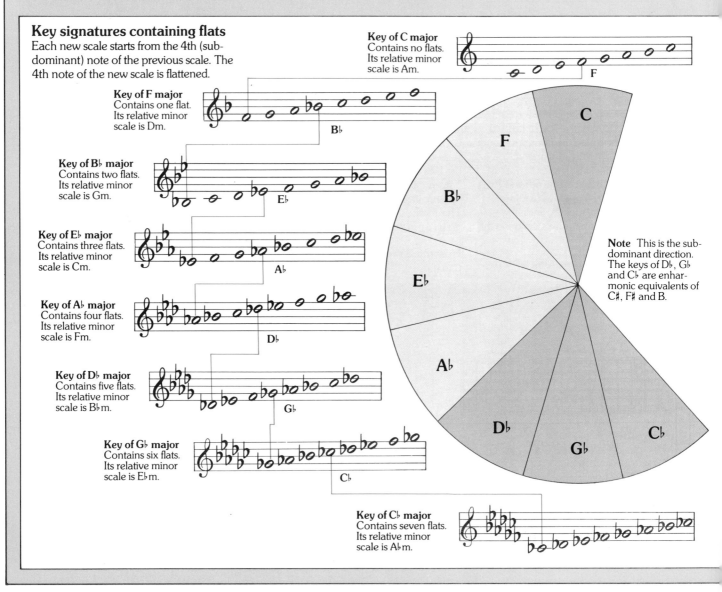

Key signatures containing flats
Each new scale starts from the 4th (sub-dominant) note of the previous scale. The 4th note of the new scale is flattened.

Key of C major
Contains no flats.
Its relative minor scale is Am.

Key of F major
Contains one flat.
Its relative minor scale is Dm.

Key of B♭ major
Contains two flats.
Its relative minor scale is Gm.

Key of E♭ major
Contains three flats.
Its relative minor scale is Cm.

Key of A♭ major
Contains four flats.
Its relative minor scale is Fm.

Key of D♭ major
Contains five flats.
Its relative minor scale is B♭m.

Key of G♭ major
Contains six flats.
Its relative minor scale is E♭m.

Key of C♭ major
Contains seven flats.
Its relative minor scale is A♭m.

Note This is the sub-dominant direction. The keys of D♭, G♭ and C♭ are enharmonic equivalents of C♯, F♯ and B.

The circle of fifths

The key signatures can be combined to form what is called the *circle of fifths*. This device is often used in music theory to illustrate the relationship of the keys.

The method by which sharp key signatures are formed can be traced by moving clockwise around the circle. Each step in the "dominant" direction is an interval of a fifth (counting up from the tonic) and involves adding one extra sharp note to the new major scale.

Moving anti-clockwise traces the formation of flat key signatures. Each step in the "sub-dominant" direction is an interval of a fifth (counting *down* from the tonic) or a fourth (counting *up* from the tonic) and involves adding one extra flat note to the new major scale.

As the circle demonstrates, in theory, it is possible to continue right around in either direction. The key of C can therefore be represented theoretically as either B♯ (with twelve sharps) of D♭♭ (with twelve flats).

Sub-dominant direction
4th (sub-dominant) note of old scale becomes 1st note of new scale. 7th (leading) note of old scale becomes 4th (sub-dominant) note of new scale and is *flattened.*

Dominant direction
5th (dominant) note of old scale becomes 1st note of new scale. 4th (sub-dominant) note of old scale becomes 7th (leading) note of new scale and is *sharpened.*

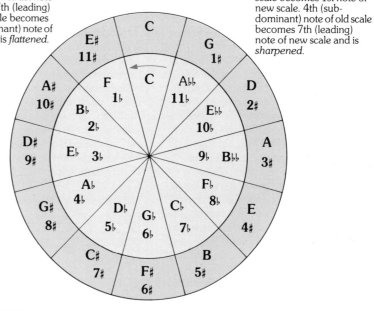

Key signatures containing sharps

Each new scale starts from the 5th (dominant) note of the previous scale. The 7th note of the new scale is sharpened.

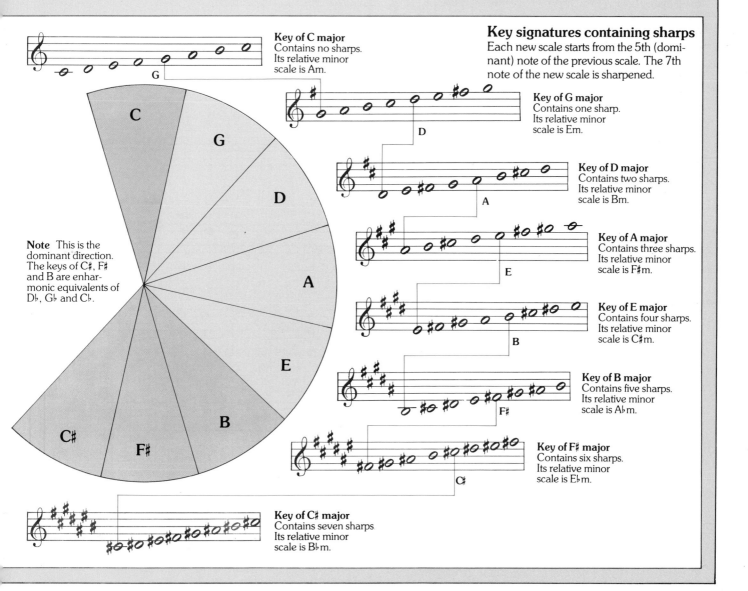

Key of C major
Contains no sharps. Its relative minor scale is Am.

Key of G major
Contains one sharp. Its relative minor scale is Em.

Key of D major
Contains two sharps. Its relative minor scale is Bm.

Key of A major
Contains three sharps. Its relative minor scale is F♯m.

Key of E major
Contains four sharps. Its relative minor scale is C♯m.

Key of B major
Contains five sharps. Its relative minor scale is A♭m.

Key of F♯ major
Contains six sharps. Its relative minor scale is E♭m.

Key of C♯ major
Contains seven sharps. Its relative minor scale is B♭m.

Note This is the dominant direction. The keys of C♯, F♯ and B are enharmonic equivalents of D♭, G♭ and C♭.

Scales and modes

The ancient Greeks are credited with having the earliest form of scales. These were named after their most important tribes – the Dorian, Phrygian, Lydian and Mixolydian. They all contained eight notes (including the octave) which were equivalent to the notes on the white keys of a keyboard, and they were written in descending order. The Dorian scale descended from E, the Phrygian from D, the Lydian from C, and the Mixolydian from B.

In the Middle Ages, these scales were adopted by musicians in the Christian Church. But, for an obscure reason, they introduced various changes: first, they reversed the order, so that the scales ascended; second, they changed the notes from which they started; and third, they substituted the term "mode" for "scale". This meant that the Greek Dorian scale became the Dorian Mode and went up from D to D, the Phrygian Mode went up from E to E, the Lydian Mode went up from F to F, and the Mixolydian Mode went up from G to G.

Furthermore, the old Greek Lydian scale, which had originally descended from C, now ascended from C and was renamed the Ionian Mode. And the Greek Mixolydian scale, which had descended from B, now ascended from B and was renamed the Locrian Mode. The scale that began on the note A was called the Aeolian Mode.

This meant that there were now seven modes – one for each of the white notes. We have already seen that the characteristic sound of any scale or series of notes is determined by its step-pattern of tone or semi-tone intervals. Since each mode has its own step-pattern, each mode has its own sound.

In the Middle Ages, the modal system was the source of melody. However, by the early sixteenth century, the increasing complexities of "polyphony" (music containing two or more harmonized melody lines) were leading to the breakdown of the modal system.

By the seventeenth century, a new harmonic language had been developed. The idea of "tonality" was expanded to include the key system (see p. 108). All music was written with a "key signature" which identified the tonic (or first) note of the scale as the "key-center" or "home key". The intervals between notes were fixed by their distance from the tonic note or key center.

At the heart of the key system lay the concept of diatonic major and minor scales. A "diatonic" scale comprises the notes proper to the key. The diatonic major scale has the same pattern of tones and semi-tones as the medieval Ionian Mode (which started on C), and the diatonic natural minor scale has the same pattern as the Aeolian Mode (which started on A). However, the resemblance is one of structure, not usage.

The modal system

A *mode* is a series of notes, like a scale, in which there is one principal note to which all the others are related. The first and last note of the octave is always the principal note in any mode. It is this note that establishes the "tonality" of the mode, and it is the step-pattern of tones or semi-tones that establishes its "modality". Take the Aeolian Mode as an example. It begins and ends on A; therefore, A is its "tonality". Its intervals are tone, semi-tone, tone, tone, semi-tone, tone, tone; therefore, this step-pattern describes its "modality".

The staves below set out the seven modes, and show from which note each one starts. You can see that because they are formed by playing only the white notes on the keyboard, each mode has its own different step-pattern. This gives it its own sound characteristic.

The C major scale (2 octaves of the white notes on the keyboard)

C D E F G A B C D E F G A B C

The Ionian Mode
From C to C.

C D E F G A B C

The Dorian Mode
From D to D.

D E F G A B C D

The Phrygian Mode
From E to E.

E F G A B C D E

The Lydian Mode
From F to F.

F G A B C D E F

The Mixolydian Mode
From G to G.

G A B C D E F G

The Aeolian Mode
From A to A.

A B C D E F G A

The Locrian Mode
From B to B.

B C D E F G A B

From modes to scales

The sound characteristic of each mode can be translated into any key as long as its original step-pattern is not altered. The scales below show the results of starting each mode on the note C.

In effect, this produces five new scales – not seven, since the Ionian and Aeolian are the same as the diatonic major and natural minor. These five new scales represent an *alternative* to the melodic and harmonic structure of the diatonic scales. In fact, modes and scales have different applications. Scales determine harmony and modes express melodic variation.

You can tell whether a mode is major or minor by looking at the interval between its 1st and 3rd notes (see p. 118). The Lydian and Mixolydian turn out to be major, and the Dorian and Phrygian are minor. The Locrian is unusual in that its tonic chord is "diminished" (see p. 121). The overall mood of the mode can be heard by playing chords built on its various steps, using only the notes which that mode contains.

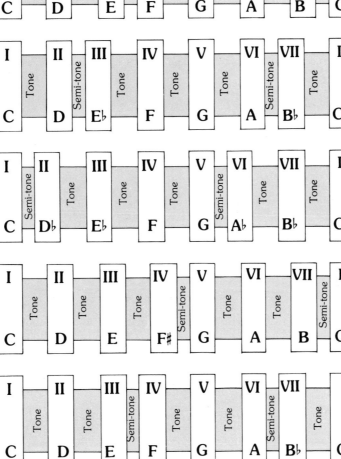
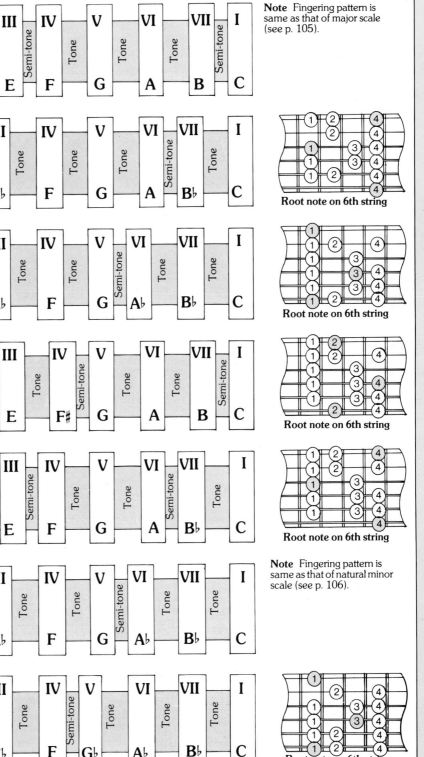

Ionian Mode (in key of C)
This mode was the predecessor of the diatonic major scale. It has the same step-pattern and therefore the same sound.

Note Fingering pattern is same as that of major scale (see p. 105).

Dorian Mode (in key of C)
This is a minor mode. It differs from the natural minor (Aeolian) scale in that the 6th note is sharpened. It suits minor chord sequences (e.g., I m, II m, III, IV, V m, and VII chords), and produces a jazz feel.

Root note on 6th string

Phrygian Mode (in key of C)
Also a minor mode, this is identical to the natural minor (Aeolian) scale except that it has a flattened 2nd note (the Db). This note is heard as a "flattened 9th" when played against a tonic minor seventh chord.

Root note on 6th string

Lydian Mode (in key of C)
This is a major scale. It differs from the diatonic major (Ionian) because it has a sharpened 4th note (the F♯). This means that it has the same notes as the major scale in the key of G – and G is the 5th (dominant) note in the C scale.

Root note on 6th string

Mixolydian Mode (in key of C)
The Mixolydian scale contains a flattened 7th note (the Bb). This is the only thing that differentiates it from the diatonic major (Ionian) scale. In fact, it is one of the most commonly used modes in blues and jazz improvisation.

Root note on 6th string

Aeolian Mode (in key of C)
This mode was the predecessor of the diatonic natural minor scale. It has the same step-pattern and therefore the same sound.

Note Fingering pattern is same as that of natural minor scale (see p. 106).

Locrian Mode (in key of C)
All the notes in this scale are flattened except for the tonic (1st) and the 4th (the F). Of the seven modes, it is the least often used in Western music, but it forms an important part of Japanese and Hindu music.

Root note on 6th string

Synthetic scales

The diatonic scales we have looked at so far — the major and three minors — are by no means the end of the story. While it is true that the major scale has dominated the theory and practice of melody and harmony, in fact, it is possible to create many other scales from the octave simply by selecting a different step-pattern from the twelve equal semi-tone intervals of the chromatic scale. Some scales that fall outside the sphere of the major and minor scales and modes are called *synthetic*. Of these, the whole-tone, the diminished and the pentatonic scales are probably the most commonly used in contemporary music. They are all explained here.

The whole-tone scale

Also known as "augmented", the *whole-tone scale* is exactly what its name implies. It divides the octave into six equal intervals of a whole tone each. There are no semi-tone intervals at all.

The whole-tone scale has a "floating" sound characteristic and establishes no specific key-center. In fact, because of its unique step-pattern, with the absence of semi-tones, it sounds the same whatever note you start from. Therefore, only two whole-tone scales are needed in order to cover all twelve keys. One starts from C, and the other starts from C#/Db. The note you choose to play first gives the scale its name.

The whole-tone scale allows harmonic transitions not possible with conventional diatonic harmony, and as such is a very useful compositional device.

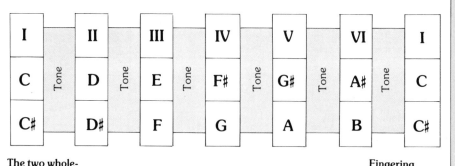

I		II		III		IV		V		VI		I
C	Tone	D	Tone	E	Tone	F#	Tone	G#	Tone	A#	Tone	C
C#		D#		F		G		A		B		C#

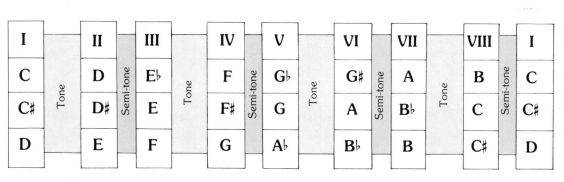

The two whole-tone scales All twelve notes in the octave are contained in these two scales. The starting note gives the name of the scale.

Fingering pattern Whole-tone scales do not really have root notes. If this pattern were used to play the whole-tone C scale, you would begin on the 3rd fret of the 5th string.

The diminished scale

This scale contains nine notes and divides the octave into eight intervals. Also called the "symmetric" scale, its step-pattern is based on alternate intervals of tone, semi-tone, tone, semi-tone, etc. Each diminished scale has four potential key-centers — the 1st, the 3rd, the 5th and the 7th notes in its scale. This means that only three diminished scales are needed in order to cover all twelve keys. One starts from C, the second starts from C#/Db, and the third starts from D. The scale that starts on C contains the same notes as the Eb, Gb and A scales; C# is the same as E, G and Bb; and D is the same as F, Ab and B (see *Diminished chords*, p. 128). The diminished is like the whole-tone scale in its potential to occupy or suggest more than one key-center. Melodies and chords built on diminished scales are very unlike the familiar melodies built on diatonic harmony, and tend to have a powerful, disorienting effect on a key-center. Playing the scales and the diminished "run" pattern shown below will illustrate this immediately.

The three diminished scales Each diminished scale has four key-centers — indicated by the 1st, 3rd, 5th and 7th notes of the scale. For example, the diminished scales of C, Eb, Gb and A all share the same notes. Three scales alone can therefore cover all twelve keys.

I		II		III		IV		V		VI		VII		VIII		I
C	Tone	D	Semi-tone	Eb	Tone	F	Semi-tone	Gb	Tone	G#	Semi-tone	A	Tone	B	Semi-tone	C
C#		D#		E		F#		G		A		Bb		C		C#
D		E		F		G		Ab		Bb		B		C#		D

Fingering pattern for diminished scale
The root note is on the 6th string. However, since diminished scales have four potential key-centers, starting this pattern on, say, D would also give the diminished pattern for F, Ab and B.

Fingering pattern for diminished "runs"
This pattern is an "arpeggio" or "horizontal" form of a diminished seventh chord. It includes only the 1st, 3rd, 5th and 7th notes of the diminished scale, separated by minor thirds.

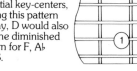

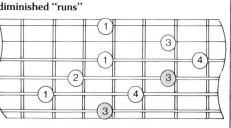

The pentatonic scales

One of the oldest and most widespread scales of all, the *pentatonic* is thought to have Mongolian and Japanese origins, and forms an important part of all Far Eastern, African and Celtic music. It is a five-note scale, and differs from the diatonic major in that two notes are left out – the 4th and 7th.

There is also a *pentatonic minor* scale. It differs from the diatonic natural minor in that two notes are again left out – this time, the 2nd and 6th. Its minor characteristic can be identified by the three semi-tone interval (a minor third) between the 1st and 2nd notes of the scale.

The two pentatonic scales share the same relationship as the diatonic major and minor scales – three semi-tones *down* from the major to the minor, and three semi-tones *up* from the minor to the major (see p. 106). So the pentatonic C scale and the pentatonic A minor scale, for example, share the same notes and intervals. Pentatonic scales are used more widely than any other synthetic (or non-diatonic) scale – in particular, for their strong melodic feel. Several popular riffs and chichés used by rock and jazz guitarists are based on a pentatonic scale.

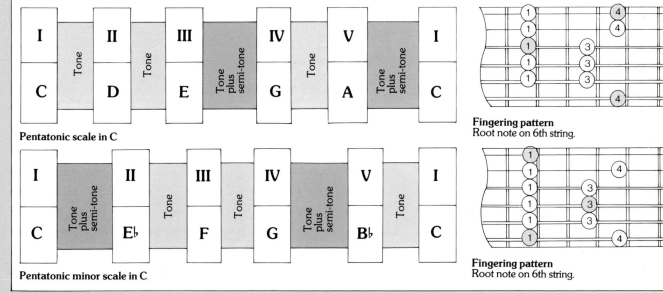

Pentatonic scale in C

I		II		III		IV		V		I
C	Tone	D	Tone	E	Tone plus semi-tone	G	Tone	A	Tone plus semi-tone	C

Pentatonic minor scale in C

I		II		III		IV		V		I
C	Tone plus semi-tone	E♭	Tone	F	Tone	G	Tone plus semi-tone	B♭	Tone	C

Fingering pattern
Root note on 6th string.

Fingering pattern
Root note on 6th string.

Other scales

The charts below illustrate four of the many other synthetic scales in use around the world. They all have a single key-center and so, although written out here in C, they can be transposed easily to any other key provided their step-pattern remains intact. In comparison with conventional Western diatonic harmony, you may find them difficult to use, since they are considered in many ways to be "dissonant". However, they represent melodic alternatives, and the best policy is to experiment with them, familiarize yourself with their sound, and, if one catches your imagination, use it to create your own distinctive chords and melodies.

Enigmatic scale in key of C Differs from diatonic major scale in its flattened 2nd note and sharpened 4th, 5th and 6th notes.

I		II		III		IV		V		VI		VII		I
C	Semi-tone	D♭	Tone plus semi-tone	E	Tone	F♯	Tone	G♯	Tone	A♯	Semi-tone	B	Semi-tone	C

Neapolitan scale in key of C Differs from diatonic major scale in its flattened 2nd and 3rd notes.

I		II		III		IV		V		VI		VII		I
C	Semi-tone	D♭	Tone	E♭	Tone	F	Tone	G	Tone	A	Tone	B	Semi-tone	C

Neapolitan minor scale in key of C Differs from diatonic major scale in its flattened 2nd, 3rd and 6th notes.

I		II		III		IV		V		VI		VII		I
C	Semi-tone	D♭	Tone	E♭	Tone	F	Tone	G	Semi-tone	A♭	Tone plus semi-tone	B	Semi-tone	C

Hungarian minor scale in key of C Differs from diatonic major scale in its flattened 3rd and 6th notes and sharpened 4th note.

I		II		III		IV		V		VI		VII		I
C	Tone	D	Semi-tone	E♭	Tone plus semi-tone	F♯	Semi-tone	G	Tone	A♭	Tone plus semi-tone	B	Semi-tone	C

THE HARMONIC GUITARIST

This section of the book is concerned with *harmony*. We have already seen, in the preceding pages of *The Melodic Guitarist*, that melody represents the horizontal principle of music. All melodies are derived from scales, and all melodies move horizontally. Harmony, on the other hand, represents the vertical principle of music. Harmony is also derived from scales, but it is concerned with the effects produced by sounding two or more notes at the same time, not one after the other. It is the study of *chords*.

This section begins with the subject of *harmonics*. The reason for this is that the phenomenon of harmonics (or "overtones" as they are often called) lies at the heart of harmony. The harmonics that are present along with the fundamental whenever a note is played are not only responsible for the tonal characteristics of the sound. They are also responsible for the particular effect created whenever two or three or four different notes are played simultaneously.

"With a note of music, one strikes the fundamental, and, in addition to the root note, other notes are generated: these are called the harmonic series ... As one fundamental note contains within it other notes in the octave, two fundamentals produce a remarkable array of harmonics, and the number of possible combinations between all the notes increases phenomenally. With a triad, affairs stand a good chance of getting severely out of hand ..."
Robert Fripp

When you play any two notes together, you are playing what is called an *interval* (see p. 118). Intervals are built from scales and differ according to the distance between the two notes. When you play more than two notes together, you are playing a *chord*. Chords are built from intervals. The simplest type of chord is the *triad* (see pp. 121-5), a three-note chord formed by stacking the 1st, 3rd and 5th notes of a scale on top of one another. This section of the book emphasizes the importance of understanding triads and will show you both how to play them and also why the four types – the major, minor, augmented and diminished – sound different.

From triads, we move on to look at slightly more complex chords – sevenths, sixths, suspended fourths, and so on – and explain how they are all built using the same principles of vertical construction, by stacking different notes of the scale one above the other. This basic principle applies to all chords. Once you have grasped it, seemingly difficult chords such as minor thirteenths, seventh diminished fifths or major ninth augmented elevenths will appear far less daunting.

"I practice all the scales. Everyone should know lots of scales. Actually, I feel there are only scales. What is a chord, if not the notes of a scale hooked together? There are several reasons for learning scales: one, the knowledge will unlock the neck for you – you'll learn the instrument; second, if I say I want you to improvise over G maj 7 +5, then go to E aug 9 −5, then to B maj 7 −5 – well, if you don't know what those chords are in scale terms, you're lost. It's not all that difficult, but you have to be ready to apply yourself ..."
John McLaughlin

Robert Fripp

The pages that follow will help you greatly increase your chord vocabulary. However, you should always bear in mind that understanding the chords is more important than simply being able to finger them. There is virtually no point in learning chords you do not know how to use. Chords are meaningless in isolation. They become interesting only when put together in sequences. This is why it is important to understand how chords move, how they create a sense of consonance, dissonance or resolution, and how chord voicings and cadences work. These principles are vital if you want to see how melody relates to chords. The thing to aim for is to know, whenever you play a chord, what notes it contains. This way, you will know, when you play a lead solo over the top which of the notes are part of the chord and which are not. Those that are not are called *passing notes*, and you should be aware of how they relate to the chord you are playing.

"I'm constantly thinking melodies. Now, to add interest to those melodies, obviously you have to know what things can be superimposed over a chord, and I will think of extended arpeggios and the upper extensions. If I'm playing very vertically, I will invariably start to include certain passing notes which imply certain scales – like a melodic minor scale against a C minor chord, or diminished scales, something like that. But I'm not thinking of a scale at that specific moment. I'm

John McLaughlin

thinking of the notes as surrounding that chord – because I know how each of the twelve notes in music sound against a C minor seventh, for instance.''

Lee Ritenour

This kind of theory always sounds more difficult than it really is. The way to master it is to play, and to think about what you are playing. Experiment with the chords that we have included, play them slowly one note at a time, and listen to the *sound* of the intervals from which they are constructed. With time, you will learn to recognize intervals instinctively.

For the sake of simplicity, the examples used in the following explanations of intervals, triads and chord-building are in the key of C major. The reason for this is that, in C major, the diatonic notes are natural, and the five chromatic notes are the five black keys on the keyboard. However, the same relationships and the same sound characteristics exist in any other key, and you should certainly make the effort to transpose them.

"I spent a lot of time teaching myself theory and harmony so I could be free to express myself on the instrument. I learned what relatives and substitutes could be played against a root of a chord, like E minor related to G, and so forth. I've also gathered all this knowledge because for ten years all I've done is play jazz, every day.''

George Benson

George Benson

The principles of harmony

There are two sets of laws governing musical sounds. One stems from the natural properties of acoustics, and the other is based on the rules of mathematics. These laws are set out below as an introduction to this section of the book. They may be difficult to absorb at first, especially if intervals and chord construction are still a mystery to you. If so, do not worry. Come back to them as you work your way through the following pages. You should then find them easier.

Every note, regardless of the instrument on which it is produced, comprises a sound spectrum or ''harmonic series''. Within this spectrum are contained the tonic, the octave and the triad intervals (see p. 116). There is a mathematical relationship between them. Any two notes an octave apart have a frequency ratio of 2:1. Two notes separated by an interval of a fifth have a frequency ratio of 3:2. And two notes a fourth apart have a frequency ratio of 3:4. The fourth and the fifth have an inverse relationship; together, they make up one octave. These ratios and relationships form the basic harmonic structure present in the nature of sound. In a sense, they can be considered to be ''the physics of the octave''.

Historically, this harmonic structure has been organized in different ways by different cultures. Western music divides the octave into twelve equal divisions of a semitone each (see p. 103). But the octave has also been divided into as few as five and as many as twenty-four divisions. These steps or increments represent different scales.

It has been suggested that the number twelve (the basis of the Western system) was derived from ancient religions or from astrology. In terms of mathematics, however, twelve is quite simply the lowest common denominator for the fractions of a half, a third and a quarter. These are the fractions represented by the primary interval ratios – the octave 2:1, the fifth 3:2, and the fourth 3:4. This is one of the logical reasons why the number twelve has a special significance in terms of the natural harmonic structure.

The interval inversion chart on p. 120 illustrates the concept of the octave as a symmetric ''sound prism''. The tritone interval is at the center, between the fourth and the fifth. It is unique in its ability to invert to itself, and can be seen as the neutral pivot on which the tonality of the octave is delicately balanced. Any vertical or horizontal combination of notes other than the tritone disturbs the balance and initiates a sense of *motion*. This motion is increased or counteracted by whatever intervals follow until it comes to rest – by resolving back to the tonic.

The further you go into a study of the principles of harmony, the more you will find that every aspect of tonal cause and effect is related to the number twelve. The following examples represent some of the many ways in which this can be demonstrated. They are presented simply to illustrate the mathematical balance that underlies the structure of Western harmony.

Interval inversions

Any interval plus the interval formed when it is inverted totals twelve semi-tones. Thus, an interval of x semi-tones will invert to an interval of $12-x$ semi-tones (see p. 120).

Triad inversions

A root position major triad spans seven semi-tones between the tonic and the 5th, five short of an octave ($7+5=12$). The first inversion spans eight semi-tones between the 3rd and the upper tonic, four short of an octave ($8+4=12$). The second inversion spans nine semi-tones between the 5th and the upper 3rd, three short of an octave ($9+3=12$). The sum of the semi-tones in all three inversions is twenty-four ($7+8+9=24$), and the sum of the semi-tones remaining from each inversion is twelve ($5+4+3=12$) (see pp. 121-2).

The four triad types

There are four different kinds of triad – the major, minor, augmented and diminished (see p. 121). Each has three inversions. The result is $12 \times 12 = 144$ triads, 36 of each type. Each note in each type of triad can perform one of three different functions (it can be the tonic, 3rd or 5th). Considering the four kinds of triad in their root positions only, this means that each note can perform twelve different functions. For all twelve notes, there are 144 different uses.

Triad harmony

The four primary triads (those built on the tonic, the 4th, the 5th and the octave) use a total of twelve notes. So do the four secondary triads (those built on the 2nd, 3rd, 6th and 7th notes of the scale). The actual notes number seven (see p. 123).

Octave divisions

An octave divided into twelve equal steps produces a chromatic scale (see p. 103). An octave divided into six equal steps produces a whole-tone scale (see p. 112). An octave divided into four equal steps produces a diminished seventh chord (see p. 128). An octave divided into three equal steps produces an augmented chord. An octave divided in half produces the tritone interval (see pp. 118-9).

Harmonics

Harmonics are an important part of every note. Each time a guitar string is struck it vibrates in a complex pattern, and the sound it generates is composed of several elements. The basic building block of the sound is the *fundamental*. This is the loudest element we hear, and the one by which we identify the pitch of the note. It is the sound generated by the string vibrating in a single loop along its entire length. At the same time, the string produces a series of *harmonics*, *overtones* or *upper partials*. These are simply tones with frequencies that are multiples of the frequency of the fundamental, and they are generated by the string also vibrating simultaneously in shorter loops. They begin one octave above the fundamental and then rise in pitch in specific intervals – the fifth, the next octave, the following third, and so on.

All musical instruments produce notes that consist of a fundamental and a number of harmonics. Together, these components of each note are known as its *harmonic series*, and, in this context, the fundamental is referred to as the *first harmonic*. The balance or blend of the fundamental and harmonics in relation to each other determines the "tone" of the instrument. In effect, the harmonic series therefore forms a unique "audio fingerprint". No two guitars – however similar – have exactly the same tone because they do not produce exactly the same balance of harmonics.

Artificial harmonics

There are several special techniques in guitar playing which enable you to sound one selected harmonic while at the same time silencing the louder fundamental and also the other harmonics. This is known as playing *artificial harmonics*.

Let's take the simplest example. By lightly fingering an open string over the 12th fret, you divide it into two equal lengths. When you then play the string, you get an artificial harmonic one octave above the open string. In the context of artificial harmonics, this octave note – not the fundamental – is called the *first harmonic*.

What happens is this. Fingering the string creates a *node* or *node point* where the string does not vibrate at all. This alters the vibration pattern that the open string would otherwise produce and stops the fundamental and other harmonics from sounding. On either side of the node, the two equal lengths of the string then vibrate out of phase with one another and produce the artificial harmonic. The points at which the string vibrates most are called the *anti-nodes*. As the drawing shows, there are several places on the string where artificial harmonics can be played.

Where to find open-string harmonics

If the length of the string is divided into two (exactly over the 12th fret), the frequency of the harmonic will be one octave higher than that of the fundamental on the open string. If you split the string length into three (exactly over the 7th or 19th fret), the frequency of the harmonic will be three times greater – one octave and a fifth above the open string. In theory, it is possible to go on producing higher and higher harmonics. In practice, you can only go so far before they become impossible to hear.

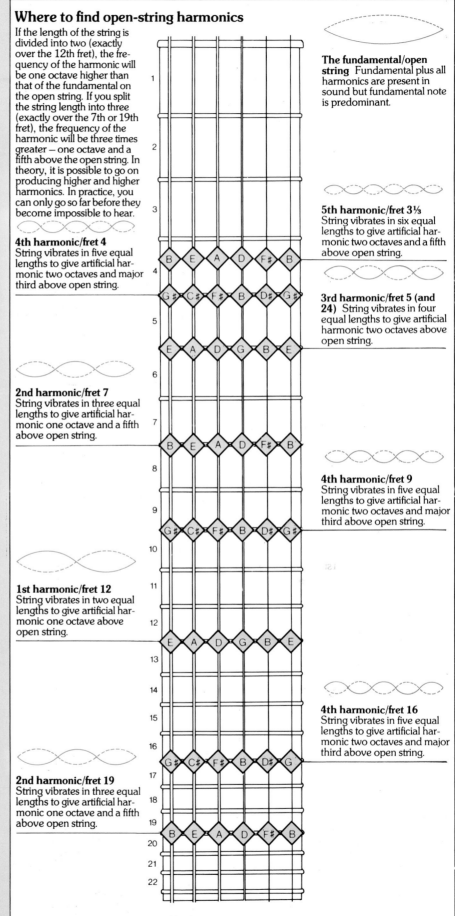

The fundamental/open string Fundamental plus all harmonics are present in sound but fundamental note is predominant.

5th harmonic/fret 3⅓ String vibrates in six equal lengths to give artificial harmonic two octaves and a fifth above open string.

3rd harmonic/fret 5 (and 24) String vibrates in four equal lengths to give artificial harmonic two octaves above open string.

4th harmonic/fret 4 String vibrates in five equal lengths to give artificial harmonic two octaves and major third above open string.

2nd harmonic/fret 7 String vibrates in three equal lengths to give artificial harmonic one octave and a fifth above open string.

4th harmonic/fret 9 String vibrates in five equal lengths to give artificial harmonic two octaves and major third above open string.

1st harmonic/fret 12 String vibrates in two equal lengths to give artificial harmonic one octave above open string.

4th harmonic/fret 16 String vibrates in five equal lengths to give artificial harmonic two octaves and major third above open string.

2nd harmonic/fret 19 String vibrates in three equal lengths to give artificial harmonic one octave and a fifth above open string.

How to play open-string harmonics

The first, second and third artificial harmonics are the easiest to play. More are available with varying degrees of practice. The right-hand technique is the same as normal: you pluck or strum the strings as usual. The left-hand technique – which is really the key to playing harmonics – differs from normal fretting in two ways. First, whichever finger you decide to use, you must only just touch the string. Do not push it down on to the fret. Second, you must place your finger directly over the fret in question, not slightly behind it as you would when playing a note normally. The only exception is the fifth harmonic – between the 3rd and 4th frets.

To get the first harmonic, place one of your left-hand fingers directly over the 12th fret. To get the second harmonic, place a finger directly over the 7th or 19th fret. For further harmonics, see the fingerboard opposite.

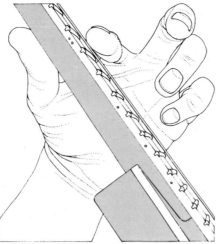

Left-hand technique
Place one left-hand finger on the string directly above the 12th fret. Pluck the string with your right hand. As soon as you feel the string being struck, remove your left-hand finger from the string.

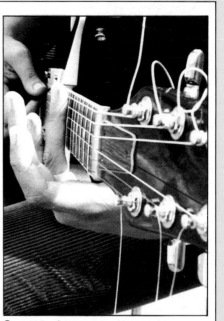

Open-string harmonics technique

How to play fretted-string harmonics

There is a classical guitar technique for playing harmonics – also applicable to steel-string guitars – in which the fingers of the right hand are used to both touch and strike the string. As shown below, you touch the "node point" of the string with the 1st finger of your right hand, and then either pluck the string with your 4th finger or strike it with your plectrum. The great advantage of this technique is that it does not restrict you to playing harmonics on open strings. Your left hand is free to fret any note you wish. As long as you place the 1st finger of your left hand lightly on the string, exactly halfway between the bridge and the fret on which you are holding down the string, you will get the octave harmonic of whatever note you are fretting. Using this method, melody or chord patterns can be picked out and played entirely in harmonics – for example, the notes of a G chord as shown below.

An alternative and favorite technique among rock and blues guitarists is that of "pinching" or "squeezing" harmonics between the right-hand thumb and the plectrum. Hold the plectrum so that it only just protrudes beyond your thumb. Then strike the string with your plectrum and thumb virtually simultaneously. The effect of your plectrum hitting the string and your thumb damping it – in the right place – produces a dynamic harmonic shift. This works better on high fretted notes as it puts stronger harmonics in range.

To begin with, try the technique by fretting the 1st string at the 12th fret. Now "pinch" the string in the way described where the 24th fret would be – that is, midway along its length. You will hear immediately when you get it right. As soon as you can produce this first octave harmonic, go up to an F, a G and so on.

Fingerstyle right-hand technique
Place the 1st finger of your right hand over the "node point" of the string and pluck it with your 4th (or 3rd) finger.

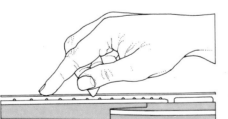

Plectrum-style right-hand technique
Use your 1st finger to touch the string lightly in the correct place and strike it with the plectrum held between your thumb and 2nd finger.

Example: arpeggio harmonic G chord

12

Left hand
Finger a G chord with your left hand as shown – pushing the strings down onto the frets.

Right hand
Using your right hand to locate the frets one octave (12 frets) higher than the fretted positions, play the notes of the G chord one at a time.

Fretted-string harmonics technique

Intervals

The difference in pitch between any two notes is called an *interval*. The interval is the same whether the notes are sounded together or one after the other.

Every different interval has its own specific sound quality. This is determined by the ratio between the frequencies of the two notes. We have seen how each note produces a harmonic series, made up of its fundamental plus a kind of "sound spectrum" of overtones or upper partials. Sounding two notes together, therefore, has the effect of combining two fundamentals and their two harmonic spectrums. The result is the creation of a third harmonic series – and it is this that is responsible for the specific sound of any interval.

In the case of two notes with the same pitch, the two harmonic series are doubled – this is called a *unison*. In the case of two notes an octave apart, the two harmonic series reinforce one another – this is the *octave*.

How intervals are named

Intervals can be identified by their position in the diatonic scale. The most fundamental of all intervals is, of course, the octave; it determines the first and last notes. All other intervals are then named according to their distance from the first note of the scale (the "tonic" or "root" note). They are called *seconds, thirds, fourths, fifths, sixths* and *sevenths*.

This system covers the eight notes (including the octave) that make up the diatonic major scale. However, as we have seen, the octave is divided into twelve semitones, producing thirteen different notes (including the octave). Since each of these has its own sound characteristic, there is a system of names which further defines each interval as being *perfect, major, minor, augmented* or *diminished*.

Of the diatonic intervals, the term "perfect" applies to the unison, the fourth, the fifth and the octave. The second, third, sixth and seventh intervals may be either "major" or "minor". The interval between the fourth and fifth is called the "tritone".

Because of enharmonic spellings, the same physical interval can have more than one name, so the tritone is called either an augmented fourth or a diminished fifth.

Here are the rules for identifying intervals.
- A major interval lowered by a semi-tone becomes a minor interval.
- A minor interval raised by a semi-tone becomes a major interval.
- A major interval raised by a semi-tone becomes an augmented interval.
- A minor interval lowered by a semi-tone becomes a diminished interval.
- A perfect interval raised by a semi-tone becomes an augmented interval.
- A perfect interval lowered by a semi-tone becomes a diminished interval.

Compound intervals

When the notes extend beyond the range of one octave, the diatonic scale numbering system simply continues.
- When the second is an octave higher, it is called a *ninth*. It is major naturally, minor if lowered, and augmented if raised.
- When the third is an octave higher, it is called a *tenth*. It can be major or minor.
- When the fourth is an octave higher, it is called an *eleventh*. It can be perfect, augmented or diminished.
- When the sixth is an octave higher, it is called a *thirteenth*. It can be major, minor or augmented.

Consonance and dissonance

The different sound quality possessed by each interval can be defined by using the terms *consonant* and *dissonant*. The reason for this is that some intervals seem to have a smooth, satisfying sound. These are the unison, the thirds, the fifth, the sixth and the octave. They are called either "open" or "soft" consonances. Others have an unsatisfying, "un-resolved" sound. These are the second and the seventh. They are called either "sharp" or "mild" dissonances. The fourth can be either consonant or dissonant. The tritone has an ambiguous quality which is considered neutral or restless on its own, but dissonant in a diatonic context.

Interval chart

	I (1st)	ii (♭2nd)	II (2nd)	iii (♭3rd)	III (3rd)	IV (4th)	Enharmonic IV+ (♯4th)
Numerical symbol	I (1st)	ii (♭2nd)	II (2nd)	iii (♭3rd)	III (3rd)	IV (4th)	IV+ (♯4th)
Degree	Tonic	Supertonic		Mediant		Sub-dominant	Tritone
Pitch in key of C	C	D♭	D	E♭	E	F	F♯
Intervals from C	C to C	C to D♭	C to D	C to E♭	C to E	C to F	C to F♯
Distance of interval	Zero	1 semi-tone	2 semi-tones	3 semi-tones	4 semi-tones	5 semi-tones	6 semi-tones
Name of interval	Unison	Minor second	Major second	Minor third	Major third	Perfect fourth	Augmented fourth
Sound characteristic	Open consonance	Sharp dissonance	Mild dissonance	Soft consonance	Soft consonance	Consonance or dissonance	Neutral or

Fingerboard intervals

Intervals are the building blocks of all chords. If you are to understand the role of intervals in harmony and chord construction, you must learn to identify their sound by ear. They are set out in the large chart below, together with the names by which they are known.

The characteristic sound of each interval is always the same, whatever the two notes involved. So a minor third from C to E♭, for example, has the same sound quality as a minor third from D to F. A pattern of inter-vals can be plotted out on the guitar finger-board. The pattern remains consistent wherever it is played. Any note can be considered as the tonic or root, and all the other intervals will then relate to this note. When playing in a specific key, the name of the key is the name of the tonic or root note.

Let's take an example. If you play the first pattern (below left) with your 1st finger on the 3rd fret of the 6th string, this identifies the tonic or root note as a G. All the other intervals then relate to G. If you start on the 5th fret, the tonic or root note will be an A. These patterns are invaluable for working out scale and chord fingerings.

Roman numerals are used to symbolize intervals in the same way as they are for chords (see p. 76). The only difference is that upper-case numerals are used specifically for major and perfect intervals, lower-case numerals are introduced for minor intervals, a plus sign means an augmented interval, and a small circle indicates a diminished interval.

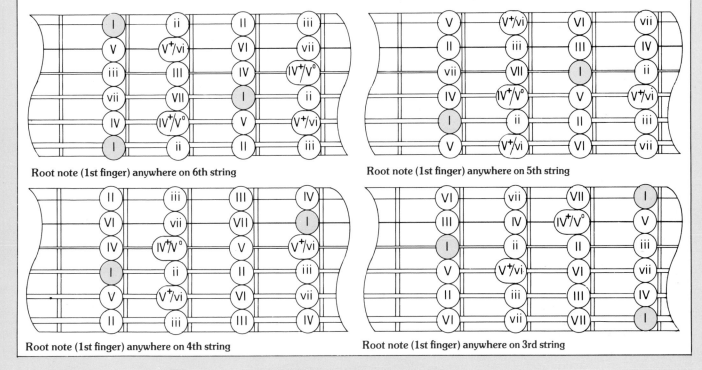

Root note (1st finger) anywhere on 6th string

Root note (1st finger) anywhere on 5th string

Root note (1st finger) anywhere on 4th string

Root note (1st finger) anywhere on 3rd string

Enharmonic		Enharmonic		Enharmonic				
V° (♭5th)	V (5th)	V+ (♯5th)	vi (♭6th)	VI (6th)	vii° (♭♭7th)	vii (♭7th)	VII (7th)	I (1st)
Tritone	Dominant	Sub-mediant				Sub-tonic	Leading note	Tonic
G♭	G	G♯	A♭	A	B♭♭	B♭	B	C
C to G♭	C to G	C to G♯	C to A♭	C to A	C to B♭♭	C to B♭	C to B	C to C
6 semi-tones	7 semi-tones	8 semi-tones		9 semi-tones		10 semi-tones	11 semi-tones	12 semi-tones
Diminished fifth	Perfect fifth	Augmented fifth	Minor sixth	Major sixth	Diminished seventh	Minor seventh	Major seventh	Octave (8va)
restless	Open consonance	Soft consonance		Soft consonance		Mild dissonance	Sharp dissonance	Open consonance

Interval inversions

An interval is said to be *inverted* when the lower note becomes the higher, or the higher note becomes the lower. In effect, this is done either by raising the lower note or by lowering the higher note one octave.

When an interval is inverted it changes and becomes a new interval with a different value. The important thing to realize about inversions is that, in relation to an octave, the new interval is symmetrically equivalent to the old one. Let's look at an example in the key of C major. Take the interval between the 1st note (C) and the 4th note (F); it is a "perfect fourth". Now invert it so that the lower note is F and the higher note is C. You will see that, in its new form, it has become a "perfect fifth".

Together, the fourth and fifth make up an octave. This means that the note F is a fourth above C and a fifth below it.

Obviously, the same thing happens if you take an interval of a perfect fifth (in the key of C major, from C to G). When you invert it, it becomes a perfect fourth. Again, the two intervals add up to an octave. The note G is a fifth above C and a fourth below it.

The rules that govern other inversions work in the same way. This allows any note in a scale to be related to the tonic note either from *above* or from *below*.

For how inversions work in terms of chords, not just two-note intervals, see opposite and p. 122.

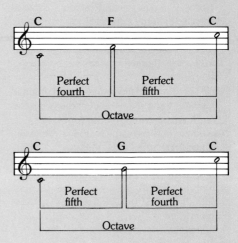

Rules governing interval inversions

When intervals are inverted their original quality of either consonance or dissonance may change. This is because the register of the two notes, and the spacing between them, has been altered. The degree of change depends on the interval in question.

We have seen that a perfect fourth becomes a perfect fifth and a perfect fifth becomes a perfect fourth. Although both remain perfect, inverting these two intervals alters their function considerably. The same

is true when a unison becomes an octave and an octave becomes a unison.

Inverting an interval of a second creates a seventh and inverting a seventh creates a second. The major and minor qualities change, but both intervals remain dissonant in character.

A third becomes a sixth and a sixth becomes a third when inverted. As before, major and minor change but both intervals remain consonant.

An augmented fourth becomes a diminished fifth when inverted, and vice versa. The sound qualities are exactly the same, however, since the intervals are enharmonic. Six semi-tones remain between the two notes, whether inverted or not.

This information is presented visually in the chart below. The scale of intervals can be considered as "pivoting" on the augmented fourth and diminished fifth, which are the same when inverted.

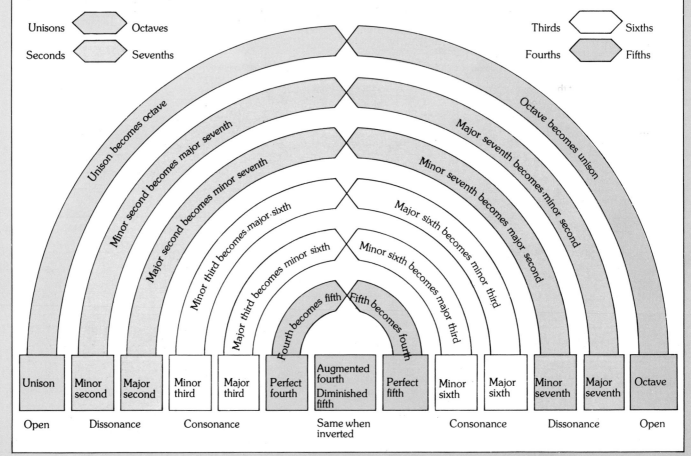

Triads

A *triad* is a simultaneous combination of three notes. It can be made up of any note plus the two notes a third and a fifth above it. This means that a triad has two intervals, each of a third. All triads are three-note chords, but not all three-note chords are triads.

The theory of triads dates back to the middle of the fifteenth century, when the diatonic major/minor tonal system was evolving. Before then, the horizontal effect of the intervals in the various "modes" (*see* p. 110) had established the tonic note and the 5th note of a scale as the most important. The triad was created when the 3rd was combined with the 1st and 5th to produce a vertical chord.

In the harmonic series of any note, the tonic is the fundamental, and the octave, the 5th and the 3rd are the most prominent "overtones" (*see* p. 116). These are the notes that make up the triad, and the reinforcement of these overtones gives it its strong sound.

The four different triads

There are four kinds of triad – major, minor, augmented and diminished. Although the intervals that make up the triad are always thirds, they differ in that they may be either major or minor thirds. They can also appear in a different vertical order.

In the context of triads (or, indeed, any chord), the tonic note is referred to as the root. Every interval has an *effect* on the sound of the chord, but it is the root that determines the chord's identity.

Major and minor triads both span an interval of a perfect fifth from the root note. It is the interval from the root to the middle note of the group (the 3rd) that determines whether they are major or minor. A major triad with a sharpened 5th is called augmented, and a minor triad with a flattened 5th is called diminished.

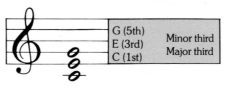

The C major triad
Derived from the 1st, 3rd and 5th notes of the diatonic major scale (*see* p. 104), the major triad consists of a minor third stacked on top of a major third. Overall this forms a perfect fifth.

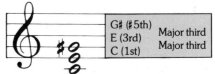

The C augmented triad
Derived from the 1st, 3rd and 5th notes of the whole-tone scale (*see* p. 112), this triad consists of two major thirds on top of one another. This forms an interval of an augmented fifth.

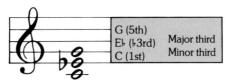

The C minor triad
Derived from the 1st, 3rd and 5th notes of the diatonic natural minor scale (*see* p. 106), the minor triad has a minor third on the bottom and a major third on top. It still forms a perfect fifth.

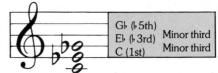

The C diminished triad
Derived from the 1st, 3rd and 5th notes of the diminished scale (*see* p. 112), this triad consists of two minor thirds which together form an interval of a diminished fifth.

Triad inversions

The four triads shown above are all in the *root position*. This means that the root or tonic note is the lowest note in the chord. If the lowest note is *not* the root, the chord is said to be *inverted* (see opposite). In this case, the term "root" may still be used to describe the lowest note – but it will no longer be the tonic.

If you take a C major root position triad and raise the tonic by an octave, the 3rd will become the lowest note. This form of the triad is called the *first inversion*. If you now raise the 3rd by an octave, the 5th will be left as the root. This form is called the *second inversion*. Repeating the process once again brings you back to the root position triad one octave higher.

In this way, it is possible to get three different "sounds" from one triad – the root position, the first inversion and the second

inversion. Because the three notes have the same key-center and tonality, whatever their arrangement, they have the same name – in the example below, C major. But, because of the influence of the root note, each inversion suggests a different "motion" and can have many different applications. An understanding of triad inversions, including where they can be played on the fingerboard, is important.

How major triad inversion works
In the root position, the tonic (C) is the lowest note. In the first inversion, the 3rd (E) is the lowest note. And, in the second inversion, the 5th (G) is the lowest note. The three forms are all C major triads, but each has a different sound and, therefore, a different use.

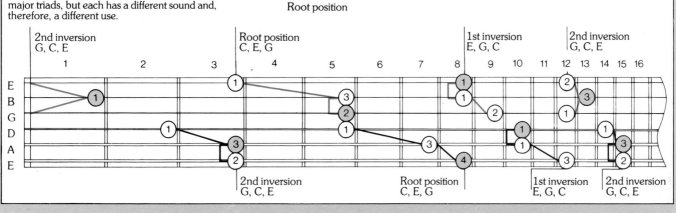

Further triad inversions

The principles of major triad inversion outlined on the previous page apply in exactly the same way to the other three kinds of triad – the minor, augmented and diminished. Each of these also has a root position, a first inversion and a second inversion. A sound knowledge of triads everywhere on the fingerboard is possibly one of the greatest assets to any guitarist wishing to work out chords and harmony. In the fingerboard drawings below and on the previous page, the triads shown are C major, A minor, C augmented and B diminished, but the shapes can be moved anywhere on the fingerboard to give triads with different names (or pitches).

It is important not only that you learn these shapes and understand how they function, but also that you work out how to find triads and their inversions on any set of adjacent strings – on the 2nd, 3rd and 4th, or on the 3rd, 4th and 5th, for example. This will give you a thorough grounding for the theory and practice of all chord work.

How minor triad inversions work
In the root position, the tonic (A) is the lowest note. In the first inversion, the 3rd (C) is the lowest note. And, in the second inversion, the 5th (E) is the lowest note. The three forms are all A minor triads, but each has a different sound.

How augmented triad inversion works
In the root position, the tonic (C) is the lowest note. In the first inversion, the 3rd (E) is the lowest note. And, in the second inversion, the 5th (G♯) is the lowest note. The three forms are all C augmented triads, but each has a different sound.

How diminished triad inversion works
In the root position, the tonic (B) is the lowest note. In the first inversion, the 3rd (D) is the lowest note. And, in the second inversion, the 5th (F) is the lowest note. The three forms are all B diminished triads, but each has a different sound.

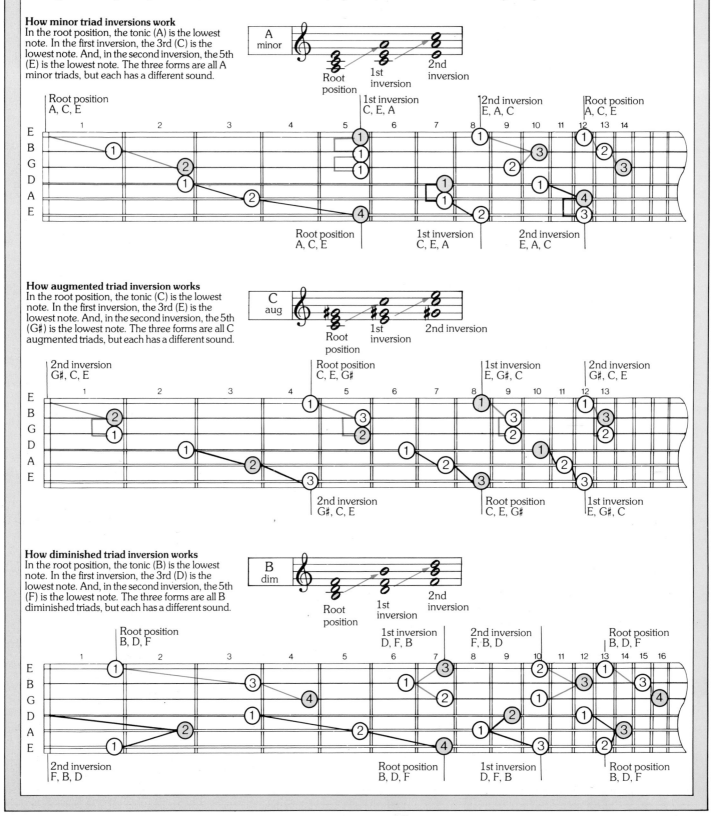

Triad doubling

The major and minor triads are the two most important basic chord forms in music. To use them in any chord in which more than three notes are sounded together requires *doubling* one or more of the three notes. Not surprisingly, the note most often doubled is the tonic. This reinforces the overall sound of the chord and stresses the key-center. Doubling the 5th strengthens the "stability" of the chord, and doubling the 3rd emphasizes the tonality (that is, whether it is major or minor).

The choice of what notes are doubled and their vertical placement creates what is considered the *voicing* of the chord. The most important notes are always the highest and lowest. When one chord changes to another in the course of a progression, the highest notes establish a melodic relationship. The root note (the lowest) determines the "inversion" of the chord.

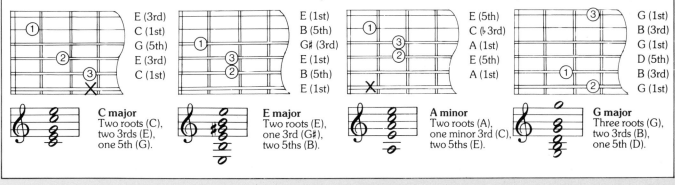

C major
Two roots (C), two 3rds (E), one 5th (G).

E (3rd)
C (1st)
G (5th)
E (3rd)
C (1st)

E major
Two roots (E), one 3rd (G♯), two 5ths (B).

E (1st)
B (5th)
G♯ (3rd)
E (1st)
B (5th)
E (1st)

A minor
Two roots (A), one minor 3rd (C), two 5ths (E).

E (5th)
C (♭3rd)
A (1st)
E (5th)
A (1st)

G major
Three roots (G), two 3rds (B), one 5th (D).

G (1st)
B (3rd)
G (1st)
D (5th)
B (3rd)
G (1st)

Building triads on the notes of a scale

In any key, there are seven *diatonic triads*. They can be formed by building two intervals of a third on each note in the diatonic scale. Only notes included in the diatonic scale are used to build the thirds. The whereabouts of the semi-tone steps will determine whether the intervals are major or minor thirds, and will therefore dictate the type of triad.

Because each note in the scale represents an interval with its own sound in relation to the tonic, so the triads built on these notes also have their own sound in relation to the tonic triad. Changing from one chord to another within the scale creates an effect of movement that is considered in terms of "tension" and "resolution" within the key. This relationship between the seven different diatonic triads creates a sense of harmony which has been a characteristic feature of almost all Western music.

The harmonized C major scale
Building diatonic triads on each note of the diatonic major scale produces the following series: I major, II minor, III minor, IV major, V major, VI minor, VII diminished. The primary chords are the I, IV and V; the others are secondary. This "harmonized" scale is shown here on the staff and the guitar fingerboard in the key of C major.

The harmonized natural A minor scale
Building triads on each note of the diatonic natural minor scale produces the following series: I minor, II diminished, III major, IV minor, V minor, VI major, VII major. Again, the primary chords are the I, IV and V. The "harmonized" scale is shown this time in the key of A minor – the relative minor of C major.

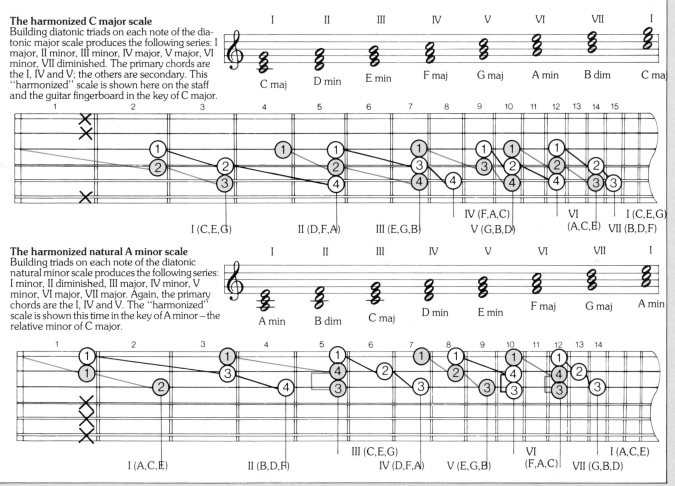

The theory of chord progressions

During the development of diatonic harmony, rules were established to govern the movement from one chord to another in progressions. These rules were based on a strict sense of consonance and dissonance (see p. 118), and their function was to organize chord changes within a key so that the tonic chord emerged clearly as the "home chord" and so that the best and most logical "horizontal" effect was created between two chords.

The role of the primary chords – the most important ones – was determined by what is called *cadence*. A cadence (from the Latin word meaning "to fall") describes a concluding phrase or a phrase suggesting conclusion. It normally occurs at or near the end of a melody or a section of music. There are four different cadences in primary chord progressions.

The *perfect cadence* is the resolution from the V (dominant) to the I (tonic) chord.

The *imperfect cadence* is the progression from the I (tonic) chord to the V (dominant). It normally occurs in the middle of a chord sequence, not at the end, and it can also be used to describe the movement of any chord to the V – usually the II, IV or VI.

The *plagal cadence* is the resolution from the IV (sub-dominant) to the I (tonic) chord.

The *interrupted cadence* is the progression from the V (dominant) to any chord other than the I (tonic). It is usually to the III, IV or VI.

In chord sequences in a major key, these cadences reflect a definite sense of motion, tension and resolution. However, in a minor key, the V (dominant) chord is a minor triad, not a major triad, and this means that it does not produce the same effect when used in cadences. It was for this reason that the 7th note in the minor scale was raised by a semi-tone to create the harmonic minor scale (see p. 107). Triads built on the notes of the harmonic minor scale could therefore produce a different series of chords: I minor,

II diminished, III augmented, IV diminished, V major, VI major, and VII diminished. The V chord was now major instead of minor, and the result was that the rules of cadences could be applied in the same way to both major and minor keys.

In traditional harmony, there is a system of general rules for how diatonic chords should be used in a progression. These rules reflect musical tastes at the time the diatonic system came into being.

- A I chord can change to any chord.
- A II chord can change to any chord except the I.
- A III chord can change to any chord except the I or VII.
- A IV chord can change to any chord.
- A V chord can change to any chord except the II or VII.
- A VI chord can change to any chord except the I or VII.
- A VII chord can change to any chord except the II or IV.

The harmonized harmonic A minor scale
In order to avoid the minor V chord that occurs when triads are built on the natural minor scale (see p. 123), the 7th note was sharpened to produce a major V chord. Using the harmonic minor scale allows primary chords in a minor key to follow the rules of cadence.

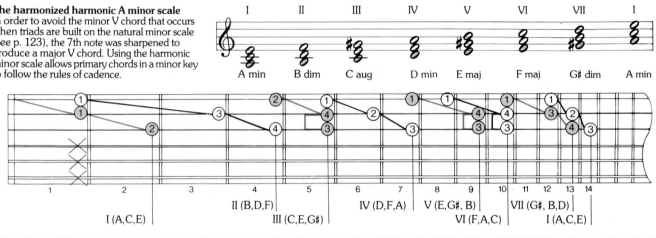

I A min · II B dim · III C aug · IV D min · V E maj · VI F maj · VII G# dim · I A min

I (A,C,E) · II (B,D,F) · III (C,E,G#) · IV (D,F,A) · V (E,G#,B) · VI (F,A,C) · VII (G#,B,D) · I (A,C,E)

How chord voicings move in progressions

The basic rules of traditional harmony are usually illustrated in "four-part" writing. Triads become four-part chords when one of the notes is doubled (see p. 123). The doubled note is traditionally either the root or the 5th. In four-part progressions, both the vertical and horizontal effect of all four notes in each chord were conventionally subject to strict regulations.

Two or three parts moving in the same direction is called *similar motion*. Two parts moving in different directions is called *contrary motion*. And one part moving while the other stays at the same pitch is called *oblique motion*. In four-part harmony, the two most important parts are the lowest and highest. In vocal writing, the lowest is the bass, the highest is the soprano, and the two in between are the tenor and alto.

Some of the rules of traditional harmony

you are likely to encounter are as follows. No two parts are allowed to move in "consecutive" fifths or octaves. Less rigidly enforced is the rule forbidding "hidden" fifths or octaves. These occur when two parts move in similar motion (up or down together) to arrive at a fifth or octave; it is permissible only when the upper voice moves by no more than a single step. Wherever possible, common notes between two chords should be in the same voice, and, ideally, the movement of each should consist of the smallest intervals possible. The jump of a tritone (three tones) was strictly forbidden.

These rules form the basic framework of traditional harmony, and were established in the sixteenth century. However, even as they were being developed, they were being broken. Anything was considered

valid as long as the sound produced had a clear harmonic motive and met with popular acceptance. As musical taste broadened to include new concepts of consonance and dissonance, the many rules forbidding specific voice and chord movements were relaxed. By including non-diatonic notes, new chords were produced, and it became possible to "modulate" to another key (see p. 138).

In the eighteenth and nineteenth centuries, the fundamental rules of chord progression revolved around the tonal pillars of the I (tonic), IV (sub-dominant) and V (dominant) chords. Looking at the interval chart on pp. 118-9, you can see that the IV and V chords balance the tonic on either side with perfect fifths. In any exploration of harmony, you will find that these relationships dominate all others.

Common or shared notes

It should now be apparent that when building triads on the notes of a major or minor scale, each note has a variety of different functions. Since any triad contains three notes – the tonic, the 3rd and the 5th – and since any note can play any of these three roles, it follows that any note can belong in three different triads.

Take a look at the harmonic A minor scale on the opposite page. The 1st note (the A) shows up immediately as being included in the three different triads – the A minor triad (I), the D minor triad (IV), and the F major triad (VI).

In the examples on the right, the C major scale and its diatonic triads are used to show how the principle is applied. The note C is already familiar as the root note of a C major triad. It is also the minor third of the sub-mediant A minor triad, and it is the perfect fifth of the sub-dominant F major triad. The examples show each of the seven diatonic notes and indicate in which three triads each note appears. By transferring these principles to theory (using Roman numerals instead of specific pitches), they may be applied to any key and will give you a sound basis for understanding chord harmony.

The tonic note (C)
The perfect fifth of the IV chord (F major).
The minor third of the VI chord (A minor).
The root of the I chord (C major).

The supertonic note (D)
The perfect fifth of the V chord (G major).
The minor third of the VII chord (B dim).
The root of the II chord (D minor).

The mediant note (E)
The perfect fifth of the VI chord (A minor).
The major third of the I chord (C major).
The root of the III chord (E minor).

The sub-dominant note (F)
The diminished fifth of the VII chord (B dim).
The minor third of the II chord (D minor).
The root of the IV chord (F major).

The dominant note (G)
The perfect fifth of the I chord (C major).
The minor third of the III chord (E minor).
The root of the V chord (G major).

The sub-mediant note (A)
The perfect fifth of the II chord (D minor).
The major third of the IV chord (F major).
The root of the VI chord (A minor).

The leading note (B)
The perfect fifth of the III chord (E minor).
The major third of the V chord (G major).
The root of the VII chord (B dim).

Choosing chords to create harmony

The principle of common notes shown above means that you can choose any one of three possible chords to use as a harmony for a particular melody note or bass note. If the bass note is C, for example, either C major, F major or A minor can be used as the chord. On pp. 121-2, we also saw that it is possible to "invert" triads. Applying this principle gives you another possibility.

The four harmonized scales below show different chord progressions for the same series of bass or root notes – in this case, the notes of the C major scale. Compare them with the triads in their natural root positions – shown in the harmonized scale on p. 123. They demonstrate how the appropriate inversion can be used to treat the same material in a number of different ways.

Harmony using primary triads
By employing inversions, a harmonized scale is constructed using only primary (I, IV and V) triads.

Harmony using primary and secondary triads
The first example shows that further variation is possible by introducing inversions of the II and VI triads. The second example employs both inversions of the I (tonic) and II (supertonic) triads. In the last harmonized scale, inversions of the subtonic triad (B♭) are used to replace the II and IV chords – although, strictly, it is outside the diatonic major scale.

Seventh chords

The evolution of triad harmony established the prominent role of the dominant (V) chord. There is a strong resolution when it is followed by the tonic (I) chord. In four-part writing an extra note evolved on top of the dominant triad. Instead of simply doubling the root, the new note was considered to be a continuation of the construction of the triad; another minor third was added on top of the fifth so that the interval between the root note and the new note was a minor seventh. This produced a four-note chord called the dominant seventh, built on the 5th note of the diatonic scale.

As shown below, there are various other types of seventh chord created by adding to the triads built on each note of the scale – in all, there are ten different kinds. However, all seventh chords must consist of a root, a 3rd, a 5th and a 7th. And, when it is in its root position, each seventh chord must comprise three vertical thirds stacked on top of one another, totaling an interval of a seventh between the bottom and top notes. The actual tonality of the thirds may be either major or minor. It is this variation that produces the ten different seventh forms.

How seventh chords are built from the diatonic major scale

Adding intervals of a third to each of the triads built on the notes of the major scale produces the following pattern: major seventh, minor seventh, minor seventh, major seventh, dominant seventh, minor seventh, half-diminished seventh.

The term *dominant seventh* came to apply not only to the chord built on the dominant note but to the type of seventh chord that it is. The usual abbreviation for a dominant seventh chord is simply to refer to it as the "seventh". Although the interval between the tonic and the extra note is a minor seventh, the term "minor seventh" is reserved for seventh chords built on a minor triad – for example, the supertonic (II), mediant (III) and sub-mediant (VI) seventh chords. The *triad* determines the name, not the interval between tonic and seventh.

When the extra note is added on top of the tonic (I) triad, it is an interval of a major seventh above the tonic note. Initially referred to as the "tonic seventh", this type of seventh chord is called a *major seventh*. The sub-dominant (IV) seventh chord is also a major seventh type.

The seventh chord built on the leading note of the scale (VII) produces an entirely new type of chord. It is made up of a major third on top of a diminished triad. This produces a minor seventh interval between the tonic note and the new note. The chord is called a *half-diminished seventh* because the triad is diminished but the seventh is not. It also has an alternative name – a "minor seventh diminished fifth".

The harmonized diatonic C major scale

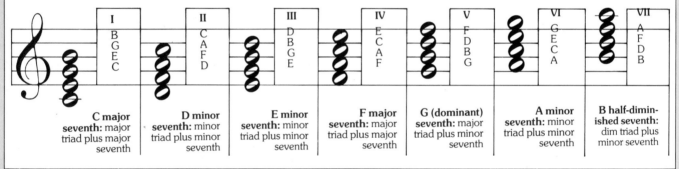

I	II	III	IV	V	VI	VII
B G E C	C A F D	D B G E	E C A F	F D B G	G E C A	A F D B
C major seventh: major triad plus major seventh	**D minor seventh:** minor triad plus minor seventh	**E minor seventh:** minor triad plus minor seventh	**F major seventh:** major triad plus major seventh	**G (dominant) seventh:** major triad plus minor seventh	**A minor seventh:** minor triad plus minor seventh	**B half-diminished seventh:** dim triad plus minor seventh

How seventh chords are built from the diatonic minor scales

Seventh chords built on the relative *natural* minor scale are identical to those derived from the major scale. Only their relative functions within the scale change. However, when the *harmonic* minor scale is used (see p. 107), three new kinds of seventh chord are produced. These are the "minor/major seventh", the "major seventh augmented fifth" and the "diminished seventh". The *minor/major seventh* is built on the 1st note of the scale, the tonic. It is made up of a major third on top of a minor triad, so the interval from the root note of the chord to the 7th note is a major seventh. The *major seventh augmented fifth*, built on the mediant (III) note of the scale, is a minor third on top of an augmented triad. From bottom to top, the interval is actually an augmented major seventh, but, because this is a potentially confusing name, it is identified as a "major seventh sharp five". The *diminished seventh*, the chord built on the leading note (VII), is a special case. It is explained in more detail on p. 128.

The harmonized harmonic A minor scale

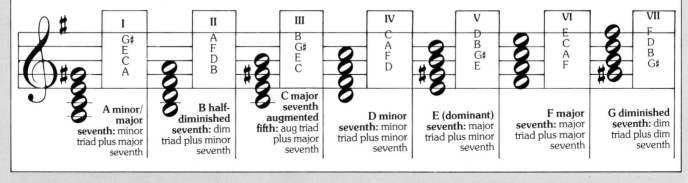

I	II	III	IV	V	VI	VII
G# E C A	A F D B	B G# E C	C A F D	D B G# E	E C A F	F D B G#
A minor/major seventh: minor triad plus major seventh	**B half-diminished seventh:** dim triad plus minor seventh	**C major seventh augmented fifth:** aug triad plus major seventh	**D minor seventh:** minor triad plus minor seventh	**E (dominant) seventh:** major triad plus minor seventh	**F major seventh:** major triad plus major seventh	**G diminished seventh:** dim triad plus dim seventh

The dominant seventh chords

The three chords included in this family are all derived from major triads plus minor sevenths. They are the *dominant seventh* (usually just called the "seventh"), the *seventh augmented fifth* (or "seventh sharp five"), and the *seventh diminished fifth* (or "seventh flat five"). The dominant seventh is formed by adding a minor seventh on top of a major triad, the seventh augmented fifth is based on an augmented triad, and the seventh diminished fifth on a diminished triad. The fingering shapes below are all "movable" forms; the name of the chord is determined by the tonic or root note. The root note is colored green.

Seventh chord fingerings
Usually abbreviated from "dominant seventh" to "seventh". Written simply as 7.

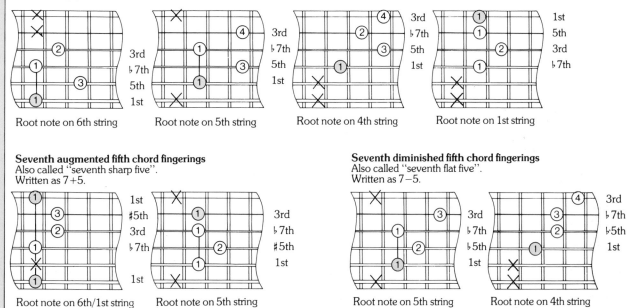

Root note on 6th string   Root note on 5th string   Root note on 4th string   Root note on 1st string

Seventh augmented fifth chord fingerings
Also called "seventh sharp five". Written as 7+5.

Seventh diminished fifth chord fingerings
Also called "seventh flat five". Written as 7−5.

Root note on 6th/1st string   Root note on 5th string   Root note on 5th string   Root note on 4th string

The minor seventh chords

There are also three chords in the minor seventh family. These are the *minor seventh* itself, the *half-diminished seventh* (or "minor seventh diminished fifth"), and the *diminished seventh*. The first two are shown here – with a choice of four different fingerings for each – and the third is dealt with separately on p. 128. The minor seventh is formed by adding a minor seventh interval on top of a minor triad. The half-diminished seventh is built on top of a diminished triad (one in which the 5th note is flattened).

Minor seventh chord fingerings
Written as m7.

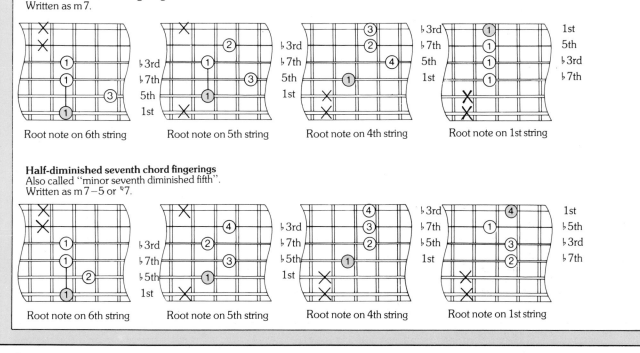

Root note on 6th string   Root note on 5th string   Root note on 4th string   Root note on 1st string

Half-diminished seventh chord fingerings
Also called "minor seventh diminished fifth". Written as m7−5 or ⌀7.

Root note on 6th string   Root note on 5th string   Root note on 4th string   Root note on 1st string

The major seventh chords

The family of major sevenths includes four different chords. These are the *major seventh* itself, the *minor/major seventh*, the *major seventh augmented fifth* (or "major seventh sharp five"), and the *major seventh diminished fifth* (or "major seventh flat five"). These chords differ from those in the other families in that they all have an interval of a major seventh between the lowest and highest notes. Chords in the dominant and minor seventh families (see p. 127) both have an interval of a minor seventh.

The four major seventh chords are shown here in various fingering shapes, with their tonic or root notes on different strings. In most cases, they can be transformed from four-note chords into six-note chords (one note for each string) by "doubling" some of the notes (see p. 123). They can be doubled, inverted and spaced in any manner without affecting the chord.

Major seventh chord fingerings
Written as maj 7 or △ 7.

Minor/major seventh chord fingerings
Written as min/maj 7.

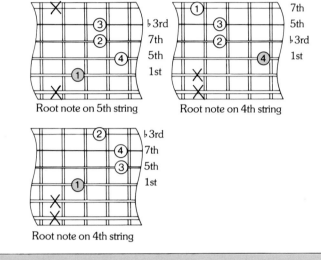

Root note on 6th string

Root note on 5th string

Root note on 4th string

Root note on 4th string

Root note on 5th string

Root note on 4th string

Root note on 4th string

The diminished chord

The seventh chord built on the leading note (VII) of the diatonic scale was considered to be an important musical discovery – the *diminished seventh*. This chord is often abbreviated to the name "diminished".

Because both the 5th in the existing triad and the new, added note are flattened, this seventh chord creates an interval of a diminished seventh to the tonic. The diminished seventh is a double flattened seventh – the enharmonic name for a major sixth (see p. 118). The most unusual feature of the diminished seventh chord is therefore the fact that it is made up of three minor thirds stacked on top of each other. And, when the tonic is doubled at the top, yet another minor third is formed. This means that, in effect, the octave is divided equally into four intervals of a minor third.

If each of the four notes (the root, the 3rd, the 5th and the 7th) is doubled in turn, so that two octaves are spanned, it is clear that any of the notes in the chord can be considered to be the root of a new chord that has exactly the same structure and tonality as the original. When viewed enharmonically, all four chords are, in fact, part of the same chord. In each inversion of the original chord, specific notes can be renamed as either the root, the 3rd, the 5th or the 7th to create the intervals necessary for forming a new diminished seventh chord.

The diminished chord was originally used to extend the properties of "resolution" that were a feature of leading note sevenths. However, it was soon realized that this was only part of its potential. Because it can be any one of four different chords, it occupies four different tonalities. This means that it is interchangeable between four separate keys, and that it represents a unique "gateway" between these keys. The sound of the chord quickly gained in popularity, and the effects it made possible opened up a new world of modulation (see p. 138).

For details of the "diminished scale" – also built on a series of minor third intervals – see p. 112.

The diminished seventh: four chords in one This example is in C and shows four inversions of a C diminished seventh chord. It illustrates the fact that, because the intervals remain the same from one inversion to the next, the notes C, E♭, G♭ and B♭♭ (A) give four diminished chords that are enharmonic equivalents of one another: they all share the same four notes.

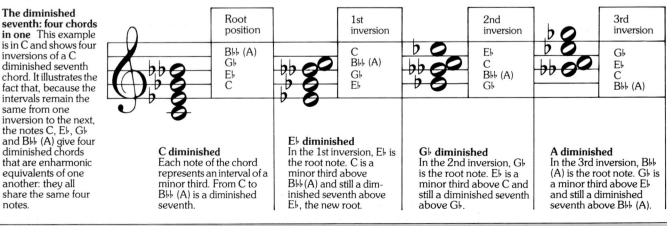

	Root position	1st inversion	2nd inversion	3rd inversion
	B♭♭ (A) G♭ E♭ C	C B♭♭ (A) G♭ E♭	E♭ C B♭♭ (A) G♭	G♭ E♭ C B♭♭ (A)

C diminished
Each note of the chord represents an interval of a minor third. From C to B♭♭ (A) is a diminished seventh.

E♭ diminished
In the 1st inversion, E♭ is the root note. C is a minor third above B♭♭ (A) and still a diminished seventh above E♭, the new root.

G♭ diminished
In the 2nd inversion, G♭ is the root note. E♭ is a minor third above C and still a diminished seventh above G♭.

A diminished
In the 3rd inversion, B♭♭ (A) is the root note. G♭ is a minor third above E♭ and still a diminished seventh above B♭♭ (A).

Major seventh augmented fifth chord fingerings
Also called "major seventh sharp five".
Written as maj 7 +5 or △7+5.

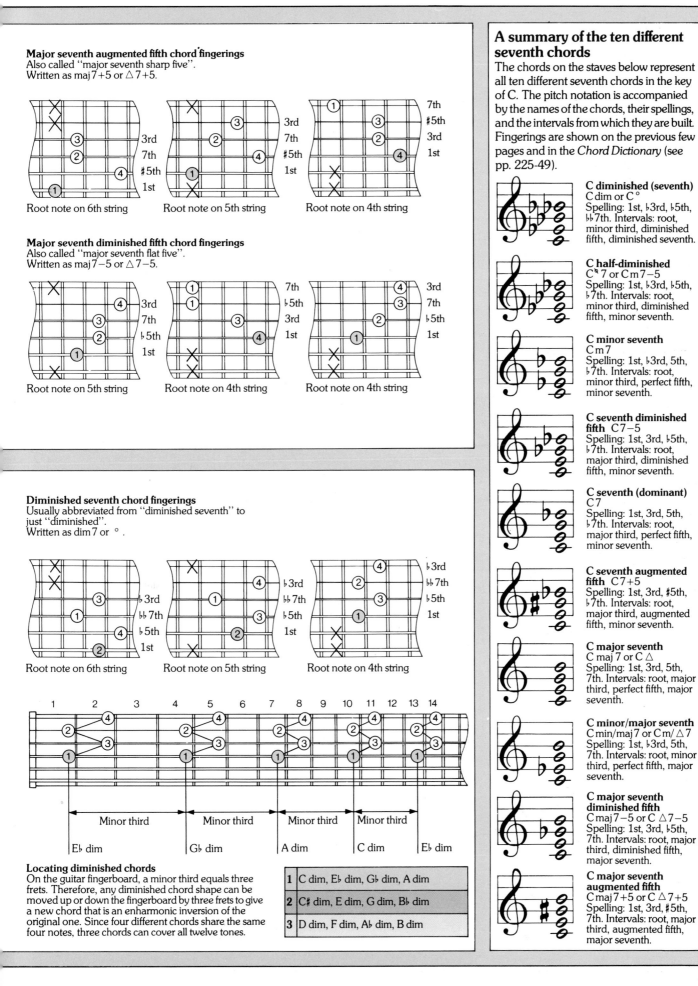

Root note on 6th string   Root note on 5th string   Root note on 4th string

Major seventh diminished fifth chord fingerings
Also called "major seventh flat five".
Written as maj 7 −5 or △7−5.

Root note on 5th string   Root note on 4th string   Root note on 4th string

Diminished seventh chord fingerings
Usually abbreviated from "diminished seventh" to just "diminished".
Written as dim 7 or °.

Root note on 6th string   Root note on 5th string   Root note on 4th string

Minor third   Minor third   Minor third   Minor third

E♭ dim   G♭ dim   A dim   C dim   E♭ dim

Locating diminished chords
On the guitar fingerboard, a minor third equals three frets. Therefore, any diminished chord shape can be moved up or down the fingerboard by three frets to give a new chord that is an enharmonic inversion of the original one. Since four different chords share the same four notes, three chords can cover all twelve tones.

1	C dim, E♭ dim, G♭ dim, A dim
2	C♯ dim, E dim, G dim, B♭ dim
3	D dim, F dim, A♭ dim, B dim

A summary of the ten different seventh chords
The chords on the staves below represent all ten different seventh chords in the key of C. The pitch notation is accompanied by the names of the chords, their spellings, and the intervals from which they are built. Fingerings are shown on the previous few pages and in the *Chord Dictionary* (see pp. 225-49).

C diminished (seventh)
C dim or C°
Spelling: 1st, ♭3rd, ♭5th, ♭♭7th. Intervals: root, minor third, diminished fifth, diminished seventh.

C half-diminished
C⌀7 or C m7−5
Spelling: 1st, ♭3rd, ♭5th, ♭7th. Intervals: root, minor third, diminished fifth, minor seventh.

C minor seventh
C m7
Spelling: 1st, ♭3rd, 5th, ♭7th. Intervals: root, minor third, perfect fifth, minor seventh.

C seventh diminished fifth C7−5
Spelling: 1st, 3rd, ♭5th, ♭7th. Intervals: root, major third, diminished fifth, minor seventh.

C seventh (dominant)
C7
Spelling: 1st, 3rd, 5th, ♭7th. Intervals: root, major third, perfect fifth, minor seventh.

C seventh augmented fifth C7+5
Spelling: 1st, 3rd, ♯5th, ♭7th. Intervals: root, major third, augmented fifth, minor seventh.

C major seventh
C maj 7 or C △
Spelling: 1st, 3rd, 5th, 7th. Intervals: root, major third, perfect fifth, major seventh.

C minor/major seventh
C min/maj 7 or C m/△7
Spelling: 1st, ♭3rd, 5th, 7th. Intervals: root, minor third, perfect fifth, major seventh.

C major seventh diminished fifth
C maj 7−5 or C △7−5
Spelling: 1st, 3rd, ♭5th, 7th. Intervals: root, major third, diminished fifth, major seventh.

C major seventh augmented fifth
C maj 7+5 or C △7+5
Spelling: 1st, 3rd, ♯5th, 7th. Intervals: root, major third, augmented fifth, major seventh.

Added ninths, suspended fourths, and sixths

We have now seen how four of the notes in the diatonic scale can be combined in various ways to form vertical chords. The 1st, 3rd and 5th notes form triads (see pp. 121-5) and the 7th note, when added to the triad, forms seventh chords (see pp. 126-9). We will now look at the remaining notes in the scale – the 2nd, 4th and 6th – and see what chords can be created by using them.

The three types of chords produced by using these notes are the "added ninths", the "suspended fourths", and the "sixths". In their root positions, these chords all remain within the span of one octave. They are the chords that we are concerned with here. However, if the notes are stacked in thirds on top of the existing chords, then chords that span more than one octave are created. When this happens, the 2nd, 4th and 6th are called the 9th, 11th and 13th respectively, and the chords are "extended" (see p. 132).

Added ninth chords

When the 2nd note of a scale is added to the major triad built on that scale's tonic note, it produces a chord made up of the 1st, 2nd, 3rd and 5th notes. Normally, it would be called a "second chord", but to avoid confusion with second inversions and with chords in which the 2nd note actually replaces the 3rd, it is referred to by its extended name – the "ninth" (the 9th note is the same as the 2nd but an octave higher). Because it is not an extended chord, this is made clear by using the prefix "added".

The 2nd note can be added to minor triads as well as to majors. In both cases, added ninths are clear, strong chords – due to the relationship of the I, II and V. In fact, the added ninth is often played without the third note. The minor added ninth features the most dissonant interval of all – the one semi-tone minor second – between the 2nd/9th note and the flattened 3rd. Yet, used creatively, this interval can produce simple chords of startling beauty, especially on the guitar.

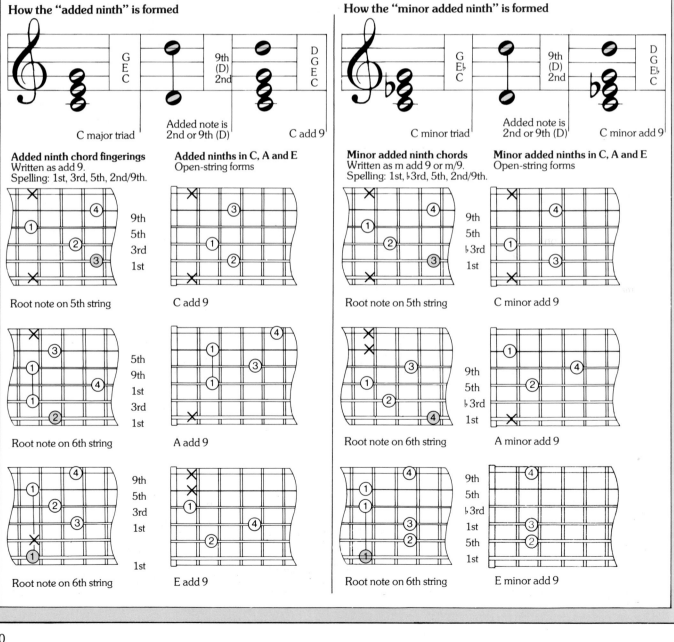

How the "added ninth" is formed

C major triad — Added note is 2nd or 9th (D) — C add 9

How the "minor added ninth" is formed

C minor triad — Added note is 2nd or 9th (D) — C minor add 9

Added ninth chord fingerings
Written as add 9.
Spelling: 1st, 3rd, 5th, 2nd/9th.

Root note on 5th string

Root note on 6th string

Root note on 6th string

Added ninths in C, A and E
Open-string forms

C add 9

A add 9

E add 9

Minor added ninth chords
Written as m add 9 or m/9.
Spelling: 1st, ♭3rd, 5th, 2nd/9th.

Root note on 5th string

Root note on 6th string

Root note on 6th string

Minor added ninths in C, A and E
Open-string forms

C minor add 9

A minor add 9

E minor add 9

Suspended fourth chords

When the 4th (sub-dominant) note of the scale is included in the major triad built on the tonic, it replaces the 3rd, and the resulting chord is called a *suspended fourth*. In fact, any chord in which the 3rd note has been replaced by the 4th is called suspended. The tension created by the 4th seeking resolution to the 3rd is clearly audible in the sound of the chord. When the 4th note replaces the 3rd in a dominant seventh chord, the new chord is called a *seventh suspended fourth*.

How the "suspended fourth" is formed

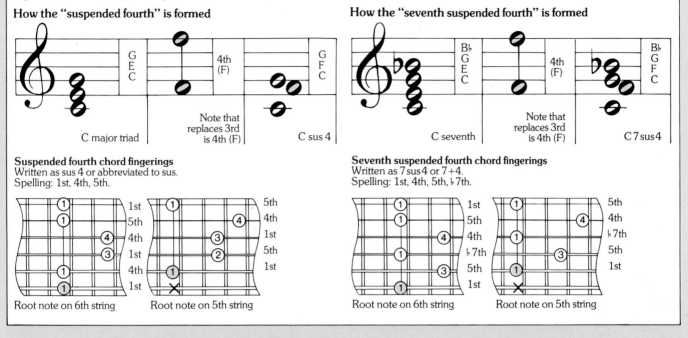

C major triad | Note that replaces 3rd is 4th (F) | C sus 4

How the "seventh suspended fourth" is formed

C seventh | Note that replaces 3rd is 4th (F) | C 7 sus 4

Suspended fourth chord fingerings
Written as sus 4 or abbreviated to sus.
Spelling: 1st, 4th, 5th.

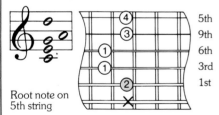

Root note on 6th string Root note on 5th string

Seventh suspended fourth chord fingerings
Written as 7 sus 4 or 7+4.
Spelling: 1st, 4th, 5th, ♭7th.

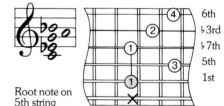

Root note on 6th string Root note on 5th string

Sixths

When the 6th note of the scale, the sub-mediant, is added to a major triad, the resulting chord is called a *sixth*. When the 6th note is added to a minor triad, it produces a *minor sixth* chord. In both cases, the 6th is an extra note, not a replacement for the 5th. The fingerings below are all movable forms; the notes on the staves show each of the various sixth chords in C.

Sixth chord fingerings
Written as 6.
Spelling: 1st, 3rd, 5th, 6th.

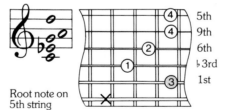

Root note on 5th string

Minor sixth chord fingerings
Written as m6.
Spelling: 1st, ♭3rd, 5th, 6th.

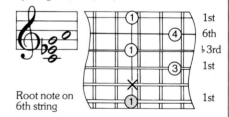

Root note on 6th string

Six nine chord fingerings
Also "major sixth added ninth". Written as 6/9.
Spelling: 1st, 3rd, 5th, 6th, 9th (i.e., 9th added to sixth chord).

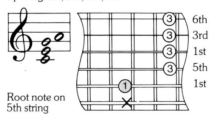

Root note on 5th string

Minor six nine chord fingerings
Also "minor sixth added ninth". Written as m6/9.
Spelling: 1st, ♭3rd, 5th, 6th, 9th (i.e., 9th added to minor sixth chord).

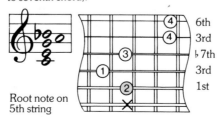

Root note on 5th string

Minor six seven chord fingering
Written as m6/7.
Spelling: 1st, ♭3rd, 5th, 6th, ♭7th (i.e., 6th added to minor seventh chord).

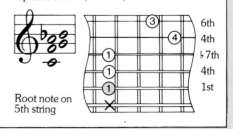

Root note on 5th string

Minor six seven eleven chord fingering
Written as m6/7/11.
Spelling: 1st, ♭3rd, 5th, 6th, ♭7th, 11th/4th (i.e., 11th added to minor 6/7 chord).

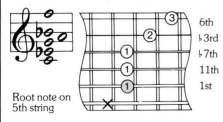

Root note on 5th string

Six seven chord fingering
Written as 6/7.
Spelling: 1st, 3rd, 5th, 6th, ♭7th (i.e., 6th added to seventh chord).

Root note on 5th string

Six seven suspended chord fingerings
Written as 6/7 sus.
Spelling: 1st, 4th, 5th, 6th, ♭7th (i.e., 4th replaces 3rd in 6/7 chord).

Root note on 5th string

Extended chords

Adding to a triad a note which is theoretically more than an octave above the root produces what is called an *extended chord*. If the 2nd note is inverted an octave above the root and added to a chord, the chord is called a *ninth*. If the 4th note an octave above the root is added, the chord is called an *eleventh*. And if the 6th note an octave above the root is added, the chord is called a *thirteenth*.

Each extended chord belongs in one of three families – the dominant, major or minor. These are produced by adding the extra note to the four-note dominant seventh, major seventh or minor seventh. The tonality of the third and seventh intervals determines the tonality of the extended chord. When both are minor, the chord belongs to the minor family. When the third is major but the seventh is minor, the chord belongs to the dominant family. And when both are major, the chord belongs to the major family.

By raising or lowering the 5th or the new, extra note, variations can be derived from the basic chord. These are called *altered chords*. However, it is vital that you learn how the basic chords function before you attempt to use the altered forms.

The three basic ninth chords

These ninths are five-note chords, all constructed by adding an extra note to the four-note seventh chords (see pp. 126-9). The new note is actually a 2nd, but because it is added *on top* of the seventh chord, a third above the 7th, it is called a 9th. The 9th, in fact, equals a 2nd plus one octave; in other words, it is the same note but, as you can see below, it is an octave higher.

All three basic ninth chords comprise four intervals of a third stacked on top of one another. They can therefore be seen as two triads, the top one anchored to the upper note of the bottom one. The sound created by varying the five notes in a ninth chord will depend on which notes are omitted or doubled, and on how the notes are spaced (i.e., the chord's "voicing").

How the "ninth" is formed

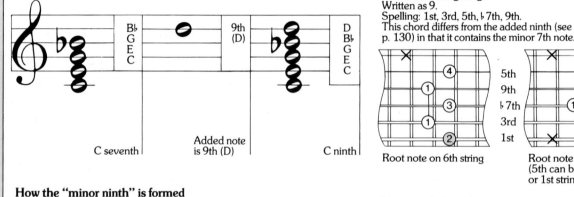

C seventh   Added note is 9th (D)   C ninth

Ninth chord fingerings
Written as 9.
Spelling: 1st, 3rd, 5th, ♭7th, 9th.
This chord differs from the added ninth (see p. 130) in that it contains the minor 7th note.

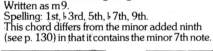

Root note on 6th string   Root note on 5th string (5th can be added on 6th or 1st string)

How the "minor ninth" is formed

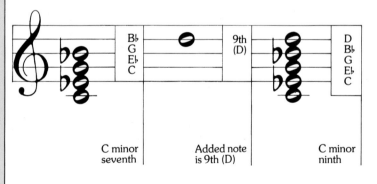
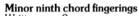

C minor seventh   Added note is 9th (D)   C minor ninth

Minor ninth chord fingerings
Written as m9.
Spelling: 1st, ♭3rd, 5th, ♭7th, 9th.
This chord differs from the minor added ninth (see p. 130) in that it contains the minor 7th note.

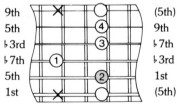
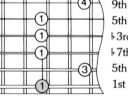

Root note on 6th string   Root note on 5th string (5th can be added on 6th or 1st string)

How the "major ninth" is formed

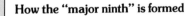
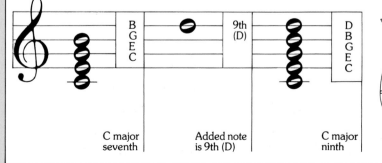

C major seventh   Added note is 9th (D)   C major ninth

Major ninth chord fingerings
Written as maj9 or △9.
Spelling: 1st, 3rd, 5th, 7th, 9th.

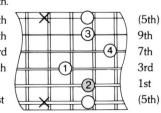
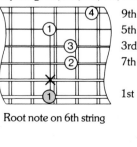

Root note on 6th string   Root note on 5th string (5th can be added on 6th or 1st string)

Altered ninth chords

Within the structure of a ninth chord each of the four notes above the root (the 3rd, 5th, 7th and 9th) may be altered: the 3rd note may be either major or minor in relation to the root; the 5th may be diminished, perfect or augmented; the 7th may be diminished, minor or major; and the 9th may be minor, major or augmented. A simple mathematical calculation shows that these permutations can produce twenty-seven different ninth chords. Many of these, however, are mis-spellings or "synonyms" (see p. 137) of other chords. Excluding the three basic chords on the opposite page, this leaves twelve altered ninth chords.

These chords can be grouped into the three families of dominants, minors and majors. The dominant family offers the greatest number of altered ninths. Eight are shown below. They can be divided into those that feature only one altered note (the 5th *or* the 9th) and those that feature two altered notes (the 5th *and* the 9th).

We have seen on p. 118 that, when the 5th note is altered, it becomes diminished if lowered by a semi-tone and augmented if raised by a semi-tone. In a chord, a diminished fifth is indicated by a minus (or a flat) sign before the five. The term "diminished" should be used only if it applies to the whole chord. An augmented fifth is indicated by a plus (or a sharp) sign before the five. A dominant ninth chord with an altered 5th note is therefore either 9−5 or 9+5.

When the 9th note is altered, the chord is named according to the four-note seventh chord that forms its foundation. The altered ninth is written after this as either −9 or +9. The term "minor ninth" and "major ninth" are generally reserved for ninth chords built on minor sevenths and major sevenths.

The 6th note of a scale can also be included in these ninth chords. However, if the 6th replaces the 7th, the chord is called a "six nine" chord (see p. 131), and if the 6th, 7th and 9th are all present, the chord is called a thirteenth (see p. 135).

The chord fingerings shown below illustrate only one of the many possible positions and voicings for each chord. The notes on the staves show the chords in C. They illustrate the construction of each chord and not the spacing of the notes and intervals in the fingerings.

Seventh flat nine chord fingering
Written as 7−9.
Spelling: 1st, 3rd, 5th, ♭7th, ♭9th.

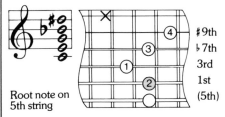

Seventh augmented ninth chord fingering
Written as 7+9.
Spelling: 1st, 3rd, 5th, ♭7th, ♯9th.

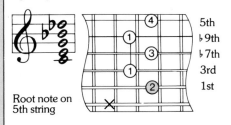

Seventh augmented ninth diminished fifth chord fingering Written as 7+9−5.
Spelling: 1st, 3rd, ♭5th, ♭7th, ♯9th.

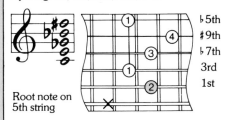

Minor ninth diminished fifth chord fingering Written as m9−5.
Spelling: 1st, ♭3rd, ♭5th, ♭7th, 9th.

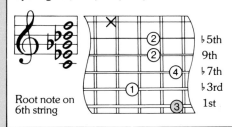

Ninth diminished fifth chord fingering
Written as 9−5.
Spelling: 1st, 3rd, ♭5th, ♭7th, 9th.

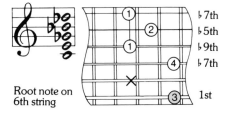

Seventh flat nine diminished fifth chord fingering Written as 7−9−5.
Spelling: 1st, 3rd, ♭5th, ♭7th, ♭9th.

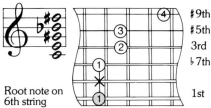

Seventh augmented ninth augmented fifth chord fingering Written as 7+9+5.
Spelling: 1st, 3rd, ♯5th, ♭7th, ♯9th.

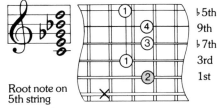

Minor/major ninth chord fingering
Written as min/maj9 or m/△9.
Spelling: 1st, ♭3rd, 5th, 7th, 9th.

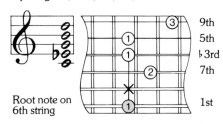

Ninth augmented fifth chord fingering
Written as 9+5.
Spelling: 1st, 3rd, ♯5th, ♭7th, 9th.

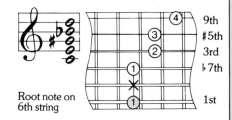

Seventh flat nine augmented fifth chord fingering Written as 7−9+5.
Spelling: 1st, 3rd, ♯5th, ♭7th, ♭9th.

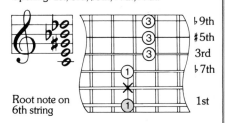

Minor seventh flat nine chord fingering
Written as m7−9.
Spelling: 1st, ♭3rd, 5th, ♭7th, ♭9th.

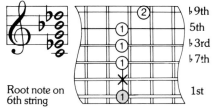

Major ninth augmented fifth chord fingering Written as maj9+5 or △9+5.
Spelling: 1st, 3rd, ♯5th, 7th, 9th.

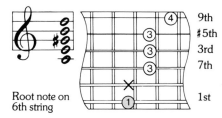

Polychords

A *polychord* is defined as two chords sounding together. Polychords are also sometimes known as "polytonal" chords. A true polychord must contain at least the basic elements of its two constituent chords. Many of the extended chords that we have already described can, in fact, be considered as polychords. Take, as an example, C major ninth (see p. 132). If you look at the notes it contains – the 1st (C), 3rd (E), 5th (G), 7th (B) and 9th (D) – you will see that these actually represent a C major triad (C, E and G) and a G major triad (G, B and D). Playing the two triads together produces the effect of *one* chord and gives the C major ninth sound.

In contemporary usage, polychords can take many forms. One of the most common involves playing a chord over a different bass note – one that is not its normal root. Chords of this kind can be considered "bi-tonal" and can best be thought of as chords with *altered* bass notes. They are indicated using two symbols separated by an oblique stroke. The first (or top) symbol represents the chord, and the second (or bottom) symbol represents the bass note. So, D/C, for example, means you should play a D major chord with a C note in the bass.

Although these are not true polychords in the strict sense (because only the root note has changed), they are widely used. They provide a way of simplifying complicated information and of specifying the notes that are to be included or omitted.

All the chords shown on this page are formed by playing a simple triad over an altered bass note – that is, over a bass note that is neither part of the triad nor the note from which the triad is normally built (see pp. 121-4). They produce a strong, clean sound in which both tonalities, the bass and the chord, can be clearly heard.

Polychords of this kind can all be analyzed and written out as extended or altered chords which have the bass note as their root. But there is an important distinction. The polychord does not contain *all* the notes included in the full extended or altered chord. The notes most often omitted from the extended chord are the 3rd and 5th.

Take C major ninth as an example again. If you leave out the 3rd (E) so that you are playing a G major triad over a C bass note, this can be indicated as the polychord symbol G/C. It is easier and more efficient than writing C maj 9 (no 3rd).

To take another similar example, it is much simpler to write D/C than C 6/9/#11 (no 3rd or 5th) when you want to indicate that a D major triad should be played over the top of a C bass note.

If you are playing rhythm guitar and you come up against one of these polychord symbols, you immediately have two options. The obvious one is simply to play the top triad together with the altered bass note. But if the bass note is being sounded clearly by either the bassist or the keyboard player, you need play only the top triad. However, you must take care to play an appropriate inversion, without altering or extending the chord.

The use of this type of polychord is on the increase in popular music. To familiarize yourself with their sound, try playing different triads over a common bass note – using an open bass string and sounding the triads on the higher strings.

Altered bass note chords

The polychords shown below are all major triads with an altered bass note. The two most commonly used are probably D/C and G/C. Although the bass note is always a C in the examples here, it can in fact be any note. Turn to the triad fingerings shown on pp. 121-2 and experiment with adding altered bass notes to them.

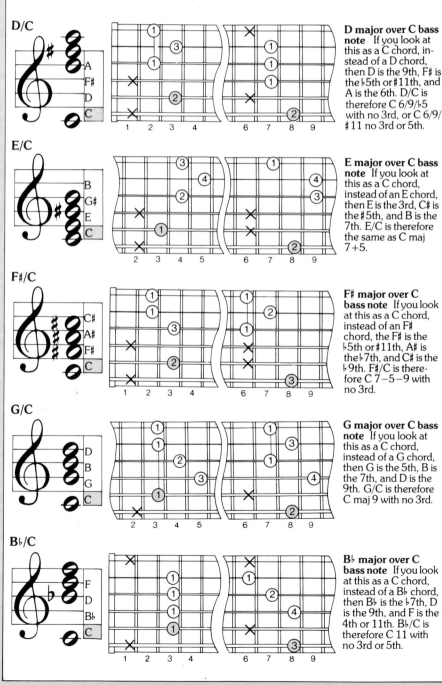

D major over C bass note If you look at this as a C chord, instead of a D chord, then D is the 9th, F# is the b5th or #11th, and A is the 6th. D/C is therefore C 6/9/b5 with no 3rd, or C 6/9/#11 no 3rd or 5th.

E major over C bass note If you look at this as a C chord, instead of an E chord, then E is the 3rd, C# is the #5th, and B is the 7th. E/C is therefore the same as C maj 7+5.

F# major over C bass note If you look at this as a C chord, instead of an F# chord, the F# is the b5th or #11th, A# is the b7th, and C# is the b9th. F#/C is therefore C 7−5−9 with no 3rd.

G major over C bass note If you look at this as a C chord, instead of a G chord, then G is the 5th, B is the 7th, and D is the 9th. G/C is therefore C maj 9 with no 3rd.

Bb major over C bass note If you look at this as a C chord, instead of a Bb chord, then Bb is the b7th, D is the 9th, and F is the 4th or 11th. Bb/C is therefore C 11 with no 3rd or 5th.

Chord synonyms

Unlike keyboard players, guitarists are limited to playing a maximum of six notes at once, and – for chord work – a minimum of three. This means that you must choose carefully which notes you play and which you omit in any given chord progression. You must also consider how what you choose to play will complement the harmonic statements of the other instruments in a band. This ability is one of the principal skills of the harmonic guitarist.

The first step is obviously a solid understanding of how extended chords are constructed and how they can be altered. As soon as you begin to explore this area, you will see that the upper notes of extended chords often form separate chords with different names (although the notes may have to be inverted and re-arranged to make this clear). These are called *synonyms*. And synonyms are two or more chords made up of the same notes but with different names.

Let's take Am7 as a simple example. It is made up of the 1st (A), ♭3rd (C), 5th (E) and ♭7th (G). If you leave out the root note, then a C major triad remains; so Am7 with no root and C major are chord synonyms. In practice, both chords are therefore interchangeable and either can be used as long as the bassist or keyboard player is clearly stating the bass note of A. This demonstrates that, if you understand the components of a chord, you will have more than one choice of harmony when playing in a band with other musicians. Due to the inherent limitations of the fingerboard, it is essential that you also understand the relationship between chords that have common or shared notes (see p. 125).

It is inevitable that, with only twelve notes to work with, there is a limit to the number of chords that can be formed without repetition, and also that all larger chords are composed of smaller ones. Because of the relationship between inverted intervals and chord construction, there are many ways in which the principles of chord synonyms can be applied. A few examples are given here to show how they work. But bear in mind that principles are useless without the ear to apply them. Unraveling the mysteries of related harmony can take years. However, once you understand even the most basic of these principles, you will find your existing chord vocabulary greatly expanded. A knowledge of chord synonyms and how they work also forms one of the necesssary skills required for chord substitution (see p. 150).

Examples of chord synonyms

Added ninths and suspended fourths
Omitting the 3rd from C add 9 produces a three-note chord called C2 (C second). If the C is inverted so that G is the root, these three notes form a G sus4 chord. (See pp. 130-31 for these chords.)
Rule *Any add 9 chord with no 3rd is the same as a sus4 chord whose root is a fifth higher.*

Added ninth suspended fourths and seventh suspended fourths This example is a variation on the one above. The 4th takes the place of the 3rd in the add 9 sus 4 chord.
Rule *Any add 9 sus4 chord is the same as a 7 sus4 chord whose root is a fifth higher.*

Six nine chords and seventh suspended fouths
Omitting the 3rd from C 6/9 and inverting the 9th (D) produces D 7 sus4. Omitting the root from C 6/9 and using the 6th (A) as a new root produces A 7 sus4. (See p. 131 for these chords.)
Rule *Any 6/9 chord with no 3rd is the same as a 7 sus 4 chord whose root is one tone higher.*
Rule *Any 6/9 chord with no root is the same as a 7 sus4 chord whose root is three semi-tones lower.*

Minor ninths and major sevenths
Omitting the root note from C m9 produces E♭ major 7. No inversion is necessary. (See p. 128 and p. 132 for these chords.)
Rule *Any minor 9 chord with no root is the same as a major 7 chord whose root is three semi-tones higher.*

Minor sevenths and sixths
Inverting the upper three notes of an Am 7 chord produces a C6 chord. (See p. 127 and p. 131 for these chords.)
Rule *Any minor 7 chord is the same as a 6 chord whose root is three semi-tones higher.*

Ninths and half-diminished chords
Omitting the root note from C9 leaves a four-note half-diminished chord with E♭ as its root. (See p. 127 and p. 132 for these chords.)
Rule *Any 9 chord with no root is the same as a half-diminished chord whose root is three semi-tones higher.*

Seventh flat nines and diminished chords
Omitting the root note from C7−9 leaves a four-note diminished chord named according to any of its four notes – E dim, G dim, B♭ dim or D♭ dim. (See p. 128 and p. 133 for these chords.)
Rule *Any 7−9 chord with no root is the same as a diminished chord rooted on any of the remaining four notes.*

Ninth diminished fifths and seventh augmented fifths Omitting the root note from C 9−5 and inverting the 3rd (E) to its enharmonic equivalent (F♭) produces G♭7+5. (See p. 127 and p. 133 for these chords.)
Rule *Any 9−5 chord with no root is the same as a 7+5 chord whose root is a diminished fifth higher.*

Ninth diminished fifths and ninth augmented fifths Inverting the various notes in C9−5 and using the 9th (D) as a new root produces D9+5. (See p. 133 for these chords.)
Rule *Any 9−5 chord is the same as a 9+5 chord whose root is one tone higher.*

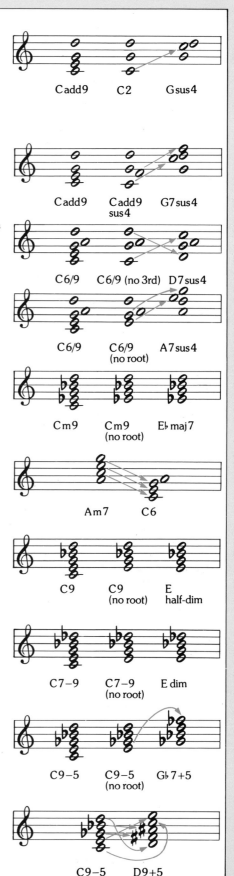

C add 9   C2   G sus4

C add 9   C add 9 sus 4   G7 sus 4

C 6/9   C 6/9 (no 3rd)   D 7 sus 4

C 6/9   C 6/9 (no root)   A 7 sus 4

C m9   C m9 (no root)   E♭ maj 7

Am7   C6

C9   C9 (no root)   E half-dim

C7−9   C7−9 (no root)   E dim

C9−5   C9−5 (no root)   G♭ 7+5

C9−5   D9+5

Modulation

Modulation can be defined as changing from one key to another in the middle of a piece of music. There are a number of rules and conventions designed to make the key change as smooth as possible.

Every major key is related to a minor key. The relative minor scale begins on the 6th note of the major scale, and the two scales share the same notes. They also share the same key signature (see pp. 108-9). For this reason, the following explanation of modulation needs deal only with major keys.

As the circle of fifths demonstrates (see p. 109), every major key is closely related to two other major keys. Only one note in their scales differs each time. These two other keys begin on the sub-dominant (4th) and dominant (5th) notes of the original key. Take the key of C major as an example: the two keys closest to it are F major and G major. F is the 4th note in the scale of C major, and G is the 5th. Only one note in the scale of F major differs from that of C major – B♭. And only one note in the scale of G major differs – F♯.

Moreover, comparing the three major scales of C, F and G reveals that the primary intervals (I, IV and V) of all three keys are related by common notes. The note C is the root in C major, the sub-dominant (4th) in G major, and the dominant (5th) in F major. The note F is the root in F major and the sub-dominant (4th) in C major. The note G is the root in G major and the dominant (5th) in C major. This pattern is repeated throughout the twelve keys, and these primary relationships allow a smooth, natural modulation.

The primary modulation chart and how to use it

The vertical block of the three chords shown on the right represents the primary interval "link" that connects the key signatures. The primary intervals are the I, IV and V. They are color-coded to indicate which note is which interval in every key. The rule when modulating from one key to another using primary interval links is: one horizontal step, then one vertical step. The chord in the vertical column is the "pivot" chord that allows the modulation.

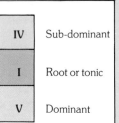

IV	Sub-dominant
I	Root or tonic
V	Dominant

Key of C♯	7 sharps		A♯	B♯	C♯	D♯	E♯	F♯	G♯	A♯	B♯	C♯	D♯	E♯	F♯
Key of F♯	6 sharps		A♯	B	C♯	D♯	E♯	F♯	G♯	A♯	B	C♯	D♯	E♯	F♯
Key of B	5 sharps		A♯	B	C♯	D♯	E	F♯	G♯	A♯	B	C♯	D♯	E	F♯
Key of E	4 sharps		A	B	C♯	D♯	E	F♯	G♯	A	B	C♯	D♯	E	F♯
Key of A	3 sharps		A	B	C♯	D	E	F♯	G♯	A	B	C♯	D	E	F♯
Key of D	2 sharps	Dominant direction	A	B	C♯	D	E	F♯	G	A	B	C♯	D	E	F♯
Key of G	1 sharp		A	B	C	D	E	F♯	G	A	B	C	D	E	F♯
Key of C			A	B	C	D	E	F	G	A	B	C	D	E	F
Key of F	1 flat		A	B♭	C	D	E	F	G	A	B♭	C	D	E	F
Key of B♭	2 flats	Sub-dominant direction	A	B♭	C	D	E♭	F	G	A	B♭	C	D	E♭	F
Key of E♭	3 flats		A♭	B♭	C	D	E♭	F	G	A♭	B♭	C	D	E♭	F
Key of A♭	4 flats		A♭	B♭	C	D♭	E♭	F	G	A♭	B♭	C	D♭	E♭	F
Key of D♭	5 flats		A♭	B♭	C	D♭	E♭	F	G♭	A♭	B♭	C	D♭	E♭	F
Key of G♭	6 flats		A♭	B♭	C♭	D♭	E♭	F	G♭	A♭	B♭	C♭	D♭	E♭	F
Key of C♭	7 flats		A♭	B♭	C♭	D♭	E♭	F♭	G♭	A♭	B♭	C♭	D♭	E♭	F♭

Modulation using primary chords

The chart on the opposite page illustrates how the primary intervals – the root or tonic (I), the sub-dominant (IV) and the dominant (V) – can be used to modulate between different keys. The relationships between the keys are those of the "circle of fifths" (see p. 109). Modulation based on these principles can work in two ways: it can either move in the dominant direction (up the chart) or in the sub-dominant direction (down the chart).

In the dominant direction, the dominant (V) of the old key becomes the root (I) of the new key. In the sub-dominant direction, the sub-dominant (IV) of the old key becomes the root (I) of the new key.

In the chart, each of the primary intervals appears in a different color. For example, in the key of C, C itself (I) is colored dark green, F (IV) is colored light green, and G (V) is colored gray. You will see that these three intervals occur throughout the chart in vertical columns. The root (I) is in the center, the sub-dominant (IV) is above it, and the dominant (V) is below it. This demonstrates that the note C, for example, is the sub-

dominant (IV) in the key of G major, the root (I) in the key of C major, and the dominant (V) in the key of F major. The vertical columns are therefore "pivots" which allow you to modulate directly from the key you are in to one of two others.

Take a simple example. Say you want to modulate from the key of C major to the key of G major. You might choose to do it one of two ways. You could change straight from C to G, since the vertical columns show that G is both the dominant (V) in the key of C and the root (I) in the key of C and the sub-dominant (IV) in the key of G. Alternatively, you could change from C to D to G. The vertical columns show that C is both the root (I) in the key of C and the sub-dominant (IV) in the key of G. Treating it as the latter, and then changing to the D, the dominant (V) in the key of G, introduces the F#, heard for the first time. This chord then resolves to G.

If you want to modulate from C to F, the same principles apply, but you move in the opposite (sub-dominant) direction. You can therefore change straight from C to F, or you can go from C to Bb (the pivot) to F.

Now take an example in which you want to modulate from your original key to one that is further away – say, from C to E. You can still use the primary intervals as your "pivot" chords and you can still follow the links indicated on the modulation chart. You might choose to do it like this: start at C and go horizontally to G; G takes you up one line; go horizontally to D; D takes you up one line; go horizontally to A; A takes you up one line; go horizontally to E (V in the key of A); E takes you up one line; go horizontally to B seventh (V in the key of E); go horizontally and resolve to E. The chord sequence is therefore C to G to D to A to E to B7 to E. You are, in effect, using primary intervals to travel around the circle of fifths in the dominant direction.

Traveling the opposite way uses the same principles. To modulate from C to Ab, for example, you might choose to go from C to F to Bb to Eb to Ab to Db to Ab.

In other words, a modulating sequence may go through several key-centers before arriving at the new key. The keys passed en route are considered transitional.

Modulation using secondary chords

In the chart opposite, the secondary chords are the ones left white. They are based on the II, III, VI and VII intervals. These, too, can act as "pivot" chords when modulating from one key to another.

Take as an example a modulation from C major to G major. The difference between the two keys is that G major contains an F# instead of an F. Of the chords built on the notes of the C major scale, three contain the note F. These are D minor, F major and B diminished. When the F changes to F# in the key of G major, these chords change to D major, F# diminished and B minor. Any of these three chords can be used as the pivot chord in a modulation from C major to G major. This might produce any of the following chord sequences:
- C to D7 to G, or
- C to F#dim to D7 to G, or
- C to Bm to D7 to G.

There is a principle here which applies to any modulation in the dominant direction. The II minor in the original key changes to major, and becomes the V chord in the new key; the IV major is sharpened by a semitone to produce a diminished chord based on the tritone, and becomes the VII chord in the new key; the VII diminished in the original key changes to minor, and becomes the III chord in the new key. The presence of the F# in these altered chords prepares the ear for the modulation to G major.

A similar principle operates for modu-

lations in a sub-dominant direction. Take as an example a modulation from C major to F major. In this case, the difference between the two keys is that F major contains a Bb instead of a B. This Bb also affects three of the chords built on the notes of the C major scale – the three that contain the note B. When the Bb is substituted, the result is that E minor changes to E diminished, G major changes to G minor, and B diminished changes to Bb major. Again, any of these three altered chords can be introduced into a C major chord progression to act as a pivot for a modulation to F major. This might produce any of the following sequences:
- C to Bb to C7 to F, or
- C to E dim to C7 to F, or
- C to Gm to C7 to F.

The "pivot" chord, in each case, precedes the dominant seventh of the new key – which then resolves to the new root or tonic.

Again, there is a principle at work which can be applied to other modulations in the sub-dominant direction. The III minor in the original key changes to diminished, and becomes the VII chord in the new key; the V major in the original key changes to minor, and becomes the II chord in the new key; the VII diminished is flattened by a semitone to produce a major chord, and becomes the IV chord in the new key. If any of these three altered chords are used in the key of C major, the presence of the Bb can suggest a sense of motion which makes for a

smooth, natural modulation to F major.

In either direction, the three altered chords may resolve directly into a progression based in the new key, or they may continue the modulation to a more remote key. In closely related keys, most chords remain unaltered – but their positions and functions in the scale change.

The study of modulation is complex. The explanations given here represent only some of the ways in which it is possible. The rules of modulation are governed not only by primary and secondary interval relationships, but also by the way in which individual notes in the chords move. Diminished (or diminished seventh) chords are particularly useful in this respect, since they can occupy four key-centers at once (see p. 128). Shown below are some other examples of modulations – all of which can be transposed to any key.

Key of C major to the key of F# major:
- C to Am to C#7 to F#, or
- C to Dm to C#7 to F#, or
- C to Bm to C#7 to F#.

Key of C major to E major:
- C to Em to B7 to E, or
- C to Am to B7 to E, or
- C to Dm to B7 to E.

Key of C major to A major:
- C to C#dim to E dim to E to E7 to A, or
- C to C dim to Eb dim to E7 to A, or
- C to D dim to F dim to A, or
- C to B dim to E7 to A.

THE ADVANCED GUITARIST

True improvisation consists of playing spontaneous variations on a musical theme. These variations are created actually during a performance. In this sense, improvisation provides a musician with an unequaled opportunity for personal expression. In contrast, unimprovised music is simply adhering note-for-note to a previously written or rehearsed arrangement.

There are essentially two ways of approaching an improvised solo: either you can start by playing the previously established melody and then go on to embellish it by altering the actual notes and the phrasing, or you can quite literally start from scratch with simply a feel or awareness of what is expected by the other musicians and by the audience.

"The only planning I do is about a minute before I play. I desperately try to think of something that will be effective, but I never sit down and work it out note for note."
Eric Clapton

"Improvisation" is a term with a wide usage: it can apply either to a player who is fluent, imaginative and truly creative, or to one who relies on a battery of standard licks that are rehearsed, memorized and then linked together. To some extent, most guitarists are a bit of both.

Playing a solo to fill a set number of bars somewhere in the middle of a song is not the same as just improvising endlessly until you are finished. In a set-piece, you would be more likely to look to the existing melody for

Jeff Beck

inspiration, and you would usually have some sort of structure to ensure that the right effect is created and that you can get out of the solo at the right place. In an extended "jam", there are few restrictions other than your own continual ability to think of fresh ideas to play. Opinions vary about which kind of solo is most valid.

"I've got no particular desire to play ten-minute solos. Those were never valid anyway in my book – never. It was just a cheap way of building up a tension in the audience ... A solo should do something; it shouldn't just be there as a cosmetic. It should have some aim, take the tune somewhere. I'm not saying I can do it, but I try and take the tune somewhere."
Jeff Beck

There is a rich tradition of guitar soloing which draws on every imaginable musical source. Two of the greatest guitar soloists, Django Reinhardt and Charlie Christian, established beyond doubt that the guitar was capable of almost anything that could be played on other instruments.

Aiming to play like Reinhardt or Christian might seem like an impossible ambition. Nevertheless, some kind of improvisation is well within the scope of every average guitarist. Approaches vary widely, and you can equally well construct a solo by connecting a series of licks or melodic phrases, by working from chord shapes, or by improvising on familiar scale patterns.

"I used to practice scales, but I think mainly in positions. I do runs that go from position to position, basically around chord shapes. I can get around pretty easily from one position to another, and on a good night it sounds pretty hot. I'll take chances. Sometimes I'll trip over myself, but most times I'm lucky."
Albert Lee

Knowing all the rock licks doesn't make you a lead guitarist, and simply being able to play any scale at blinding speed will rarely produce a good solo. The most common mistake made by aspiring guitarists is that of using a solo as a showcase for their technique. This is partly forgivable, since, as a guitarist, hearing a brilliant solo that is beyond your own ability is always impressive, but it will make little sense to the majority of an audience. A good solo, like any good art, stands out because it communicates. The secret is to *listen* – not only to your own playing and to the playing of the other musicians in the band, but to anything and everything.

"Listening to as many guitar solos as possible is the best method for someone in the early stages. But saxophone solos can be helpful. They're interesting because they're all single notes, and therefore can be repeated on the guitar. If you can copy a sax solo you're playing very well, because the average saxophonist can play much better than the average guitarist."
Ritchie Blackmore

Eric Clapton

Single-string lead techniques

One of the special features of the guitar is that – more than most other instruments – it allows you to manipulate the sound after a note has been played. With your left hand holding down a specific note, you have a choice of various special techniques which you can use to modify and control the sound as the note rings, or which you can use to go to the next note you want to play. These techniques can be divided into four broad categories – hammers, slides, bends, and vibrato. The first three are principally ways of changing the pitch without having to fret a new note and strike the string again – as you would normally have to. The fourth, the vibrato, is a technique that adds the guitarist's personal signature to the overall sound.

We have included these single-string techniques here, in the section on improvisation, for two reasons. First, because they are an essential part of the lead guitarist's repertoire. And, second, because each technique has almost as many variations as there are guitarists. They form the basis of innumerable, individual tricks and licks that are an important and characteristic part of the *sound* of improvised guitar.

Hammering techniques

All these techniques involve sounding two or more notes while striking the string only once. They include hammer-ons, hammer-offs or pull-offs, and trills.

Hammer-ons

The simplest way to observe the effect of a *hammer-on* is with an open string. Play an E on the open 1st string and then, without striking the string again with your right hand, bring the 1st finger of your left hand firmly down onto the 1st fret. The note will keep ringing, but the pitch will rise from E to F.

Try the same thing with your 2nd finger on the 2nd fret (F♯), your 3rd finger on the 3rd fret (G), and your 4th finger on the 4th fret (G♯).

The effect of the hammer-on depends on two things: the length of time you leave

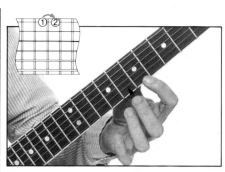

Hammering on from a fretted note

Pull-offs

Also called "hammer-offs", *pull-offs* are hammer-ons in reverse. This time, you start by playing a fretted note and then go down either to an open string or to a lower fret. The pitch of the note therefore drops.

Pull-offs require more care than hammer-ons if both notes are to be heard clearly. You must pull your left-hand finger away sharply and at an angle of about 45 degrees so that your fingertip virtually "plucks" the string and keeps the new note ringing. If you pull off too slowly or at the wrong angle, you will not catch the string and the second note will not sound clearly.

Pulling off from a fretted note to an open string is relatively easy, since you can move your whole hand. Pulling off from one fretted note to a lower fretted note needs more practice. There is less room for movement and more risk of accidentally hitting another string, yet your finger must pull off with enough force to sound the new note at the same volume.

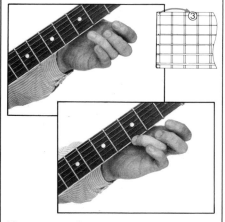

Hammering on from an open string

between playing the open string and hammering on with your left hand, and the speed and force with which you bring down your finger onto the ringing string.

Hammering on from a fretted note is essentially the same – although there is obviously a limit of around four frets, the span of the left hand in any one position. By starting with a note held down by your 1st finger, and then hammering on with each successive finger, it is possible to play four ascending notes with only one stroke of the right hand.

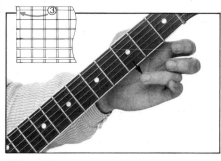

Pulling off from an open string

Pull-offs over four frets allow you to play four descending notes with only one stroke of your right hand. Start with all four fingers of your left hand on one string, with one finger per fret. Play the note held down by your 4th finger, and then pull off each finger in succession until the note held down by your 1st finger is left ringing. Four-fret pull-offs can be combined very effectively with four-fret hammer-ons. A descending pull-off using the 1st, 3rd and 4th fingers is a common lick that features in many blues and rock solos.

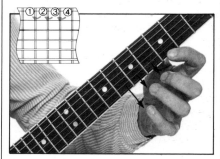

Pulling off with all four fingers

Trills

Alternating rapidly between the same two notes is called a *trill*. It is best done by fretting the lower of the two notes, playing it once, and then hammering quickly and regularly on and off the note above it. The string should keep ringing clearly.

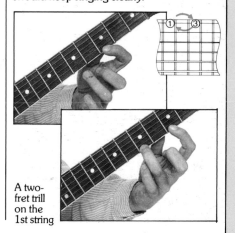

A two-fret trill on the 1st string

Slides

Slides are similar to hammer-ons and pull-offs in that more than one note is sounded but the string is only struck once. They differ in that *every* note between the first and last can be heard.

A slide is easier to perform on a guitar than on most other instruments; indeed, on some, it is impossible. Slides are best done with the 2nd or 3rd finger of your left hand, since this leaves your 1st and 4th fingers free to continue playing in either direction at the end of the slide.

Generally, ascending slides are easier than descending slides. This is because, as you slide your finger *up* the string, the volume tends to increase. No special skill is required other than accuracy; in other words, you should be able to stop exactly where you want to, without falling short of, or overshooting, the final fretted note. When you slide your finger *down* the string, you will find that you need more pressure to ensure that the last note rings properly.

Finger pressure is the key to sliding notes, whether ascending or descending. You must learn to release the grip of your left hand on the guitar neck so that the finger you are actually using is the only point of firm contact. When your finger reaches the note to which you are sliding, the rest of your left hand — especially your thumb — should tighten up on the guitar neck. This acts as a brake against the motion of your hand, and it should happen just before the

last note is sounded so that, from that moment, your left hand is once again in a stable playing position. You can, if you wish, finish the slide with a "vibrato" since this helps to keep the note ringing.

Sliding chords

The guitar is the only instrument on which it is possible to slide an entire chord up and down. Again, it is relatively easy when ascending but quite difficult when descending more than a couple of frets.

The principle of sliding chords is the same as that of single notes, but more control is required to keep all your fingers in the right place and to maintain each individual note of the chord. To start with, try sliding a simple F major shape (played on the top four strings) up and down over the space of one or two frets. Concentrate on keeping the chord under control, and avoid using so much pressure that you hurt your fingers. When you have mastered this, move on to various other full, six-string barre shapes. Ninth chords (see p. 132) are ideal for sliding, and can produce a jazz or funk feel.

The most effective chord slides are over an interval of a fourth (5 frets), a fifth (7 frets) and an octave (12 frets). Sliding fifths — especially with chords played on the lower strings — are a common feature of heavy metal; the sustain and distortion make it easier to ascend and descend than it is if you hear only the pure sound of the strings.

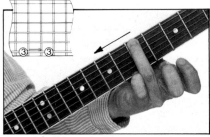

A two-fret slide on the 6th string

Sliding an entire ninth chord shape

String bending

This is one of the most basic of all techniques. It is used to some degree by virtually *every* guitarist playing a melody line or a lead break, and it is one of the most recognizable characteristics of modern guitar styles. James Burton, the pioneering country and rock session guitarist, is often credited as one of the first influential players to use string bending to alter one note in a chord. It was originally employed to imitate the sound of pedal-steel and bottleneck guitarists, and, as such, has its roots in blues and country music. Over the years, the technique has also been one of the major factors in the use of progressively lighter-gauge strings (see p. 163).

On modern electric guitars, the top three strings are the ones most commonly used for string bending — although, for special effects, any string can be bent. Usually, the pitch of the bent note is raised by the equivalent of one fret (semi-tone), two frets (tone) or three frets (tone and a half). It is possible to bend a string so that the pitch of the note rises by four frets (two tones), but this requires very light-gauge strings and considerable finger strength.

The most common problem associated with string bending is keeping the strings in tune. In general, bending a string beyond a tone tends to de-tune it — although this depends on the age of the string, whereabouts on the fingerboard you play the bend, how hard you strike the string with your right hand to begin with, how much finger pressure you apply, and, of course, exactly how far you bend the note. The way to avoid your strings de-tuning is to pay special attention to how they are wound on to the tuning heads, and to "stretch" them thoroughly when they are new (see p. 165).

3rd-finger bends

For beginners, the 3rd finger is the easiest to use for string bending. The leverage between your 3rd finger and your thumb will give you the pressure you need, especially if you hook your thumb over the top of

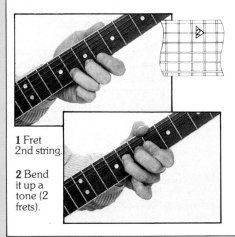

1 Fret
2nd string.

2 Bend
it up a
tone (2
frets).

Vibrato

Putting a slight "waver" into a note is called *vibrato*. It amounts to a rapid and slight variation in pitch. Vibrato increases a note's sustain and can add expression and feeling to the simplest melody or lead line. It is a technique that can be used in any situation, but is particularly effective when combined with string bending: you bend a string up, and apply vibrato when you reach the note you are bending to.

There are various ways of achieving vibrato, and *every* guitarist's method is slightly different. However, there are two basic techniques — horizontal and vertical

movement. The traditional method is the horizontal one. You move the whole of your left hand sideways (parallel to the guitar neck) while holding a note or chord. This is probably easier if you relax or even remove your thumb from the back of the neck. The contact between your finger and the string does not actually change, but the effect of it rolling back and forth produces a subtle variation in pressure that creates the vibrato.

The vertical technique is more often used with single-string bends. It, in fact, involves bending the string very slightly but very quickly up and down.

the neck. You should hold down the string with the middle of your fingertip so that it doesn't slide out underneath or catch on your fingernail.

On most guitars, the 2nd and 3rd strings are the easiest to bend. Although it can be bent in either direction, pushing a string upwards (towards the bass strings) generally gives you better control than pulling it down (towards the treble strings). When you push a string up, your whole hand can get behind it; when you pull a string down, one finger has to do all the work.

Two of the most important things on which to concentrate are pitch and noise. It is vital that, when you bend a string, it goes up to exactly the right pitch. Bending to a note that does not quite reach the desired pitch almost always sounds awful. How far you have to bend a string to get the note you want depends on the string gauge. It is not something you can measure, and only your ear will tell you whether you are getting it right. However, practicing and *listening* will

A semi-tone (1-fret) bend

A whole-tone (2-fret) bend

A 3 semi-tone (3-fret) bend

A 4 semi-tone (4-fret) bend

soon give you the feel of the relationship between pressure and pitch.

Accidentally hitting other strings with the finger that is doing the bending can result in unwanted noise. It can ruin a perfectly good solo. There are several ways to cut out unwanted noise. One is to deaden other nearby strings by muting them with your 1st or 2nd finger, behind the fret on which the string is being bent. Another is to push the nearest strings clear with the protruding tip of the finger that is doing the bending.

Muting unused strings with 1st finger

Hooking 3rd finger beneath unused strings

Bends using your other fingers

Once you can control bends of up to three semi-tones with your 3rd finger, it is time to learn how to use the others. As with all guitar techniques, being able to use all your fingers equally well will increase your versatility.

Your 2nd finger should not prove too difficult once you have adjusted your hand so that your thumb still provides a fulcrum for the necessary leverage. Bends with your 1st finger can present problems: first, the fulcrum of your thumb is not as effective; second, you have no finger free to deaden strings behind the bend; third, you usually need your 1st finger to play other notes either immediately before or after the bend. However, you should be able to use your 1st finger for bends of at least a semi-tone on the 2nd and 3rd strings. Fourth finger bends are obviously more difficult, since the 4th finger is much weaker than the others.

Descending string bends

All string bends can be done equally effectively in reverse. In other words, you start with a string bent up to a higher note, strike it, and then let it "relax" back to its normal pitch. The *effect* is of a single note falling in pitch. As when bending notes up, you can vary the speed at which the pitch drops. Descending string bends sound particularly

good if you put a vibrato on the note you bend down to.

The technique demands a good feel for tension and pitch, since you have to guess just how far to bend the string. You don't hear the note until it has been played. The answer is to practice, first with a one-fret bend, then with two, and then with three, to learn the differences in feel. Try playing a single note and bend it up and down two or three semi-tones while it is sounding. Remember that the tension differs from string to string.

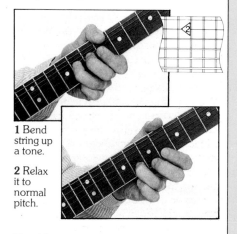

1 Bend string up a tone.

2 Relax it to normal pitch.

Double-string bends

It is possible to bend two strings at once to produce a slightly discordant effect which can nevertheless sound good in the right context. The most common double-string bends are on the 2nd and 3rd strings, bending both strings from the same fret, and on the 1st and 2nd strings, bending the 2nd string from one fret higher than the first. Both are illustrated here.

However, the technique is usually more effective if one string is bent and the other isn't. Common clichés employing this are shown on p. 145.

Bending 2nd and 3rd strings together

Bending 1st and 2nd strings together

Blues and rock guitar licks

Despite the fact that improvisation imposes no limits on what a guitarist can play, there is a strong tradition of popular guitar soloing. Certain licks and runs, established during the period when blues was evolving to rock, have become well-known clichés, and still form the basis of many lead solos. Of course, they are often adapted, changed, re-ordered, and used in a variety of different ways, according to the requirements of the music and the skill of the individual guitarists. But they are worth learning if only to understand how rock guitar solos are put together. Exactly when and where to use them is something that can be understood only by listening to how they

sound in the context of the ideas they connect. You should consider them as springboards to take you somewhere, not as thematic ideas in their own right. Once you have mastered them, you are quite free to throw them out altogether, and play something completely different. Remember that little individuality can be expressed simply by playing clichés.

Forms of improvisation can be found in black American music of around the turn of the century. This music, and the expressive qualities that it contained, formed the basis for the spirit of improvisation in both jazz and rock styles. Traditionally, a blues solo contains a minimum of notes. It is the way the notes are played that produces the effect and creates the feeling of the blues. Rock guitarists have, in general, retained the essence of this approach but have expanded the formula – largely by introducing a feeling of speed and excitement.

The runs and licks in the following pages are just some of the elements that go into the making of a "classic" rock solo. Remember that there are no strict rules. Experiment with the examples given and try to see why and where they might work. Learn the basic fingering patterns and use them to invent your own lead lines.

Basic fingering patterns

By combining the notes that feature most often in a variety of soloing styles, it is possible to come up with a series of fingering patterns that you can use as the basis for your own solos. These are shown below –

one set of patterns for major solos and one for minor solos. We have plotted them here in the key of A, but you should learn to transpose them and to play them in as many different positions and situations as possible.

ible. They can be played in either ascending or descending order, and you can combine them in any way that gives you the right sound. Some notes can be left out, and others can be added.

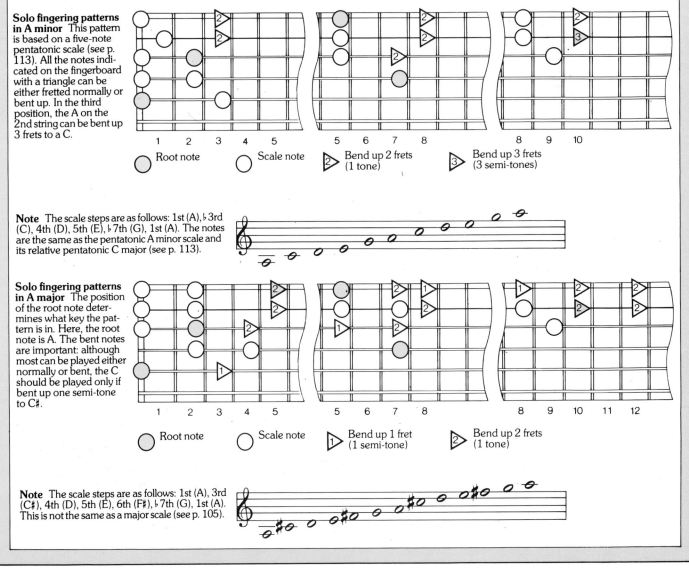

Solo fingering patterns in A minor This pattern is based on a five-note pentatonic scale (see p. 113). All the notes indicated on the fingerboard with a triangle can be either fretted normally or bent up. In the third position, the A on the 2nd string can be bent up 3 frets to a C.

○ Root note   ○ Scale note   ▷2 Bend up 2 frets (1 tone)   ▷3 Bend up 3 frets (3 semi-tones)

Note The scale steps are as follows: 1st (A), ♭3rd (C), 4th (D), 5th (E), ♭7th (G), 1st (A). The notes are the same as the pentatonic A minor scale and its relative pentatonic C major (see p. 113).

Solo fingering patterns in A major The position of the root note determines what key the pattern is in. Here, the root note is A. The bent notes are important: although most can be played either normally or bent, the C should be played only if bent up one semi-tone to C♯.

○ Root note   ○ Scale note   ▷1 Bend up 1 fret (1 semi-tone)   ▷2 Bend up 2 frets (1 tone)

Note The scale steps are as follows: 1st (A), 3rd (C♯), 4th (D), 5th (E), 6th (F♯), ♭7th (G), 1st (A). This is not the same as a major scale (see p. 105).

Basic licks

String bending is an important factor in all rock solos, and it is one of the things that most strongly contributes to the sense of speed and the feeling that the guitarist creates. There are certain recognizable licks built around simple string bends which can serve as a starting point for discovering others of your own.

One of the most common of all licks is played on the top two strings (example 1).

One string is bent up and the other is fretted normally. There are two different places where this lick can be played within the context of one chord.

A variation of this technique can be played using three strings (example 2). Fret the 1st and 2nd strings in the same place, but hold them both down with your 4th finger. Use your 3rd finger to hold down the 3rd string one fret lower. Play all three strings (together or separately) and bend the 3rd string up one tone. The sound this lick produces is similar to a pedal-steel guitar.

Two further licks exploit the major third relationship of the 3rd and 2nd strings (G and B). Examples 3 and 4 both feature bending the 3rd string up by a tone (2 frets) to produce the same note as the one you are holding on the 2nd string. The two strings can be played at once or one after the other.

Example 1
In key of A, hold down 1st string on either 12th fret (note will be 5th/E) or 3rd fret (note will be ♭7th/G). Bent note goes up from 2nd to major 3rd, or from 4th to 5th note of key.

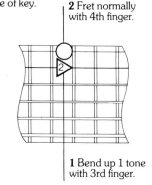

2 Fret normally with 4th finger.

1 Bend up 1 tone with 3rd finger.

Example 2
In key of A, hold down 1st string on 5th fret (note will be 1st/A). Bent note on 3rd string goes up from 2nd to major 3rd in key.

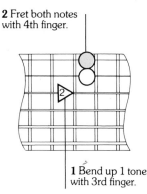

2 Fret both notes with 4th finger.

1 Bend up 1 tone with 3rd finger.

Example 3
In key of A, hold down 2nd string on 5th fret with 1st finger (note will be 5th/E). Bent note goes up from 4th to 5th note in key.

2 Fret normally with 1st finger.

3 Hammer on and off with 4th finger.

1 Bend up 1 tone with 3rd finger to sound in unison with 2nd string.

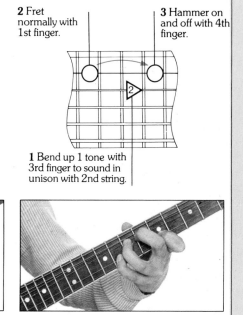

Example 4
In key of A, hold down 1st string on 5th fret (note will be 1st/A). Bent note on 3rd string goes up from 4th to 5th note in key.

2 Fret both notes with 1st finger.

3 Hammer on and off with 4th finger.

1 Bend up 1 tone with 3rd finger to sound in unison with 2nd string.

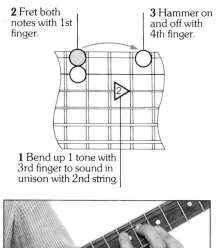

Example 5
In key of A, hold down 2nd string on 5th fret with 3rd finger (note will be 5th/E). Bent note goes up from 2nd to major 3rd in key.

3 Fret normally with 1st finger.

2 Fret normally with 3rd finger.

1 Bend up 1 tone with 2nd finger.

Example 6
In key of A, hold down 1st string on 5th fret (note will be 1st/A). Bent note on 3rd string goes up from 4th to 5th note in key.

3 Fret normally with 1st finger.

2 Fret normally with 3rd finger.

1 Bend up 1 tone with 2nd finger.

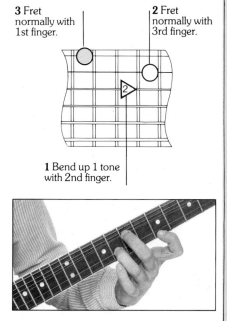

Ascending runs with 3rd-finger slides

To get from one position to another in the middle of a solo requires planning. Ideally, you should know the fingerboard well enough to give yourself plenty of options. So it is worth learning the ascending runs shown below. They are both based on pentatonic scales (see p.113). Written out here in the keys of E major and E minor, they both cover the three octaves of the first twelve frets. By beginning from a different root note, they can, of course, be transposed to other keys. The basic fingering pattern remains the same; it is simply shifted intact up the fingerboard. The major run is often used in rock and country music, and the minor run in rock or jazz solos.

Both runs demonstrate a way of traveling smoothly and quickly up the fingerboard by sliding. In this case, the slide is done with the 3rd finger. Options are given which allow you to vary the fingering slightly when you cross from the 3rd to the 2nd string, or from the 2nd to the 1st string. It is important to remember that a certain series of notes can be played in many different ways. The choice is up to you. Any difficult line can be made relatively easy when you locate the best fingering for it.

Obviously, what goes up must come down. Unfortunately, descending on the guitar is not quite as easy as ascending. For this reason, you may have to work out variations on these fingering patterns in order to run down the fingerboard as quickly as you can go up. Including pull-offs may be one answer (see p.141).

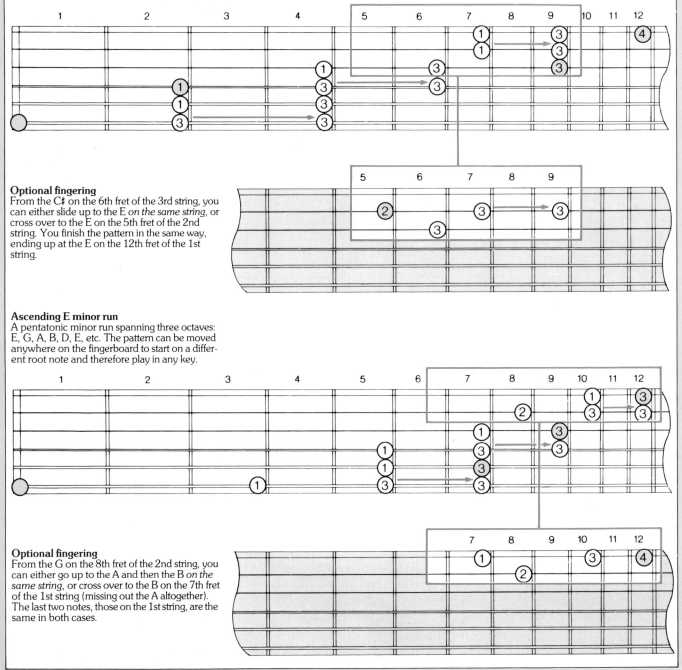

Ascending E major run
A pentatonic major run spanning three octaves: E, F♯, G♯, B, C♯, E, etc. The pattern can be moved anywhere on the fingerboard to start on a different root note and therefore play in any key.

Optional fingering
From the C♯ on the 6th fret of the 3rd string, you can either slide up to the E *on the same string*, or cross over to the E on the 5th fret of the 2nd string. You finish the pattern in the same way, ending up at the E on the 12th fret of the 1st string.

Ascending E minor run
A pentatonic minor run spanning three octaves: E, G, A, B, D, E, etc. The pattern can be moved anywhere on the fingerboard to start on a different root note and therefore play in any key.

Optional fingering
From the G on the 8th fret of the 2nd string, you can either go up to the A and then the B *on the same string*, or cross over to the B on the 7th fret of the 1st string (missing out the A altogether). The last two notes, those on the 1st string, are the same in both cases.

Ascending runs with 4th-finger slides

Because it is so important that you should be able to play any run or scale in various different fingerings, two ascending runs in which the 4th finger not only starts the pattern but also slides to the next position are included here. The obvious advantage of this kind of fingering pattern is that it leaves you well placed to switch immediately to a fixed barre position – when playing a chord,

for example. The patterns are plotted out here in A major and A minor. They are, in fact, simply a diatonic major scale (see p. 104) and a natural minor scale (see p. 106) spread out horizontally up the length of the fingerboard. They can easily be transposed to any other key by moving the whole pattern up or down to a new root note. As with ascending runs where the 3rd finger slides,

you will have to adapt the fingering for a descending run.

It is good practice to be as comfortable with these patterns as with other scale fingerings. They will give you extra flexibility when working out solo lines. In classical guitar studies, all major and minor scales are practiced starting from each finger, in every possible position.

Ascending A major run

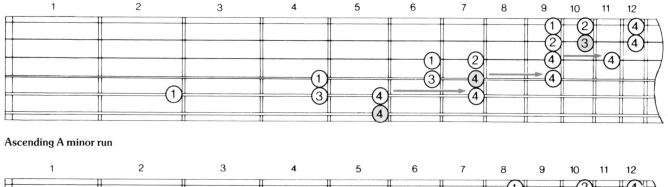

Ascending A minor run

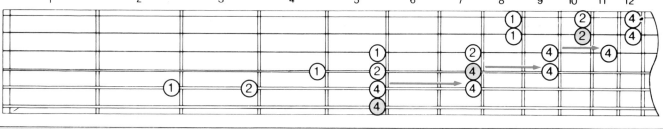

Ascending runs from fixed barre positions

One of the most effective ways of increasing speed and fluency is to learn fast runs from a fixed 1st-finger barre. All the notes other than those held by the barre are either hammered on or pulled off (see p. 141). This means that, when ascending and hammering on, you strike only the notes held by the barre. When descending, you strike only the notes held by your other fingers and pull off to those held by the barre.

Besides speed, one of the chief advantages of a fixed barre is that it reduces fret chatter behind the notes. You can see this for yourself by first playing a selection of notes anywhere between the 7th and 12th frets using normal fingering, and then playing them using a fixed barre. You should notice immediately how much clearer the overall sound is and how you are making more efficient use of your left hand. These are

among the reasons why the fixed barre technique is one of the principal features of classical left-hand posture.

The illustrations below show four fixed runs – in major and minor keys, and with the root note on the 6th and 5th strings. They are all movable forms, and, by adapting the fingering patterns to different chord inversions, they can be shifted up and down the fingerboard to play in any key you wish.

Major run with root note on 6th string
The pattern contains the dominant (or minor) seventh instead of the major seventh. In the key of C, this is B♭ instead of B.

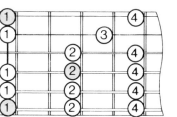

Major run with root note on 5th string
As above, this pattern contains the flattened 7th note of the major scale.

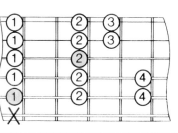

Minor run with root note on 6th string
The pattern contains a raised 6th note. In the key of A, this is F♯ instead of F.

Minor run with root note on 5th string
This pattern skips the 6th note of the scale altogether. In A natural minor, this would be F.

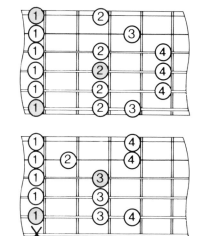

Chord substitution

The term *chord substitution* is something of a misnomer that throws many guitarists off the path to understanding what is, in fact, a relatively easy principle. Essentially, chord substitution is no more than the introduction of *variations* on an existing chord sequence. Once you understand the principles by which certain chords can be substituted for others, you will see that chord substitution offers a means of expression similar to that of improvisation. Whereas a guitarist improvising a solo is developing new melodic ideas, a rhythm guitarist substituting chords is experimenting with new harmonic ideas.

We have already seen that any chord progression consists of a succession of tonic or root notes (see p. 125). It is the notes stacked vertically above these that create the chords and "harmonize" the succession of root notes. Unless you intend to rearrange the original progression completely, these root notes always remain the same in their relation to time and melody. It is the other notes, the ones that create the chord harmony, which you alter in the process of chord substitution.

Chord substitution can work in two different ways: you can either choose to *change* some of the existing chords, or you can choose to *add* extra chords to the progression with which you start.

Changing existing chords

In a progression consisting of fairly simple chords, it is possible to extend or alter the chords you are given to produce a different type of harmony for what is essentially the same basic idea. A simple A minor chord, for example, could well become an A minor seventh, an A minor added ninth, a G suspended fourth, a C sixth, or a C major seventh. In the following pages, we will explain how this works, but, in each case, the substitution does not change the basic function of the A minor chord. You are simply choosing a different series of notes to create a new harmony for the root note of A. In other words, you are going beyond thinking of the chord just as an A minor triad.

Adding extra chords

Employing the same principle of introducing extended or altered chords that represent variations on the basic harmony, you can use the space or time between existing chord changes to play new chords chosen to complement the original progression. Taken to its logical extreme – as it is in some jazz styles – this can produce a progression in which you change chord on *every* beat of the bar.

The principles of substitution

Both the approaches to substitution outlined above – changing existing chords or introducing new ones to connect them – rely on your ability to create additional harmony. This works in two ways – vertically and horizontally. The vertical effect is determined by what notes you add on top of the root note. The horizontal effect is determined by when you play them.

When one chord changes to another, the two different root notes dominate the sound. The root note is always the strongest element in the chord, and the effect of the chord change depends on the interval between the two root notes. However, the other notes in each chord – called the "upper voices" – also play an important part. Of these, the highest note is the most prominent. In any chord progression, the changing top note of each chord can be heard as a melodic line. Of couse, when two chords share the same root note (as in a change from C major to C seventh, or C minor sixth to C minor seventh), then any change in the upper voices is more noticeable. In fact, harmonic variety can be achieved by changing just one note.

It is important both that you *understand* how chords are constructed and that you can *hear* how a chord changes when one or more of its constituent notes are altered. This lies at the heart of all chord substitution.

There are two further requirements. First, an understanding of how chords are generally divided into three families: major, minor and dominant. Chords are categorized according to whether the 3rd is major or minor (see p. 121) and whether the 7th is major or minor (see p. 127). The second requirement is a thorough grasp of "synonyms" – chords with the same notes but different names (see p. 137).

The only rules that exist in chord substitution are those of good taste, and these can only be determined by your own ear. The field is therefore open to experiment. However, there are some pointers, based on the principles of resolution, that should give you an indication of what is likely to work and what is not. It is these that we deal with in the following pages.

Substituting a dominant seventh chord

The simplest example of substitution occurs when you play a dominant seventh chord instead of a major chord – for example, a C seventh instead of a C major. However, this is not something that can be done randomly. There are some situations where it is appropriate, and others where it isn't. What is important is the context: you must learn to recognize what role the chord has (whether it is the I, IV, V or whatever) and to consider what chord it is going to change to.

Take a simple example of a chord change from C major to F major. There are two bars, with four beats in each. For the first bar you play C, and for the second bar you play F. For the substitution, you could play C seventh instead of C on the third and fourth beats of the first bar. The chord progression therefore becomes C major to C seventh to F major.

If you are in the key of F, the C is the dominant (V) chord and the F is the tonic (I)

chord. When C resolves to F, a "perfect cadence" is observed (see p. 124). The root note descends by a fifth. Adding the extra note to the C major creates the C dominant seventh and enhances the sense of resolution.

If you are in the key of C, on the other hand, the C is the tonic (I) chord and the F is the sub-dominant (IV) chord. The root note ascends by a fourth. In this case, C seventh is actually a "tonic seventh" (built on the 1st, not the 5th, note of the scale), but it is still a dominant seventh *type* chord, and it resolves to F in the same way.

In each case, whether the root note goes up or down, substituting the dominant seventh is a way of *extending* the original chord. The dominant seventh acts as a "passing chord". There is a general rule here: *a dominant seventh can be formed on any chord when the root note of the next chord is a fourth higher or a fifth lower.*

Original progression

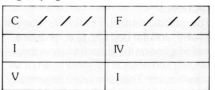

Substitution

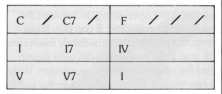

Principle Because F is a fourth above C or a fifth below it, the dominant seventh can be substituted in the first bar; in other words, C seventh can be played instead of C major to connect the two chords. This principle applies whether the progression shown above is in the key of C or the key of F.

Substituting minor seventh and dominant eleventh chords

A seventh chord acting as the dominant (V) chord in a progression presents you with the possibility of two common substitutions – a minor seventh or a dominant eleventh. In both cases, the dominant seventh is not completely replaced by the new chord; it is preceded by it. In other words, you are introducing an extra chord.

Take a simple example in the key of C – a chord progression from C major to F major to G seventh to C major. G seventh is the chord to focus on. It is a dominant seventh type and it is acting as the dominant (V) chord in the key.

Minor seventh substitutions

To substitute a minor seventh, you would replace the first and second beats on G seventh with two beats of D minor seventh. In other words, you substitute a minor

seventh built on the note one fifth higher than that of the dominant seventh chord. This minor seventh is, in fact, the supertonic (II) chord of whatever key you are playing in. The rule is therefore as follows: *any dominant seventh chord can be preceded by a minor seventh chord built on a root note a fifth higher.*

Dominant eleventh substitutions

Substituting a dominant eleventh works in the same way but is, if anything, even easier since the root note does not change. Using the same chord progression as an example, you would replace the first and second beats on G seventh with two beats of G eleventh. The rule is therefore: *any dominant seventh chord can be preceded by a dominant eleventh chord built on the same root.*

The interesting thing about the dominant eleventh is that it can be considered as a "polychord". If you turn to p. 136, you will see that B♭/C is basically C eleventh. It therefore follows that you can think of G eleventh as the polychord F/G – that is, F major played over a G bass note. This makes what is happening in the substitution more obvious: you are changing from F major to F major with a G in the bass, and then to G seventh.

It is possible to use both minor seventh and dominant eleventh substitutions in the same progression. Our third example illustrates this. The first two beats on the G seventh are replaced by two beats on G eleventh (or F/G), and the last two beats of F major are replaced by D minor seventh. It is worth noting that D minor seventh is actually the relative minor of F.

Original progression

C / / /	F / / /	G7 / / /	C / / /
I	IV	V7	I

Substitution

C / / /	F / / /	Dm7 / G7 /	C / / /
I	IV	IIm7 V7	I

Substituting a minor seventh

Principle The first two beats of G seventh (which is the dominant chord) are replaced by D minor seventh – the minor seventh chord built on the note a fifth higher than the root note of the original chord.

Original progression

C / / /	F / / /	G7 / / /	C / / /
I	IV	V7	I

Substitution

C / / /	F / / /	G11 / G7 /	C / / /
I	IV	V11 V7	I

Substituting a dominant eleventh

Principle This time, the first two beats of G seventh are replaced by G eleventh – the dominant eleventh chord built on the same root note. G eleventh is, in fact, the same as the polychord F/G (see p. 136).

Original progression

C / / /	F / / /	G7 / / /	C / / /
I	IV	V7	I

Substitution

C / C7 /	F / Dm7 /	G11 / G7 /	C / / /
I I7	IV IIm7	V11 V7	I

Substituting a dominant seventh, a minor seventh and a dominant eleventh

Principle This example illustrates all the three principles we have looked at so far – substituting dominant sevenths, minor sevenths and dominant elevenths. The newly introduced chords are C seventh, D minor seventh and G eleventh. The chord diagrams below illustrate one way in which the complete progression might be played.

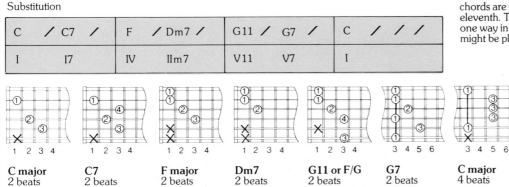

| C major 2 beats | C7 2 beats | F major 2 beats | Dm7 2 beats | G11 or F/G 2 beats | G7 2 beats | C major 4 beats |

Extending and altering dominant chords

In theory, any simple chord can be "extended" to a ninth, eleventh or thirteenth form (see pp. 132-5). In practice however, the chords most frequently involved in substitutions come from the dominant family. All dominant chords contain a minor third *and* a minor or flattened seventh. There is scope for "altering" the remaining notes: the 5th can be sharpened to produce a seventh augmented fifth chord or flattened to produce a seventh diminished fifth (see p. 127); and the 9th can be sharpened to produce a seventh augmented ninth or flattened to produce a seventh flat nine (see p. 133). Essentially,

What to do when a dominant chord is followed by one a fourth higher

Take as an example a bar of C followed by a bar of F. Here, C is about to change to a chord a fourth higher. You might decide to treat this first by substituting C ninth for the C and F seventh for the F. You could then introduce an altered chord – a C seventh augmented ninth or a C seventh flat nine – for the last two beats of the C ninth bar. In other words, you are altering the ninth of a dominant chord. Alternatively, you could start by substituting C seventh for the C and F major seventh for F. You could then alter

Original progression

| C | / | / | / | F | / | / | / |

Substitution

| C9 | / | C7+9 | / | F7 | / | / | / |

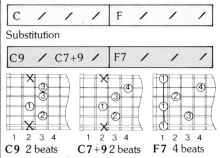

C9 2 beats   C7+9 2 beats   F7 4 beats

Principle C seventh augmented ninth can be substituted for the last two beats of the dominant chord C ninth, since it is followed by a chord a fourth higher.

Original progression

| C | / | / | / | F | / | / | / |

Substitution

| C9 | / | C7–9 | / | F7 | / | / | / |

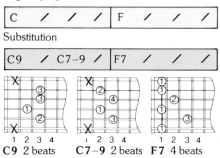

C9 2 beats   C7–9 2 beats   F7 4 beats

Principle C seventh flat nine can be substituted for the last two beats of the dominant chord C ninth, since it is followed by a chord a fourth higher.

Original progression

| C | / | / | / | F | / | / | / |

Substitution

| C7 | / | C7+5 | / | FΔ7 | / | / | / |

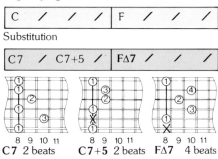

C7 2 beats   C7+5 2 beats   FΔ7 4 beats

Principle C seventh augmented fifth can be substituted for the last two beats of the dominant chord C seventh, since it is followed by a chord a fourth higher.

What to do when a dominant chord is followed by one a semi-tone lower

This is the second situation where substituting altered dominant chords is possible. Take as an example a bar of C followed by a bar of B (in the key of F major). In this case, C is about to change to a chord one semi-tone lower. The same rules apply to this situation as they do to those above – where the dominant chord is followed by one a fourth higher. The dominant chord can be substituted for an extended one with various altered notes. In the examples below, the altered chord completely replaces the

Original progression

| C | / | / | / | B | / | / | / |

Substitution

| C7+9 | / | / | / | B7 | / | / | / |

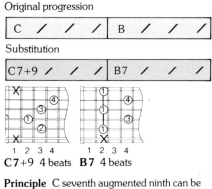

C7+9 4 beats   B7 4 beats

Principle C seventh augmented ninth can be substituted in the first bar, since it is followed by a chord a semi-tone lower.

Original progression

| C | / | / | / | B | / | / | / |

Substitution

| C7–9 | / | / | / | B9 | / | / | / |

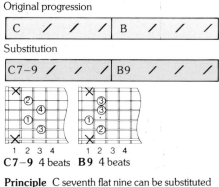

C7–9 4 beats   B9 4 beats

Principle C seventh flat nine can be substituted in the first bar, since it is followed by a chord a semi-tone lower.

Original progression

| C | / | / | / | B | / | / | / |

Substitution

| C7+5 | / | / | / | B6 | / | / | / |

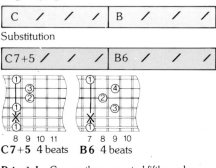

C7+5 4 beats   B6 4 beats

Principle C seventh augmented fifth can be substituted in the first bar, since it is followed by a chord a semi-tone lower.

Substituting minor "passing chords"

We have already seen on p. 151 how minor seventh chords can be used as substitutes in certain circumstances – in particular, how the supertonic (II) minor chord can be used to prepare a dominant (V) chord. Minor chords built on the mediant (III) note and on the sub-mediant (VI) note of the scale can also be introduced into simple chord sequences to add variety and sometimes to produce scale-like progressions. Take a simple example of a change from C to F. As a I to IV progression, it can be treated by substituting a D minor (the II chord) in the second half of the bar of C and an E minor (the III chord) in the first half of the bar of F. The two minor chords act as "passing chords" and serve to connect the two original chords. The sequence can be varied still further by substituting an A minor chord. This is the VI chord, the relative minor of C. Minor chords can be altered in substitutions. The most common alteration is to play the chord with a diminished fifth. For example, in a II–V–I progression such as D minor to G seventh to C major, the last two beats of D minor could be played as a D minor diminished fifth (Dm–5) or as a D half-diminished (Dm7–5).

Original progression

| C | / | / | / | F | / | / | / |
| I | | | | IV | | | |

there are two situations where these chords can be substituted. First, when a dominant chord is followed by one that is a fourth higher, and, second, when it is followed by one that is a semi-tone lower.

the C seventh. In both cases, the rule is as follows: *a chord with an altered fifth or ninth can be substituted for a dominant chord if the next chord is a fourth higher.*

Original progression

C	/	/	/	F	/	/	/

Substitution

C7	/	C7–5	/	F9	/	/	/

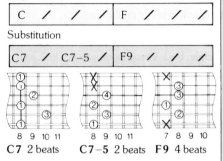

C7 2 beats   **C7–5** 2 beats   **F9** 4 beats

Principle C seventh diminished fifth can be substituted for the last two beats of the dominant chord C seventh, since it is followed by a chord a fourth higher.

original. The rule is as follows: *a chord with an altered fifth or ninth can be substituted for a dominant chord if the next chord is a semi-tone lower.*

Original progression

C	/	/	/	B	/	/	/

Substitution

C7–5	/	/	/	B7	/	/	/

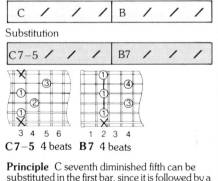

C7–5 4 beats   **B7** 4 beats

Principle C seventh diminished fifth can be substituted in the first bar, since it is followed by a chord a semi-tone lower.

Inserting new dominant chords

If you come across either of the situations described opposite – that is, a dominant chord followed by one either a fourth above or a semi-tone below – you have another option besides that of simply using an extended or altered version of the original chord. You can substitute in its place a dominant chord built on a root note that is a flattened fifth higher. As before, this new chord can be of any kind – extended or altered – as long as it comes from the dominant family, not from the majors or minors. Usually, it is a "partial" substitution. It does not replace the first chord completely but is played on the last two beats of the bar. In other words, it is introduced between the two original chords and acts as a link between them.

The rule is as follows: *when a dominant chord is followed by one either a fourth above or a semi-tone below, a new dominant chord built on a root note a flattened fifth above the first can be substituted.* The chord progressions shown here illustrate two examples of each situation. They work because, in the first case, C is a fourth above G (the chord it follows) and, in the second case, B♭ is a semi-tone below G.

Introducing a new dominant chord when the root note goes up by a fourth

Original progression

G	/	/	/	C	/	/	/

Substitution/example 1

G7	/	C♯9	/	C7+9	/	/	/

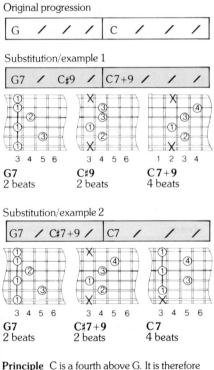

G7 2 beats   **C♯9** 2 beats   **C7+9** 4 beats

Substitution/example 2

G7	/	C♯7+9	/	C7	/	/	/

G7 2 beats   **C♯7+9** 2 beats   **C7** 4 beats

Principle C is a fourth above G. It is therefore possible to build a new dominant chord on C♯ – the root note a flattened fifth above G – and substitute it for the last two beats in the bar of G. The new chord can be extended and/or altered – to C♯ ninth or C♯ seventh augmented ninth, for example, as here – as long as it is dominant.

Introducing a new dominant chord when the root note goes down by a semi-tone

Original progression

G	/	/	/	G♭	/	/	/

Substitution/example 1

G7	/	D♭7	/	G♭7	/	/	/

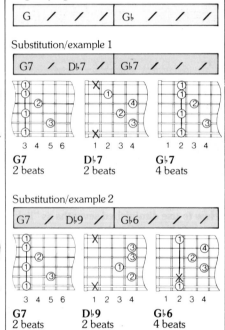

G7 2 beats   **D♭7** 2 beats   **G♭7** 4 beats

Substitution/example 2

G7	/	D♭9	/	G♭6	/	/	/

G7 2 beats   **D♭9** 2 beats   **G♭6** 4 beats

Principle G♭ is a semi-tone below G. It is therefore possible to build a new dominant chord on D♭ – the root note a flattened fifth above G – and substitute it for the last two beats of the bar of G. The new chord can be simply a dominant D♭7 or extended to a D♭9, for example, as long as it remains dominant.

Three examples of how to substitute minor chords

Principle The supertonic (II) minor chord is substituted for the last two beats of C, and the mediant (III) minor for the first two beats of F.

Substitution/example 1

C	/	Dm	/	Em	/	F	/
1		IIm		IIIm		IV	

Principle The relative minor (VI) chord is substituted for the last two beats of C, and the supertonic (II) minor chord for the first two beats of F.

Substitution/example 2

C	/	Am	/	Dm	/	F	/
I		VIm		IIm		IV	

Principle The relative minor (VI) chord is again substituted in the first bar. This time, however, the mediant (III) minor chord replaces the first two beats of F.

Substitution/example 3

C	/	Am	/	Em	/	F	/
I		VIm		IIIm		IV	

Power chords and fret tapping

The "Power Chord" has been used by almost all of the great blues and rock guitarists in one form or another. Players with such diverse styles as John Lee Hooker, Chuck Berry, Pete Townshend, Jimmy Page, Jimi Hendrix, Eddie Van Halen, and Steve Vai have all used power chords to great effect. Understanding the elementary theory of the power chord unlocks many of the mysteries of rock music and its related forms. A power chord is also sometimes known as a "5 chord" or "5th", for example, "E5" or "E 5th".

The elementary building block for the power chord is the pairing of the root note and its perfect fifth. Since musical convention teaches that the foundation for all harmony is the major or minor triad, some theorists regard the 5th chord as being in some way invalid, simply because it does not contain a major or minor 3rd. However, the fact remains that this family of chords has become an essential part of rock and other related playing styles and is widely used by both guitarists and keyboard players.

Fret tapping is a lead guitar technique that is often used in conjunction with power chords. It combines standard left hand hammer-ons and pull-offs with right hand versions of the same technique to create phrases that can be repeated on their own, integrated into longer phrases and solos, or used to play arpeggiated chords.

Fret tapping was first popularized in the late seventies by Eddie Van Halen who has continued using it to stunning effect. Among the best-known examples of the technique are his solos on "Eruption", and Michael Jackson's "Beat It". It was quickly adopted by many guitarists and has now become a standard playing technique.

One of the more advanced forms of fret tapping can be heard in the playing of jazz guitarist Stanley Jordan. His solo performances combine tapping the melody with his right hand, whilst hammering-on chords and bass lines with his left hand.

Power Chords

By examining the first position standard E chord (right) we can see what separates a 5th chord from others. The first note of the chord is the root note E. The second note of the chord is B which is a perfect fifth above the E. Play the two together and we have an E5 or E 5th chord. Even this basic combination of two notes has a powerful sound which when played on an electric guitar is ideally suited to blues, rock and heavy metal.

If we now play all three bottom strings of the basic E chord we have the next development of the power chord which consists of the notes E and B plus an E one octave higher than the root. Whereas basic power chords consist of a root note with the perfect fifth note above it, more extensive power chords simply repeat the same two notes further up the scale.

As we have already seen on page 121, a major triad consists of the root note of a scale, the major or minor 3rd and then the 5th. Power chords do not include the 3rd or the 10th (the same note as a 3rd played an octave higher). Because of the absence of the 3rd and the 10th, 5th chords can be played with both major and minor sounding melody lines and chords. They also work with other scales that do not include the 3rd or 10th notes.

Returning to the basic E major chord, if we play the fourth string the note fretted at the first fret is G sharp and immediately gives the chord a major sound. If the string is played open the note is G, creating an E minor chord.

As the E5 chord chart on the right shows, fretting the string at the fourth fret creates a second B note. The full six string E5 chord, therefore, consists of E, B, E, B, B, E. This is a six note power chord. The fact that there are two B notes of identical pitch being played next to each other is quite acceptable and gives the six string power chord its characteristic depth.

Single note runs or arpeggios which do not include the 3rd or 10th notes and fret tapping are techniques frequently used with power chords.

Other keys

The first position E, G, A, C and D power chords shown on the right all consist of root and perfect fifth notes repeated in varying orders. They are shown next to the first position major chords from which they are derived. The notes to be played are indicated on the chord chart in green. The numbers in the circle show which fingers should be used. An "X" indicates that the string should be muted. Where strings are muted, the nearest finger leans over slightly to stop the string from sounding.

Variations

Playing just 5th chords can sometimes sound repetitive. Additional tone colours can add interest and variation without detracting from the basic tonality or sound. For example, the third type of chord shown is the 5th chord with the 2nd interval added. Chords that do not incorporate the major or minor 3rd notes of the scale are often also used in conjunction with power chords. Because of the simplicity of the two and three-note structure of power chords, many players have used them combined with melody figures. Muting strings with the left and right hands to prevent unwanted notes from sounding is of prime importance when power chords are being used.

Just listen to players like Jimi Hendrix, Steve Vai and Eddie Van Halen. Underestimate the effectiveness of the simple power chord at your peril.

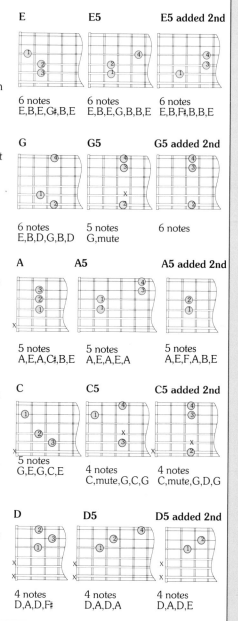

E	E5	E5 added 2nd
6 notes E,B,E,G♯,B,E	6 notes E,B,E,G,B,B,E	6 notes E,B,F♯,B,B,E

G	G5	G5 added 2nd
6 notes E,B,D,G,B,D	5 notes G,mute	6 notes

A	A5	A5 added 2nd
5 notes A,E,A,C♯,B,E	5 notes A,E,A,E,A	5 notes A,E,F,A,B,E

C	C5	C5 added 2nd
5 notes G,E,G,C,E	4 notes C,mute,G,C,G	4 notes C,mute,G,D,G

D	D5	D5 added 2nd
4 notes D,A,D,F♯	4 notes D,A,D,A	4 notes D,A,D,E

Movable power chords

Power chords are popular not only because of their effectiveness but because many of the two and three note forms are so easy to play. The same rules that apply to the E chords described on page 156 apply to the movable chords based on the barre F and B flat chords shown here. Playing the bottom two or three notes of each of these chords gives the 5th chords. As these movable barre chords can be played all the way up the fretboard, a large number of power chords can be devised for virtually all keys. Heavy metal would not exist without this family of chords. The fingerings are given as a guide and can, if necessary, be adjusted to suit the sequence being played.

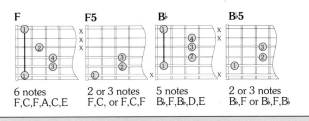

F
6 notes
F,C,F,A,C,E

F5
2 or 3 notes
F,C, or F,C,F

B♭
5 notes
B♭,F,B♭,D,E

B♭5
2 or 3 notes
B♭,F or B♭,F,B♭

Fret tapping technique

The basic technique is relatively easy to develop. Fret tapping is based on the hammering-on and pulling-off of notes – both techniques that have been at the heart of rock guitar playing for many years. Once the basics have been mastered, fret tapping equips a guitarist to play impressively fast and exciting solos with relative ease.

The left-hand hammer-on and pull-off techniques are both as described in detail on page 140. To hammer-on a note, the impact of the left hand finger striking or "hammering" the string and pushing it down into contact with the fret causes the note to sound. To execute a pull-off, instead of lifting the finger directly off the string, the finger is moved slightly across the string in a downwards direction just before being lifted off the string.

Right hand technique

The right hand hammer-on also causes a note to sound in exactly the same way as a left hand hammer-on. Whilst there are a number of different approaches, many guitarists using this technique prefer to rest their right hand thumb on the edge of the fretboard to provide a steady anchor for the hand. As the right hand moves up and down the fretboard to reach different frets, the thumb simply slides along the edge of the fretboard.

The right hand pull-off technique differs from the left hand version only in that the slight movement of the finger across the string as it is lifted off is in an upwards rather than a downwards direction.

The type of single string fret tapping shown in the exercise below involves three notes. The bottom note is usually either played on an open string or – as in the exercise – is a fretted note for which a left hand finger stays in position on the string throughout the entire phrase.

The exercise

Basic positioning
Place the first finger of the left hand on the top E string at the 7th fret with the third finger poised an inch or so above the same string at the 9th fret ready to play. Rest the right hand thumb on the edge of the fretboard with the first finger poised an inch or so above the string ready to hammer-on just below the 12th fret.

The hammer-on
Hammer-on the first note at the twelfth fret with the right hand index finger. The note played is E. Just before you execute the pull-off – by moving the finger slightly sideways across the string before actually lifting it quickly off the string – place the third finger on the string at the 9th fret so that the note – a C sharp – sounds.

The pull-off
Execute a left hand pull-off with the third finger of the left hand: the B note, being fretted at the 7th fret, will sound. Once you have begun to master the technique practise playing the phrase slowly and evenly, repeating it as a continuous flow of notes. You will soon find the speed will come quite naturally.

Other approaches

It is also possible to use the fret tapping technique with chords. Two notes will be played on each string.

First hold down any chord, preferably near the nut, when first trying this technique. The basic idea is to play a right hand hammer-on and pull-off with the right hand finger on each string in turn. By executing the hammer-on and pull-off twelve frets above the fret for each note of the chord, you will be playing the same notes as are present in the chord, plus the same notes one octave higher. If you are playing a G chord and fingering the first string at the third fret and hammering-on and pulling-off at the 15th fret, the hammer-on will sound the higher G note and the pull-off will sound the G one octave lower.

Right hand tapping opens whole new areas for the guitarist in that it increases the melodic possibilities of the instrument. Whereas many have mainly used the technique to be visually impressive, it can be used to play melodic runs and arpeggios that are not otherwise possible on the guitar. A good approach, following the examples of players like Steve Vai and Joe Satriani, is to look for new musical ideas that can be played incorporating right hand tapping with other techniques rather than playing a tapped riff and then reverting to "normal" playing. Eddie Van Halen has further developed his own playing technique by fret tapping with his right hand both above *and* below the notes being played with his left hand.

Alternative tunings

The method we now use to tune the guitar – E, A, D, G, B, E from 6th string to 1st – is a convention that has developed over the centuries. Custom and practice have shown that it provides an acceptable range, a convenient placing of the intervals, and a manageable choice of basic chord fingerings. Of course, it is not the only system. There are countless other ways in which the strings can be tuned.

Alternative tunings generally fall into one of two categories. They are either "open" tunings, which means that the strings are tuned to sound a chord when they are all played open or unfretted, or they are adaptations of the standard tuning and are designed to feature one or more open strings as part of the piece for which they are used. Alternative tunings occur widely in folk, blues and ragtime styles, and, particularly, in bottle-neck or slide playing (see p. 160).

The tunings illustrated here are presented as a selection of those used most often. You should remember that they are only suggestions. The field is wide open to experiment and to the discovery of new sounds.

Ry Cooder, renowned for his slide playing, much of which features alternative tunings

Open tunings

When the guitar is re-tuned so that you can play a chord on the open strings, this is known as an *open tuning*. The most common are open G (also known as "slack key", "Spanish" or "Hawaiian"), open D, open E and open C. These tunings give open-string chords of G major, D major, E major and C major respectively. One of the chief advantages of an open tuning is that other chords can be played simply by using a 1st-finger barre across all six strings, placed at any fret. In open G, for example, a 1st-finger barre on the 2nd fret will give the chord A major. You will, of course, have to discover fingerings for other chords yourself. A few examples in open G and open D are given below.

When choosing an open tuning, it is always better to go for one in which the altered strings are tuned *down*. Tuning strings *up* can break them.

Open G tuning ("slack key")					
6th	5th	4th	3rd	2nd	1st
D	G	D	G	B	D

How to tune
6th string *down* to D.
5th string *down* to G.
4th string as normal.
3rd string as normal.
2nd string as normal.
1st string *down* to D.

Open D tuning					
6th	5th	4th	3rd	2nd	1st
D	A	D	F♯	A	D

How to tune
6th string *down* to D.
5th string as normal.
4th string as normal.
3rd string *down* to F♯.
2nd string *down* to A.
1st string *down* to D.

Three chord shapes in open G tuning

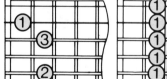

C major   D seventh   A major

Three chord shapes in open D tuning

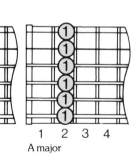

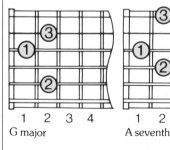
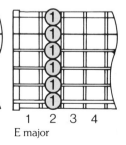

G major   A seventh   E major

Open E tuning					
6th	5th	4th	3rd	2nd	1st
E	B	E	G♯	B	E

How to tune
6th string as normal.
5th string *up* to B.
4th string *up* to E.
3rd string *up* to G♯.
2nd string as normal.
1st string as normal.

Open C tuning					
6th	5th	4th	3rd	2nd	1st
C	G	C	G	C	E

How to tune
6th string *down* to C.
5th string *down* to G.
4th string *down* to C.
3rd string as normal.
2nd string *up* to C.
1st string as normal.

Modal tunings

So-called *modal tunings* are, in a sense, "open" tunings. When all six strings are played open, the sound is of a suspended fourth chord (see p. 131). This gives a very distinctive feel and is ideal for fingerstyles. The example below shows a D modal tuning. It differs from open D in that the 3rd string remains on G instead of being tuned down to F♯. This means that the strings give the notes D (the 1st note in the scale of D major), G (the 4th note) and A (the 5th note). Together, the 1st, 4th and 5th produce a suspended fourth chord.

D modal tuning					
6th	5th	4th	3rd	2nd	1st
D	A	D	G	A	D

How to tune
6th string *down* to D. 5th string as normal. 4th string as normal. 3rd string as normal. 2nd string *down* to A. 1st string *down* to D. All modal tunings contain the 1st, 4th and 5th notes of the major scale in the key that gives them their name. In D modal, these notes are D (1st), G (4th) and A (5th).

Dropped tunings

A *dropped tuning* is the simplest and probably the most frequently used of all alternative tunings. Essentially, it involves lowering the pitch of just one or two of the strings. The most useful of all is dropped D: it is exactly the same as the standard E, A, D, G, B, E tuning except that the 6th string is lowered by a tone to D. It therefore sounds the same as the open 4th string but an octave lower in pitch. Dropped D tuning is ideal when playing in the key of D, since it means that the open 6th string can be used to play the bass. Alternating between the D on the 6th string and the D on the 4th string can produce an attractive rhythmic "drone" which underpins a melody played on the top strings. It is also useful when playing in the key of A, since the open 5th string acts as the bass for the tonic chord of A and the open 6th string for the sub-dominant chord of D. Dropped tunings are often used in blues for these reasons.

There is a variation on dropped D tuning that tunes the 2nd string down from B to A. It therefore sounds the same as the A on the open 5th string but an octave lower.

Dropped D tuning					
6th	5th	4th	3rd	2nd	1st
D	A	D	G	B	E

How to tune
6th string *down* to D. 5th string as normal. 4th string as normal. 3rd string as normal. 2nd string as normal. 1st string as normal. Tune either by lowering the 6th string so that it is an octave below the open 4th string or by lowering it so that the 7th fret on the 6th string gives the same note as the open 5th string.

Dropped D variation					
6th	5th	4th	3rd	2nd	1st
D	A	D	G	A	E

How to tune
6th string *down* to D. 5th string as normal. 4th string as normal. 3rd string as normal. 2nd string *down* to A. 1st string as normal. The variation on standard dropped D tuning lies in the fact that the 2nd string is tuned down from B to A.

Crossnote tunings

Open tunings in which the open-string chord is minor instead of major are called *crossnote tunings*. They differ from the ordinary open tunings in that one string is lowered by a semi-tone. This gives the minor third interval that characterizes minor chords. Thus, in crossnote D the 3rd string is tuned down to F instead of F♯, and in crossnote E the 3rd string remains at G instead of being tuned up to G♯. In both cases, fretting the 3rd string at the 1st fret will raise the open chord from a minor to a major.

Crossnote D tuning (open D minor)					
6th	5th	4th	3rd	2nd	1st
D	A	D	F	A	D

How to tune
6th string *down* to D. 5th string as normal. 4th string as normal. 3rd string *down* to F. 2nd string *down* to A. 1st string *down* to D.

Crossnote E tuning (open E minor)					
6th	5th	4th	3rd	2nd	1st
E	B	E	G	B	E

How to tune
6th string as normal. 5th string *up* to B. 4th string *up* to E. 3rd string as normal. 2nd string as normal. 1st string as normal.

Miscellaneous tunings

Example 1 is sometimes called "sawmill" tuning. It is in fact a G modal tuning – and differs from open G in that the 2nd string is tuned up to C. Examples 2 and 3 are variations on other D tunings. Example 4 is slightly more unusual. It involves tuning the 2nd string down from B to A and the 3rd string down three semi-tones from G to E. Example 5 is the same as 4 but with the 6th string dropped to D.

Example 1 ("sawmill")					
6th	5th	4th	3rd	2nd	1st
D	G	D	G	C	D

How to tune
6th string *down* to D. 5th string *down* to G. 4th string as normal. 3rd string as normal. 2nd string *up* to C. 1st string *down* to D.

Example 2					
6th	5th	4th	3rd	2nd	1st
D	A	D	G	B	D

How to tune
6th string *down* to D. 5th string as normal. 4th string as normal. 3rd string as normal. 2nd string as normal. 1st string *down* to D.

Example 3					
6th	5th	4th	3rd	2nd	1st
D	A	D	F♯	B	D

How to tune
6th string *down* to D. 5th string as normal. 4th string as normal. 3rd string *down* to F♯. 2nd string as normal. 1st string *down* to D.

Example 4					
6th	5th	4th	3rd	2nd	1st
E	A	D	E	A	E

How to tune
6th string as normal. 5th string as normal. 4th string as normal. 3rd string *down* to E. 2nd string *down* to A. 1st string as normal.

Example 5					
6th	5th	4th	3rd	2nd	1st
D	A	D	E	A	E

How to tune
6th string *down* to D. 5th string as normal. 4th string as normal. 3rd string *down* to E. 2nd string *down* to A. 1st string as normal.

Bottleneck and slide guitar

Bottleneck and *slide* are terms often used interchangeably for a style of guitar playing in which the strings are "stopped" by a small metal or glass tube held in the left hand or slipped over one of the left-hand fingers. Strictly speaking, "bottleneck" refers to glass, and "slide" refers to metal, but the technique is the same in both cases.

Slide guitar originated in America, in and around the Mississippi Delta. It was Negro music, with its roots in the tradition of black slavery and therefore linked strongly to the evolution of the blues. At the outset, it was an attempt to imitate the expressiveness of the human voice. The term "bottleneck" comes from the fact that the earliest slides were made from the broken-off necks of beer bottles. Due to the Hawaiian influence, the first slide players laid their guitars flat across their laps with the strings facing upwards. They used anything from penknives to cigar tubes as makeshift slides. Later, when the slide was worn over one finger, the guitar was held in the normal way.

The history of slide guitar playing begins with some of the great American blues musicians – Charley Patton, Son House, Mississippi Fred McDowell, Big Joe Williams, Bukka White, Robert Johnson, Blind Lemon Jefferson, Leadbelly, Blind Willie McTell and Blind Boy Fuller. They created the style, set the standards, and passed on what they knew to the second generation – guitarists such as Muddy Waters and, primarily, Elmore James. They, in turn, took slide playing into the electric blues era and influenced the rock guitarists we now associate most strongly with slide playing – Eric Clapton, the late Duane Allman, the late Lowell George (of Little Feat), Rory Gallagher and Ry Cooder.

How to use a slide

It is in fact quite easy to make your own glass slide from the neck of a bottle, or improvise a metal one from a piece of tubing, but ready-made slides are available in most guitar shops and are not expensive. Metal and glass slides produce different sounds, so experiment with both to see which you prefer. The same goes for whether you choose to wear the slide on your 3rd or 4th finger. One advantage in wearing it on your 4th finger is that it leaves three other fingers free to play chords. A guitar with a high action is best for slide since it reduces the likelihood of fret buzz. The slide merely rests on the strings; it is *not* used to push them down to the frets. For this reason, it should come to rest directly over the frets, not slightly behind them. Many of the most effective slide guitar effects are created with open or dropped tunings (see p. 158), which allow whole chords to be slid up or down.

Slide technique
This close-up shows the left hand of Mississippi Fred McDowell, one of the greatest and earliest slide players. He wears an original glass bottleneck on his 3rd finger.

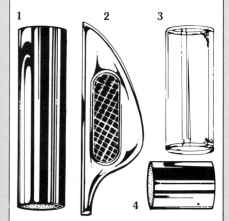

Four different types of slide
1 Full-length polished metal slide. **2** Metal lap slide used when guitar is rested flat on knees. **3** Glass slide. **4** Short polished-metal slide.

Big Joe Williams playing a 9-string Harmony Sovereign with a metal slide on his 4th finger.

GUITAR MAINTENANCE AND CUSTOMIZING

The information in this chapter should give you a good understanding of how to care for your guitar, how to set it up properly so that it plays well, and what to look for when buying a new one. It should also enable you to diagnose faults at an early stage and take the appropriate action before the situation gets progressively worse and more and more expensive to deal with. Although any vintage or valuable guitar in need of repair should be given to a specialist, there are many simple maintenance and repair jobs that can be carried out on more modest instruments by almost anyone willing to take time and care. If you are reasonably good with your hands, follow the instructions carefully and you should have no problems. But remember that many of the guitars which finally arrive on the professional repairer's workbench have been bodged by their owners and are often sadly beyond practical repair. Guitar electronics is also within the scope of the amateur. These pages contain all the basic information needed to open up a whole world of experimentation – from installing or re-wiring pick-ups to building a pre-amp. The growth of guitar customizing and "spare-part guitar surgery" has been astounding in the past few years. Nowadays, this can mean anything from fitting a special strap button to assembling a complete guitar from parts bought over the counter at a local music store. This chapter will tell you what's available, how to choose what you need, and how to fit what you've bought.

Strings

In the past, guitar strings were made of either wire or gut (called "cat gut" but, in fact, almost always the intestines of sheep). However, modern guitar strings divide into two basic types – steel and nylon. Steel strings are used on electric guitars and on flat-top and arch-top acoustics; nylon strings are used on classical and flamenco guitars.

Most guitars are strung with a set of six strings, each of a different thickness and each tuned to a different pitch. Of these six, the 1st and 2nd strings are "plain", and the 4th, 5th and 6th strings are "wound". On electric guitars, the 3rd string may be either plain or wound. Twelve-string guitars, of course, have twelve strings, normally tuned in pairs and octaves (see p. 68).

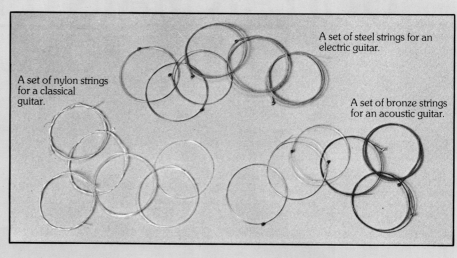

A set of nylon strings for a classical guitar.

A set of steel strings for an electric guitar.

A set of bronze strings for an acoustic guitar.

String types

Because it is impractical to make thick plain strings, the mass of the bass strings is increased by wrapping lengths of extra "wire" around a central core. These are *wound* strings. The central core may be either round or hexagonal. With steel strings, the core is made of steel; with nylon strings, the core is made of nylon.

The material from which the wire winding is made varies: they can be roughly classified as "white" or "silver" metal (stainless steel, nickel, nickel alloy, silver-plated copper) or "gold" or "yellow" metal (bronze, brass and various alloys). Either white or yellow strings can be used on acoustic guitars – although most players prefer the yellow bronze or brass strings. Only certain strings can be used on electric guitars with magnetic pick-ups. These are the magnetically responsive white metal ones. Neither yellow metal strings nor nylon strings will work with a magnetic pick-up. A guitar with a contact transducer or microphone can be fitted with any type of string.

The shape or profile which the winding gives the wound string varies according to whether the string is roundwound, flatwound or groundwound.

Roundwound strings

These are the most commonly used strings. To produce the bottom three (or four) wound strings, the steel or nylon core is wrapped round with a long, continuous length of round wire. The winding is done

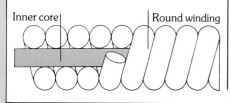

Inner core | Round winding

automatically, by a machine that spins the central core. Roundwound strings produce a good tone and volume, and when new give a clear ring suitable for both acoustic and electric guitars.

Flatwound strings

Also known as "tapewound" strings, flatwounds have a far smoother surface than that of roundwound strings. This is because the winding is made not from round wire

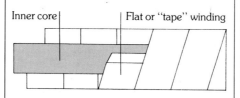

Inner core | Flat or "tape" winding

but from flat metal tape or ribbon.

Flatwound strings were designed to overcome the problem of "finger squeak" – the noise produced when the guitarist's left hand moves up and down the fingerboard while in contact with the strings. The smooth, flat surface of flatwound strings helps to reduce this noise.

Flatwounds have a more mellow sound than roundwound strings and are therefore

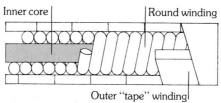

Inner core | Round winding

Outer "tape" winding

often preferred by jazz players. They tend not to be popular with rock guitarists, chiefly because they lack the bright, percussive tone of roundwounds – and also because

they tend not to last so well.

Some flatwound strings are made with both a round *and* a flat winding. The round winding goes on first and is then covered with a flat ribbon winding. Usually known as "compound flatwounds", these strings are sometimes used by jazz players.

Groundwound strings

These strings are an attempt to combine the different advantages of roundwound and flatwound strings. They are made in the same way as roundwound strings – that is, a round wire is wrapped around the core – but the winding is then ground down and polished so that the protrusions are removed and a flattened surface is left. Different makes are ground to different degrees. Groundwound (or "half-flat") strings therefore give some of the bright tone quality, projection and sustain of roundwounds while also offering the smoother feel of flatwounds.

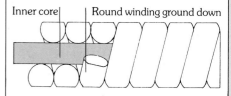

Inner core | Round winding ground down

Silk and steel strings

Sometimes called "compound strings", these are something of a special case, since the inner core is made of a combination of steel and silk. The two treble strings are plain, unwound steel. But the four bass strings comprise a steel core wrapped first with a fine layer of silk fiber and then with a regular metal winding. For use only on acoustic guitars, these strings have a sound and feel between that of steel and nylon.

String gauges and tension

The pitch of the note produced by a guitar string depends on three things: the tension placed on it (this is controlled by the tuning heads); the length of its vibrating section (determined by the distance between the nut and saddle); and its *mass*. When both the diameter and weight of a guitar string are increased, so is its mass. If two strings of equal length are placed under equal tension, the one with the greater mass will vibrate at a slower rate and produce a lower note. In short, this is why the bass strings get progressively heavier and thicker.

Steel-string diameters are expressed as *gauges* – usually measured as fractions of an inch. Sets of strings are graduated so that their tension is as consistent as possible when they are in tune and so that they offer an even resistance when fretting notes with the left hand. They are available in sets, usually labelled "heavy", "medium", "light", "extra light" and "ultra light". Manufacturers' names for these basic sets may vary and you may find an intermediate set such as "medium light". Strings are also available individually – in almost all practical gauges – so you can make up your own combination if you wish.

Changing the strings on your guitar from one gauge to another will affect its sound and "feel". Light-gauge strings are easier to push down onto the frets (since the tension is lower) and make note bending easier. However, they can be hard to keep in tune, they give less volume and sustain, and you may find that you tend to bend strings out of tune accidentally when playing chords. For the same reasons, using a set of heavy-gauge strings has all the opposite effects. The guitar may be slightly harder to play, but the strings will distort less when playing chords, will hold their pitch better, and will give longer sustain and more volume.

Classical nylon strings are available in different "tensions" as well as gauges. Varying the type of nylon will give a "hard", "medium" or "light" action. Flamenco strings (which are sometimes red) are generally "hard" since this suits the sound of flamenco music, the faster technique and the lower action of the guitars.

String gauges A comparison of typical sets.

Note W = wound 3rd string.

Ultra light		Extra light		Light		Medium		Heavy	
	.008		.010		.011		.013		.014
	.010		.014		.015		.017		.018
	.014		.020W		.022W		.026W		.028W
	.022		.028		.030		.034		.040
	.030		.040		.042		.046		.050
	.038		.050		.052		.056		.060

Why do strings break?

Guitar strings can and do break for any of the following reasons.

● The string is over-tensioned. Guitar strings are designed to be tuned to concert pitch (see p. 69). They can be tightened only a little higher before there is a risk of them breaking or of the excessive tension distorting or damaging the guitar neck.

● The older a string, the more likely it is to break. Less elasticity, combined with wear and rust caused by sweat from the fingers, will weaken strings and may eventually cause them to snap.

● Strings are often broken by heavy right-hand technique, particularly hard strumming. This can cause the string to break at any point along its length. While many lead guitarists hardly ever break strings, some rhythm players – especially those who play hard – regularly do.

● A kink in a string can cause a weak spot. Before it breaks, it can be seen and felt as a small bump. When fitting strings, take care not to fold them back on themselves, since this is what causes the kinks.

● Sharp edges on the saddle, nut or tuning head capstans can cause strings to break. Check where the string has broken and file down any sharp edges.

How can I make strings last longer?

Strings stretch during their lifetime. They slowly lose their elasticity and their tone quality decreases. Eventually, they will stretch no more. Old, fully stretched strings produce notes which are no longer rich in harmonic overtones. As a result, the guitar becomes harder to tune and the sound is dull and lifeless.

Strings also wear, particularly at the points where they make contact with the frets. Wound strings suffer most; they develop "flat spots" where the undersides

Flat spot   Dirt and rust

of the windings are worn flat. Flat spots and broken windings will both impair tone, while the latter will also cause string "buzz".

With time, strings can become tarnished, dirty and rusty. Dirt and grease from sweaty hands build up quickly on the strings, especially on the undersides and between the windings. For this reason, you should clean and dry your strings immediately after playing (see p. 177).

"Snapping" the strings is a pro's trick which sometimes helps to dislodge dirt from beneath the windings. One at a time, pull each string away from the fingerboard and allow it to snap back. Repeat this a few times with each string.

"Boiling" the strings is an amateur's trick occasionally employed by impoverished professionals. The old strings are taken off the guitar and simply boiled in a pan of water for a few minutes to remove grease and dirt. Although this will never make the strings sound new again, some people claim that it gives them a slightly brighter tone.

Just how long you can expect a set of strings to last depends on several factors. A guitar player who works four hours a night, six nights a week, in a sweaty, smoke-filled club will get through far more sets of strings than someone who plays a twenty-minute party piece a couple of times a year. The more you sweat, the shorter the life of your strings. If you play hard with your right hand and fret notes heavily with your left, the same thing applies: you will wear out strings quickly.

How often you should change strings is also up to you. Some professional guitarists fit a new set of strings each night they play. Many amateurs, on the other hand, leave the same set on their guitar for years and regard replacing them as an unnecessary and exceptional circumstance.

Many people love the bright, "zingy" sound of new strings that have just been fitted. Most experienced guitarists, however, prefer the slightly more "played-in" sound that comes after playing for a couple of hours or so.

Fitting strings

Guitar manufacturers often advise you to fit new strings one at a time. The idea is that removing all the old strings at once will release the tension on the neck and risk it distorting. In fact, this is unlikely. What is more important, perhaps, is to de-tune the strings at a similar rate so that the tension on the neck is reduced evenly.

Occasionally, strings break while they are being tightened, and the whiplash of the sharp ends can be dangerous. For this reason, keep your face away from the string while you are tuning it up to pitch.

Never tune your strings more than a tone above concert pitch. Not only does this increase the chance of them breaking, it also exerts an excessive strain on the neck and may distort or damage it. Fitting one string at a time helps to avoid this, since you always have the other strings as an indication of the right pitch.

When you string any guitar, you can expect that by the time you have tuned the last string the first one you fitted will have gone down in pitch. New strings always take a couple of

days to stretch so that they stay reasonably in tune (see opposite).

Loose guitar strings are in fact quite easily damaged. They are usually sold coiled in separate envelopes, and when taking them out of their packets you should be careful not to get kinks in them. This will weaken them and may also hurt your left-hand fingers.

Various methods for fitting both steel and nylon strings are shown on these pages. It is most important that you *never* put steel strings on a classical or flamenco guitar. Nylon strings exert far less tension than steel, and classical and flamenco instruments are simply not constructed to withstand the extra forces. Putting steel strings on them will almost certainly damage the neck and, possibly, the soundbox.

You can, if you wish, put nylon strings on a steel-string guitar. There is little point, however, since their stronger, heavier construction means that the nylon strings will produce less volume and a tone which is neither as percussive as that of steel strings nor as rich as when they are fitted to a classical guitar.

Guitar stringwinders
A stringwinder is a gadget that slips over the button on the tuning head and enables you to wind the strings on or off the capstans quickly and easily. If several neat coils of string are wound onto the capstan, the extra string length will facilitate fine tuning and place a more even tension on the tuning head.

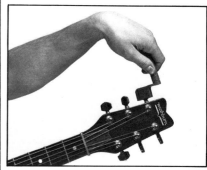

Using a stringwinder

Fitting steel strings to an acoustic guitar

Almost all steel strings have a small knob or ball attached to one end. This anchors the string to either the bridge or tailpiece, and it is the end that you should attach first. On most flat-top guitars, the strings are secured at the body by bridge pins. Bridge pins are tapered – as are the holes into which they fit – so that they will stay in place when pushed home. On most arch-tops, the strings are

attached to a tailpiece, not to the bridge. They each pass through a hole or slot large enough to allow the string through but not the knob on the end. The strings then simply pass over the bridge and saddle without being attached to them at all.

At the head of the guitar, the strings are secured to the tuning head capstans. Allow some slack so that they can be wound

around a couple of times before passing through the hole in the capstan. To prevent the treble strings from slipping, you may thread them once through the hole, once around the capstan, and then through the hole a second time. Tidy the ends and prevent them from rattling while you are playing by coiling them around or clipping them off with pliers or wire cutters.

Removing bridge pins
The pins can be removed by gently prising them out with a coin or nail file. This is done *after* the string has been slackened.

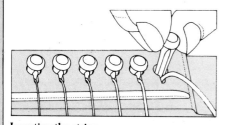

Inserting the string
The knob on the end of the string *must* be pushed to one side by the bridge pin, otherwise it will pull straight out again as the string is tightened. Bend the knob slightly to one side as it goes in.

Attaching the strings to the tuning heads

1 Bring the string over the nut and up the center of the head. Wind it over the *top* of the capstan, towards the edge.

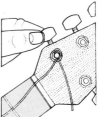

2 Thread the end of the string through the hole, pull it outwards and begin tightening the button to take up the slack.

3 Continue winding so that the string coils neatly onto the capstan and the final wrap lies close to the head.

Fitting strings to an electric guitar

In the case of solid-body electrics, the strings are attached to the tuning heads in the same way as they are for steel-string acoustics. At the body, the fixing method varies with the design of the guitar. Sometimes the strings are secured by means of a tailpiece, sometimes a combined bridge and tailpiece, and sometimes they pass right through the body. The principle is usually the same: the string is threaded through a hole or slot small enough to retain the knob on the end of the string.

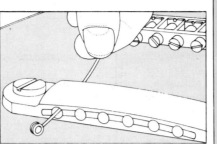

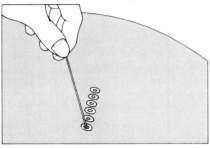

Through-the-body attachment
1 The strings are threaded through from the back of the body and are anchored to a bridge plate.

Tailpiece attachment
Electric guitars with tailpieces are simple to re-string. The ball-ends of the strings secure them in position at the holes in the tailpiece.

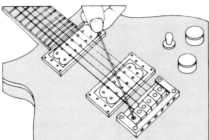

2 The strings are then pulled out from the front, up and over the bridge assembly, and are then fixed to the tuning head capstans.

"Stretching" the strings

Many guitarists, especially those new to performing in public, fit new strings too soon before a gig and consequently suffer severe tuning problems. If new strings must be fitted a few hours before a performance, playing them in or thoroughly stretching them as shown below will help to keep them in tune.

How to stretch strings
Tune the new string up to pitch, then pull it about an inch (2.5 cm) away from the guitar. It will have dropped in pitch slightly. Tune it back up and repeat until stretching it no longer puts it out of tune.

Fitting nylon strings to classical and flamenco guitars

Nylon strings have no ball-ends. Instead, they are fixed to the bridge with a simple knot. The wound bass strings usually have a loop made from the central nylon strands at one end. Originally, this was hooked onto the tailpieces fitted to early, rare instruments. The loop end is always the one which should be secured to the bridge since the last 2-3 in. (5-7.5 cm) of the string are usually more pliable and therefore easier to tie. There are various methods of tying the knot (see below), but in each case you should have only a short end of loose string left at the bridge. If the end is too long, it may rattle against the soundboard.

Flamenco guitars sometimes have wooden tuning pegs instead of geared tuning heads (see p. 43). The pegs stay in place because, like bridge pins, they have a taper fit. To replace a string, the peg must be pulled out slightly so that it can be turned. It is then pushed back to form a tight fit once the string is up to the right pitch. As there is no gearing, your fingers have to hold the tension that the string exerts on the peg until the peg is pushed back in. This is not easy and requires some practice.

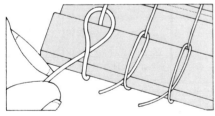

Tying a single loop knot
Thread end of string through bridge hole. Pass pliable end over top of bridge and under string. Make single loop knot and tighten.

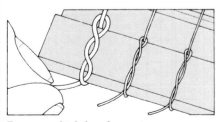

Tying a multiple loop knot
Begin in same way as above, leading string through, over bridge and under itself. This time, make two loop knots, threading string under, over and under itself.

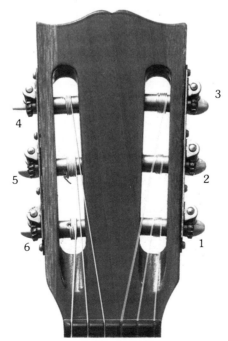

Attaching the strings to the tuning heads

1 Bring the string over the nut and up the center of the head. Thread it through the hole in the capstan from the top to the bottom.

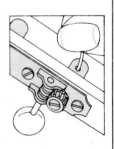

2 Bring the end of the string over the top of the capstan and pass it underneath itself.

3 Begin winding so that the string wraps neatly round the capstan as you take up the slack and come up to pitch.

Setting the action

The *action* of a guitar can be defined as its "playability". It determines how much pressure you have to exert on the strings in order to press them down on to the frets.

The strings on any guitar are always closest to the 1st fret and furthest away from the highest fret. So there is always a slight increase in the amount of pressure needed to fret strings as you go higher up the fingerboard. A guitar is said to have "good" action if it is possible to play in any position on the neck without having to exert any more than this slight increase in finger pressure – in other words, if the action is consistent. A guitar with "bad" action is noticeably more difficult – sometimes almost impossible – to play above the first few frets.

"High" or "low" action describes the actual distance between the top of the frets and the bottom of the strings. In general, a guitar with a low action is easier to play than one with a high action. However, if the action is *too* low, the strings may rattle against the frets and cause "fret buzz". A very low action also tends to reduce the guitar's volume and can impair its tone slightly. For this reason, and to prevent string rattle, you will probably

do best with a guitar that has its action set fairly high if you strum hard.

Most guitars, especially those in the cheaper price range, do not have their action set anywhere near the optimum. This can be very discouraging for beginners. Some simply give up learning to play because certain notes are too hard to fret or because "barre" chords are too difficult. Those who persevere on guitars with bad action risk developing faults in their technique that may be hard to correct later. Because bad action makes notes hard to fret, there is a tendency to tense up the left hand and also fret too heavily – even after graduating on to a better guitar.

How the action is adjusted

The action of any guitar is determined by the construction of the instrument, the condition of the neck and body, the scale length (see p. 40), the gauge of the strings, and the distance between the top of the frets and the bottom of the strings.

"Setting the action" is the term used for altering the distance between the frets and the strings. This adjustment can be done in any of four ways: by raising or lowering the bridge or

saddle; by altering the height of the nut; by adjusting the dip in the neck; and by changing the height or profile of the frets. The methods by which these adjustments are made are covered in the following pages. They should only be attempted *after* you have ruled out distortion and checked the glued joints between the guitar neck and body.

Sets of steel strings of different gauges will almost certainly have an effect on the profile of the guitar neck. The heavier the gauge of the strings, the greater the tension required to bring them up to pitch and the more strain is exerted on the neck. If the action of your guitar is correctly set for light-gauge strings, a change to a heavy-gauge set will probably mean that you will have to re-adjust the action slightly.

Many professional guitarists have their guitars set up by a specialist maker or repairer who will watch the guitarist playing in order to assess how high or low to set the action. The adjustment may take anything from a few minutes to a few hours, depending on what needs to be done. There may even be a "second fitting" after the guitar has been set up once and then played in for a while.

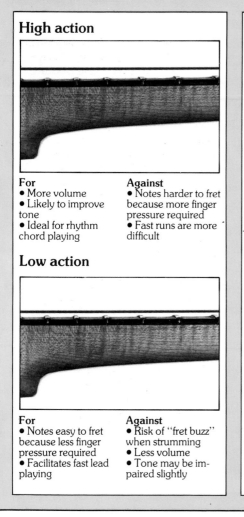

High action

For
• More volume
• Likely to improve tone
• Ideal for rhythm chord playing

Against
• Notes harder to fret because more finger pressure required
• Fast runs are more difficult

Low action

For
• Notes easy to fret because less finger pressure required
• Facilitates fast lead playing

Against
• Risk of "fret buzz" when strumming
• Less volume
• Tone may be impaired slightly

Measuring the action

It is possible to measure the action on a guitar, but the adjustments are usually infinitesimally small and most guitarists and repairers are therefore concerned more with "feel" than with precise dimensions. Setting the action is normally a question of trial and error.

However, the figures given here can be taken as a rough guide. Action measurements are taken from at least two points on each string – usually at the 1st fret and at the "body fret" (the fret where the fingerboard joins the guitar body). Guitar necks are actually designed to have a slight dip (see p. 168). The action is always a little higher at the body fret to allow for the wide loop in which the string vibrates when played open or when low fretted notes are sounded.

The action is higher for the bass strings than it is for the treble strings. This, too, is to take account of the bass string's larger vibration loop.

All action measurements should be taken with the strings at concert pitch, although they may need to be slackened off while adjustments are made. The action at the body fret can be measured using a "feeler gauge" or by improvising one from several small pieces of card. The action at the 1st fret should be only slightly higher than the action at the 2nd fret when the string is held down on the 1st fret.

Action at 1st fret

Action at body fret

A guide to action measurements
Measurements are for "medium" action. Adding or subtracting 1/64 in. (0.4 mm) will change the action to "high" or "low".

Type of guitar	Body fret	
	Bass E	Treble E
Electric	6/64 in. 2.38 mm)	4/64 in. (1.59 mm)
Flat-top acoustic	8/64 in. (3.18 mm)	6/64 in. (2.38 mm)
Classical	10/64 in. (3.97 mm)	8/64 in. (3.18 mm)

Adjusting the height of the nut

To set the action correctly, you *must* check the nut. Although you can sometimes *improve* the action simply by adjusting the bridge, you will never set up the guitar properly if the strings are too high or too low at the nut.

If your guitar has a "zero fret" (see p. 41), the action at that end of the neck should be correct – unless the frets need attention (see p. 170). If not, it may be that the grooves or notches in the nut are too high and that, as a result, the strings rest on the nut and not on the zero fret. This would put the intonation out as well. As long as the grooves in the nut are lower than the top of the zero fret, no problems should arise.

On guitars without a zero fret, the height of the nut is more critical. If the strings are set too high at the nut, you will find it hard to push them down onto the first two or three frets. A simple test will establish whether the nut is at fault. Play the guitar on and around the first three frets – including a bar F chord. Now put a capo on the 1st fret and play the same fingerings as before. If the guitar is much easier to play with the capo on, the action is too high.

The solution is usually to make the grooves in the nut a little deeper so that the strings sit closer to the fingerboard. Needle files and thin saw blades can be used for cutting the notches. However, be careful. The job must be done with precision. First, it is all too easy to make the grooves too deep. If this happens, you will get fret buzz and have to start all over again with a new nut. Second, the grooves should be semi-circular, providing a dish-shaped recess for each string to sit in, and should be of exactly the right diameter for each string. If they are too wide the string may rattle or slip out of position, and if they are too deep the tone

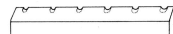

Groove height
Notches should be semi-circular, with no more than half the string's circumference below the top of the nut.

Nut profile
A curved fingerboard needs a curved nut. Otherwise, the strings will be closer to the fingerboard in the center than at either edge.

will be impaired. Third, if the fingerboard is curved across the frets, the nut should have the same profile so that the height of all six strings will be correct. Fourth, because the scale length begins at the front of the nut, it is important that the grooves slope down slightly towards the head.

If the strings are set too low at the nut, they will rattle or buzz against the frets when you play them open (unfretted). The remedy is to fit a new nut. In most cases, the nut is lightly glued in position. Removing it is fairly simple, although it should be done with care. The glued joint can usually be freed by gently tapping the nut so that it comes out sideways, using a light hammer and a piece of wood to cushion the impact of the blows.

It is possible to make a temporary adjustment by putting thin veneers of wood or shims of plastic underneath the old nut to raise its overall height. But a new nut is better. Like saddles, nuts are made from plastic, ivory or bone (or in the case of some electric guitars, brass). Ivory is the best choice but may be difficult to obtain. New nuts must have grooves cut in them (see left) to match the guitar's string spacing.

Adjusting the height of the bridge

Since almost all electrics and many acoustic guitars have adjustable bridges, raising or lowering the height of the saddle is the most obvious way of adjusting the action. However, this should be done only *after* you have checked neck and body joints, the fret profile and dip in the neck, and the nut height. If any of these are at fault, no amount of bridge adjustment will improve the guitar's playability.

Electric guitars with bridges based on the design of the Fender Stratocaster can be adjusted by means of small Allen screws.

The two-footed adjustable bridge commonly fitted to f-hole arch-top guitars, and the "Tune-O-Matic" bridge fitted to most

Gibsons and many other electrics, both work in the same way. At each end of the saddle, there is a knurled metal adjuster threaded onto a metal shaft. When one adjuster is screwed up or down it raises or lowers its side of the saddle. With bridges of this type, you should adjust the height of the bass strings first and the height of the treble strings afterwards. You will find that you have to de-tune the strings in order to relax the tension on the saddle when raising it.

Guitars with fixed bridges – classical, flamenco and some flat-tops – are not so easily adjusted. The bridge is glued to the face of the soundboard. However, the saddle, over which the strings pass, sits in a

groove in the bridge and is usually held in position only by string tension. Once the strings have been loosened, the saddle comes out of its slot easily and can be re-shaped, re-positioned or replaced.

If the action is too low, you can insert thin "shims" of wood or veneer beneath the saddle to increase the string height. Alternatively, you can make a new saddle from a fresh piece of plastic, ivory or bone.

If the action is too high, you can either shave off the base of the saddle slightly or make the grooves in which the strings sit slightly deeper – in the same way as for the nut (see above). Take care not to damage the saddle's tight fit.

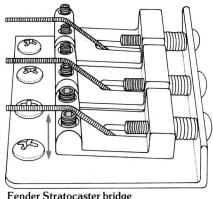

Fender Stratocaster bridge

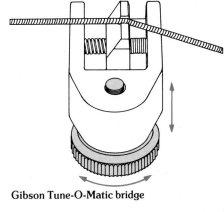

Gibson Tune-O-Matic bridge

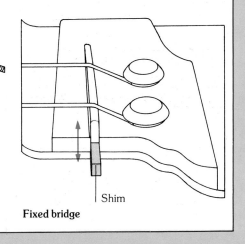

Shim

Fixed bridge

Adjusting the neck

Nine times out of ten, problems with the action of guitars can be traced to neck distortion of one kind or another. If a guitar is knocked about and not treated with care, the action will almost certainly suffer. Even the most expensive instrument is liable to distort if exposed to extreme changes in temperature or humidity.

It is impossible to set the action correctly if the joint between the neck and body is faulty (see p. 172) or if the shape of the neck itself is either "twisted", "bowed" or "warped". If the neck is badly distorted, the guitar will need the attention of a maker or repairer. However, if it is only slightly out of true and if it has an adjustable truss rod, you may be able to adjust it yourself. Only the very cheapest guitars – those that border on being toys – are so badly constructed that the action cannot be set in order and the instrument put in good playing condition.

It is a popular fallacy that all guitar necks should be perfectly straight. It is true that the fingerboard and the tops of the frets are usually level when first made but, as soon as the guitar is strung and the strings are tuned up to pitch, the tension should curve the neck very slightly – giving it a concave profile rather like an archer's bow. This has a beneficial effect on both the tone and the action: you are more likely to get a clean, ringing note and less likely to get fret buzz, because the dip in the neck corresponds to the point on the length of the open string where it vibrates in its widest arc.

Guitars fitted with adjustable truss rods (see p. 39) allow you to adjust the dip in the neck and therefore to compensate for the tension of the strings you select. They are also useful for any minor adjustments to the neck that may become necessary as a result of changes in humidity and temperature or the aging of the instrument. Adjustable truss rods are fitted inside the guitar neck, below the fingerboard. One end is fixed (usually secured to the body of the guitar) and the other is threaded to accept a nut and washer. Because there is more wood in front of the rod than behind it, tightening the rod will reduce the dip in the neck and loosening the rod will increase the dip. Initially, before the guitar leaves its maker, the neck should be put under some compression – by tightening the adjusting nut on the rod – to act against the pull of the strings and to produce exactly the right amount of dip.

Most steel-string guitars (electric as well as acoustic) have adjustable truss rods of this type. However, Martin guitars do not, and several other famous makes have rods which work on different principles. Gretsch, for example, has fitted a geared arrangement in several of their guitar necks. Every guitar with an adjustable truss rod should be supplied with information on how to use it, but, if in doubt, always check with the manufacturer.

Guitars that do *not* have an adjustable truss rod must be taken to a professional repairer if the neck develops a bow, warp or twist. Correction of the fault may involve taking the neck apart, replacing or repairing certain parts, and then re-building it.

Adjusting the truss rod

Adjustable truss rods must always be used with great care. They are purely for *small* alterations in the dip of the neck. It is another popular fallacy that they can easily correct any degree of bow or warp. On anything other than a cheap copy guitar, you should attempt only very slight adjustments. Many guitar necks are ruined through incorrect truss rod adjustment, and any major alterations should be put in the hands of an experienced guitar repairer.

The actual dimensions of the dip in a neck depend on the type of guitar, the gauge and tension of the strings, and the way the instrument is played. Classical, flamenco, arch-top, flat-top and solid-body electric guitars all have different characteristics and will require different settings. Some makers and repairers do not take measurements at all, but instead work solely on visual assessment and "feel". However, as a general rule, the dip in the neck should measure about 1/64 in. (0.4 mm). If it is more than 1/32 in. (0.79 mm), it should probably be reduced slightly by adjusting the truss rod.

Before attempting any adjustment, check the maintenance instructions provided with the guitar to ensure that a standard type of truss rod is fitted. Then go over the joints between the neck and the body, and fit a new set of strings and bring them up to concert pitch.

There are two methods of measuring the dip in the neck. The first is as follows. Put a capo on the 1st fret and then hold down the bass E (6th) string one fret above the body fret. The string will then be in a perfectly straight line between these two frets. To check how much the neck dips, measure the distance between the bottom of the string and the top of the fret furthest from it. This will be the 5th, 6th, 7th or 8th fret, depending on the type of guitar and on the construction of the neck.

The second method is essentially the same but involves using a metal straight edge instead of the string itself. The metal edge is laid along the top of the frets and the dip measured as above.

If the dip is insufficient, increase it by rotating the adjusting nut on the truss rod by an eighth of a turn in an anti-clockwise direction. This will loosen the compression on the rod so that the string tension increases the "bow" of the neck very slightly. Take another measurement and, if the dip is still too shallow, give the nut another eighth of a turn. If you find that you have to turn the truss rod more than one complete rotation, consult a repairer before going any further. It is almost certain that some more major

Measuring the dip in the neck
If you have no straight edge to lay along the top of the frets, use the guitar strings themselves. Put a capo on the 1st fret and hold the string down on the fret one above the body fret. The dip in the neck is measured at its maximum, usually somewhere between the 5th and 8th frets.

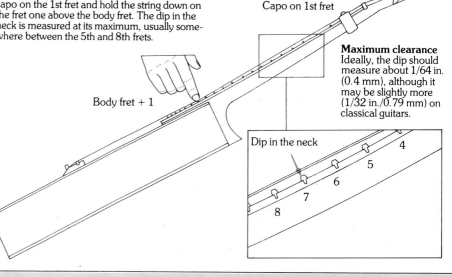

Capo on 1st fret

Body fret + 1

Maximum clearance
Ideally, the dip should measure about 1/64 in. (0.4 mm), although it may be slightly more (1/32 in./0.79 mm) on classical guitars.

Dip in the neck

Checking for a twisted neck

A twisted neck causes some of the frets — or, at least, parts of them — to be too close to the strings and others to be too far away. In other words, you may get fret buzz on some parts of the fingerboard while the action will be too high elsewhere.

You can check for a twist in the neck by "sighting a line" down the length of the fingerboard. The frets and the gaps should be perfectly parallel. If they are not, the neck is twisted and will need attention from a repairer before the action can be set. Some Rickenbackers and other guitars have "double adjustable truss rods" inside the neck which can be used to correct minor faults of this kind.

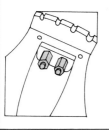

Dual truss rods
Rickenbacker builds all their guitar necks with two adjustable truss rods. Each side can be adjusted separately so that it does not put the other out of alignment.

Correct
Frets perfectly parallel with one another indicate that neck is not twisted.

"Sighting a line"
Close one eye and look down the length of the neck towards the body. Hold the guitar at an angle which makes the frets look like sleepers on a railway track, with the gaps only just visible between.

Incorrect
Frets out of line with one another indicate that neck is twisted.

---

repair will be required.

If the dip is too great, first loosen the strings and then rotate the adjusting nut clockwise by an eighth of a turn. This will tighten the compression on the rod, thus straightening the neck against the pull of the strings and reducing the dip. Re-tune the strings, bringing them back up to pitch, and check the dip again. If it is still too great, repeat the operation — again going no further than one complete turn of the nut. Putting too much compression on the truss rod has often been known to break it.

Increasing the dip in the neck
If the dip in the neck is too shallow, the strings will be too close to the fingerboard and will probably cause fret buzz. To increase the dip, loosen the truss rod (anti-clockwise) so that compression on the neck is reduced.

When you have adjusted the dip between the neck and the bass E (6th) string, move on to the other side of the fingerboard and check the measurement from the treble E (1st) string. It can afford to be slightly smaller since the treble string does not vibrate in such a wide arc as the bass string.

Because the fingerboard above the body fret is usually secured to the body of the guitar, and the fingerboard below it is attached to the neck, there is sometimes a slight high point at the body fret. This does not usually present any problem.

Note In these drawings the bow and warp of the neck have been exaggerated for the purpose of explanation. Badly distorted necks cannot be repaired by adjusting the truss rod.

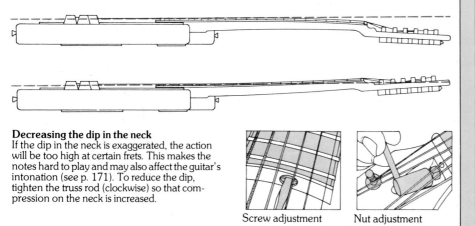

Decreasing the dip in the neck
If the dip in the neck is exaggerated, the action will be too high at certain frets. This makes the notes hard to play and may also affect the guitar's intonation (see p. 171). To reduce the dip, tighten the truss rod (clockwise) so that compression on the neck is increased.

Screw adjustment

Nut adjustment

Neck tilt

With classical, flamenco and flat-top guitars, the fingerboard is usually more or less parallel with the face of the soundboard. Many electric guitars, however, have necks that tilt back slightly. This increases the space between the top of the body or soundboard and the bottom of the strings and provides sufficient room for mounting the pick-ups.

Most arch-top guitars also have tilted necks. This developed as a design feature of the instrument when it first appeared in the 1920s. The guitars were then played acoustically and players wanted as much volume as possible. Tilting the neck increases the height of the bridge — and this, in turn, increases the acoustic volume of the guitar. Some arch-top guitars have detachable necks which allow the angle of the tilt to be adjusted.

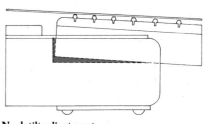

Neck tilt adjustment
Solid-body electrics with bolt-on necks can have "shims" (small pieces of wood veneer) inserted to adjust the neck angle. Some Fenders have their own built-in "Micro-Tilt" adjustment (see p. 51).

Fret care

Frets, which are cut from continuous lengths of metal "fretwire", are available in various shapes and sizes. In the early days of steel-string acoustic guitars, the tops of the frets were often fairly high off the fingerboard and somewhat square in profile. But, because guitarists felt that this slowed down their left-hand technique, there was a trend towards much lower frets. As an example, Gibson's Les Paul Custom, introduced in 1954, was nicknamed the "Fretless Wonder" because its frets were so low (see p. 58)

More recently, slightly higher, more rounded frets have become popular on many electric guitars. They are still fast, but they make left-hand note-bending much easier. There is less friction because the tips of the left-hand fingers do not come into such close contact with the fingerboard and because there is more room to get a good "grip" on the string.

Leveling frets

When the strings are de-tuned and the tension on the neck is released, the tops of the frets should be in a straight line. If one fret is still higher than the others, the strings may well rattle against it and cause fret buzz. To find the fret or frets causing the problem, simply play each note on the string in question, moving up the fingerboard. As soon as you play a note *without* a buzz, you will have identified the fret immediately below it as the offender.

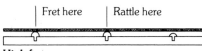

Fret here | Rattle here

High frets
A high fret protrudes above the line of the others and will cause a rattle if you fret notes below it.

If the fret is not loose in its groove, if the action has been set correctly and if you have checked that the neck is not distorted, the fret must be too high. The answer is to level it down, and the procedure is as follows.

Loosen or remove the strings. Protect the wood of the fingerboard with masking tape and the face of the soundboard where the fingerboard ends with a piece of cardboard. Protect the nut with a piece of plastic or more tape so that you do not damage it while working. The tops of the protruding frets should be leveled with a very fine file about 10 in. (25 cm) long or with a carborundum stone. You must take care to exert an even pressure on the file or stone all the time and work along the length of the fingerboard. Work slowly and keep checking that you are not filing the frets too low.

The frets you have filed down will have a shiny, flat top surface and must now be "re-shaped" to the same rounded profile as the other frets. This is usually done using a small fine file – preferably a specially curved "fret file". The job is then finished by very carefully buffing the frets with fine-gauge wire wool or glasspaper.

On steel-string guitars, frets that have had grooves or notches cut in them by the strings can be ground down in the same way – although, in this case, *all* the frets must be filed to a new, uniform level, and badly worn frets will have to be replaced.

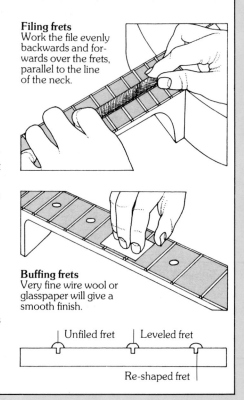

Filing frets
Work the file evenly backwards and forwards over the frets, parallel to the line of the neck.

Buffing frets
Very fine wire wool or glasspaper will give a smooth finish.

Unfiled fret | Leveled fret

Re-shaped fret

Re-fitting loose frets

Loose frets can affect intonation and tone, and can cause unwanted buzzes and rattles. They must be removed and either re-fitted or replaced. The job is tricky but within the capabilities of anyone prepared to take the necessary care.

The "tang" or stem of fretwire has small protrusions which grip the sides of the slot in the fingerboard when the fret is hammered into place. A filler (glue or polish) is then used to fill in the spaces between the fret and the wood of the fingerboard and to prevent rattles. Before a fret can be removed, this filler must be softened – either with steam, hot water on a rag, or a soldering iron run carefully along the fret. A special pair of flat-nosed pliers, a chisel or a knife with a thin blade can then be used to extract the fret. Frets are in fact easy to remove. The difficulty lies in avoiding damage to the fingerboard – and the only answer is to work with care.

It should be possible to re-fit the same fret if you roughen the tang so that it will grip firmly. Give it a coat of white glue or white polish before gently tapping it back into place. Putting a slight curve on the fretwire will help to seat the ends correctly. If the tangs will not bite, you must make a new fret or go to a repairer.

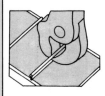

Removing frets
Guitar repairers often use a pair of pliers specially adapted for the job so that the jaws sit level on the surface of the fingerboard.

Re-shaping frets
Old frets can be re-fitted if the tangs are hammered and the bottom of the fret splayed out to give a good grip.

Filing down protruding frets

Sometimes the ends of the frets stick out slightly from the sides of the fingerboard. Brand new guitars may be faulty in this respect if they have not been properly finished, and on older instruments a slight shrinkage of the wood in the fingerboard may have the same effect. Protruding frets make a guitar uncomfortable – sometimes even painful – to play, and the sharp ends should be filed down.

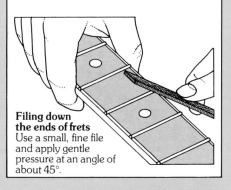

Filing down the ends of frets
Use a small, fine file and apply gentle pressure at an angle of about 45°.

Setting the intonation

The *intonation* of a guitar is said to be correct when – once the open strings are tuned to concert pitch – the notes fretted at every point on the fingerboard all have the right pitch. That is to say, they are neither sharp nor flat.

Intonation is always a problem with guitars. Every time you fret a note, you stretch the string and increase its tension slightly as you push it down towards the fingerboard. This sharpens the pitch of the fretted note. It is more noticeable on a guitar with a high action and its effect increases with the thickness (gauge) of the strings. The result is that notes go progressively out of tune as you move up the fingerboard. If an open G chord sounds fine, but a barre G chord on the 10th fret sounds awful, then the guitar's intonation needs adjusting.

Assuming that the frets have been properly fitted in the right positions, that the neck is not distorted, and that the action is set correctly, the fault will almost certainly lie with the condition or length of the strings.

Old, tarnished or dirty strings can never be expected to play in tune. They will stretch with age, and dirt or damage will inhibit the notes' "harmonic series". The first thing to do before attempting to check the guitar's intonation is, therefore, to fit a new set and tune them up to concert pitch.

The length of the vibrating strings is determined by the guitar's *scale length* – the distance from the nut to the saddle (see p. 40). Increasing the scale length – by slightly more for the bass strings – will cancel out the rise in pitch of fretted notes.

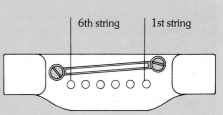

Slanted bridge
The bass strings, which go out of tune the most when fretted, are longer than the treble strings.

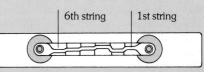

Compensating bridge
Each string has a different length. The 6th string is furthest from the nut and the 3rd string closest to it.

Checking the intonation

Tune the guitar to concert pitch and check the intonation of each string separately. First play the note on the 12th fret (one octave above the open string), then play the 12th fret harmonic (also an octave above the open string). The technique for playing harmonics is described on p. 116. If both notes have exactly the same pitch, the intonation is correct. If the pitch of the fretted note is higher than that of the harmonic, the scale length of the string is too short and the saddle should be moved away from the nut. If the pitch of the fretted note is lower than that of the harmonic, the scale length is too long and the saddle must be moved towards the nut so that the pitch of the fretted note is raised.

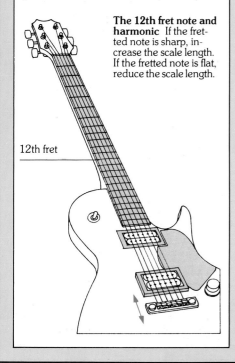

The 12th fret note and harmonic If the fretted note is sharp, increase the scale length. If the fretted note is flat, reduce the scale length.

12th fret

Adjusting the saddle

Classical, flamenco and most flat-top steel-string guitars have bridges which do not allow adjustment of the scale length – although most of them are "slanted" to improve intonation. If a slight adjustment is necessary, it may be possible by re-shaping the profile of the top of the saddle to increase or reduce the length of the vibrating string. If this is the case, however, you should probably take the guitar to an experienced repairer.

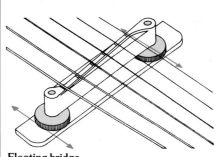

Floating bridge
The bridge is not fixed to the soundboard but is held in place only by the downward pull of the strings. If the intonation needs adjusting, set the bridge position for the treble E (1st) string first.

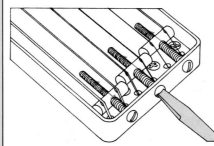

Fender Telecaster bridge
The bridge on a Telecaster allows the scale length of the strings to be adjusted in pairs. The strings to check and adjust are the treble E (1st), the D (4th) and the bass E (6th).

Almost all arch-top guitars and also most electrics have bridges that are adjustable both for string height and string length. This means that the action and the scale length – the two factors which most affect intonation – can be adjusted in relation to one another. Arch-tops usually have a floating bridge which can be moved freely backwards and forwards. Sometimes, there will be a mark on the soundboard indicating the correct position for the bridge.

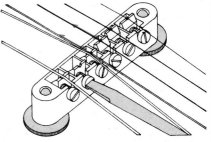

Gibson Tune-O-Matic bridge
Each string sits on a small metal insert that acts as its own saddle. These can be moved backwards and forwards individually by means of small adjustment screws.

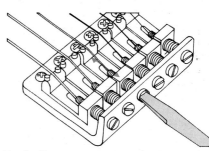

Fender Stratocaster bridge
Small screws mounted on the fixed base plate control the position of the separate saddle for each string. With bridges such as this, the string lengths need be set in no particular order.

Simple guitar repairs

If a guitar has been badly damaged or if it needs a complicated repair, you will probably need the skill and experience of a specialist repairer. However, some repairs can be made quite easily by any inexperienced player willing to work patiently and carefully. The most common of these are described here. They rarely require more than the right glue and a range of suitable clamps.

In essence, the procedure for repairing wood fractures, cracks and broken joints is always the same. The surfaces to be joined should marry up well and should be clean before the work begins. A liberal coating of glue should be applied to one or both surfaces (according to the glue manufacturer's instructions), and the surfaces should then be evenly and snugly pressed together.

When the pieces are aligned correctly, they should be clamped or secured in place, and any excess glue should be wiped away. The space between the two glued surfaces should be visible only as a hairline crack. If the repair is likely to be placed under stress when the guitar is re-strung and tuned up, it should be left for at least 24 hours for the glued joint to dry thoroughly.

Checking neck and bridge joints

The joints most likely to suffer with time are those between the neck and the body of the guitar and those between the bridge and the soundboard.

If the neck is of the glued-on type, the dovetail joint by which it is attached to the body is sometimes pulled open by the tension of the strings. If there are any signs of cracks appearing between the two, the guitar should be placed in the hands of a professional repairer.

Bridge joints are also placed under stress by string tension. If the bridge is glued to the face of the soundboard — as on classical, flamenco and flat-top guitars — it may either begin to pull away or distort the soundboard. And on guitars where the strings are anchored to a tailpiece, the soundboard may be pushed downwards, causing an indentation in the top of the guitar.

Distorted soundboards should be repaired professionally, but, if the bridge is simply peeling away, you may be able to prise it off carefully and re-glue it yourself.

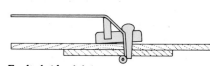

Faulty bridge joint
A gap may appear between the bridge and soundboard if the tension of the strings is pulling the glue joint apart.

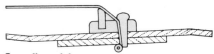

Soundboard distortion
String tension acting on the glued bridge may sometimes pull the soundboard out of shape and affect the action.

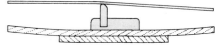

Soundboard indentation
On a guitar with a tailpiece, the downward pressure of the strings passing over the bridge may indent the soundboard.

Glues and clamps

The glue that guitar-repairers traditionally use is animal-based and called *hide glue* — although it may also be referred to as "Scotch", "cabinet-maker's", "gelatine" or "violin-maker's" glue. It can be used either hot or cold, and is sold in solid or powder form. It is also available as "fish glue", in which case it is fish- not animal-based.

Hot hide glue is the best. It is usually soaked in water and then heated to the required working temperature — either in an electric glue pot or a double boiler. The temperature and degree of dilution vary from repairer to repairer and job to job.

Hide glues have been used by instrument-makers for hundreds of years. Though not as strong as some modern adhesives, hide glues dry very hard and give a more rigid joint than more elastic resin glues. They also offer the advantage that the consistency can be controlled by varying the ratio of water to glue. Moreover, it is possible to separate a hide-glue joint. An eye dropper or teaspoonful of warm water, a controlled jet of steam, or a heated knife blade slipped into the joint will usually break the seal. However, it might take half an hour or so for the glue to soften; time and patience are therefore essential.

Unfortunately, hide glues are not perfect. They are vulnerable to moisture in the air and to extremes of temperature. They are also popular with colonizing fungus spores that may set up home in a glued joint and will eventually weaken it.

Because all hide glues are quite time-consuming to prepare and sometimes difficult to obtain, *white woodworking glues* are used extensively throughout the industry — including guitar mass production. When set, white glue is softer and more elastic than hide glue, and some people feel this impairs the acoustic tone. Some makers are therefore happy to use white glue for joints such as the one between the neck and finger-board, but prefer to use a traditional hide glue for the construction of the soundbox.

Modern "miracle" glues — those that set in a few seconds — are suitable for thousands of applications, but not for guitar repairs. The speed with which they bond and the fact that they are almost impossible to take apart mean that their use is very limited.

Both hide and white glues begin to set after a few minutes. They will then take several hours to dry completely and form a good bond. Excess glue forced out of cracks or joints as pressure is applied to them should be removed immediately with a damp cloth. In most cases, the repair will have to be clamped while the glue sets. As clamps are available in various shapes and sizes, make certain you have the right one for the job.

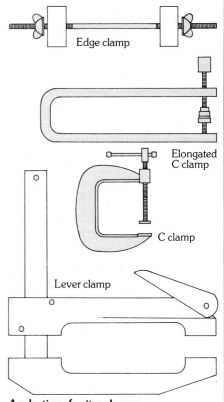

A selection of guitar clamps
While glued joints are setting, a light, even pressure is required. Take care to use the correct clamps and not to overtighten them — otherwise you may damage the guitar still further.

Repairing a broken joint

Dropping or knocking a guitar will produce undue strain on the wooden joints. White glues are usually stronger than the woods they bind together, so the wood is likely to fracture before the joint gives way, but hide glues are fairly brittle and can break more easily. They can also be weakened by excess damp, extremes of temperature or attack by fungus spores.

If the joint has only partially come away, it must be dismantled and reset. One of the best methods is to apply small amounts of hot water to soften the glue – this may take half an hour or so. Once the glue is soft, the two pieces of wood can be pulled carefully apart. Scrape off the old glue while it is still soft, and, if water has been used, allow the wood to dry out thoroughly before re-gluing.

Although "keying" (or roughening) of the two surfaces to be joined is common practice among repairers who use traditional hide glues, wooden synthetic resin woodworking glues will work well with smooth surfaces. Once the new glue has been applied, the joint should be pressed gently together and clamped until set. Any glue that seeps out should be wiped off.

Repairing fractured wood

Wood fractures usually occur as a result of the guitar being dropped, knocked over or struck. Breaks of this kind tend to happen if a guitar is left propped up against a wall or speaker cabinet; the slightest vibration will send the guitar crashing to the floor.

One of the most common fractures occurs when the neck breaks somewhere between the nut and the first two machine heads – that is, at its weakest point. This is more likely with electric guitars (which are heavier than acoustics) and with any guitar

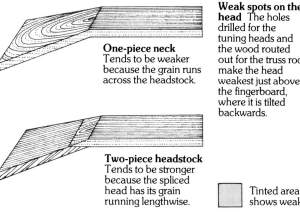

One-piece neck
Tends to be weaker because the grain runs across the headstock.

Two-piece headstock
Tends to be stronger because the spliced head has its grain running lengthwise.

that has a one-piece neck and truss rod.

If the wood has only partially split, or if it has broken into two separate pieces which can be fitted snugly together, the repair may be quite easy. As long as the two pieces of wood are aligned carefully and accurately, a simple gluing and clamping operation will be all that is required.

However, if the wood has splintered or broken so that the surfaces cannot be married up perfectly, the repair should be handed over to a professional.

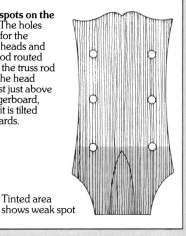

Weak spots on the head The holes drilled for the tuning heads and the wood routed out for the truss rod make the head weakest just above the fingerboard, where it is tilted backwards.

☐ Tinted area shows weak spot

Repairing splits and cracks

Splits and cracks in the woodwork are, once again, most often caused by accidentally dropping the guitar. But this kind of damage can also be the result of the wood aging and changing its shape, or of the guitar being exposed to extremes of temperature and humidity. The thinner timbers of the soundbox are the most liable to split or crack, particularly if the wood originally used for the construction of the guitar was of low quality or poorly seasoned.

When making the repair, the most important thing is to align correctly the pieces of wood on either side of the crack and maintain this alignment while you make a tight, solid glued joint. This will almost certainly mean using a system of clamps or weights. It may also involve using "cleats" or "studs". These are thin slivers of wood which help to reinforce the crack and keep the wood aligned correctly. They are "patched" over the crack on the inside of the soundbox,

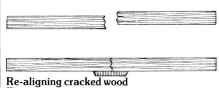

Re-aligning cracked wood
The two pieces of wood on either side of a crack or split are usually out of alignment. Cleats or studs attached to the underside will help to keep them together correctly.

Diamond cleats

Rectangular cleats

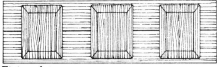

Fixing cleats
Cleats should be shaved or beveled at the edges and glued over the inside of the crack with their grain running perpendicular to that of the damaged wood.

with their grain running at right angles to the wood of the guitar. In some cases, you may be able to work through the soundhole, using probes and an inspection light.

If you are willing to take the extra trouble, hot hide glue is the best sort to use for repairing cracks. It should be warmed until quite runny and then rubbed into the split with a piece of cloth. Apply the glue from the outside and work it in between the two edges of wood until it can just be seen on the inside. This will be sufficient.

Sometimes, a split may occur around the sides of an acoustic guitar soundbox. This can be treated in the same way, by working

glue into the crack and clamping the linings until set. Decorative edging that has come loose can be re-glued with hide glue or white glue if made of wood. But, if the edging is plastic, you should use an ordinary cement-type adhesive.

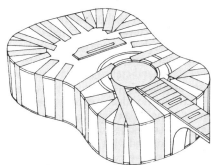

Re-gluing edging
While the glue dries, plenty of sticky tape can be used to keep the edging in place.

Repairs to simple splits and cracks are within the scope of most people and details of refinishing are given on pp. 174-6. However, serious damage – a large crack or chip with a missing piece or a broken strut, for example – should be given to a repairer. The same is true for any repair work, however minor, that needs doing to valuable or older guitars.

Applying the finish

Whether you are using a spray or working by hand with a brush or rubber, finishing should always be carried out in a warm, dry environment. Some finishes are highly inflammable and may give off toxic fumes, so take precautions.

Make sure that the surface of the wood is perfectly smooth, and that all traces of stripper (which may attack the new finish) have been removed. Give several thin coats in preference to fewer, heavier applications. To familiarize yourself with a new technique, try it out first on a spare piece of wood – discarded furniture is ideal – before starting work on the guitar.

Lacquer, shellac and varnish can be applied with a soft, purpose-made varnishing brush no more than 1 in. (2.5 cm) wide. Buy a new brush rather than using an old one which you have previously used with a different kind of finish. To avoid overloading, dip only the tip of the bristles into the finish, and apply with regular, even strokes that follow the grain of the wood. Apply successive coats, sanding down in between until you have a smooth finish. Then give a couple of final coats without sanding.

Spray finishing

With practice, you can use spraying to give fine control, allowing you to achieve an even and regular finish. Industrial equipment gives the highest gloss, although you can use an artist's airbrush or a rented spraygun/compressor unit suitable for home use to achieve good results. Aerosol sprays are cheap and can give a passable finish if used with care.

Working into the light
If you work with your light source positioned so that the surface of the guitar catches the light, you will find it easy to spot any blemishes or irregularities in the finish.

Work on a dry day so that moisture in the air does not spoil the finish and slow down drying. Keeping the gun square-on to the surface, spray at a regular distance to give an even coating. Start moving the gun before you release the jet, otherwise the fluid may spurt and form blobs, and keep it moving at a constant rate. Spray thinly, and wear a face mask at all times.

Wood stains

Most people prefer to retain the attractive natural appearance of good quality timbers such as rosewood, mahogany, maple and spruce by using only a simple, clear finish. As woods like these have become expensive and harder to find, however, substitute timbers have been used – often with great success – by many makers. These woods are frequently stained in order to enhance their appearance, as well as to give the traditional look of dark fingerboard, ribs and back against a light-colored soundboard.

Stains can be bought in a variety of solid and liquid forms, and can be applied at any one of several stages in the finishing process. For example, a stain can be applied directly to the bare wood to darken it before finishing begins, using a brush, rag or rubber. It can also be added to grain filler to match a tone or color, or it can be mixed with the finish itself. Different shades of varnish and French polish are available and are ideal for darkening existing finishes.

Since stain can sink deeper into some parts of the wood than others, care is needed in order to achieve an even tone. Generally speaking, it is best to use stain only when you wish to match an existing color. Stained wood does not look as attractive as natural wood when finished.

French polishing

This technique must be used with great care, but results can be superior to brush finishing. You can use the method to apply other finishes besides French polish itself.

Take a piece of lint-free cotton or cloth 3-6 in. (7.5-15 cm) square. Dip a small ball of cotton into a tray of finish, shake off the excess, and then wrap it inside the cloth to form a pad or rubber. Apply coats of finish thinly. When the entire surface is covered, leave it to dry thoroughly and then give it a light rubbing down with garnet paper. Apply the next coat, repeating the process until a smooth, even finish is achieved. Finally apply two or three coats along the grain. If the rubber starts to stick or bind on the surface, add a drop of linseed oil to the pad.

If you want the highest possible gloss, add some methylated spirit to the finish before the final coats. Add more spirit to each coat and then finish off with a single coat of spirit on its own. For a matte finish, omit the spirit and simply burnish the surface with a soft, dry cloth.

Sanding down between coats
After each layer of finish has been applied, it should be sanded down, using fine abrasive paper, before the next coat goes on. This technique is sometimes known as "cutting back".

Final rubbing down and polishing

Before giving a finish a final rub-down, it is best to put the instrument to one side for a week or so to dry. The exact drying time will depend on the type of finish you have used and the method you employed, as well as the temperature and humidity of the surroundings.

Rub down using very fine grades of abrasive paper or wire wool. Some makers use 1000 or even 2000 grit when the instrument demands a first-class finish. Wet-and-dry papers are also useful, because they have less of a tendency to become clogged. They are commonly applied using water as a lubricant, although sometimes lemon oil is used instead.

Rubbing and polishing compounds are available in either paste or liquid form. A rubbing compound paste contains a grinding agent which you rub evenly over the surface of the finish. Different grades are made, from coarse to fine, so make sure you buy the latter for work on guitars. Smoothing compounds are sold at motor parts dealers, as they are often used in restoring vehicle finishes which have lost their original high gloss.

Guitar care and travel

Always keep your guitar in its case when you are not using it, and clean the strings with a dry cloth as soon as you finish playing. This will remove any dirt, moisture or sweat and, more than anything else, will help make the strings last longer. It is also a good idea to wipe down the body and neck, including any metal parts – especially gold plating, which may tarnish if it is not kept clean.

Cleaning and polishing your guitar

Combined cleaner-polishers such as those made for use on household surfaces are suitable for all modern synthetic guitar finishes. Creams are probably better than aerosols since there is a danger that the spray will get into the pick-ups or tuning heads.

Guitars with a traditional finish such as French polish *must* be cleaned with a cream. The solvents used in aerosols have been known to have a harmful effect on these finishes. Some major guitar manufacturers market their own brands of hand-applied cream cleaner-polishers.

French-polish finishes can also be cleaned and polished with beeswax, although many French polishers recommend that you simply wipe the surface with a damp cloth and a little vinegar or lemon oil, and then buff it up with a dry, soft cloth.

Varnished or lacquered fingerboards can be treated with the same cleaner-polisher as the rest of the guitar. But oiled fingerboards – such as those traditionally fitted to classical guitars – and oiled-wood bodies should be cleaned and oiled two or three times a year with linseed oil. This is rubbed into the wood, working with the grain, using fine-grade wire wool. A good time to do this is when you are changing strings.

It is worth noting that, if the guitar finish is scratched or damaged so that the wood shows through, the cleaner will penetrate the surface. Repair blemishes before applying any cream or aerosol.

Storing your guitar

Although a fairly constant temperature of 20-21°C (68-70°F) is desirable, it is more important to avoid sudden changes and extremes of temperature and humidity. Never leave a guitar near a radiator, close to hot water pipes, or in a damp cellar or basement.

Classical guitars are more vulnerable than other types to changes in humidity – as are old or antique instruments. If you intend to keep one in a centrally heated room, you should invest in a "room humidifier" to prevent the air from becoming too dry.

During most normal use, a guitar should be kept at concert pitch so that there is an even tension on the strings. But if you intend to store a guitar for a lengthy period, you should de-tune *all* the strings and release the tension from the neck completely.

Traveling with your guitar

Advice about taking a guitar on a plane varies from airline to airline. Essentially, there are only two options: it either travels with you in the cabin – in which case you may have to book a seat for it – or it goes in the hold with the luggage. If the flight is not full, however, you may be allowed to take your guitar on board with you and store it in a closet in the cabin. Airline staff try to be as helpful as possible, but obviously fare-paying passengers take priority. Guitars are frequently damaged in cargo holds. A proper flight case is the only way to give guaranteed protection. Even hardshell cases are often smashed, while a soft fabric or plastic case will mean almost certain disaster.

When traveling by road or rail, lay the guitar flat so it cannot fall forward. Avoid putting a heavy amp or speaker where a sudden jolt could tip it onto your guitar. Remember that guitar cases are very recognizable, and will readily attract thieves.

Guitar cases

Cheap fabric or plastic guitar cases give little protection other than keeping dust and rain off. Hardshell cases made from wood or fiberglass are essential if you intend to travel with your guitar. The inside of the case is usually covered with a soft felt or velvet-like material to protect the finish, and there is sometimes additional foam padding between the casing and the inner lining. A spare strings compartment is often positioned to give support to the neck and to stop movement once the case is closed.

If the case supplied with the guitar is unsatisfactory, buy one which fits the instrument as closely as possible, to stop it moving around in transit. Acoustic guitar cases usually follow the contours of the instrument. Because solid-bodies are considerably smaller, electric guitar cases are often oblong. It is quite easy to make an oblong case yourself, but it may not be much cheaper than buying one ready-made.

A good hardshell case not only protects a guitar from knocks but also from excessive moisture and damp. An excessively warm, dry environment can be just as harmful, causing cracks and warping. Some owners of expensive, hand-made classical guitars put a small "guitar humidifier" in the string compartment of the case to ensure that the air is not too dry.

Touring bands and musicians usually invest in a complete set of "flight cases" for their equipment. These are similar to oblong hardshell cases but are larger, heavier and much more robust.

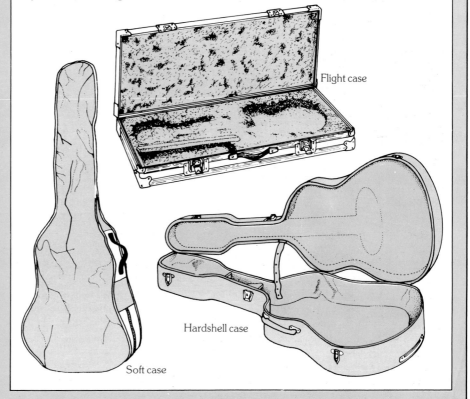

Flight case

Hardshell case

Soft case

Custom and customized guitars

A *custom* guitar is, strictly speaking, one that has been made to order or modified to suit a particular musician's requirements. Such instruments can either be hand-built or they can be standard production-line models which have been changed in some way by the manufacturer in response to a specific request. However, some makers also use the term loosely to distinguish between the basic production model and an instrument which has certain non-standard features. In the Gibson Les Paul range, for instance, the Les Paul Custom originally had three humbucker pick-ups and a special black finish which set it apart from other models.

A *customized* guitar is one which the owner has altered, or has had altered, to meet his own needs. Sometimes the modification is largely cosmetic, as with the use of brass control knobs to enhance the appearance of the instrument. More often, the motive is to combine the distinctive features of guitars made by different manufacturers to improve the sound and playing qualities. A custom modification which has been popular for many years is to fit a Gibson "PAF" humbucking pick-up (see p. 195) to the neck pick-up position of a Stratocaster. The Gibson pick-up can then be used on its own, or in conjunction with the two Fender single-coil pick-ups.

The growth of independent custom parts makers such as Schecter and DiMarzio in recent years has meant that guitarists are now able to improve or upgrade almost any type of instrument – Japanese copy guitars, for instance. Some players indeed prefer the tailor-made sound they can achieve with such instruments to the familiar, off-the-shelf properties of mass-produced guitars.

Hand-built guitar
Tony Zemaitis specializes in custom guitars. His early patrons included Keith Richards and Ron Wood. This guitar features an original Gibson "PAF" humbucking pick-up, and was given special mother-of-pearl inlays to the order of ex-Whitesnake guitarist, Micky Moody.

Spare parts and kits

Fender and Gibson have, for many years, produced a wide range of replacement parts for their guitars. Apart from the products of makers like Grover and De Armond, however, quality spares such as tuning heads and clip-on pick-ups have not always been so readily available. It was not until the growth of interest in customizing in the 1970s that alternative, custom parts could easily be bought over the counter. It was then that major custom parts makers such as

DiMarzio, as well as smaller, specialist firms such as Seymour Duncan, began to offer precision equipment at reasonable prices. Seymour Duncan, himself, had made an extensive study of vintage pick-ups and had perfected the art of making them to match the requests of knowledgeable guitarists seeking particular vintage rock sounds, most of which could be traced back to the early products of Gibson or Fender. By the end of the 1970s, the range had been ex-

tended by companies such as Schecter Guitar Research, Mighty Mite and DiMarzio, among others, to include items such as tuning heads and bridges. The range has now become so extensive that it is possible to buy a complete set of guitar parts in a do-it-yourself kit form.

These kits and parts are still, by and large, based on Gibson Les Paul and Explorer guitars, Fender Telecasters, Stratocasters, and Jazz and Precision basses.

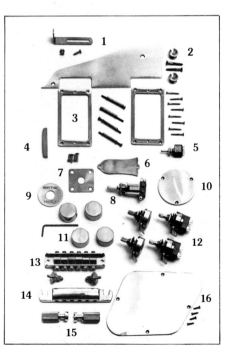

Guitar kit (*left*)
This is a replica Stratocaster in kit form from Mighty Mite. The body comes ready-sealed and primed, thus cutting down preparatory finishing work.

Custom spares (*right*)
Like several other makers, Mighty Mite offers a full range of high-quality fittings for custom guitars. This is their "Les Paul" range.
1 Fingerplate and mount. **2** Strap buttons. **3** Pick-up mounting rings. **4** Nut.
5 On–off switch.
6 Truss rod cover.
7 Jack plate. **8** Three-way switch with **9** mounting plate and **10** cover. **11** Control knobs. **12** Pots.
13 Bridge. **14** Tailpiece. **15** Studs.
16 Control cover back plate.

Custom modifications

The "spare-part surgery" market was mainly developed by American companies catering to guitarists who sought to enhance the performance of their instruments. In the early 1970s the emphasis was on quality, and this contrasted with the attitude of Japanese guitar-makers at the time.

Taking their chances with patent legalities, the Japanese had flooded the market with blatant copies of the most popular Gibson and Fender guitars. While some of these copies represented a genuine attempt at producing a replica that was as good as the original in every way, many more were made to be sold at very low prices, with a production and sound quality to match.

These Japanese copies brought electric guitars within almost everyone's reach, and even their rough sound quality found its adherents. Nevertheless, the higher-priced, better-made copies proved very popular, especially since musicians discovered that they could readily be upgraded by customizing. Tuning heads and pick-ups were often of inferior quality, but with replacement spares from the American parts-makers' catalogues they could easily be rebuilt into high-quality instruments.

It is now common practice to use a Japanese copy guitar as the basis for a series of custom modifications. Replacement pick-

Pick-up modification
Rory Gallagher's Fender Esquire, as originally built, had only one single-coil pick-up in the bridge position. This has now been augmented by two new single-coils.

ups, bridges and hardware are based closely on the Fender, Gibson and (among others) Rickenbacker originals. Necks and bodies are also available if you wish to build up the whole guitar from scratch. If you take care over the work, you can produce a viable alternative to the "real" guitar, or you can improvise – building a guitar which will give a new range of characteristics.

Kit-built guitars
One of several similar instruments owned by Pete Townshend, this "Telecaster" was built entirely with Schecter parts. Though the basic assembly of a kit-built guitar is relatively easy, a great deal of care must be taken with setting the intonation and action. For instance, if you decide to fit a Fender-style single-coil pick-up to a Gibson model, you may have problems with setting the height of the strings in relation to the pick-up, or in matching the string spacings with individual pick-up pole pieces. Though many kits and parts are of excellent quality – as good as, if not better than, the products of established makers – they will be of little use if the basic guitar (a cheap Japanese copy, for instance) has faults which cannot be eradicated. The body or neck of a cheap guitar may be badly designed or made, in which case it may be impossible to get a good sound from the instrument, no matter how good the replacement parts.

Fitting new nuts and saddles

Most production-made acoustic and electric guitars have synthetic or plastic nuts; acoustics usually have a saddle made of a similar material. Only better-quality guitars have bone, ivory or – in the case of electrics – brass nuts, which give a better tone and are less prone to wear.

If you want to upgrade your guitar you can buy slightly oversized pieces of bone or (more rarely) ivory from guitar shops and instrument-makers' suppliers, which you can then cut and file to the exact shape and size required. Brass nuts made by Mighty Mite, Schecter, and other customizing suppliers are made to suit stock models of electric guitars.

To fit a replacement nut, first remove the strings from the guitar, relaxing the tension gradually on all the strings at the same time so as not to put an uneven strain on the neck. If the finish has coagulated around the nut, scrape it off carefully with a knife. The nut will probably be held in place simply by a couple of spots of glue, in which case you can tap away gently at the sides of the nut with a hammer until the glue cracks. Hold a piece of wood against the nut to cushion the blows. If the nut is any more than slightly recessed, or if it will not come loose readily, you may damage the guitar by using force to remove it, and the job should really be given to a repairer to handle.

Saw the new nut to the rough shape of the old one, and then give it its final shape using fine, flat files. To finish, smooth down with 400-600 grit wet-and-dry abrasive paper before applying a burnishing cream or fine rubbing compound. The new nut should be glued in place with a couple of spots of epoxy resin; if you use too much, the nut may prove difficult to remove at a later stage. When the adhesive has set, you can cut grooves for the strings in the nut with fine needle files. Their depth determines the action of the guitar (see p. 167). Cutting too deeply will cause fret buzz.

If you are replacing a saddle, again use the original as a guide to shape and size. The saddle is usually held in its groove in the bridge solely by the downward tension of the strings.

Fitting replacement tuning heads

To make tuning easier and more accurate, many people like to upgrade their guitars by fitting better-quality tuning heads. The best kind are the low-geared, enclosed, self-lubricating tuning heads of the type made by Schaller and Grover.

If you wish simply to replace heads which are worn or damaged, try to get an identical set from the maker of your guitar. If this is not possible, take the guitar or the old tuning heads along with you to a music shop. Look for a set that calls for the least amount of drilling of new holes in the head of the guitar. Tuning heads on two mounting plates, each with three machines, can be difficult to replace because, unless the new set has the same spacing between the capstans, the holes will have to be re-drilled. If this is the case, it is often better to replace them with the individual type, which also tend to be of higher quality.

Gradually reduce the tension on the strings and then remove the old tuning heads. If the old fixing holes do not match up, they must be filled. This is best done by plugging with small, matchstick-like strips of wood with a point at one end. Use a hardwood which matches the headstock. Put a good covering of glue (white woodworking glue will suffice) onto each piece and push them into the hole one by one. When the hole is almost full, tap the last strips of hardwood in place with a small hammer. After the glue has set, trim off the excess with a sharp knife, and touch up the spots with the appropriate finish.

Carefully mark the position of the new fixing screws and drill a pilot hole with a small hand drill or bradawl. Do not over-tighten the screws or you may strip the thread in the hole. If this happens, plug the hole and start again.

To prevent wear, good-quality tuning heads have some type of sleeve or collar arrangement through which the capstan passes. If they are a tight fit, these sleeves can sometimes be simply tapped into position, and will stay firmly anchored. Otherwise, you will have to drill a bigger hole through the headstock. Use a hand drill and a drilling stand to ensure accuracy.

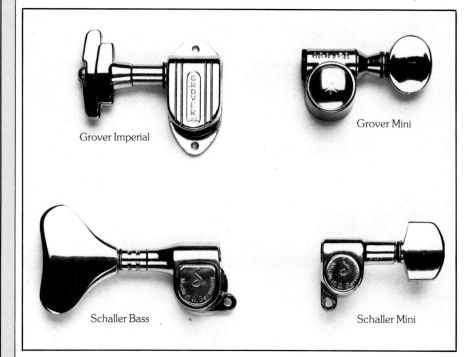

Grover Imperial

Grover Mini

Schaller Bass

Schaller Mini

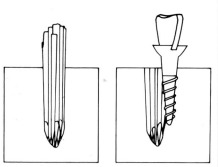

Filling screw holes
If the old holes are not covered by the machine heads, or if they are too close to the new positions, they should be filled. Plug the hole with pointed strips of hardwood which have been liberally coated with glue. Use the same technique to give grip to screws if the old holes are too large for them.

Tuning heads
The Grover Imperial has a gear ratio of 14:1 for very fine tuning. The smaller Grover model has a 12:1 ratio with sealed lubrication. Note the size difference compared to the butterfly-shaped Schaller machine head for bass guitars. Schaller's self-locking Mini is designed for guitarists who prefer a smaller and lighter machine head.

Fitting replacement bridges

Removing and replacing the glued-on bridge of an acoustic guitar is a tricky job which you should only attempt if you have an aptitude for working with wood. If not, you should entrust the job to an experienced maker or repairer. The bridge of an electric guitar is a more straightforward proposition. Fitting a new bridge can give better string-height and intonation adjustment, while a heavy brass bridge will markedly increase the sustain. You can also fit a Fender-type tremelo/bridge unit to many other makes of guitar. Choose the new bridge carefully, checking that it will give you the required string height after allowing for the size of the pick-ups.

If the new bridge is of the relatively simple surface-fixing type, and the intonation of your guitar was correct with the old one, use the position of the existing saddle (rather than the bridge itself) as a guide for fixing. Most quality bridges have a lengthwise adjustment, which allows you to set the individual scale length of each string independently. The ideal bridge position should therefore give you maximum scale-length adjustment in both directions. If you position the bridge so that the intonation of the top E string is correct (see p. 171), you will have an equal amount of back and forward adjustment.

Surface-fixed bridges may be secured either by screws or, more likely, by a bolt-and-stud arrangement, in which the body is fitted with sunken metal studs into which are screwed the bolts securing the bridge or tailpiece. If the new fixing positions do not align with the old ones, or if the fixings have a different thread, you will need to change the studs. A special tool is available for removing them. The hole should then be filled. You can cut a length of dowel of the right diameter, or you can use a special plug-cutting tool of the appropriate size. Glue the new plug into the hole and, when it

is dry, trim the plug and smooth down to a level surface. To drill the new hole, make a small pilot hole and then drill with progressively larger bits until you have reached the correct size for the new plug. This can now be tapped into place; its fluted sides will grip the wood firmly.

As far as the guitar's appearance is concerned, it is best to find a replacement bridge which covers the old, plugged

mounting holes. If this is not possible, you should sand down the plug till it is level with the surface of the guitar body and then touch it up (as outlined on p. 175) to match the existing finish. This technique will be satisfactory for a guitar with an opaque finish, but unfortunately with a natural finish there is little you can do other than ensuring that the grain of the plug matches the direction of the grain on the body.

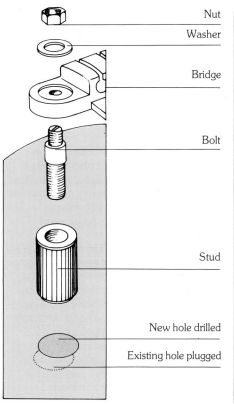

Bridge mounting
In the diagram above, the old stud holes have been filled in and new ones drilled. The stud (a screw-threaded brass collar with fluted sides) is tapped into position. A brass bolt is screwed into the stud and the bridge is mounted on this. It is then secured by a nut and washer.

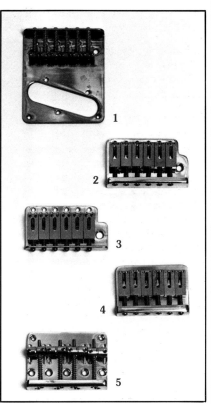

Replacement bridges
These are solid brass bridges for Fender guitars. **1** Bridge plate for a Telecaster. **2-3** Trax bridge for Stratocaster, with tremolo facility. **4** Stratocaster Trax bridge. without tremolo. **5** Bridge for Precision and Jazz model bass guitars.

String bender

Also known as a "pull-string", this is a mechanical system of levers and springs which allows you to raise the pitch of the top E or B string, according to type. It simulates some pedal-steel guitar techniques. The rods and springs are fitted into a cavity in the guitar body, and a pivoting arm is connected to the string at the bridge. A second arm is attached to the strap button, so that pushing down on the guitar at this point raises the pitch by a tone. Palm pedals such as those made by Bigsby also allow you to raise one or two notes without affecting others, whereas a tremolo arm alters the pitch of all six strings.

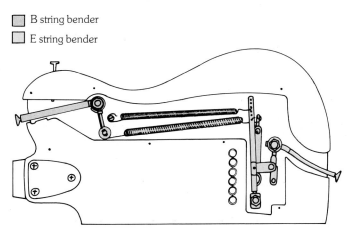

☐ B string bender
☐ E string bender

Parsons-White string bender
This Telecaster is custom-fitted with two benders, one working on the B string and the other on the top E. The device was invented by Gene Parsons and the late Clarence White when they were members of the Byrds. Though effective, the string bender requires considerable skill to make full use of its potential.

A guide to guitar electronics

The basic function of an electric guitar pick-up is remarkably simple. The pick-up generates a small alternating current (AC) across its windings when the strings are played, and this signal is subsequently amplified (see pp. 52-3). You could plug the pick-up directly into an amplifier and the sound of the guitar would come through perfectly clearly, though with no variation in volume or tone, other than that achieved by adjusting the amplifier's controls. The controls wired into so-called "passive" guitar circuits simply enable you to modify the alternating current output from the pick-up in order to give variations of tone and volume. They work by altering and controlling the voltage, amperage and wattage of the signal generated by the pick-up before it is directed to the input of the amplifier.

Volume controls (potentiometers or "pots") control the amount of electrical energy delivered. Tone controls (incorporating potentiometers and capacitors or coils) modify the frequency distributions within the AC signal from the pick-up in a way which enables you to vary its harmonic content or balance.

"Active" guitar circuits make use of a battery-powered pre-amplifier mounted on the guitar itself. This permits tone settings to be cut or boosted by wider margins than are possible with passive circuits, which rely purely on power from the amplifier. All current in passive guitar circuitry is AC. Direct current (DC) is only present in active circuits.

Bearing in mind the increasing sophistication of guitar electronics, and the fact that you may wish to add electrical components to your guitar or make repairs and modifications, it is a good idea to have a working technical knowledge of the subject. In the following pages, we have assumed no prior knowledge of electronics. We therefore begin with a general introduction to electricity, electrical components and wiring diagrams, and follow with some practical information on soldering and screening before going on to look at particular guitar circuits.

What is electricity?

Electricity is a force which arises from the fundamental properties of matter, which is made up of atoms. The outer bands of some atoms are incomplete and unstable. As a result, electrons (elementary particles of atoms) within these bands can be made to pass from atom to atom and form a flow known as *electrical current*. Substances which have incomplete outer shells, permitting the passage of electrons, are called *conductors*.

Other substances – such as silicon – are formed in groups of atoms that have stable outer shells which block the passage of electrons. These are *non-conductors* or *insulators*. There are also *semi-conductors*, consisting of substances which, although normally insulators, are deliberately contaminated with atoms whose unstable outer shells permit a flow of electrons. As a result, electrons can be made to pass through a semi-conductor in a controlled fashion. The ability to regulate and modify the characteristics of a current by means of semi-conductors is an all-important part of electronic circuitry.

An electrical current flows through a conductor when a source of electrons is connected to one end and an "electron sink", into which the current is absorbed, is connected to the other. For example, a wire connected between the positive and negative poles of a battery will cause the electrons to flow from the minus connection to the plus connection. The pressure which pushes electrons through a conductor is called the *voltage*, and it is measured in volts, millivolts, etc. The quantity of electrons flowing through a conductor is called the current, and it is measured in amps, milliamps, etc. The power in the circuit is dependent on both the amperage and voltage and is measured in watts, milliwatts, etc. Voltage is multiplied by amperage to determine wattage.

To prevent connecting wires from melting, the flow of current must be controlled. This can be done by inserting a *resistor* into the circuit. As its name implies, this is a component with a more or less specific resistance to the flow of current. Resistance is measured in ohms (Ω). Ohm's law states that voltage = resistance × current. Conductors – even wiring components – have a very slight resistance to the flow of current, but no significant effect is likely to be noticed over short conductor lengths.

Reading wiring diagrams

Electrical wiring diagrams can, at first sight, appear frighteningly complicated. They are, however, quite simple to read. Each component in a circuit is represented by a standard symbol (see opposite). Intercommunications between components – which are either wires or copper tracks on a printed circuit board – are shown by solid, unbroken lines joining the component symbols together.

Wiring diagrams are generally arranged with the signal input or generation shown on the left of the diagram and the output shown on the right. So the signal flows from left to right. Across the bottom of the diagram, is the earth or "zero volts" line, while across the top is the DC (positive or negative) power line that powers the circuit. AC flows from left to right, while DC flows from top to bottom.

The components built into an electrical circuit are represented in wiring diagrams by standardized symbols. There are many variations of the basic types of components used in guitar and amplifier circuitry. One capacitor, for instance, can look totally different from another, in spite of the fact that they both perform the same function. Allowing for different values and tolerances, there are literally thousands of components to choose from. For the inexperienced, identifying components can be a problem at first. One reason is that the wiring diagram symbols for components are based on their internal structure, not their outward appearance.

On the opposite page are set out all the wiring diagram symbols you are likely to encounter, together with illustrations showing what the components actually look like.

Electronic abbreviations	
V	Volts
A	Amps
W	Watts
F	Farads
Ω	Ohms
H	Henries
Hz	Hertz (cycles per second)
K	Kilo (× 1,000)
M	Mega (× 1,000,000)
m	Milli (÷ 1,000)
µ	Micro (÷ 1,000,000)
p	Pico (÷ [1,000,000 × 1,000,000])

Electrical symbols

1 Fixed resistor.

2 (a) Variable resistor. **(b)** Potentiometer. (Both knob controlled.) **(c)** Pre-set variable resistor. **(d)** Pre-set potentiometer. (Both screwdriver controlled.)

3 Ganged variable resistors or potentiometers (two pots on one spindle).

4 (a) Capacitor (any non-polarized type). **(b)** Electrolytic capacitor. **(c)** Tantalum capacitor.

5 Fuse.

6 (a) Mono jack socket. **(b)** Stereo jack socket. **(c)** Stereo jack socket with one make switch. **(d)** Stereo jack socket with one break switch.

7 Coaxial socket.

8 (a) One-way (single-throw) switch. **(b)** Two-way (double-throw) switch.

9 Semi-conductor diode.

10 (a) P-N-P transistor. **(b)** N-P-N transistor.

11 (a) n-channel junction field effect transistor (J-FET). **(b)** p-channel FET. **(c)** n-channel I G FET. **(d)** p-channel I G FET.

12 (a) Diode valve. **(b)** Triode valve. **(c)** Tetrode valve. **(d)** Pentode valve.

13 (a) Wires crossed but not connected. **(b)** Wires connected.

14 (a) Earth connection. **(b)** Chassis. **(c)** Terminal.

15 Battery.

16 Microphones.

17 Loudspeaker.

18 Transformer.

19 Iron-cored choke or inductance.

Electrical components

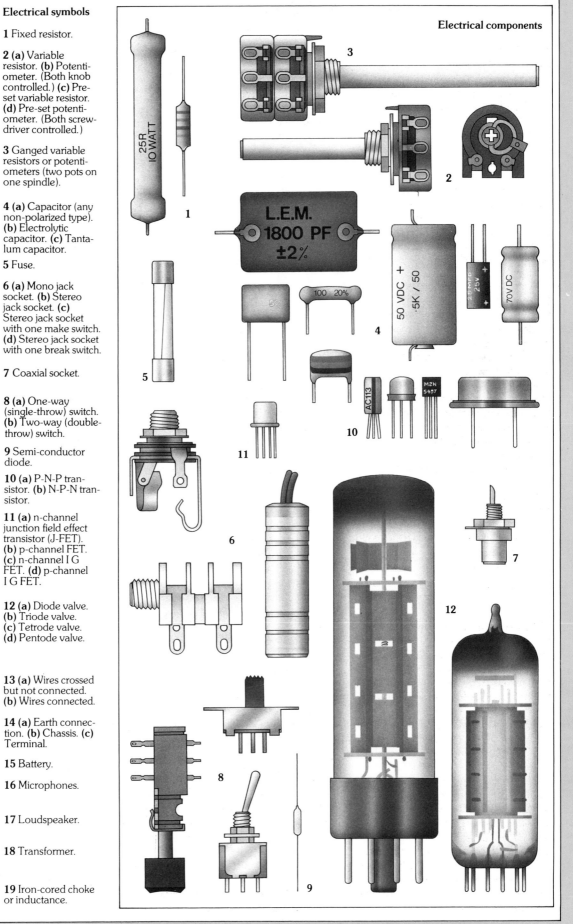

Choosing tools

Shown here is a selection of tools which should enable you to carry out almost any electrical work. You will find it useful to have two soldering irons, one for general work and the other for cases where heavy-duty soldering is involved. The multimeter is an invaluable item for measuring electrical currents and also enables you to carry out a large number of routine checks on electrical equipment. Your multimeter should be capable of measuring ohms from zero to 1 megohm and AC/DC volts from zero to at least 500 volts.

1 Multimeter.
2 Spanner with multiple jaws, used for potentiometer mounting nuts, etc.
3 Small electrical screwdriver.
4 Medium-sized, general-purpose screwdriver.
5 Cross-head screwdriver.
6 Small snipe-nosed or needle-nosed pliers.
7 Wire strippers with adjustable stop fitted to close over a cable so only the insulation is cut, the core remaining undamaged.
8 Wire cutter with sharpened tip. End cutters are the most useful type. The jaws are hollowed out for holding terminals.
9 40-60 W soldering iron for heavy-duty soldering, such as attaching earth leads to pot casings.
10 15-25 W soldering iron for most general work. Fit a 1 amp fuse in the plug of your soldering iron. Larger sizes of fuse may make the iron dangerous. Soldering irons are sometimes supplied with interchangeable tips of different sizes and shapes.

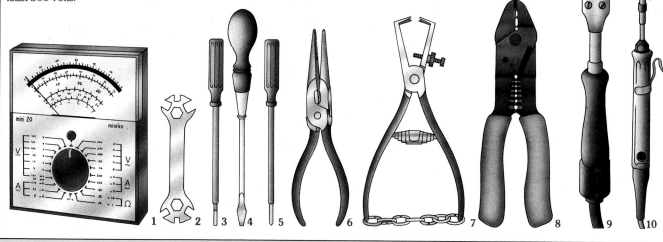

Soldering

Solder is an alloy which when heated – usually with an electric soldering iron – will melt so that it can be applied to two pieces of metal to make a fairly strong bond between them. The bonding occurs during the few seconds that the solder takes to cool. Solder is conductive, which means that it will carry electrical current. It is therefore ideal for many electrical connections of a semi-permanent nature, since the connection can easily be dismantled with the application of more heat from a soldering iron. This, of course, is useful for repair work.

You must always use an electrical solder in conjunction with flux. Flux cleans the surface of pieces of metal which are to be joined together. It is needed because many metals oxidize when exposed to air, and the layer of oxidation left on the surface makes the joint weak and unreliable. Flux chemically removes this layer and prevents any re-oxidation during the soldering process.

The best type of solder to use in guitar and electronic work is that which has a built-in core or cores of flux. Remember that certain metals and metal platings will not accept solder: aluminum, for instance, needs a special purpose-made solder. Note, however, that plumbing solder is entirely unsuitable for any form of electrical soldering work.

Soldering is a relatively simple process and, in the long run, it is no more difficult to solder well than it is to solder badly. Since badly soldered joints will let you down sooner or later, it is only sensible to use the correct techniques from the outset.

For general-purpose work a 15–25 watt soldering iron with interchangeable tips is ideal. It is a good idea to have a second soldering iron of a fairly high power – 40–60 watts – to tackle those jobs involving soldering wires to larger pieces of metal which absorb far more heat: when you have to solder an earth connection to the outer casing of a pick-up, for example.

Selecting the size of tip to be used is simple. Choose the one with a tip contact size closest to the size of the joint to be made. Never change the tip of an iron while it is still plugged in or while it is still hot.

An important part of soldering is the technique of "tinning" the tip of the soldering iron bit before and after use to prevent it from becoming corroded and eventually unusable. Each time the soldering iron is switched on, hold the solder against the contact surface of the tip until the solder melts, giving the tip a thin coating. Surplus solder should always be removed from the tip by means of a quick wipe with a piece of damp foam, sponge or rag. Hot solder should never be shaken or knocked off, because of the risk of damage to the iron, as well as the danger from flying molten metal.

After tinning, the iron should be used immediately. If you delay for even a couple of minutes, the iron should be wiped clean and tinned once again. Failure to do this will result in partially oxidized – and consequently much weakened – solder being applied to the joint. It is also sensible to do all pre-soldering preparation (cutting to length and stripping of wires, labeling of contacts, etc.) before switching on the iron.

Metal surfaces to be joined together should be clean, bright, dry and grease-free.

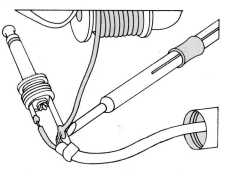

Soldering a jack plug connection
Use soldering iron to heat metal surface. Apply solder to connection, letting it flow over joint. Remove iron to let solder solidify.

Preparing screened cables for connections

Screened cable consists of one or more insulated central cores of wire around which a further screen of wires is wrapped or braided. A final external layer of insulation (rubber, plastic or fabric) encloses the complete cable. The central core is used to carry the signal transmitted from component to component, or for external connections such as the one between guitar and amplifier. The screening is connected to the earth side of the guitar's circuitry so that any rogue interference is sent to earth. Avoid the cheap, thinner types of wrapped screened cable; braided screen cables are far superior. For quality work such as recording – when it is desirable to keep background noise and interference to the minimum – "low-noise" screened cable is recommended.

To prepare wrapped screen cable for connections, use wire strippers or a sharp knife to remove 2 in. (5 cm) of the outer insulation. Unwind the screening wires and twist them into a core. Strip back about ½–1 in. (1.2–2.5 cm) of the insulation around the central core or cores. Insulate the part of the screening which is exposed, leaving ½ in. (1.2 cm) bare for the connection. Finally, tin the ends of the wires to be connected.

With braided cable, you should first remove about 2 in. (5 cm) of the outer insulation, and then push the braiding back from the cable end to form a bulge where the outer insulation now ends. Using a small screwdriver, push the wires aside and carefully part the braiding in the area of the bulge so that the insulated central core can be pulled through. Stretch out the braiding again into a fairly straight core, insulate the exposed screening and tin the ends.

Low-noise cables have an additional black layer of conductive synthetic material between the screening and the insulation around the central core or cores. As this layer is conductive and in contact with the main screening , it must be cut back so as not to short-circuit the signal connections carried by the central core or cores.

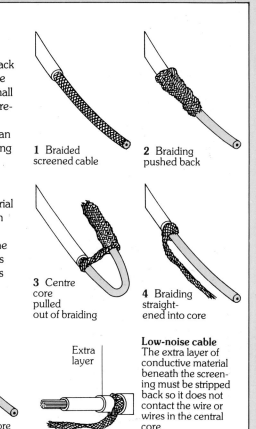

1 Braided screened cable

2 Braiding pushed back

3 Centre core pulled out of braiding

4 Braiding straightened into core

Extra layer

Low-noise cable
The extra layer of conductive material beneath the screening must be stripped back so it does not contact the wire or wires in the central core.

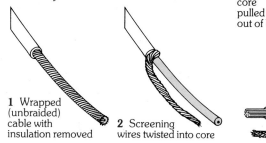

1 Wrapped (unbraided) cable with insulation removed

2 Screening wires twisted into core

When all the pre-soldering preparatory work has been carried out, the parts to be joined together should be tinned. This is done by applying heat directly to the parts being soldered, with the tip of the iron in contact with the cleaned metal surface. The solder is applied directly to the metal, not melted on the tip of the soldering iron first. Never carry a big blob of solder to the metal on the tip of the iron. Use the minimum amount of solder necessary to plate just the pieces of metal being joined. Now bring the parts together and, if possible, crimp wires to terminals to make a joint which is sound before it is soldered. Now apply the iron and add solder until it has flowed over the entire joint. Take the soldering iron away from the joint and allow it to cool, while at the same time ensuring that no movement of the components or wires occurs. A good soldered joint is bright and shiny. A crystalline or dull gray appearance implies that there was movement before the solder solidified, or that the solder has oxidized. In both cases, the joint must be completely re-soldered.

All components can be damaged by heat from a soldering iron, so it is wise only to apply the soldering iron to the joint for the minimum amount of time, without rushing the job.

Wiring an electric guitar circuit

In the following pages we shall explain the stages of installing the necessary circuitry for an electric guitar, beginning with a single pick-up plus tone and volume controls, and then going on to cover more sophisticated arrangements.

The physical layout of the components inside the guitar body will, of course, vary from make to make. For example, some solid-body guitars have recesses behind the fingerplates, and all the circuitry, except for the pick-up, can be fitted to the fingerplate itself. Other solid-body guitars have access plates at the back. Arch-top, hollow-body, f-hole guitars, on the other hand, do not have this recess and are best wired up by making up the circuit in the form of a wiring "harness" or "loom".

This is done by first deciding where to locate the components on the guitar, cutting all the connecting wires to the appropriate length, and then installing the assembly as a complete unit. (Some connections may have to be made once the components are fitted.) The wiring harness is then fed into the soundbox of the guitar through the openings in the body. A little maneuvring and ingenuity (particularly in assessing the length of connecting wires) may be called for, depending on the design of the actual guitar.

"Screening" or "shielding" is the part of the guitar circuitry which reduces the amount of rogue interference picked up from outside sources such as radio waves. Many guitars employ no shielding materials other than those already built into the actual components and connecting wires. Though many manufacturers make guitars with circuits of this type, they are not ideal, since they leave the ends of wires, solder tags, capacitors and other components unshielded (see above for details of using screened cables).

Copper foil – available through some metal merchants or electrical components dealers – and purpose-made electrical shielding tape with an adhesive backing are the best types of material to use for lining a solid-body cavity. They can also be used to line the underside of plastic and synthetic fingerplates.

Also available are special screening paints – such as those that are carbon-based – but they must be used with great care if the shielding effect is to be consistent. The same must be said of domestic aluminum-based cooking foil, which some people use in the same way as copper foil.

Whatever materials or methods you employ, all shielding must be connected to the earth side of the guitar circuit.

How electric guitars are wired

Pick-ups and their associated controls form the heart of any electric guitar's sound characteristics. Though it is possible to make a modest adjustment to this by fitting custom brass hardware, it is really only through working on the actual electrical circuitry of the guitar that you can exploit its full potential.

In this section, the basic principles of pick-up and allied technology explained on p. 52 are developed to show you how, by making certain adjustments or by adding extra components, you can substantially alter the sound characteristics of your guitar. There are also

full notes on how to make checks to ensure that your equipment is functioning correctly. We begin with the rudimentary single pick-up circuit and then move on to more involved work. The pick-ups in this section are all single-coil types. Twin-coil "humbuckers" are dealt with on p. 194.

The single pick-up guitar is, in reality, something of a rarity. The only production guitars nowadays which do not have two or more pick-ups are either vintage models or the very cheapest "beginner's" guitars. While it is unlikely, then, that you would want to

make such a guitar yourself, it is important to understand the principle and assembly of the single pick-up wiring circuit. This is because the seemingly complicated circuitry involved in a two and three pick-up guitar is, in effect, a multiplication of the basic single pick-up circuit — with the addition of option switches that determine whether the pick-ups are used singly or in combination, in series or in parallel, and in or out of phase with one another. If you can grasp the basics of a single pick-up, you should have little difficulty in progressing to more sophisticated circuits.

A single pick-up guitar circuit

The single pick-up circuit shown below involves the following components: the pick-up itself, a capacitor, two potentiometers, screened cable, and a ¼in. (6mm) mono jack socket.

The potentiometers used in the tone and volume controls are shown with the same value of 500 K log. This means that they have a maximum resistance value of 500 Kilohms and that they are the logarithmic rather than linear type. They are good general-purpose pots which will work quite well in most passive guitar circuits.

If the value of the pot is too low, it will prevent your guitar from delivering the maximum volume of which it is capable, while too high a value will result in a loss of control sensitivity. In other words, your volume and tone controls will seem to have no effect over part of their range. The optimum result is – like so many things in electronics – a compromise. When it comes down to component values, the influencing factors should be the type and style of music you are playing as well as the situations in which you are playing it.

The capacitor is used in conjunction with one of the pots to form the tone control. This is, in effect, a treble-cut control. The capacitor's job is to set a frequency below which the tone control pot has no effect, but above which operation of the pot will progressively increase the proportion of high frequencies in the signal from the pick-up that it sends to earth.

The smaller the value of the capacitor, the higher the frequency "roll-off" point will be, and vice versa. To put it another way, the higher the value of the capacitor, the less noticeable it will be when high frequencies are sent to earth. The control will not cut off much treble. The lower the value of the capacitor, the more effective the tone control will be. It will cut off more of the treble.

The procedure for wiring a single pick-up guitar circuit is simplicity itself. As the

diagrams show, a screened lead comes from the pick-up to the volume pot, and another screened lead runs from the volume pot to the jack socket. The tone control is connected to the capacitor and an earth wire. Having prepared the ends of the screened leads as shown on p. 185, make the earth connections to the volume pot and solder them carefully. Then connect the short earth wire to the tone pot.

The next step is to solder the earth connections to the metal covers of the pots. You may need a more powerful soldering iron for this job, and, on some pots, you may have to use an aluminium solder. If you are unable to get a strong joint between the

earth wires and pot casings in this way, try wrapping a piece of bare wire several times through the shake-proof washer on the pot spindle and solder the other end of the wire to the earth tag on the pot.

Now attach and solder the cores of the two screened cables to the volume pot. Lastly connect the .02μF capacitor and the jack socket. Check the sound of the guitar both with and without the optional additional .001μF capacitor shown below. You can just crimp the wire for this component on to the volume control until you have decided whether or not you like the effect. If you then decide to keep it, the connections must be soldered.

Components of single pick-up circuit with volume and tone controls

Note Wires to earthed terminals on pots are extended past the terminals and soldered onto the cases of the pots as part of the necessary screening.

Treble by-pass capacitor
This capacitor is optional. It will give improved treble at lower volumes, but at full volume it will have no effect.

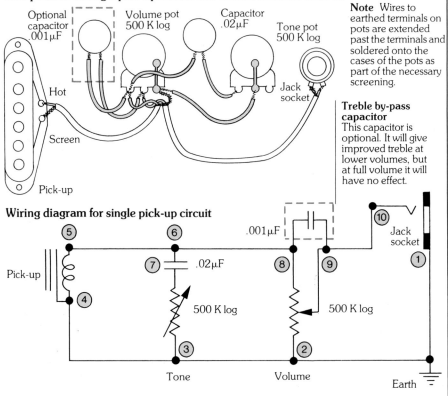

Wiring diagram for single pick-up circuit

A two pick-up guitar circuit

The sound characteristics of an electric guitar are partially generated by the position of the pick-up under the strings – in the same way that different sounds can be produced from an acoustic guitar by playing at the bridge or directly above the soundhole. A single pick-up guitar, such as a Fender Esquire or Gibson Les Paul Junior, has a perfectly adequate sound, but because of the fixed position of the pick-up the only tonal variation comes from adjusting the tone control settings.

By using two pick-ups, you can amplify sound from two different sections of the strings. Either coil used on its own will give its own distinctive sound, or you can use the two pick-ups in phase together to produce a third variation in tone. By fitting the *phase switch* shown as an alternative in the diagram below, you can use the coils out of phase with one another, thus creating four basic options for single-coil pick-ups.

As can be seen from the wiring diagram,

the two pick-up circuit is, in effect, two single pick-up circuits wired in parallel, with the addition of a three-position selector switch. Consequently, apart from the switching, you can follow the basic wiring procedure described opposite.

A useful addition to wiring circuits of this type is the *coil tap*. This is attached to an extra output connection on the pick-up,

located in the center of the coil. By wiring in a two-way switch, you can either use the pick-up as usual or you can take the output from one of the normal connections at either end of the pick-up and the center coil-tap connection. This will effectively halve the impedence of the coil. The lower tap output produces a much cleaner tone with more high frequencies.

Components of twin pick-up circuit with individual volume and tone controls

Note The wiring for a two pick-up circuit is basically a duplication of the one opposite. The optional phase switch (inside the blue dotted line) can be added to pick-up 1.

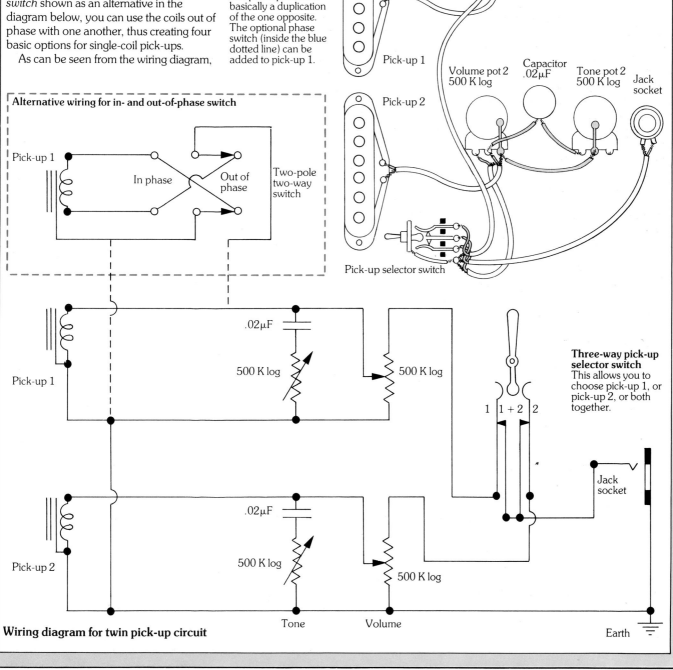

Alternative wiring for in- and out-of-phase switch

Three-way pick-up selector switch
This allows you to choose pick-up 1, or pick-up 2, or both together.

Wiring diagram for twin pick-up circuit

A three pick-up guitar circuit

The use of a third single-coil pick-up dramatically increases the scope for tonal variations. Each single-coil pick-up can be used individually – giving three options – or any pair can be used in phase – giving three more options. Pairs can also be used out of phase with one another, producing a further three variations, while all three can be combined in phase to make an extra option. Bearing in mind the additional possibility of using all three pick-ups together, but with any one out of phase with the other two, there is a potential for many different switching positions, each with its own tonal characteristics.

With humbuckers (see p. 194), the choice can be almost infinite. If all the end connections for both coils are accessible, you have no less than six options for each pick-up. You can wire a humbucker to use either coil on its own, or with both coils in series (in or out of phase), or with both coils in parallel (again either in or out of phase). It should be pointed out, however, that some of these wiring options may negate the hum-canceling properties of the pick-ups. The sound potential for three humbuckers, therefore, is enormous – as it would also be with three single-coil pick-ups fitted with "coil taps" (see p. 187). Of course, with this degree of choice the differences between tones may be so subtle that, in practice, they can scarcely be detected.

Wiring diagram for three pick-up multi-operation circuit

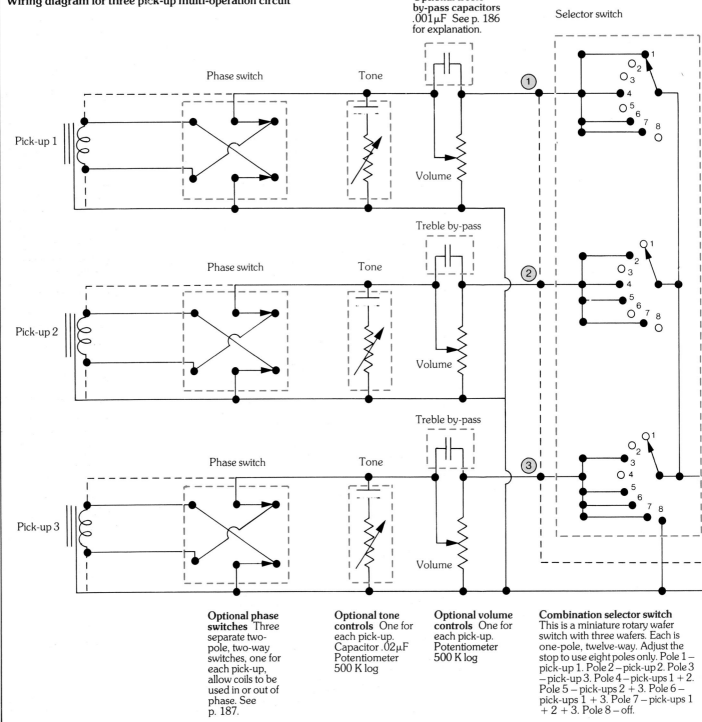

Optional phase switches Three separate two-pole, two-way switches, one for each pick-up, allow coils to be used in or out of phase. See p. 187.

Optional tone controls One for each pick-up. Capacitor .02μF Potentiometer 500 K log

Optional volume controls One for each pick-up. Potentiometer 500 K log

Combination selector switch This is a miniature rotary wafer switch with three wafers. Each is one-pole, twelve-way. Adjust the stop to use eight poles only. Pole 1 – pick-up 1. Pole 2 – pick-up 2. Pole 3 – pick-up 3. Pole 4 – pick-ups 1 + 2. Pole 5 – pick-ups 2 + 3. Pole 6 – pick-ups 1 + 3. Pole 7 – pick-ups 1 + 2 + 3. Pole 8 – off.

An important practical consideration is to think how you can accommodate all the necessary pick-up switches on one guitar. You may also find it difficult to remember how to select an individual sound from the hundreds available to you with such a set-up. Some degree of compromise is therefore necessary. The best thing to do is to experiment with different circuit connections to your switches until you get the results that you want.

Note All optional features are shown inside blue dotted lines. If they are not used, you should complete the black dotted circuitry. Individual volume controls can be used to fulfill the functions of the individual selector switches, which can then be left out (link points 1, 2, 3 and 4). However, a master volume control is useful if these selector switches are omitted. A master tone control may replace or supplement individual tone controls. If you fit treble by-pass filters to one or more of the individual volume controls, then you must also fit one to the master volume control.

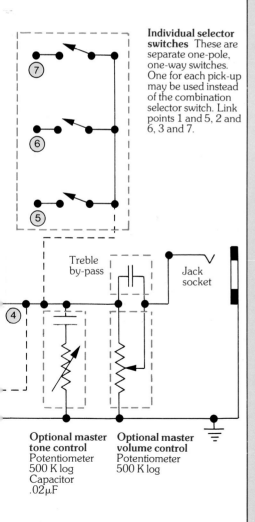

Individual selector switches These are separate one-pole, one-way switches. One for each pick-up may be used instead of the combination selector switch. Link points 1 and 5, 2 and 6, 3 and 7.

Treble by-pass

Jack socket

Optional master tone control
Potentiometer 500 K log
Capacitor .02 µF

Optional master volume control
Potentiometer 500 K log

Fault diagnosis

Use the table below as a guide to isolating faults which cannot be traced to the amplifier or lead. A number of faults can be located by testing the circuit with a multimeter, as detailed on the following pages.

Faults invariably occur when you least expect them to, so it is a good idea to follow the example of many roadies and make regular, systematic checks on your equipment. Always carry essential spares.

Fault	Remedy	Fault	Remedy
No output		**Hum or noise on output**	
Broken or detached internal wire	Find and replace broken wire or connection.	Earth line broken	Trace and repair break.
Short circuit	Locate short circuit and insulate or replace faulty wire or component.	Faulty screening	Use only high-quality braided screen cable. Screen the control compartment with copper foil, etc.
Pick-up, switch or volume control faulty	Replace faulty component. A faulty pick-up is likely to be nothing worse than a broken connection to the coil.	Local interference, especially on single-coil pick-up	This can be difficult to deal with. Interference can be mains or ether-borne. Mains filters can reduce interference to some extent, but the best solution is suppression at source , assuming you can gain access to this. Many venues today have a three-phase mains supply, so make sure your equipment is not plugged into the same phase as any lighting circuits which are often a prime cause of mains interference. Ether-borne interference, such as radio waves, can be even more troublesome. Try different locations and orientations of your equipment to minimize this, or short radio frequencies to earth before they can cause trouble. This can be done by inserting 250 µF capacitors in suitable places: between the pick-up hot wire(s) and earth; between the core and screen of your jack leads (you can easily fit a capacitor inside the jack plug); between grid and earth on all input and high-gain valves in the amp or the equivalent parts of a transistor amp. Note that capacitors used to modify amps in this way must be high-voltage working types with very low leakage, otherwise you will create problems worse than the ones you are trying to solve. Radio frequencies on valve grids can show up as excessive distortion.
Low output			
Section of pick-up wiring short-circuited	Simple single-section pick-ups should be replaced. Twin-coil or tapped-coil pick-ups are likely to be short-circuited at one of the internal connection points.		
Aged or faulty solder joint	Remove old solder with de-soldering braid and re-solder.		
Dirty switch	Clean with switch-cleaner.		
Muffled output			
Too high a value capacitor in tone control	Fit correct value capacitor. If in doubt, a 0.02 µF capacitor is generally satisfactory.		
Short circuit across tone pot	Find and remove cause of short circuit.		
Tone control acts as volume control			
Capacitor short circuited	Replace faulty capacitor.		
Capacitor has too large a value	Replace with correct value capacitor.		
Controls reversed			
Control wired wrong way round	Reverse connections to end of potentiometer track.		
Crackly or distorted output			
Faulty soldering (dry joint)	Remove old solder with de-soldering braid and re-solder.		
Dirty or loose pots or switches	Clean with switch-cleaner and re-solder.		
Worn jack plug	Replace socket.		
Poor-quality screened cable	Replace with high-quality cable.		

Testing components, connections and circuits

Over the next few pages are outlined a number of simple tests that should enable you to locate, diagnose and repair the faults that are most likely to stop an electric guitar from working properly. Some faults can be traced by sight or touch: for instance, soldered connections that have broken, or screws that have worked loose. There are, however, many other faults – such as damaged wires and components – which cannot be traced in the same way and require the use of special test equipment.

Most test equipment is costly, but it is possible to buy relatively inexpensively an accurate and efficient "multimeter", or "multi-tester" as it is sometimes called. This will enable you to carry out a number of useful tests and measurements; indeed it is impossible to carry out some circuitry work without using such a device. Very cheap meters are not recommended, both because they tend to be inaccurate (their own resistance is often low, and this will upset voltage readings), and because they may offer only a limited range of measuring facilities. Choose a meter which will measure from zero ohms to one megohm, and AC/DC volts from zero to 500 volts.

Safety precautions

Testing or metering any form of mains-powered equipment carries with it the risk of electrocution. This warning applies particularly to amplifiers, where very high (and potentially lethal) voltages are involved. None of the tests described in the following pages are to be used on equipment while it is still connected to the mains supply, or on any other devices (guitars, leads or pedals) while plugged into such equipment.

How to use a multimeter

Initially, your biggest problem is likely to be learning how to use the meter. At first glance, the multitude of markings and figures can be very confusing. However, here we shall only be using the meter for simple, basic tests, such as measuring resistance and measuring AC and DC voltage. For this reason, some of the controls normally found on a multimeter have been omitted from the diagram below, since they will not be used in the tests.

For this type of work, a multimeter with an indicator needle and scales is best. Meters with digital readouts can give very accurate readings but, if the voltage is fluctuating or if the resistance varies, you may see only a blur of unreadable figures. The way in which the needle moves across the scale can be useful information in itself.

Two test leads, sometimes called "banana jack leads", are usually supplied with the meter. One end of each lead is plugged into the meter, while the probes at the other ends are placed in contact with the component or connection being tested or measured. The function switch and range selector on the meter must be set according to the requirements of the test.

Zeroing the meter

Before carrying out any tests, you should first zero the meter. This involves getting the indicator to point to 0, showing that there is no resistance to the flow of current between the probes. Set the function switch to ohms and the range selector to the most sensitive setting (R × 1). Plug the test leads into the meter (the red lead always goes into the socket marked +) and touch the tips of the probes together. The needle should swing across the ohms scale, from maximum resistance to no resistance (zero). If this doesn't happen, turn the adjustment screw until it does.

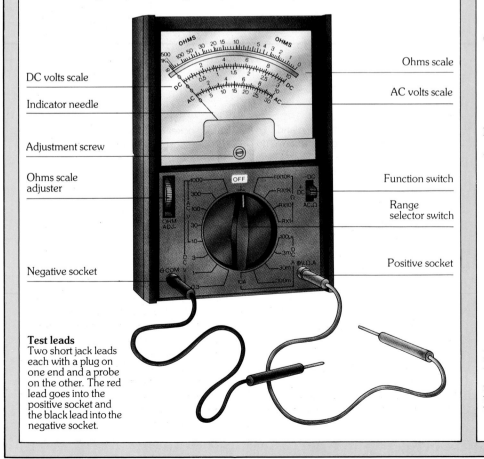

Test leads
Two short jack leads each with a plug on one end and a probe on the other. The red lead goes into the positive socket and the black lead into the negative socket.

- DC volts scale
- Indicator needle
- Adjustment screw
- Ohms scale adjuster
- Negative socket
- Ohms scale
- AC volts scale
- Function switch
- Range selector switch
- Positive socket

Range selector at R × 1

How to zero the meter
Function switch at ohms. Range selector at R × 1. Touch the two probes together and, if necessary, alter the ohms scale adjuster until the needle aligns exactly with 0 (zero ohms) on the ohms scale.

Testing a guitar lead

This is a test to ensure that the connections and cable of a standard screened mono guitar lead are not faulty. It will establish whether there is a short circuit between the outer screening and the central wire. This particular fault is caused by damage to the insulation between the earthing and the central core, and it allows electrical contact between the two. A short circuit can also occur in the region of the jack plug connecting tags or in the jack plug itself. The test measures the resistance to the flow of current in the lead.

Plug the test leads into the meter and set the range selector to its most sensitive setting. With the meter we are using as an example, use the R × 1 setting. As a result, a reading of 1 on the ohms scale will indicate a resistance of 1 ohm in the subject under test.

Testing for a short circuit

Zero the meter as described on the opposite page. Place one probe in contact with the earth sleeve of one of the jack plugs and the other in contact with the end central wire connection, as shown in the diagram below.

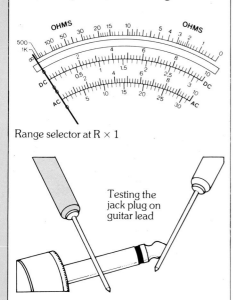

Range selector at R × 1

Testing the jack plug on guitar lead

The needle should point to the top end of the scale, indicating infinite resistance. If it does, there is no short circuit between the earth and central core connections allowing current to pass between them.

If the needle moves away from the top of the scale, this indicates a decrease in resistance. Current is able to pass between the earth and the central core. There is therefore a short circuit either through the insulation or between the internal connections of the jack plug. You should remedy this by repairing the insulation or replacing the faulty components.

If the original problem is that the sound of the guitar keeps cutting out intermittently,

and you suspect the lead may be at fault, pull the lead about in different directions while you are testing it. This should soon indicate whether a short circuit is causing the guitar to cut in and out.

Checking the plug connections

To check the central core connection of the lead, place the probes in contact with the jack plug end connections. Use the same settings as before. The needle should move from the high end of the scale to indicate

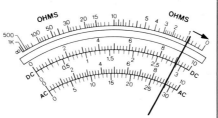

Range selector at R × 1

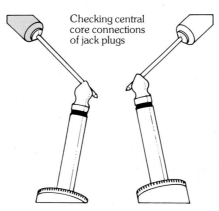

Checking central core connections of jack plugs

almost zero resistance to the flow of current (1 ohm or less is acceptable). The small resistance allows an unrestricted flow of current, so the lead is functioning correctly.

If the needle remains at the high end, indicating infinite resistance, then there is no flow of current. This means that there is a break in the connections or wires.

Repeat the above procedure, but this time place the probes in contact with the earth sleeve connections of each jack plug. This is to check that the screening and screen contacts are all in order. A reading of 0 (zero ohms) indicates that the connection is good. Less than 1 ohm is still acceptable.

If any fault is detected through these tests, you can narrow down its actual location by unscrewing the casing of the jack plugs and testing in the same way as before. Some faults can be isolated by taking readings from the point at which the wires are soldered onto the connecting tags.

Now that you have tested a guitar lead, you can apply the same principle and use the same method to test any lead, connection or passive resistive component.

Testing a mains lead

It is easy to test mains leads that have a plug (which goes into a wall socket) at one end and a cable socket (which plugs into the piece of equipment) at the other. If you think that the lead is malfunctioning, the first thing to test is probably the fuse. Set

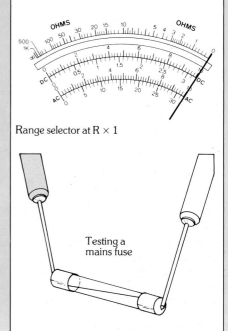

Range selector at R × 1

Testing a mains fuse

the function switch to ohms, and the range selector to R × 1. Zero the meter, and place the two probes in contact with opposite ends of the fuse. If the needle stays at the high end of the scale, indicating infinite resistance, the connection has broken and the fuse has blown. If the indicator swings across to measure zero, the fuse is good.

Assuming no problems with the fuse, the next thing is to test the lead for a short circuit. Set and zero the meter as above. Place one probe in the earth socket of the cable socket and the other in contact with the live socket. A reading of infinite ohms indicates that there is no short circuit.

Now repeat the check, but with one probe in the earth socket and the other in the negative socket of the cable socket. Analyze the readings as above. Finally, make the test with one probe in the positive socket and the other in the negative.

If the lead is not short-circuiting, you can go on to test the connections. Keeping the settings as above, zero the meter. Place one probe inside the earth socket of the cable socket and the other probe in contact with the earth pin on the plug at the other end of the lead. If the meter shows infinite resistance, there is a fault. If it registers zero or slightly above, the connection is in good order.

Repeat the process, checking first the positive connections and then the negative connections.

Checking the output signal

If there is no volume at all when the guitar is plugged into an amplifier, there may be no output signal coming from the guitar itself. First, make sure that the lead is functioning correctly (see p. 191). Then set the range selector to the most sensitive setting on the AC volts scale; with the meter shown, this is ACV 10. Plug the tested jack lead into the guitar output socket, and place one probe in contact with the center connection of the jack plug at the other end of the lead. Place the second probe in contact with the earthing sleeve of the same plug.

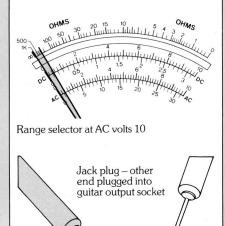

Range selector at AC volts 10

Jack plug – other end plugged into guitar output socket

As the output from the guitar is relatively small – in the region of 50-200 millivolts – even with the meter at its most sensitive setting, the needle will kick only very marginally at the bottom of the volts scale. To get the maximum output, turn the volume control full up and turn the treble and bass controls to maximum. Get someone else to play repeated chords with a plectrum, or use crocodile clips for the connections so you can play the guitar yourself. With all but the cheapest and least sensitive of meters, the output should be sufficient to nudge the indicator needle on the scale.

If there is plainly no output signal, you should locate the source of the fault by going through the circuit-testing procedure outlined on the opposite page. Once you have found the faulty component or connection, you should replace it with one which is working. You should then be able to plug the guitar into the amplifier and find that it is working normally.

Testing a pick-up

Testing the performance characteristics of a pick-up requires sophisticated measuring equipment capable of measuring AC impedance at all frequencies. This is beyond the scope of a multimeter. However, you can still use your meter to check that the pick-up is functioning, and also to measure its resistance. Because there is a correlation between its resistance and its AC impedance, this can give you a useful rule-of-thumb guide to the pick-up's.

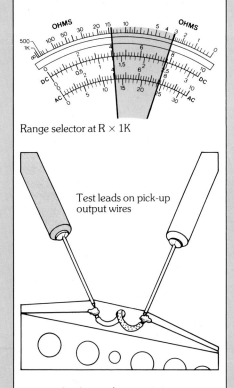

Range selector at R × 1K

Test leads on pick-up output wires

tone and volume characteristics.

If the pick-up is wired into the circuit, you must first disconnect it. Set the meter's function switch to ohms (which will also measure DC resistance) and the range selector to a setting which can cope with between 3 and 14 K (R × 1 K is shown here). Zero the ohms scale, and place each test probe in contact with a pick-up output wire.

Generally, the resistance will lie between 3 K and 14 K. A pick-up with a 3 K resistance will have a very clear tone, but will not be capable of producing as much volume as a 12 K pick-up, which will have a correspondingly warmer tone as treble frequencies are increasingly impeded.

You can use DC resistance measurements to identify the coil-tap connection of a pick-up (if one is fitted). The coil-tap will have a lower resistance than the normal pick-up connections (see p. 187).

Testing components

These tests can be used to measure the resistance of components such as pots, capacitors and resistors. Their resistance values will affect their operation.

Testing pots

As we have seen (p. 186) a 500 K log pot is a good, general-purpose component for installation in guitar circuits. Here is a test for checking the efficiency of such a pot.

Set the function switch to ohms, and the range selector to R × 10 K. Zero the meter. Place the test probes in contact with the two

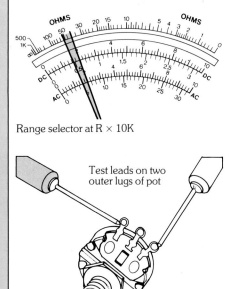

Range selector at R × 10K

Test leads on two outer lugs of pot

outer lugs of the pot. Pots commonly used in guitar circuits usually have the resistance marked on the casing, along with a tolerance expressed as a percentage. Therefore, a pot marked 500 K (20%) should ideally have a maximum resistance of 500 K, but in practice may vary between 400 K and 600 K. Pots with 10%, 5% and 1% tolerances are also available, but 20% is the most common figure. If the needle shows a reading above 600 K, or whatever the upper tolerance limit may be, you should replace the pot. The resistive track has probably been damaged.

Now check from one outer lug to the central lug. Use crocodile clips to leave your hands free. Rotate the spindle smoothly from one end of its range to the other. As you do so, the indicator needle should also move smoothly from zero to the maximum value of the pot, or vice versa. Repeat this procedure, this time checking the other outer lug with the center lug.

If the needle kicks during either of these tests, the pot may be dirty and you should clean it with special switch cleaner. If the needle still kicks, replace the pot.

Testing resistors

Whereas pots present variable resistance to the flow of current, resistors have just one set value which you can easily check by setting the function switch and selector as

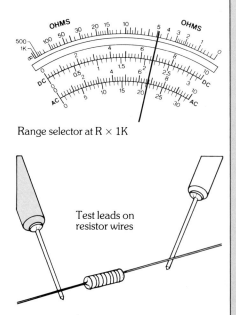

Range selector at R × 1K

Test leads on resistor wires

above and placing the probes in contact with the wires of the resistor. There is a standard, color-coded identification system for resistor values.

Testing capacitors

Specialized equipment is needed to test the actual capacitance of a capacitor; a multimeter cannot be used for this. However, the multimeter is useful for other tests on capacitors. If your guitar's tone control is totally ineffective, it may have gone "open circuit", meaning that the capacitor has a broken internal connection and must be replaced. If the tone control starts to act on both tone and volume, and then gradually loses its ability to alter the tone, the capacitor may be going "leaky" internally. Eventually it is likely to short circuit and behave purely as a volume control.

To test a capacitor, set the function switch to ohms, and the range selector to the highest ohms setting (R × 10 K here). Zero the meter and, if the capacitor is in a circuit, disconnect one wire. Place the probes in contact with the capacitor's wires. If the needle kicks momentarily across part of the scale and then returns slowly and smoothly to infinite ohms, then the capacitor is functioning correctly. If the needle stays on infinite ohms, then the capacitor has a broken connection; it should therefore be replaced. If the needle kicks across the scale but does not return to infinite ohms, the capacitor is leaking. A zero reading shows that the capacitor has short-circuited.

Testing a passive guitar circuit

The circuit test described here is for a single pick-up guitar (see p. 186); as we have seen, this is the basis for more complicated configurations, such as two and three pick-up circuits, and you can follow the same basic procedure for testing each of them.

The numbers refer to the test points on the circuit, shown in circles on the diagram. When testing the actual components, it is sometimes necessary to disconnect them by detaching one connection. Because these components behave as resistors wired in parallel, you may in some circumstances get a false reading if you do not do this.

Set the meter function switch to ohms, and the range selector to its most sensitive setting (R × 1 here). Zero the meter. Place the black (negative) probe in contact with point 1 (the outer screening connection of the jack socket); as it will remain in this position through most of the tests, you can use crocodile clips to hold it in place. Place the red (positive) probe in contact with point 2 (the earth tag of the volume pot). A reading of zero ohms indicates that the connection between the outer jack socket screening and the volume control is good. A reading of 1 ohm or more suggests a badly soldered connection or wire, which you should repair. A reading of infinite ohms indicates a broken or disconnected wire.

Now move the red probe so it is in contact with point 3, the earthed tag of the tone control. Interpret the readings as above. If no fault is indicated, move the red probe to point 4 (the earthed output of the pick-up). If this is satisfactory, turn the guitar volume control to the fully off position, and place the red probe in contact with point 9 (the center tag of the volume control pot). Interpret the readings as above.

Now place the red probe in contact with point 10, and set the treble control to maximum. Operate the volume control through its range while watching the needle's movements. A zero reading throughout indicates a short circuit between the wire joining points 9 and 10 and the

earth wire. A reading of zero at the top and bottom of the scale with a reading of about half the value of the pot in between suggests a short circuit between the wire connecting point 5 (the hot connection of the pick-up) to point 8 (the third tag of the volume pot) and the earth wire. If the pot is operating correctly, with no short circuits, the needle will move smoothly across the scale. You will not, however, be able to read the value of the pot correctly, since it is wired in parallel with the pick-up. To do this, you should disconnect at either point 8 or 2 and then carry out the potentiometer value test described on the opposite page.

Having reconnected the pot, you can now continue with the circuit test. Leaving the volume pot set at maximum, the black probe in contact with point 1, and the red probe in contact with point 10, operate the treble control through its range. A zero reading indicates that the capacitor has short-circuited and must be replaced. If, the tone control does not work, then you should check the capacitor for an "open circuit".

To test the junction between the capacitor and the tone control pot, place the red probe in contact with point 7. Operate the control through its range. If the needle moves slowly from zero to the value marked on the pot, then all is in order. A reading of infinite ohms, though, indicates that the resistive track inside the pot is broken; zero ohms throughout indicates that the pot has short-circuited.

For the remaining tests you should unclip the black probe from point 1, and place it in contact with point 10 instead. Place the red probe in contact with point 5, and operate the volume pot from minimum to maximum through its range. A high reading, dropping smoothly to zero, shows that it is functioning correctly. If infinite ohms is indicated, the connection between points 5 and 8 is broken. A reading of 1 ohm suggests a suspect solder connection. To test the pick-up itself, disconnect one contact and proceed as described on the opposite page.

Wiring diagram for single pick-up passive guitar circuit
See p. 186 for an explanation of this circuit.

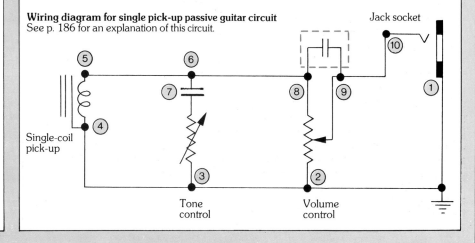

Humbucking pick-ups

Until now, we have been dealing only with single-coil pick-ups and how they are wired. Humbuckers, described on p. 53, contain two coils instead of one. Each coil has its own set of pole-pieces which are in contact with a single, central magnet. This means that, in effect, the humbucker can also be considered as though it were two separate pick-ups in one body. The fact that these two coils are wired in series and out of phase with one another means that mains hum or background noise picked up by the coils — not by the magnets — is cancelled out. Humbuckers have a characteristically warmer tone than single-coil pick-ups.

Wiring humbuckers

Humbuckers offer a wide variety of wiring options. One unit can be used either as a true humbucker, with its two coils in series, or as two separate single-coil pick-ups, with the coils working separately or together, in or out of phase. These different combinations can produce a formidable range of sounds.

Humbuckers can be bought already fitted with a four-core screened cable. This allows you immediate access to the individual coils and makes any or all of the above configurations possible. The first thing to do is to identify each of the four core wires. This is quite simple if you use a multimeter (see pp. 190-93). To establish which wires come from the ends of the two coils, set your meter to read ohms and take readings until you have identified the two pairs. You must now find out which of each pair is the hot wire. To do this, set your meter to its smallest AC volts setting. Connect the ends of one coil to the meter, and tap the pick-up pole-pieces gently with a screwdriver blade. As you do so, you should see the needle of the meter kick slightly – either up or down off the scale. If the needle seems to kick down, reverse the connections to the meter. When you are quite certain that the needle is kicking upwards, the red wire of your meter will be connected to the hot wire of the coil. Repeat this procedure for the two wires from the other coil.

Humbuckers fitted with only a single-core screened cable can, with care and patience, be modified to produce the four separate core wires necessary for the options shown in the circuit below. However, you will have to open your pick-up to locate the connections. Unfortunately, this means unsoldering the pick-up cover from its base. The best way to do this is to use "de-soldering braid", which is flux-impregnated braided wire. Hold it against the solder you want to remove, and place a soldering iron on top of it to heat both the braid and the joint. The braid will take up the solder, and the cover will come free.

When the cover is off, you will see that there is insulation tape wrapping both coils together. Unwind the tape so that you can get to the soldered connection joining the two coils. Open this joint, so that the two ends become two of your cores. The third core wire will lead from the end of one of the coils to an earth connection on the pick-up base plate. This, too, should be disconnected. The fourth and final core wire is the one connected to the existing single-core cable. Detach this one as well.

Now connect the four ends that you have freed to the cores of the new four-core cable, and connect the screen wire of the cable to the base.

If you cannot get hold of four-core screened cable, you can use two lengths of two-core. Be sure, however, to connect the screen wire to the pick-up base (at one end) and to the potentiometer (at the other end) on only one of the two lengths. Leave the screen wire on the other length unconnected at the pick-up end.

Some humbuckers are available with wired-in "coil taps" (see p. 187). This increases their versatility still further, since each section of each coil can be used separately. Coil-tapped humbuckers have six core wires. When you come to identify which wires are connected to which coil, you will, of course, find that there are two sets of three linked wires. Of each three, one leads to one end of the coil, one leads to the other end, and one (the "tap") comes from the center of the coil. If you use a meter to test each set of three wires in pairs (1 and 2, 2 and 3, 1 and 3), you will find that one pair has twice the resistance of the other two pairs. This pair will be connected to each end of the coil. The remaining one will be the coil-tap wire.

Wiring diagram for multi-option humbucker wiring

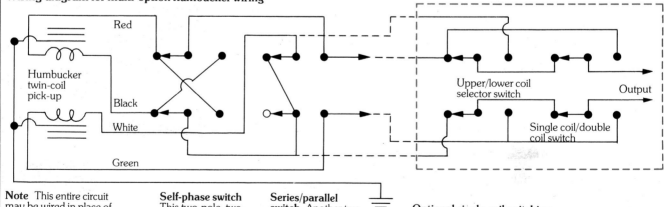

Note This entire circuit may be wired in place of any of the single-coil pick-ups in previous diagrams (see pp. 186-9). However, the hum-canceling property of the pick-up will not operate in all switch positions. The colors are based on the DiMarzio code.

Self-phase switch This two-pole, two-way switch puts the two coils of the pick-up either in or out of phase with one another.

Series/parallel switch Another two-pole, two-way switch changes the normal series wiring of the two coils to parallel.

Optional single-coil switching The two switches shown above allow you to choose between using only one or using both of the humbucker's coils. The selector switch chooses which of the two coils operates when you are switched to single coil. A simpler arrangement can be made by inserting a one-pole, one-way switch into the green wire. This will function as a single-coil switch when the series/parallel switch is set to parallel. When series is selected, it becomes an on/off switch.

Buying pick-ups

The two things that most affect the tone of pick-ups are the strength of the magnets and the way in which the coils are made.

In general, the stronger the magnet, the louder the sound and the more the treble frequencies are accentuated. Although magnets become gradually weaker over a period of years, this is not always regarded as a drawback. In fact, such is the demand for the sound of "vintage" pick-ups that the American manufacturer Seymour Duncan artificially "ages" the magnets in some of the pick-ups he makes. In recent years, manufacturers such as Alembic have begun using ceramic or piezo magnets. These are cheaper, more permanent and give a higher output.

Pick-up coils differ from one type to another in terms of the gauge of wire used and the number of turns or windings. Both these factors affect the impedance of the pick-up. Thin wire has a greater resistance to the flow of current than thick wire. Increasing the number of windings gives the coil a higher impedance and produces more volume – but a reduction in overall clarity because of the decrease in treble response.

The working impedance of a pick-up is difficult to measure without sophisticated equipment. For this reason, it is common practice when assessing a pick-up's likely performance to measure the coil's resistance to DC (see p. 192). However, some people regard the *resonant peak* or *resonant frequency* as the best indication of what a pick-up will actually sound like. A resonant peak occurs at the point in the audio spectrum where a pick-up is at its most efficient in reproducing the sound of the guitar. A graph showing a pick-up's frequency response would rise gradually before reaching a fairly sharp peak (representing the resonant peak) and would then fall off. If a pick-up has a resonant peak towards the higher end of its frequency spectrum, it will emphasize trebles. If the peak is lower down its frequency spectrum, then mid-range frequencies will be emphasized. Using a larger number of coil windings or weaker magnets will lower the resonant peak of the pick-up. Conversely, fewer windings or stronger magnets will result in a higher peak. Strong magnets can, however, inhibit or "choke" string vibration.

This all amounts to the fact that pick-up specifications can be, at the best of times, confusing and, at the worst, misleading. Judging a pick-up by its sound and by measuring its resistance to the flow of DC will give you the best indication.

Gibson pick-ups

The Gibson company has been making guitar pick-ups since the 1930s (see p. 54). However, perhaps the most famous of all their pick-ups are the "PAF" humbuckers fitted to Les Pauls between 1957 and 1960 (PAF stood for "patent applied for"). Something of a legend has grown up around these pick-ups, and originals are highly prized. Gibson makes a current PAF model (see below) as well as many other humbuckers.

Gibson "PAF" humbucker

Gibson "Velvet Brick" humbucker

Custom pick-ups

Replacement pick-ups have played a prominent part in the custom-parts industry during the last ten years or so. Companies such as DiMarzio, Schecter, Mighty Mite, Seymour Duncan and Bill Lawrence now produce a wide variety of different pick-ups which vary in specification and design. It is now possible to simulate the vintage sounds of early Gibson and Fender pick-ups, or to switch instantly from the bright, clean sound of the classic single-coil to the fattest, dirtiest distortion of a powerful humbucker.

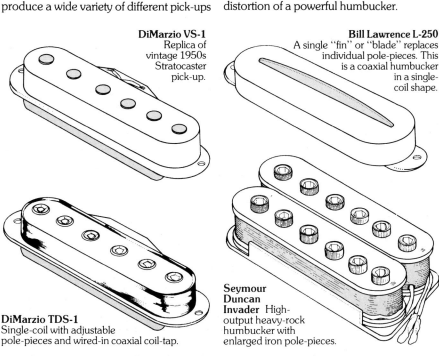

DiMarzio VS-1
Replica of vintage 1950s Stratocaster pick-up.

DiMarzio TDS-1
Single-coil with adjustable pole-pieces and wired-in coaxial coil-tap.

Bill Lawrence L-250
A single "fin" or "blade" replaces individual pole-pieces. This is a coaxial humbucker in a single-coil shape.

Seymour Duncan Invader High-output heavy-rock humbucker with enlarged iron pole-pieces.

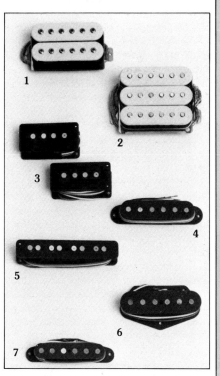

Mighty Mite pick-ups
1 Distortion humbucker with split-coil wiring. 2 Motherbucker triple-coil pick-up. 3 Offset single-coils for Precision-style bass. 4 Strat pick-up. 5 Lead pick-up for Jazz-style bass. 6 Lead pick-up for Tele. 7 Rhythm pick-up for Tele.

Active guitar circuitry

All the circuits discussed previously have been *passive*. There are, however, *active* guitar circuits as well. In electronics, an active circuit is one which includes a device that introduces *gain* (see p. 202) or allows current to flow in one direction only.

Active circuitry allows you to get a consistently high output signal, whatever type of pick-up is used. This is achieved by means of a *pre-amplifier*, which amplifies the signal from the pick-up. Boosting the signal level reduces the risk of extraneous noise being picked up by the guitar lead, improves the signal-to-noise ratio when pedals are in use, and makes it easy to drive a valve amplifier into distortion. Active circuitry also lets you fit comprehensive tone controls of almost any level of sophistication – as well as many effects available as foot pedals – to your guitar.

Early pre-amps based on a single transistor suffered from the fact that, while guitar pick-ups and amplifiers are high-impedance units, transistors work better in low-impedance circuitry. Though the high-impedance *field effect transistor* is simple, cheap and performs tolerably well, today's trend is to use integrated circuits (ICs) in the form of an *operational amplifier*. When ICs containing several operational amplifiers are used, highly complex circuits can be constructed in a very small space. Operational amplifiers amplify the difference between voltages fed to their two inputs. Either input can, however, be set at a fixed reference voltage and a signal applied to the other input. If this signal is fed to the non-inverting (positive) input, the output waveform will be in phase with the input waveform. If applied to the inverting (negative) input, the output will be 180 degrees out of phase. As it stands, the gain of the operational amplifier is unusably large; to bring it under control, some of the output is returned to the input in such a way as to subtract from the input (this is called *negative feedback*).

Building a pre-amplifier

This pre-amp uses a non-inverting circuit to preserve the phase relationship of the signal whether the unit is switched in or out of the circuit. It is constructed on "Veroboard", a readily available plastic board drilled every 0.1 in. (2.5 mm) and faced with copper strips on one side, which serves as a printed circuit. To build this pre-amp, your board should have 14 strips of 13 holes; identify these with letters and numbers respectively as in the diagram (right) where the strips on the reverse run left to right.

The first stage is to cut the strips into sections. Drill behind points A5, D9, E7, G7, H3, I8, J8 and K8. Assemble the components in the order suggested in the table. Bend the leads to fit through the holes and trim so about 1/8 in. (3 mm) protrudes. Bend these stubs flat along the copper strips and solder in place, being careful not to bridge the strips with solder. If the switch terminals are too large to fit through the holes, solder on short lengths of wire and feed these through instead. The potentiometer adjusts the gain of the unit to give an output of between twice and ten times the level of the input signal. The type used here is a 20-turn cermet preset resistor; it takes 20 turns of the screw to adjust from the minimum to maximum settings, thus giving precise adjustment. Set this to give the greatest distortion you wish to use. Turning down the volume on the guitar will give you the option of a clean sound or any amount of distortion up to the maximum you have set.

To fit the unit to your guitar, drill a ¼ in. (6 mm) hole through the fingerplate and mount the switch through this. Detach the coaxial lead to the output socket from the volume control, and solder in its place a suitable length of coaxial, taking it to the unit's input terminals (E1 core, A1 screen). Rewire the lead to the output socket to the output terminals (E13 core, A13 screen).

Replace the output jack socket with a stereo jack socket using the sleeve and tip connections for the screen and core respectively of the signal cable. Solder a separate wire from the ring connection on the stereo jack socket to point L1. The unit is switched on whenever the guitar is plugged in; the switch merely takes it in or out of the circuit.

Component layout (top view)

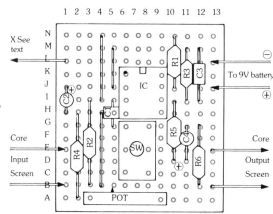

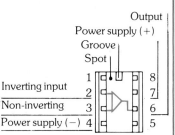

Output
Power supply (+)
Groove
Spot

Inverting input	1	8
Non-inverting	2	7
Power supply (−)	3	6
	4	5

Operational amplifier (top view)
The device is in an 8-pin dual in-line (DIL) plastic package. Orientate the pins (un-numbered) by the spot above pin 1 or the groove between pins 1 and 8. The TL 071 version recommended has FET inputs and low noise and distortion.

Components list and assembly sequence

Location	Diagram	Component
H/I/J/K 6 and 9	IC	IC socket (8-way low-profile DIL) with TL 071 (or 741 or 748) IC
J10–N10	R1	470K resistor, 5%, carbon film, ¼ watt
B3–I3	R2	470K resistor, 5%, carbon film, ¼ watt
I11–M11	R3	100K resistor, 5%, carbon film, ¼ watt
A2–H2	R4	10K resistor, 5%, carbon film, ¼ watt
D10–I10	R5	1K resistor, 5%, carbon film, ¼ watt
B12–G12	R6	100K resistor, 5%, carbon film, ¼ watt
B4–H4, I4–N4, J5–M5	–	Wire links (use offcuts from resistor wires)
G5–I5	C1	.022 µF capacitor (polyester or polystyrene)
H1–J1 (+)	C2	10 µF 25V DC capacitor (tantalum)
I12–M12	C3	100 pF capacitor
D11(+)–G11	C4	10 fd 25V DC capacitor (tantalum)
C/E/G 6 and 8	SW	DPDT miniature toggle switch
A3, A8, B5	POT	VRI 50K linear potentiometer
J13(+), L13	–	Battery connector for PP3 (9V)

PERFORMANCE TECHNOLOGY

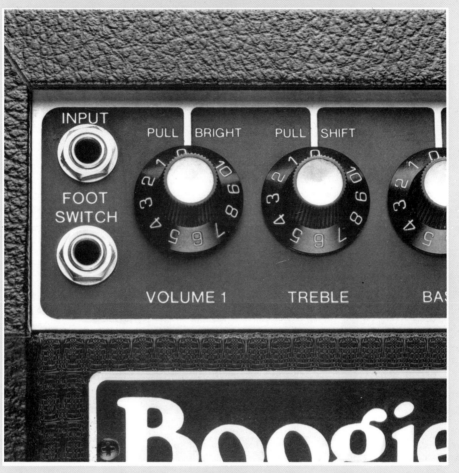

Apart from when playing an acoustic instrument to a handful of people, the guitarist will, to some degree, become involved with performance technology. Here we have brought together live performance and recording simply because much of the same equipment is used for both functions. Getting to grips with the basics of using amplifiers, microphones, mixing consoles, and sound processing will provide any guitarist with an insight into the process of recording and live performance. Certainly some techniques are different in the studio, but the only fundamental difference is that sound recording equipment is used to capture performances for repeated playback and, depending on the technical sophistication of the equipment, allows for some layering and further crafting of the sound. This section of the book provides both the acoustic and electric guitar player with the hands-on information needed both to perform and record their music. It also contains everything the guitarist needs to know to communicate with sound engineers, recording engineers, and record producers, *and* maintain a level of understanding and control at all levels of performance.

The role of the electric guitar amplifier

An electric guitar relies on amplification to increase the signal generated by the pick-ups when the instrument is played. The guitar cannot be connected directly to a loudspeaker because it takes more energy to drive the moving parts of a speaker than the vibration of the strings can generate across the windings of the pick-up. Therefore an amplifier has to be used.

An amplifier takes electrical power from an external source (either an outlet or battery) and uses the signal voltage derived from the guitar to control the delivery of that power to the speaker. The amplifier enables you to modify tone and volume, and to add effects like distortion and echo.

Amplifiers can be powered by valve or transistorized "solid state" circuitry. At the time when the electric guitar came to prominence in the fifties and early sixties, all amplifiers were valve-powered. Solid state technology was not widely used until the late sixties and early seventies. Its ability to reproduce faithfully and amplify sound with greater reliability soon led to solid state technology virtually replacing valves in hi-fi amplifiers and other electronic devices.

Initially, solid state circuitry was embraced by guitar amplifier manufacturers but it soon became evident that the humble valve amplifier was an essential part of the character of the classic electric guitar sound.

During the seventies and eighties, as solid state electronics continued to evolve, a hybrid technology combining valve and solid state circuitry was developed.

Amplifiers maintaining some desirable aspects of the valve sound while employing a certain amount of solid-state circuitry were developed producing sounds that were quite acceptable to some guitarists.

By the end of the 1980s all the major manufacturers of classic guitar amplifiers had returned to the traditional but costly valve technology for their top line ranges of amplifiers. Famous players like Eric Clapton and Brian May use either vintage or new valve-powered amplifiers.

By 1990 several leading manufacturers had evolved a range of hybrid amplifiers using a combination of valve and solid state technology to produce more affordable amplifiers. These have found acceptance among many aspiring guitar players.

The classic Brian May sound *(left)*
Although Queen's Brian May has 12 Vox AC 30 combo amplifiers on stage, only the bottom four are used. The signal from his guitar goes into a pedalboard, through a treble booster, a Fox phase pedal, and then a second treble booster with an overload switch. A switching unit directs the signal to one AC 30 to produce the main guitar sound. The second amplifier receives the same signal via a chorus with a 19 milliseconds delay and sweep to give a stereo effect. The remaining two amplifiers receive the guitar signal via a pair of delays or pitch changers.

Valves

Valves or "tubes" work on the thermionic principle. A low voltage is passed through the heater filament which heats up the cathode. This makes it possible for the electrons to flow between the cathode and anode, so causing a current to flow from the power supply, through the valve and back to the power supply. The voltage signal from the guitar is fed to the control grid, where it regulates the flow of current between anode and cathode. As the controlling voltage rises and falls, so the flow of current rises and falls. The restrictive effect of the resistors feeding anode and cathode causes a voltage fluctuation to appear at X and Y as a result of the variation in current flow. The voltage fluctuation is large compared to that on the control grid, so amplification is achieved. The amplified signal can be taken from either X or Y. The signal at X is 180 degrees out of phase with that at Y.

With heavy use, valves need replacing frequently. Mechanical shock may cause the glass envelope to fracture and destroy the vacuum. Cracking of the glass may also occur as a result of a sudden

How a valve amplifier works

The diagram on the right shows the various stages involved in the operation of a typical valve amplifier equipped with two input channels.

The quality of the *power supply* governs the efficiency of all subsequent links in the chain. No matter how good the rest of the circuitry, the amplifier's performance will suffer if the power supply is sub-standard. At this preparatory stage, power taken from the AC outlet is transformed to a higher voltage and rectified to DC current through valve or semi-conductor diodes. A network of resistors, capacitors and an inductor finally smooths the direct current and supplies different voltages to the various amplification stages.

The *first stage*, or *pre-amplifier*, consists of a single valve and all of its associated components. These apply a fixed voltage gain to the input signal from the guitar, i.e., they amplify the signal voltage.

The *tone and volume controls* often use a passive network of resistors and capacitors similar to the controls on a guitar. Some amplifiers have active controls which affect the gain of the second stage at suitable frequencies.

The *second stage* consists of one valve which, like the first stage, is a voltage amplifier. Its function is to make good the

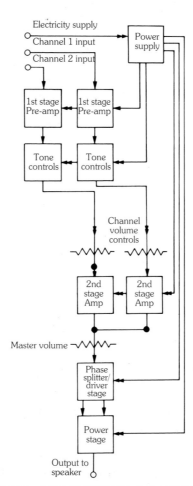

loss of signal voltage inherent in the use of passive tone controls, and in some cases to give additional voltage gain.

The *master volume* is a passive control that acts on the overall signal level delivered from every one of the input channels to the amplifier.

The *power amplifier* consists of three stages: the phase splitter (sometimes known as the inverter), the driver, and the power stage. The phase splitter delivers two output signals, one of which is 180 degrees out of phase with the other. The voltage of these signals is amplified by the driver stage. The two valves employed in the phase splitter are often used to achieve this amplification themselves, and so the two stages can be combined. In the majority of amplifiers, the valves used up to this point in the circuit are triodes. However, in order to make space savings, double triodes are usually employed, since they combine the function of two valves in a single unit. Therefore, the function of one valve in theory may, in practice, be carried out by half a valve; the remaining capacity might then be used for other purposes.

In the *power stage*, one or more pairs of valves (usually pentodes) are used to convert the large signal voltage into a large current flow. This current is drawn through the output transformer before finally being delivered to the loudspeaker.

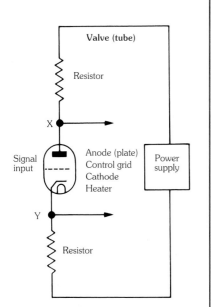

temperature change. Another hazard is "microphony," caused by internal parts of the valve becoming loose enough to respond to vibration that can modulate the electrical signal, making the valve behave like a microphone.

Transistors

Transistors consist of layers of different semi-conductor materials deposited on top of one another. Many contain toxic chemicals, so it is unwise to open them up to see how they are made.

Unlike valves, transistors do not need heaters to make them work. Current flows from the power supply through the transistor, between the emitter and collector, and then back to the power supply. The fluctuating voltage of the signal from the guitar pick-up or microphone, applied to the base, controls the flow of current between emitter and collector. As with valves, the resistors feeding these cause current fluctuations to appear as voltage fluctuations at points X and Y. Amplifiers taking their output from point X are called "common emitter amplifiers," while those taking their output from Y are called "emitter follower amplifiers."

Transistor failure is almost always caused by the failure of associated components. This can mean that incorrect voltages or polarities are applied to the transistor or that there is an attempt to pass too much current through it.

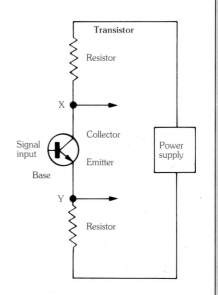

A short-circuiting of the loudspeaker connections on a transistor amplifier will cause instant failure of the output transistors because too much current will be drawn through them. Many modern transistor amplifiers now feature special circuitry to protect against this happening.

Speakers

Both the sound quality and volume of a speaker is governed by its efficiency, its size and its compatibility with other speakers. Its efficiency – the energy output from the amplifier which is converted into sound – governs the volume possible from an amplifier of a given power output.

The speakers or "drivers" that have been used most successfully for guitar amplification are either 10 inches (25.5 cm) or 12 inches (30cm) in diameter. A single amplifier may drive one, two, four or eight speakers of this size.

Speakers used in concert sound systems are usually arranged so that the smallest speakers handle the high frequencies, the middle-sized speakers handle mid and low range frequencies and bass or sub-bass cabinets handle the lowest frequencies. Separate amplifiers are employed to drive the different frequency speakers, or "crossover units" may be used to split the sound into frequency bandwidths.

How a loudspeaker works

A guitar pick-up or a microphone generates a low level signal of AC (alternating current) electricity. This signal is then fed to the input of an amplifier where its strength is dramatically increased. This is necessary because no microphone or guitar pickup can generate enough power to drive a loudspeaker on its own. The output signal from the amplifier is delivered to a "voice coil" wound around the neck of the cone and positioned between the poles of the magnet. The signal causes the coil to generate a magnetic field which interacts with the field of the fixed, permanent magnet in the speaker. When the voltage is rising on the voice coil, it is pushed away from the magnet, and thus the diaphragm moves forwards. With a falling voltage, the reverse occurs. The back-and-forth movement of the diaphragm causes the cone to vibrate on its suspension (by which the cone is held in place at each end). This movement causes compression and rarefaction (or expansion) of surrounding air which simulates the soundwaves that originally generated the signal from the pick-up or microphone. But because the signal strength has been multiplied by the amplifier, greater volumes of air are moved by the speaker with the result that the sound is amplified. The degree to which the unit can move forwards is deliberately limited, and if the speaker is forced to exceed this limit (if an input signal greater than its handling capacity is applied, for instance), then damage may occur to the cone which may even break loose from its suspension.

Bass speakers
Tina Weymouth, the former bass player with the Talking Heads, uses a system that includes a pair of 15 inch (38 cm) speakers. Though such large speakers can handle bass frequencies well, a certain loss of definition occurs. This can be compensated for by putting part of the amplifier output through additional smaller speakers, which are better able to produce a crisply defined sound. Note that only one of the twin speakers has been miked into the sound reinforcement system: both of them produce the same sound, so it is only necessary to mike one of them.

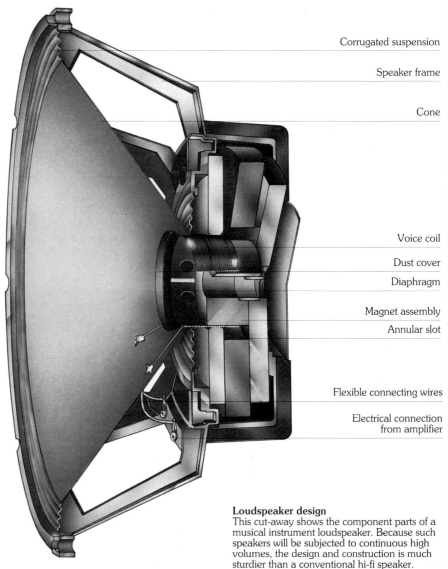

Corrugated suspension

Speaker frame

Cone

Voice coil

Dust cover

Diaphragm

Magnet assembly

Annular slot

Flexible connecting wires

Electrical connection from amplifier

Loudspeaker design
This cut-away shows the component parts of a musical instrument loudspeaker. Because such speakers will be subjected to continuous high volumes, the design and construction is much sturdier than a conventional hi-fi speaker.

Guitar amplifier characteristics

As described on page 116, notes played on a guitar have a fundamental tone and a harmonic series of tones at higher frequencies but of lower intensity. The more complex that harmonic series, the richer the sound of the note. A note played on an unamplified solid body electric guitar is not nearly as rich in harmonics as a note played on an acoustic guitar. A valve amplifier adds harmonic content to the signal it receives. Also, the harder it is driven by being played louder, the more the harmonic content is increased. That's one of the main reasons why, apart from wanting to be heard above the drummer, electric guitar players like to play loud. If the valve guitar amplifier had been invented after the solid state amplifier instead of the other way around, the most appropriate name for it would be "the amplifying harmonic processor." Guitar amplifier designers have exploited this harmonic characteristic in order to produce amplifiers which enhance the signal from an electric guitar's pickup to give the rich, powerful and emotive sound that is an integral part of the playing of guitarists like Eric Clapton, Jimi Hendrix, Jeff Beck, and Eddie Van Halen.

Solid state amplifiers have very different characteristics to valve amplifiers – unless special circuitry is used, they amplify the signals fed into them far more faithfully.

Distortion

Two types of distortion can occur with valve amplifiers. At lower volumes and when the circuitry is just beginning to be driven hard, smooth and musical harmonic distortion occurs. When the amplifier circuitry is overloaded even more, the sound starts to break up. This type of sound is an essential part of a number of guitar sounds, the best known being heavy metal and heavy rock. At the extreme it is referred to by a number of highly descriptive names including "shredder" and "crunch" sound. Both types of distortion, or a mixture of the two can be achieved by using an amplifier at high volume levels. Alternatively it may be induced by boosting the signal from the guitar before it is sent to the channel input on the amplifier.

Frequently, external pre-amplifiers which deliberately overload the amplifier by increasing the gain delivered to the channel input are used to create a distortion effect. They can be solid state or valve powered, located on the guitar as part of the instrument's circuitry, in a foot pedal, or in a rack-mounting device.

Input and output levels

For many guitarists, the power output is the first consideration when comparing amplifiers. However, in practical terms, the input to the amplifier is also significant.

Input sensitivity

The sensitivity of an amplifier refers to the minimum voltage of input signal required to achieve the maximum specified power output from the amplifier (with the volume control at maximum and the tone controls set flat – giving neither boost nor cut). Thus it is easier to overdrive an amplifier with a low input sensitivity (eg, 9 mV) in order to produce distortion.

Power output

The amount of amplification you may need will depend on factors such as the size of the venue, the type of mixing, the room's acoustics, the general sound level. A 50-100 watt combo will give you sufficient volume on its own at small venues, and, when necessary, you can always increase your volume by miking up the combo through the PA or sound-reinforcement system at larger gigs. Using a powerful stack in a small club can be a problem, particularly if you want an overdriven sound, because the volume needed to achieve this may be too much for the audience. In this case, the answer might be to use the amplifier with just one 4x12 cabinet and a pre-amp to achieve the overdriven sound.

There are several systems by which power output can be assessed, but the most useful is the RMS (root mean square) method. This indicates the sustained power load that the amplifier is capable of handling at various frequencies. Some manufacturers, however, invite confusion by using a variety of systems in their performance statistics. Terms such as "music power" and "peak watts" can give misleadingly high figures, since they may refer not to sustained output over several cycles, but to momentary peaks of high energy at a particular frequency. It is quite possible that an amplifier rated at 100 watts by such a system may, in practice, be drowned out by an amplifier rated at only 50 watts on the more meaningful (and universal) RMS system.

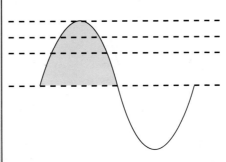

Peak power
RMS (root mean square) power
Average power

Zero

Power ratings
Each system bases power output ratings on different sections of the sine wave.

Matching speakers to the amplifier

Valve amplifiers must be matched to the impedances of the speakers used. These are normally either 8 Ohms or 15–16 Ohms. The different ways of connecting speakers to achieve specific impedances are shown on the right. Valve amplifiers must never be switched on when they are not connected to speakers, otherwise the output transformer and output valves may be damaged.

Transistor amplifiers are more robust – most quality models are immune to both short and open circuits on the speaker outputs. A minimum speaker impedance is normally quoted which will give the greatest output at acceptable distortion levels. Fitting speakers with a higher impedance will result only in reduced output – although it might also result in reduced levels of distortion. If there is no standby switch on the amplifier it is always a good policy to turn the volume down to zero before switching on.

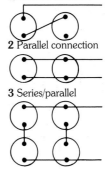

1 Series connection

2 Parallel connection

3 Series/parallel

Impedance
(1), combined impedance is the sum of the individual impedances. In (2), total impedance R of speakers r1 and r2 is calculated thus:
$$\frac{1}{R} + \frac{1}{r1} = \frac{1}{r2}$$
With four speakers of equal impedance connected as in (3), the combined impedance is equal to the impedance of a single speaker.

Channel gain

Some guitar amplifiers with more than one input channel are designed to provide different overall gain features. The higher-gain channel will have the greater sensitivity and overload at lower signal levels. Since the overall gain difference will almost certainly be caused by an alteration to the gain achieved by the first valve, the possibility of causing distortion in the first valve increases. This is desirable because if you can distort the first valve you can have an overdriven valve sound at any volume setting.

Switch-on characteristics

Valve amplifiers require a minute or two to warm up to operating temperature. The standby switch found on many valve amplifiers disconnects the high operating voltages from the valve but leaves the low-voltage heater supply fully connected. This allows the amplifier to be held, fully warmed up, ready for instant use.

Transistor amplifiers respond instantly when switched on, and require no warm-up period. However, the initial surge of electricity rushing into the amplifier circuitry, charging the capacitors, and establishing operating voltages throughout the circuit, causes a rushing noise or thump to be heard from the speakers. This is unpleasant and, in the case of high-powered amplifiers, can actually cause damage to the speakers. To avoid this happening, many amplifiers incorporate automatic circuitry that inhibits the delivery of power to the speakers for a few seconds.

MESA/Boogie

Vox AC 30

Fender twin reverb

Other Features

Some of the more expensive top-line valve amplifiers like MESA/Boogie and Soldano are designed to survive excessive punishment on the road. They are therefore built to extremely rugged specifications.

A useful feature to look out for is the ability to switch channels and to have a mix of channels. Foot switches that achieve this can be especially useful when playing live.

Some guitar amplifiers also offer true stereo. They are, in fact, separate amplifiers each with separate speakers all within one cabinet. They only really come into their own in a recording situation when used to add dimension to the stereo picture.

Fender produce amplifiers that can offer a variety of valve sounds in addition to their own traditional sound. A good example is Fender's "The Twin," a version of the famous "Twin Reverb" which has a Fender sound on one channel and a variety of overdrive sounds on the other.

MIDI amplifier control

Musical Instrument Digital Interface (MIDI) is a computer communication standard agreed between synthesizer manufacturers to allow their products to interface or "talk" to each other. MIDI can be used with amplifiers to allow the guitarist to store "patches" of volume, tone, and sound effect settings.

MIDI itself does not interface with the amplifier's power circuitry. A small computer memory with a battery back-up retains the settings even when the amplifier is switched off. MIDI digitally controls the amplifier settings and should not be confused with the actual amplification circuitry.

Most MIDI-equipped amplifiers allow the guitarist to create more than enough patches for most likely applications. For example, in a live situation, instead of having to remember the different settings required for each song, the guitarist can store the settings as a series or "chain" of patches and switch from one patch to another with a single control on the amplifier or a footpedal.

MIDI has become an increasingly popular interfacing system both for recording and live applications. It allows an off-stage technician to adjust on-stage equipment remotely. Alternatively, a lighting rig could be interfaced so that when a guitarist changes amplifier patches, control lighting effects would change accordingly.

By setting MIDI-controlled effects units to the same MIDI channel number as an amplifier, they can be programmed to change settings simultaneously with the amplifier, thus simplifying life on stage.

Rack Mounting Amplifiers

Rack mounting amplifiers are designed to fit into a standard 19 inch (48cm) racking unit. A unit consists of a pair of purpose-made, metal rack strips. The amplifier, like all standard racking devices, can vary in height in multiples of one unit or "1U." Each unit measures 1.75 inches (4.5cm) high and is bolted onto the front of the rack unit. Musicians involved in recording and live performance often prefer to have their amplifier fitted in a rack along with pre-amps and effects that will be used on stage and in the recording studio.

Top session players sometimes have a rack mounting system built into a flight case to give maximum protection in transit. Such systems have the advantage of being quick to set up, as equipment in the rack can be permanently connected and ready for use.

A rack that is deeper than necessary for your initial requirements will leave space for equipment that you may want to add at a later stage.

The seduction of new technology can sometimes lure a guitarist away from the most practical solutions. Rack systems will grow in weight as more units are added and they can become rather awkward for one person to transport.

Marshall stack

Rack-mounting
MESA/Boogie and Marshall, among others, offer rack mounting versions of their equipment. MESA/Boogie offer the option of a "retro kit" to allow combo amps to be converted for rack mounting.

Sound processing

Any device used to change or color sound, from a simple guitar pedal to the most complex studio multiple effect unit, falls under the general heading of sound processing. Despite the vast array of exotic gadgets the guitarist is likely to be confronted with, they all alter sound in one or more of four ways.

Volume and *gain* controls allow the loudness of an amplified sound to be varied and at extremes driven into *distortion*.

Equalization and *tone* controls change the character of the sound by boosting or cutting some of the frequencies.

Time-based effects allow delayed copies of a signal to be used to create a variety of different effects.

Pitch change effects allow the pitch of a note to be made higher or lower.

MIDI (see page 203) plays an important role in sound processing in that a lot of amplification, sound processing, and recording equipment can be programmed to carry out a number of different tasks during a performance or recording.

Producers use compression, limiting, gating, and expansion just as creatively as effects that change sound in a more obvious way. Clever use of such devices adds greatly to the impact and dynamics of most recorded music we hear.

Equalizers

An equalizer is a group of tone controls that allow adjustment to the full frequency range of an incoming signal in a number of separate bands. A simple equalizer would consist of control knobs for bass, middle and treble ranges, usually with a central 0 dB setting. Turning the knob clockwise boosts the frequency; turning it counterclockwise cuts the frequency.

Sweep equalizers

Although some amplifier designs incorporate as many as three mid-range tone controls, a more elaborate method frequently used on mixing desks and available also as a foot pedal is to have one or two *sweep frequency controls*. A sweep equalizer has the usual lift/cut control, but also an additional control which allows you to shift the centre frequency of the control up or down the audio spectrum to a higher or lower frequency. This more flexible arrangement allows more accurate adjustment. The turnover frequency of treble and bass controls is also often sweepable on mixing desks.

On amplifiers fitted with two sweep frequency controls and two lift/cut controls, dramatic effects can be achieved if the area of operation of the controls is overlapped. A *wah-wah pedal* is simply a sweep equalizer with a fixed amount of lift.

Parametric equalizers

Parametric equalizers (as sweep equalizers are sometimes incorrectly termed) in fact have an additional control, the "bandwidth" or "Q" control. "Q" refers to the steepness of the slope on each side of the centre frequency. On cheaper parametric equalizers you simply switch from "low Q" to "high Q", but the best have a totally variable "Q" control (which allows you to select a suitable bandwidth) and also a frequency control as on a sweep equalizer, permitting precise shaping of the sound.

One way in which a parametric equalizer can be used on stage as well as in the studio is to remove a small peak of accentuated

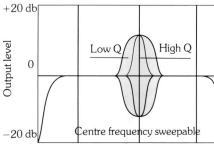

Effect of parametric equalizer
The area shaded grey shows the effect range of the mid-lift and cut of the parametric at low Q (wide bandwidth setting). Increasingly, Q narrows the bandwidth. The area shaded blue shows a typical maximum Q setting.

Amplifier, volume and tone controls

Altering the frequency curve of an amplifier is achieved by the use of tone (or equalization) controls. The simplest tone controls act on the extremities of the audio frequency spectrum, namely the bass and treble. In a passive guitar circuit, the controls cut or reduce these frequencies. The tone controls on active guitar circuits, amplifiers and mixing desks, on the other hand, are also able to lift and increase these frequencies. The typical effect of these controls is shown in the graph below. The frequency at which the tone controls begin to take effect (X and Y on the graph) is known as the "turnover point". The curve which they produce is called the "slope".

A more sophisticated system can be produced by adding one or more mid-range controls, often termed "presence controls" by manufacturers. The effect of a mid-range control is shown in the second graph.

Some amplifiers also feature a *bright channel*. This is an additional channel which

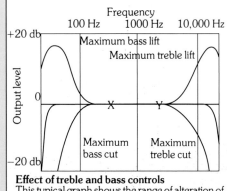

Effect of treble and bass controls
This typical graph shows the range of alteration of the output levels achieved by these controls. The dotted line shows the effect of setting an intermediate bass and treble cut.

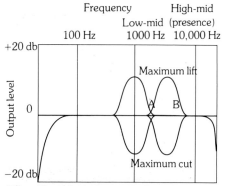

Effect of mid-frequency controls
Similarly, this shows the effect on mid-frequencies of two typical mid-range controls. The dotted line shows the effect of combining a small cut on one with a large lift on the other.

Volume control
This controls the volume on channel A. The knob is pulled out to boost the mid-range sound.

Tone controls
Treble, middle and bass controls provide equalization on Channel A. The treble control can be pulled out to give added brightness.

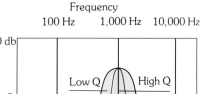

frequencies. In the studio, the peak might merely affect one note, or a group of notes, by making them louder, but on stage it may cause them to feed back. In both cases, a single note would require a high Q, whereas a group of notes is more likely to need the wider frequency bandwidth cut of a low Q.

Graphic equalizers
Originally designed for studio use, *graphic equalizers* can now be found on guitar amplifiers, foot pedals and domestic stereo systems. Technically more complex than parametric equalizers, they are paradoxically much easier to operate and can, if they offer sufficient facilities, do the job of all other kinds of equalizer.

The graphic equalizer uses sliding controls called "faders" arranged with their tracks parallel to one another. Each fader controls a particular band of frequencies and is labelled with the centre frequency of that band. This may cover a full octave, a half, or a third, or even a sixth of an octave. Obviously, the more faders the equalizer has, the greater its versatility, although this creates design problems in trying to keep noise and harmonic distortion down to acceptable levels.

If you look at the fader knobs on a graphic equalizer as though they were points on a graph, and think of the curving line that would link them all together most smoothly, then this would recreate exactly the type of graph used to illustrate the effects of an equalizer. This is the feature that makes a graphic equalizer so easy to use, and also explains its name.

Filters
Filters can be designed to remove or to pass any desired frequency or band of frequencies, although high-pass and low-pass filters are the types most frequently encountered. High-pass filters resemble basscut controls: all frequencies above their turnover frequency remain unchanged, while frequencies below the turnover point are sharply reduced. The chief difference is that the slope of the filter is generally invariable and much steeper than that of the bass control. A similar comparison can be made between the standard treble control and a low-pass filter.

Graphic equalizer
The design of this graphic equalizer shows clearly how frequency response can be visibly shaped by adjusting the faders, each of which controls a particular band of frequencies. Small graphic equalizers are also available in pedal form, typically having between six and ten faders, operating across proportionally broader frequencies but giving less precise control.

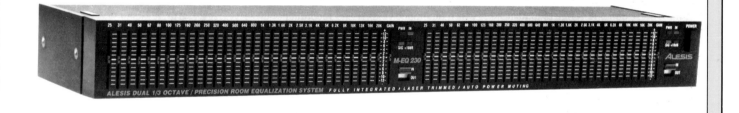

has an increased treble response, generally achieved by simply introducing a treble bypass capacitor wired to the channel volume control in the same way as is shown on the passive guitar circuits (see pp. 186-9).

In recent years, tone controls on amps have become increasingly comprehensive, allowing greater flexibility and giving the opportunity of "shaping" the sound far more precisely. It is not uncommon for modern amps to have built-in equalizers – simpler versions of the one shown above.

Input jacks and channel selector
The high and low inputs differ in sensitivity by 12 db. Either channel can be selected to give different sound characteristics.

Gain control
This adjusts the gain when using channel B. Pulling the knob out boosts the mid-range.

Master volume control
This control alters the volume of channel B, and can be used in conjunction with the gain control to vary distortion.

Tone controls
These act in the same way as those for Channel A.

Parametric equalizer
Level, Q and frequency controls divide up the audio spectrum into small bands for precise adjustment.

Built-in amplifier controls
These are the controls of a Yamaha G100-212 combo amplifier rated at 100 watts RMS and using two 12 in. (30 cm) speakers. The unit has two input channels: high (channel A) and low (channel B).

Reverb control
With this control the ratio of direct and delayed sound can be adjusted (see p. 209).

Sound processing effects

The majority of sound processing effects are available as foot pedals. The guitar lead is plugged directly into the pedal's input socket and another lead is inserted between the output of the pedal and the amplifier input. When additional pedals are added, a simple pedal board can keep them together on stage and make them more convenient to use.

Generally speaking, foot pedals are made from lower quality components than their more expensive studio equivalents. For this reason, they can create a considerable amount of background noise. The simplest way to remove or reduce the noise is to use a noise gate as the last link in the chain before the signal is directed to the amplifier.

Rack mounting sound processors are generally of a higher quality than foot pedals. Some guitarists have a series of effects mounted in a rack together with their amplifiers allowing settings to be saved as MIDI patches which can then be selected from the front panel. MIDI interfaces also allow stage technicians or engineers to control the patch changes.

Inputs and outputs

A simple processor like a foot pedal has a single input for the guitar and an output for connection to the amplifier or mixing console. Many of the better quality sound processors also operate in stereo. The most common use of stereo with guitars is to have one direct or clean signal that is not changed, whilst the other goes through the effect. Stereo effects are often used to enhance a recording – using the pan settings to place the two signals left and right can create a spacial effect.

Many rack mounting units are multiple processors that offer the equivalent of directing a guitar signal through up to a

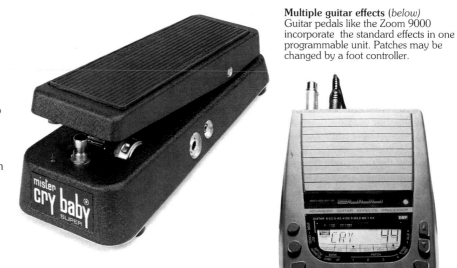

Multiple guitar effects (*below*)
Guitar pedals like the Zoom 9000 incorporate the standard effects in one programmable unit. Patches may be changed by a foot controller.

Wah wah pedal (*above*)
Used to great effect in the sixties by Jimi Hendrix, the wah wah enjoyed a new lease on life in many of the late eighties "rave" bands.

Rack-mounted sound processing (*above*)
Reasonably priced rack-mounted multiple effects units are capable of simultaneously providing

dozen different types of sound processing effect at the same time.

Mixing consoles and some amplifiers have independent sockets which allow a signal to be sent to a sound processor. The output to the effect is called the "send" while the input coming back is the "return."

high-quality digital versions of all of the most commonly used sound processing effects.

They are also referred to as "auxilliary," "ancillary," or "insert points."

Signal level matching

Mixing consoles, some sound processors, and amplifiers have "gain" controls that allow inputs and outputs to be matched.

A piece of equipment that has a gain control may have a warning LED which lights up when a signal input overloads and is likely to be causing unwanted distortion. If the light stays on continuously while a signal is being received, this will almost certainly mean a high input signal level is causing unwanted and discernible distortion. If the light occasionally blinks this indicates peaks on which distortion is occurring but that are undetectable to the human ear. Such momentary flashes are often desirable as they indicate that a full input signal is being retrieved.

Some sound processors and effects units have a "mix" control which can be used to adjust the relative output levels of the clean or "direct" signal and the processed signal.

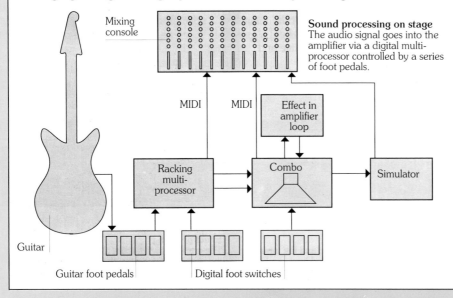

Mixing console

Sound processing on stage
The audio signal goes into the amplifier via a digital multi-processor controlled by a series of foot pedals.

MIDI

MIDI

Effect in amplifier loop

Racking multi-processor

Combo

Simulator

Guitar

Guitar foot pedals

Digital foot switches

Natural echo and reverberation

Throughout the history of recording, echo and reverberation have been found attractive and flattering to sound.

A natural *echo* occurs when a sound is bounced or reflected off a surface distant from the source of the sound. The fact that the sound takes some time to travel through the air causes the delay in hearing the echo. Because traveling through the air reduces the energy of the sound-wave and the reflective surface also absorbs some of that energy, an echo is always quieter or lower in volume than the original sound.

Reverberation occurs when a sound made in an enclosed space is reflected off walls or other surfaces a number of times before dying away. Because the multiple reflections start before the original sound has died away, reverberation is heard as part of the original sound. It can be heard to continue after the end of the original sound because the soundwaves may bounce back and forth many times before dying out.

Reverberation can develop into an unpleasant phenomenon called a "standing wave" which occurs when certain frequencies continue bouncing back and forth

between two parallel surfaces after the rest of the reverberation has died away. Facing walls of professional recording studios are frequently deliberately built very slightly out of parallel to avoid standing waves.

In purpose-built recording studios, natural reverberation can last for around 500 milliseconds (half a second). Large studios used for recording full orchestras have even longer reverberation times.

Natural reverberation continues to be used in recording studios but digital reverb and echo is now widely used both for playing live and studio recording.

Delaying sound electronically

Digital delay units are the simplest and most economic method of creating delayed effects and reverberation. However, whereas top players continue to use vintage technology amplifiers, most use modern digital delay effects.

There are some exceptions. Some re-issues of vintage guitar amplifiers feature spring reverb units, the best-loved being made by Hammond. Recording studio EMT valve plate reverberation is also preferred by some recordists for its individual warm sound.

In the pre-digital fifties and sixties, tape echo was widely used. A signal was recorded onto one machine which usually had tape joined in a loop. By altering the distance between the record head and one or more playback heads, the time by which the repeat echos were delayed could be controlled.

Phase shifting and flanging

Phasing is the name given to the characteristic sound heard when a delayed copy of a signal is heard almost immediately after the original sound: the delay is so short that only a single sound is heard. Phase cancellation is what actually occurs. When the copy is played back after a slightly longer delay, a

metallic sound known as *flanging* occurs. Phasing and flanging effects occur with delays of between 10 and 12 milliseconds.

During the 1960s, phasing was achieved by playing back two copies of a recording on two different tape machines running at slightly differing speeds. By gently pressing a finger on one of the tape reels and slowing it down, the signal was delayed and made to go "out of phase" with the other

Delay pedal
Adjustments can be made to the rate (speed of repetition), intensity (strength of the delayed signal), and depth (amount of delay).

tape. As the finger was released the tape machine took up the slack, first traveling faster to catch up. Due to the slowing down and catching up, the delayed recording slipped in and out of phase. Today, guitar and other effects units simulate this effect electronically.

Automatic double-tracking (ADT)

Double-tracking is an effect achieved by recording a guitar line or vocal part on one track and then recording the same thing in unison on a second track. The slight differences in the performance create the effect of the two parts being played in unison. Ken Townsend of Abbey Road Studios devised a system of recording the same vocal performance on two different tape machines and then playing one back slightly later than the other, thus inventing "automatic double-tracking." Since then, both analogue and digital circuitry has been designed to simulate this effect. The automatic double-tracking effect works with delays of between 25 and 35 milliseconds, working particularly well at around 27 to 28 milliseconds.

Modulation and pitch changing

Tape delay techniques involving changing tape speeds create slight changes in pitch which often enhance effects. A *chorus* effect is created by delaying several ADT copies of a signal to varying degrees. The effect works particularly well when slight pitch changes are introduced. Digital and analogue processors have been designed to introduce controllable pitch changes.

Digital technology allows far greater manipulation of sound than tape recorders or analogue circuitry. The amount a signal can be delayed is infinitely variable as are pitch changes. The harmonizer is used to alter the pitch of an incoming signal. Thus a guitarist can set a harmonizer so that the guitar part is accompanied by a harmony.

Phase relationship
Phasing depends on the splitting of the signal (the one that comes from a guitar pick-up, for example) into two. If the signals remain perfectly in time or in phase with each other, no change will be heard. When the signal drifts in and out of phase, cancellation will cause tonal changes, particularly between 90 and 180 degrees out-of-phase.

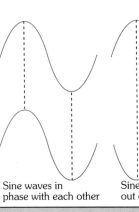

Sine waves in phase with each other

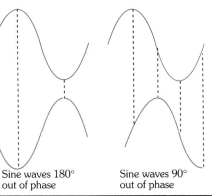

Sine waves 180° out of phase

Sine waves 90° out of phase

Mixing consoles

"Mixing desks" or "consoles" allow signals from microphones, instruments and their amplification to be brought together, treated with sound processing and effects equipment and "balanced" or "mixed." Mono, stereo or quadrophonic mixes can then be amplified through a sound system or recorded. During multitrack recording, signals can be recorded separately with or without sound processing and effects which can be added later during a final mixdown. Although consoles, with their vast rows of knobs, buttons, faders and indicator lights, may appear to be extremely complex, they repeat a number of facilities on a number of identical vertical "channels."

Mixing consoles provide the user not only with an extremely creative tool with which to sculpture sound, but also a detailed map that shows how each sound is being altered. It should be remembered that this is only a guide for working towards an overall sound. Irrespective of technical considerations, for the ultimate judgements regarding sound, the musician, sound engineer or producer must use the most sophisticated audio equipment at their disposal, namely their ears.

Monitor man
Top American monitor sound engineer Michael L. Parker of Maryland Sound is seen here at the controls of a Ramsa monitor console. Mike has supplied the on-stage sound for Great White, Striper, Smokie Robinson, Soul to Soul, and many others.

Frequency response

Sound equipment is judged on its ability to handle sounds with a fundamental frequency of between 20 hertz (20 cycles per second) and 20 kilohertz (20,000 cycles per second). Acoustic instruments start producing sounds distinguishable as musical pitches at between 30 and 300 hertz. Although church organs and synthesizers can produce sounds with a musical pitch below 30 hertz, most sounds in that frequency range are perceived as rumble or hum.

Though some instruments can produce notes which have harmonics with a pitch of 20 kHz and beyond, human hearing tails off at 17 or 18 kHz. This is borne out by the fact that although U.K. stereo BBC FM radio broadcasts sound clear and bright to most people, they never broadcast at above 15 kHz. Also, even the best analogue cassette recorders can only record frequencies below 15 kHz, therfore all analogue portastudio recordings will have a limited frequency range.

Professional quality audio equipment is judged by its capability to reproduce sound between 20 Hz and 20 kHz at an even level. However, as the above figures indicate, equipment with lower specifications can often prove adequate for many musical applications.

"In-line" and "split" consoles

All mixing desks, from the small personal mixers used on stage to the computerized consoles used in top recording studios, generally fall within two main categories: they are referred to as being either "split console" or "in-line."

The "split console" has separate sets of input as well as output or "monitor" channels. Split consoles are usually designed with the input channels on the left and the output channels to the right. A central area is usually occupied by one master output channel or several output channels which allow selections of input channels to be manipulated as "groups." The "in-line" console has switching that allows the input channel and monitor or output controls to be laid out in the same vertical line.

The "split" console design is favored by some as being easy to use as all input and output channel settings can be easily assessed from a visual point of view. They are also useful during a recording mixdown because tape monitor channels can be used for line level inputs from drum machines, synthesizers and samplers which can be synchronized to a multitrack tape machine. The split design can also be useful for providing independent monitor mixes to musicians on stage.

Technology has narrowed the differences between in-line and split consoles. However, broadly speaking, the split console design can be advantageous when additional inputs might be useful during a mixdown or when a number of different mixes are needed for monitoring purposes.

Console configurations

An "input channel" accepts incoming signals from microphones, musical instruments, sound processors, and effects units. A "bus" is the name given to a set of connections within a console which provide the main audio outputs from a console. A

Input channels | Monitor channels
Group channel | Master channel

Split console concept
Dedicated input and output channels are all housed within the same console.

Console features

Besides the basic input channels, a major feature of all consoles is the "grouping" together and mixing down of a number of input signals into groups. For both live performance and recording, once a group of sounds have been balanced they often have to be manipulated together. For example, grouping is ideal for drum kits and percussion. Once the relative levels between the signals (which might come from microphones, drum machines, samplers or other sources) have been balanced they can be controlled with one level fader on a group channel.

Live performance monitoring consoles have most output groups so as to give musicians individual mixes in their monitors. "Master" channels also allow sound processing like compression to be used on a stereo mixdown signal. The fader on an output master channel is also used for a fade-out at the end of a track.

Foldback and talkback

"Foldback" is the name sometimes used to describe the monitor systems that allow musicians to hear themselves, other musicians or the signal from a recorder through monitor speakers or headphones or earsets. The speaker systems in recording studio control rooms are usually referred to as monitors, as are those used by musicians on stage.

A "talkback" system is used to allow verbal communication between musicians and sound engineers when they would otherwise be too far apart to hear each other or, as in recording studios, may even be acoustically and visually isolated.

The more comprehensive consoles made for concert sound and recording studios are constructed with a "frame" into which the appropriate "channel modules" are fitted. By making a number of types of frames and modules, console manufacturers can meet the requirements of live performance, recording, broadcast and various sound-to-picture applications. Also if a fault occurs channel modules can be removed and replaced or serviced.

Patch bay and console matrix

A patch bay may be either a separate unit or built into the console. In its simplest form an audio "patch bay" is a network of connections beneath a surface on which pairs of rows of sockets are mounted. By bringing all equipment to such a patch bay, any connection can be easily made without the need for getting to awkwardly situated output and input sockets. Also a signal chain can be quickly altered.

If a piece of equipment has to be inserted on one bus, the connection can be made by inserting short patch cables. When a plug is inserted in any socket, because it is "normalled" the usual or normal connection is broken. Cables with identical plugs on each end are used to make connections between the various pieces of equipment.

More advanced designs can use solid state switching. MIDI patch bays allow MIDI-controlled devices to be interfaced in similar ways. Sometimes a patch bay may be referred to as a "matrix."

Digital consoles

In 1992, Neve launched the Capricorn computer-automated and digital signal path recording console. With dramatically improved signal-to-noise ratio and zero channel crosstalk, infinite configuration possibilities, and improved sound quality, the Neve Capricorn has set a new standard in recording consoles.

recording console referred to as a 16/8/2 configuration has 16 input channels, an 8 track bus to connect to an 8 track recorder and a stereo bus mixing bus. A live sound 24/3 console has 24 inputs, a stereo output bus, and an additional mono output bus. This three-path bus could provide a left and

SSL G Series recording console
Solid State Logic's G Series computer-controlled analogue signal path recording console set new standards for recording and automated mixing.

right sound system with an additional central mono output used for a speaker array that would only be used for vocals.

Recording consoles are configured to match the recording medium they are to be used with. For larger concert systems, which amplify instruments as well as voices, separate front-of-house and monitor consoles would be employed.

Console requirements

For small venues with an audience in the low hundreds, a simple console that mixes any instruments and voices to be amplified through the PA system can be used. This type of console can be operated by a musician on stage or by someone acting as a balance engineer off stage where the sound from the PA system can be better heard. More complex versions of this type of console may send individual mixes to musicians on stage by means of a monitor section.

At larger live music venues it is more usual to have a "front-of-house" console used to mix the sound the audience hears and a separate monitor console which is used to send individual mixes to the musicians on stage. As musicians rely on hearing high quality sound on stage, front-of-house and monitor consoles generally deliver the same level of quality of sound but with different channel combinations and connection possibilities.

Microphone and line level inputs

The signal from a microphone, electric guitar or any other electronic device has an "impedance" value. This is the amount by which that device impedes or resists the flow of electrical current. Impedance is measured in Ohms: the value will appear suffixed by the Greek letter omega (Ω). As a guide, the impedance of an input should be between five and ten times greater than the impedance of the output signal.

The input channels on a comprehensive mixing console will each have two types of input, one to accept signals from low impedance microphones and the other to accept higher impedance signals at "line level" from sound processing units, outboard equipment, synthesizers, and drum machines.

The majority of microphones of a sufficiently acceptable quality for musical applications are low impedance. High quality studio microphones most frequently have an impedance of 200 Ohms. A few operate at 50 Ohms and some as high as 600 Ohms. So, broadly speaking, good quality low impedance microphones have impedances between 50 & 600 Ohms and most professional models are 200 Ohms. Line outputs from outboard effects and synthesizers tend to have much higher impedance outputs measured in thousands (1000 Ohms = 1 kOhm), rather than hundreds of Ohms.

Both types of input will have a fine tuning adjustment. It may be called a "trim pot," "coarse attenuator" or a "gain control." They may have a variety of different markings but most will have a central 0 dB setting with "–" signal cutting settings to the left, and "+" signal boosting settings to the right. A "pad" switch gives the added option of altering the gain of a microphone input by a set amount. For example a + or – 20 decibel switch would be called a 20 dB pad.

Some condenser microphones require 48 volt power. A console's "phantom power" switch directs such power down a microphone line or the microphone might have its own power supply.

The inputs on a console might accept standard unbalanced RCA phono plugs, unbalanced mono jack plugs, balanced line jack plugs, or balanced line XLR

The Pan control
The Pan facility, found on all mixing consoles, controls the position of the sound in the stereo field. The increasing sophistication of cinema sound systems has resulted in the evolution of a number of alternatives to traditional stereo sound for which panning is absolutely crucial.

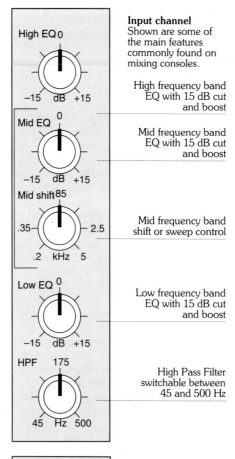

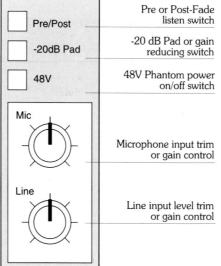

Input channel
Shown are some of the main features commonly found on mixing consoles.

High frequency band EQ with 15 dB cut and boost

Mid frequency band EQ with 15 dB cut and boost

Mid frequency band shift or sweep control

Low frequency band EQ with 15 dB cut and boost

High Pass Filter switchable between 45 and 500 Hz

Pre or Post-Fade listen switch

-20 dB Pad or gain reducing switch

48V Phantom power on/off switch

Microphone input trim or gain control

Line input level trim or gain control

Pan pot controlling stereo position in mix

connectors. When there is a choice, a balanced line will give a better quality of signal. Additionally, XLR connectors are far more robust and therefore more reliable that other connectors.

The long vertical sliding controls, usually found at the bottom of the console, are known as "Faders." They control the overall volume level and usually have a 0 dB setting with "+" boost settings marked above, and "–" cut settings marked below.

Pan control
A "Pan" pot positions a sound at a specific place in the "stereo picture." The central "0" position sends an equal level of the signal to both the left and right stereo speakers making the sound appear to come from the central position between them. Turning the control to one of the extreme positions will direct the signal to either the left or the right speaker.

Using the seven settings on the pan pot shown in the diagram it would be possible to create an audio impression of a row of seven singers standing in a straight line between the left and right stereo speakers.

Post or after-fade listen, pre-fade listen, solo, and mute
A "pre-fade listen" switch allows a signal coming into the console to be monitored for quality even before it has passed through the fader, whereas switching to "post-fade listen" allows monitoring after the fader and usually in its stereo position.

Different consoles have various types of "solo" cut switches which allow the input on a channel to be heard with all other sound on adjacent channels muted.

"Mute" is a common term in sound technology for preventing the signal from a channel from being heard without disturbing the actual channel level settings. Mute or solo switches are to be found in a number of forms.

Some recording consoles may also have a switch that toggles between an "input" and a "tape" setting to give the option of hearing the sound from a particular input *before* it reaches the tape recorder, or when it comes *from* the tape recorder.

Equalization
All equalizers are tone controls which reduce or boost selective "bandwidths" in the audible spectrum. The simplest form of equalizer or "EQ" section to be found on consoles typically consists of three controls which operate on three "bandwidths" within the audible spectrum of sound. There is very little difference between such an equalizer section and the three tone controls for bass, mid (or presence), and

treble found on some guitar amplifiers. The input channel illustrated has the additional facility of a "sweep" control on the Mid EQ. The fixed LOW EQ operates on bass frequencies below 100 Hz and the fixed HI EQ on treble frequencies above 10 kHz. The MID EQ sweep control allows its bandwidth to be moved anywhere between 200 Hz and 5 kHz. All three controls can cut or boost their bandwidth by up to 15 dB. This is a simple EQ section of the type that might be found on a good quality home studio console or portastudio.

Professional studio consoles might have five fixed band EQ controls plus several sweep and parametric equalizers. On a professional recording session a recordist may also decide to use additional outboard equalization for a particular sound or effect. When first getting a sound from an input all equalizer controls should be set to their central (0 dB) setting. Experienced recordists sometimes prefer to use a choice of microphone, placement technique, and careful exploitation of its characteristics whenever possible, in preference to equalization. Therefore, in some cases, little or no equalization may be necessary.

High pass and low pass filters
High and low pass filters are also equalizers. A high pass filter allows all frequencies above a certain point to pass through it whereas all frequencies below that point will not. A high pass filter may just have one fixed pass cut-off frequency.

Filters cut off with frequencies at a slope but quite sharply. The one illustrated (HPF) is switchable between 45 and 500 Hz. A high pass filter can be used to reduce ambient traffic and train noise, sound transferred to a microphone through its stand, close vocal "popping" or any other unwanted low frequency noise that could

be picked up by the microphone. Low pass filters may be found on some high quality consoles but, in musical situations, they do not have as many applications as high pass filters.

Effects send and return
"Auxiliary," "ancillary," "insert points," and "effects send and return" are names applied to the inputs and outputs on a channel that allow the signal to be routed through sound processing and effects equipment and returned to the console.

Insert points may be found at various points in the channel's signal path because a sound processor may have a different impact if inserted at different points in the signal path: directly before or after the equalizer section are popular insert points.

Sends and returns may also have their own gain controls which allow incoming and outgoing signal levels to be adjusted.

Phase switch
A phase switch is a feature not found on all consoles. It simply reverses the positive and negative connections of the input. This may be used if, for example, it is discovered that the cable of a microphone has been accidentally wired with the connections the wrong way round.

Other input channel features
There are many other facilities to be found on mixing consoles, particularly the top makes like Neve, SSL, and DDA. Some of them may feature built-in sound processing facilities like compressors and limiters. However, the majority of the features listed above will appear on virtually all consoles, although some may be given different names in manufacturer's attempts to bestow their consoles with magical capabilities.

Universal level method
Matching a console input with an input signal is a vital but nonetheless extremely simple operation. Too high a signal can cause distortion or damage a console's circuitry whereas too low a signal may not even be audible with the fader at maximum.

Matching the incoming signal with the console input and setting approximate recording levels are both part of the same process. For example, with a microphone on an acoustic guitar, first set the trim pot and the fader at their lowest settings. Plug the microphone into the appropriate input. Ask the guitarist to play and gradually bring the fader up to 0 dB. Adjust the trim pot until the record level meter indicates an average level of 0 dB, or just above. The input is then matched and an approximate record level has been set.

Some recording equipment may have just mic and line inputs, or a general purpose input. Bass and electric guitars can be be plugged directly into a line level input. Because guitar pick-ups usually have a higher impedance than line level devices, they may first need to be routed through a "Direct injection" box (see p. 217).

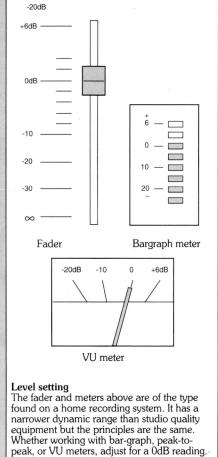

Fader   Bargraph meter

VU meter

Level setting
The fader and meters above are of the type found on a home recording system. It has a narrower dynamic range than studio quality equipment but the principles are the same. Whether working with bar-graph, peak-to-peak, or VU meters, adjust for a 0dB reading.

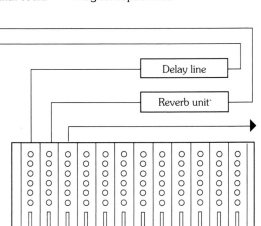

Using input channels as returns
Directing a signal back to a console via a channel input will allow greater control over that signal than if brought back via a return input.

Delay line

Reverb unit

213

Working on stage

In order to perform at their best, a group of musicians must be able to hear themselves adequately. They also need to feel comfortable about the quality and level of the sound that both they and their audience are hearing.

There may seem to be little in common between a small amplification system used in a small bar and the huge sound system used by a stadium band to satisfy an audience of tens-of-thousands. Yet for both applications, and for the wide range of possible permutations in between, the same basic guidelines apply.

The terminology is sometimes confusing regarding sound systems. A PA or "Public Address" system is generally the smaller type of sound system, sometimes also used to amplify people speaking or making a public address or to amplify a singer's voice. "Sound Reinforcement" is the term used to describe larger systems designed for use by bands when both the sound of voices and instruments is amplified.

Sound reinforcement
In the sixties, bands used stacks for the guitarists and a modest PA for the vocalists. Today, even in small clubs, the whole group sound usually goes through a PA system controlled by a sound engineer.

Basic set-up

In a relatively small venue a band can play quite well together using individual amplifiers for guitars, keyboards and bass and a PA or sound system to amplify signals from microphones. With three or so musicians using separate amplifiers of between 30 and 100 watts, a PA sound system rated between 300 and 500 watts should handle vocals quite well. A PA rated at anything lower than around 200 watts would not allow vocals to be heard clearly and consistently. Whereas guitar amplifiers are designed specifically to give an added sound character, good PA systems are intended to amplify in much the same way as hi-fi systems. That is to say that they should amplify the signals fed to them without colouring or altering the sound. Such an amplifier is described as having a "transparent" sound.

Speakers should be connected with unscreened twin-core cable. Specialist electronics suppliers usually stock a range of purpose made cables. Care should always be taken to ensure speaker cabinets are connected in phase with all "+" and "−" connections matching. Otherwise sound quality will be lost and bass frequencies reduced. Guitar, bass guitar and keyboard amplifiers will bring the level of the amplified instruments up to the acoustic sound level of the drum kit using the amplifier volume controls to achieve an acceptable balance.

The phenomenon that largely dictates how on-stage equipment is set up and used is unwanted "feedback." Guitar pick-ups and microphones can cause feedback, with microphones usually proving the most sensitive to the problem and the most troublesome. Feedback is the loud and usually unpleasant howl or whistle heard when a microphone or guitar pick-up starts to re-amplify the sound coming from its own loudspeakers. In many live sound situations, the microphone's input controls can be used to keep levels just below the point at which feedback occurs.

To minimize feedback problems in a practical way while at the same time optimizing the amplification and PA system, the familiar set-up of "backline" and the PA system is the most widely used. Amplifiers for electric instruments including guitar, bass, and keyboards are set up in a row with the drum kit facing the audience, to form what is referred to collectively as the "backline."

By placing PA or sound system speaker enclosures to the extreme left and right of the stage area and just in front of the microphones, feedback is minimized. Feedback can be reduced to managable

levels by keeping microphone levels as low as possible, and keeping the microphones as far away, and as far behind the main PA speakers as is practical.

A problem often experienced by bands using small PA systems is that they cannot hear the singer sufficiently well on stage. The PA system projects the sound into the audience area but on stage the sound level of the backline drowns out the vocal. If small PA "monitor speakers" are introduced and placed on stage and facing towards the stage, a better on-stage sound balance can be achieved. The small PA systems described so far, with power amplifiers of a few hundred watts, are used in small clubs in which the backline can generate sufficient levels.

For all their apparent complexity, larger "sound reinforcement" or concert "sound systems" all work on similar principles. These larger systems are likely to be rated from between 1 to 2 kilowatts (1000 watts = 1 kilowatt or 1 kW) up to 500 kilowatts. These larger concert sound systems actually consist of two separate systems, one being the "FOH" (front-of-house) system and the other a separate "monitor" system. All the instruments are amplified through the main front-of-house system while the monitor engineer has the option of feeding whatever instruments or voices that are required to the individual musician's monitor systems on stage. The front-of-house console is positioned amongst the audience so that the engineer operating it can hear the same sound as most of the audience. The monitor console is positioned as close to the band as possible so that the monitor engineer gets some idea of the sound on stage and can communicate with the musicians and stage crew in order to overcome any problems that might arise during the performance. Bands that are working to a budget might have to make do with one console that provides both the front-of-house and monitor sound, possibly without the capability of giving the musicians individually tailored mixes.

Front-of house and monitor system

The system shown is for a four-piece band consisting of guitarist, bass guitarist, drummer and vocalist. More complex systems for larger line-ups would simply increase the number of microphones and monitor speakers and probably entail some direct injection connections from some instruments or their amplifiers.

Five microphones are in use. Two overhead microphones are held above the drum kit to provide a stereo mix. (In practice there would probably be at least

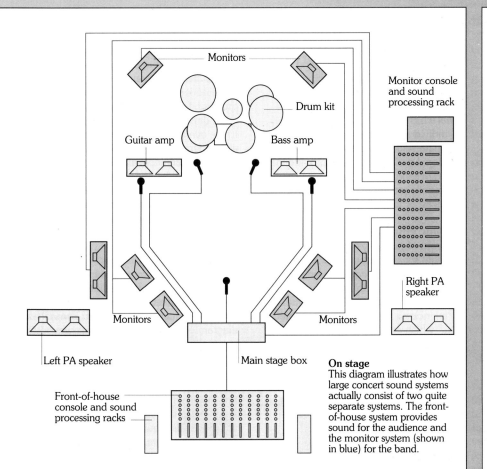

Monitors
Drum kit
Guitar amp
Bass amp
Monitor console and sound processing rack
Right PA speaker
Monitors
Monitors
Left PA speaker
Main stage box
Front-of-house console and sound processing racks

On stage
This diagram illustrates how large concert sound systems actually consist of two quite separate systems. The front-of-house system provides sound for the audience and the monitor system (shown in blue) for the band.

Using MIDI on stage

There are many switching applications for MIDI on stage. Bands using backing tapes can make particular use of MIDI because a sequence of instructions can be recorded or stored on computer so that, during a performance, sound and lighting effects can be triggered automatically. Being able to call up pre-set patches for sound processors at the touch of a single switch allows the performing musician and the sound engineer to devote their thoughts to the more creative aspects of a performance.

Direct injection

"Direct injection" or "DI" is the technique of connecting the output from a guitar's pick-up directly into an input channel of a mixing console. The output from some instruments can match the input on the console, but frequently a special DI box is needed. Guitars usually have a high impedance output and a DI box facilitates impedance matching with the console's input.

If a guitarist's on-stage amplification adds color or character to the sound, a "speaker simulator" is a much better alternative to direct injection. A speaker simulator is a sound processor which takes a signal from a guitar amplifier and processes it to simulate the sound of a speaker cabinet without spending time miking up the cabinet. The signal from the simulator is fed directly into a mixing console. Advantages include consistent sound quality both live and in the studio, not picking up unwanted noise or sound from other instruments and, because there is no microphone, there is no risk of unwanted feedback.

Feedback-assisted sustain

Like a microphone, an electric guitar and its pick-ups can "feed back" the sound coming from its own amplifier to create a feedback loop.

The art of playing with feedback is to find positions on stage where sustain can be induced without the guitar's pick-ups causing an unwanted whistle. The guitar's body and strings will then vibrate in sympathy with soundwaves from the amplifier, creating a feedback loop that can be used to make notes sustain indefinitely. A good string muting technique is essential to ensure that only the desired strings sound.

Eric Clapton uses feedback so that it counteracts friction in the guitar, creating a constant feedback loop. Brian May uses a higher level of feedback so that the guitar is almost bursting into sound of its own accord.

one further microphone on the snare drum and another on the bass drum.) One microphone is placed 2 or 3 inches from one of the speakers of the guitar amplifier. The same cabinet miking is used on the bass guitar amplifier and there is one microphone for a lead vocalist.

All the microphones are connected via their individual cables to the "main stage box." The main stage box splits the signal from each microphone in order to have two outputs for each microphone. A multicore cable then takes a complete set of microphone inputs to the front-of-house console while another multicore cable takes a duplicate set to the monitor console.

The front-of-house engineer has the responsibility for balancing the sound the audience hears, using one mix. The monitor engineer has the responsibility for keeping all the individual musicians on stage happy by giving them the best possible sound balance, with the option of giving them all individual mixes if they wish. If it were not for the monitors in this set-up the band would be likely to have problems. The guitarist and drummer would probably not be able to hear the bass player very well and everyone on stage would be lucky if they were able to hear the vocalist very well. In those circumstances, the band could be quite

badly put off and as a result not give the best of performances.

In this monitor set-up the lead vocalist has monitors 1 and 2 close by which would probably both have the same mix. Having two monitors would allow the vocalist to move around to a certain extent while still being able to hear clearly. The guitarist and bass guitarist would hear a combination of the mix from individual monitors (3 & 4) and their own amplifiers. Because drummers generate a considerable amount of sound around themselves it is quite usual for them to have two monitors (5 & 6).

The larger sidefill monitors would allow the guitarist, bass guitarist and vocalist to still hear an acceptable balance at various postions towards the front of the stage. As a rule, on-stage monitor levels should be kept to the minimum necessary to keep the musicians happy.

The quality of front-of-house sound can be seriously spoiled if for instance a drummer's kit microphones are picking up sound from his monitors. Every microphone will pick up overspill from other instruments and their amplifiers. The approach should always be to minimize such problems by keeping microphones as close to their sound sources as possible.

Microphone technique

Here we look at various ways of inputting guitar sounds to recording and live performance equipment using microphones.

Musicians can easily develop a good working knowledge of microphones by thinking of them as being unidirectional or omnidirectional, and by employing the close, natural and ambient approach to microphone placement.

There is more scope for creative technique in the recording studio. The high volumes of sound on stage invariably limit miking to close positions.

Though described in guitar terms, the principles explained here can be applied to recording voices and all other instruments.

Miking acoustic guitars

A round soundhole acoustic guitar will be loudest close to the soundhole and have the most balanced close mic sound in front of the soundhole and bridge area. By moving a microphone towards the bell of the instrument, the bass will tend to be accentuated, and the treble accentuated by miking the narrower part of the body closest to the headstock. Microphones placed near the neck of the instrument will accentuate any left hand finger noises, fret buzz and string rattle. Close miking near to the soundhole will accentuate right hand picking sounds.

Two, three or even more close microphones can be used together and the sound balanced at the console, possibly with signals from mid-distance and distant ambient microphones.

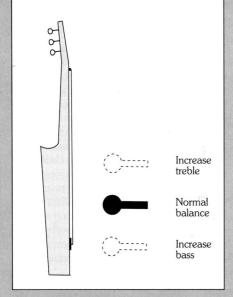

- - - - Increase treble

● Normal balance

- - - - Increase bass

Microphone placement

The character of an amplified or recorded sound can be changed greatly according to the position of the microphone in relation to the source of the sound and the distance between the two. As a microphone is placed closer or further way from the sound source, characteristic changes are continous and gradual. However as a guide we can divide microphone placement into three types, "close," mid-distance "natural," and distant "ambient" miking.

Close miking

Close miking will usually involve placing microphones 12 inches (30 cm) or less away from the instrument. To a certain extent, the instrument will sound very close and unnatural because direct soundwaves from the instrument will dominate and be much louder than any

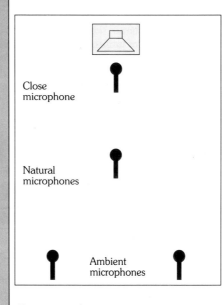

Close microphone

Natural microphones

Ambient microphones

Basic principles
Close, natural, and ambient positioning is shown in relation to a speaker cabinet.

soundwaves bounced back from walls, ceilings, and other reflective surfaces. A natural sound can be achieved with a close microphone by adding reverb or delay. When several instruments are being played at the same time, close miking minimizes the sound leakage from other instruments and amplifiers.

When miking an acoustic guitar, the player will nearly always move his instrument while playing, therefore microphones should never be placed so close as to interfere with such movements or those of the player's hands. No sound engineer worth his salt would inhibit a musician by placing microphones uncomfortably close, no matter how technically desirable it may be.

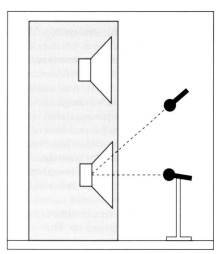

Miking a cabinet
A system used by many guitarists incorporates two microphones, one off-set at a 45° angle.

For live performance, a close mike on a guitar speaker cabinet is usually placed between 2 or 3 inches (5 and 7.5 cm) in front of the center of one speaker cone or possibly slightly off center. A close mike could be placed further away from the speaker cone when recording if the guitar is being tracked alone or is sufficiently acoustically isolated from other instruments that are being played at the same time.

The Shure SM57 is a classic and versatile instrument microphone which is frequently used for close miking a guitar cabinet. For his 1992 world tour, Eric Clapton used an SM57 placed between 2 and 3 inches (5 and 7.5 cm) away from one of the speaker cones on his Marshall 4x12. For recording the "Unlawful Carnal Knowledge" album, Eddie Van Halen used two SM57s.

A directional microphone is usually the obvious choice for close miking. It will pick up the sound predominantly from the source it is pointed directly at and give far better separation from other nearby instruments or amplifiers. A non-directional microphone could be used if the instrument was being tracked individually during a multitrack session. Then some of the reflections from boundary and other surfaces might add an attractive quality to the sound. It is possible that a close mike could distort if the sound from a speaker cabinet simply exceeds the dynamic range of the microphone. The answer might be move the microphone further away from the cabinet, reducing the volume of the amplifier, or trying a combination of both.

Natural miking

Natural miking is usually achieved by placing microphones between 2 and 8 feet (0.7 and 2.4 metres) away from the instrument or the speaker cabinet in a medium-sized room. This is the area in which soundwaves from the instrument still dominate but those reflected off walls and other surfaces will also be picked up making the sound quite natural. At this point a directional or non-directional microphone, or a combination of both may sound best.

Ambient miking
Ambient miking is usually achieved at distances greater than 10 feet (3 meters) and right up to walls and other boundary surfaces of a room. Pressure zone microphones (PZMs) are designed to be used attached to walls and similar reflective surfaces and are an obvious choice for ambient miking. Again, directional, non-directional or a mixture of both may be used. Signals from ambient microphones are mixed in with close, natural microphone signals or a combination of both.

The precise areas in which close, natural and ambient microphone sounds will occur will vary according to the loudness of the sound source, the size of room and the reflective characteristics of the boundary surfaces. In general a good close mike sound will sound too close and flat to be used without delay or reverberation, or without being mixed in with the signal from natural and ambient microphones. A good natural microphone will sound acceptable on its own. A good ambient microphone signal will simply sound too distant and lacking in power to be used without being mixed in with natural or close mike signals.

An electric guitar amplified through a 100 watt stack playing at full volume will sound close everywhere in a small bedroom, whereas an acoustic guitar might be inaudible from the back rows of a large stadium venue. Accepting that changes are gradual, the fact remains that the concept of close, natural and ambient miking is at the heart of all good microphone techniques and can be applied to any live performance or recording situation to some degree. The one qualification to this statement is that with loud and amplified music when several instruments are played at the same time (as opposed to "track-laying" one instrument at a time in recording), close miking positions are mostly used.

The guitarist who understands the concept of close, natural, and ambient microphone placement and the nature of directional and non-directional microphones will almost always be able to achieve a good sound in the recording studio or at a live venue.

The Vortex
Record producer Chris Tsangarides, who has worked with Thin Lizzy, Gary Moore, Bruce Dickenson and many other major names, devised his own unique "Vortex" system for recording lead guitar overdubs.

Acoustic screens are set up in a "V" formation directing the sound from a guitar combo amplifier or stack towards one end of the studio. By using close, mid-distance, and ambient miking, the signals from the microphones can be recorded on separate tracks and treated in a variety of different ways during a mixdown. For example, the microphone positions could be emphasized in the stereo picture: the ambient mikes could be placed extreme left and right, the mid-distance mikes left-center and right-center, and the close mike in the center.

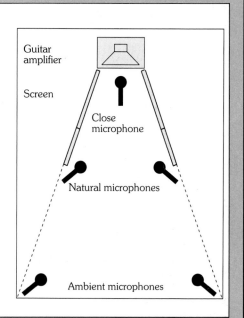
Guitar amplifier

Screen

Close microphone

Natural microphones

Ambient microphones

Acoustic isolation and tracklaying
The aim with multitrack recording is to have as clean a signal on each track with as little spillage of other instruments as possible. This gives maximum flexibility during the mixing process when the various tracks are all mixed down to a final mono or stereo master recording. In a recording situation this could be overcome by recording each instrument onto a separate track one at a time. Technically this is fine if the musicians are happy with this way of working. But many groups want to play at least some of the instruments together, particularly bass, drums, and any others that contribute to the fundamental feel and rhythm of the piece of music. So it is common practice to record the bass, drums, rhythm guitar, and similar instruments together as a "backing track." As this can be quite strange for the musicians, a singer may record a guide vocal just so that everyone doesn't get lost. Then instruments such as lead guitar can be individually tracked on afterwards.

Separation
The difficulty is in achieving separation between the instruments recorded together on the backing tracks. In the professional recording studio the ideal technical solution is to record the musicians playing in different rooms or playing areas which are acoustically isolated. But again vital feel might be lost as it can be difficult for the musicians to hear each other through headphones, though with experience this becomes less of a problem. By placing acoustic screens around the different instruments and their

amplifiers and by using close miking technique, a workable degree of separation can be achieved. When several instruments are played together in a room it is inevitable that there will be some leakage of sound but as long as this is kept down it is not likely to be problematic.

Multiple techniques
At times, inspiration can be a limited commodity in the recording studio. When the guitarist or any other performer comes up with that one astounding take that seems to have an unrepeatable quality, it had better be captured on tape.

An interesting technique is to have the guitar signal routed to a number of separate amplifiers, each with different tonal characteristics, for example, a Vox AC30, Marshall, and a MESA/Boogie. Each amplifier's cabinet is close-miked and recorded onto a separate track. This prevents the need for a performance to be duplicated if, at a later stage, a preference for a different amplifier sound arises.

There is also the additional alternative of mixing the sound of all three amplifiers. There are endless permutations to this approach. Even if the guitarist has only one amplifier, as well as close, natural, and ambient miking, there are the possibilities of mixing in the signal from a speaker simulator, or, as is common practice when recording the bass guitar, a direct injection signal (see page 217).

It should be remembered that in a home recording environment, the use of ambient microphones may be limited because the acoustics will not be as good as in a professional recording studio.

Recording media

Much live performance equipment is very similar to that used in the recording process. Essentially the only difference is that a form of recording media is added at the end of the chain.

The options when recording are analogue recording to magnetic tape, digital recording to magnetic tape or a computer memory storage device, or sequencing which involves recording MIDI events which will, when played back, cause a number of synthesizers, samplers or electronic sound modules to play back a musical performance. No matter how complex the recording system, it will either be an analogue tape recorder, a digital recorder, a sequencer, or any combination of the three systems.

The recording process

The first step in making a recording is to pick up the sound of each instrument on a microphone. Several microphones may be used on one instrument or, conversely, one microphone may be used to record several instruments in turn. Signals from the microphone are passed to a mixing console where, along with the input from any directly injected instruments, they may be subjected to any desired sound processing. Each instrument is then recorded on magnetic tape at the optimum recording level; if facilities permit, each instrument will be allotted its own track on the tape.

When the recording of the individual tracks has been completed, the multitrack master tape must then be "mixed down" to stereo. To do this, the tracks are fed back into the mixing console where they are balanced against each other, given further sound processing, and then "reduced" to stereo. This is fed into a stereo (two-track) tape recorder to produce the master tape from which all subsequent copies will be made.

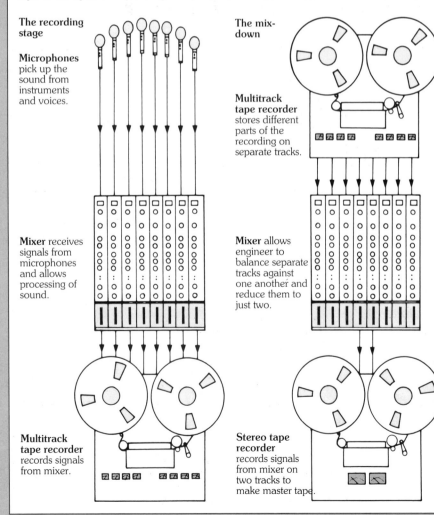

The recording stage

Microphones pick up the sound from instruments and voices.

Mixer receives signals from microphones and allows processing of sound.

Multitrack tape recorder records signals from mixer.

The mix-down

Multitrack tape recorder stores different parts of the recording on separate tracks.

Mixer allows engineer to balance separate tracks against one another and reduce them to just two.

Stereo tape recorder records signals from mixer on two tracks to make master tape.

Digital versus analogue

Digital recordings do not suffer from tape hiss, the continuous background noise heard on analogue tape even when no sounds have been recorded on it. Various "noise reduction" systems, Dolby being the most widely used, reduce analogue tape hiss considerably. Professional studio systems such as Dolby SR reduce the unwanted noise to an almost inaudible level.

Dynamic range

The reduction of tape hiss also increases the "dynamic range" of a recording. The dynamic range is limited by the highest signal that a tape can record without distortion and the quietest sound that can be heard above any backgound noise such as tape hiss. The dynamic range of a recorder is also commonly referred to as the "signal-to-noise" ratio. The majority of popular music is performed within a fairly narrow dynamic range, so by simply recording with the loudest parts of the music just below the point at which distortion starts, the effect of tape hiss will be minimized and a full-sounding recording will be achieved. Classical

MIDI

"MIDI" stands for Musical Instrument Digital Interface. It is a relatively simple computer language devised during the early 1980s to allow synthesizers and sequencers made by different manufacturers to operate together. MIDI was subsequently found to be a very useful system for controlling sound processors, effects units, samplers, amplifiers, and settings on mixing desks.

MIDI is so versatile that sequencing recorders like Cubase and C-Lab's Creator can be used to record and edit complete musical performances without the tape recorder.

MIDI Channels

There are 16 "MIDI channels" which allow up to 16 totally separate streams of data to be sent down a single MIDI connecting cable. For example, for general applications this means that the same stream of data can be sent to a drum machine set to receive data on Channel 1 and a bass synthesizer set to receive data on Channel 2. By setting the two devices to receive on their own channels they do not react to MIDI messages intended for the other device.

music has a far greater dynamic range than most popular music and can benefit greatly from the wider signal-to-noise ratio of digital recording.

A major advantage digital tape recording has over analogue is that a recording can be copied many more times before there is a noticeable loss in sound quality.

An advantage of using analogue tape in popular music is what is sometimes referred to as "tape compression." Frequently when the sound of a musical instrument is compressed by an actual compressor the performance sounds more punchy and has greater impact.

Since the early days of rock'n'roll, recordists have found that by recording the very highest level that analogue tape will accept without the onset of unpleasant distortion, "tape saturation" occurs. Part of the effect is that the tape compresses the signal which is often found to give recorded rock music more impact. The effect is achieved by recording just above the safe recording level indicated by the meters. Some engineers and producers refer to it as "recording in the red."

High quality "live" stereo recordings can be achieved either by taking direct inputs from a console or by using a pair of microphones to record a performance acoustically. In both cases, a digital machine will offer the better recording quality. Live recordings from a console to a DAT machine simply involve making the appropriate connections and recording with an average level at 0dB with momentary peaks slightly higher.

Multitrack analogue and digital recording is at the heart of the creative process. The Fostex 280 "portastudio" is an all-in-one mixing console and analogue recorder which can be used to try out new ideas and make demonstration recordings.

Professional recording studios equipped with digital machines such as the Sony PCM 3348 48-track free the musician from virtually all creative constraints.

The "Portastudio"
When Teac introduced the first "Portastudio", few anticipated the speed that the 4-track cassette format would dominate the home recording market. Since then, major manufacturers such as Fostex have successfully produced their own variations. The use of noise reduction systems like Dolby C and DBX make high-quality recordings possible with care.

How MIDI works

There are four "MIDI modes" which can be used to suit a number of situations: the most frequently used is "Mode 3 Omni off/Poly on." "Omni off" means a sound module will only respond to messages on the MIDI channel it is set to, whereas "Omni on" means messages on *all* channels will be responded to. "Poly on" means that the sound module can play polyphonically (with more than one note sounding at the same time).

The other three modes are "Mode 1 – Omni On/Poly," "Mode 2 – Omni On/Mono" and "Mode 4 – Omni off/Mono" which can be used to suit specific system needs. In Mode 4 – Omni off/Mono, a multi-timbral module which can sound several different voices at one time can receive several monophonic solo lines and play them each with a different voice. This is very useful with a MIDI guitar controller because the module automatically receives information on separate MIDI channels, allowing each of the six strings of a MIDI guitar controller to be received on separate MIDI channels. If the sound module is set to receive MIDI channel 1, the data from the other strings will automatically be received

on channels 2, 3, 4, 5 & 6. This is essential for guitar controllers to ensure that, for example, pitch bend instructions only act on one voice. Alternatively, a multi-timbral sound module could be set to receive on separate MIDI channels.

Voice messages cause a sound module to play its notes. The "note-on" message indicates the start point, a "pitch" message provides pitch value, a "velocity" message controls the note volume and a "note-off" message will stop the note playing.

Controller changes can be used to control pitch and modulation. They can also send voice program information to a sound module or may instruct the module to switch from one sound to another.

A *MIDI patch* is simply a specified group of settings. On an amplifier this might be stored EQ settings. On a multi-timbral synthesizer a patch could consist of dozens of settings such as reverberation, pitch bend rate, and stereo position.

MIDI interfaces

MIDI-controlled equipment has din plug sockets which allow them to interface and send and receive data: the "MIDI in" sockets accept incoming instructions; the

"MIDI out" sockets allow instructions to be sent to sound modules and other MIDI controllable devices; the "MIDI thru" sockets – found on some equipment – allow information to be relayed through to another MIDI device.

It is possible to link MIDI equipment in one continuous "daisy chain," but the more additional devices are added, the greater the chance of noticeable timing delays occuring at the end of the chain.

MIDI songs

MIDI songs are a sequence of instructions that are constructed on a sequencer which can be saved to disc and reloaded into the same sequencer or another compatible sequencer at a later time.

Song position pointers are numbered positions in a MIDI sequence. They allow a sequencer to control the playback of a number of MIDI devices from any point in a song without having to re-set each of the devices individually. Song position pointers are extremely convenient in that they allow the user to play back a particular section of a MIDI song without necessarily having to hear the whole song from the beginning each time.

Guitar synthesizers

In the past, the guitar synthesizer or MIDI guitar controller has been the cause of much confusion amongst guitarists. During the 1980s, adventurous players like Andy Summers of the Police managed to coax a range of exciting sounds from the various Roland systems. In the jazz arena, Pat Metheny pioneered new means of expression using a Roland controller with the NED Synclavier digital synthesis and recording system. However, exotic devices like the SynthAxe and Stepp digital guitar proved too complex or expensive for guitarists to adopt.

By the end of the 1980s, Roland had refined their guitar synthesizer system to such a degree that it is now on a par with keyboard technology, allowing the guitarist to use MIDI to control sound modules at a reasonable cost.

The key to successful use of guitar synthesis is to think of the guitar synth as an additional means of expression, not a direct replacement for the guitar itself.

Roland guitar synthesizer

The Roland system is made up of two units, the GK-2 and the GR50. The GK-2 consists of a pick-up and a combined connection and switching unit, both of which can be attached to any guitar by means of adhesive or small screws. The MIDI pick-up is positioned beneath the strings in the same general area as a normal magnetic pick-up, allowing the guitar to be used normally or as a controller that sends digital data from each of the six strings to the GR-50 rack module. The guitar and synthesizer can be used simultaneously.

The GR-50 is a rack-mounting sound module with Roland D Series LA synthesis containing 128 preset voices, 63 preset rhythm and percussion sounds, and 64 programmable sounds. MIDI messages can also be sent from the GR-50 to any other MIDI device which has the capability to receive MIDI. The system works on a "pitch-to-MIDI" principle where the pick-up detects the frequency of each note played and converts it into digital data, responding also to normal playing techniques like note bending and vibrato. The data from the GR-2 pick-up is converted to MIDI by the GR-50 unit.

Roland GK-2 (*left*) The Roland GK-2 synthesizer driver consists of a pitch-sensing pick-up and a combined connection and switching unit. It can be fitted to any guitar with small screws, or alternatively adhesive pads, to avoid defacing valuable instruments.

Roland GR-50 (*below*) This rack-mounting sound module converts the information from the GK-2 to MIDI.

There is a slight delay while the system detects the pitch of the note. This is sometimes noticeable on the lower notes. MIDI pitch change can be used to overcome this problem to a certain extent.

"Patches" are programmable on the GR-50 to allow different sounds to be assigned to each string with other variables like pitch, though the system comes with a range of presets.

MIDI system control

This system shows how a synthesizer keyboard and a guitar equipped with the Roland GK-2 and GR-5O could be used with a computer running a MIDI sequencing program, an additional sound module, and a sampler. The MIDI connections for this system could be made in a number of other ways. This avoids the use of MIDI thru sockets (to avoid time delays) and allows tracks to be recorded onto the sequencer from the guitar or keyboard utilizing their own sound modules. Most of the current sound modules have stereo or multiple audio outputs as shown.

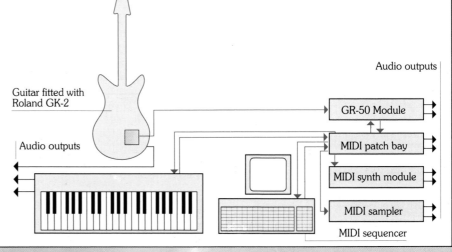

Guitar fitted with Roland GK-2

Audio outputs

Audio outputs

GR-50 Module

MIDI patch bay

MIDI synth module

MIDI sampler

MIDI sequencer

THE CHORD DICTIONARY

This Chord Dictionary is designed to serve two purposes: first, as a reference section to be used with the *Playing the guitar* chapter, second, as a collection on popular sounds.

It is not a complete catalogue of guitar chords. Instead, we have chosen just 23 chords in each of the twelve keys. The choice is, of course, subjective, but by and large these 23 chords are the first ones that the average guitarist is likely to encounter when playing with other musicians.

The first five chords in each key – the major, the seventh, the minor, the minor seventh and the major seventh – are the "workhorses" which guitarists use most often. The other eighteen are those most frequently combined with the first five; they form an introduction to more sophisticated chords. At first, some of these may sound awkward. But, once you begin to play them in context with other chords, as part of a progression,

they will sound better, make more sense and gradually become part of your repertoire.

How to use the Dictionary

Each chord is identified first by its symbol

Cmaj7 (C△7)

then by its full name

C major seventh

and then by its spelling

1st(C), 3rd (E), 5th (G), 7th (B).

The spelling tells you which notes make up the chord and at what intervals they occur in the diatonic major scale of the key.

The fingerboard is divided into three sections to show three positions in which each chord can be played. The top E string is at the top of the drawing and the bottom E string is at the bottom. The head of the guitar is on the

left; the bridge is on the right. In other words, you are seeing the fingerboard as if you were looking down at it while playing. Quite simply, the numbered green circles tell you where to put your fingers. The unnumbered white circles indicate extra notes which you can add once you know the basic chord. Strings without a circle are played open (unfretted) unless they have an "X" on them – in which case you do not play them at all.

Chords can be played on the guitar in an almost infinite variety of "voicings". Over the range of the twelve keys, this results in thousands of fingering positions. Getting to grips with the full harmonic potential of the fingerboard is a lifetime's study. Therefore, in this book, we have put more emphasis on *understanding* chords than on simply learning them by rote. A full explanation of chords together with additional forms that do not appear in the Dictionary is set out on p. 121-37.

Example: Cmaj7 in three positions

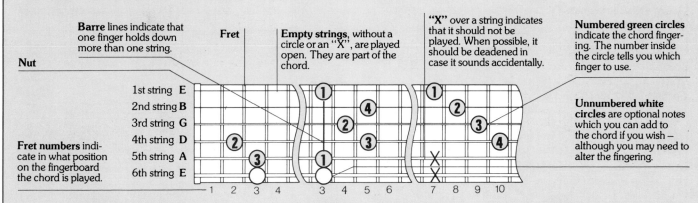

Barre lines indicate that one finger holds down more than one string.

Nut

Fret

Empty strings, without a circle or an "X", are played open. They are part of the chord.

"X" over a string indicates that it should not be played. When possible, it should be deadened in case it sounds accidentally.

Numbered green circles indicate the chord fingering. The number inside the circle tells you which finger to use.

1st string E
2nd string B
3rd string G
4th string D
5th string A
6th string E

Fret numbers indicate in what position on the fingerboard the chord is played.

Unnumbered white circles are optional notes which you can add to the chord if you wish – although you may need to alter the fingering.

First position
Follow the green circles: 2nd finger on 4th string, 2nd fret; 3rd finger on 5th string, 3rd fret (root note C); 1st, 2nd and 3rd strings are played open. Do not play 6th string unless you fret the extra G.

Second position
This is a "barre chord". 1st finger holds down both 1st and 5th strings on 3rd fret. Follow green circles for 2nd, 3rd and 4th fingers. You may add optional G on 6th string by extending barre.

Third position
In this form, the root note C is on 4th string, 10th fret. As before, numbered green circles show fingering position. 5th and 6th strings are not played.

Choosing the best fingering

The point of knowing at least three forms for each chord is so that you can interchange them. When you are playing a chord sequence, a form fairly high up the fingerboard may be much easier to get to than one at the bottom, down near the nut. Moreover, the different forms do not sound the same. Play them one after the other until you can hear the difference, and practice moving from one to the next – the smoother the better.

Most of the chord forms are "root positions" – that is, the lowest note is the root note of the chord. Once these forms have been learned, you should find it easy to move

them up and down the fingerboard so that you can play the same chord in different keys (see p. 82). Sometimes the fingering of these basic forms can be altered slightly to accommodate open strings, to add optional notes or to substitute a different bass note.

Diminished chords occupy four "key-centers" and augmented chords occupy three. This means that one chord shape can be played in either three or four different places on the fingerboard. These chords are therefore a special case, and you should read the section on p. 128 to see how they work.

When playing chords consisting of more

than four notes, you may not be able to play all the elements of the chord. In this case, you must select which notes to omit. Use the chord spelling to see which are the most important notes and experiment with different fingerings. Because the notes you choose will affect the sound of the chord, base your decision on the following factors: the arrangement of the notes in relation to one another (the bottom and top notes are predominant in the sound); the strings you wish to use; the position on the fingerboard; the function that the chord is to have between two others; and for how long it is to be heard in a progression.

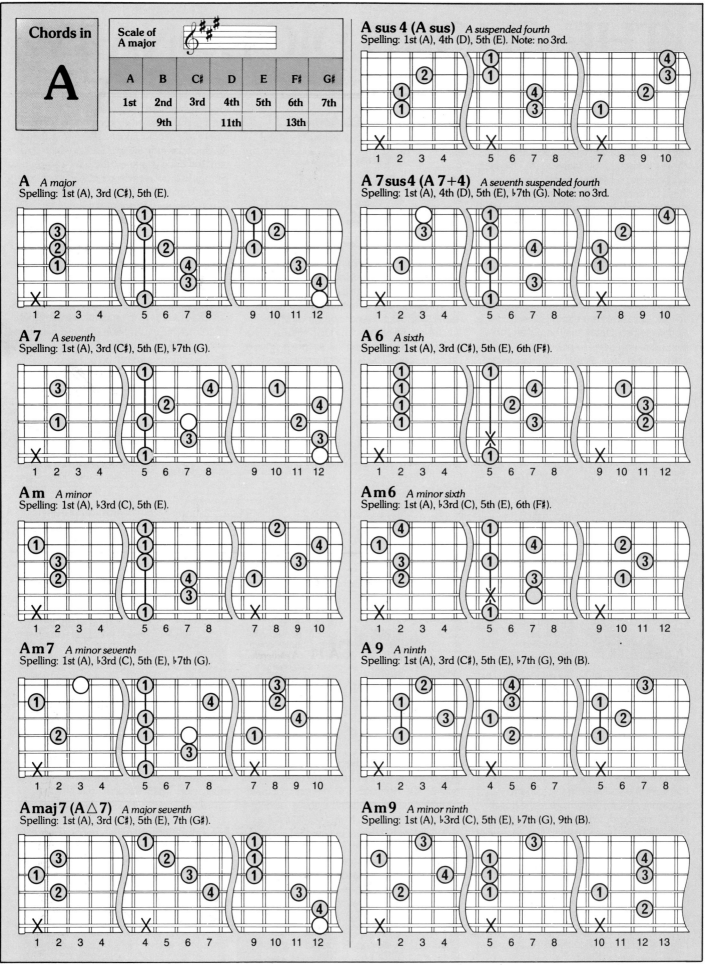

Chords in A

Scale of A major

A	B	C#	D	E	F#	G#
1st	2nd	3rd	4th	5th	6th	7th
	9th		11th		13th	

A *A major*
Spelling: 1st (A), 3rd (C#), 5th (E).

A 7 *A seventh*
Spelling: 1st (A), 3rd (C#), 5th (E), ♭7th (G).

A m *A minor*
Spelling: 1st (A), ♭3rd (C), 5th (E).

A m7 *A minor seventh*
Spelling: 1st (A), ♭3rd (C), 5th (E), ♭7th (G).

A maj7 (A△7) *A major seventh*
Spelling: 1st (A), 3rd (C#), 5th (E), 7th (G#).

A sus 4 (A sus) *A suspended fourth*
Spelling: 1st (A), 4th (D), 5th (E). Note: no 3rd.

A 7 sus4 (A 7+4) *A seventh suspended fourth*
Spelling: 1st (A), 4th (D), 5th (E), ♭7th (G). Note: no 3rd.

A 6 *A sixth*
Spelling: 1st (A), 3rd (C#), 5th (E), 6th (F#).

A m6 *A minor sixth*
Spelling: 1st (A), ♭3rd (C), 5th (E), 6th (F#).

A 9 *A ninth*
Spelling: 1st (A), 3rd (C#), 5th (E), ♭7th (G), 9th (B).

A m9 *A minor ninth*
Spelling: 1st (A), ♭3rd (C), 5th (E), ♭7th (G), 9th (B).

226

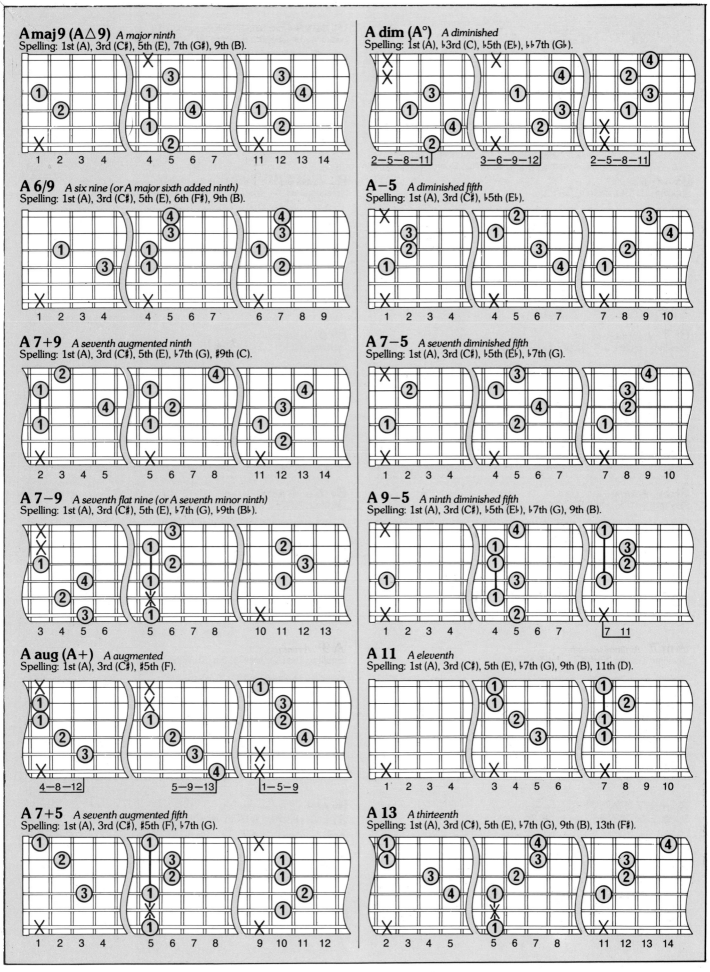

A maj9 (A△9) *A major ninth*
Spelling: 1st (A), 3rd (C#), 5th (E), 7th (G#), 9th (B).

A 6/9 *A six nine (or A major sixth added ninth)*
Spelling: 1st (A), 3rd (C#), 5th (E), 6th (F#), 9th (B).

A 7+9 *A seventh augmented ninth*
Spelling: 1st (A), 3rd (C#), 5th (E), ♭7th (G), #9th (C).

A 7−9 *A seventh flat nine (or A seventh minor ninth)*
Spelling: 1st (A), 3rd (C#), 5th (E), ♭7th (G), ♭9th (B♭).

A aug (A+) *A augmented*
Spelling: 1st (A), 3rd (C#), #5th (F).

A 7+5 *A seventh augmented fifth*
Spelling: 1st (A), 3rd (C#), #5th (F), ♭7th (G).

A dim (A°) *A diminished*
Spelling: 1st (A), ♭3rd (C), ♭5th (E♭), ♭♭7th (G♭).

A−5 *A diminished fifth*
Spelling: 1st (A), 3rd (C#), ♭5th (E♭).

A 7−5 *A seventh diminished fifth*
Spelling: 1st (A), 3rd (C#), ♭5th (E♭), ♭7th (G).

A 9−5 *A ninth diminished fifth*
Spelling: 1st (A), 3rd (C#), ♭5th (E♭), ♭7th (G), 9th (B).

A 11 *A eleventh*
Spelling: 1st (A), 3rd (C#), 5th (E), ♭7th (G), 9th (B), 11th (D).

A 13 *A thirteenth*
Spelling: 1st (A), 3rd (C#), 5th (E), ♭7th (G), 9th (B), 13th (F#).

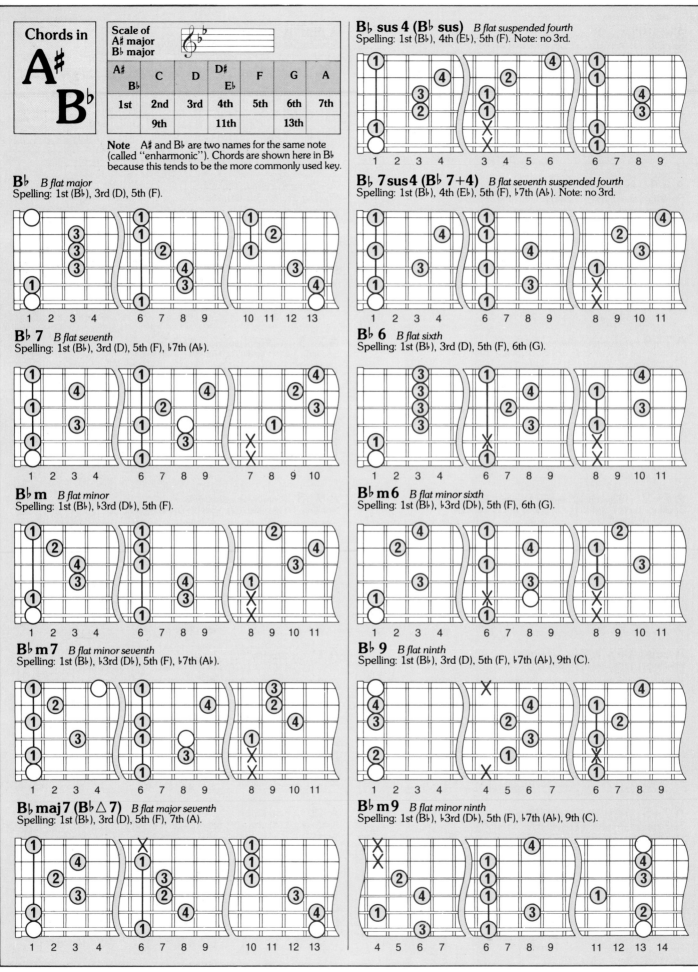

Chords in A♯ B♭

Scale of A♯ major B♭ major						
A♯ B♭	C	D	D♯ E♭	F	G	A
1st	2nd	3rd	4th	5th	6th	7th
	9th		11th		13th	

Note A♯ and B♭ are two names for the same note (called "enharmonic"). Chords are shown here in B♭ because this tends to be the more commonly used key.

B♭ *B flat major*
Spelling: 1st (B♭), 3rd (D), 5th (F).

B♭ 7 *B flat seventh*
Spelling: 1st (B♭), 3rd (D), 5th (F), ♭7th (A♭).

B♭ m *B flat minor*
Spelling: 1st (B♭), ♭3rd (D♭), 5th (F).

B♭ m 7 *B flat minor seventh*
Spelling: 1st (B♭), ♭3rd (D♭), 5th (F), ♭7th (A♭).

B♭ maj 7 (B♭△7) *B flat major seventh*
Spelling: 1st (B♭), 3rd (D), 5th (F), 7th (A).

B♭ sus 4 (B♭ sus) *B flat suspended fourth*
Spelling: 1st (B♭), 4th (E♭), 5th (F). Note: no 3rd.

B♭ 7 sus 4 (B♭ 7+4) *B flat seventh suspended fourth*
Spelling: 1st (B♭), 4th (E♭), 5th (F), ♭7th (A♭). Note: no 3rd.

B♭ 6 *B flat sixth*
Spelling: 1st (B♭), 3rd (D), 5th (F), 6th (G).

B♭ m6 *B flat minor sixth*
Spelling: 1st (B♭), ♭3rd (D♭), 5th (F), 6th (G).

B♭ 9 *B flat ninth*
Spelling: 1st (B♭), 3rd (D), 5th (F), ♭7th (A♭), 9th (C).

B♭ m9 *B flat minor ninth*
Spelling: 1st (B♭), ♭3rd (D♭), 5th (F), ♭7th (A♭), 9th (C).

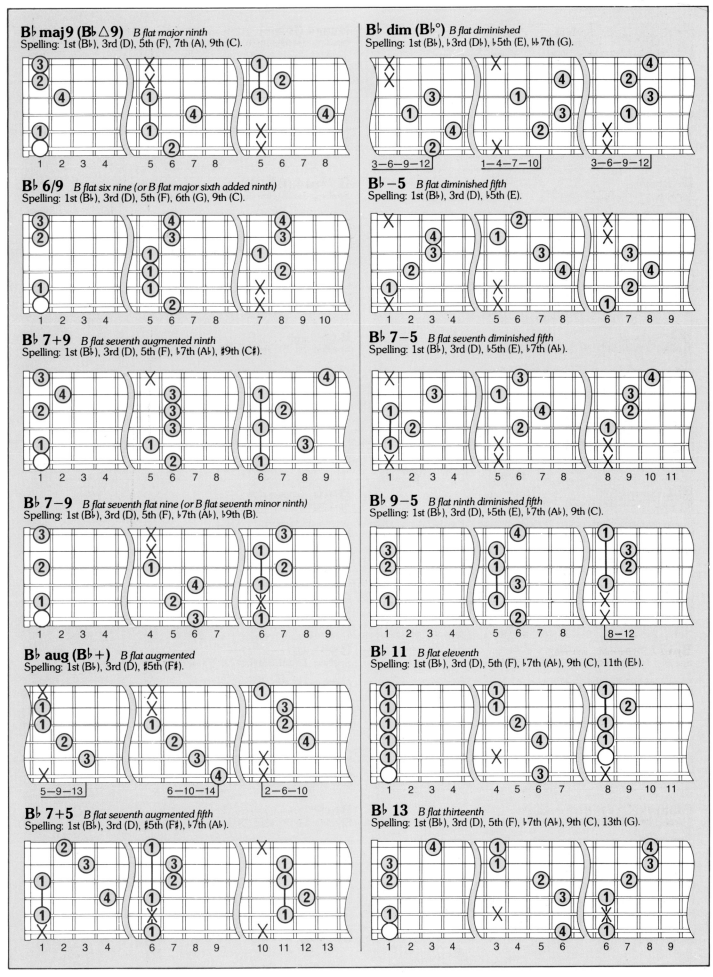

B♭ maj9 (B♭△9) *B flat major ninth*
Spelling: 1st (B♭), 3rd (D), 5th (F), 7th (A), 9th (C).

B♭ 6/9 *B flat six nine (or B flat major sixth added ninth)*
Spelling: 1st (B♭), 3rd (D), 5th (F), 6th (G), 9th (C).

B♭ 7+9 *B flat seventh augmented ninth*
Spelling: 1st (B♭), 3rd (D), 5th (F), ♭7th (A♭), ♯9th (C♯).

B♭ 7−9 *B flat seventh flat nine (or B flat seventh minor ninth)*
Spelling: 1st (B♭), 3rd (D), 5th (F), ♭7th (A♭), ♭9th (B).

B♭ aug (B♭+) *B flat augmented*
Spelling: 1st (B♭), 3rd (D), ♯5th (F♯).

B♭ 7+5 *B flat seventh augmented fifth*
Spelling: 1st (B♭), 3rd (D), ♯5th (F♯), ♭7th (A♭).

B♭ dim (B♭°) *B flat diminished*
Spelling: 1st (B♭), ♭3rd (D♭), ♭5th (E), ♭♭7th (G).

B♭ −5 *B flat diminished fifth*
Spelling: 1st (B♭), 3rd (D), ♭5th (E).

B♭ 7−5 *B flat seventh diminished fifth*
Spelling: 1st (B♭), 3rd (D), ♭5th (E), ♭7th (A♭).

B♭ 9−5 *B flat ninth diminished fifth*
Spelling: 1st (B♭), 3rd (D), ♭5th (E), ♭7th (A♭), 9th (C).

B♭ 11 *B flat eleventh*
Spelling: 1st (B♭), 3rd (D), 5th (F), ♭7th (A♭), 9th (C), 11th (E♭).

B♭ 13 *B flat thirteenth*
Spelling: 1st (B♭), 3rd (D), 5th (F), ♭7th (A♭), 9th (C), 13th (G).

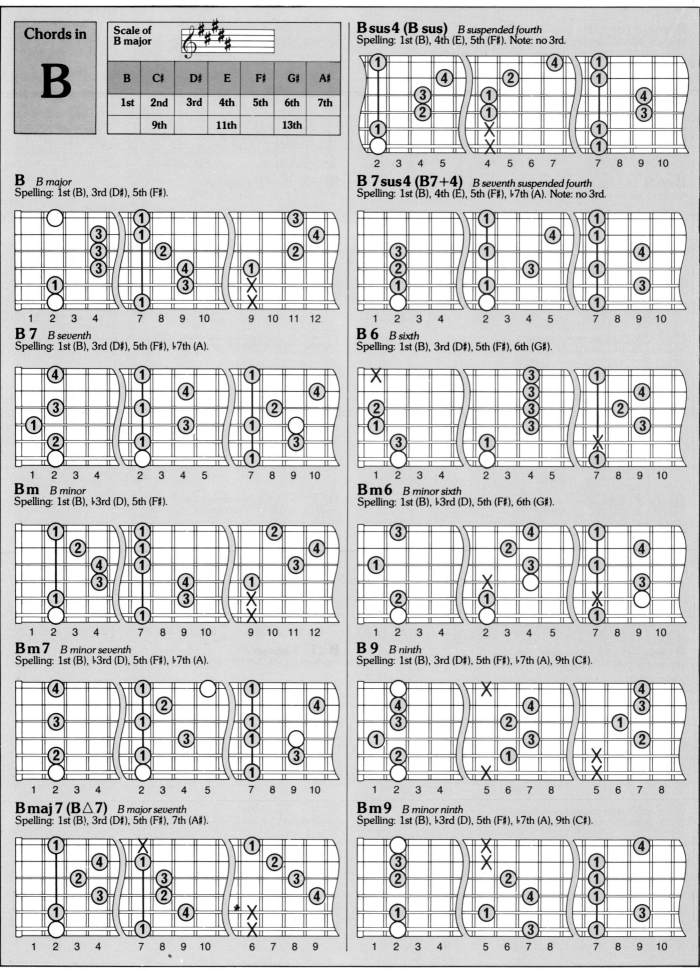

Chords in

B

Scale of B major						
B	C#	D#	E	F#	G#	A#
1st	2nd	3rd	4th	5th	6th	7th
	9th		11th		13th	

B *B major*
Spelling: 1st (B), 3rd (D#), 5th (F#).

B 7 *B seventh*
Spelling: 1st (B), 3rd (D#), 5th (F#), ♭7th (A).

B m *B minor*
Spelling: 1st (B), ♭3rd (D), 5th (F#).

B m 7 *B minor seventh*
Spelling: 1st (B), ♭3rd (D), 5th (F#), ♭7th (A).

B maj 7 (B△7) *B major seventh*
Spelling: 1st (B♭), 3rd (D#), 5th (F#), 7th (A#).

B sus 4 (B sus) *B suspended fourth*
Spelling: 1st (B), 4th (E), 5th (F#). Note: no 3rd.

B 7 sus 4 (B7+4) *B seventh suspended fourth*
Spelling: 1st (B), 4th (E), 5th (F#), ♭7th (A). Note: no 3rd.

B 6 *B sixth*
Spelling: 1st (B), 3rd (D#), 5th (F#), 6th (G#).

B m 6 *B minor sixth*
Spelling: 1st (B), ♭3rd (D), 5th (F#), 6th (G#).

B 9 *B ninth*
Spelling: 1st (B), 3rd (D#), 5th (F#), ♭7th (A), 9th (C#).

B m 9 *B minor ninth*
Spelling: 1st (B), ♭3rd (D), 5th (F#), ♭7th (A), 9th (C#).

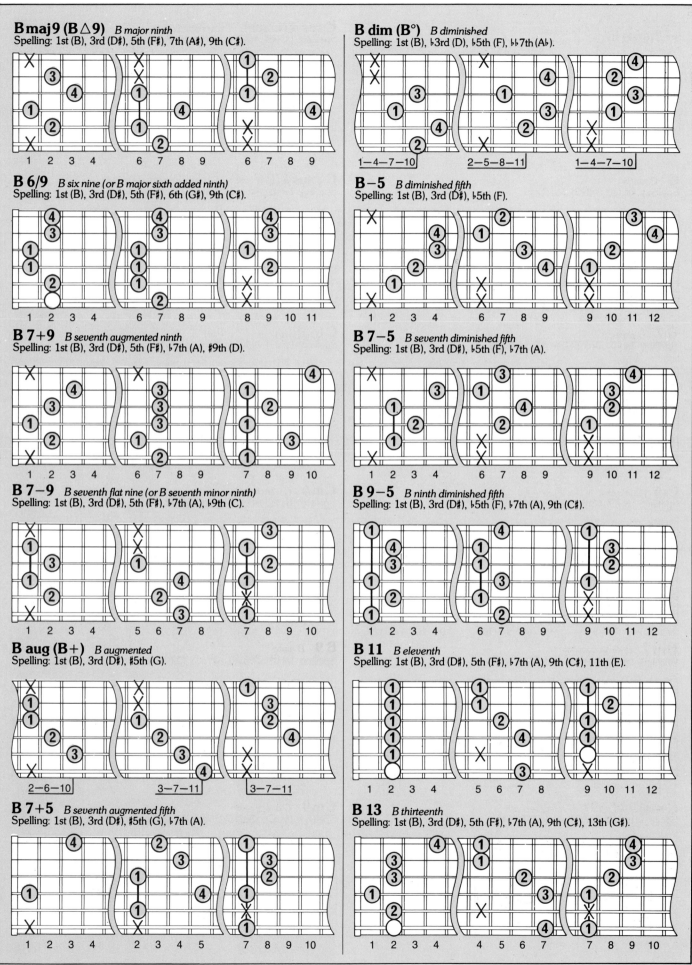

Bmaj9 (B△9) *B major ninth*
Spelling: 1st (B), 3rd (D♯), 5th (F♯), 7th (A♯), 9th (C♯).

B 6/9 *B six nine (or B major sixth added ninth)*
Spelling: 1st (B), 3rd (D♯), 5th (F♯), 6th (G♯), 9th (C♯).

B 7+9 *B seventh augmented ninth*
Spelling: 1st (B), 3rd (D♯), 5th (F♯), ♭7th (A), ♯9th (D).

B 7−9 *B seventh flat nine (or B seventh minor ninth)*
Spelling: 1st (B), 3rd (D♯), 5th (F♯), ♭7th (A), ♭9th (C).

B aug (B+) *B augmented*
Spelling: 1st (B), 3rd (D♯), ♯5th (G).

B 7+5 *B seventh augmented fifth*
Spelling: 1st (B), 3rd (D♯), ♯5th (G), ♭7th (A).

B dim (B°) *B diminished*
Spelling: 1st (B), ♭3rd (D), ♭5th (F), ♭♭7th (A♭).

B−5 *B diminished fifth*
Spelling: 1st (B), 3rd (D♯), ♭5th (F).

B 7−5 *B seventh diminished fifth*
Spelling: 1st (B), 3rd (D♯), ♭5th (F), ♭7th (A).

B 9−5 *B ninth diminished fifth*
Spelling: 1st (B), 3rd (D♯), ♭5th (F), ♭7th (A), 9th (C♯).

B 11 *B eleventh*
Spelling: 1st (B), 3rd (D♯), 5th (F♯), ♭7th (A), 9th (C♯), 11th (E).

B 13 *B thirteenth*
Spelling: 1st (B), 3rd (D♯), 5th (F♯), ♭7th (A), 9th (C♯), 13th (G♯).

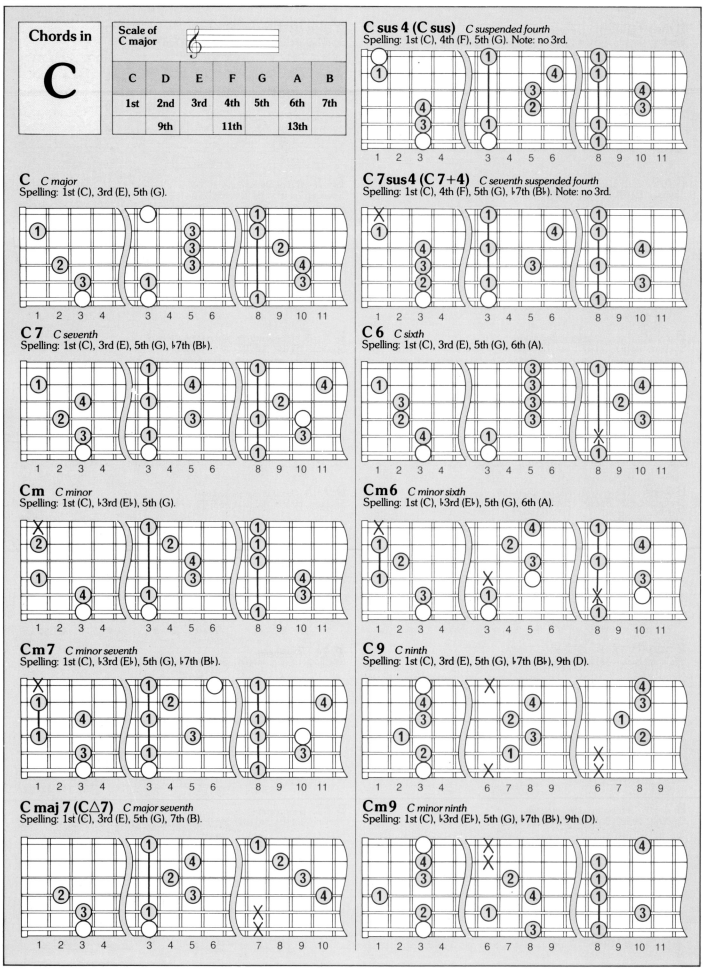

Chords in C

Scale of C major						
C	D	E	F	G	A	B
1st	2nd	3rd	4th	5th	6th	7th
	9th		11th		13th	

C *C major*
Spelling: 1st (C), 3rd (E), 5th (G).

C 7 *C seventh*
Spelling: 1st (C), 3rd (E), 5th (G), ♭7th (B♭).

Cm *C minor*
Spelling: 1st (C), ♭3rd (E♭), 5th (G).

Cm 7 *C minor seventh*
Spelling: 1st (C), ♭3rd (E♭), 5th (G), ♭7th (B♭).

C maj 7 (C△7) *C major seventh*
Spelling: 1st (C), 3rd (E), 5th (G), 7th (B).

C sus 4 (C sus) *C suspended fourth*
Spelling: 1st (C), 4th (F), 5th (G). Note: no 3rd.

C 7 sus 4 (C 7+4) *C seventh suspended fourth*
Spelling: 1st (C), 4th (F), 5th (G), ♭7th (B♭). Note: no 3rd.

C 6 *C sixth*
Spelling: 1st (C), 3rd (E), 5th (G), 6th (A).

Cm 6 *C minor sixth*
Spelling: 1st (C), ♭3rd (E♭), 5th (G), 6th (A).

C 9 *C ninth*
Spelling: 1st (C), 3rd (E), 5th (G), ♭7th (B♭), 9th (D).

Cm 9 *C minor ninth*
Spelling: 1st (C), ♭3rd (E♭), 5th (G), ♭7th (B♭), 9th (D).

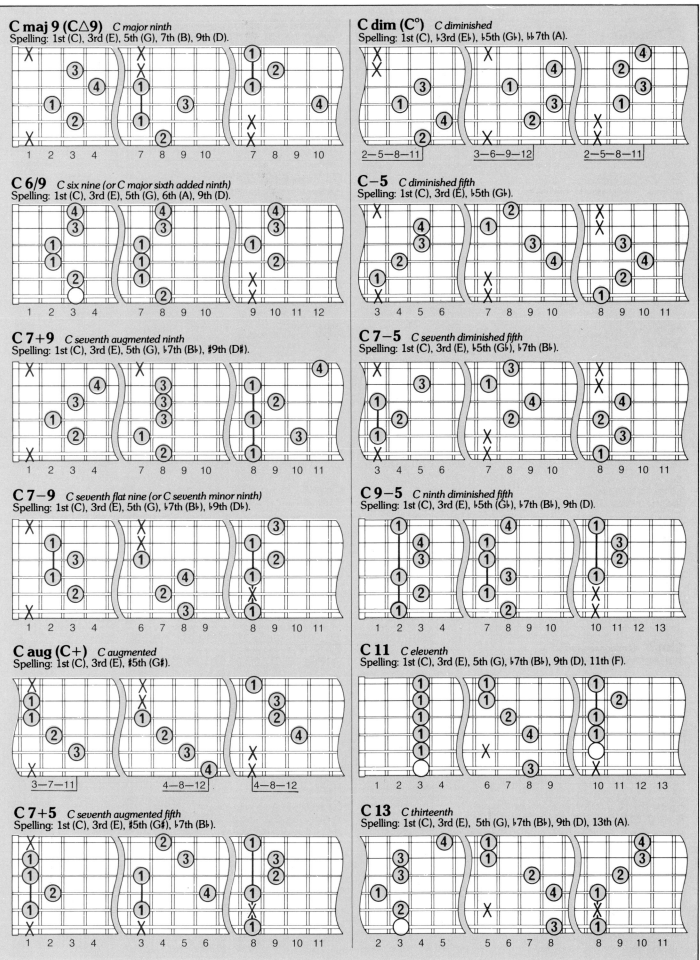

C maj 9 (C△9) *C major ninth*
Spelling: 1st (C), 3rd (E), 5th (G), 7th (B), 9th (D).

C 6/9 *C six nine (or C major sixth added ninth)*
Spelling: 1st (C), 3rd (E), 5th (G), 6th (A), 9th (D).

C 7+9 *C seventh augmented ninth*
Spelling: 1st (C), 3rd (E), 5th (G), ♭7th (B♭), #9th (D#).

C 7−9 *C seventh flat nine (or C seventh minor ninth)*
Spelling: 1st (C), 3rd (E), 5th (G), ♭7th (B♭), ♭9th (D♭).

C aug (C+) *C augmented*
Spelling: 1st (C), 3rd (E), #5th (G#).

C 7+5 *C seventh augmented fifth*
Spelling: 1st (C), 3rd (E), #5th (G#), ♭7th (B♭).

C dim (C°) *C diminished*
Spelling: 1st (C), ♭3rd (E♭), ♭5th (G♭), ♭♭7th (A).

C−5 *C diminished fifth*
Spelling: 1st (C), 3rd (E), ♭5th (G♭).

C 7−5 *C seventh diminished fifth*
Spelling: 1st (C), 3rd (E), ♭5th (G♭), ♭7th (B♭).

C 9−5 *C ninth diminished fifth*
Spelling: 1st (C), 3rd (E), ♭5th (G♭), ♭7th (B♭), 9th (D).

C 11 *C eleventh*
Spelling: 1st (C), 3rd (E), 5th (G), ♭7th (B♭), 9th (D), 11th (F).

C 13 *C thirteenth*
Spelling: 1st (C), 3rd (E), 5th (G), ♭7th (B♭), 9th (D), 13th (A).

233

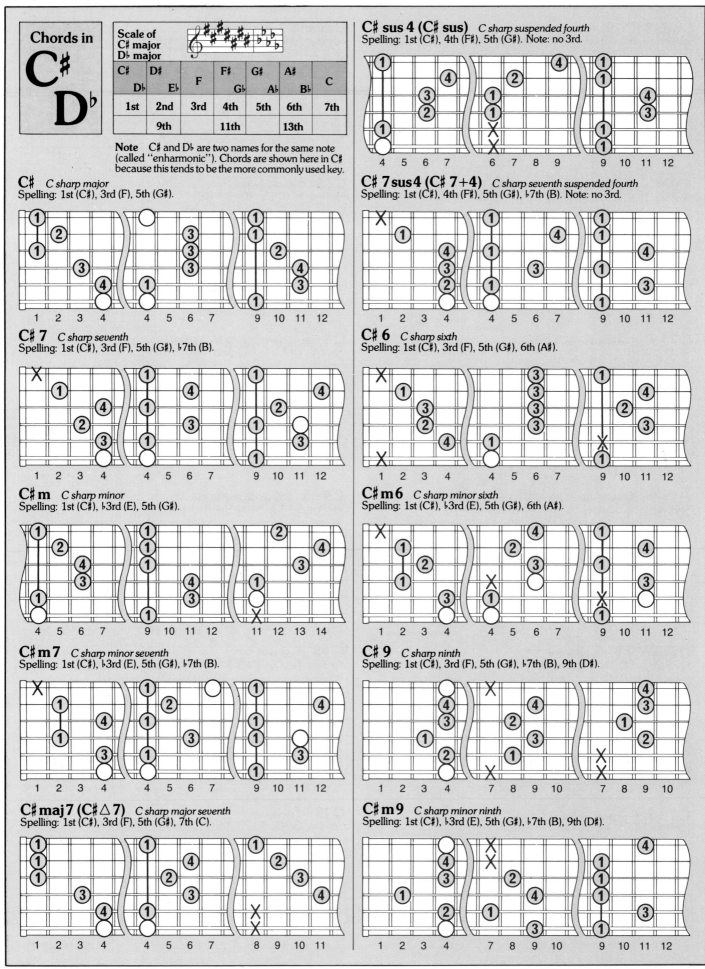

Chords in **C♯ D♭**

Scale of
C♯ major
D♭ major

C♯	D♯	F	F♯	G♯	A♯	C
D♭	E♭		G♭		A♭	B♭	
1st	2nd	3rd	4th	5th	6th	7th
	9th		11th		13th	

Note C♯ and D♭ are two names for the same note (called "enharmonic"). Chords are shown here in C♯ because this tends to be the more commonly used key.

C♯ *C sharp major*
Spelling: 1st (C♯), 3rd (F), 5th (G♯).

C♯ 7 *C sharp seventh*
Spelling: 1st (C♯), 3rd (F), 5th (G♯), ♭7th (B).

C♯ m *C sharp minor*
Spelling: 1st (C♯), ♭3rd (E), 5th (G♯).

C♯ m 7 *C sharp minor seventh*
Spelling: 1st (C♯), ♭3rd (E), 5th (G♯), ♭7th (B).

C♯ maj 7 (C♯△7) *C sharp major seventh*
Spelling: 1st (C♯), 3rd (F), 5th (G♯), 7th (C).

C♯ sus 4 (C♯ sus) *C sharp suspended fourth*
Spelling: 1st (C♯), 4th (F♯), 5th (G♯). Note: no 3rd.

C♯ 7 sus 4 (C♯ 7+4) *C sharp seventh suspended fourth*
Spelling: 1st (C♯), 4th (F♯), 5th (G♯), ♭7th (B). Note: no 3rd.

C♯ 6 *C sharp sixth*
Spelling: 1st (C♯), 3rd (F), 5th (G♯), 6th (A♯).

C♯ m 6 *C sharp minor sixth*
Spelling: 1st (C♯), ♭3rd (E), 5th (G♯), 6th (A♯).

C♯ 9 *C sharp ninth*
Spelling: 1st (C♯), 3rd (F), 5th (G♯), ♭7th (B), 9th (D♯).

C♯ m 9 *C sharp minor ninth*
Spelling: 1st (C♯), ♭3rd (E), 5th (G♯), ♭7th (B), 9th (D♯).

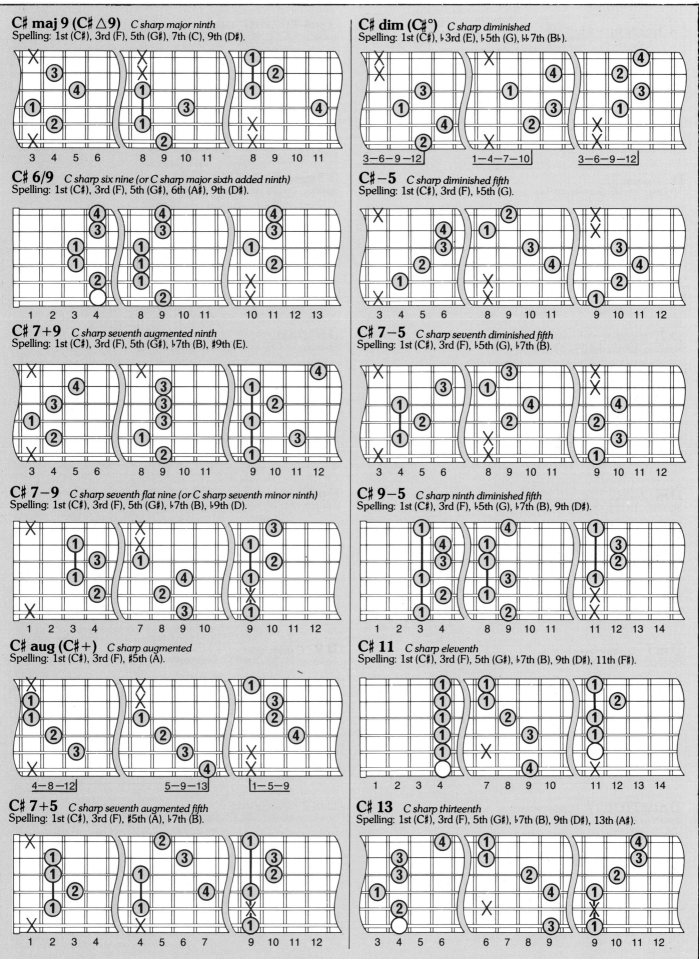

C♯ maj 9 (C♯△9) *C sharp major ninth*
Spelling: 1st (C♯), 3rd (F), 5th (G♯), 7th (C), 9th (D♯).

C♯ 6/9 *C sharp six nine (or C sharp major sixth added ninth)*
Spelling: 1st (C♯), 3rd (F), 5th (G♯), 6th (A♯), 9th (D♯).

C♯ 7+9 *C sharp seventh augmented ninth*
Spelling: 1st (C♯), 3rd (F), 5th (G♯), ♭7th (B), ♯9th (E).

C♯ 7−9 *C sharp seventh flat nine (or C sharp seventh minor ninth)*
Spelling: 1st (C♯), 3rd (F), 5th (G♯), ♭7th (B), ♭9th (D).

C♯ aug (C♯+) *C sharp augmented*
Spelling: 1st (C♯), 3rd (F), ♯5th (A).

C♯ 7+5 *C sharp seventh augmented fifth*
Spelling: 1st (C♯), 3rd (F), ♯5th (A), ♭7th (B).

C♯ dim (C♯°) *C sharp diminished*
Spelling: 1st (C♯), ♭3rd (E), ♭5th (G), ♭♭7th (B♭).

C♯ −5 *C sharp diminished fifth*
Spelling: 1st (C♯), 3rd (F), ♭5th (G).

C♯ 7−5 *C sharp seventh diminished fifth*
Spelling: 1st (C♯), 3rd (F), ♭5th (G), ♭7th (B).

C♯ 9−5 *C sharp ninth diminished fifth*
Spelling: 1st (C♯), 3rd (F), ♭5th (G), ♭7th (B), 9th (D♯).

C♯ 11 *C sharp eleventh*
Spelling: 1st (C♯), 3rd (F), 5th (G♯), ♭7th (B), 9th (D♯), 11th (F♯).

C♯ 13 *C sharp thirteenth*
Spelling: 1st (C♯), 3rd (F), 5th (G♯), ♭7th (B), 9th (D♯), 13th (A♯).

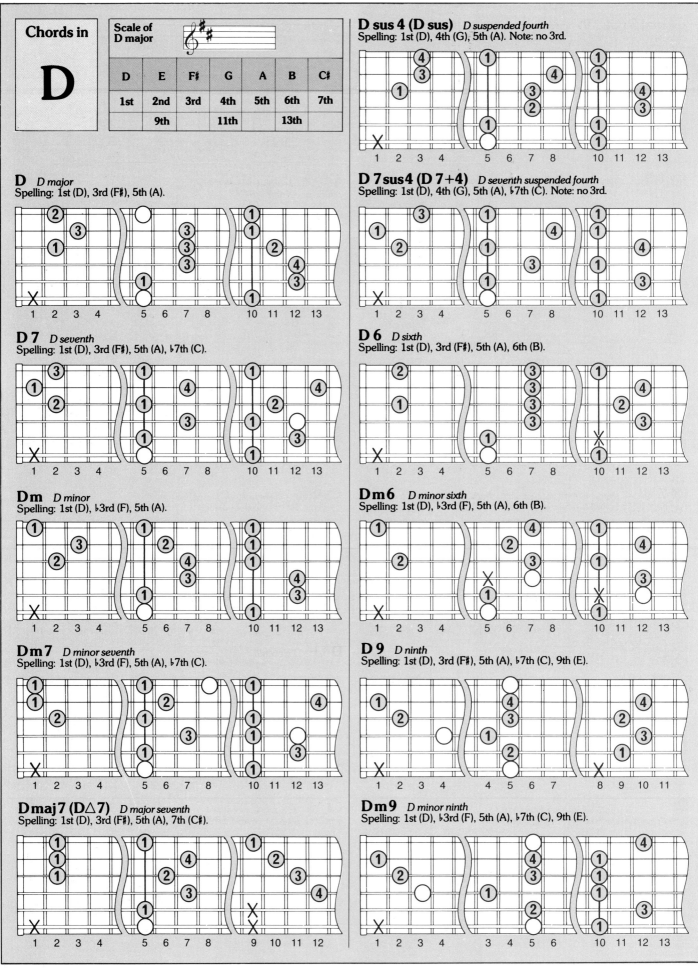

Chords in **D**	Scale of D major						
	D	**E**	**F#**	**G**	**A**	**B**	**C#**
	1st	2nd	3rd	4th	5th	6th	7th
		9th		11th		13th	

D sus 4 (D sus) *D suspended fourth*
Spelling: 1st (D), 4th (G), 5th (A). Note: no 3rd.

D *D major*
Spelling: 1st (D), 3rd (F#), 5th (A).

D 7 sus 4 (D 7+4) *D seventh suspended fourth*
Spelling: 1st (D), 4th (G), 5th (A), ♭7th (C). Note: no 3rd.

D 7 *D seventh*
Spelling: 1st (D), 3rd (F#), 5th (A), ♭7th (C).

D 6 *D sixth*
Spelling: 1st (D), 3rd (F#), 5th (A), 6th (B).

Dm *D minor*
Spelling: 1st (D), ♭3rd (F), 5th (A).

Dm6 *D minor sixth*
Spelling: 1st (D), ♭3rd (F), 5th (A), 6th (B).

Dm7 *D minor seventh*
Spelling: 1st (D), ♭3rd (F), 5th (A), ♭7th (C).

D 9 *D ninth*
Spelling: 1st (D), 3rd (F#), 5th (A), ♭7th (C), 9th (E).

Dmaj7 (D△7) *D major seventh*
Spelling: 1st (D), 3rd (F#), 5th (A), 7th (C#).

Dm9 *D minor ninth*
Spelling: 1st (D), ♭3rd (F), 5th (A), ♭7th (C), 9th (E).

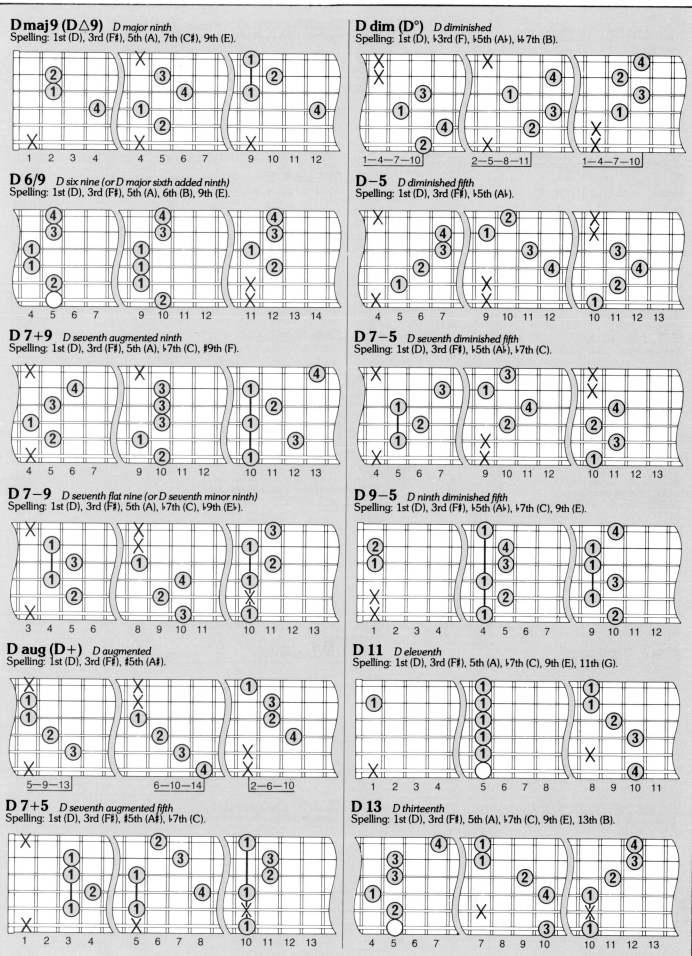

Dmaj9 (D△9) *D major ninth*
Spelling: 1st (D), 3rd (F♯), 5th (A), 7th (C♯), 9th (E).

D dim (D°) *D diminished*
Spelling: 1st (D), ♭3rd (F), ♭5th (A♭), ♭♭7th (B).

D 6/9 *D six nine (or D major sixth added ninth)*
Spelling: 1st (D), 3rd (F♯), 5th (A), 6th (B), 9th (E).

D−5 *D diminished fifth*
Spelling: 1st (D), 3rd (F♯), ♭5th (A♭).

D 7+9 *D seventh augmented ninth*
Spelling: 1st (D), 3rd (F♯), 5th (A), ♭7th (C), ♯9th (F).

D 7−5 *D seventh diminished fifth*
Spelling: 1st (D), 3rd (F♯), ♭5th (A♭), ♭7th (C).

D 7−9 *D seventh flat nine (or D seventh minor ninth)*
Spelling: 1st (D), 3rd (F♯), 5th (A), ♭7th (C), ♭9th (E♭).

D 9−5 *D ninth diminished fifth*
Spelling: 1st (D), 3rd (F♯), ♭5th (A♭), ♭7th (C), 9th (E).

D aug (D+) *D augmented*
Spelling: 1st (D), 3rd (F♯), ♯5th (A♯).

D 11 *D eleventh*
Spelling: 1st (D), 3rd (F♯), 5th (A), ♭7th (C), 9th (E), 11th (G).

D 7+5 *D seventh augmented fifth*
Spelling: 1st (D), 3rd (F♯), ♯5th (A♯), ♭7th (C).

D 13 *D thirteenth*
Spelling: 1st (D), 3rd (F♯), 5th (A), ♭7th (C), 9th (E), 13th (B).

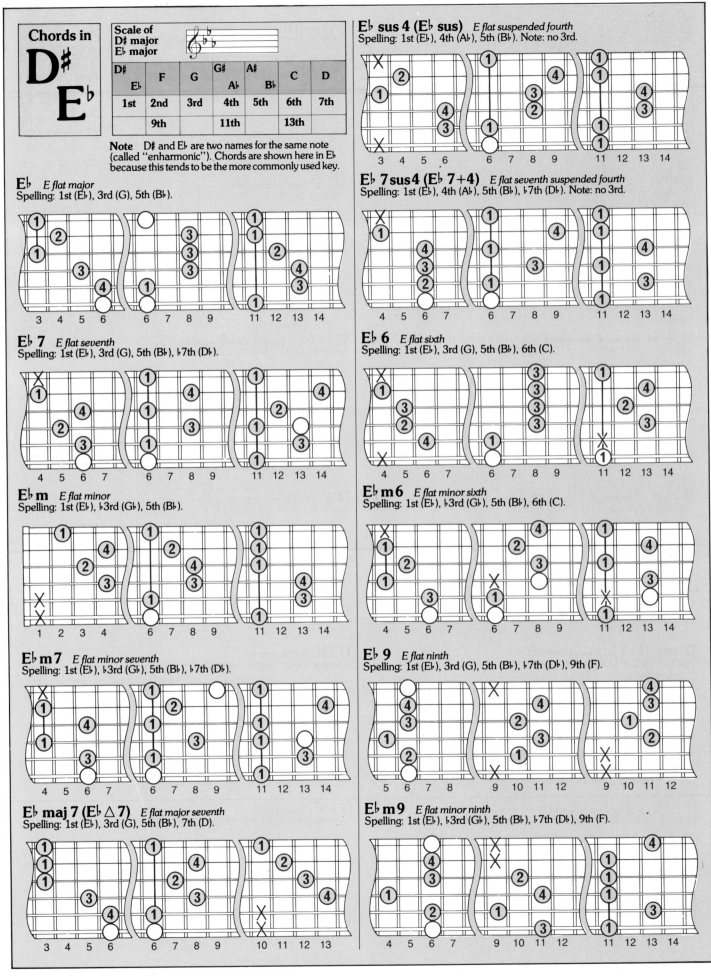

Chords in D♯ E♭

Scale of D♯ major E♭ major							
D♯ E♭	F	G	G♯ A♭	A♯ B♭	C	D
1st	2nd	3rd	4th	5th	6th	7th
	9th		11th		13th	

Note D♯ and E♭ are two names for the same note (called "enharmonic"). Chords are shown here in E♭ because this tends to be the more commonly used key.

E♭ *E flat major*
Spelling: 1st (E♭), 3rd (G), 5th (B♭).

E♭ 7 *E flat seventh*
Spelling: 1st (E♭), 3rd (G), 5th (B♭), ♭7th (D♭).

E♭ m *E flat minor*
Spelling: 1st (E♭), ♭3rd (G♭), 5th (B♭).

E♭ m7 *E flat minor seventh*
Spelling: 1st (E♭), ♭3rd (G♭), 5th (B♭), ♭7th (D♭).

E♭ maj 7 (E♭ △ 7) *E flat major seventh*
Spelling: 1st (E♭), 3rd (G), 5th (B♭), 7th (D).

E♭ sus 4 (E♭ sus) *E flat suspended fourth*
Spelling: 1st (E♭), 4th (A♭), 5th (B♭). Note: no 3rd.

E♭ 7sus4 (E♭ 7+4) *E flat seventh suspended fourth*
Spelling: 1st (E♭), 4th (A♭), 5th (B♭), ♭7th (D♭). Note: no 3rd.

E♭ 6 *E flat sixth*
Spelling: 1st (E♭), 3rd (G), 5th (B♭), 6th (C).

E♭ m6 *E flat minor sixth*
Spelling: 1st (E♭), ♭3rd (G♭), 5th (B♭), 6th (C).

E♭ 9 *E flat ninth*
Spelling: 1st (E♭), 3rd (G), 5th (B♭), ♭7th (D♭), 9th (F).

E♭ m9 *E flat minor ninth*
Spelling: 1st (E♭), ♭3rd (G♭), 5th (B♭), ♭7th (D♭), 9th (F).

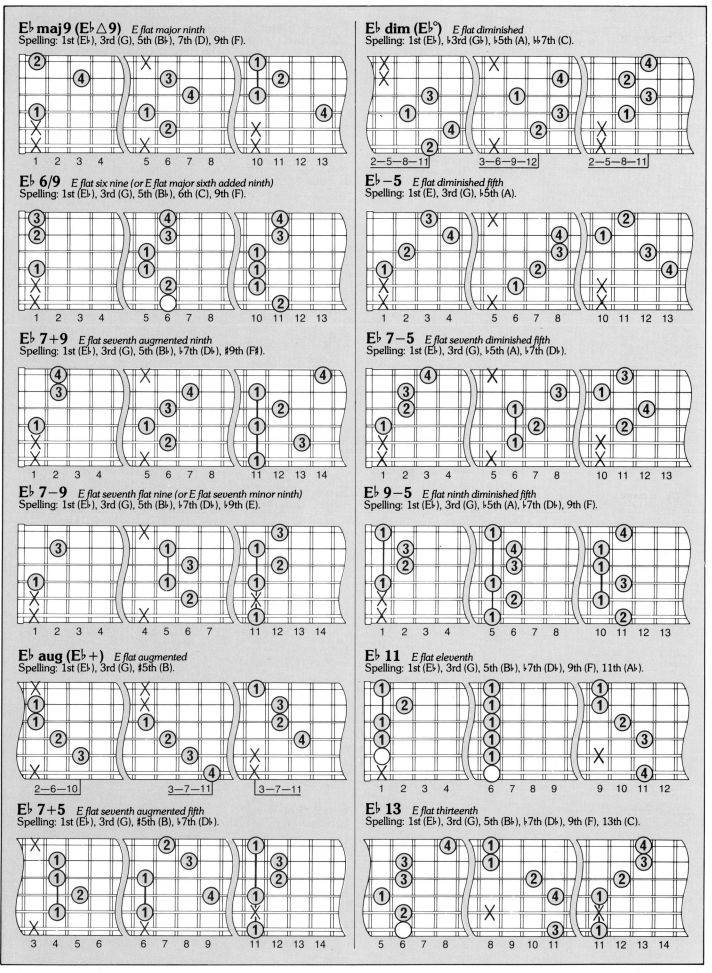

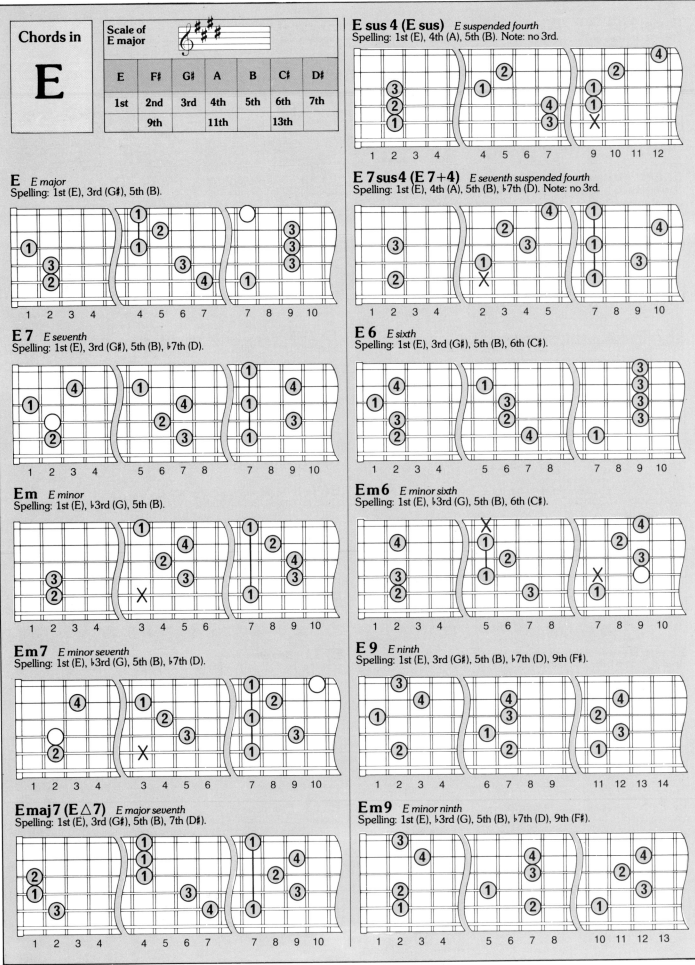

Chords in

E

Scale of E major						
E	F#	G#	A	B	C#	D#
1st	2nd	3rd	4th	5th	6th	7th
	9th		11th		13th	

E *E major*
Spelling: 1st (E), 3rd (G#), 5th (B).

E 7 *E seventh*
Spelling: 1st (E), 3rd (G#), 5th (B), ♭7th (D).

Em *E minor*
Spelling: 1st (E), ♭3rd (G), 5th (B).

Em7 *E minor seventh*
Spelling: 1st (E), ♭3rd (G), 5th (B), ♭7th (D).

Emaj7 (E△7) *E major seventh*
Spelling: 1st (E), 3rd (G#), 5th (B), 7th (D#).

E sus 4 (E sus) *E suspended fourth*
Spelling: 1st (E), 4th (A), 5th (B). Note: no 3rd.

E 7sus4 (E 7+4) *E seventh suspended fourth*
Spelling: 1st (E), 4th (A), 5th (B), ♭7th (D). Note: no 3rd.

E 6 *E sixth*
Spelling: 1st (E), 3rd (G#), 5th (B), 6th (C#).

Em6 *E minor sixth*
Spelling: 1st (E), ♭3rd (G), 5th (B), 6th (C#).

E 9 *E ninth*
Spelling: 1st (E), 3rd (G#), 5th (B), ♭7th (D), 9th (F#).

Em9 *E minor ninth*
Spelling: 1st (E), ♭3rd (G), 5th (B), ♭7th (D), 9th (F#).

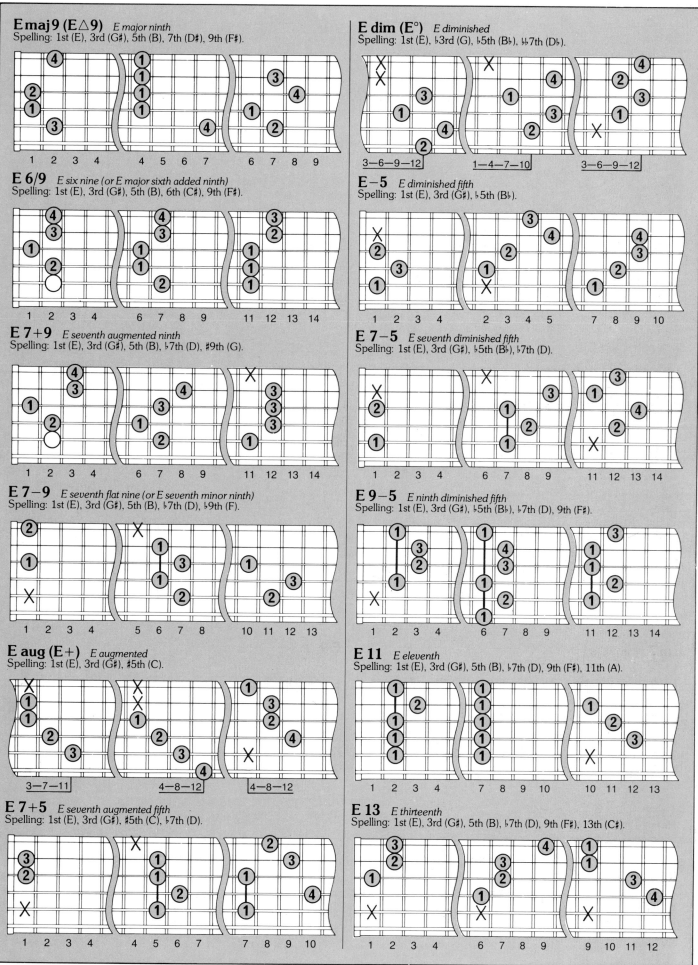

E maj 9 (E△9) *E major ninth*
Spelling: 1st (E), 3rd (G♯), 5th (B), 7th (D♯), 9th (F♯).

E 6/9 *E six nine (or E major sixth added ninth)*
Spelling: 1st (E), 3rd (G♯), 5th (B), 6th (C♯), 9th (F♯).

E 7+9 *E seventh augmented ninth*
Spelling: 1st (E), 3rd (G♯), 5th (B), ♭7th (D), ♯9th (G).

E 7−9 *E seventh flat nine (or E seventh minor ninth)*
Spelling: 1st (E), 3rd (G♯), 5th (B), ♭7th (D), ♭9th (F).

E aug (E+) *E augmented*
Spelling: 1st (E), 3rd (G♯), ♯5th (C).

E 7+5 *E seventh augmented fifth*
Spelling: 1st (E), 3rd (G♯), ♯5th (C), ♭7th (D).

E dim (E°) *E diminished*
Spelling: 1st (E), ♭3rd (G), ♭5th (B♭), ♭♭7th (D♭).

E−5 *E diminished fifth*
Spelling: 1st (E), 3rd (G♯), ♭5th (B♭).

E 7−5 *E seventh diminished fifth*
Spelling: 1st (E), 3rd (G♯), ♭5th (B♭), ♭7th (D).

E 9−5 *E ninth diminished fifth*
Spelling: 1st (E), 3rd (G♯), ♭5th (B♭), ♭7th (D), 9th (F♯).

E 11 *E eleventh*
Spelling: 1st (E), 3rd (G♯), 5th (B), ♭7th (D), 9th (F♯), 11th (A).

E 13 *E thirteenth*
Spelling: 1st (E), 3rd (G♯), 5th (B), ♭7th (D), 9th (F♯), 13th (C♯).

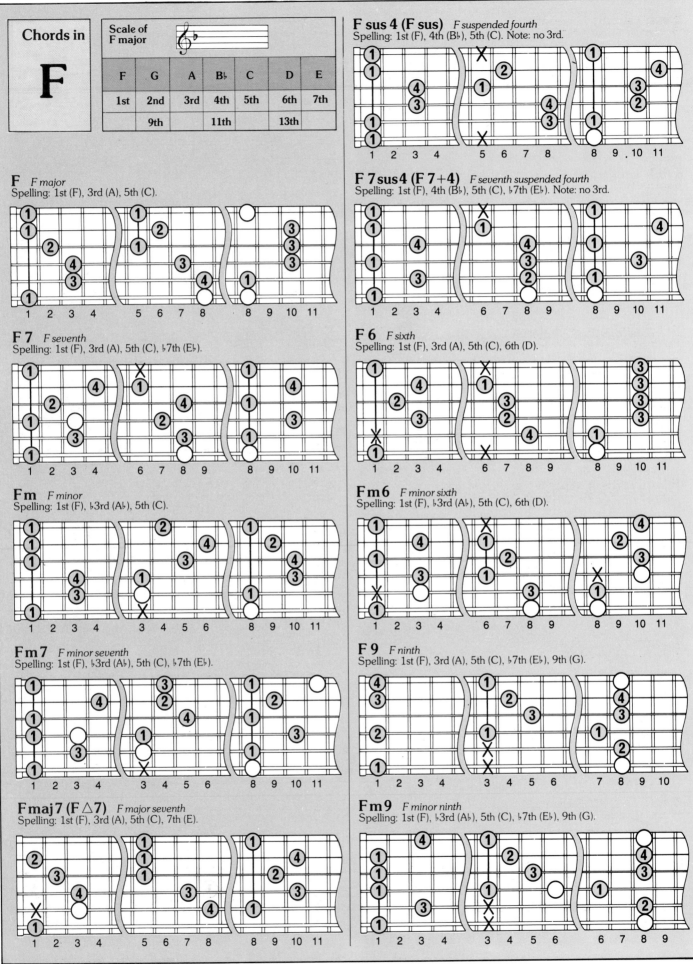

Chords in

F

Scale of F major						
F	G	A	B♭	C	D	E
1st	2nd	3rd	4th	5th	6th	7th
	9th		11th		13th	

F *F major*
Spelling: 1st (F), 3rd (A), 5th (C).

F 7 *F seventh*
Spelling: 1st (F), 3rd (A), 5th (C), ♭7th (E♭).

Fm *F minor*
Spelling: 1st (F), ♭3rd (A♭), 5th (C).

Fm7 *F minor seventh*
Spelling: 1st (F), ♭3rd (A♭), 5th (C), ♭7th (E♭).

Fmaj7 (F△7) *F major seventh*
Spelling: 1st (F), 3rd (A), 5th (C), 7th (E).

F sus 4 (F sus) *F suspended fourth*
Spelling: 1st (F), 4th (B♭), 5th (C). Note: no 3rd.

F 7sus4 (F 7+4) *F seventh suspended fourth*
Spelling: 1st (F), 4th (B♭), 5th (C), ♭7th (E♭). Note: no 3rd.

F 6 *F sixth*
Spelling: 1st (F), 3rd (A), 5th (C), 6th (D).

Fm6 *F minor sixth*
Spelling: 1st (F), ♭3rd (A♭), 5th (C), 6th (D).

F 9 *F ninth*
Spelling: 1st (F), 3rd (A), 5th (C), ♭7th (E♭), 9th (G).

Fm9 *F minor ninth*
Spelling: 1st (F), ♭3rd (A♭), 5th (C), ♭7th (E♭), 9th (G).

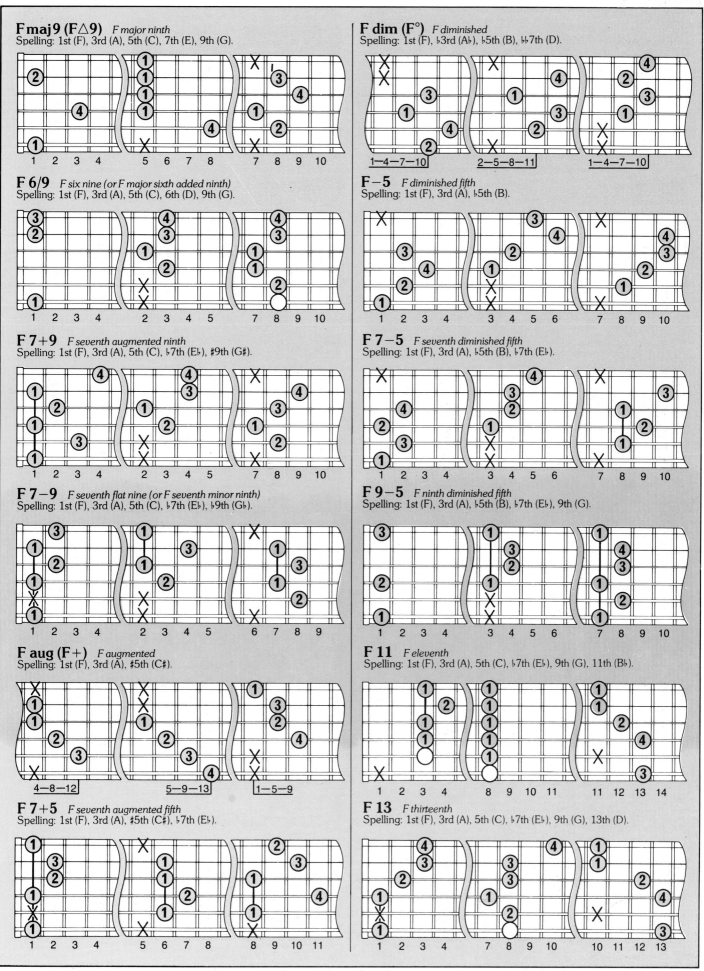

Fmaj9 (F△9) *F major ninth*
Spelling: 1st (F), 3rd (A), 5th (C), 7th (E), 9th (G).

F 6/9 *F six nine (or F major sixth added ninth)*
Spelling: 1st (F), 3rd (A), 5th (C), 6th (D), 9th (G).

F 7+9 *F seventh augmented ninth*
Spelling: 1st (F), 3rd (A), 5th (C), ♭7th (E♭), ♯9th (G♯).

F 7−9 *F seventh flat nine (or F seventh minor ninth)*
Spelling: 1st (F), 3rd (A), 5th (C), ♭7th (E♭), ♭9th (G♭).

F aug (F+) *F augmented*
Spelling: 1st (F), 3rd (A), ♯5th (C♯).

F 7+5 *F seventh augmented fifth*
Spelling: 1st (F), 3rd (A), ♯5th (C♯), ♭7th (E♭).

F dim (F°) *F diminished*
Spelling: 1st (F), ♭3rd (A♭), ♭5th (B), ♭♭7th (D).

F−5 *F diminished fifth*
Spelling: 1st (F), 3rd (A), ♭5th (B).

F 7−5 *F seventh diminished fifth*
Spelling: 1st (F), 3rd (A), ♭5th (B), ♭7th (E♭).

F 9−5 *F ninth diminished fifth*
Spelling: 1st (F), 3rd (A), ♭5th (B), ♭7th (E♭), 9th (G).

F 11 *F eleventh*
Spelling: 1st (F), 3rd (A), 5th (C), ♭7th (E♭), 9th (G), 11th (B♭).

F 13 *F thirteenth*
Spelling: 1st (F), 3rd (A), 5th (C), ♭7th (E♭), 9th (G), 13th (D).

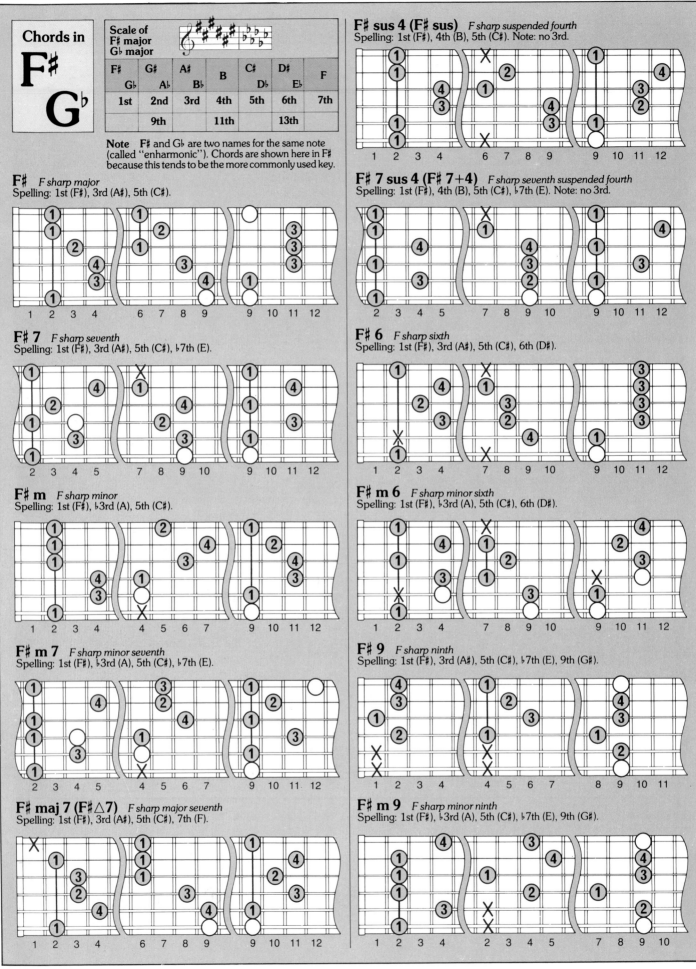

Chords in
F♯
G♭

Scale of
F♯ major
G♭ major

F♯ G♭	G♯ A♭	A♯ B♭	B	C♯ D♭	D♯ E♭	F
1st	2nd	3rd	4th	5th	6th	7th
	9th		11th		13th	

Note F♯ and G♭ are two names for the same note (called "enharmonic"). Chords are shown here in F♯ because this tends to be the more commonly used key.

F♯ *F sharp major*
Spelling: 1st (F♯), 3rd (A♯), 5th (C♯).

F♯ 7 *F sharp seventh*
Spelling: 1st (F♯), 3rd (A♯), 5th (C♯), ♭7th (E).

F♯ m *F sharp minor*
Spelling: 1st (F♯), ♭3rd (A), 5th (C♯).

F♯ m 7 *F sharp minor seventh*
Spelling: 1st (F♯), ♭3rd (A), 5th (C♯), ♭7th (E).

F♯ maj 7 (F♯△7) *F sharp major seventh*
Spelling: 1st (F♯), 3rd (A♯), 5th (C♯), 7th (F).

F♯ sus 4 (F♯ sus) *F sharp suspended fourth*
Spelling: 1st (F♯), 4th (B), 5th (C♯). Note: no 3rd.

F♯ 7 sus 4 (F♯ 7+4) *F sharp seventh suspended fourth*
Spelling: 1st (F♯), 4th (B), 5th (C♯), ♭7th (E). Note: no 3rd.

F♯ 6 *F sharp sixth*
Spelling: 1st (F♯), 3rd (A♯), 5th (C♯), 6th (D♯).

F♯ m 6 *F sharp minor sixth*
Spelling: 1st (F♯), ♭3rd (A), 5th (C♯), 6th (D♯).

F♯ 9 *F sharp ninth*
Spelling: 1st (F♯), 3rd (A♯), 5th (C♯), ♭7th (E), 9th (G♯).

F♯ m 9 *F sharp minor ninth*
Spelling: 1st (F♯), ♭3rd (A), 5th (C♯), ♭7th (E), 9th (G♯).

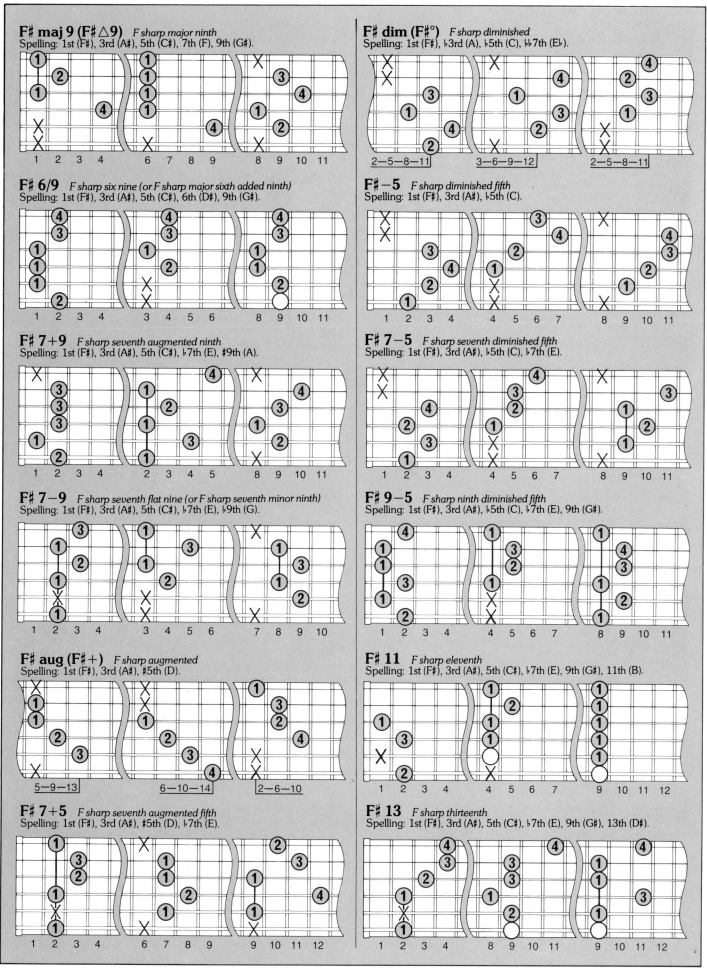

F♯ maj 9 (F♯△9) *F sharp major ninth*
Spelling: 1st (F♯), 3rd (A♯), 5th (C♯), 7th (F), 9th (G♯).

F♯ 6/9 *F sharp six nine (or F sharp major sixth added ninth)*
Spelling: 1st (F♯), 3rd (A♯), 5th (C♯), 6th (D♯), 9th (G♯).

F♯ 7+9 *F sharp seventh augmented ninth*
Spelling: 1st (F♯), 3rd (A♯), 5th (C♯), ♭7th (E), ♯9th (A).

F♯ 7−9 *F sharp seventh flat nine (or F sharp seventh minor ninth)*
Spelling: 1st (F♯), 3rd (A♯), 5th (C♯), ♭7th (E), ♭9th (G).

F♯ aug (F♯+) *F sharp augmented*
Spelling: 1st (F♯), 3rd (A♯), ♯5th (D).

F♯ 7+5 *F sharp seventh augmented fifth*
Spelling: 1st (F♯), 3rd (A♯), ♯5th (D), ♭7th (E).

F♯ dim (F♯°) *F sharp diminished*
Spelling: 1st (F♯), ♭3rd (A), ♭5th (C), ♭♭7th (E♭).

F♯−5 *F sharp diminished fifth*
Spelling: 1st (F♯), 3rd (A♯), ♭5th (C).

F♯ 7−5 *F sharp seventh diminished fifth*
Spelling: 1st (F♯), 3rd (A♯), ♭5th (C), ♭7th (E).

F♯ 9−5 *F sharp ninth diminished fifth*
Spelling: 1st (F♯), 3rd (A♯), ♭5th (C), ♭7th (E), 9th (G♯).

F♯ 11 *F sharp eleventh*
Spelling: 1st (F♯), 3rd (A♯), 5th (C♯), ♭7th (E), 9th (G♯), 11th (B).

F♯ 13 *F sharp thirteenth*
Spelling: 1st (F♯), 3rd (A♯), 5th (C♯), ♭7th (E), 9th (G♯), 13th (D♯).

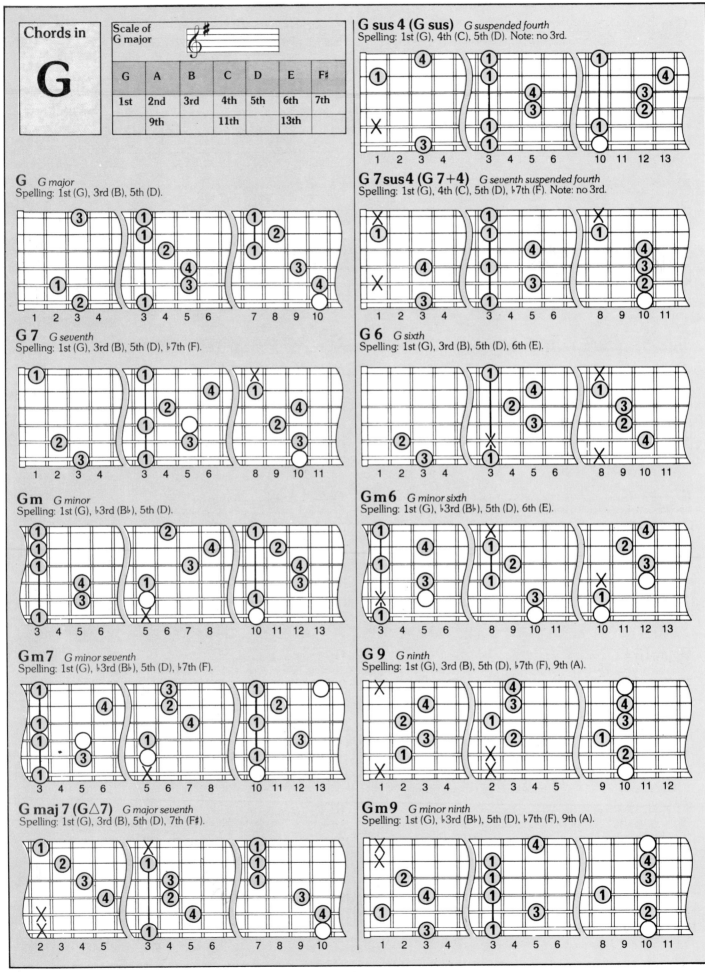

Chords in G

Scale of G major	G	A	B	C	D	E	F#
	1st	2nd	3rd	4th	5th	6th	7th
		9th		11th		13th	

G *G major*
Spelling: 1st (G), 3rd (B), 5th (D).

G 7 *G seventh*
Spelling: 1st (G), 3rd (B), 5th (D), ♭7th (F).

Gm *G minor*
Spelling: 1st (G), ♭3rd (B♭), 5th (D).

Gm 7 *G minor seventh*
Spelling: 1st (G), ♭3rd (B♭), 5th (D), ♭7th (F).

G maj 7 (G△7) *G major seventh*
Spelling: 1st (G), 3rd (B), 5th (D), 7th (F#).

G sus 4 (G sus) *G suspended fourth*
Spelling: 1st (G), 4th (C), 5th (D). Note: no 3rd.

G 7 sus 4 (G 7+4) *G seventh suspended fourth*
Spelling: 1st (G), 4th (C), 5th (D), ♭7th (F). Note: no 3rd.

G 6 *G sixth*
Spelling: 1st (G), 3rd (B), 5th (D), 6th (E).

Gm6 *G minor sixth*
Spelling: 1st (G), ♭3rd (B♭), 5th (D), 6th (E).

G 9 *G ninth*
Spelling: 1st (G), 3rd (B), 5th (D), ♭7th (F), 9th (A).

Gm9 *G minor ninth*
Spelling: 1st (G), ♭3rd (B♭), 5th (D), ♭7th (F), 9th (A).

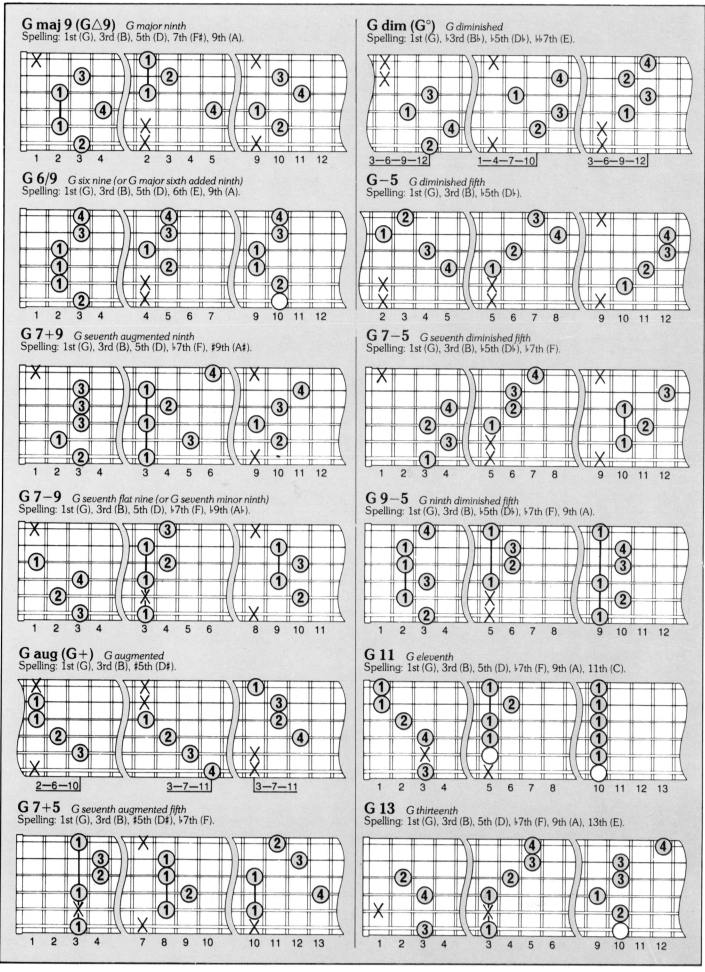

G maj 9 (G△9) *G major ninth*
Spelling: 1st (G), 3rd (B), 5th (D), 7th (F#), 9th (A).

G 6/9 *G six nine (or G major sixth added ninth)*
Spelling: 1st (G), 3rd (B), 5th (D), 6th (E), 9th (A).

G 7+9 *G seventh augmented ninth*
Spelling: 1st (G), 3rd (B), 5th (D), ♭7th (F), #9th (A#).

G 7−9 *G seventh flat nine (or G seventh minor ninth)*
Spelling: 1st (G), 3rd (B), 5th (D), ♭7th (F), ♭9th (A♭).

G aug (G+) *G augmented*
Spelling: 1st (G), 3rd (B), #5th (D#).

G 7+5 *G seventh augmented fifth*
Spelling: 1st (G), 3rd (B), #5th (D#), ♭7th (F).

G dim (G°) *G diminished*
Spelling: 1st (G), ♭3rd (B♭), ♭5th (D♭), ♭♭7th (E).

G−5 *G diminished fifth*
Spelling: 1st (G), 3rd (B), ♭5th (D♭).

G 7−5 *G seventh diminished fifth*
Spelling: 1st (G), 3rd (B), ♭5th (D♭), ♭7th (F).

G 9−5 *G ninth diminished fifth*
Spelling: 1st (G), 3rd (B), ♭5th (D♭), ♭7th (F), 9th (A).

G 11 *G eleventh*
Spelling: 1st (G), 3rd (B), 5th (D), ♭7th (F), 9th (A), 11th (C).

G 13 *G thirteenth*
Spelling: 1st (G), 3rd (B), 5th (D), ♭7th (F), 9th (A), 13th (E).

247

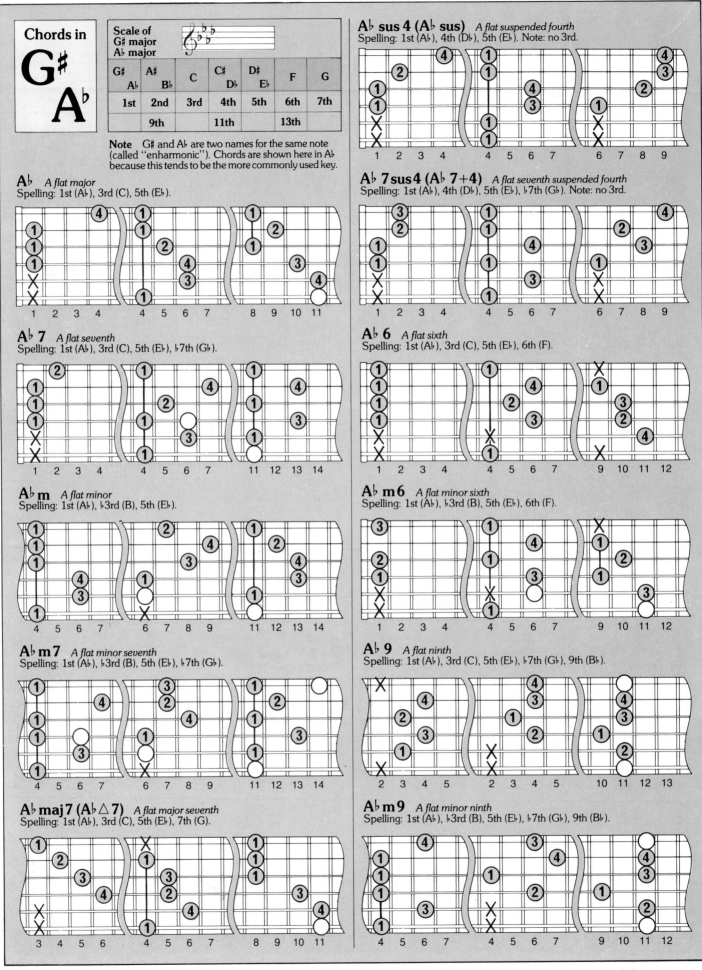

Chords in G♯ / A♭

G♯ / A♭	A♯ / B♭	C	C♯ / D♭	D♯ / E♭	F	G
1st	2nd	3rd	4th	5th	6th	7th
	9th		11th		13th	

Scale of G♯ major / A♭ major

Note G♯ and A♭ are two names for the same note (called "enharmonic"). Chords are shown here in A♭ because this tends to be the more commonly used key.

A♭ *A flat major*
Spelling: 1st (A♭), 3rd (C), 5th (E♭).

A♭ 7 *A flat seventh*
Spelling: 1st (A♭), 3rd (C), 5th (E♭), ♭7th (G♭).

A♭ m *A flat minor*
Spelling: 1st (A♭), ♭3rd (B), 5th (E♭).

A♭ m7 *A flat minor seventh*
Spelling: 1st (A♭), ♭3rd (B), 5th (E♭), ♭7th (G♭).

A♭ maj7 (A♭△7) *A flat major seventh*
Spelling: 1st (A♭), 3rd (C), 5th (E♭), 7th (G).

A♭ sus 4 (A♭ sus) *A flat suspended fourth*
Spelling: 1st (A♭), 4th (D♭), 5th (E♭). Note: no 3rd.

A♭ 7sus4 (A♭ 7+4) *A flat seventh suspended fourth*
Spelling: 1st (A♭), 4th (D♭), 5th (E♭), ♭7th (G♭). Note: no 3rd.

A♭ 6 *A flat sixth*
Spelling: 1st (A♭), 3rd (C), 5th (E♭), 6th (F).

A♭ m6 *A flat minor sixth*
Spelling: 1st (A♭), ♭3rd (B), 5th (E♭), 6th (F).

A♭ 9 *A flat ninth*
Spelling: 1st (A♭), 3rd (C), 5th (E♭), ♭7th (G♭), 9th (B♭).

A♭ m9 *A flat minor ninth*
Spelling: 1st (A♭), ♭3rd (B), 5th (E♭), ♭7th (G♭), 9th (B♭).

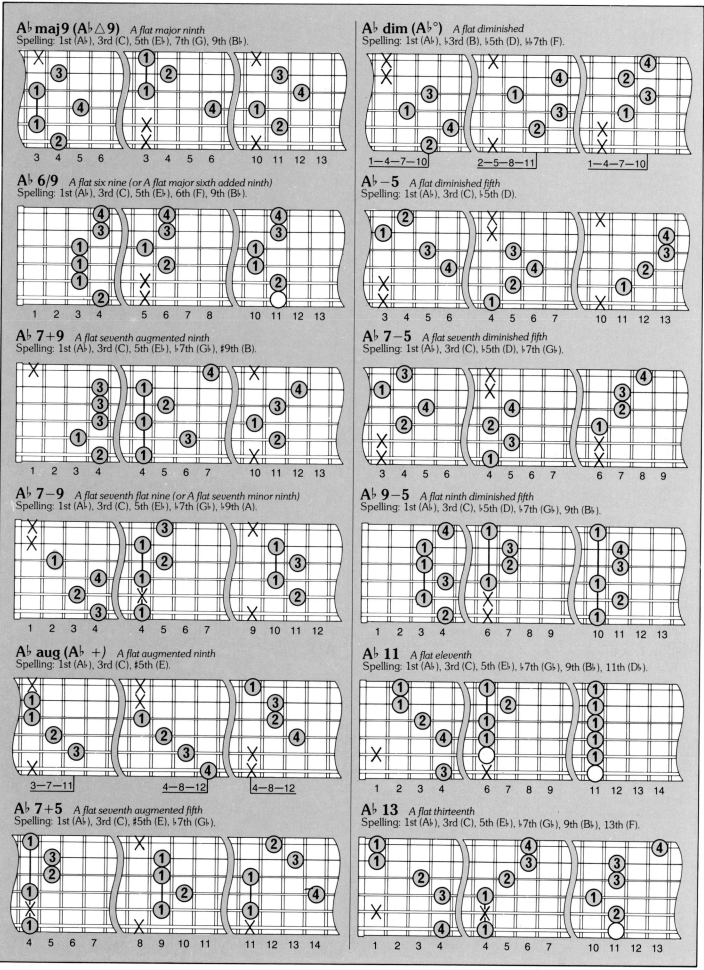

A♭ maj9 (A♭△9) *A flat major ninth*
Spelling: 1st (A♭), 3rd (C), 5th (E♭), 7th (G), 9th (B♭).

A♭ 6/9 *A flat six nine (or A flat major sixth added ninth)*
Spelling: 1st (A♭), 3rd (C), 5th (E♭), 6th (F), 9th (B♭).

A♭ 7+9 *A flat seventh augmented ninth*
Spelling: 1st (A♭), 3rd (C), 5th (E♭), ♭7th (G♭), ♯9th (B).

A♭ 7−9 *A flat seventh flat nine (or A flat seventh minor ninth)*
Spelling: 1st (A♭), 3rd (C), 5th (E♭), ♭7th (G♭), ♭9th (A).

A♭ aug (A♭ +) *A flat augmented ninth*
Spelling: 1st (A♭), 3rd (C), ♯5th (E).

A♭ 7+5 *A flat seventh augmented fifth*
Spelling: 1st (A♭), 3rd (C), ♯5th (E), ♭7th (G♭).

A♭ dim (A♭°) *A flat diminished*
Spelling: 1st (A♭), ♭3rd (B), ♭5th (D), ♭♭7th (F).

A♭ −5 *A flat diminished fifth*
Spelling: 1st (A♭), 3rd (C), ♭5th (D).

A♭ 7−5 *A flat seventh diminished fifth*
Spelling: 1st (A♭), 3rd (C), ♭5th (D), ♭7th (G♭).

A♭ 9−5 *A flat ninth diminished fifth*
Spelling: 1st (A♭), 3rd (C), ♭5th (D), ♭7th (G♭), 9th (B♭).

A♭ 11 *A flat eleventh*
Spelling: 1st (A♭), 3rd (C), 5th (E♭), ♭7th (G♭), 9th (B♭), 11th (D♭).

A♭ 13 *A flat thirteenth*
Spelling: 1st (A♭), 3rd (C), 5th (E♭), ♭7th (G♭), 9th (B♭), 13th (F).

249

Index

Acknowledgments

Author's acknowledgments
First edition
I would like to extend my personal thanks to:
Alan Buckingham, Ron Pickless, Nick Harris, Tim
Shackleton; Felicity Bryan; Brian Gascoigne;
Isaac Guillory; Alastair Crawford; David
Wernham, Pete Wingfield, Frank Richmond and
Dave Almond; Andy Summers, Phil Palmer, Mo
Foster and Phil Childs; Tony Zemaitis, Chris
Eccleshall, Mike Cameron and Tom Mates;
Richard Elen and Noel Bell; Angus Robertson;
Tony Bacon; Gwen Alexander; Dave Peterson;
Dave Green; Christine Keiffer; Trevor Newman;
Trevor Cash; London Rock Shop; Kelly Pike;
Mike Wilkie of Epic Records Ltd; Hugh Attwool;
Ritchie Gold; Andy's Guitar Workshop.

Revised edition
Special thanks to Terry Burrows for efforts above
and beyond; Christopher Davis; Jane Laing;
Claire Legemah and all at Dorling Kindersley.
Caroline Begrave of Curtis-Brown Ltd; Lee
Dickson – guitar technician to Eric Clapton;
Brian "Jobby" Zellis – guitar technician to Brian
May; Steve Flood of Master Rock studios; Fostex
UK; Sony Broadcast & Communications UK;
Solid State Logic; Brüel and Kjaer; Chris Solbé of
Nick Hopewell-Smith Associates; Tom Nolan of
the Fender A & R Centre; Mark Smith of Rose-
Morris; Roger Lindsay; John "Boy" Blyth; David
Alison; Simon Turnbull, Neil Mooring and Alan
Hud of John Hornby Skewes; Simon Alexander,
Steve Yelding and Robin Figg of Jim Marshall
(Products) Ltd; Johnny Joyce of Aria (UK) Ltd;
Britannia Row productions/Sales.

Dorling Kindersley would like to thank the
following for their help in the preparation of this
book: Warren Mitchell and Gordon Dungate;
Geoff Dann; Steve Gorton; Judith More and
Sarah Moule for picture research; Max Kay; Mark
Richards, Calvin Evans, Phil Wilkinson, Del
Brenner and Lesley Gilbert; Roddy MacDonald,
Steve Parker and Gary Marsh; Enca of Keith
Altham Publicity; David S. Harding; Mike
Longworth; David Seville; M. J. Summerfield;
Wayne Floyd Edwards of Rose Morris; Stuart
Sawney and Robb Davenport; Nick Martin;
Anthony Macari; Music Lab; Watkins Electric
Music (WEM); Ken Achard; Roland (U.K.); Rocky
Roadshow; MCMXCIX; Drawmer; Ralph Dunlop
of Sound Technology; Rhiannon of Cheetah
International; Jon Lewin of Making Music; Simon
Hopkins of Virgin; Marc Snelling of Strings and
Things; Tony Barrett of Rockstar.

We would also like to thank the many readers
who have taken the trouble to pass on their
comments to us over the past ten years.

Picture sources
B&K 214
Daily Telegraph Colour Library 43
Geoff Dann 41, 48(l), 68-69, 71-75, 82-85, 87,
141-3, 145, 148, 162, 164, 165, 166, 169
Decca Records 17(l)
Ralph Denyer/Performance Technology 6(l),
23(l), 24, 28, 200, 202, 211, 216
Philip Dowell 33, 49, 65, 161
Drawmer 206
E. F. R. Guitars/Geoff Dann 46, 47(l), 48(r),
56-57, 60, 61(cl, b), 62(l, c), 174, 176, 178(t),
179(t).
E. F. R. Guitars/Jack Durrant 38, 47(l), 54, 59,
62(r), 63.
Fender 202(bc)
Fostex (UK) 222
Gibson/Rosetti 195(t)
Jazz Music Books 8, 9(l), 100.
JHS 208(c)
London Features International 7, 10, 15(t), 16,
18, 20, 22, 25, 30(r), 31(t), 88(t), 102, 114-5,
140, 158.
Marshall 202(br), 203
C. F. Martin Organization 37, 45.
MCMXCIX 208(tr)
Melody Maker 15(b)
Neumann 214
Ian O'Leary/Chandler Guitars 179b
Pictorial Press 21(r), 23(r), 26,
David Redfern 11, 12, 13, 17(r), 19, 31(b),
32(b), 66, 101.
Relativity Records 32(t)
Rex Features 27
Rockstar/Tony Barrett 14
Rocky Roadshow 202 (bl)
Roland (UK) 224
Rosetti 178(b), 180-181, 195(b).
Shuttlesound 219
Solid State Logic 211(r)
Sony Music Entertainment Inc 9(r)
Sound Technology 89, 204
Strings and Things 208(tl)
Summerfield 34, 47(bc), 61(t).
Tandy 214
Graham Tucker 29(t)
Virgin Records 29(b)
Vox 61(cr), 198, 200(bl)
Valerie Wilmer 160
Frank Zappa 21(l)

Key: t=top, c=center, b=bottom, l=left,
r=right.

Text quotations
GPI Publications Cupertino, California.
Reprinted with permission: p.66 Howard Roberts
(*Rock Guitarists*, vol. I); p.66 Ted Nugent (*Rock
Guitarists*. vol. 2); p.88 Keith Richards (*The
Guitar Player Book*, Nov. 1977 p.88 Pete
Townshend (*Guitar Player* magazine. July 1981
); p.102 Frank Zappa (*The Guitar Player Book*,
Jan. 1977); p.114 John McLaughlin (*The Guitar
Player Book* Feb. 1975); p.114-15 George
Benson (*The Guitar Player Book*, Jan. 1974);
p.140 Eric Clapton (*Guitar Player* magazine, July
l981); p.140 Jeff Beck (*Guitar Player* magazine,
July 1981); p.140 Ritchie Blackmore (*Guitar
Player* magazine, July 1981); p.156 Howard
Roberts (*Rock Guitarists*, vol. I); p.157 Albert Lee
(*Guitar Player* magazine, May 1981).
Sphere Books, London. Reprinted with
permission, p.10-11 Chuck Berry (*The Rolling
Stone Interviews*, vol. 1, by Patrick William
Salvo). ©1981, Rolling Stone Press .
Omnibus Press, London. Reprinted with
permission: p.26 Jimi Hendrix (*Hendrix: A
Biography* by Chris Welch).

Illustrators John Bishop, Gary Marsh, Hayward
and Martin, Alun Jones, Kong Kang Chen and
Nick Harris.

Computer graphics Terry Burrows and Claire
Legemah.

Photographic services W. Photo, Negs and
Photo Summit.

Reproduction F. E. Burman Ltd and Dot
Gradations Ltd.

Typesetting Rowland Phototypesetting (London)
Ltd. (original edition).

MASTERING APPLEWORKS

MASTERING APPLEWORKS™

ELNA TYMES

SYBEX®

Berkeley • Paris • Düsseldorf • London

Book design by Ingrid Owen

Apple, Apple IIe, Apple IIc, AppleWorks, Quick File, Imagewriter, and ProDOS are trademarks of
Apple Computer, Inc.
DIF is a trademark of Software Arts, Inc.
VisiCalc is a trademark of VisiCorp.

SYBEX is not affiliated with any manufacturer.

Every effort has been made to supply complete and accurate information. However, SYBEX assumes
no responsibility for its use, nor for any infringements of patents or other rights of third parties which
would result.

Library of Congress Card Number: 84-51794
ISBN 0-89588-240-x
Printed by Haddon Craftsmen
Manufactured in the United States of America
10 9 8 7 6

ACKNOWLEDGMENTS

No book like this gets done by a single person, working without help. I am indebted to:

Chuck Murphy, for bringing me to SYBEX, Jim Hill, for pushing through the contract and finding me the necessary hardware, David Kolodney, for a prudent red pencil and thoughtful questions, Karl Ray and Rudy Langer, for help at the last minute, Don Field of Apple Computer, for answering my questions and updating my software, and Charles, Adrian, and Robin, for letting me write on sunny summer weekends without complaining about Mom's misplaced priorities.

Palo Alto, California
October 1, 1984

AUTHOR'S NOTE

This book teaches you about AppleWorks, an integrated program. The chapters in this book give you some examples of what you can do with each of the component programs—word processor, spreadsheet, and data base—and then show you how to use them together. The Appendix, A Basic Business Toolkit, gives you a collection of spreadsheet models that you can type into your Apple IIe or IIc and use right away.

The book is oriented toward the needs of the businessperson, and uses examples drawn from the business world.

CONTENTS

CHAPTER 4

The Word Processor

CHAPTER 5

Printer Options

CHAPTER 6

The Spreadsheet

CHAPTER

87

The Data Base

CHAPTER

109

Cutting and Pasting

CHAPTER 121

Putting it all Together

CHAPTER 143

More About Printing

APPENDIX 149

A Basic Business Toolkit

WHAT IS APPLEWORKS?

IS APPLEWO

CHAPTER

AppleWorks is an integrated program that combines three of the most widely used types of applications software: word processing, spreadsheet manipulation of data, and data base management.

Word processing allows you to write letters, articles, memos, proposals, or reports, and then to format them to suit your purposes and print them. However, because you store the text magnetically on a diskette, you can print your document again as many times as you wish; you can revise it without retyping the whole text and print it again; and you can keep several different versions of your document for later use, knowing that each version is available whenever you need it.

A spreadsheet program allows you to manipulate rows and columns of numbers to create such standard financial reports as income statements, balance sheets, and cash flow statements, as well as do projections, perform complex calculations, prepare invoices and quotations, and keep statistical records. A spreadsheet program also lends itself to "What if?" analyses, allowing you to change one item and see what impact that change has on the rest of your calculations. Like a word processor, a spreadsheet program allows you to store your spreadsheet on a diskette, and then print it at will. You can store your "What if?" changes on the same diskette and use them to illustrate how the different assumptions can alter the results.

A data base manager lets you organize information into convenient segments that can be sorted and recalled in a variety of useful ways. A good example of a non-computer data base is a desktop card file of clients: you can sort the cards alphabetically by name; select them by telephone area code, zip code, or company product; and you can augment the basic data with comments. A data base manager lets you set up your data in such a way that you can sort, select, and rearrange the information to suit your needs. And, because the data is stored on a diskette, you can update it whenever you like and never lose the original information. Further, you can print out the results of each sorting in a separate, formatted report without altering the information in the data base.

An integrated package combines two or more applications functions into one program, so that you can move easily between the functions without having to switch diskettes or be concerned about one program not being able to use the files from another. The commands and other methods used to communicate with the user are also consistent between the programs, so you only have to learn one set of conventions. Once you've learned how to use one program, it's easy to learn and become proficient in the others.

Most applications programs for microcomputers produce files that cannot be used by other applications programs. For instance, most word processors cannot handle a spreadsheet file, and vice versa. Unfortunately, the real world sometimes requires that you produce a report or some other form of document that necessitates going back and forth between the different programs. When you get ready to produce the final document, you may have to physically cut and paste printed reports from one program into the printed text from another.

Because AppleWorks combines a word processing program, a spreadsheet program, and a data base manager program, you can move easily from one function to another without worrying about file compatibility. This means that you can include a budget forecast in the middle of a report, provide a list of potential customers in a proposal, add explanatory text to a monthly sales chart, or set up a financial model using data stored in your data base files. All of this without changing diskettes or moving out of the AppleWorks program.

For instance, suppose you had written a letter to a customer (Figure 1.1) and you needed to use just the schedule from the letter in an internal memorandum.

In many word processing situations, you'd need to retype the schedule in the internal memo. With AppleWorks, you can use the "cut and paste" facility to copy the schedule from the letter into the memo, as in Figure 1.2. All this with a couple of keystrokes.

But that's not all that Appleworks can do. How about transferring information from a spreadsheet to the middle of a letter or proposal? Figure 1.3 is a word processed proposal incorporating a chart that was generated by the spreadsheet program.

Figure 1.4 is an example of a letter incorporating information from a data base file containing customer information.

July 28, 1984

Adrian Thomas
Sports World, Inc.
445 Scripps Ave.
Palo Alto, Ca. 94367

Dear Mr. Thomas:

Thank you for your order for our Model 4350 Timing and Display System. As you know, it is one of the most accurate systems in the world, capable of measuring lap times in thousandths of a second.

The system will be delivered and set up according to the schedule below. Please note that there is a one month break-in period, during which our service people will be on call every day of the week to come out and fix any part of the system that doesn't work. Note also that there is a training session for the people you will use as timers. We will hold the training session at your facility for up to ten people, at no additional charge. You indicated you'd like to hold the session before the end of the break-in period. Please contact the head of our customer service department, Don Burden, to arrange the time and date of this training session.

	SCHEDULE
April 5	Site visit, Engineering Dept. (for measurement of facilities).
April 16	Site plan delivered to customer for approval; permit application delivered to City.
April 19	Customer-requested changes incorporated in plans; City notified.
April 30	City approvals expected.
May 8	System installation at customer site; demonstration to facility manager and staff; begin one-month break-in period.
May 15	Field service checkup of system.
June 8	Customer acceptance of system.

Thank you again for your order.

Yours truly,

P. K. O'Meagher

Figure 1.1: Letter to a customer including schedule (shaded portion).

The customer file, a portion of which is used in the letter, would probably contain addditional information, such as address, date and amount of last order, and the total amount of purchases to date. With AppleWorks, you can excerpt portions from your data base file, sort and format them as you choose, and then "cut and paste" them into your word processed letter or report.

How about using information from your data base in a spreadsheet? AppleWorks makes that easy too. Suppose, for example, you had a data base file like the one in Figure 1.5.

To: Don Burden
From: P. K. O'Meagher
Re: Model 4350 System order for Sports World
March 28, 1984

As you can see from the schedule below, we have some work to do. I know you don't have the training program ready—we've never had a customer who wanted one before—but he bought it and now we have to deliver it.

Here's the schedule:

SCHEDULE

April 5   Site visit, Engineering Dept. (for measurement of facilities).

April 16   Site plan delivered to customer for approval; permit application delivered to City.

April 19   Customer-requested changes incorporated in plans; City notified.

April 30   City approvals expected.

May 8   System installation at customer site; demonstration to facility manager and staff; begin one-month break-in period.

May 15   Field service checkup of system.

June 8   Customer acceptance of system.

I can meet with you and George Ebey from Engineering on Friday, March 30 at 9:30 to go over what the system does and what Sports World's expectations are about training. I can also probably help you write and print a nice little handout to supplement your class if you and George can define what all the system will do. But let's get our collective act together quickly.

Figure 1.2: Memorandum incorporating the schedule from Figure 1.1.

THE AMES PROJECT

The 1984 Olympic Games in Los Angeles generated a great deal of interest in and enthusiasm for a number of sports, including bicycling. Reports from our retail customers indicate a considerably increased demand for all types of bicycle accessories, including sport-specific clothing.

We have been experiencing some difficulties with these items, especially the cycling shirts and pants. Our retailers report that the wool knits have stretched and become misshapen in washing—the seams have even come apart. As one means of offering our customers higher quality merchandise, we are investigating the possibility of manufacturing the clothing ourselves.

Below is a preliminary cash flow projection showing the income and expenses that would be involved in such a venture. We have assumed that we could use the spare capacity available in our swim and tennis apparel manufacturing facility in Tucson, Arizona. Product launching would be during the fall, a traditionally slow time for cycling gear. This together with startup costs, will keep our net income for the first quarter low. However, as the chart shows, net income from this project alone is likely to experience a healthy growth.

	Ames Project Cash Flow Projection			
	First Quarter	Second Quarter	Third Quarter	Fourth Quarter
Income	100,000	115,000	132,250	152,087.50
Cost of Sales	10,000	11,500	13,225	15,208.75
Cost of Goods	50,000	57,500	66,125	76,043.75
Operating Expenses	10,000	11,500	13,225	15,208.75
Net Income	30,000	34,500	39,675	45,626.25
Taxes	14,700	16,905	19,440.75	22,356.86
Carryfwd. Profits	0	15,300	32,895	53,129.25
Cumulative Profits	15,300	32,895	53,129.25	76,398.63

The Cost of Sales is our estimate of what it would cost to find and use reps, and the Operating Costs is an estimate of this project's share of plant overhead. The Cost of Goods figure would probably be proportional to sales, since we already have idle time on the equipment in place.

While this is just a preliminary study, we feel it is promising enough to warrant more investigation by the Product Marketing group.

Figure 1.3: Word processed letter incorporating a spreadsheet chart (shaded portion).

Now suppose you want to use that same information in a spreadsheet to compute the value of your inventory. Of course, you could retype the data into a spreadsheet. Far more convenient is AppleWorks' ability to transfer information from the data base to a spreadsheet. Once it is there, you can add the appropriate formulas to come up with the inventory valuation shown in Figure 1.6

March 30, 1984

Fred Olson, vice-president
First City Bank
855 Main Street
Belmont, Ca. 94083

Dear Mr. Olson:

Thank you for spending time with us yesterday and reviewing our proposal for an extension of our credit line. As you know, when the timing is right for a new product line—as we believe it is for our own line of bicycle clothing—it is important to move quickly.

In addition to the other documents you requested, you asked for a list of our customers whom you could contact as references. Please feel free to call the following:

Customer Name	Phone Number	Contact Person
The Bike Rack	619 555 1357	Don Burwell
Speedo Bike Stores, Inc.	408 555 1352	Adrian Jeremy
Novus Sport Shops	415 555 8297	Charles Prael
Sports Emporium	206 555 4399	Robin Weberg
A-1 Sporting Goods Stores	206 555 4466	Chris Davis

Since the idea of manufacturing our own line of bicycle clothing was initially sparked by the enthusiasm of our retailers, we feel sure their comments will add credibility to our assessment of this market.

If we can provide any more information, please don't hesitate to call us.

Yours truly,

Charles Everett, Director of Marketing

Figure 1.4: Word processed letter incorporating information from the data base program (shaded portion).

Item Name	M/F	Size	Color	Number in Stock	Date Rcd.
Pegasus Shirt	M	S	blue/yellow	200	1/25/84
Pegasus Shirt	M	M	blue/yellow	300	1/25/84
Pegasus Shirt	M	L	blue/yellow	250	1/25/84
Pegasus Shirt	M	XL	blue/yellow	100	1/25/84
Alligator Shirt	F	S	red/black	70	2/15/84
Alligator Shirt	F	M	red/black	100	2/15/84
Alligator Shirt	F	L	red/black	55	2/15/84
Cycling pants	M	28	black	35	1/31/84
Cycling pants	M	30	black	42	2/6/84
Cycling pants	M	32	black	27	2/6/84
Cycling pants	M	34	black	36	2/6/84
Cycling pants	M	36	black	29	1/31/84
Cycling pants	M	38	black	23	1/31/84
Cycling pants	M	40	black	12	1/31/84

Figure 1.5: Data base file for inventory.

Item Name	M/F	Size	Color	Number in stock	@	Value
Pegasus Shirt	M	S	blue/yellow	200	12.14	2428.00
Pegasus Shirt	M	M	blue/yellow	300	12.14	3642.00
Pegasus Shirt	M	L	blue/yellow	250	12.14	3035.00
Pegasus Shirt	M	XL	blue/yellow	100	12.14	1214.00
Alligator Shirt	F	S	red/black	70	10.74	751.80
Alligator Shirt	F	M	red/black	100	10.74	1074.00
Alligator Shirt	F	L	red/black	55	10.74	590.70
Cycling pants	M	28	black	35	20.55	719.25
Cycling pants	M	30	black	42	20.55	863.10
Cycling pants	M	32	black	27	20.55	554.85
Cycling pants	M	34	black	36	20.55	739.80
Cycling pants	M	36	black	29	20.55	595.95
Cycling pants	M	38	black	23	20.55	472.65
Cycling pants	M	40	black	12	20.55	246.60
Total value of inventory						16927.70

Figure 1.6: Inventory valuation spreadsheet using information from the data base file in Figure 1.5.

Later on in this book we'll show you with simple, step-by-step instructions how all these different kinds of data transfers are done. But first we need to look at how you can get started using AppleWorks.

GETTING STARTED

CHAPTER 2

Apple Computer, with its legendary attention to making life easy for the computer user, has made it a breeze to get up and running on AppleWorks.

If you haven't discovered the *AppleWorks Tutorial* in the material that came with your AppleWorks program, take time now to find it. The Tutorial takes you on a guided tour of AppleWorks, using the Startup, Program, Sample Files, and Apple Presents diskettes. You will also find that the *Reference Manual* is very handy for explaining why things work the way they do, and for showing the functions of the menus and commands.

In case you want a brief introduction to AppleWorks, without going through the tutorial that Apple provides, this chapter will discuss a few introductory matters.

What Equipment Is Necessary?

AppleWorks runs on an Apple IIe or IIc computer. With the IIe, it also needs the Apple 80-column Text Card (the extra 64k of memory is recommended). This card goes in the large auxiliary slot.

You will also need:

- a video monitor;
- for the Apple IIe, one or more Apple disk drives with the controller card in slot 6 (a second disk drive is recommended for either the Apple IIe or IIc);
- two or more blank, formatted disks (see page 19) so that you can make copies of your Startup and Program disks; and
- a printer, with the printer interface card in slot 1.

Starting the Program

After checking to see that your computer is configured as it should be (see "Equipment Checklist," page xiii in the *AppleWorks Tutorial*), perform the following steps:

1. Insert the AppleWorks Startup diskette into Drive 1.

2. Turn on the monitor and the computer. If the computer is already on, press Control-Open-Apple-Reset simultaneously.

3. The Apple opening screen appears briefly, then is replaced by the AppleWorks title screen, which includes this message at the bottom:

   Place the AppleWorks PROGRAM disk in Drive I and press Return.

4. Take the Startup diskette out of Drive 1 and replace it with the AppleWorks Program diskette, then press Return. A GETTING STARTED screen will appear with this message at the bottom:

   Type today's date or press Return:

   (After the diskette has been used once, the last date of use appears here on this line.)

5. Type in the date, using slashes to separate month, day, and year. This date will be "stamped" for future reference on any files you create in this session. Once you have typed in the date, press Return. A screen will appear with the following menu:

   Path: P2/FEB

   Main Menu

   1. Add files to the Desktop.

   2. Work with one of the files on the Desktop.

   3. Save Desktop files to disk.

   4. Remove files from the Desktop.

   5. Other activities.

   6. Quit.

This is the first of AppleWorks' menus, and is referred to as the Main Menu, since any use of files eventually returns you to it. Notice that it appears within a drawing in the shape of a file folder.

File folders are the symbols used for manipulating your files in Appleworks' Desktop (see Figure 2.1). The Desktop is analogous to your own desk: it is where you do your work. When you are through with a project for the time being, you put the papers associated with it back in the file folder and either leave it handy on your deskstop, or else store it away in a file drawer.

You do the same sort of thing electronically with AppleWorks' Desktop, spreading out on your screen the files you want to work with and storing the rest away on your diskette. Just as you can have more than one folder open on your desk, you can use the Desktop to shuffle information electronically from one file to another. When you are through, you put all the files away and clear your desk. In the next chapter we'll look at the Desktop in more detail.

Using Return and Escape

You choose an item on an AppleWorks menu by moving the cursor (the shaded bar) up or down the list until it is over the item you want, then pressing Return. This causes the selected command to be executed.

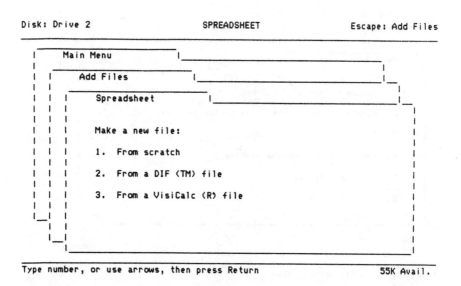

```
Disk: Drive 2                  SPREADSHEET              Escape: Add Files
 _____
I      Main Menu            I_____
I    _____I                                          I
I  I    Add Files          I_____I__
I  I  _____I                                            I
I  I  I  Spreadsheet       I_____I__
I  I  I                                                                 I
I  I  I  Make a new file:                                               I
I  I  I                                                                 I
I  I  I  1.  From scratch                                               I
I  I  I                                                                 I
I  I  I  2.  From a DIF (TM) file                                       I
I  I  I                                                                 I
I  I  I  3.  From a VisiCalc (R) file                                   I
I  I  I                                                                 I
I__I  I                                                                 I
   I  I                                                                 I
   I__I                                                                 I
      I_____I

Type number, or use arrows, then press Return                 55K Avail.
```

Figure 2.1: The Desktop screen with overlapping file folders.

To try this out right now, press the down-arrow key until the shaded bar is over Quit. Press Return to execute the Quit command. The screen will ask you if you really want to Quit. Since we have other things to do with the Main Menu in this chapter, type an N or press Return to indicate No, you don't really want to quit.

Notice that the shaded bar now jumps back to the top item on the list, Add files to the Desktop. Whenever you return to the Main Menu, the shaded bar will appear over the first item, as shown in Figure 2.2.

What happens if you make a mistake and want to go back to the previous menu for another try? In most cases, you can simply press the Escape key. This action cancels the previous command, and returns you to the menu you just left. In general you can see where Escape will take you by looking at the upper-right corner of the screen.

Let's try out the Return and Escape keys. Since the shaded bar is still over the first item, Add files to the Desktop, we can execute that command by pressing Return. We're not actually going to add any files at this point; we just want to see how Return and Escape can move us from menu to menu.

Your screen now displays the Add Files menu (Figure 2.3) as a list of items on a second file folder that overlays the Main Menu folder. In the upper-right corner of the screen are the words Escape: Main Menu.

```
Disk: Drive 2                    MAIN MENU
_____
  |_____|
  |   Main Menu              |_____|
  |                                                              |
  |                                                              |
  |   1.  Add files to the Desktop                               |
  |                                                              |
  |   2.  Work with one of the files on the Desktop              |
  |                                                              |
  |   3.  Save Desktop files to disk                             |
  |                                                              |
  |   4.  Remove files from the Desktop                          |
  |                                                              |
  |   5.  Other Activities                                       |
  |                                                              |
  |   6.  Quit                                                   |
  |                                                              |
  |_____|

_____
Type number, or use arrows, then press Return        ∂-? for Help
```

Figure 2.2: The Main Menu screen with item 1 highlighted.

Since we are not adding files at this point, press Escape and notice that the Add Files menu disappears and the Main Menu replaces it.

As long as you are executing one of the Main Menu's commands and not using one of the three applications programs, pressing Return will cause another file folder with a menu on it to appear, overlaying the previous one. Pressing Escape causes the program to "back up" to the previous folder.

Using the Arrow Keys

You'll use the arrow keys (located at the lower-right of your keyboard) to move the cursor to a new position. Generally, you use the up-arrow and down-arrow keys to move the shaded bar cursor up and down a menu list. When you go past the top or bottom of a menu, the shaded bar cycles around to the other end.

If you try to use the right-arrow or left-arrow key in a situation where only the up-arrow or down-arrow key is appropriate, your computer will beep at you, indicating that this key is not correct.

```
Disk: Drive 2                    ADD FILES              Escape: Main Menu
_____
   |_____|
   | Main Menu               |_____
   |  _____                               |
   | |   Add Files                  |_____|_
   | |                                                               |
   | |                                                               |
   | |      Get files from:                                          |
   | |                                                               |
   | |   1.  The current disk: Drive 2                               |
   | |   2.  A different disk                                        |
   | |                                                               |
   | |      Make a new file for the:                                 |
   | |                                                               |
   | |   3.  Word Processor                                          |
   | |   4.  Data Base                                               |
   | |   5.  Spreadsheet                                             |
   |_|                                                               |
   |                                                                 |
   |_____|

_____
Type number, or use arrows, then press Return              55K Avail.
```

Figure 2.3: The Add Files menu.

Using the Cursors

There are three kinds of cursors in AppleWorks.

- The shaded bar, used for selecting items on the menus
- The blinking rectangle, called the *overstrike cursor*
- The blinking underline, called the *insert cursor*

The shaded bar is used only for selecting commands from a menu. The blinking rectangle and blinking underline are used to edit existing text. In both cases the cursor shows where the next character you type is going to appear. With the rectangle the new character will overstrike (replace) an existing character. With the underline the new character is *inserted* and existing text is moved to the right to make room for it.

Once you have started up by entering the date, you can change back and forth between the two cursors whenever you like: just type Open-Apple together with the letter E. AppleWorks always gives you the insert cursor to start out.

Deleting Characters

If you wish to erase characters, you can do so easily with the *Delete key*. Each time you press Delete, the character to the left of the cursor disappears, and the text to the right moves over to fill in the space. You can delete all the text from the cursor on to the end of the entry or line by pressing the *Control key* together with the letter Y.

The Open-Apple Key

AppleWorks uses the Open-Apple key, in combination with other characters, to perform special functions. For instance, we mentioned above that you press Open-Apple together with the letter E to change back and forth between the two cursors. There are other commands that use the Open-Apple key in the same sort of way, and they will be explained as they come up.

Getting Help Quickly

Sooner or later you will reach a point where you are in the midst of doing some work and you find that you need to use a command but can't remember the right keys for it. What to do? You can stop what you're doing and look up the answer. Or you can use the Help command.

From anywhere in AppleWorks, pressing Open-Apple with the **?** key will get you a screenful of information, usually relating to exactly the kind of work you are doing. The screen will display tips on relevant commands, or file usage, or something that lays out the options open to you right where you are. Once you've read the screen and decided what to do, simply press Return to get back to where you were before.

Quitting the Program

When it's time to end a session, the orderly way to shut down the program is to use the Quit command on the Main Menu. You can, of course, simply turn the computer off, but you shouldn't: if you've been using the Desktop, you'll lose all of the files you've worked on if they haven't been "saved," (see page 26) and you may cause other problems with Desktop files.

To stop AppleWorks and close out any open files, be sure the Main Menu is on your screen (use the Escape key if you're not already there), move the shaded bar to Quit and press Return. When the screen asks you if you really want to quit, type Y for yes. You'll be asked to specify what you want done with each of the files you've used during this session, throw it out, save it on this disk or on a different one, or replace an existing file with a newer version. If you have used no files, as has been done in this chapter, this part is skipped over.

You will now see a ProDOS prompt like this:

ENTER PREFIX (PRESS "RETURN" TO ACCEPT)
/SAMPLES

Instead of the word SAMPLES, however, you will find whatever name has been given the current disk.

At this point, you are back in the Apple operating system, and you can either shut down the computer (turn off the power switch in back, then turn off the monitor) or specify a new application by giving its pathname.

THE DESKTOP

CHAPTER 3

We looked at the Desktop briefly in the last chapter. Now we'll go into some more detail. As we stated before, the Desktop is where you do your work. You use an application program, such as the word processor, spreadsheet, or data base manager, on the Desktop, with files you either create from scratch or which you have previously stored.

The Desktop is actually a program for handling your files that allows you to do your work electronically in somewhat the same way you actually work with papers on top of your desk.

AppleWorks assumes you are of the "clean desk" mentality, and presents you with a list of things you can do when you start the program. In this respect, it is a bit like your desk was when you first started a job—there was a clean surface, and you spent your first hours learning how to use the information tools that were available to you. This is analogous to the Main Menu of AppleWorks: the basic tool set is listed there.

In this chapter we'll go over the tools of the AppleWorks kit.

Formatting a Disk

You can't store files unless you have a properly formatted diskette to work with, so let's look at how you format a disk:

1. Call up the Main Menu and choose item 5. Other Activities.

2. The Other Activities Menu will appear on the screen. Choose item 5. Format a blank disk. (The disk needn't actually be blank, but formatting will erase any information it currently contains.)

3. The Disk formatter screen shown in Figure 3.1 will appear. Give your diskette a name as instructed. You have up to 15 characters to work with, but you don't have to use them all. Type something that will be easy to remember, such as SAMPLE, or MINE. Press Return.

4. You will now see this message:

   **The disk to be formatted should
   be in the disk drive NOW.**

   Insert the disk and press the Space Bar.

5. The disk drive will make some noises and eventually will stop. This message will appear:

   Successfully formatted.

6. You now have a properly formatted data diskette. Press the Space Bar again if you wish to format another disk. Otherwise, put the Appleworks Program disk back in Drive 1, and press Escape twice to get back to the Main Menu. We are ready to create some sample files.

```
Disk: Drive 2                    DISK FORMATTER         Escape: Other Activities
_____
 I      _____I_____
 I     Main Menu                 I                                       I
 I     I_____I_
 I     I   Other Activities     I                                        I_
 I     I  _____
 I     I I   Disk formatter     I                                            I_
 I     I I                                                                    I
 I     I I                                                                    I
 I     I I   The formatter will use the disk drive                           I
 I     I I   shown on the top line of the screen.                            I
 I     I I                                                                    I
 I     I I   A disk name consists of up to 15 letters,                       I
 I     I I   numbers, and periods.  The first character                      I
 I     I I   must be a letter.                                               I
 I     I I                                                                    I
 I     I I                                                                    I
 I__I I                                                                    I
    I  I                                                                    I
    I__I                                                                    I
       I_____I
_____
Type a disk name:                                              55K Avail.
```

Figure 3.1: The Disk formatter screen.

AppleWorks Files

AppleWorks uses two kinds of files:

- *program files,* which contain the word processor, spreadsheet, data base manager, and utilities; and
- *data files,* which are the files (letters, spreadsheets, etc.) you create using the applications programs.

The program files are stored on the Program diskette which you received as part of the AppleWorks package. They are in a special programming language, and need not be changed in any way.

You own data files can be in any of several formats:

- ASCII, which consists of the alphabet, numbers, punctuation, and special characters. This is the way that all word processing files, and most data base and spreadsheet files are written.
- DIF [tm] (Data Interchange Format) files, which are files that have been translated into a standard format such that unrelated programs can share data. A spreadsheet or data base program, for instance, that is not part of AppleWorks could produce a DIF file, which could then be used by the AppleWorks spreadsheet or data base manager.
- Quick File [tm] files are the result of the Quick File data base program (not included with AppleWorks).
- VisiCalc files are the result of using the spreadsheet program VisiCalc [tm], and then "printing" the resulting worksheet into a disk file.

Active files are the result of AppleWorks' *loading* one of your files into the Desktop so that information in it can be changed, or so that the file itself can be used or manipulated (renamed, saved, deleted). *Inactive files* are those that are available to the program on your diskette, but have not been loaded into the Desktop because they aren't required for whatever operation you are currently doing.

Each file must have a unique filename, using up to 15 characters. The name must begin with a letter, and may use upper- or lowercase letters, numbers, spaces, and periods. No other characters are allowed.

You can have as many AppleWorks files as you want on your data diskette; however the program can only handle 140k *bytes* or characters (about 70 double-spaced pages of text) on a diskette. If you are using a ProDOS hard disk, you can have up to 130 AppleWorks files per ProDOS subdirectory.

Backing Up Your Files

Almost every computer book stresses the importance of backing up your files. This means simply that you store a duplicate version of your file on a separate diskette in a different location, so that if something happens to the disk you're working on you will not have lost the information.

Most users get really tired of seeing the same admonition in book after book about the importance of backups. Experienced computer users frequently develop an "It'll never happen to me— I'm careful!" attitude that serves them well—until, one day:

> a well intentioned friend accidentally spills coffee on your desk, soaking your diskette,

> or a freak electrical storm causes a power surge that catches your computer up and running with the only copy of your data files in the midst of being run,

> or you are taking work home with you, in the form of a couple of diskettes, and you leave them on the seat beside you during the hot drive home, only to discover when you try to run them that you've essentially fried your data.

You can add your own poignant scenarios. The point is that it is important to make duplicate copies of files that are valuable to you— including the AppleWorks diskettes and your data diskettes. Use DOS 3.3 COPYA or the ProDOS Filer on the ProDos User's Disk to make your copies; the user's manual for your system explains how to make the copies.

Adding Files to the Desktop

When you create a file, you automatically add it to the Desktop. We're going to create some empty files, just to show how to work with the commands on the Main Menu, but you can follow the same procedure when you create your actual word processor, spreadsheet, or data base files. To start with let's make an empty word processor file:

- On the Main Menu, choose 1. Add files to the Desktop.

- The Add Files screen, shown in Figure 3.2, will appear. From this screen choose 3. Word Processor.

- You will now see the Word Processor menu, shown in Figure 3.3. The cursor is on the first choice, 1. From scratch, and that's what we want, so press the Return key.

- The line at the bottom of the screen will now ask:

  Type a name for this new file.

  The name can be up to 15 characters long, and can use uppercase or lowercase letters, as well as numbers, periods, and spaces (it must start with a letter). Let's use the name WPTEST. Type the file name and press Return.

- Now you are shown the opening, empty Word Processing screen, as in Figure 3.4, with your file name in the line at the top of the screen. Since we aren't really going to create a document (we'll do that in Chapter 4), we'll leave this file empty and return to the Main Menu. To do that, press Escape.

When the Main Menu appears, the shaded bar is on the Add Files line again. We're going to create another empty file, so press Return to take this option.

```
Disk: Drive 2                    ADD FILES              Escape: Main Menu
_____

  I    Main Menu          I_____
  I   _____ I                                       I
  I  I   Add Files        I_____ I__
  I  I                                                              I
  I  I                                                              I
  I  I      Get files from:                                         I
  I  I                                                              I
  I  I      1.  The current disk: Drive 2                           I
  I  I      2.  A different disk                                    I
  I  I                                                              I
  I  I      Make a new file for the:                                I
  I  I                                                              I
  I  I      3.  Word Processor                                      I
  I  I      4.  Data Base                                           I
  I  I      5.  Spreadsheet                                         I
  I_I                                                               I
    I                                                               I
    I_____I

_____
Type number, or use arrows, then press Return              55K Avail.
```

Figure 3.2: The Add Files screen.

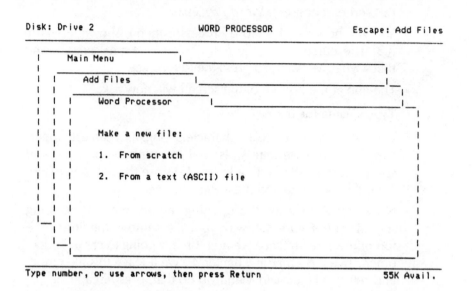

```
Disk: Drive 2                   WORD PROCESSOR              Escape: Add Files
_____
|      Main Menu            |_____
|                          |                                         |
|  |     Add Files           |_____|_
|  |                        |                                        |_
|  |  |   Word Processor       |_____|_
|  |  |                                                               |
|  |  |                                                               |
|  |  |   Make a new file:                                            |
|  |  |                                                               |
|  |  |   1.  From scratch                                            |
|  |  |                                                               |
|  |  |   2.  From a text (ASCII) file                                |
|  |  |                                                               |
|  |  |                                                               |
|  |  |                                                               |
|__|  |                                                               |
   |__|                                                               |
      |                                                               |
      |_____|
_____
Type number, or use arrows, then press Return              55K Avail.
```

Figure 3.3: The Word Processor menu.

```
File: WPTEST                    REVIEW/ADD/CHANGE          Escape: Main Menu
=====|====|====|====|====|====|====|====|====|====|====|====|====|====|===
```

```
-------------------------------------------------------------------------
Type entry or use ? commands        Line 1   Column  1       ?-? for Help
```

Figure 3.4: The opening Word Processing screen.

The screen now shows you the Add Files menu once more. This time, we want to create a new file for the Data Base program, so choose 1. Add files to the Desktop. When the Add Files menu appears, choose 4. Data Base.

When asked what kind of file you want to create, choose 1. From scratch. For the file name, type DBTEST and press Return. This time you'll be shown the opening Data Base screen. Again, since we are not actually going to use the Data Base program just yet, return to the Main Menu by pressing Escape three times.

Go on now to create an empty Spreadsheet file, going through the same procedure we have used for the Word Processor and the Data Base programs. When you're done, return to the Main Menu.

Listing the Files on the Current Disk

When you need to know what files are on your data disk, you can easily get a list of them. This section shows you how. Be sure the Main Menu is on the screen. Choose 5. Other Activities. When the Other Activities menu appears, choose 2. List all files on the current disk drive.

You'll be shown the list of files on the current data disk, starting with those in AppleWorks format. With a single drive system, you will need to take out the Program disk and replace it with your data disk. With a two-drive system or a hard disk, AppleWorks will automatically look on the drive you have specified as your standard data disk location. Other files will be listed alphabetically after the AppleWorks files, and identified as either Subdirectory or Other. If there are more than 10 files, you'll see the word *more* at the bottom of the screen. You can see the rest of the files by pressing the down-arrow key.

If you do have files noted as Subdirectory, these were created under ProDOS and are, in fact, the names of subdirectories containing further files. To see those files, change the location of your default data disk to a ProDOS prefix that includes the name of the subdirectory, then list those files.

When you are finished checking your file directory, return to the Other Activities menu by pressing the Escape key.

Working with an Existing File

Be sure the Main Menu is on your screen. Choose 2. Work with one of the files on the Desktop. The screen now looks like Figure 3.5.

Choose WPTEST and you will see the opening screen of the Word Processor, with the file name WPTEST indicated in the top line. If we had entered text when we created this file, that text would also be displayed. The blinking underline is in the upper-left corner, waiting for you to enter something.

Type something. It can be "This is a test" or anything else you'd like to say. When you are through, press Escape. This puts your newly revised document in temporary storage on the Desktop, much as if you'd slipped a note into a folder you intended to come back to later. By pressing Escape, you perform an action that is equivalent to closing the file folder, but not putting it away. You can come back to precisely this spot in your file and continue working on it any time before you quit the session or save this file.

So now you have three files on your Desktop: a Word Processing file which has some text in it, and a Spreadsheet file and a Data Base file that are empty. All are available to you immediately on the Desktop.

Saving a Desktop File on Disk

You may wish to save one of your files on disk before you finish working with the rest of them on the Desktop. Or you may, for safety's

```
Disk: Drive 2               MAIN MENU              Escape: Main Menu
_____

 I    Main Menu            I_____
 I                         I                                      I
 I                         I                                      I
 I   1.  Add files to the Desktop                                 I
 I                                                                I
 I   --> Work with one   _____                   I
 I                       I     Desktop Index   I                  I
 I   3.  Save Desktop    I---------------------I                  I
 I                       I 1.   WPTEST     WP  I                  I
 I   4.  Remove files    I 2.   SSTEST     SS  I                  I
 I                       I 3.   DBTEST     DB  I                  I
 I   5.  Other Activit   I_____I                  I
 I                                                                I
 I   6.  Quit                                                     I
 I                                                                I
 I_____I


_____
Type number, or use arrows, then press Return          55K Avail.
```

Figure 3.5: The Main Menu with Desktop Index.

sake, want to save one of your Desktop files even though you continue to work on it.

As a safety precaution, AppleWorks writes the new version of your file on disk before it deletes a previous one. That way, if anything goes wrong with the actual writing of the new file, the old one is still intact. Only when the disk writing process has been successfully completed does AppleWorks go ahead and delete the old file. Thus one of the things you should keep in mind when your disk is beginning to get full is that AppleWorks will need enough room to store both the old and new versions of the file.

To save a file, call up the Main Menu and choose 3. Save Desktop files to disk. You'll see the Save Files menu shown in Figure 3.6.

Use the arrow keys to move the shaded bar to the file you want to save. In this case, we're going to save WPTEST, so you don't have to move the bar at all. To save the file simply press the right-arrow key, then Return. When you are asked how you want to save the file, specify that it is to be on the current disk. If you have a single drive system you'll be prompted to put your Data disk in Drive 1 before the information can be saved. With a two drive system this prompt will not appear. Don't forget to press Return.

```
Disk: Drive 2                  SAVE FILES              Escape: Main Menu
_____

 |    Main Menu         |_____
 |    _____|                                          |
 | |    Save Files      |_____|__
 | |    Name            Status      Document type    Size           |
 | |    ==============================================              |
 | |    WPTEST          New         Word Processor   1K             |
 | |    SSTEST          New         Spreadsheet      1K             |
 | |    DBTEST          New         Data Base        1K             |
 | |                                                                |
 | |                                                                |
 | |                                                                |
 | |                                                                |
 | |                                                                |
 | |_|                                                              |
 |   |                                                              |
 |___|_____|
_____
Use Right Arrow to choose files, Left Arrow to undo          55K Avail.
```

Figure 3.6: The Save Files menu.

Now where are we? We have the file WPTEST saved on disk, and all three of our files active on the Desktop. We can modify them, or delete them, or even save them on another disk if we wish.

Deleting a File from the Desktop

Just as when the top of your desk occasionally gets too full for you to find anything, so you will sometimes have to clean up the Desktop. You can save a file on disk and delete it from the Desktop. Or you can delete the file, without saving it, though AppleWorks will ask you first if you really mean to do that.

Let's try deleting a file from the Desktop.

Be sure the Program disk is in Drive 1 (for a single drive system), and that the Main Menu is on your screen. Choose 4. Remove files from the Desktop. AppleWorks then displays the Remove Files menu shown in Figure 3.7.

Since we already saved WPTEST, it's a logical one to delete. But let's also delete SSTEST at the same time. Press the right-arrow key to choose WPTEST, then use the arrow keys to highlight SSTEST and use the right-arrow key to choose it as well. Then press Return.

```
Disk: Drive 2               REMOVE FILES              Escape: Main Menu
 _____
 I    Main Menu              I_____
 I                           I                                        I
 I   I  Remove Files         I_____I_
 I   I  Name                 Status      Document type     Size      I
 I   I  ===============================================================
 I   I  WPTEST               Saved       Word Processor    1K        I
 I   I  SSTEST               New         Spreadsheet       1K        I
 I   I  DBTEST               New         Data Base         1K        I
 I   I                                                               I
 I   I                                                               I
 I   I                                                               I
 I   I                                                               I
 I   I                                                               I
 I_I                                                               I
     I                                                             I
     I_____I

 Use Right Arrow to choose files, Left Arrow to undo        54K Avail.
```

Figure 3.7: The Remove Files menu.

Because you are indicating that you want to discard a file without saving it (SSTEST), AppleWorks gives you the option of saving it first. (Notice that, since you've already saved WPTEST, AppleWorks doesn't question your judgment there.) But we have decided to do without SSTEST, so choose 3. Throw out the new file. When AppleWorks asks if you really want to do this, answer Y. AppleWorks will return you to the Main Menu.

Quitting AppleWorks—Round 2

We discussed quitting the program at the end of the last chapter, and since we hadn't created any files yet, it was quite straightforward. Now that we have one file saved and another still on the Desktop, quitting is not quite so simple. But AppleWorks is still looking out for your welfare, so the few extra steps required should be considered as a safety measure.

On the Main Menu choose 6. Quit. When AppleWorks asks you if you really want to quit, answer by typing Y. Here's where AppleWorks handles some housekeeping for you.

You still have one file left on your Desktop, and you haven't told AppleWorks what to do with it. You can:

1. Save the file on the current disk (along with WPTEST).

2. Change to a different disk or directory. You'll have to specify which one.

3. Discard the file. You'll be asked if you really want to do that, as you were in the Remove File menu.

If you reconsider and do want to save the file, choose the first or second option. If you decide to discard the file, choose the third option. If you choose 3. and *then* change your mind, type N when asked if you really want to go ahead with this; you'll be given the same three choices again.

Since you have an empty file in DBTEST, there's no need to save it, choose 3. Throw out the new file. Answer Y when asked to verify your choice. You will now have exited the AppleWorks program, and see the following message on your screen:

ENTER PREFIX (PRESS "RETURN" TO ACCEPT)

/APPLEWORKS/

At this point, you may turn off the machine or go on to another application.

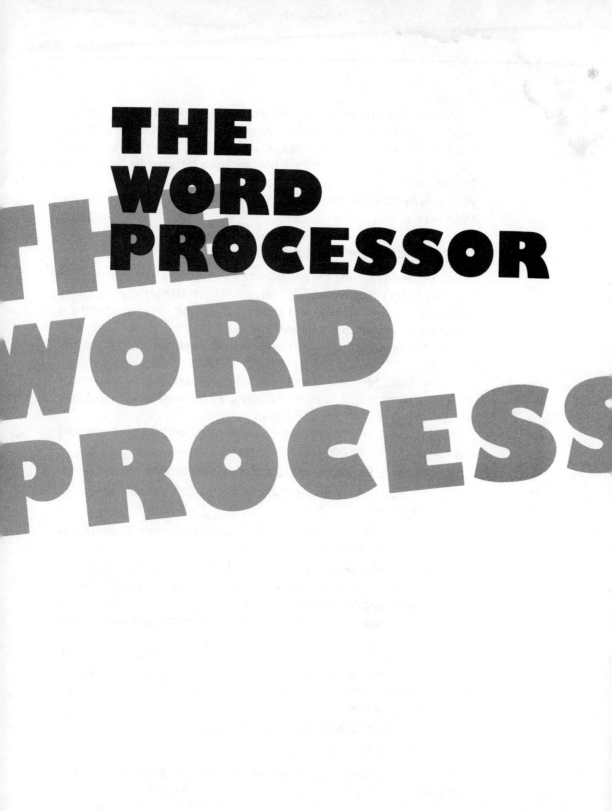

THE
WORD
PROCESSOR

CHAPTER 4

No doubt you've been in situations like these:

- You've just finished typing a 5-page report. Checking for typographical errors, you discover that you repeated a sentence from the bottom of one page on the top of the next.
- You've just finished typing a business proposal when you discover that your addition was wrong; you need to reword some of the concluding paragraphs.
- You've embarked on a sales campaign where letters need to be individually typed, but most of the content of each can be substantially the same.

AppleWorks' word processor allows you to catch your errors and fix them without retyping before you print a document. It also gives you the flexibility to use a document as a kind of standard form, and print it out repeatedly, each time modifying only certain portions of it as needed.

What distinguishes AppleWorks' word processor from others is the fact that it is integrated with the two other programs in the package—the spreadsheet and the data base. You can transfer information from one program to another without ever leaving AppleWorks. You do this with the Desktop's cut-and-paste capabilities, which we'll discuss in Chapter 8.

Creating a Document with the Word Processor

In this chapter, we are going to show you how to construct, edit, and save a document using the AppleWorks word processor. Our sample is going to be the letter that we looked at in Chapter One from a sports clothes company to its customers.

Boot up the AppleWorks program and progress through the opening commands until you have the Main Menu on your screen. Since this will be a new file, choose 1. Add files to the Desktop. Now choose to create a new file for the Word Processor from scratch. Give it the name CYCLELETTER. The opening Word Processor screen appears, and looks like Figure 4.1.

The line at the top of the screen gives you some status information about the program:

- The file you're currently working on is called CYCLELETTER.
- You can review, add to, or change the contents of the file.
- If you press Escape, you will be returned to the Main Menu.

The broken line under that is called the Ruler, and shows you where the tab stops are. You can change the tab stops, and later in this chapter we'll show you how.

The insert cursor is blinking on the far left of the next line under the ruler.

The dashed line near the bottom of the screen shows you how much text you can see at once. You can fit 20 lines on your screen at once. When you get to the 21st line, the top line will scroll off the top of the

```
File: CYCLELETTER             REVIEW/ADD/CHANGE             Escape: Main Menu
=====|====|====|====|====|====|====|====|====|====|====|====|====|====|===
```

```
------------------------------------------------------------------------
Type entry or use ä commands        Line 1  Column  1        ä-? for Help
```

Figure 4.1: The opening Word Processor screen.

screen so that you are still looking at 20 lines of text. You can scroll up and down in your letter by using the up-arrow and down-arrow keys.

The bottom line on the screen is used for helpful information. Right now the item on the left tells you what kinds of entries you can make. The item in the middle tells you where you are in the document, and the entry on the right shows you what keys to press if you'd like to see some helpful tips about the program.

Entering Information

You're going to enter the following sample letter, as shown here, in the file CYCLELETTER. But there are few things you should know before you start typing:

- There are two kinds of cursors: the blinking underline is the insert cursor, and the blinking rectangle is the overstrike cursor. The insert cursor, which is normally used, means that whatever you type will be inserted at the point where the cursor is located and existing text will move over to make room. The overstrike cursor means that whatever you type will replace the text that is already there. You get from one kind of cursor to the other by pressing the Open-Apple key together with the letter and E.

- You can move the cursor up and down from line to line with the up-arrow and down-arrow keys.

- You can move the cursor horizontally, one character at a time, by using the right-arrow and left-arrow keys.

- You can move the cursor to the next tab stop by pressing the TAB key.

- You can move the cursor to the right one *word* by pressing the Open-Apple and right-arrow keys, or to the left one word by pressing the Open-Apple and left-arrow keys. By holding down the keys, the cursor will continue moving in that direction until you release the keys.

- You can move the cursor up to the top of the screen and then up another 20 lines by pressing the Open-Apple and up-arrow keys, or down the same amount by pressing the Open-Apple and down-arrow keys.

- You can delete the character to the left of the cursor by pressing the Delete key.

- You can delete the rest of line to the right of the cursor by pressing Control and the letter Y.

- You can mark a block of text to be deleted by moving the cursor to the beginning or end of the block, typing Open-Apple and the letter D, then moving the cursor to the other end of the block. AppleWorks will highlight the block thus enclosed. When the entire block that you want to delete is highlighted, press Return. AppleWorks will close up the remaining text.

- When AppleWorks gets to the end of a line with a word not completed, it will move the word to the beginning of the next line. You do not have to press Return, unless you want to go to a new line *before* reaching the end of the previous line. This feature is called *Word Wrap.*

- When you press Return while entering text, the cursor automatically moves to the far left of the next line, just the way the carriage return works on an electric typewriter. Use Return at the end of a paragraph, or the end of a partial line, such as the lines in an address.

Typing the Sample Letter

With the blinking underline in the upper-left corner of the blank word processor screen, type the following letter:

September 25, 1984

Charles Anderson
Cycle World, Inc.
149 Woodside Road
Redwood City, CA 94644

Dear Mr. Anderson:

As you know, U.S. attention to the sport of cycling was heightened by the performance of American athletes in the recent Olympic cycling events. We feel this is the major reason for the dramatic surge in orders for cycling clothing and accessories in the past two months. While we anticipated a somewhat higher demand, we did not expect to be swamped with orders as we have been in the last five weeks.

As a result, we have been unable to meet our customers' orders as promptly as we expected. We have been negotiating with our current manufacturers, and now feel we can keep pace with the demand. We will complete your order within the next two weeks, and ship it to you no later than three weeks from now. We hope your customers will understand that the delay is due to overwhelming demand.

Yours truly,

Linda Smith-Gorski

Your most recent order to us was as follows:

Amount	Item	Size
20	Men's black cycling shorts	S
50	Men's black cycling shorts	M
40	Men's black cycling shorts	L
10	Pegasus shirts: blue/yellow	S
30	Pegasus shirts: blue/yellow	M
20	Pegasus shirts: red/yellow	M
20	Pegasus shirts: blue/yellow	L
20	Pegasus shirts: red/yellow	L
10	Pegasus shirts: red/yellow	XL
35	Waist packs	one size

Your letter is 48 lines long, and so it won't all fit on the screen at once. To see the rest of the letter, use the up-arrow and down-arrow, or use the Open-Apple with the up-arrow and down-arrow. If you have made errors, correct them with the keystrokes explained above.

Searching for Information

Occasionally it is important for you to be able to find where in a document you put a particular piece of information. AppleWorks will search it out for you. For instance, if you were suspicious of the way you might have spelled the word "cycling," you could search for it this way:

1. Position the cursor at the top of the area where the word may have occurred.

2. Press the Open-Apple and F keys. The line at the bottom of the screen says

   Find? Text Page Marker Case sensitive text Options for printer

3. Since you want to find only a single word (*Text* can mean a single word or several words) and the word Text is highlighted, press Return.

4. The line now asks

   Find what text?

5. Type the word 'cycling' exactly as it occurs and press Return.

6. The first instance of the word in the letter is highlighted, and the line at the bottom of the screen asks

   Find next occurrence? No Yes

7. If you were sure there was only one occurrence, you could choose the No option. But since you used the word more than once, use the right-arrow to choose Yes and press the Return key.

8. Repeat step 7 until the computer beeps and the line comments

   Not found, press Space Bar to continue.

   How else could you use the Find command?

- If you choose Page, you can jump to a particular page in a document.
- If you choose Marker, you can jump to a preplaced marker— especially handy in a long document.
- If you choose Case sensitive text, the program will search for the words only where they are capitalized or lowercase as you specify, rather than for all occurrences of the words.
- If you specify Options for printer, you will see the list of printer options overlaying your text, and you'll be asked to specify which printer option is to be found. This is especially useful for situations where you need to change a margin, or mark an area for subscripts or superscripts.

Replacing Information

Sometimes you need to replace text within a document. AppleWorks lets you replace one, several, or all occurrences of a string of text within a document with a new string. You can replace all occurrences automatically or have the program check with you about each one. Both the new and old strings can be up to 30 characters long.

Suppose, for example, you've finished typing your letter and are about to send it out, when you discover that Mr. Anderson didn't order the Pegasus shirts at all: the model he ordered was Mercury. What do you do? You could use the cursor and the Delete key to delete each reference to Pegasus, retyping each one as Mercury. Or you could use AppleWorks' search and replace function. It's a whole lot easier to do the latter.

To replace all instances of the word Pegasus, follow these steps:

1. Position the cursor at the beginning of the area where the word Pegasus occurs.

2. Since you want to *replace* the word, you'll need to switch cursors. Press Open-Apple and E to use the overstrike cursor.

3. Press the Open-Apple and R keys.

4. The line at the bottom of the screen asks

   Replace? Text Case sensitive text

   The word Text is highlighted, and since that is the option we want, press Return.

5. AppleWorks now asks

   Find what?

   and offers the previous character string as a suggestion. Type the word Pegasus, and press Return.

6. Now the line asks

   Replace with what?

7. Type the word Mercury and press Return.

8. The line now asks

   Replace? One at a time All

   Since you want to replace all occurrences of Pegasus with Mercury, use the right-arrow key to move the highlighting to All and press Return.

Notice on your screen that all the places that used to say Pegasus now say Mercury. If you had chosen One at a time, Appleworks would have highlighted each occurrence of the word Pegasus, and asked you if you wanted to replace that one.

Moving Text

You can move blocks of text within an AppleWorks file, or to or from the Clipboard. We'll look at moving text within a file in this chapter, and at moving text to and from the Clipboard in Chapter 8.

Sometimes when you are through typing a letter or a report, and you're looking at the first draft, you realize that a section would make more sense if it were placed differently. If you were just using a typewriter, this would entail retyping at least the page or pages affected, or sometimes most or all of the document. With AppleWorks, a few keystrokes will move the section and print out the revised text.

Let's see how the Move command works with our sample letter. We'd like to move the order summary up into the body of the letter, right after the second paragraph. Follow these steps:

1. Move the cursor to the first character of the area you want to move. In this case, that's the letter Y in Your.

2. Press Open-Apple and M.

3. The line at the bottom of the screen asks

   Move Text? Within document To clipboard (cut) From clipboard (paste)

   Since you want to move the text within the document, and the highlighting is on that choice, simply press Return. (Apple-Works now shows you the text with all carriage returns and printer commands displayed, normally they are not shown.)

4. Move the cursor to the last character of the area you want to move. Notice that as you move the cursor, the area thus enclosed appears highlighted. If you want to use a blank line at the beginning or end of your block, be sure to move the cursor so that the blank line falls within the highlighting.

5. Press the Return key. This locks-in the block to be moved.

6. Now move the cursor to the point where the block is to go (notice that the cursor is invisible within the highlighting). Press Return and the block is moved.

7. At this point, you may have to adjust the spacing, inserting a space or blank line or remove one. But any spacing within a

paragraph is done for you, automatically, so that right and left margins are observed. The area that used to contain the block of information is closed up, although you may have to adjust the spacing here as well.

Now your letter looks like Figure 4.2.

September 25, 1984

Charles Anderson
Cycle World, Inc.
149 Woodside Road
Redwood City, CA 94644

Dear Mr. Anderson:

As you know, U.S. attention to the sport of cycling was heightened by the performance of American athletes in the recent Olympic cycling events. We feel this is the major reason for the dramatic surge in orders for cycling clothing and accessories in the past two months. While we anticipated a somewhat higher demand, we did not expect to be swamped with orders as we have been in the last five weeks.

As a result, we have been unable to meet our customers' orders as promptly as we expected. We have been negotiating with our current manufacturers, and now feel we can keep pace with the demand.

Your most recent order to us was as follows:

Amount	Item	Size
20	Men's black cycling shorts	S
50	Men's black cycling shorts	M
40	Men's black cycling shorts	L
10	Pegasus shirts: blue/yellow	S
30	Pegasus shirts: blue/yellow	M
20	Pegasus shirts: red/yellow	M
20	Pegasus shirts: blue/yellow	L
20	Pegasus shirts: red/yellow	L
10	Pegasus shirts: red/yellow	XL
35	Waist packs	one size

We will complete your order within the next two weeks, and ship it to you no later than three weeks from now. We hope your customers will understand that the delay is due to overwhelming demand.

Yours truly,

Linda Smith-Gorski

Figure 4.2: The cycle letter after block move.

Copying Blocks of Information

Sometimes it's convenient to be able to copy text from one place to another within a document. You can do this in AppleWorks by using the Copy command. This differs from Move in that the text remains intact in its original location, as well as appearing in the new location.

The Copy command is particularly useful if you are using standard phrases or paragraphs, known as *boilerplate text,* or if you are setting up tables or charts with the same or similar headings and spacing.

The Copy command works in much the same way as the Move command:

1. Move the cursor to the first character of the block of text you want to copy.

2. Press Open-Apple and C.

3. The line at the bottom of the screen asks

   Copy Text? Within document To clipboard (cut) From clipboard (paste)

   To copy text within the document, simply press Return. (The carriage returns and printer commands are displayed.)

4. Move the cursor to the last character of the area you want to copy. As you move the cursor, the area thus enclosed is high-lighted.

5. Press Return. This locks-in the block to be copied.

6. Now move the cursor to the point where the text is to be copied and press Return. The block is copied.

Using Markers

Markers are handy to use when you're working with a large document and need to jump around. With AppleWorks, you can set one or more markers, go away and do something else, and then come back to one of your preset markers for further work. Markers are not characters that actually print; they are only used to spot the cursor.

To set a marker, follow these steps:

1. Move the cursor to the location where you want the marker to be placed.

2. Press Open-Apple and the letter O (not zero). The printer options menu will appear, overlaying your text on the screen.

3. Type SM (for Set Marker) and press Return.

4. Type the number of the marker (any number between 1 and 254) and press Return. You will see the note

– – – – – –Set a Marker:

followed by the number you designated. The number appears above the marked point in the text.

5. Press the Escape key. Your text returns as it normally appears, without the printer options menu or hidden characters.

Now suppose you have moved somewhere else in the document and wish to return to one of your markers. Here's how:

1. Press Open-Apple and F.

2. The bottom line on the screen will ask

Find? Text Page Marker Case sensitive text Options for printer

Use the Right-arrow key to position the highlighting over the word Marker, then press Return.

3. The bottom line now asks

Marker number?

4. Type the number of the marker you want to return to, and press Return.

5. You'll also be asked if you want to find the next occurrence of the same number. Answer N. Then your text will appear with the marker and hidden characters showing. To return your text to its normal condition, without removing the marker, press Escape.

Tabs

The Ruler line at the top of the word processor screen shows you where the tabs are set. Each vertical line represents one tab stop. All new documents have tabs set every five spaces.

To set or clear a tab, follow these steps:

1. Press Open-Apple and T. The cursor moves to the far left of the Ruler line.

2. Use the right-arrow and left-arrow to move the cursor to wherever you want to set or clear a tab stop.

3. To set a tab at this location, type S. To clear a tab here, type C. To remove all existing tabs, type R.

4. If you wish to continue setting or clearing tabs, move the cursor to the appropriate spots and type the correct letter for what you want to do. When you are through setting and clearing tabs, press Escape.

Changing the Name of Your File

Suppose you want to keep two versions of the same file. You can't call them the same name—AppleWorks wouldn't know which one you want when you ask for it by name. But you can change the name of the version you're using on the Desktop, and keep the stored version under its old name on your data disk.

To change the name of the file you're currently using on the Desktop, follow these steps:

1. Press Open-Apple and N.

2. The bottom line will ask

   Type filename: [**your current file name appears here**]

3. Type the new name of the file. Notice that as you type it, the old filename is pushed to the right until there are 15 characters showing. Then as you type more letters, any characters over 15 are chopped off. To totally eliminate any characters of the old filename, type spaces to the right to total 15 characters.

4. Press Return.

Summary

There you have it! You've used AppleWorks' word processor to create a letter. You've learned how to move the cursor within your text, and how to edit your text by inserting and deleting items. You've moved a block and you've learned how to copy a block. You've learned how to search for a string, and how to replace it with new string. You've learned how to set and find markers, and how to set and clear tabs, and you've learned how to change the name of the file you're working on. That's a lot!

Now all that remains is to save your file. You can do that by returning to the Main Menu and using 3. Save Desktop files to disk, as we discussed in Chapter 2, or you can save your file in the Quit process as we outlined in Chapter 3.

PRINTER
OPTIONS

CHAPTER 5

In a few instances in the last chapter, you used a command that caused the Printer Options menu to appear, overlaying the text that had been on your screen. We didn't explore that menu at the time, but in this chapter we will.

The printer options allow you to specify such things as margins, line spacing, indents, justification or centering, headers and footers, page numbering, underlining, boldface, subscripts, and superscripts.

Some printer options remain in effect until you change them. Others hold only until the end of the paragraph or line you're working on, or until you stop them, whichever is sooner. Still others are used to communicate information to the printer—such as skipping lines—but do not do anything to the text you see on the screen.

How to See the Printer Options

Any time you are in the AppleWorks word processor, and you want to see the printer options, press Open-Apple and the letter O (not zero). The Printer Options menu will appear (see Figure 5.1), overlaying your text on the screen. (Your text is still there—it will reappear in full when you close up the Printer Options menu by pressing the Escape key.)

To request one of the Printer Options, follow these steps:

1. Before calling up the options menu, position the cursor where you want the option to take effect. If you want the option to apply to the entire document, move the cursor to the top of your document, using Open-Apple and the number 1.

2. Press Open-Apple and O (not zero). This causes the Printer Options menu to be displayed.

3. Type the code for the printer option you want. Press Return.

4. Type the new value if AppleWorks asks for one. This can be like the marker numbers we discussed in the last chapter, or it can be a measurement, such as 1 inch or 1.5 inches. If you are typing a whole number, such as 1 inch, you don't have to type the decimal part.

5. Specify any other printer options you want. Press Return after each one.

6. When you are through with the printer options, press Escape.

Notice that, when the Printer Options menu is on your screen, your text is displayed with the normally hidden control characters visible. Thus you can see exactly where your printer option control characters go, and what they affect.

Default Values

Certain options and values, such as margin widths are in effect for a new file at the outset. These are the *default values* set up automatically by AppleWorks. They are displayed in the shaded bar at the top of the

```
File: CYCLELETTER                PRINTER OPTIONS        Escape: Review/Add/Change
=====|====|====|====|====|====|====|====|====|====|====|====|====|====|===
```

```
       PW=8.0   LM=1.0   RM=1.0  CI=10  UJ   PL=11.0  TM=0.0  BM=2.0  LI=6  SS
Option:                       UJ: Unjustified      GB: Group Begin      BE: Boldface End
                              CN: Centered         GE: Group End        +B: Superscript Beg
PW: Platen Width              PL: Paper Length     HE: Page Header      +E: Superscript End
LM: Left Margin               TM: Top Margin       FO: Page Footer      -B: Subscript Begin
RM: Right Margin              BM: Bottom Margin    SK: Skip Lines       -E: Subscript End
CI: Chars per Inch            LI: Lines per Inch   PN: Page Number      UB: Underline Begin
P1: Proportional-1            SS: Single Space     PE: Pause Each page  UE: Underline End
P2: Proportional-2            DS: Double Space     PH: Pause Here       PP: Print Page No.
IN: Indent                    TS: Triple Space     SM: Set a Marker     EK: Enter Keyboard
JU: Justified                 NP: New Page         BB: Boldface Begin
```

Figure 5.1: The Printer Options Menu.

menu. Until you change them, these values are:

Platen Width: 8.0 inches	(this is the width of your paper)
Left Margin: 1.0 inches	(measured from the paper's left edge)
Right Margin: 1.0 inches	(measured from the paper's right edge)
Characters per Inch: 10	(measured horizontally)
Unjustified	(you'll have a "ragged" right margin)
Page Length: 11.0 inches	(including top and bottom margins)
Top Margin: 1.0 inches	
Bottom Margin: 2.0 inches	
Lines per Inch: 6	
Single Space	

If you change any printer options, they will apply to this file only, and will not affect any other word processor files on the Desktop. Depending on the option, some can be stored with the file, but others will disappear when the session ends or you remove the file from the Desktop.

The discussion below groups the options under common headings, and does not reflect the order in which they appear on the screen.

Horizontal and Vertical Spacing

The three options that control horizontal spacing are platen width, left margin, and right margin.

Platen Width (PW) means the distance the print head travels across the page when printing. The print head should stop at the left edge of the paper. This number (maximum 13.2 inches, default 8 inches) should be equal to or less than the platen width you set permanently with the Other Activities menu option 7. Specify information about your printer(s). (This also has a default value of 8 inches.)

Left Margin (LM) is the width of the left margin in inches, measured from the left edge of the paper to the first character of text. (Maximum 9 inches, default 1 inch.)

Right Margin (RM) is the width of the right margin in inches, measured from the last character on a right justified line to the right edge of the paper. (Maximum 9 inches, default 1 inch.)

Subtract your right and left margin widths from the platen width to get the width of your text. Multiply that by the number of characters per inch (discussed below) to get the number of characters per line of your text.

The eight options that control vertical spacing are paper length, top margin, bottom margin, single, double, or triple spacing, lines per inch, and skipping lines.

Paper length (PL) is the height of the paper you are using, in inches. (Maximum 25.4 inches, default 11 inches.)

Top Margin (TM) is the length in inches from the top of the paper to the first line of printing. (Maximum 9 inches, default 0 inches.) If you use a tractor-feed printer you should reset this. If you have a sheet-fed printer, you should use the default value and position the sheet so that the print head is exactly where you want the first line to be. Any header is printed on the first line after the top margin, and is followed by two blank lines before beginning the page text.

Bottom Margin (BM) is the length in inches from the last line of printing to the bottom of the paper. (Maximum 9 inches, default 2 inches.) The page number and any footers are printed on the last line before the bottom margin, but are preceded by two blank lines, so any text stops at least three lines before the bottom margin.

Single, Double, and Triple Space (SS, DS, or TS) control how much white space there is between lines of printed text. You can change the spacing wherever you want in a document. (Default: single spacing.) All text is displayed on your screen as single spaced; double and triple spacing take effect only when you print.

Lines per Inch (LI) determines how many single spaced lines of print will appear per vertical inch. You can specify 6 or 8 (default: 6).

Skip Lines (SK) is the number of lines the printer should leave blank at a specified point to leave room for something not handled by Apple-works, such as an illustration. The most lines you can skip is the number of lines on your page.

You can determine the number of potential lines on your page by subtracting the top and bottom margin from the page length, then multiplying the result by the number of lines per inch. To determine the number of lines for any given page, of course, you will have to adjust for headers and footers, subtract any lines skipped, and adjust for any double or triple spacing.

The print density options also affect horizontal spacing, but in another way. The print density options include the number of Characters per Inch (CI), and two kinds of Proportional Spacing (P1 and P2).

The Characters-per-Inch option and Proportional Spacing options work together to produce different effects, and these in turn depend on the kind of printer (dot matrix or letter-quality) that you have.

With the Characters-per-Inch option, you can specify that your printer print from 4 to 24 characters per inch. If you wish non-proportional spacing, ignore the P1 and P2 options; each character will take up the same amount of horizontal space, whether the letter is wide (like an m) or narrow (like an i). With a dot matrix printer, a higher number of characters per inch will result in thinner, more dense-appearing text. With a letter-quality printer, such as a Daisy wheel printer, you will have to change the print wheel to the same "pitch" or number as you have specified in order to have the characters print correctly. If you choose a print density your printer doesn't have, AppleWorks uses the last one specified.

The Proportional Spacing options work with the Characters-per-Inch option to determine how text is spread across each line. If you use proportional spacing, AppleWorks assumes you want each line right- and left-justified, and tries to spread the spacing between words (for letter-quality printers) or between letters (for dot-matrix printers) equally. Examples of how these options work with different printers are shown in the AppleWorks *Reference Manual,* pages 140 and 141.

Indenting

Indenting is a useful feature when you want to set off several lines or paragraphs from the rest of the text. We've used indenting many times in this book, when we list instructions, for example. To illustrate,

> this is an indented paragraph, the purpose of which is simply to demonstrate how an indent can be used.

> You can indent just the left margin, as we have done above, or you can indent just the right margin, or you can indent both the left and right margins, as in this paragraph.

> You can create hanging paragraphs like this, where the first line is flush with the left margin , but succeeding lines are indented a specified number of spaces.

> • You can also create list-like paragraphs or sentences by preceding each sentence with a •.

- The "bullets" preceding each set of sentences make the set stand out from the rest of the text.

To use the indenting feature,

1. Have the cursor on the last character before the paragraph or sentence to be indented. Press Open-Apple and the letter O.

2. Change the left and/or right margins if you need to. Remember, all text will be right-and left-justified according to the new margins until you reset them again.

3. Type IN (for Insert) and press Return.

4. Type the number of spaces you want to indent succeeding text. Press Return.

5. Press the Escape key.

Type your indented text, including any bullets or hanging paragraphs. You may want to combine indenting with tabs to create the proper look. When you are finished, reset things by following these steps:

1. Have the cursor on the last character before normal text is to resume. Press Open-Apple and the letter O.

2. Type IN and press Return.

3. Type 0 (zero) as a value for the Indent, and press Return.

4. Reset any margins you may have changed.

5. Press Escape.

Justifying

Word processing text is either left-justified, right- and left-justified, or centered. You can specify any of these options.

The default for this option in AppleWorks is left-justified text. Our sample letter to cycle clothing retailers shows an example of this. All lines are flush with the left margin, but they end on the right wherever the last full word ends, thus producing a *ragged-right* margin. This paragraph is an example of a ragged-right margin. To specify this kind of right margin, either use the default, or specify UJ (for UnJustified) in the Printer Options.

Sometimes you prefer that your text have lines that end flush with the right margin. This is called Right-Justified, and to get it, you specify

JU in the Printer Options. This paragraph, like most of the text in this book, is set Right-Justified. AppleWorks distributes the spaces between words so that the last word in each line always ends at the right margin.

The last option in this category is *centering*. The lines in this
paragraph show you an example of text that is centered. To
center a line, or a set of lines, type CN when you set
Printer Options. All lines, from this point on until you reset
(by specifying JU or UJ), will be centered, much like the
lines in this paragraph have been centered.

Whatever justification option you use will remain in force until you change it.

Headers and Footers

Headers and *footers* are handy reference aids in large documents. They help a reader flipping through pages tell what section he is in without referring back to a table of contents.

A header looks like this:

Chapter 1   Getting Started

Text text text text text text text text text text text text text text text text text text text text text text text text text text text text text text text text text text text text text text text

And a footer looks like this:

Text text text text text text text text text text text text text text text text text text text text text text text text text text text text text text text text text text text text text text text text

Page 15   Getting Started

You will have to sacrifice some lines of text on each page to fit in either headers or footers. The one-line header (which can contain the page number) goes on the first printing line of each page, and is followed by two blank lines before the text begins. The one-line footer (which also can contain the page number) appears on the bottom printing line of the page. AppleWorks skips two lines after the last line of text before printing the footer.

For instance, suppose you have set your page length to 11 inches, and you have accepted the default top and bottom margins of 1 and 2 inches, respectively. Here's how to calculate how many lines of text you will have to work with after you add a header and a footer:

Page length:	11 inches
Top margin:	− 1 inch
Bottom margin:	− 2 inches
	————
Available for text:	8 inches
Lines per inch:	x 6
	————
	48 lines
Header	− 1
blank lines	− 2
	————
	45 lines
Footer	− 1
blank lines	− 2
	————
Remaining for text:	42 lines

In the example above, we used AppleWorks default values. You may wish to create more room for text when you use headers and footers by reducing the amount of space for top and bottom margins, or by specifying just a header or a footer, but not both.

To add a header or footer, follow these steps:

1. Position the cursor correctly for the header or footer. If you want a header, the cursor must be at the top of the page. If you want a footer, the cursor can be anywhere on the page. In either case, the cursor must be on the page where the header or footer is to start.

2. Press Open-Apple and the letter O.

3. Type HE for a header, or FO for a footer, and press Return.

4. Press Escape. Notice that the label

    − − − −**Page Header**

          or

    − − − −**Page Footer**

    appears where the information is supposed to go, and that the cursor is at the left margin, directly under the reminder.

5. Type the header or footer as if it were a line of text, complete with proper spacing and justification. Whatever follows the Page Header or Page Footer reminder will print as the page header or footer.

Notice also that the letter on your screen contains this information as if it were part of the text. When printed, neither of the reminders will appear, only the text you specified.

The header or footer will continue to appear on each succeeding page until you tell it to stop. You stop a header or footer by calling up the Printer Option menu, specifying header or footer, and instead of text, pressing the Return key to create a blank line. The reminders – – – – Page Header or – – – – Page Footer will continue to appear on your screen, but they will have no effect.

You can also use page numbers in a header or footer. We'll discuss that below in the section on Pagination.

Boldface and Underlining

You can use *boldface* or *underlines* with one word, several words, or even a whole paragraph. In each case, you'll need to put *control characters* before and after the text you want to give special treatment. **This is an example of boldface,** and this is an example of underlining.

To boldface a word or set of words, follow these steps:

1. Position the cursor on the first letter of the first word you want to put in boldface.
2. Press Control and the letter B together.
3. Move the cursor to the first character (or space) after the word or words to be in boldface.
4. Again, press Control and the letter B together.

To underline a word or set of words, follow the same instructions, but substitute Control-L for Control-B in steps 2 and 4.

You can also use the Printer Options menu to boldface or underline. When you are asked for the option, type BB for Boldface Begin, BE for Boldface End, UB for Underline Begin, and UE for Underline End.

Both methods will place a caret (^) before and after the word or words affected.

Notice that, until you tell AppleWorks to stop boldfacing or underlining, it will continue to do so. When using these options, be sure to use the control characters in pairs, one to begin and one to end.

Subscripts and Superscripts

A *subscript* is a piece of information, like the 2 in H_2O, that is printed below the line of normal text. A *superscript* is a similar piece of information, usually a letter or number such as an exponent, like the 2 in X^2, that is printed above the line of normal text.

To specify text that is to be superscripted or subscripted, follow these steps:

1. Position the cursor on the first character that is to be superscripted or subscripted.

2. Press Open-Apple and the letter O.

3. Type +B for Superscript Begin, or −B for Subscript Begin. Then press Return.

4. Press Escape.

5. AppleWorks puts a caret (^) just before the first superscripted or subscripted character. All succeeding characters are superscripted or subscripted until AppleWorks encounters the stop character, or until you enter a carriage return.

6. To stop the superscripting or subscripting, position the cursor on the first character past the character that is superscripted or subscripted.

7. Press Open-Apple and the letter O.

8. Type +E for Superscript End or −E for Subscript End. Press Return.

9. Press Escape.

A caret will appear on your screen wherever you inserted a +B, −B, +E, or −E.

Pagination

AppleWorks allows you to use its automatic pagination or to specify page numbers yourself. You indicate where the number should appear (such as in a header or footer). You may also force a page break or indicate blocks of text that shouldn't be separated by a page break.

To Calculate Page Numbers

At any time in a document, you can pause and let AppleWorks break your text up into pages. It calculates pages according to a set of internal rules:

- No *widows or orphans*. That is, text will not be broken so that the first line of a paragraph is left by itself on the bottom of a page, nor will the last line of a paragraph be put by itself on the top of the next page. If AppleWorks gets to the bottom of the page and finds it can't fit at least two lines of a new paragraph on the page, it moves the entire paragraph to the next page. If it sees that only the last line of the current paragraph is going on the next page, it moves the next-to-last line to the next page too, to "keep the last line company."

- If you *specified* a page break, however, you won't be over-ruled.

- If you specified that a certain block of text remain intact, it won't be broken to create a new page. If necessary, the whole block will go on a fresh page, even if this leaves the previous page short.

If you don't care where the pages break (for instance, you're working with a first draft), print the document and let AppleWorks determine page breaks and page numbers. It will display a broken line across the screen to indicate where each page break will occur. (The line, of course, doesn't actually print.)

To specify page numbering, follow these steps:

1. Before you print your document, press Open-Apple-K (for calculate).

2. Choose the type of printer you'll be using and press Return.

Now you can check on page breaks by using the arrow keys to scroll through the document. If you now make any changes to text (that is, if you change anything after AppleWorks has specified page numbers), the page breaks disappear. Then you should calculate new ones.

Specifying a Fresh Page

When you want to control page breaks yourself, use the New Page option. Follow these steps:

1. Position the cursor on the line that you want to be at the top of the new page.

2. Press Open-Apple and the letter O.

3. Type NP (New Page) and Return.

4. Press Escape.

AppleWorks won't overrule your page breaks, but it will break text between them if it is more than one page long. If you specify a page break in the middle of a paragraph, AppleWorks will assume you made a mistake and will break the page at the beginning of that paragraph. If you do want to force a new page in the middle of a paragraph, place the cursor *exactly* where you want the paragraph to end, press Return to insert a carriage return, and then specify a new page as directed above.

Grouping Information

Occasionally you will want to tell AppleWorks to keep certain text together as a block, but otherwise to apply its own pagination rules. This block might be a list of instructions, a special note, information for a title page, a section of a table of contents, etc. This facility is called *Grouping.*

To establish a Group, follow these steps:

1. Position the cursor on the first line of the group.

2. Press Open-Apple and the letter O.

3. Type GB (Group Begin) and press Return.

4. Move the cursor to the line *following* the last line of the group.

5. Press Open-Apple and the letter O again.

6. Type GE (Group End) and press Return.

Assigning Page Numbers

When you want to specify that a particular page should have a certain number, and subsequent pages are to be numbered accordingly, use the Page Number option. This option overrides AppleWorks' page numbering scheme.

1. Position the cursor anywhere on the page to which you're going to assign a number.

2. Press Open-Apple and the letter O.

3. Type PN (Page Number) and press Return.

4. Type the page number you want (any number from 1 to 512) and press Return.

Printing Page Numbers

Pages are not normally printed with page numbers under Apple-Works. You have to specify that page numbers are to be printed. They can appear in a header or a footer, or in the text. To cause page numbers to be printed:

1. Position the cursor wherever you want the page number to be printed. This is likely to be somewhere in your header or footer, or in a line by itself at the bottom of a page.
   If it's in a header or footer, it will be somewhere in the line you enter below the reminder – – – – Page Header or – – – – Page Footer.

2. Type the word Page (or PAGE or Pg.) if you want that included as part of the page number. Then press the Space Bar so that there is a space between the word and the page number.

3. Press Open-Apple and the letter O.

4. Type PP (for Print Page number) and press the Return key. Apple-Works inserts a caret in that spot, but prints the page number there, either the one it calculates or the one you specify.

Summary

This chapter has looked at the printer options available under Apple-Works. Using one or more of these options, you can control how your file will look when printed. All of these features can be implemented through the Printer Options menu, which appears as an overlay on your screen when you type Open-Apple and the letter O. Default values for some of these options are given in the status line when you first see the Printer Options menu.

THE
SPREADSHEET

CHAPTER

If you've ever worked with a budget, and tried to forecast what would happen over time if various different assumptions were true, you will understand the value of a spreadsheet program. For instance, let's look at the following:

Assumptions:

1. You have a 4-unit apartment building, with four identical units. They currently rent for $500 a month each.

2. Your expenses are as follows:
   Operating Expenses $200
   Taxes and Insurance $300
   Mortgage Payments $900

A six-month budget forecast for the operation of this building might look like this:

	JAN	FEB	MARCH	APRIL	MAY	JUNE
Income	2000	2000	2000	2000	2000	2000
Operating Expenses	200	200	200	200	200	200
Taxes and Insurance	300	300	300	300	300	300
Mortgage Payments	900	900	900	900	900	900
Profit (monthly)	600	600	600	600	600	600
Profit (cum.)	600	1200	1800	2400	3000	3600

Now let's change one of your assumptions. Suppose that one of your tenants moved out in February, and you had to repaint the apartment and replace the carpet at a cost of $1200. Because of the work, you had to keep the apartment vacant for a month, foregoing $500 in income. Now what does your forecast look like?

	JAN	FEB	MARCH	APRIL	MAY	JUNE
Income	2000	1500	2000	2000	2000	2000
Operating Expenses	200	1400	200	200	200	200
Taxes and Insurance	300	300	300	300	300	300
Mortgage Payments	900	900	900	900	900	900
Profit (monthly)	600	<1100>	600	600	600	600
Profit (cum.)	600	<500>	100	700	1300	1900

Now suppose you decided to raise the rents $50 per unit in May. What would your forecast look like then?

	JAN	FEB	MARCH	APRIL	MAY	JUNE
Income	2000	1500	2000	2000	2200	2200
Operating Expenses	200	1400	200	200	200	200
Taxes and Insurance	300	300	300	300	300	300
Mortgage Payments	900	900	900	900	900	900
Profit (monthly)	600	<1100>	600	600	800	800
Profit (cum.)	600	<500>	100	700	1500	2300

A spreadsheet program is ideal for this kind of *What if?* analysis. Once set up, the spreadsheet instantly calculates and displays the effects of different assumptions on a set of data.

You can enter text, numbers, or formulas in your spreadsheet. In the example above, text would be the row labels *Income, Operating Expenses, Taxes and Insurance,* and the like. The numbers are the figures shown. The formulas, which are not displayed, control the calculations on the numbers you enter. The example above employs the formula

> Income
> − Operating Expenses
> − Taxes and Insurance
> − Mortgage Payments
> ――――――――――――――
> Profit

When you create a spreadsheet, you set up your columns and rows to contain the information the way you want to see it displayed, then you enter your data and formulas, and choose formats for the numbers (dollars and cents, integers, decimals, or percentages). You can manipulate the data with your own formulas, or choose from a selection of standard formulas, or *functions,* such as Sum, Square Root, and Count. You can print the spreadsheet by itself or "Cut and Paste" it into a word processor document.

This chapter will take you through the construction of a sample spreadsheet, explaining the commands and how they affect the information you enter.

Creating a Spreadsheet

Although we're going to make up a small spreadsheet, AppleWorks can handle up to 127 columns and up to 99 rows. Columns are identified by a letter code:

> A through Z, then
> AA through AZ, then
> BA through BZ, then
> CA through CZ, then
> DA through DW.

Rows are simply identified by number.

Each box where a column crosses a row is called a *cell.* As a general rule, if your Apple computer has a 64K memory you can have a spreadsheet with about 1800 filled cells; if your Apple has a 128K memory you can have about 6000 filled cells.

The first question for you to answer is what kind of information you want your spreadsheet to provide. A simple listing of information you already have, presented in a clear format? A calculation of answers you really don't know? Is it to be set up so that you can change one piece of data and watch how that changes the rest?

Our small sample spreadsheet is going to produce a cash flow projection for the Ames project. You want to know if, over the course of a year, it is likely to be a profitable venture. How do you approach the problem?

What do you already know about the project?

1. You know the basic formula:

   Income − Expenses = Profit

2. You know that income is going to be small at the beginning, but is likely to grow by 15% per quarter.

3. You have three kinds of expenses:

> *Cost of Sales:* commissions and other expenses related to actually selling the product

> *Cost of Goods:* what the raw materials and labor cost that are required to produce the product

> *Operating Expenses:* the project's fair share of company overhead, maintenance, and other factors.

4. You'll assume that taxes on any profits will be at 49%.

5. You'll want to plow the profits back into the project until the end of the year.

6. You're going to want to see the results for each fiscal-year quarter, as well as cumulatively for the entire year.

You can picture your spreadsheet right now. It will have a title across the top, labels on the left for each row, and four columns of quarterly data. You'll group the expense items together, and the bottom line will show totals for each column. That last figure will also be used to add in to the income figure in the next column to the right, so that the bottom figure in the rightmost column will show a cumulative total for the year.

OK, let's get the spreadsheet program into the AppleWorks. With the Main Menu showing on your screen, do the following:

1. Choose 1. Add files to the Desktop.

2. When the Add Files menu appears, choose 5. Make a new file for the Spreadsheet.

3. When the Spreadsheet menu appears, choose 1. From scratch. (You'll be creating a brand new spreadsheet.)

4. When asked, type the file name. We'll use the name CASHFLOW. Then press Return.

Now you see a blank spreadsheet on the screen, awaiting your entries.

(*NOTE:* We are going to construct a small spreadsheet, using data and formulas, and then modify it in several ways. If at any time you want to leave the program before we finish, save your worksheet by pressing Open-Apple and the letter S. You will need to remove the program diskette and replace it with your data disk to complete the Save operation, but your worksheet-in-progress will then be on your disk so that you can come back to it whenever you are ready.)

Default Options

Before you start entering data, you should know that AppleWorks lets you choose among several different formats for your numbers and labels, as well as several different column widths.

Unless you change them, the following are the default options:

- All labels will be left-justified.
- All numbers will be displayed just as you type them, if the column is wide enough.
- All columns are 9-characters wide.
- All calculations will be performed automatically, as the data is entered.
- Calculations will be performed from the top down in columns and then across rows.

Labels and Their Formats

In a spreadsheet, all values that aren't numbers or formulas are considered *labels*. Labels can be titles at the top of the page, or column titles or row titles, or even non-numeric information you enter into a cell in the middle of your spreadsheet. AppleWorks doesn't do much with labels; it will not add $100 to a cell containing the entry "John Smith".

We're going to assume, for simplicity's sake, that you want all the labels in your sample spreadsheet left-justified. That means you can go along with AppleWorks' default values for labels.

So let's get started. Using the arrow keys, move the shaded-bar cursor to cell D1 (that's column D, row 1) type

Ames Project

and press Return. If you make a mistake in typing, you can correct it *before* you press Return by using the Delete key and retyping. (Don't use the arrow keys, or you'll just enter your misspelled word into another cell.)

You can also use two special cursors, the blinking bar and the blinking rectangle, to change your entry. The blinking bar is an insert cursor: whatever you type replaces the information to the right of the cursor and moves everything else farther to the right to make room for it. Whatever you type with the blinking rectangle, the overstrike cursor, replaces the information under the cursor. You get from one kind of cursor to the other by pressing Open-Apple-E.

Move the cursor to D2 and type

Cash Flow Projection

and press Return.

Now that we have the title on our spreadsheet, let's set up the columns. You'll need to reserve columns A, B, and C to hold the row labels, so move the cursor to D3. Column D will hold the first quarter's figures, Column E will hold the second quarter's, and so on.

Type the word First in cell D3 and press Return. Then move the cursor to cell D4 and type Quarter and press Return. Use rows 3 and 4 for the column headings of columns E, F, and G, and enter Second Quarter, Third Quarter, and Fourth Quarter in those three columns. When you're done, the top half of your spreadsheet should look like Figure 6.1. If it doesn't, press Open-Apple-E, move the cursor to problem items and retype them correctly.

Next, we're going to label the rows. Move the cursor to cell A5. You'll be at the left edge of your spreadsheet. Type the first row heading:

Income

and press Return. Next move the cursor down a row to A6 and type

Cost of Sales

```
File: spread1              REVIEW/ADD/CHANGE           Escape: Main Menu
========A========B========C========D========E========F========G========H====
 1|                        Ames Project
 2|                        Cash Flow Projection
 3|                        First    Second   Third    Fourth
 4|                        Quarter  Quarter  Quarter  Quarter
 5|
 6|
 7|
 8|
 9|
10|
11|
12|
13|
14|
15|
16|
17|
18|
-----------------------------------------------------------------------------
G4: (Label) Quarter

Type entry or use a commands                          a-? for Help
```

Figure 6.1: The top rows of the sample spreadsheet.

and press Return. Then move the cursor down another row to A7 and type

Cost of Goods

and press Return. Now move the cursor down to A8 and type

Operating Expenses

and press Return. Notice that this row label went to the right edge of Column B. That's why we didn't start the data columns until column D.

Now you want to skip a line (so that you can enter tally lines for the Net Income before taxes). Move the cursor down to A10 and type

Net Income

and press Return. Net income is what you have after you've subtracted all of your expenses from your income. (It isn't really "profits" until you've subtracted taxes.)

Line 11 is for taxes. In cell A11 type

Taxes

and press Return. Then skip a line (for the tally lines again) and move the cursor to cell A13. Here's where your profits will show up, so type

Net Profits

and press Return. Now your spreadsheet should look like this:

```
File: spread2              REVIEW/ADD/CHANGE ·              Escape: Main Menu
========A=========B========C========D========E========F========G========H====
   1 |                     Ames Project
   2 |                     Cash Flow Projection
   3 |                     First    Second   Third    Fourth
   4 |                     Quarter  Quarter  Quarter  Quarter
   5 | Income
   6 | Cost of Sales
   7 | Cost of Goods
   8 | Operating Expenses
   9 |
  10 | Net Income
  11 | Taxes
  12 |
  13 | Net Profits
  14 |
  15 |
  16 |
  17 |
  18 |
------------------------------------------------------------------------------
A13: (Label) Net Profi

Type entry or use a commands                             a-? for Help
```

Figure 6.2: The sample spreadsheet with all labels in place.

Numbers and Their Formats

AppleWorks recognizes a value as a number if it begins with a digit 0 through 9, a plus sign (+), a minus sign (−), or a decimal point (.). Added symbols like dollar signs and percent marks are added automatically if the number is formatted correctly; you don't enter these characters.

The cell indicator in the entry line tells you what kind of format your number has, and what value is being stored in that cell. For instance, if cell G5 has been formatted to be

Dollars, two decimal places

and you enter 155.46, the cell will show the value as $155.46; if, however, the same cell has been formatted to be

Fixed, one decimal place

and you enter the same value, the cell will show the value as 155.4.

AppleWorks recognizes both standard values—those that apply to all values in the worksheet—and individual cell values. Possible number formats include the following:

Format	Description	Example
Fixed	Contains a fixed number (0–7) of decimal places.	123 45.678
Commas	Puts a comma between thousands. Negative amounts are in parentheses. Contains a fixed number (0–7) of decimal places.	2,468 (1,357) 98,765.43
Dollar	Same as comma, but with a dollar sign before each amount.	2,468 (1,357) $98,765.43
Percent	Multiplies the number in the cell by 100 and displays it with fixed number (0–7) of decimal places and a percent sign.	123% 42.5% 3.566%
Appropriate	AppleWorks attempts to display numbers exactly

the way you typed them in. Numbers are right justified with a blank in the leftmost position of all columns. Trailing zeroes after the decimal point are dropped.

Standard   Restores the cells in the group you specify to the worksheet standard values.

You set individual cell number formats by typing Open-Apple-L, and then specifying the layout you want, then specifying the cells which are to have formats different from the rest of the worksheet.

Getting Back to Our Example: Entering Numbers

The Ames project now needs some numbers. Let's start with the ones for the first quarter. The numbers will be placed in the appropriate cells in column D.

We're going to assume that you can produce $100,000 in sales during the first quarter of the project. So, position the cursor in cell D5, type

    100000

and press Return. The number appears on the worksheet as you typed it. So far so good.

Next item is the Cost of Sales. Let's assume that this will be 10% of the income for the product. So position the cursor in cell D6, type

    10000

and press Return.

Next we have to deal with the Cost of Goods. We'll assume that the product costs 50% of the income. Position the cursor in cell D7, type

    50000

and press Return.

Finally you need to enter your proposed Operating Costs. Let's assume that your overhead is going to be very low, say $10,000. Position the cursor in D8 and enter

    10000

Now you have your basic numbers entered for the first quarter.

Formulas

Formulas are another type of value. These are mathematical statements that calculate numbers; they are stored in the cells, though normally only the results show on the screen. Each time the worksheet is calculated (either automatically or manually), the result is recalculated.

A formula consists of two or more of the following:

Numbers
Arithmetic operators
+ add
− subtract
∗ multiply
/ divide
^ exponent
Pointers to other cells, such as + E6 or + F10
One or more built-in functions, such as @SUM or @INT

Formulas must begin with a plus sign (+), a minus sign (−), a decimal point, the digits 0–9, a left parenthesis, or the @ sign. The following are examples of legitimate formulas:

+ D5 − G6
− E7 + 2 ∗ E8
144 + F10
(D4 ∗ D7) − E8
@SUM(E5 . . . E9)

Built-In Functions

AppleWorks provides a number of functions that can simplify your work. These built-in functions can be used by name, rather than laboriously typing in every arithmetic operator needed to accomplish the same task. The functions provided in AppleWorks are listed below, with a brief explanation for each. Notice that each function must begin with the @ sign. Where the function is followed by a word in parentheses, this means that you must supply something, such as a number, one or more cell addresses, or a list of values along with the function. Whatever you supply must be enclosed in parentheses, and there must be no spaces in the expression.

Function	What it does
@ABS(*value*)	Absolute value of the single value noted

@AVG(*list*)	Calculates the arithmetic mean of the values in the list. The list can contain numbers or cell addresses, or a combination of both.
@CHOOSE (*cell,list*)	Evaluates the value in the cell to see whether it is equal to 1, 2, or 3. For example, if cell D6 contains the expression @CHOOSE(E6,50,60,70), cell E6 is evaluated to see if it contains a 1, 2, or 3. If it contains a 1, the value 50 is displayed in D6. If it contains a 2, the value 60 is displayed in that cell. If it contains a 3, the value 70 is displayed in D6. If the cell noted contains a 0 or a negative number, or if its value is greater than any of the numbers in parentheses, the expression is evaluated as NA.
@COUNT(*list*)	Counts the number of non-blank entries in the list.
@ERROR	Causes the value ERROR to be displayed in the cell where it is entered, and in all cells referring to it. Helpful in @LOOKUP and @IF functions.
@IF(*list*)	The @IF function is evaluated this way:

@IF(*expression,value1,value2*)

The expression is a logical formula, and is evaluated as being True or False. If it is true, value1 is used where the @IF function is located; if it is false, value2 is used. The logical operators you can use in the expression are:

LT	less than
<=	less than or equal to
>	greater than
>=	greater than or equal to
=	equal to
<>	not equal to

Some examples of the @IF function are:

@IF(A5 = 1,D5,D5 − 6)

@IF(D5>D6,10,20)
@IF(G7<>10,G8,G9)

@INT(value)

Displays only the integer part of the value.

@LOOKUP(list)

The @LOOKUP function is evaluated this way:

@LOOKUP(*value,range*)

The @LOOKUP function uses the values in two adjacent rows or columns and a search value to determine a result. It searches the row (or column) you specified as the range for the largest value equal to or less than the value you specified, and displays the corresponding value in the row immediately below (or column immediately to the right of) the search range. The values in the search range must be in ascending order.

If the search value is smaller than the first entry in the search range, NA is returned. If the search value is larger than any value in the search range, the last value in the search range is returned.

For example, suppose you use the function thus:

@LOOKUP(45,D5 . . . G5)

The search value is 45, and the range refers to row 5, columns D through G, which are set up as follows:

	D	E	F	G
row 5	20	30	40	50
row 6	3	5	7	9

The value returned for the @LOOKUP function is 7.

@MAX(*list*)

Returns the largest value in the list.

@MIN(*list*)	Returns the smallest value in the list.
@NA	Used where you will need a value that isn't available yet. When AppleWorks calculates values that refer to cells that contain @NA, the result is NA, which helps you keep track of values that haven't yet been entered.
@NPV(*value*)	The @NPV function is evaluated this way:
	@NPV(*interest rate, range*)
	This function calculates the value of a series of future cash flows. The interest rate is the discount rate, or cost of money used to discount the future cash flows, and the range is a series of cells that contain the amount of the cash payments.
@SQRT(*value*)	Returns the square root of the value.
@SUM(*list*)	Returns the sum of the values in the list.

Back to Our Example: Determining Net Income

Move the cursor to cell D10. Here you could enter a number, the result of subtracting the Cost of Sales and the Cost of Goods from Income, but that would defeat the purpose of a spreadsheet program. What you want is to create a formula that allows you to plug in any values for cells D5, D6, D7, and D8 and get the answer in cell D10 calculated for you.

There are two ways to do it, one using a simple formula, the other using a function.

The simple formula is

D10 = D5 − D6 − D7 − D8

If you wish to type this version in, type only what's to the right of the = sign. Remember to start your formula with a **+** so that the program knows this is a formula and not a label.

The version that uses a function looks like this:

D10 = D5 − (@SUM(D6 . . . D8))

In essence, the equation says to subtract the sum of the values in cells D6 through D8 from the value in D5. If you use this version, start your entry with a + as above, and type only the right side of the equation. Notice that you have two sets of parentheses, each requiring both a left and a right parenthesis. This is perfectly legitimate; it is also a common source of errors, as it is easy to overlook the need to match each left parenthesis with a right parenthesis.

Type either the simple formula or the version that uses the function into cell D10 and press Return.

Computing Net Income after Taxes

We're almost done. We still have to deal with taxes. Remember we assumed that the tax rate for this venture was going to be 49%. Again, we can calculate this with a formula.

Position the cursor in cell D11 and enter

.49*D10

The result, $14,700, will appear in D11.

One more calculation: we have to subtract the Taxes in D11 from the Net Income shown in D10 in order to determine Net Profits. We'll use a formula for this. Position the cursor in D13 and enter

+D10-D11

Your projected profit for the first quarter is $15,300.

We still need to put in the tally lines in rows 9 and 12. We'll use a string of minus signs for the tally line. But if we don't tell AppleWorks that the minus signs are really part of a label, AppleWorks will consider it a formula and, finding no numbers, will report an error. So to specify that this string of characters should be considered a label, start with a quotation mark ("). Then type the string:

" _ _ _ _

(Once you've typed the double quote, you can simply hold down the minus sign key until the cell is filled.) Type this string of characters into cells D9 and D12.

Your worksheet now looks like Figure 6.3.

Inserting and Deleting Information

You can insert and delete information in your worksheet by row or column, or by groups of rows or columns. You can also *blank* the contents of cells without deleting the cells themselves. You can blank entire rows or columns, or even the entire worksheet.

Inserting

You can insert a maximum of nine blank columns or rows into your worksheet with AppleWorks. This allows you to rearrange your worksheet while you are working with it, or to use an existing worksheet as a template for a new one.

To insert a column:

1. Position the cursor in the column that will be to the left of the new column.

2. Press Open-Apple and the letter I.

3. Select Columns when you are asked.

4. Type the number of columns you want inserted, and press Return.

The new, blank columns will be inserted to the right of the column containing the cursor, and all existing columns to the right will be relettered to take the new columns into account. Any formulas referring to cells in the relettered columns will be adjusted automatically to reflect the columns' new letter.

If you want to add columns beyond the last column on an existing worksheet, don't use the Insert command. Instead, simply move the cursor to the new column on your screen, and begin typing. The new information will be appended to the worksheet when you store it.

```
File: spread3              REVIEW/ADD/CHANGE              Escape: Main Menu
=======A========B========C========D========E========F========G========H====
  1|                       Ames Project
  2|                       Cash Flow Projection
  3|                       First    Second   Third    Fourth
  4|                       Quarter  Quarter  Quarter  Quarter
  5|Income                 100000
  6|Cost of Sales          10000
  7|Cost of Goods          50000
  8|Operating Expenses     10000
  9|                       ----------
 10|Net Income             30000
 11|Taxes                  14700
 12|                       ----------
 13|Net Profits            15300
 14|
 15|
 16|
 17|
 18|
---------------------------------------------------------------------------
D13: (Value) +D10-D11

Type entry or use @ commands                              @-? for Help
```

Figure 6.3: Sample spreadsheet with the First Quarter complete.

To insert a row:

1. Position the cursor in the row that will be above the new row.
2. Press Open-Apple and the letter I.
3. Select Rows when you are asked.
4. Type the number of rows you want inserted, and press Return.

The new, blank rows will be inserted immediately below the column containing the cursor, and all existing rows below it will be renumbered to take the new rows into account. Any formulas referring to cells in the renumbered rows will be adjusted automatically to reflect the renumbering.

New rows below the last existing row may be appended by simply positioning the cursor and making entries.

Deleting

Columns and rows may be deleted from the worksheet on the screen in much the same way as they are inserted.

To delete a set of columns:

1. Position the cursor in the leftmost column of the set that is to be deleted.
2. Press Open-Apple and the letter D.
3. Select Columns when you are asked.
4. Type the number of columns you want deleted, counting the one where the cursor is located, and press Return.

As with inserting, columns which were to the right of the deleted set of columns are relettered, and the formulas within them are adjusted. AppleWorks displays ERROR in those cells which contain formulas with references to cells in the now-deleted columns.

To delete a set of rows:

1. Position the cursor in the top row of the set that is to be deleted.
2. Press Open-Apple and the letter D.
3. Select Rows when you are asked.
4. Type the number of rows you want deleted, counting the one where the cursor is located, and press Return.

Existing rows are renumbered and formulas adjusted. ERROR is reported in cells containing references to deleted rows.

Blanking

Rather than deleting columns or rows, with the resulting adjustment of formulas, you can blank columns or rows, an individual cell or block of cells, or even an entire worksheet with the Blank command.

To blank a cell:

1. Move the cursor to the cell.
2. Press Open-Apple and the letter B.
3. When asked, choose Entry, and press Return.

Any data that was in the cell disappears. If any formula refers to this cell, the value it will see is zero. If you have protected this cell with Open-Apple-L and protection set to Yes, the cell cannot be blanked. If you set protection to labels only or values only, the cell is blanked.

To blank a column or row:

1. Move the cursor to any cell in the row or column you want to blank.
2. Press Open-Apple and the letter B.
3. When asked, choose either Rows or Columns, and press Return.

The same conditions apply to blanked rows and columns for individual cells.

To blank a block of cells:

1. Move the cursor to the upper-left corner of the rectangular block involved.
2. Press Open-Apple and the letter B.
3. When asked, choose Block. Don't press Return yet.
4. Use the arrow keys to move the cursor so that it highlights the area in which you want information blanked. Then press Return.

The same conditions apply to cells in a blanked block of cells as are true for an individual cell.

Moving Columns and Rows within a Spreadsheet

You may wish to move a row or column of information to another location within your worksheet. AppleWorks makes this easy to do with the Move command.

You can move up to 125 columns or up to 250 rows within your worksheet be performing the following steps:

1. Move the cursor to the top row or leftmost column of the group of rows or columns you want to move.

2. Press Open-Apple and the letter M.

3. When asked, specify Within Worksheet.

4. When asked, specify either Columns or Rows.

5. Use the arrow keys to move the cursor so that the rows or columns you wish to move are highlighted. Then press Return.

6. Move the cursor to the place where you want the moved columns or rows to go: the moved columns will be inserted to the left of the cursor; moved rows will be inserted above the cursor. Press Return.

AppleWorks closes up the space left vacant by the move, and adjusts the column letters and row numbers accordingly. Formulas are adjusted to take the move into account so that all formulas still refer to the cells they referred to originally.

Copying

One of the great timesaving features of AppleWorks is its ability to let you type something once, then use the Copy command to duplicate the contents in other cells with just a few keystrokes. The copied information can be an exact duplicate, or it can be adjusted so that it is relative to its new location. Furthermore, you can copy the contents of one cell into a single cell or many cells, or you can copy the contents of one row or column into one or many rows or columns. However you can't copy the contents of a row into a column, or vice versa.

To copy information from one place to another, use the following steps:

1. Move the cursor to the cell you wish to copy. If you're copying a row, move the cursor to the leftmost or rightmost cell in the row. If you're moving a column, move the cursor to the top or bottom cell in the column.

2. Press Open-Apple and the letter C.

3. When asked, choose Within Worksheet.

4. Use the arrow keys to move the cursor so that all the cells you wish to copy in this operation are highlighted. Then press Return.

5. Now move the cursor to the cell you're copying to. If you're copying cells to a row or column, move the cursor to the left-most cell of the row or the top cell of the column to receive the data.

6. If you're making only one copy of your data, just press Return. If you're making more than one copy, type a period, then use the arrow keys to move the cursor so that all of the cells to receive copies of the data are highlighted. Then press Return.

7. If your copy operation involves formulas, the screen will then ask you if you want to make an *exact* copy of each cell. This allows you to tell AppleWorks that some of the information in your formulas is relative, while some is exactly the same. The screen shows you the referenced cells in the entry line as you proceed, and you can choose No Change (type N) or Relative (type R) for each reference.

Cells to receive the copied information must be contiguous—you can't use a single copy operation to copy data to B4, C6, and D8 all at once. However, you can use three separate copy operations to accomplish this.

Back to the Example: Using the Copy Command

When we last used it, our example had a complete set of data and formulas for the first quarter (see Figure 6.3).

But we wanted to do a full four-quarter projection. We'll prepare that now, using the Copy command.

We can use all of the data we entered for the first quarter, with some modification. For instance, we assumed that Income would grow by 15% per quarter. And since all of our Costs were a percentage of income, we can use the same formulas. However, in the first quarter we didn't enter the data as formulas, so we'll have to do that here.

Since Income for the second quarter is going to be 15% more than income for the first quarter, move the cursor to cell E5, and type the formula

+D5 +(.15*D5)

Income for the third and fourth quarters is again going to increase 15% per quarter, so we can copy the formula from the second quarter into these cells:

1. Press Open-Apple and the letter C.
2. Choose Within Worksheet.
3. Press Return.
4. Move the cursor to cell F5 and type a period. Then move the cursor to cell G5 and press Return.
5. When the screen asks No Change or Relative, move the highlighted block to Relative, and press Return. The screen then asks about D5. Again, move the highlighted block to Relative and press Return.

You can now check on the formulas in cells F5 and G5. Cell F5 contains the formula +E5+(.15*E5), and cell G5 contains the formula +F5+(.l5*F5).

Next we have to enter the formulas for Costs. Using the same percentages we used for the first quarter, type the following formulas into cells E6, E7, and E8 respectively:

```
+.1*E5
+.5*E5
+.1*E5
```

And since these can be copied to the third and fourth quarter just as Income was, follow the same steps as were shown above for copying Income. The worksheet should now look like Figure 6.4.

We still have to finish the bottom of the worksheet. To draw in the tally lines, position the cursor in cell D9 and follow these steps:

1. Press Open-Apple and the letter C.
2. Choose Within Worksheet.
3. Press Return.
4. Move the cursor to cell E9 and type a period. Then use the arrow key to move the cursor to G9, and press Return.

To draw the second tally line, follow these steps:

1. Position the cursor in cell D9.
2. Press Open-Apple and the letter C.
3. Choose Within Worksheet.

4. Press Return.

5. Move the cursor to cell D12 and type a period. Then use the arrow key to move the cursor to G12 and press Return.

We still must copy the Net Income, Taxes, and Net Profits formulas across into the other quarters. Use the following steps to copy the formulas, one row at a time, from cells D10, D11, and D13 into the other three columns:

1. Press Open-Apple and the letter C.

2. Choose Within Worksheet.

3. Press Return.

4. Move the cursor to the cell for the second quarter and type a period. Then move the cursor to the cell for the fourth quarter and press Return.

5. Each time the screen asks you No Change or Relative, choose Relative.

The all-but-complete worksheet shown in Figure 6.5 should now appear.

One item is still missing: while the net profits appear for each quarter, they are not carried forward to add to the net profits for the next quarter.

We can rememdy this by inserting a line below the Taxes row to

```
File: spread4                  REVIEW/ADD/CHANGE              Escape: Main Menu
========A=======B=======C=======D=======E=======F=======G=======H====
  1 |                        Ames Project
  2 |                        Cash Flow Projection
  3 |                        First    Second   Third    Fourth
  4 |                        Quarter  Quarter  Quarter  Quarter
  5 |Income                   100000   115000   132250  152087.5
  6 |Cost of Sales             10000    11500    13225  15208.75
  7 |Cost of Goods             50000    57500    66125  76043.75
  8 |Operating Expenses        10000    11500    13225  15208.75
  9 |                        ---------
 10 |Net Income                30000
 11 |Taxes                     14700
 12 |                        ---------
 13 |Net Profits               15300
 14 |
 15 |
 16 |
 17 |
 18 |
--------------------------------------------------------------------
D13: (Value) +D10-D11

Type entry or use ∂ commands                         ∂-? for Help
```

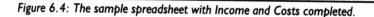

Figure 6.4: The sample spreadsheet with Income and Costs completed.

show Carryforward Profits. To insert the line, follow these steps:

1. Move the cursor to any cell in row 12.

2. Press Open-Apple and the letter I.

3. Choose Rows.

4. Type 1, then press Return.

5. When the new blank line appears as line 12, move the cursor to cell A12, type

   Carryforward Profits

   and press Return.

6. Type a 0 as the value for cell D12.

7. Edit the formula in cell D14 to read

   +D10 − D11 + D12.

8. To carry forward the previous quarter's profits, move the cursor to cell E12 and type

   +D14

9. Copy the formula in cells D14 and E12 into the cells to the right.

```
File: spread5                    REVIEW/ADD/CHANGE              Escape: Main Menu
========A========B========C========D========E========F========G========H====
 1|                        Ames Project
 2|                        Cash Flow Projection
 3|                        First    Second   Third    Fourth
 4|                        Quarter  Quarter  Quarter  Quarter
 5|Income                  100000   115000    132250 152087.5
 6|Cost of Sales            10000    11500     13225 15208.75
 7|Cost of Goods            50000    57500     66125 76043.75
 8|Operating Expenses       10000    11500     13225 15208.75
 9|                        ------------------------------------
10|Net Income               30000    34500     39675 45626.25
11|Taxes                    14700    16905  19440.75 22356.86
12|                        ------------------------------------
13|Net Profits             15300    17595  20234.25 23269.38
14|
15|
16|
17|
18|
---------------------------------------------------------------------------
G13: (Value) +G10-G11

Type entry or use a commands                             a-? for Help
```

Figure 6.5: The all-but-complete sample spreadsheet

10. Recalculate the results by pressing Open-Apple and the letter K.

When finished, your worksheet looks like Figure 6.6.

Playing "What If?" with Your Worksheet Values

Now that your worksheet is set up, you can easily adjust one value and see how it affects the rest. For instance, let's vary a few of our assumptions.

One of the first assumptions was that profits would grow by 15% per quarter. What if they were to grow by 20% per quarter instead? What would the worksheet look like then? It's easy to find out. Simply follow these steps:

1. Move the cursor to cell E5, which contains a formula.

2. Edit the formula so that it reads

   +D5+(.2*D5)

3. Copy the newly edited cell contents into F5 and G5.

4. To see the results, press Open-Apple and the letter K.

Your worksheet now looks like Figure 6.7.

```
File: spread6                    REVIEW/ADD/CHANGE              Escape: Main Menu
========A=========B=========C=========D=========E=========F=========G=========H====
  4|                             Quarter  Quarter  Quarter   Quarter
  5|Income                        100000   115000   132250 152087.5
  6|Cost of Sales                  10000    11500    13225 15208.75
  7|Cost of Goods                  50000    57500    66125 76043.75
  8|Operating Expenses             10000    11500    13225 15208.75
  9|                             ------------------------------------
 10|Net Income                     30000    34500    39675 45626.25
 11|Taxes                          14700    16905 19440.75 22356.86
 12|Carryforward Profits               0    15300    32895 53129.25
 13|                             ------------------------------------
 14|Net Profits                    15300    32895 53129.25 76398.63
 15|
 16|
 17|
 18|
 19|
 20|
 21|
------------------------------------------------------------------------------------
G14: (Value) +G10-G11+G12

Type entry or use @ commands                              @-? for Help
```

Figure 6.6

Another assumption was that Operating Expenses would be 10% of Income. What if you were able to hold Operating Expenses to a flat figure per quarter, say $12,500? What would your worksheet look like this time?

This is also easy to see. Follow these steps:

1. Move the cursor to cell D8, and type in the value 12500.
2. Copy the contents of D8 into the three cells to the right.
3. Press Open-Apple and the letter K to recalculate.

Now your worksheet looks like Figure 6.8.

Printing Your Worksheet

If you intend to hand your worksheet to anyone else, you'd better make a hard copy of it on your printer. We'll assume you've already set up your printer as noted in the previous chapter, so you're all set.

But how does AppleWorks know what to print?

You specify exactly what parts of your spreadsheet are to be printed.

Part of specifying what's to be printed involves telling your printer about the width of your spreadsheet. You have already set up your printer for a line length of a certain number of characters. Now you need to check your spreadsheet to be sure its data will fit within that line length.

1. Press Open-Apple and the letter P.

```
File: spread7                    REVIEW/ADD/CHANGE                Escape: Main Menu
=======A=======B=======C=======D=======E=======F=======G=======H====
  1 |                           Ames Project
  2 |                           Cash Flow Projection
  3 |                           First    Second   Third    Fourth
  4 |                           Quarter  Quarter  Quarter  Quarter
  5 |Income                      100000   120000   144000   172800
  6 |Cost of Sales                10000    12000    14400    17280
  7 |Cost of Goods                50000    60000    72000    86400
  8 |Operating Expenses           10000    12000    14400    17280
  9 |                           ------------------------------------
 10 |Net Income                   30000    36000    43200    51840
 11 |Taxes                        14700    17640    21168  25401.6
 12 |Carryforward Profits             0    15300    33660    55692
 13 |                           ------------------------------------
 14 |Net Profits                  15300    33660    55692  82130.4
 15 |
 16 |
 17 |
 18 |
------------------------------------------------------------------------
G14: (Value) +G10-G11+G12

Type entry or use ᗺ commands                              ᗺ-? for Help
```

Figure 6.7: *The sample spreadsheet with a 20%-per-quarter Profit increase*

2. Specify how much of your worksheet you want to print by typing the first letter of your option (All, Rows, Columns, or Block). You want All, so type A, then press Return.

3. Check the information on the Print menu that tells you how wide your report will be. If it's too wide, press Escape to return to the Review/Add/Change menu so you can replan your report. You have a 63-character line length, enough for most printers. If your printer can't handle that, use the Columns option specified in step 2 above, and print only the number of columns that will fit on your printer. Then come back and redefine the area to be printed as the remaining columns, and print those.

4. Assuming your printer can handle the entire worksheet, choose the printer as the device where you want your worksheet printed.

5. AppleWorks asks you how many copies you want. Type 1 and press Return.

You can stop printing at any time by either one of two methods:

1. If you press Escape, you will stop printing and return to the Review/Add/Change menu. This enables you to change line length or other page characteristics.

```
File: spread8                REVIEW/ADD/CHANGE              Escape: Main Menu
========A========B========C========D========E========F========G========H====
  1|                         Ames Project
  2|                         Cash Flow Projection
  3|                         First     Second    Third     Fourth
  4|                         Quarter   Quarter   Quarter   Quarter
  5|Income                    100000    120000    144000    172800
  6|Cost of Sales              10000     12000     14400     17280
  7|Cost of Goods              50000     60000     72000     86400
  8|Operating Expenses         12500     12500     12500     12500
  9|                         -----------------------------------------
 10|Net Income                 27500     35500     45100     56620
 11|Taxes                      13475     17395     22099   27743.8
 12|Carryforward Profits           0     14025     32130     55131
 13|                         -----------------------------------------
 14|Net Profits                14025     32130     55131   84007.2
 15|
 16|
 17|
 18|
-------------------------------------------------------------------------------
G14: (Value) +G10-G11+G12

Type entry or use a commands                                 a-? for Help
```

Figure 6.8: The sample spreadsheet with Operating Expenses held flat.

2. If you press the Space Bar, printing will pause. You can start it again by pressing the Space Bar a second time.

Saving Your Worksheet

Now that you've finished constructing a worksheet, you'll want to save it. And because you are still using the AppleWorks Desktop, saving a file is admirably simple:

1. Return to the Main Menu by pressing Escape.

2. Use the down-arrow key to highlight the item that says "Save Desktop files to disk." Then press Return.

3. The screen now displays the SAVE FILES menu. The last file you used is CASHFLOW, your spreadsheet file. Use the arrow keys to be sure it is highlighted, then press Return.

4. The screen now gives you some options for what you want to do with this file. Since you want the first choice, "Save the file on the current disk," press Return.

5. On a one-drive system, remove the Program diskette from the disk drive at this point, replace it with your working diskette, and press Return.

6. You can quit now, if you wish, by choosing the Quit option on the Main Menu, once the file is saved.

Your worksheet is now safely stored on your disk, under the name CASHFLOW. You can retrieve it and modify it any time you wish, or make a copy of it to use for a different worksheet.

Summary

In this chapter, you have learned how to use AppleWorks to construct a worksheet, and how to modify it to play "What if?" While we dealt with a simple cash flow projection, your projects can be much more complex.

This chapter has deliberately not been a complete exercise of the spreadsheet commands in AppleWorks. A complete list can be found in the AppleWorks manual. Rather, this chapter has focussed on showing you how you can use AppleWorks to construct and then use a spreadsheet to solve your problems.

What is a Data Base Program?

A *data base* is an organized collection of information. It is organized according to some structure, usually one you set up or one that is widely accepted. An example of a data base that you might set up yourself would be a list of marketing prospects, with their names, addresses, and phone numbers, titles, areas of responsibility, and comments. An example of a data base with a more conventional format would be a payroll file, showing employee ID number, name and address, exemptions, kinds of deductions, pay rate, hours worked, and year-to-date calculations.

A *data base program*, also called a data base manager, is a program that allows you to sort through your information and report it in various formats that you or the program specify. In other words, it lets you pick through and rearrange the information in a given file and then display it in the way you want.

Creating a Data Base File

Your AppleWorks data base file will consist of *categories, records,* and *entries*. A *category* is a group of similar things, such as office equipment, depreciable items, vendors of a particular kind of product, or payroll information. A *record* is all the information about one of those things, such as the purchase record and warranty information about a copier, the date and amount of purchase and any related information about a depreciable item such as a piece of capital equipment, or the name, address, phone number, and ordering information for a vendor. An *entry* is one piece of information in a record, such as the serial number of the copier, the date of purchase of the piece of capital equipment, or the phone number of the vendor.

The file will also have a name, just as your word processing and spreadsheet files have names. Let's call this one DBSAMPLE.

To create a data base file from scratch, follow these steps:

1. With the Main Menu on the screen, select 1. Add files to the Desktop.

2. On the next menu, choose to create a new file for the data base.

3. On the next menu, select 1. From scratch.

4. The line at the bottom of the screen asks you for a file name. Type DBSAMPLE and press Return. (As with the other file names, this one can be up to 15 characters long, must start with a letter, and can contain uppercase and lowercase letters, numbers, periods, and spaces.)

Now you see the opening screen for the data base program. It looks like Figure 7.1.

The cursor is over the first letter of the word Category. What you are now expected to do is start listing your categories for this new file. Oho! This means we have to think through what kinds of information we're going to put in this file.

```
File: DBSAMPLE            CHANGE NAME/CATEGORY     Escape: Review/Add/Change



Category names
=================================================================
Category 1                       |
                                 | Options:
                                 |
                                 | Change category name
                                 | Up arrow    Go to filename
                                 | Down arrow Go to next category
                                 | ∂-I        Insert new category
                                 |
                                 |
                                 |
                                 |
                                 |
                                 |
-----------------------------------------------------------------
Type entry or use ∂ commands                        55K Avail.
```

Figure 7.1: The opening data base screen.

Let's create a customer list, and indicate things like the date and amount of last order, and dollar volume ordered to date, along with the customer name, address, phone number, and contact person. Each of the items we just listed will be a category and will receive a name. All of the information about a particular customer will be a record. And each piece of information about the customer will be an entry.

Probably the easiest way to approach constructing a data base file is to think of all the possible ways you may want to sort the information. Each item you would want to sort for should then become a category. For instance, you will probably want an alphabetical list of your customers. Therefore, one of your categories will be the customer name. You may want to sort by address, by city, by state, or by zip code. Each of those should be a category. So should phone numbers. And since you may want to keep in close contact with those customers who regularly place large orders, you'll want to be able to sort by date of last order and by amount. Since very large accounts sometimes make large but infrequent purchases, you'll want to be able to sort by dollar volume to date. And when you print the list of customers, sorted whichever way you choose, you will probably also want to show the contact person—so that's another category.

Category names can be up to 20 characters long, and can be uppercase or lowercase. However, there can be no numbers, spaces, or periods in a category name. You can get around that by running two or more words together, as we will do below.

One important note to remember before we start entering category names: unless you use the overstrike cursor, you'll wind up with "Category 1" as part or all of a category name. So press Open-Apple and the letter E to change to the overstrike cursor.

Our category names will be as follows:

CustomerName
Address
City
State
ZipCode
PhoneNumber
ContactPerson
DateLastOrder
AmountLastOrder
PurchasesThisYear

Type each of these category names in, pressing Return key after each name. If you misspell a category name but haven't yet pressed Return, use Delete to backspace over the mistaken character, then type the correct spelling. If you want to erase the entire name and start over, press Escape. If you have pressed Return, you'll need to use the up arrow to go back to the entry and overtype the correct name. The up arrow and down arrow can be used to move up and down the list of category names. Press Open-Apple and the letter I to insert a category name ahead of the one where the cursor is located, or press Open-Apple and the letter D to delete the category name in the same line as the cursor. (The reminder on the top line, and the messages on the right side of the screen tell you what you can do as you're entering the names.)

NOTE: If you use a category name that has the word *date* or *time* in it, AppleWorks will convert entries in that category to standard date or time format.

When you have correctly typed in the category names, press Escape. Your list of categories disappears and the screen message shown in Figure 7.2 comes up.

```
File: DBSAMPLE              REVIEW/ADD/CHANGE              Escape: Main Menu


Category names
==============================================================================


                   This file does not yet contain
                   any information. Therefore, you
                   will automatically go into the
                   Insert New Records feature.




------------------------------------------------------------------------------
Press Space Bar to continue                                     55K Avail.
```

Figure 7.2: The data base Review/Add/Change screen.

That's right—you have no records in this file, yet. We'll show you how to add them in a bit.

If you aren't interested in learning about using ASCII text files, DIF files, or QuickFiles (TM) as your data base files, skip ahead to the section titled "Creating Records."

Using Other Files as Input

You can use certain types of other files as input for your data base files. But there are restrictions. We'll discuss them in this section.

ASCII Text Files

You can use as input for the AppleWorks data base an ASCII text file created by programs like the Apple Pascal Editor, Apple Writer, or some data base systems. The formatting restrictions are:

1. Each entry in the file has to be on a separate line, and end with a carriage return.

2. Entries have to be grouped by record, and be in the same order throughout the file.

3. Text files on DOS 3.2 or 3.3 disks must be converted to Pro-DOS format in order to function with AppleWorks.

To use an ASCII file as a data base file, follow these steps:

1. Start with adding a new data base file as usual. When asked on the data base new file menu what kind of file to create, select 2. From a text (ASCII) file.

2. On a single-drive system you'll be asked for the path name. Type the complete path name (which includes the ProDOS identifier, any subdirectory name, and file name) and press Return key. (On the Apple IIe, you'll be asked for this information after the next step.

3. When asked, type the number of categories in each record and press Return.

4. You'll be asked for the new file name. This is the name under which the file will be stored in AppleWorks, and it must follow the AppleWorks file name conventions. Type the name and press Return.

5. All of your categories on the file will be named Category 1, Category 2, etc. To rename them, press Open-Apple and the letter N, then follow the screen instructions.

DIF Files

DIF files generally come from VisiCalc or similar programs, and can be used as the source of a data base file. However, to use a DIF file in AppleWorks' data base program, the DIF file must have been created using the C (column-wise) option so that the information for each record is grouped together.

To create an AppleWorks data base file using a DIF file as a source, follow the instructions above for ASCII files. The same limitations about ProDOS formats, path names, and AppleWorks file names apply. As with ASCII files, the categories will be given general names that you may change with the Open-Apple-N command.

Quick Files

You can also use a Quick File as a source for your data base file. If you specify it, AppleWorks retrieves the Quick File catalog from the disk in the current drive. You select the file you want, and AppleWorks simply adds it to the Desktop. Follow the instructions for ASCII files and DIF files.

Creating Records

Assuming you still have the screen showing your category names in front of you, you should see the line at the bottom saying "Press Space Bar to continue." Press the Space Bar so we can begin entering records into our file. The screen now looks like Figure 7.3.

Type information for each item, ending each entry with Return. You can use up to 76 characters for each item. Either make up your own data or use the five records we show you below:

CustomerName: The Bike Rack
Address: 434 Mission Valley Blvd.
City: Coronado
State: Calif.
ZipCode: 90245
PhoneNumber: 619 555 1357
ContactPerson: Don Burwell

DateLastOrder: 4/23/84
AmountLastOrder: $1580
PurchasesThisYear: $5332

CustomerName: Speedo Bike Stores Inc.
Address: 1535 Stevens Creek Blvd.
City: San Jose
State: Calif.
ZipCode: 95123
PhoneNumber: 408 555 1352
ContactPerson: Adrian Jeremy
DateLastOrder: 6/15/84
AmountLastOrder: $7565
PurchasesThisYear: $25,642

CustomerName: Novus Sport Shops
Address: 2553 Post St.
City: San Francisco
State: Calif.
ZipCode: 94159
PhoneNumber: 415 555 8297
ContactPerson: Charles Prael
DateLastOrder: 6/8/84
AmountLastOrder: $6833
PurchasesThisYear: $21,446

CustomerName: Sports Emporium
Address: 3447 1st Ave. S.
City: Seattle
State: Wash.
ZipCode: 98102
PhoneNumber: 206 555 4398
ContactPerson: Robin Weberg
DateLastOrder: 5/29/84
AmountLastOrder: $2588
PurchasesThisYear: $20,466

CustomerName: A-1 Sporting Goods Stores
Address: 256 6th Ave.
City: Edmonds
State: Wash.
ZipCode: 98133
PhoneNumber: 206 555 4466

ContactPerson: Chris Davis
DateLastOrder: 4/27/84
AmountLastOrder: $3577
PurchasesThisYear: $7849

Nearly everybody makes errors when typing, and AppleWorks has a few special keystrokes that help you clean up your mistaeks—er, make that mistakes.

- The insert cursor is indicated by the blinking underline. The overstrike cursor is indicated by the blinking rectangle. Use whichever one is appropriate to what you need to do, and change between them by pressing Open-Apple-E.

- Press Delete to remove the character to the left of the cursor.

- Press Escape to restore the former entry.

- Use the arrow keys to move the cursor past characters without changing them.

- Press Control-Y-Return to erase the rest of an entry beyond the cursor. Pressing Return in a data base entry doesn't truncate the rest of the entry (the way it does in the word processor).

```
File: dbsample              INSERT NEW RECORDS      Escape: Review/Add/Change



Record 1 of 6
===============================================================================
CustomerName: -
Address: -
City: -
State: -
ZipCode: -
PhoneNumber: -
ContactPerson: -
DateLastOrder: -
AmountLastOrder: -
PurchasesThisYear: -




------------------------------------------------------------------------
Type entry or use a commands                                  54K Avail.
```

Figure 7.3: The data base Insert New Records screen.

• You can create standard values (values that will be used for all entries in a particular category —such as the same state in an address) by pressing Open-Apple and the letter V. (Be sure you are in the Review/Add/Change or Insert New Records menu.) The screen then shows you a record with any previously established standard values. Type the standard value for the categories you wish, ending each by pressing Return. When you're done, press Escape to return to where you were. For each category in which you typed a standard value, that value appears in every record. If you want to remove a standard value, press Open-Apple-V, position the cursor on the category whose standard value you want to remove, then press Control-Y and Return. The standard value disappears from all entries in that category.

You can also use standard values selectively. Establish the standard value first, then edit those individual records where the standard value isn't applicable.

When you have finished entering your records, press Escape. AppleWorks presents the records in Single Record format, as shown above. (The Multiple Record format will be discussed below.)

Notice that when your record is displayed the dates are changed to month/day/year format. AppleWorks does this automatically if you have the word "date" in your category name.

You can skim through your records by using the up arrow and down arrow to go from category to category. When you reach the bottom (or top) of a record, pressing the down arrow (or up arrow) will cause the next (or last) record to be displayed. If you decide to change the information in an entry, use the right arrow or left arrow to position the cursor properly, change to the overstrike cursor if necessary (by pressing Open-Apple-E), and type the correction.

Press Escape to return to the Main Menu.

Single and Multiple Record Layout

As you entered your records, you were shown the categories for one record. When you finished, the screen showed you the entire record, but one record at a time. AppleWorks refers to this as *Single Record Layout.*

You can also see your records in *Multiple Record Layout.* In this format, you can browse through all of your records, and see them in tabular form by category. Each record appears in one row, with some of the entry information beneath the appropriate category name at the top of the column.

To see your records for the file DBSAMPLE in Multiple Record Layout, press Open-Apple and the letter Z. Your screen will look like Figure 7.4.

Moving the Cursor

Once your records are created, you can move the cursor from record to record, or from entry to entry, or even by character within an entry.

The following table shows you what keystrokes are required to move the cursor in both Single and Multiple Record Layouts:

Press These Keys	**For This Result**
TAB	Move the cursor to the next entry
Open-Apple-TAB	Move the cursor to the last entry
right arrow	Move the cursor right one character within an entry.
left arrow	Move the cursor left one character within an entry.
down arrow	Move the cursor down one category.
up arrow	Move the cursor up one category.
Open-Apple and up arrow	For Single Record Layout: Display the previous record in the file, leaving the cursor in the same category.
	For Multiple Record Layout: Move the cursor to the top of the previous screenful of records.

Open-Apple and down arrow	For Single Record Layout: Display the next record in the file, leaving the cursor in the same category.
	For Multiple Record Layout: Move the cursor to the bottom of the next screenful of records.

Inserting Records

Now you have a completed data base file. But suppose you want to add another record. What do you do? While you can insert new entries in Multiple Entry Layout, the character limitations in the display make it difficult to know how correct your information is. Therefore, it is recommended that all record insertion be done in Single Entry Layout. You can always check your insertion by switching back to Multiple Entry Layout with the Open-Apple-Z command.

To insert a new record, be sure you are in Single Entry Layout. Then press Open-Apple and the letter I. You'll be shown the blank Categories screen you worked with before. Enter the information, category by category, pressing Return after each one. When you reach the end of the new record, press Return to bring back the blank Categories

```
File: dbsample              REVIEW/ADD/CHANGE              Escape: Main Menu

Selection: All records


CustomerName    Address        City           State        ZipCode
=====================================================================
The Bike Rack   434 Mission Val Coronado       Calif.       90245
Speedo Bike Sto 1535 Stevens Cr San Jose       Calif.       95123
Novus Sport Sho 2553 Post St.  San Francisco  Calif.       94159
Sports Emporium 3447 1st Ave. S Seattle        Wash.        98102
A-1 Sporting Go 256 6th Ave.   Edmonds        Wash.        98133




----------------------------------------------------------------------
Type entry or use ⌂ commands                        ⌂-? for Help
```

Figure 7.4: The data base Multiple Record Layout.

screen so you can add more new records. When you are through entering the new information, press Escape. AppleWorks returns you to the place you were when you pressed Open-Apple-I.

The new records will be inserted immediately before the record the cursor was on when you pressed Open-Apple-I. If you need to reorder the records, consult the section below on Moving Records.

If you want to append new records to the end of your file, you need to take one extra step to get past the last record. Move the cursor to the last record in the file. Then press Open-Apple and the down arrow. AppleWorks asks you if you want to insert new records, so answer Yes and the screen will show you a blank Categories screen. You can then proceed as above.

Deleting Records

While you can delete records in either Multiple or Single Record Layout, it's faster to do so in Multiple Record Layout, because you can skim through the entire file quickly.

To delete records,

1. Place the cursor on the first record you want to delete.

2. Press Open-Apple and the letter D. The record will be highlighted.

3. If the other records you want to delete are grouped together, use the arrow keys to highlight the entire block. When the highlighting encloses all the records in a group that you want to delete, press the Return key. The records will disappear and the remaining records will close up the space.

If you want to delete all of the records in a file but keep its structure, you have to work around an AppleWorks' rule that you can't delete every record in a file. The way you do that is to create a blank record as the first record in the file. (Be sure you are in Multiple Record Layout.) Then move the cursor to the second record, press Open-Apple-D, then Open-Apple-9 and then Return. All records but the first are deleted, and you're left with a blank record in which you can enter new information.

Copying Records

You can copy one record, a group of records, or an entry within a record.

To copy a complete record from one place in the data base to another, or to several places:

1. Be sure you are in the Review/Add/Change menu. (You can be in either Single or Multiple Record Layout.) Position the cursor anywhere in the record to be copied.

2. Press Open-Apple and the letter C.

3. When asked

   Copy? Current record To clipboard (cut) From clipboard (paste)

   choose Current record.

4. Type the number of copies you want, and press Return.

The copied records will be inserted immediately after the original. If you don't want them there, use the To clipboard and From clipboard commands (discussed below) to move them to the appropriate location.

The Copy command used with a single record is a good way to duplicate a record that will be, with few exceptions, the same. By making a number of copies, you can then edit only those categories that are different for each record, rather than typing the record in from scratch each time. This is an alternative to the use of standard values.

To copy a group of records from one place to another:

1. Be sure you are in the Review/Add/Change menu and in Multiple Record Layout.

2. Put the cursor on the first record of the group you want copied.

3. Press Open-Apple and the letter C.

4. Choose To clipboard (cut).

5. Use the arrow keys to move the highlighting so that all the records you want to copy are enclosed in highlighting.

6. Press Return. The records will be copied to the Clipboard.

7. Now move the cursor to the position where the copied records are to be inserted. They will be put just ahead of the record on which you place the cursor.

8. Press Open-Apple-C. Then choose From clipboard (paste). The records will be copied from the Clipboard into this position.

You can also copy a portion of one record into the record below it.

1. Be sure you are in Multiple Record Layout.

2. Position the cursor on the entry below the one you wish to copy.

3. Press Open-Apple and single quote ('). Be sure not to press Shift while doing this.

The entry above will be copied into the same position in the current record.

Moving Records

It's easy to move records within your data base. All you need to do is use the Clipboard. If you think of how you would move a batch of information from an actual printed page to another one, you get a picture of how AppleWorks lets you move information: first you cut out the information you want to move (you do this by highlighting the block of records), then you put the cut-out piece in a safe, temporary place (the Clipboard), then you pick up the page where you want the information to go (you designate it by moving the cursor there), and you paste the information in place (using the Paste command).

The steps are simple:

1. Be sure you are in Multiple Record Layout.
2. Press Open-Apple and the letter M.
3. Choose To clipboard (cut).
4. Use the arrow keys to highlight the records that are to be moved. When you have highlighted all of the group, press Return. The records are temporarily moved to the Clipboard.
5. Move the cursor to the place in the data base where the records are to be inserted. Remember, they will go just ahead of where the cursor is located.
6. Press Open-Apple-M. When asked, choose From clipboard (paste). The records will be inserted where you specified.

If you forget to paste your records in place, when you leave Apple-Works, the program will remind you that you still have information on the Clipboard. If you ignore this, the data will be discarded. However, you can reenter the appropriate program at that time and paste the information it in place.

Sorting Through Your Data Base

One of the biggest values in having a data base is that you can sort through it in different ways. With AppleWorks, you can ask the program to find a certain piece of information, or to find all records with a certain sequence of characters, or even to find all records in which conditions A *and* B, or A, B, *and* C occur.

You can also rearrange your records by the values in certain entries, or even rearrange the structure of the records in your entire file.

There are two ways to search for specific information in your data base file. One way is to use the Find command, and the other is to change the Record Selection Rules.

Using the Find Command

With the Find command, you ask AppleWorks to search all of the records in your file for a particular string of characters. The program will then look through all the entries for each record in your file and report any records that have the character string you specified.

To use the Find command,

1. Press Open-Apple and the letter F.

2. Type the character string you want to search for. AppleWorks will display any record that contains the character string.

This Find feature is particularly useful when you are searching for a name, where you know part of the name but not all of it. For instance, suppose you remember that you recently had an important phone conversation with one of your suppliers, and you talked with somebody whose first name was Robin, but you couldn't remember the last name or the company. Here's what you'd do:

1. Press Open-Apple-F.

2. The screen indicates

   Find all records that contain

   and the lower line says

   Type comparison information:

3. Type the name Robin and press Return.

4. The screen will then show you the first part of the record that contained the name Robin. In this case, Robin Weberg was the contact person for the Sports Emporium in Seattle, so you see the customer name, address, city, state, and zip code for that store, in Multiple Record Layout. To see the rest of the record for Sport Emporium, you can change back to Single Record Layout by pressing Open-Apple-Z.

Be sure that the character string you are looking for is exactly what you want, or AppleWorks may find things you didn't expect to see. For instance, if you were to specify that you were looking for the name Ian, the program would show you the record for Speedo Bike Stores, because the contact person there has the name Adrian, which contains the character string *ian*.

You can be more specific in your searches by using the Record Selection Rules.

Changing Record Selection Rules

When you set up your file, the record selection rule automatically used is to select all records. This means that all of your records are displayed. (You can verify this by looking at the screen when the Review/Add/Change menu is displayed. The second line says Selection: All records.) You can be much more selective about what is displayed by changing the selection rules, and specifying that only records meeting certain criteria should be displayed.

The general procedure for changing the selection rules are:

1. Press Open-Apple and the lettter R.

2. You'll be shown your list of categories. Pick the one on which you wish the program to do its first sort. (For instance, if you want to look for all records with an address in California, select State.) Press the Return key when you're done.

3. Now the screen shows you a list of comparisons. Choose the one you want. (To choose states with an address in California, choose equals.) Then press Return.

4. The comparisons disappear and the bottom line asks you to type what the computer is to look for. (In this case, type Calif.) Press Return.

5. If this is all you wish to compare for, press Escape However, if you wish to add one or two comparisons, choose one of the connectors (and, or, through) and repeat steps 2, 3, and 4 to finish your selection rule.

AppleWorks scans your data base file and picks out all the records matching your selection criteria, then it displays them on the screen. Once the records are there, you can move them around, edit, insert, delete, and restructure them.

When you want to return to the normal record format, press Open-Apple-R, and choose Yes to indicate that you want to display all records.

Reordering Your Records

You can rearrange the order of your records by sorting on the values of entries within a category, you can change the format you see on the screen, and you can change the file structure itself by adding or deleting categories or by changing the name of the file or any of your categories.

To rearrange your records according to a value in one of your categories,

1. Move the cursor (use the TAB key) to any entry in the category by which you wish to sort.

2. Press Open-Apple and the A key.

3. Your list of records will disappear, and you'll be asked how you want to arrange the entries in this category. (Your choices are forward or reverse alphabetical order, or forward or reverse numerical order.) Pick the appropriate one and press the Return key. Your records will appear on the screen, sorted in the order you requested.

Note that you can sort on several categories, if you do it sequentially. Sort on the least important one first, then the next least important, and so on, ending with the most important one.

AppleWorks' sorting formula takes special characters into account, too. These are listed on page 61 of the *AppleWorks Reference Manual.* Generally speaking, most special characters precede numbers in sorting, and numbers precede alphabetical characters. AppleWorks makes no distinction between uppercase and lowercase letters.

Changing the Format of Records on Your Screen

In addition to changing from Multiple to Single Record Layout or vice versa (with the Open-Apple-Z command), you can alter the way records are displayed on your screen with the Layout command. What appears depends on whether you are already in Single or Multiple Record Layout.

To change the displayed layout of your records (Note: not the stored version):

1. Press Open-Apple and the letter L.

2. Your options for moving categories around are displayed near the top of the screen.

   If you are in Multiple layout, you can use the arrow keys to move the cursor to other categories, and use the Open-Apple in combination with other keys (as explained on pages 62 through 64 of the *AppleWorks Reference Manual*) to switch categories, increase or decrease the width of the column for each category, or insert or delete categories.

   If you are in Single layout, you use the arrow keys to move the cursor, and the Open-Apple and arrow keys to move categories.

3. When you have finished arranging your display, press Escape.

NOTE: While you can save the new layout (type Open-Apple-S), if you later change a file's structure by inserting or deleting a category, you will lose your customized layout. However, you can also save the new layout on paper by asking for a hard copy of it (type Open-Apple-H) once you have your screen set up the way you want it.

Changing a File's Structure

AppleWorks' flexible approach to data base structure allows you to set up your file one way, use it for a while, then later modify its structure as the need arises to add or subtract categories. You can even change the file's name.

To change the file structure or name,

1. Be sure you are in the Review/Add/Change menu. Then press Open-Apple and the letter N.

2. You'll be shown the Single Record Layout, and the right side of the screen shows you your first options, which are to change the file name (note that you can type the new name over the old one on the bottom line of the screen), or to proceed to the categories (by pressing Return).

3. If you press Return, you'll be shown some other options: changing the category name, going back to the file name, moving the cursor to the next category, or inserting or deleting a category. If you move the cursor down a category, the up arrow then moves you to the previous category. If you move the cursor all the way to the bottom of the list of categories, you can add new categories.

4. When you're finished fixing the file, press Escape.

Printing a Report

OK, you've got your data base categories shuffled around to the way you want them. But sooner or later you're going to have to create a printed report with some of this information. AppleWorks lets you create two general styles of reports, *table-style* and *label-style,* and to tailor the format and information in the reports that you print.

Table-style reports look something like the Multiple Record Layout on your screen: category names are at the top of each column, and the entries for each record (in the order you choose) run horizontally. This style of report is especially good for presenting short pieces of information in a summary form.

Label-style reports, on the other hand, look more like the Single Record Layout, in that the entries for a record appear on the left side of the page. You could use a label-style report to produce a set of mailing labels. Label-style reports are also good when your data base file has entries consisting of lengthy comments that couldn't fit into one column in a table-style report.

Both kinds of reports require that you spend some time thinking about what you want displayed in your printed report. Do you want all of the data in your file, or just some of it? Should it appear in the order in which it is stored, or should the records be sorted to reflect some other order? Do you want the category names printed or not? What are you going to name your report? You probably have more data than can easily fit on a single page. If you are going to print a table-style report, how many characters per line do you have to work with? If you're going to print a label-style report, will you have a page break in the middle of a record, or does it matter?

Probably the most efficient use of your time right now is to spend some time looking over the Print Options chapter (Chapter 5) again, to determine the limitations of your page. Among the things to note are the line length in characters, the page length in lines, and any other factors that may affect how much information you can fit on one page.

Next, go over the information in this chapter on Sorting Through Your Records. Decide which information you want to present in your report, and in what order. You will have to select it in the process of setting up your report.

Finally, choose which style of report you're going to want: table-style or label-style.

Table-style Reports

To create a table-style report:

1. Be sure you are in the Review/Add/Change menu. Then press Open-Apple and the letter P.

2. Select 2. Create a new "tables" format.

3. When asked, specify the report name. This will be used as the report's file name so that you can retrieve the format and use it again. You can use up to 19 letters, numbers, or special characters.

4. The menu now shows what you can do to rearrange the information in your file. Different keystrokes let you move the cursor, change column width, switch columns, delete columns, insert previously deleted columns, sort through your records, change the record selection rules, right-justify some of your information, add or change report names or titles, and create categories that calculate and display results based on data in other columns.

   The bottom of the menu shows three records from your file, so that you can see what will happen to the records and you change your report around.

5. When you are ready to print the report, press Open-Apple-P.

Label-Style-Report

To create a label-style report:

1. Be sure you are in the Review/Add/Change menu. Then press Open-Apple and the letter P.

2. Select 3. Create a new "labels" format.

3. When asked, type the report name.

4. The screen shows you the format in which your current records will be printed in a label-style report. The bottom line indicates how many lines each record will use in printing.

5. To see the options you have for rearranging the information in your report, press Open-Apple and the ? key. (You don't have to press shift.) Similar to the options available with a table-style report, various keystrokes let you move the cursor, insert a spacing line, delete a line or a category, left-justify certain categories, change the report name or title, sort through your

records, change the record selection rules, and print the report.

In the table-style menu, however, you can have either your format *or* the list of options on the screen, but not both. To go from the options list to your format, press the Space Bar. Press Open-Apple-? to see the options list.

6. When your report is arranged the way you want it, press Open-Apple-P to print it.

With either table-style or label-style formats, you should check the printer options menu at least once before you actually print the report. While most of the printer options menu covers the same material we discussed in Chapter 5, you also have five extra options in printing a report. These allow you to insert special codes for the printer, to print a dash when the entry is blank, to print a report header on each page, to omit a line when all entries on the line are blank, and to maintain the same number of lines for all records printed. Choose from these options before you press Open-Apple-P.

Saving Formats

Once you have created a report format, it is saved under the name you gave it. You can retrieve the format at a later time, rearrange the information again, print a new report—perhaps with new data. If you want to use the old format but with new information, you can duplicate the format and give the duplicate a different name, thus creating a new report file. You can, of course, erase the format any time you wish.

These options are available under the Report Menu, which you can get from the Review/Add/Change Menu by pressing Open-Apple-P.

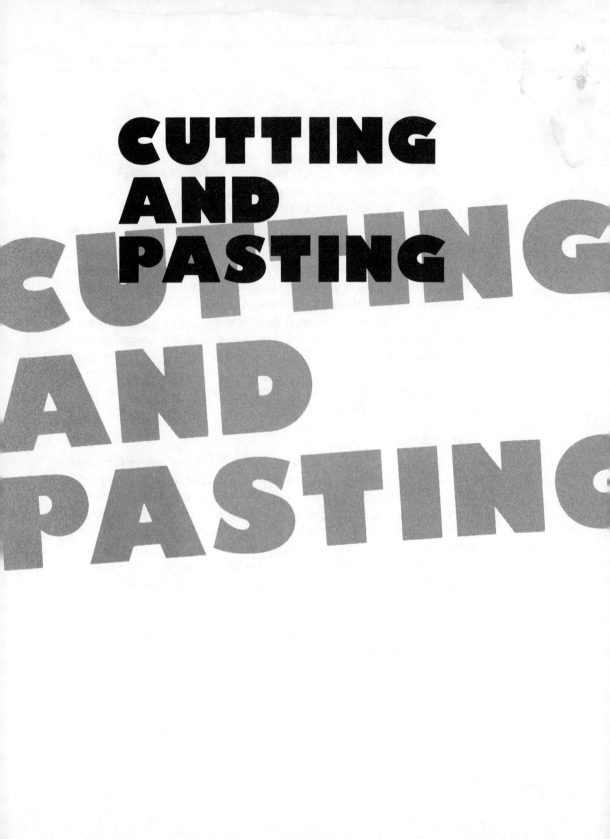

CUTTING
AND
PASTING

CUTTING
AND
PASTING

CHAPTER 8

To cut and paste in AppleWorks, you mark the information you want to transfer ("cutting"), store it temporarily in a safe place (the Clipboard), fetch the file you want to put it in, and transfer the information from the clipboard to the new position ("pasting").

For instance, you can use AppleWorks to transfer several paragraphs from one report into another. You can also put an entire spreadsheet in a written proposal or letter. You can put a copy of an edited data base table in a project summary or proposal. And you can move or copy word processor files, data base records, or spreadsheets to other files of the same type.

The Clipboard

The Clipboard is the temporary holding area for information that is being moved or copied from one file to another. It can hold 250 lines of information. All data involved in a cut and paste operation must go through the Clipboard.

When you *move* information, the information disappears from the original file. However, if you *copy* the information, the original file remains intact. (You can also move information from a file to the Clipboard, then *copy* it to a destination file; this leaves a copy on the Clipboard for another use.) When you print data base or spreadsheet information to the Clipboard, and then move it to a word processor file, the original information remains in the source file, and the printed version disappears from the Clipboard, but appears in the word processor file.

Some words of warning: moving or copying information to the Clipboard, or moving information from the Clipboard, erases what previously was there. And when you quit AppleWorks, anything left on the Clipboard disappears.

Word Processor Documents

You can transfer information between the word processor and different types of files in the following ways:

From Word Processor Files:	*To* Word Processor Files
To Word Processor Files:	*From* Word Processor Files
	From Spreadsheet Files (printed)
	From Data Base Files (printed)

You cannot transfer information from a word processor file to either a data base file or a spreadsheet file because the internal formats do not allow it.

In the rest of this chapter, we will speak of *source* and *destination* files. Source files, for our purposes here, will be those you get information from, i.e., files from which you "cut" information. Destination files will be those where the information is put, i.e., files in which you "paste" information.

From a Word Processor File to Another Word Processor File

To move or copy information where both the source file and the destination file are word processor files, follow these steps:

1. Be sure you are in the Review/Add/Change menu for the file from which you wish to "cut" information. Place the cursor at the beginning of the area you wish to "cut."

2. Press Open-Apple-M to move the information to the Clipboard (deleting it from the source file), or Open-Apple-C to copy the information to the Clipboard (leaving the original in place in the source file).

3. The bottom line of the screen asks you where you want to move or copy the text. Choose To clipboard (cut).

4. Move the cursor so that the block of text you want to move or copy is enclosed in highlighting. Then press Return.

5. Press Open-Apple-Q to see the Desktop Index. If your destination file is there, choose it. If not, add the file to the Desktop with the Main Menu, then choose it.

6. Move the cursor to the place in the destination file where you want the information moved or copied. If you want to move the information out of the Clipboard, press Open-Apple-M. If

you want to leave a version of it on the Clipboard (for use with yet another file, for example), press Open-Apple-C.

7. The line at the bottom of the screen asks you where you want to put the information. Choose From clipboard (paste). Apple-Works puts the information in the destination file.

Note that you can also use this form of cut and paste to move or copy information within a word processor file. You simply need not fetch another file (step 5 above).

From a Spreadsheet File to a Word Processor File

To move or copy spreadsheet information to a word processor document, you need to format the spreadsheet, print it to the Clipboard, and then incorporate the printed version in the word processor document.

1. Get the spreadsheet file which is to serve as the source file. Edit the information you want to print so that it will fit into the line length of the word processor (75 characters per line, including spaces).

2. Press Open-Apple-P to indicate you want to print the report.

3. Choose what you want to print, and highlight the area.

4. Choose the Clipboard as the destination. Include a date for the report header, if necessary.

5. When AppleWorks tells you the information has been transferred to the Clipboard, press Open-Apple-Q to see the Desktop Index. Choose your destination word processor file.

6. Position the cursor in the word processor document where you want the spreadsheet information to go, and press Open-Apple-M if you want to move the information from the Clipboard to the destination document, or Open-Apple-C if you want to leave a copy of it on the Clipboard.

7. Choose From the clipboard (paste).

The spreadsheet information appears in your word processor document. Note that the data is there, but not the formulas.

If you weren't careful about the line length of your spreadsheet data, you may have lines that exceed the length used with the word processor. That's not a fatal error, however, since you can always edit the information with word processing commands to fit within the line length. When a spreadsheet line is too long for the word processor, the portion of the line left over appears on the line below.

From a Data Base File to a Word Processor File

To move or copy information from a data base file to a word processor document, you have to print a data base report to the Clipboard, then move or copy the printed report to the word processor document.

1. Get the data base file you wish to use as your source, and create the report format you want for your data. Be aware that the line length of your report must fit within the 75 character line length of the word processor document, or the portion of each line that is too long will appear on a line below.

2. Press Open-Apple-P to print the report, and indicate the Clipboard as the destination. Include the report date in the header, if necessary.

3. When AppleWorks tells you the information has been transferred to the Clipboard, press Open-Apple-Q to see the Desktop Index. Choose your destination word processor file.

4. Position the cursor in the word processor document where you want the data base information to go, and press Open-Apple-M if you want to move the information from the Clipboard to the destination document, or Open-Apple-C if you want to leave a copy of it on the Clipboard.

5. Choose From the clipboard (paste).

As with the spreadsheet information, if your line length was too long for the word processor document, the portion of the line left over will appear as a new line. However, you can edit the data base report that is now included in the word processor document so that the information fits.

Spreadsheet Documents

We have looked at cutting and pasting information from a spreadsheet file into a word processor file. This section will use the Clipboard to transfer information from one spreadsheet to another, or to transfer spreadsheet information to a data base file.

From One Spreadsheet File to Another

To move or copy information from one spreadsheet file to another:

1. Get the file you want to use as your source file.

2. Move the cursor to any cell in the top row of the group of rows you want to move or copy.

3. Press Open-Apple-M if you want to move the group (deleting it from the source file), or Open-Apple-C if you want to copy it.

4. When asked for the destination, choose To clipboard (cut).

5. Move the cursor so that the rows you want to transfer are enclosed in highlighting. Then press Return.

6. When AppleWorks tells you the information has been transferred to the Clipboard, press Open-Apple-Q to see the Desktop Index. Choose your destination spreadsheet file.

7. Position the cursor in the destination spreadsheet where you want the transferred information to go, and press Open-Apple-M if you want to move the information from the Clipboard to the destination document, or Open-Apple-C if you want to leave a copy of it on the Clipboard.

8. Choose From the clipboard (paste).

From a Spreadsheet File to a Data Base File

To transfer information from a spreadsheet to a data base file, you need to print your information to a DIF file, then retrieve the file through the Desktop and transfer it to your data base by creating a new data base file.

Transferring information from a spreadsheet to a data base file bypasses the Clipboard, but is equivalent to a copying operation, in that the DIF file stays where it is written, but a copy of it is sent to the destination data base file.

NOTE: The following information is not covered in the AppleWorks User Guide or Reference Manual. While the author has indicated here steps that made the operation succeed, this procedure has never been formally tested by Apple Computer.

To transfer information from a spreadsheet to a data base file,

1. Get the spreadsheet file you want to work with, and be sure you are in the Review/Add/Change menu.

2. Format the report the way you want, then press Open-Apple-P.

When you are asked about what to print, indicate what you want.

3. When asked where you want to print the report, select 6. A DIF(TM) file on disk.

4. The bottom line of the screen will ask you about DIF order. Choose Rows.

5. The bottom of the screen will now ask you for the path name. Be careful what you do here. If yours is a single-drive system, you will need to remove the AppleWorks program disk and replace it with your data disk—there will be no message telling you to do this. If yours is a two-drive system, or a system with a hard disk, be sure that the default data drive is correctly specified and that you know the volume name exactly.
   Type the complete path name in the format

   /volumename/filename
                or
   /volumename/subdirectoryname/filename

   and press Return. The file will be written, in DIF file format, on whatever disk is in the disk drive, if yours is a one-drive system, or on the data disk if you are using more than one drive. Unless you have specified the volume name correctly, you will get error messages. The file name should be something new, but meaningful so that you will recognize it as a DIF file. (It will not show up as an AppleWorks file, and will be noted only as an OTHER type of file when you look at the disk directory in AppleWorks.) When you have finished typing the path name, press Return and the file will be written.

6. You'll be returned to the spreadsheet screen. Exit this by pressing Escape three times to take you back to the Main Menu.

7. If yours is a single-drive system, the bottom line will now ask you to put the AppleWorks program disk back in Drive 1. Do so and press Return.

8. You now have a new file on your data disk, one which Apple-Works doesn't officially recognize. In order to use it with your data base program, you have to create a new data base file. So choose 1. Add files to the Desktop.

9. Choose to make a new file for 4. Data Base. When asked, indicate that you want to make a new file 4. From a DIF (TM) file.

10. You'll now be asked for the path name. Again, be very careful. If you're using a single drive system, take out the AppleWorks Program disk and replace it with your data disk. In any case, type the complete path name and press Return.

11. When AppleWorks finds the DIF file, it will ask you for a file name since you have indicated you'll be using it to create a new data base file. Type a name for this new data base file, and press Return.

12. If yours is a single drive system, you'll now be asked to replace the data disk with the Program disk. Do so and press Return.

13. The DIF file containing your spreadsheet information appears arranged in Multiple Record Layout. Notice that the columns have been given category names of Category 01, Category 02, etc. If you want different category names, you can edit them.

Data Base Documents

Earlier we looked at transferring information from a data base file to a word processor file. In this section, we will show you how to transfer information from one data base file to another, and from a data base file to a spreadsheet.

From One Data Base File to Another

You can move up to 250 records from one data base file to another, or within a data base.

1. Be sure you are in the source file you want to use, and in the Review/Add/Change menu and Multiple Record Layout.

2. Place the cursor on the top record you want to move or copy.

3. Press Open-Apple-M to move the record or Open-Apple-C to copy it.

4. When asked for the destination, choose To clipboard (cut). Then move the cursor so that all the records you want to transfer are enclosed in highlighting, and press Return.

5. Press Open-Apple-Q to see the index of files on the Desktop. Choose your destination data base file.

6. Use the Multiple Record Layout with the destination file, and move the cursor to the point where you want to transfer the

information from the Clipboard. The transferred information will be inserted just ahead of the record where the cursor is located.

7. Press Open-Apple-M to move the record from the Clipboard or Open-Apple-C to copy it. Choose From clipboard (paste).

From a Data Base File to a Spreadsheet

You can transfer information from a data base file to a spreadsheet file by printing a data base report to a DIF file, then writing the DIF file to a newly created spreadsheet file.

When creating the printed data base report, be aware of the fact that spreadsheet columns are normally 9 characters wide, so information in your data base report that is in wider columns won't appear when you transfer the DIF file. (The information in wider columns is still there—you just have to alter the spreadsheet to make the relevant columns wider.)

Transferring information from a data base file to a spreadsheet file bypasses the Clipboard, but is equivalent to a copying operation, in that the DIF file stays where it is written, but a copy of it is sent to the destination spreadsheet file.

NOTE: The following information is not covered in the AppleWorks User Guide or Reference Manual. While the author has indicated here steps that made the operation succeed, this procedure has never been formally tested by Apple Computer.

To transfer information from a data base file to a spreadsheet,

1. Get the data base file you want to work with and be sure you are in the Review/Add/Change menu and in Multiple Record Layout.

2. Format the report the way you want, and when you are done, print the report using Open-Apple-P. When asked where you want to print it, select 7. A DIF (TM) file on disk.

3. The bottom of the screen will now ask you for the path name. Be careful what you do here. If yours is a single-drive system, you will need to remove the AppleWorks program disk and replace it with your data disk—there will be no message telling you to do this. If yours is a two-drive system, or a system with a hard disk, be sure that the default data drive is correctly specified and that you know the volume name exactly.

   Type the complete path name in the format

/volumename/filename

or

/volumename/subdirectoryname/filename

and press Return. The file will be written, in DIF file format, on whatever disk is in the disk drive, if yours is a one-drive system, or on the data disk if you are using more than one drive. Unless you have specified the volume name correctly, you will get error messages. The file name should be something new, but meaningful so that you will recognize it as a DIF file. (It will not show up as an AppleWorks file, and will be noted only as an OTHER type of file when you look at the disk directory in AppleWorks.) When you have finished typing the path name, press Return and the file will be written.

4. If yours is a single-drive system, the bottom line will now ask you to put the AppleWorks program disk back in Drive 1. Do so and press Return.

5. You'll be returned to the data base report screen. Exit this by pressing Escape three times to take you back to the Main Menu.

6. You now have a new file on your data disk, one which Apple-Works doesn't officially recognize. In order to use it, you have to create a new spreadsheet file. So choose 1. Add files to the Desktop.

7. Choose to make a new file for 5. Spreadsheet. When asked, indicate that you want to make a new file 2. From a DIF (TM) file.

8. You'll now be asked for the path name. Again, be very careful. If you're using a single-drive system, take out the AppleWorks Program disk and replace it with your data disk. In any case, type the complete path name and press Return.

9. When AppleWorks finds the DIF file, it will ask you for the new file name since you have indicated you'll be using it to create a new spreadsheet file. Type a name for this new spreadsheet file, and press Return.

10. If yours is a single-drive system, you'll now be asked to replace the data disk with the Program disk. Do so and press Return.

11. The DIF file containing your data base report appears arranged in the spreadsheet columns. Notice that if your report columns

were wider than 9 characters, information in columns is truncated to fit. The information is actually still there and you can see it by widening the columns with the Spreadsheet Layout (Open-Apple-L) commands.

Notice also that the category names are not there. Only the data has been transferred. If you want the category names, you can insert a row and type them in.

PUTTING IT ALL TOGETHER

CHAPTER

What's the use of having an integrated program unless you use it to have different kinds of files "talk" to each other?

This chapter will give you some examples of situations where the ability to get back and forth between applications within AppleWorks will be very handy.

The following types of information transfer within AppleWorks will be shown in this chapter:

1. Word Processor document to Word Processor document
2. Spreadsheet file to Spreadsheet file
3. Data Base file to Data Base file
4. Spreadsheet report to Word Processor document
5. Data Base report to Word Processor document
6. Spreadsheet report to Data Base file
7. Data Base report to Spreadsheet file

Word Processor Document to Word Processor Document

Every company has a situation like this one: The company sales force, with the assistance of product people, pounds the pavement and knocks on doors and eventually manages to place an order. In this case, let's assume it's an order for something that needs to be produced. Figure 9.1 is the confirmation letter as written by the salesperson.

That's how the schedule is presented to the customer. Inside the company, of course, it's a different matter. Ms. O'Meagher is now faced with making sure that the company engineering department puts the system together on time, that the field service people are ready to

July 28, 1984

Adrian Thomas
Sports World, Inc.
445 Scripps Ave.
Palo Alto, Ca. 94367

Dear Mr. Thomas:

Thank you for your order for our Model 4350 Timing and Display System. As you know, it is one of the most accurate systems in the world, capable of measuring lap times in thousandths of a second.

The system will be delivered and set up according to the schedule below. Please note that there is a one month break-in period, during which our service people will be on call every day of the week to come out and fix any part of the system that doesn't work. Note also that there is a training session for the people you will use as timers. We will hold the training session at your facility for up to ten people, at no additional charge. You indicated you'd like to hold the session before the end of the break-in period. Please contact the head of our customer service department, Don Burden, to arrange the time and date of this training session.

SCHEDULE

April 5	Site visit, Engineering Dept. (for measurement of facilities).
April 16	Site plan delivered to customer for approval; permit application delivered to City.
April 19	Customer-requested changes incorporated in plans; City notified.
April 30	City approvals expected.
May 8	System installation at customer site; demonstration to facility manager and staff; begin one-month break-in period.
May 15	Field service checkup of system.
June 8	Customer acceptance of system.

Thank you again for your order.

Yours truly,

P. K. O'Meagher

Figure 9.1: Letter to customer with schedule.

handle it, and in particular that Mr. Burden's training program is ready when the customer is ready. As ammunition, she needs to enclose the schedule the customer has agreed to. With AppleWorks, she can simply use the cut and paste facility to do this. Here's what she does:

1. First, she saves both the letter to Mr. Thomas and the memo under separate file names. (You can do this quickly by pressing Open-Apple-S.)

2. Both files have been created on the Desktop, hence are still there even though she saved them. (If you quit after saving the files, you'll need to get them back onto the Desktop.) She presses Open-Apple-Q to see the Desktop Index. Then she moves the highlighted block to the file name of the file containing the letter to Mr. Thomas and presses Return. The customer letter is displayed on her screen.

3. Now she moves the cursor to the first letter of the word SCHEDULE, and presses Open-Apple-C.

4. She selects To clipboard (cut).

5. She moves the cursor so that the highlighting encloses the whole schedule, including the line for June 8. Then she presses Return. The schedule is now copied to the Clipboard.

6. She presses Open-Apple-Q to see the Desktop Index again, and moves the highlighting to the file name of the file containing the memo. Then she presses Return.

7. The internal memo is now on her screen. She moves the cursor to the spot where she wants the schedule to appear and presses Open-Apple-M. On the bottom line, she selects From clipboard (paste).

8. The schedule is inserted in the memo. All she needs to do now is save the newly edited file and print it, and she's done. Her internal memo now looks like Figure 9.2.

And that's how easy it is to move text from one word processor document to another with AppleWorks.

In summary, you create and save both files; being sure both are on the Desktop, "cut" the section you want out of one and save it on the Clipboard while you go get the other file; then move or copy it to the new file. Depending on whether you have moved or copied the "cut" information, you may have also removed it from the source document, or left a copy of it on the Clipboard.

Spreadsheet File to Spreadsheet File

Suppose you had a working spreadsheet and wanted to use the same format with another spreadsheet. AppleWorks lets you do this without ever leaving the program.

For example, remember the Ames Project we constructed in Chapter 6? That's a fairly useful format. Suppose you needed to justify the first quarter figures, by showing a month-by-month cash flow projection for the first quarter. You could use the same column and row arrangement, but change the column headings and the data for each column.

To: Don Burden
From: P. K. O'Meagher
Re: Model 4350 System order for Sports World
March 28, 1984

As you can see from the schedule below, we have some work to do. I know you don't have the training program ready—we've never had a customer who wanted one before—but he bought it and now we have to deliver it.

Here's the schedule:

SCHEDULE

April 5	Site visit, Engineering Dept. (for measurement of facilities).
April 16	Site plan delivered to customer for approval; permit application delivered to City.
April 19	Customer-requested changes incorporated in plans; City notified.
April 30	City approvals expected.
May 8	System installation at customer site; demonstration to facility manager and staff; begin one-month break-in period.
May 15	Field service checkup of system.
June 8	Customer acceptance of system.

I can meet with you and George Ebey from Engineering on Friday, March 30 at 9:30 to go over what the system does and what Sports World's expectations are about training. I can also probably help you write and print a nice little handout to supplement your class if you and George can define what all the system will do. But let's get our collective act together quickly.

Figure 9.2: Memorandum containing schedule from Figure 9.1.

First off, get the Ames Project worksheet. If you've stored it on your data disk, it's a simple matter to retrieve it. From the Main Menu, add it to the Desktop. If you haven't stored it, create it. When done, your Ames Project worksheet should look like Figure 9.3.

Now, follow these steps to create a new, month-by-month worksheet in the same format:

1. With the Ames Project spreadsheet on your screen, press Open-Apple-C. Choose To clipboard (cut).

2. Use the cursor so that highlighting encloses all of the rows with information: rows 1 through 14. Then press Return.

3. Press Escape to return to the Main Menu.

4. Select 1. Add files to the Desktop.

5. Create a new spreadsheet file and give it a name.

6. Press Open-Apple-C. This time, choose From clipboard (paste).

7. If you have more than one item on the clipboard, you will need to choose the appropriate one. Otherwise, your Ames Project spreadsheet automatically appears on your screen, under the file name you gave the newly created spreadsheet file.

```
File: spread7              REVIEW/ADD/CHANGE              Escape: Main Menu
========A========B========C========D========E========F========G========H====
  1 I                      Ames Project
  2 I                      Cash Flow Projection
  3 I                      First    Second   Third    Fourth
  4 I                      Quarter  Quarter  Quarter  Quarter
  5 IIncome                100000   120000   144000   172800
  6 ICost of Sales          10000    12000    14400    17280
  7 ICost of Goods          50000    60000    72000    86400
  8 IOperating Expenses     10000    12000    14400    17280
  9 I                      -----------------------------------
 10 INet Income             30000    36000    43200    51840
 11 ITaxes                  14700    17640    21168  25401.6
 12 ICarryforward Profits       0    15300    33660    55692
 13 I                      -----------------------------------
 14 INet Profits            15300    33660    55692  82130.4
 15 I
 16 I
 17 I
 18 I
-------------------------------------------------------------------------
G14: (Value) +G10-G11+G12

Type entry or use @ commands                            @-? for Help
```

Figure 9.3: The Ames Project worksheet.

8. To make this a month-by-month spreadsheet, edit the word "Quarter" and make it into Month for columns D, E, and F. Then change the column heading "Fourth Quarter" to "First Quarter." Next, edit the formulas in column G so that the entries in G5, G6, G7, and G8 sum up the values in columns D, E, and F for that row. This can be either in the form @SUM(D5 . . F5) or +D5+E5+F5. Leave rows 9 through 14 alone, since they either contain tally lines or formulas, both of which you can use.

9. Now you're ready to play "What if?" with your new spreadsheet. The data showing on the spreadsheet is from the quarterly spreadsheet, and shows a quarterly income of $100,000. If you want to create this sum in column G, you can enter three amounts in columns D, E, and F that add up to $100,000, say 10,000 in column D, 30,000 in column E, and 60,000 in column F. Note that you are directly entering data over the formulas that were used in columns E and F, and that until the data replaces the formulas, the formulas affect columns to the right.

10. Once you've finished with row 5, move on to enter data in rows 6, 7, and 8. In each case, column G will reflect the sum of the previous three columns.

Figure 9.4 shows how one version of this month-by-month spreadsheet looks.

You can modify the data in rows 5, 6, 7, and 8 any way you wish, and notice the "ripple" effect of each change as the numbers in the rest of the spreadsheet are automatically recalculated.

When you are through playing "What if?" save the spreadsheet, by pressing Open-Apple-S and following the instructions.

Data Base File to Data Base File

Frequently, you need information about your customers in more than one place, and in more than one format. You can use the information in one data base file to develop the information you need in the other file.

As with the spreadsheet, AppleWorks requires that records in both files be in the same format. If they are not, you need to create a blank, interim file where you can do your editing of source records so that they will conform to the format of the destination file. This section will show you how to do that.

In most companies, the accounting department and the marketing and sales department work together fairly closely: one is concerned with implementing the contracts that the other one acquires. Once that is done, accounting records can show the marketing and sales force trends or patterns in customers' orders.

For instance, let's assume that you want to set up some accounting records based on the customer information in the file used as an example in Chapter 7. Since the information needed by accounting is a bit different from that needed by marketing, we know that the two files will use different formats. However, much of the information is common to the two files.

An efficient way to proceed is to set up a duplicate file of the source information but with a different name, then add the categories you want and delete the categories you don't want. Once the new file is set up, transferring information from the original source file to the destination file will require the use of an interim file, as mentioned above, for editing.

```
File: preliminaryames          REVIEW/ADD/CHANGE              Escape: Main Menu
========A========B========C========D========E========F========G========H====
   1 |                         First Quarter - Ames Project
   2 |                         Cash Flow Projection
   3 |                                                   First
   4 |                         Month 1  Month 2  Month 3  Quarter
   5 |Income                     10000    30000    60000   100000
   6 |Cost of Sales               1000     3000     6000    10000
   7 |Cost of Goods              25000    15000    10000    50000
   8 |Operating Expenses          3000     3500     3500    10000
   9 |                         ----------------------------------
  10 |Net Income                -19000     8500    40500    30000
  11 |Taxes                      -9310     4165    19845    14700
  12 |                         ----------------------------------
  13 |Net Profits               -9690     4335    20655    15300
  14 |
  15 |
  16 |
  17 |
  18 |
------------------------------------------------------------------------------
G13: (Value) +G10-G11

Type entry or use ∂ commands                              ∂-? for Help
```

Figure 9.4: The month-by-month Ames Project spreadsheet.

The information in the original marketing file had the following categories:

Customer Name
Address
City
State
Zip Code
Phone
Contact person
Date last order
Amount last order
Purchases this year

The information needed in the accounting file will be the following:

Customer Name
Address
City
State
Zip Code
Phone
Date last order
Amount last order
Invoice number
Invoice date
Date paid

Notice that much of the information is the same, but there are several categories that are different.

To create the new accounting file, first you have to create an empty file that has the same categories as the source file. Since you'll have to use the same categories, get the source file on your screen and note on a piece of scratch paper what the categories are. Then create the new file, using the Add files to the Desktop option on the Main Menu to create a data base file from scratch.

When you are asked for the new categories, type in the category names you noted. (Be sure to press Open-Apple-E to change to the overstrike cursor.) You don't have to spell the category names exactly the same, but the entries will be inserted into the new file in the same order as the old. When you get to the end of the old category names, type in the new ones, in any order. Thus your new file's categories will look like this:

> Customer Name
> Address
> City
> State
> Zip Code
> Phone
> Contact person
> Date last order
> Amount last order
> Purchases this year
> Invoice number
> Invoice date
> Date paid

Follow these steps to get information from the marketing file into your new file:

1. Press ESC to get back to the Review/Add/Change menu.

2. Press Open-Apple-Q to see the Desktop Index.

3. Select your marketing file. The screen will show you the marketing file in Multiple Record Layout.

4. Press Open-Apple-C to copy the records to the Clipboard, and choose To clipboard (cut).

5. Move the cursor so that all of the records are highlighted, then press Return.

6. Press Open-Apple-Q to see the Desktop Index again and choose your accounting file.

7. Since your accounting file is empty, you'll see a warning notice. Press the Space Bar as requested, and you'll see an empty record, with all of your categories, in Single Record Layout.

8. Press Open-Apple-Z to change to Multiple Record Layout. When you see this format, with a dash in each category, press Open-Apple-C and choose From clipboard (paste) to get the marketing records from the Clipboard. The marketing file information will then be loaded into the new file.

9. To create the file organization you want, you'll now need to use the File Name command. Press Open-Apple-N to do this.

10. The file layout changes to Single Record Layout, but with only the category names shown. Delete the categories "Contact Person" and "Purchases to Date" and notice that the categories you added, Invoice Number, Invoice Date, and Date Paid, are shown below.

11. When you have the categories arranged the way you want, press Escape. You'll have to indicate cursor direction before you can leave the Layout menu, but once you've selected that, press Return. The new file, in Multiple Record Layout, appears on your screen. But since you can only see the first part of it, press Open-Apple-Z to see a record with the new categories.

12. Move the cursor down to the Invoice Number category, and type in an invoice number. Then press Return to move to the next category, and type in an invoice date. Press Return and type in a date for Date Paid. Note that you can leave this entry blank, indicating an unpaid bill. You can then sort on this category to determine your Accounts Receivable.

13. Repeat Step 12 for all of the records in your accounting file, and you'll have it all set up.

When you add records to the marketing file and want to add them to the accounting file, or vice versa, create an interim file, using the method noted above. Edit the category organization with the Open-Apple-N command, then use the Clipboard's cut and paste capabilities to copy the information to the destination file.

Spreadsheet Report to Word Processor File

Next to transferring information between two word processing files, probably the easiest interprogram transfer to imagine is from a spreadsheet to a word processed text. However, this transfer is rather difficult to accomplish unless you're using an integrated package like Apple-Works. In a nonintegrated environment, you usually have to generate the spreadsheet, cut it to size, type the word processed document leaving space for the cut-out spreadsheet, then literally paste the spreadsheet into the blank space in the word processed printout.

With AppleWorks it is so much easier. You can do either the word processor document or the spreadsheet first, then format a report from the spreadsheet that will fit within the page width and length boundaries of the word processor document, then use the Clipboard to transfer the spreadsheet report to the word processor file. When you print the word processor document, the spreadsheet information appears exactly where you positioned it.

To see how this is done, let's use as a sample a report that includes in it the quarter-by-quarter projection of the Ames Project discussed earlier in this chapter and developed in Chapter 6. We'll assume that you have the Ames Project spreadsheet file stored on your data disk.

To see how this transfer works, create the word processor file shown in Figure 9.5.

When you have finished typing the letter, save it by pressing Open-Apple-S. Follow the instructions, and when the save is complete, press Open-Apple-Q to see the Desktop Index and fetch the Ames Project spreadsheet. You may have to press Escape to retrieve the file from your data disk if you haven't used it lately.

THE AMES PROJECT

The 1984 Olympic Games in Los Angeles generated a great deal of interest in and enthusiasm for a number of sports, including bicycling. Reports from our retail customers indicate a considerably increased demand for all types of bicycle accessories, including sport-specific clothing.

We have been experiencing some difficulties with these items, especially the cycling shirts and pants. Our retailers report that the wool knits have stretched and become misshapen in washing—the seams have even come apart. As one means of offering our customers higher quality merchandise, we are investigating the possibility of manufacturing the clothing ourselves.

We have done a preliminary cash flow projection showing the income and expenses that would be involved in such a venture. We have assumed that we could use the spare capacity available in our swim and tennis apparel manufacturing facility in Tucson, Arizona. Product launching would be during the fall, a traditionally slow time for cycling gear. This together with startup costs, will keep our net income for the first quarter low. However, as our analysis shows, net income from this project alone is likely to experience a healthy growth.

The Cost of Sales is our estimate of what it would cost to find and use reps, and the Operating Costs is an estimate of this project's share of plant overhead. The Cost of Goods figure would probably be proportional to sales, since we already have idle time on the equipment in place.

While this is just a preliminary study, we feel it is promising enough to warrant more investigation by the Product Marketing group.

Figure 9.5: The Ames Project letter.

Once you have added it to the Desktop, follow these steps:

1. Figure out how many characters wide your spreadsheet is. Since you constructed it with the standard column width of 9 characters per column, and you have a 7-column spreadsheet, you have 63 characters of information per line. However, your word processor default line length is 60 characters. If you try to incorporate the spreadsheet as it is, you'll wind up with the data from column G forming a new line in the word processor.

   To compensate for that, you can make some minor modifications to the spreadsheet, or you can change the line length of the word processor. Let's do the former.

2. Since the only thing in column C is the latter part of the row heading "Carryforward Profits," we could eliminate that column, then edit the heading to fit within columns A and B. Place the cursor in column C, press Open-Apple-D and choose Columns. (column C will be highlighted). Press Return.

3. Move the cursor to A12 and retype the row heading as "Carryfwd. Profits".

4. Press Open-Apple-P to indicate you want to print a report. Select ALL since you want to print the entire report.

5. Select the Clipboard as the place where you want to print the report.

6. When asked for the date, press Return. Then read the message and press the Space Bar.

7. Press Open-Apple-Q to see the Desktop Index again.

8. Choose the file name you gave the word processor document when you created it. The document appears on the screen.

9. Insert an extra line of space between the third and fourth paragraphs by positioning the cursor on the blank line after the third paragraph, and pressing Return. The spreadsheet information will be inserted just above the cursor.

10. Press Open-Apple-M to move the spreadsheet report from the Clipboard to the word processor document. It appears on your screen. Note that the first three lines include the name of the file, a page number, and a blank line and that these precede what was the first line of your spreadsheet. Use the editing capabilities of the word processor to remove this information.

Now your report looks like Figure 9.6.

THE AMES PROJECT

The 1984 Olympic Games in Los Angeles generated a great deal of interest in and enthusiasm for a number of sports, including bicycling. Reports from our retail customers indicate a considerably increased demand for all types of bicycle accessories, including sport-specific clothing.

We have been experiencing some difficulties with these items, especially the cycling shirts and pants. Our retailers report that the wool knits have stretched and become misshapen in washing—the seams have even come apart. As one means of offering our customers higher quality merchandise, we are investigating the possibility of manufacturing the clothing ourselves.

Below is a preliminary cash flow projection showing the income and expenses that would be involved in such a venture. We have assumed that we could use the spare capacity available in our swim and tennis apparel manufacturing facility in Tucson, Arizona. Product launching would be during the fall, a traditionally slow time for cycling gear. This together with startup costs, will keep our net income for the first quarter low. However, as the chart shows, net income from this project alone is likely to experience a healthy growth.

Ames Project Cash Flow Projection

	First Quarter	Second Quarter	Third Quarter	Fourth Quarter
Income	100,000	115,000	132,250	152,087.50
Cost of Sales	10,000	11,500	13,225	15,208.75
Cost of Goods	50,000	57,500	66,125	76,043.75
Operating Expenses	10,000	11,500	13,225	15,208.75
Net Income	30,000	34,500	39,675	45,626.25
Taxes	14,700	16,905	19,440.75	22,356.86
Carryfwd. Profits	0	15,300	32,895	53,129.25
Cumulative Profits	15,300	32,895	53,129.25	76,398.63

The Cost of Sales is our estimate of what it would cost to find and use reps, and the Operating Costs is an estimate of this project's share of plant overhead. The Cost of Goods figure would probably be proportional to sales, since we already have idle time on the equipment in place.

While this is just a preliminary study, we feel it is promising enough to warrant more investigation by the Product Marketing group.

Figure 9.6: The Ames Project letter with spreadsheet "pasted" in.

Data Base Report to Word Processor Document

Even if you use AppleWorks mostly for word processing, it's nice to have some of your data base files available at the touch of a few keys. Information in a data base file can be sifted and compressed into a form that can be used in a letter or report.

For instance, suppose you needed to provide some references when you apply for a business loan: you could as in the example below, go to your marketing file and format a list of companies with whom you do business, the phone number and contact person for each, and include it all quickly and easily in your letter to the bank. All without ever leaving AppleWorks.

Begin by typing the letter in Figure 9.7, and saving it on your data disk.

The information you want to insert is in your marketing data base file. To format it properly and then transfer to this document, follow

March 30, 1984

Fred Olson, vice-president
First City Bank
855 Main Street
Belmont, Ca. 94083

Dear Mr. Olson:

Thank you for spending time with us yesterday and reviewing our proposal for an extension of our credit line. As you know, when the timing is right for a new product line—as we believe it is for our own line of bicycle clothing—it is important to move quickly.

In addition to the other documents you requested, you asked for a list of our customers whom you could contact as references. You will find a list enclosed.

Since the idea of manufacturing our own line of bicycle clothing was initially sparked by the enthusiasm of our retailers, we feel sure their comments will add credibility to our assessment of this market.

If we can provide any more information, please don't hesitate to call us.

Yours truly,

Charles Everett, Director of Marketing

Figure 9.7: Letter to the bank.

these steps:

1. Press Open-Apple-Q to see the Desktop Index. Choose your marketing data base file if it is already listed there. If it hasn't yet been loaded, you may need to return to the Main Menu and add it to the Desktop.

2. When your marketing data base file appears on the screen, press Open-Apple-P. When asked, indicate that you are going to create a new "tables" format, then give this report a name. You'll be shown the list of options you can use in creating your table.

3. Reformat your records so that the screen only shows you the customer name, phone number, and contact person. You will need to use the delete keystroke, Open-Apple-D, to remove the columns not needed for this report, and the Open-Apple and arrow keys to widen the columns so that the entire customer name and contact person's name will fit. You may also want to add a space or two between the columns. However, be aware of the fact that your word processor document's line length is 60 characters—you don't want to have your records spill over onto a new line.

4. When your report is formatted the way you want it, press Open-Apple-P again. When asked where you want to print, indicate the Clipboard. You can simply press Return when asked about the date.

5. When you get the message that the report has been printed on the Clipboard, press the Space Bar, then press Open-Apple-Q to see the Desktop Index again.

6. Choose the file name under which you stored your letter to the bank. When it appears on your screen, move the cursor to the blank line above the third paragraph.

7. Press Open-Apple-M, and choose From clipboard (paste). The edited data base report appears on your screen, inserted between the second and third paragraphs. The first three lines contain information you may want to edit out before printing and saving the letter. You may also wish to edit the category names. The final version of the letter looks like Figure 9.8.

All that remains is for you to save the new version of the letter and print it.

Data Base File to Spreadsheet File

You can even do inventory statements with AppleWorks, using a data base file to store the information. Then, when you want to do a statement of the value of your inventory, you can simply transfer the results to a spreadsheet and do your calculations there.

March 30, 1984

Fred Olson, vice-president
First City Bank
855 Main Street
Belmont, Ca. 94083

Dear Mr. Olson:

Thank you for spending time with us yesterday and reviewing our proposal for an extension of our credit line. As you know, when the timing is right for a new product line—as we believe it is for our own line of bicycle clothing—it is important to move quickly.

In addition to the other documents you requested, you asked for a list of our customers whom you could contact as references. Please feel free to call the following:

Customer Name	Phone Number	Contact Person
The Bike Rack	619 555 1357	Don Burwell
Speedo Bike Stores, Inc.	408 555 1352	Adrian Jeremy
Novus Sport Shops	415 555 8297	Charles Prael
Sports Emporium	206 555 4399	Robin Weberg
A-1 Sporting Goods Stores	206 555 4466	Chris Davis

Since the idea of manufacturing our own line of bicycle clothing was initially sparked by the enthusiasm of our retailers, we feel sure their comments will add credibility to our assessment of this market.

If we can provide any more information, please don't hesitate to call us.

Yours truly,

Charles Everett, Director of Marketing

Figure 9.8: Letter to the bank with references from data base.

For instance, suppose you had the following information (representing part of your inventory) set up as a data base file:

Item Name	M/F	Size	Color	Number in Stock	Date Rcd.
Pegasus Shirt	M	S	blue/yellow	200	1/25/84
Pegasus Shirt	M	M	blue/yellow	300	1/25/84
Pegasus Shirt	M	L	blue/yellow	250	1/25/84
Pegasus Shirt	M	XL	blue/yellow	100	1/25/84
Alligator Shirt	F	S	red/black	70	2/15/84
Alligator Shirt	F	M	red/black	100	2/15/84
Alligator Shirt	F	L	red/black	55	2/15/84
Cycling pants	M	28	black	35	1/31/84
Cycling pants	M	30	black	42	2/6/84
Cycling pants	M	32	black	27	2/6/84
Cycling pants	M	34	black	36	2/6/84
Cycling pants	M	36	black	29	1/31/84
Cycling pants	M	38	black	23	1/31/84
Cycling pants	M	40	black	12	1/31/84

To send this information to a spreadsheet, follow these steps:

1. Create a report, using the Open-Apple-P keys and using a "table" style of report.
2. Format the report, increasing the column width for the column headed "Item Name", and reducing the column width for the columns headed "M/F" and "Size."
3. Press Open-Apple-P again, and choose the DIF file as the destination.
4. *You will not be prompted for this:* If yours is a single-drive system, remove the Program diskette and insert your data diskette.
5. Type the complete path name, beginning with a slash and including the new file name you're giving the DIF file.
6. If you have a single-drive system, remove the data diskette, insert the Program diskette, and press Return.
7. Press Escape three times to get you back to the Main Menu.
   NOTE: If you can't remember the name of your DIF file, here is where you should choose Other Activities, then List All Files. The DIF files will be listed below the AppleWorks files.

8. Since you haven't created your spreadsheet file yet, choose 1. Add files to the Desktop.

9. Choose to make a new spreadsheet file from a DIF file.

10. If you are using a single-drive system, remove the Program disk and insert the data disk.

11. Type the DIF file's complete path name, including the beginning slash and volume name.

12. Once you have typed it correctly, you will be asked for a name for this new file. This is the name you'll be giving the spreadsheet.

13. The DIF file will be loaded into the spreadsheet form. You'll want to edit the file, making the "Item Name" column wider, and probably the "M/F" and "Size" columns smaller. For these purposes, you'll also want to delete the "Date Rcd." column.

14. Since DIF files don't come with column headings, insert two rows at the top of the spreadsheet, and use them to label the columns.

15. Since you're going to use this spreadsheet to come up with a valuation for your inventory, label columns F and G "Cost" and "Value" respectively.

16. Insert cost figures into the Cost column. You can use the ones we show in the example, or make up your own.

17. In cell G3, type the formula +E3*F3. This multiplies the contents of the cell in column E by the contents of the cell in column F.

18. Use Open-Apple-C to copy the formula into the other cells in column G. Be sure to specify that the values are relative. The results will show the value of each item.

19. At the bottom of the spreadsheet, in cell A18, type

    Total value of inventory

    and type the formula @SUM(G3 . . . G16) into cell G16. When you press Return, the total value of your inventory will be determined and displayed here. Your spreadsheet will now look something like this:

Item Name	M/F	Size	Color	Number in stock	@	Value
Pegasus Shirt	M	S	blue/yellow	200	12.14	2428.00

Pegasus Shirt	M	M	blue/yellow	300	12.14	3642.00
Pegasus Shirt	M	L	blue/yellow	250	12.14	3035.00
Pegasus Shirt	M	XL	blue/yellow	100	12.14	1214.00
Alligator Shirt	F	S	red/black	70	10.74	751.80
Alligator Shirt	F	M	red/black	100	10.74	1074.00
Alligator Shirt	F	L	red/black	55	10.74	590.70
Cycling pants	M	28	black	35	20.55	719.25
Cycling pants	M	30	black	42	20.55	863.10
Cycling pants	M	32	black	27	20.55	554.85
Cycling pants	M	34	black	36	20.55	739.80
Cycling pants	M	36	black	29	20.55	595.95
Cycling pants	M	38	black	23	20.55	472.65
Cycling pants	M	40	black	12	20.55	246.60
Total value of inventory						16927.70

Your total inventory value figure can, of course, be used elsewhere, such as in a balance sheet. When you bring in new inventory at a different price, you can use this method to value it, then compare it with the value of the inventory shown here, and thus determine which should be sold first.

Spreadsheet File to Data Base File

One of the nice things about having a data base nearby, with its record and entry manipulation features, is that you can send a spreadsheet to the data base for reorganizing, then transfer the reformatted data back to the spreadsheet.

For instance, suppose you have the following accounts receivable file set up on a spreadsheet. Because you are going to be going through a DIF file and then into a data base file, you'll need to have constructed it so that there is one complete entry per column. This means that Column A needs to be widened (using the Open-Apple-L command) to 18 characters, and Column B needs to be widened to 12 characters.

Supplier	Phone	30 days	60 days	90 days	Total
Miller Supplies	803 555 1446	4057	0	1255	5312
Western Distributing	408 555 3355	0	336	3305	3641
A-1 Sporting Goods	206 555 6988	1055	1105	0	2160

Berkeley Sports	415 555 0666	0	3380	0	3380
Corona Wholesalers	619 555 6332	7882	4355	855	13092
Dolan Distribution	408 555 3355	2333	1440	0	3773
Emeryville Pkg.	415 555 4228	0	1446	1770	3216
Ferris/Grant	206 555 6640	770	355	226	1351
Hudson River Sprt.	914 555 2113	9935	0	0	9935
International Whl.	415 555 4322	0	8994	6715	15709
Jackson Lake Sprt.	307 555 6332	335	0	0	335
Kerry Corp.	408 555 7900	1335	0	0	1335
Michigan Sports	615 555 3998	290	3556	0	3846
New Mexico Supp.	505 555 2200	1443	0	355	1798
Olson May Co.	213 555 6620	8835	7725	0	16560
Park City Sports	801 555 3877	0	2440	0	2440

Now suppose you have an accounting person who needs to call the companies on this list, but wants to use a discount long distance phone line that gives no particular break on calls that are local to the 415 or 408 area. She needs to have the list sorted into local and non-local phone numbers, where local calls have the prefix 415 or 408.

You can't do this on a spreadsheet. But you can with the Apple-Works data base program. How? Glad you asked.

1. With the complete spreadsheet on your screen (and stored on disk beforehand), position the cursor at the first data entry—in this case, cell A3. Press Open-Apple-P and choose Block, then use the cursor to highlight all of the data (but not the column headings).

2. Indicate you want to print the report on a DIF file. Specify Column order.

3. Give the complete path name, including the name of the data disk and the new file name for the DIF file. It will probably help if you write down the path name. Remember to start the path name with a slash if yours is a single-drive system. *Remember to insert your data disk before you press Return.* Once the file has been recorded, reinsert the Program disk.

4. Exit to the Main Menu by pressing Escape, and choose to Add a file to the Desktop. You wish to create a data base file, using a DIF file as input.

5. Give the path name when prompted. Remember to insert the data disk before you press Return if yours is a single-drive system. Once the file has been loaded, reinsert the Program disk, and give the newly created data base file a name.

6. The spreadsheet data now appears on your screen in Multiple Record format. Note that there are no category labels except "Category 01", "Category 02," etc. However, it's easy to see that Category 02 contains the phone numbers.

7. Press Open-Apple-R (for record selection). Move the highlighted bar to Category 02 and press Return.

8. Since you want to select those records beginning with the 415 or 408 prefix,
   a. Select 8. begins with.
   b. Type 415 and press Return.
   c. Select 2. or
   d. Select Category 02.
   e. Select 8. begins with.
   f. Type 408 and press Return.

   Notice that your rules for selection are displayed at the top of the screen. You're through specifying rules, so press Escape.

9. The list that appears on your screen is those items from your original spreadsheet list that had phone numbers beginning with the prefix 415 or 408. If you want, you can now format and print a report to hand to your accounting person, or you can simply use the screen to help you mark up your printed spreadsheet report.

MORE
ABOUT
PRINTING

CHAPTER 10

You've set up your files and created the kind of word processing, spreadsheet, or data base report you want. Now you need to print it. Chapter 5 told you how to set up your pages so that you could print in the format you wanted; this chapter will tell you how to get that information communicated to your printer or other output device.

Printing to a Printer

You can configure your version of AppleWorks to recognize up to three different printers from a list of standard or custom printers. The default printer for AppleWorks is the Apple Dot Matrix Printer, but the program easily recognizes printer characteristics from the list below:

Apple Daisy Wheel Printer
Apple Silentype (TM)
Apple Imagewriter
Epson (TM) MX series
Epson MX series with Graftrax +
Epson RX series
Epson FX series
Qume (TM) Sprint 5
Qume Sprint 11

And if your printer isn't on the list above, you can still use it by defining your printer as a Custom Printer and specifying certain information about it. (You can have only one custom printer, however.)

If you aren't going to use an Apple Dot Matrix Printer, you'll need to remove it as the default, and add whatever other printers you'll be using. You can see what printers your version of AppleWorks currently expects to see by selecting 5. Other Activites on the Main Menu, then selecting 7. Specify information about your printer(s). The Change printer specifications section shows you the printers your program is currently configured for.

It's not difficult to change this printer list. The AppleWorks menus are fairly complete and helpful. However, before you start, you will need to know these things about your printer:

1. The slot number (inside your Apple IIe or IIc) to which you attach the cable that connects your printer to the computer.

2. Does it automatically insert a Line Feed character after each Carriage Return character it gets from the computer, or does the computer need to send it a Line Feed?

3. Does it accept a command telling it to go to the top of the page? (These are also called *form feed* commands.)

4. Does it automatically stop at the end of each page (so you can insert a new sheet of paper or tear off the printed sheet)?

5. What is the platen width of the printer? (It has to be as wide as or wider than the page width you specified in Chapter 5.)

If you are adding a custom printer, you will also need to know the following:

6. The codes necessary to specify the characters per inch you want your printer to produce.

7. The codes necessary to specify the number of lines per inch you want your printer to produce.

8. The codes necessary to get your printer to recognize commands to print boldface, subscript, superscript, or underlines.

Once you know this information, follow the instructions on the screen and enter the appropriate data. We won't go into it in detail here because there are too many different types of printers.

Note that, if you are entering information about a custom printer, you can't leave the menu by pressing Escape. The only way out is to type a caret (^). If you make a mistake, type a ^ and answer the question you are defining, then answer NO to the question "Is this OK?"

Changing Printer Specifications

You can easily substitute a new printer for one of the previous ones. Use the Change printer specifications command to identify which printer you want to change and what you're substituting, then give the specifications that are different.

Printing to the Clipboard

You've already seen (in Chapter 8) how to print to the Clipboard. You use this method as an interim step in getting spreadsheet or data base information into a word processor document.

Generally, what you do when you print to the Clipboard is to format a report from either the Spreadsheet or Data Base program, then use the print capabilities of those programs to send the formatted report to the Clipboard. Once there, the report can be included, formats and all, within a word processor document and the entire document printed with the Word Processor's print program.

Printing to the Screen

Once in a while, in the data base program, it is handy to check on how your report will look before you actually print it. On those occasions, you can choose to print to the screen. Your report will appear on the screen exactly as it would look if it were printed (in other words, minus the formatting instructions and special keystrokes).

To use this capability, when you are through formatting your data base report and you press Open-Apple-P the second time, specify 4. The screen as the location where you want to print the report.

Quick Printing

If you want a quick copy of what's on your screen, special characters and all, press Open-Apple-H. You'll get an exact copy of what is currently on your screen, printed on the printer designated as the default.

Printing to Disk

With most computer systems, you can create a Print File by printing a report or some other document to disk, and then copying the Print File directly to disk. You can do the first part of that with AppleWorks; however, the second part must be done outside of AppleWorks.

When an AppleWorks report is printed on disk, it contains all of the formatting information and printer codes that it would contain if it were being sent to a printer. But AppleWorks can't use it any more. You can then print the file using some other program that can copy the Print file to an actual printer.

To do this, you'll need to add a printer (preferably the same one you normally use) and assign it to disk when you add it. Thus the print codes will be the same for when you print to the printer, and when you print to disk.

Printing to an ASCII File

You can print a word processor document, a spreadsheet report, or a data base report to an ASCII file. In some ways, this is like printing to a Print File, as discussed above. You specify the ASCII file as the destination when you go to print, and the file gets "printed" on disk. However, when you print to an ASCII file, you lose the special printing codes and printer options, such as boldface or underline. The carriage returns are used in the file as follows:

- Word processing files will contain the same carriage returns you placed in the original document.

- Spreadsheet reports will have a carriage return after each cell.

- Data base reports will have a carriage return after each entry.

Note that you can use a spreadsheet ASCII file as a source for a data base file.

Printing to a DIF File

In AppleWorks, you can print to a DIF file from either the Spreadsheet or Data Base programs. This allows you to use the output of these two programs in yet other programs.

A BASIC BUSINESS TOOLKIT

APPENDIX

This Appendix presents 20 useful models, constructed with the spreadsheet part of AppleWorks. You can use these models by entering the data, cell by cell, as shown in the listing accompanying each model. With each model there is a brief explanation to tell you how the model works and how you might want to tailor it to your own needs.

These models are also available for sale on diskette. Write to Elna Tymes at P.O. Box 51432, Palo Alto, California 94303 for information.

ACCOUNTS RECEIVABLE

Accounts receivable represent those customers who owe you money for goods or services you have provided to them. In other words, you have extended credit to them. If you let these accounts go too long without collection, you may not have enough money to pay your own bills.

This model shows your company's accounts receivable, aged by the number of months since you billed the customer. This sort of model is very handy for letting you know who is paying their bills in a timely manner and who is not.

Each month, you enter your receivables here. When you extend credit to a new customer, insert a row with his name in column A, and the amount for the current month in column D. When he pays his bill, delete the row. Each month, add the items in column F to the total in column G, then blank out the block of data in column F below the column heading and above the tally line, and move the data from the same rows in columns D and E to columns E and F. You'll then have a blank column D, ready for this month's receivables.

The "Total" column (column H) automatically gives you the total for each customer, and the "Totals" line (row 18 in this model) shows you the totals for each month.

ACCOUNTS RECEIVABLE

Use the Layout command to format the block of columns D through
H, rows 7 through 18 as value format, fixed, with 1 decimal
place.

```
A1   ACCOUNTS RECEIVABLE
A2   September 30, 1984
D3   "  Current
D4   "  (Under 30
E4   "  30 to 60
F4   "  60 to 90
G4   "  Over 90
A5   Account Name
D5   "   Days
E5   "   Days
F5   "   Days
G5   "   Days
H5   "   Total
A6   "=========          Copy this to B6 through H6.
A7   Adams Printing
D7   866
E7   106
F7   0
G7   0
H7   @SUM(D7..G7)      Copy this formula to H8 through H16,
                          with all cell references relative.
A8   Barkley Advertising
D8   0
E8   888
F8   422
G8   0
A9   Chippendale Corp.
D9   924
E9   0
F9   0
G9   334.01
A10  Dover Bros. Freight
D10  3437
E10  0
F10  0
G10  0
A11  Emery Supplies
D11  326
E11  113
F11  0
G11  0
A12  Fairmeadow School
D12  270.75
E12  0
F12  0
G12  0
A13  Gunn High School
D13  270.75
E13  0
F13  0
G13  0
A14  Harris Color Supplies
 14  2288.55
E14  0
F14  505
G14  0
A15  Inter-City Express
```

```
D15 446
E15 153.44
F15 0
G15 452
A16 Jackson Hearing Center
 16 654
E16 0
F16 0
G16 0
D17 " --------              Copy this to E17 through H17.
A18 Totals
D18 @SUM(D7..D16)           Copy this formula to E18 through H18,
                            with all cell references relative.
```

ACCOUNTS RECEIVABLE
September 30, 1984

Account Name	Current (Under 30 Days	30 to 60 Days	60 to 90 Days	Over 90 Days	Total
Adams Printing	866.00	106.00	0.00	0.00	972.00
Barkley Advertising	0.00	888.00	422.00	0.00	1310.00
Chippendale Corp.	904.00	0.00	0.00	334.01	1238.01
Dover Bros. Freight	3437.00	0.00	0.00	0.00	3437.00
Enery Supplies	326.00	113.00	0.00	0.00	439.00
Fairmeadow School	270.75	0.00	0.00	0.00	270.75
Gunn High School	76.60	0.00	0.00	0.00	76.60
Harris Color Supplies	2288.55	0.00	505.00	0.00	2793.55
Inter-City Express	446.00	153.44	0.00	452.00	1051.44
Jackson Hearing Center	654.00	0.00	0.00	0.00	654.00
Totals	9268.90	1260.44	927.00	786.01	12242.35

BALANCE SHEET

This shows a very simple balance sheet for a company that makes gadgets. Most of the basic elements of a balance sheet are shown here.
Any balance sheet is constructed along the principle:

Assets = Liabilities + Equity

Clearly, the higher the assets and the lower your liabilities, the more equity you have. Note that there are different kinds of assets—current and fixed—and different kinds of liabilities—current and longer term. "Retained earnings" is what is left over as profits at the end of a fiscal year, and maybe either distributed as dividends to those who hold shares of the company's equity, or converted to more equity.

```
BALANCE SHEET

C1   Balance Sheet
C2   Acme Gadget Co.
C3   June 30, 1984
A5   ASSETS
A6   "  Cash
E6   11509
A7   "   Accounts Rec.: Trade
E7   406259
A8   "   Accounts Rec.: Other
E8   2477
A9   "   Inventory
E9   245755
A10  "   Other Current Assets
E10  15299
E11  "---------
A12  "  Total Current Assets
F12  @SUM(E6..E10)
A14  Plant and Equipment
E14  7409
A15  Notes Receivable
E15  25688
A16  Prepaid Items
E16  8667
E17  "---------
F18  @SUM(E14..E16)
F19  "---------
A20  Total Assets
F20  @SUM(F12..F18)
A22  LIABILITIES AND EQUITY
A24  "  Accounts payable
E24  187805
A25  "  Notes Payable (Short)
E25  26447
E26  "---------
A27  "  Total Current Liabilities
F27  @SUM(E24..E25)
A29  Accrued Liabilities
A30  "  Commissions
```

```
E30 28034
A31   Taxes Payable
E31 57994
A32 " Other Accruals
E32 16743
E33 "---------
F34 @SUM(E30..E32)
A35 Long Term Notes
E35 26064
A35 Other Liabilities
E36 13209
E37 "---------
F38 @SUM(E35..E36)
F39 "---------
A40 Total Liabilities
F40 @SUM(F27..F39)
A42 Stockholders' Equity
E42 +F45-E43
A43 Retained Earnings
E43 269623
E44 "---------
A45 Total Equity
F45 +F47-F40
F46 "---------
A47 Tot. Liabilities & Equity
F47 +F20
```

```
                    Balance Sheet
                    Acme Gadget Co.
                    June 30, 1984


        ASSETS
          Cash                          111509
          Axxounts Rec.: Trade          406259
          Accounts Rec.: Other            2477
          Inventory                     245755
          Other Current Assets           15299
                                      ---------
          Total Current Assets                      781299

        Plant and Equipment              7409
        Notes Receivable                25688
        Prepaid Items                    8667
                                      ---------
                                                     41764
                                                   ---------
        Total Assets                                823063


        LIABILITIES AND EQUITY

          Accounts Payables             187805
          Notes Payable (Short)          26447
                                      ---------
          Total Current Liabilities                 214252
```

```
         Accrued Liabilities
            Commissions               28034
            Taxes Payable             57994
            Other Accruals            16743
                                    ---------
                                                102771
         Long Tern Notes              26064
         Other Liabilities            13209
                                    ---------
                                                 39273
                                              ---------
         Total Liabilities                      356296

         Stockholders' Equity        197138
         Retained Earnings           269629
                                    ---------
         Total Equity                            466767
                                              ---------
         Tot. Liabilities & Equity               823063
```

BREAKEVEN ANALYSIS

This simple model is used to determine the quantity of a particular item you must sell, at a given price, in order to match the cost of producing that item. Given the data shown here, the breakeven point is somewhere between 7000 and 8000 units, probably about 7700 units. (The precise formula is 7000 + 2250/3250 × 1000.)

Costs are of two types: fixed and variable. Fixed costs are things that you must pay, regardless of how much you produce, and include things like rent, utilities, equipment, depreciation, office salaries, certain taxes, office supplies, and things like that. Variable costs are those directly related to the production of each item, and include manufacturing and assembly labor, parts and materials, the cost of inventory, and things of that nature.

This model is ideally suited to playing "What if?" because of its formulas and the way it is set up. Change one number in the Assumptions section and the entire model changes. Change the numbers for Units Sold and the model changes again.

```
BREAKEVEN ANALYSIS

A1   BREAKEVEN ANALYSIS
A3   Assumptions
A5   Fixed Costs:
C5   25000
A6   Variable Costs:
C6   1.07
D6   " per item
A7   Net sales price:
C7   4.32
D7   " per item
A9   Units sold
C9   5000
D9   6000
E9   7000
F9   8000
G9   9000
A11  Sales
C11  +C7*C9          Copy this formula into D11 through G11, with
                     the reference to C7 fixed and to C9 relative.

A12  Variable costs
C12  +C6*C9          Copy this formula into D12 through G12, with
                     the reference to C6 fixed and to C9 relative.

A13  Fixed costs
C13  through G13     Copy the contents of C5 here, fixed.
C14  " --------      Copy this into D14 through G14.
A15  Net income
C15  +C11-C12-C13    Copy this formula into D15 through G15, all
                     cell references relative.
```

```
BREAKEVEN ANALYSIS

Assumptions:

Fixed Costs:        25000
Variable Costs:      1.07 per item
Net sales price:     4.32 per item

Units sold           5000     6000     7000     8000     9000

Sales               21600    25920    30240    34560    38880
Variable costs       5350     6420     7490     8560     9630
Fixed costs         25000    25000    25000    25000    25000
                   -------- -------- -------- -------- --------
Net income          -8750    -5500    -2250     1000     4250
```

BUDGETED VS. ACTUAL EXPENSES

Budgets are an exercise in restricted fantasy: you put down the figures you think you're going to be able to spend for a set of items over the next year, and plot them out month by month.

The gotchas come when you get around to spending the money. Can you in fact get the items you budgeted at the price you indicated? Has the demand pattern shifted without a compensating shift in your budget? Most companies are reasonably tolerant of small budget deviations, but the trouble comes when the actual expenses are considerably different from what was budgeted.

This model helps you see trouble coming on a month-by-month basis. That is, it will usually be trouble if you are far over budget. It probably won't be trouble if you're under budget, or very close to your predictions.

You can use the same model from month to month, blanking out the numbers in columns D, E, F, and G on last month's model and filling in the new data.

BUDGETED VS. ACTUAL EXPENSES

Use the Layout command to specify the block of columns D, E, F, G, and H, rows 8 through 24 as number format, fixed, with 2 decimal places.

```
A1    BUDGETED VS. ACTUAL EXPENSES
A2    Publications Department
A3    September, 1984
D4    "      Sept.
E4    "      Sept.
F4    "        YTD
G4    "        YTD
H4    "     Annual
A5    Account
D5    "     Actual
E5    " Budgeted
F5    "     Actual
G5    " Budgeted
H5    "     Budget
A6    "---------         Use the Copy command to copy A6 to B6 through
                         H6.
A7    Employee Costs
A8    "    Salaries
D8    10553.44
E8    10800
F8    20733.94
G8    21000
H8    98000
A9    "  Payroll Taxes, etc.
D9    467.78
E9    500
```

```
F9   1223.15
G9   2000
H9   30000
A11  Outside Labor, Services
A12  "  Writers, Editors
D12  1820
E12  1000
F12  2140
G12  2500
H12  15000
A13  "  Artists, Designers
D13  1220
E13  1000
F13  2250
G13  2000
H13  12000
A14  "  Temp. Word Processing
D14  422
E14  500
F14  959
G14  1000
H14  6000
A16  Computer Equipment
D16  112
E16  1000
F16  1766.33
G16  2000
H16  10000
A17  Office Equipment
D17  537.88
E18  400
F18  614.87
G18  800
H18  5000
A19  Supplies
D19  522.77
E19  500
F19  956.63
G19  1000
H19  6000
A20  Printing
D20  1255.53
E20  800
F20  1866.44
G20  1400
H20  6000
A21  Travel
D21  25.88
E21  350
F21  557.44
G21  700
H21  4000
D22  "  --------         Copy D22 into E22 through H22.
A23  Total Expenses
D23  @SUM(D8..D21)
F23  @SUM(F8..F21)
H23  @SUM(H8..H21)
E24  @SUM(E8..E21)
G24  @SUM(G8..G21)
```

```
BUDGETED VS. ACTUAL EXPENSES
Publications Dept.
September, 1984
                              Sept.     Sept.       YTD       YTD    Annual
Account                      Actual  Budgeted    Actual  Budgeted    Budget
-------------------------------------------------------------------------------
Employee Costs
  Salaries                 10553.44  10800.00  20733.94  21000.00  98000.00
  Payroll Taxes, etc.        467.78    500.00   1223.15   2000.00  30000.00

Outside Labor, Services
  Writers, Editors           1820.00   1000.00   2140.00   2500.00  15000.00
  Artists, Designers         1220.00   1000.00   2250.00   2000.00  12000.00
  Temp. Word Processing       422.00    500.00    958.00   1000.00   6000.00

Computer Equipment           112.00   1000.00   1766.33   2000.00  10000.00
Office Equipment             537.88    400.00    614.87    800.00   5000.00
Supplies                     502.77    500.00    956.63   1000.00   6000.00
Telephone                    224.66    300.00    436.78    600.00   3600.00
Printing                    1255.53    800.00   1866.44   1400.00   6000.00
Travel                        25.88    350.00    557.44    700.00   4000.00
                          --------  --------  --------  --------  --------
Total Expenses             17141.94             33503.58            191600.00
                                     17150.00             35000.00
```

CASH FLOW PROJECTION

This is another of the basic financial statements that shows a business entity's health. Your company may have a wonderful balance sheet, and an income statement for the year that shows a healthy net profit, but the cash flow may kill the business in the meantime.

Cash flow statements are useful for finding out when you're going to need to borrow from someone—the owner, the bank, a friend or two—in order to keep merchandise or services flowing to customers.

In this example, we are looking at three months for Acme Gadget Co. Notice that there is a negative cash flow (look in cell D29) for the month of October. Likewise, there is a negative cash flow for December, but a positive cash flow in November. This particular period started with a "kitty" of $2000, so that when the negative cash flow came, there was money available to cover it.

The reasons behind the negative cash flow are found in the figures used in the "Assumptions" part of the model. You can change these figures, and note the effect rippling through the spreadsheet. In particular, the figures for Receivables reflect an application of the 30-day, 60-day, and 90-day percentages (in that order), and all shown here include assumptions about the sales for the three months prior to this quarter. You may also want to use an Income Tax percentage other than 35%.

Once past the "Assumptions," most of the model is formulas, except for the figures used for sales, for loan payments, and for the Beginning Cash Balance in October. Figures are also used in the Receivables area to compensate for no Sales figures for prior months.

```
CASH FLOW

Do a Layout command for the Block of columns D through G, rows 14
through 26, fixed with 0 decimal places (to create whole
numbers).

C1    CASH FLOW ANALYSIS
C2    Acme Gadget Co.
C3    Second Quarter, 1984
A5    ASSUMPTIONS
D6    Receivables: % of
A7    Cost of Goods is
E7    Sales
A8    60
B8    "% of sales
```

```
D8   Cash
E8   30
D9   "30-day
E9   45
A10  Operating Expenses are
D10  "60-day
E10  20
A11  15
B11  "% of sales
D11  90-day
E11  5
A12  "---------
B12  through G12                Use the Copy command to copy A12 here
D13  "      Oct.
E13  "      Nov.
F13  "      Dec.
G13  "      Total
A14  Sales
D14  11576
E14  12762
F14  14071
G14  @SUM(D14..F14)
A16  Cash
D16  +E8/100*D14
E16  +E8/100*E14
F16  +E8/100*F14
G16  @SUM(D16..F16)
A17  Receivables
D17  4500+1800+400
E17  +(E9/100*D14)+2000+500
F17  +(E9/100*E14)+(E10/100*D14)+500
G17  @SUM(D17..F17)
D18   through  G18           Use the Copy command to copy D12 through
                             G12 here.
A19  Total Cash Receipts
D19  +D16+D17
E19  +E16+E17
F19  +F16+F17
G19  @SUM(D19..F19)
A21  Cost of Goods
D21  +A8/100*D14
E21  +A8/100*E14
F21  +A8/100*F14
G21  @SUM(D21..F21)
A22  Operating Expenses
D22  +A11/100*D14
E22  +A11/100*D15
F22  +A11/100*D16
A23  Loan Payments
D23  1000
E23  1000
F23  1000
G23  @SUM(D23..F23)
A24  Income Taxes
D24  .35*(D19-D21-D22-D23)
E24  .35*(E19-E21-E22-E23)
F24  .35*(F19-F21-F22-F23)
G24  @SUM(D24..F24)
D25  through G25             Use the Copy command to copy D12 through
                             G12 here.

D25  @SUM(D21..D24)
E25  @SUM(E21..E24)
F25  @SUM(F21..F24)
G25  @SUM(D25..F25)
```

```
A28  Beginning Cash Balance
D28  2000
E28  +D31
F28  +E31
A29  Net Cash This Period
D29  +D19-D26
E29  +E19-E26
F29  +F19-F26
G29  @SUM(D29..F29)
D30  through G30          Use the Copy command to copy D12 through
                          G12 here.

A31  Ending Cash Balance
D31  +D28+D29
E31  +E28+E29
F31  +F28+F29
```

```
                    CASH FLOW ANALYSIS
                    Acme Gadget Co.
                    Second Quarter, 1984

ASSUMPTIONS
                         Receivables:  % of
Cost of Goods is                       Sales
        68% of sales     Cash            30
                         30-day          45
Operating Expenses are   60-day          20
        15% of sales     90-day           5
-----------------------------------------------------------
                         Oct.    Nov.    Dec.    Total
Sales                    11576   12762   14071   38409

Cash                     3473    3829    4221    11523
Receivables              6700    11709   8558    26967
                         -----------------------------------
Total Cash Receipts      10173   15538   12779   38490

Cost of Goods            7872    8678    9568    26118
Operating Expenses       1736    1914    2111    5761
Loan Payments            1000    1000    1000    3000
Income Taxes             -152    1381      35    1264
                         -----------------------------------
Total Cash Disbursements 10456   12973   12714   36143

Beginning Cash Balance   2000    1717    4282
Net Cash This Period     -283    2564    -194    2088
                         -----------------------------------
Ending Cash Balance      1717    4282    4088
```

COST OF GOODS SOLD

This simple model shows you how to compute the cost of one month's production. It assumes you can do an inventory valuation each month, producing a figure like the one you see here. The other figures are taken from various expense statements.

The way the model works is very easy to understand: start with the previous month's inventory valuation, subtract the cost of materials and labor and any other cost of sales, add back in the cost of samples and returns, and then subtract the current month's inventory valuation.

```
COST OF GOODS SOLD

A1   COST OF GOODS SOLD
A3   Value of Inventory
A4   "   8/31/84
D4   60836
A6   Materials Purchased
D6   158124
A7   Labor (incl. taxes)
D7   14064
A8   Adjustments:
A9   "  Samples
D9   415
A10  "  Returns
D10  663
A11  Other Costs of Sale
D11  7347
D12  "---------     Copy this to D17.
A13  Subtotal
D13  +D4+D6+D7-D9-D10+D11
A15  Value of Inventory
D15  86036
A16  "   9/30'84
A18  Cost of Goods Sold
D18  +D13-D15
```

```
COST OF GOODS SOLD
Value of Inventory
    8/31/84                       60836

Materials Purchased              158124
Labor (incl. taxes)               14064
Adjustments:
    Samples                         415
    Returns                         663
Other Costs of Sale                7347
                               ---------
Subtotal                         239293

Value of Inventory                86036
    9/30/84
                               ---------
Cost of Goods Sold               153257
```

INCOME STATEMENT

This spreadsheet shows a very simple income statement for Acme Gadget Co. for the fiscal year July 1, 1983, through June 30, 1984. An income statement, like a balance sheet, is one of the basic financial statements that describes the relative economic health of a business. But an income statement is concerned with where a company got its money (from sales of products, as shown in this example, or from services or other sources), and how it spent it.

The categories used here are fairly standard ones. You could create an income statement for a particular month, with the same labels.

Note that we have only one line for Operating Expenses. Many businesses find it useful to break down operating expenses into categories like Marketing, Adminstration, Manufacturing, Engineering, etc.

Note also that we have assumed an income tax rate of 35%. Depending on your situation, your rate may be higher or lower, or you may want a more elaborate calculation.

```
INCOME STATEMENT

C1   Income Statement
C2   Acme Gadget Co.
B3   Fiscal Year 7/1/83 - 6/30/84
A5   INCOME
A6   " Sales
E6   713834
A7   " Less Discounts
E7   6674
E8   "---------
A9   " Net Sales
E9   +E6-E7
A11  EXPENSES
A12  Cost of Goods
E12  205833
E13  "---------
A14  Gross Margin
E14  +E9-E12
A16  Operating Expenses
E16  82559
E17  "---------
A18  Net Operating Income
E18  +E14-E16
A20  Income Taxes
E20  .35*E18
E21  "---------
A22  Net Income After Taxes
E22  +E18-E20
```

```
                        Income Statement
                        Acme Gadget Co.
                  Fiscal Year 7/1/83 - 6/30/84

        INCOME
          Sales                                   713834
          Less Discounts                            6674
                                                ----------
          Net Sales                              707160

        EXPENSES
        Cost of Goods                            205833
                                                ----------
        Gross Margin                             501327

        Operating Expenses                        83559
                                                ----------
        Net Operating Income                     417768

        Income Taxes                             146218.8
                                                ----------
        Net Income After Taxes                   271549.2
```

VALUE OF INVENTORY

This model allows you to keep track of your inventory, as well as the amount of capital you have invested in it.

For each item you stock, keep track of the number of units used each month and the number added, and assign a per-unit value to each. If you do this monthly, you can use the "Current Number" from last month as this month's "Number Last Mo." The formulas in columns F and H compute the number remaining at the end of the month and the value for each kind of item, as well as a monthly total value.

```
INVENTORY VALUATION

Use the Layout command to format the block of columns G and H,
rows 5 through 27, as number format, fixed, with 2 decimal
places.

A1    INVENTORY VALUATION
A2    "9/30/84
C2    "    Number
D2    "      Used
E2    "     Stock
F2    "   Current
G2    "      Item
H2    "     Total
C3    " Last Mo.
D3    " This Mo.
E3    "     Added
F3    "    Number
G3    "     Value
H3    "     Value
A4    PARTS
A5    Base plates
C5    120
D5    115
E5    20
F5    +C5-D5+E5          Copy this formula into F6 through F25.
G5    .63
H5    +F5*G5             Copy this formula into H6 through H25.
A6    Stuffed pc boards
C6    155
D6    134
E6    95
G6    .87
A7    Cases
C7    244
D7    105
E7    30
G7    .23
A8    Cords
C8    46
D8    115
E8    120
```

```
G8   .89
A10  PACKAGES
A11  Boxes
C11  477
D11  143
E11  0
G11  .06
A12  Labels
C12  1023
D12  144
E12  0
G12  .02
A14  SUPPLIES, MISC.
A15  Solder, rolls
C15  25
D15  32
E15  10
G15  2.35
A16  Tape, rolls
C16  34
D16  14
E16  6
G16  1.98
A18  WORK IN PROGRESS
A19  Boards on base
C19  23
D19  110
E19  100
G19  2.50
A20  In case, no cord
C20  44
D20  109
E20  99
G20  3.75
A22  FINISHED GOODS
A23  Assembled units
C23  78
D23  67
E23  95
G23  7.65
A24  In boxes
C24  155
D24  166
E24  112
G24  9.50
A25  In shipping carton
C25  120
D25  288
E25  240
G25  10.50
H26  "---------
H27  @SUM(H5..H25)
```

```
INVENTORY VALUATION
9/30/84            Number     Used     Stock    Current     Item      Total
                 Last Mo.  This Mo.    Added    Number     Value     Value
PARTS
Base plates          120       115       20        25       .63      15.75
Stuffed pc boards    155       134       95       116       .87     100.92
Cases                244       105       30       169       .23      38.87
Cords                 46       115      120        51       .09       4.59

PACKAGES
Boxes                477       143        0       334       .06      20.04
Labels              1033       144        0       889       .02      17.78

SUPPLIES, MISC.
Solder, rolls         25        32       10         3      2.35       7.05
Tape, rolls           34        14        6        26      1.98      51.48

WORK IN PROGRESS
Boards on base        23       110      100        13      2.50      32.50
In case, no cord      44       109       98        33      3.75     123.75

FINISHED GOODS
Assembled units       78        67       95       106      7.65     810.90
In boxes             155       166      112       101      9.50     959.50
In shipping carton   120       288      240        72     10.50     756.00
                                                                 ---------
                                                                   2939.13
```

MAIL-ORDER CAMPAIGN

Ever wonder if one particular advertising method works better than others? This model evaluates the effectiveness of a mail-order campaign, using the summer catalog and the dollar volume of sales it generated over the summer.

It measures effectiveness as a function of whether the sales generated were more than the amount budgeted for production and mailing of the catalog and for the manning of a special phone. Column C presents the costs of producing the catalog and handling the special phone. The sales figures are shown in row 13. The campaign is deemed to be a success if the figure in D16, multiplied by the budgeted percent in D17, is greater than the costs shown in C14. In this case the campaign was a success.

```
MAIL ORDER CAMPAIGN

C1   MAIL ORDER CAMPAIGN
C3   Summer Catalog
F5   Responses:
A6   Costs
E6   "      May
F6   "      June
G6   "      July
H6   "    August
A8   Mailing lists
C8   4250
A9   Printing
C9   850
D9   " No. calls
E9   7033
F9   3744
G9   3698
H9   8067
A10  Postage
C10  850
D10  " Avg.size
A11  Special phone
C11  325
D11  " of order
E11  74.21
F11  46.62
G11  45.11
H11  81.53
A12  Labor
C12  4800
E12  " --------          Copy this to F12 through H12 and C13.
D13  " Total
E13  +E9*E11            Copy this formula to F11 through H11,
                        with both cell references relative.
```

```
A14 Total
C14 @SUM(C8..C12)
A16 Total sales, this period:
D16 @SUM(E13..H13)
A17 "% budgeted for catalog:
D17 1.5
E17 "%
A18 Difference
D18 +(D17/100*D16)-C14
```

```
                   MAIL ORDER CAMPAIGN

                   Summer Catalog

                                       Responses:
Costs                             May      June     July    August

Mailing lists        4250
Printing              850 No.Calls  7033    3744     3698     8067
Postage               425 Avg.size
Special phone         325 of order 74.21   46.62    45.11    81.53
Labor                4800          --------  -------- -------- --------
                     --------  Total 521919  174545   166817   657703
Total               10650

Total sales, this period:   1520984
% budgeted for catalog:         1.5%
Difference                    12165
```

MOVING AVERAGES

Moving averages are a statistical measure that gives you some flexibility in determining averages for a period. They are especially useful in determing whether the average use of something over a period of time is due to seasonal or periodic fluctuations, or if there is a genuine pattern of growth or decline.

In this model, we are looking at the average miles per month driven by a small delivery van. Two kinds of moving averages are computed: 6-month and 12-month. The 12-month moving average gives you a feeling of overall use of slightly more than 2400 miles per month. The 6-month moving average, however, seems to indicate a bit of a slump that may have been caused by market conditions.

This sort of statistical measure is helpful in the case of a vehicle for computing when to schedule maintenance, new tires, engine overhaul, and costly replacements. However, any regular usage figure (such as output from a factory line, or utility usage) can be tracked by moving average calculations.

```
MOVING AVERAGES

C1    MOVING AVERAGES
D3    "    6 Mo.
E3    "    6 Mo.
F3    "   12 Mo.
G3    "   12 Mo.
D4    "   Moving
E4    "   Moving
F4    "   Moving
G4    "   Moving
A5    Year
B5    "   Month
C5    Mi.Driven
D5    "   Total
E5    " Average
F5    "   Total
G5    " Average
A6    "---------           Copy this to B6 through G6
A7    "1983
B7    April
C7    2254
B8    May
C8    2536
B9    June
C9    2563
D9    @SUM(C7..C12)       Copy this formula to D10 through D21,
                          with all cell references relative.
E9    +D9/6               Copy this formula to E10 through E21,
                          with the reference to D9 relative.
B10   July
C10   2445
```

```
B11 August
C11 2144
B12 September
C12 2663
F12 @SUM(C7..C18)          Copy this formula to F13 through F17,
                           with all cell references relative.
G12 +F12/12                Copy this formula to G13 through G17,
                           with the reference to F12 relative.

B13 October
C13 2366
B14 November
C14 2673
B15 December
C15 2733
A16 "1984
B16 January
C16 2445
B17 February
C17 2029
B18 March
C18 2377
B19 April
C19 2511
B20 May
C20 2735
B21 June
C21 2049
B22 July
C22 2268
B23 August
C23 2287
B24 September
C24 2855
```

MOVING AVERAGES

Year	Month	Mi.Driven	6 Mo. Moving Total	6 Mo. Moving Average	12 Mo. Moving Total	12 Mo. Moving Average
1983	April	2254				
	May	2536				
	June	2563	14605	2434		
	July	2445	14717	2453		
	August	2144	14854	2476		
	September	2663	15024	2504	29228	2436
	October	2366	15024	2504	29485	2457
	November	2673	14909	2485	29684	2474
	December	2733	14623	2437	29170	2431
1984	January	2445	14768	2461	28993	2416
	February	2029	14830	2472	29136	2428
	March	2377	14146	2358		
	April	2511	13969	2328		
	May	2735	14227	2371		
	June	2049	14705	2451		
	July	2268				
	August	2287				
	September	2855				

DEPARTMENTAL SHARE OF OVERHEAD COSTS

Any department in a company, in addition to having to justify its own costs, must be prepared to shoulder a share of the general overhead costs of maintaining a facility. This model shows you one approach to a budget that allocates a percent of the overhead costs to a particular department.

The percentage this department must bear is shown in G3. The total overhead costs for the company are shown in column G, and this department's share, on a month-by-month basis, is shown in column H.

```
OVERHEAD COSTS

A1   DEPARTMENTAL SHARE OF OVERHEAD COSTS
F2   "     Dept.
A3   Marketing Department: Budget Year 1984
F3   "      Share
G3   23
H3   "%
H4   "   Monthly
B5   "        Rent
C5   "      Util.
D5   "      Phone
E5   " Security
F5   " Salaries
G5   "     Total
H5   "      Share
A6   January
B6   7200                    Copy this to B7 through B17.
C6   1200
D6   650
E6   1000                    Copy this to E7 through E17.
F6   8400
G6   @SUM(B6..F6)            Copy this formula to G7 through G17,
                             with all cell references relative.
H6   +G3*G6/100              Copy this formula to H7 through H17,
                             with references to G3 fixed and to G6
                             relative.
A7   February
C7   1200
D7   650
F7   8400
A8   March
C8   1100
D8   750
F8   8400
A9   April
C9   1000
D9   750
F9   9700
A10  May
C10  900
D10  750
F10  9700
A11  June
C11  900
```

```
D11 800
F11 9700
A12 July
C12 900
D12 800
F12 10600
A13 August
C13 900
D13 750
F13 10600
A14 September
C14 900
D14 800
F14 10600
A15 October
C15 1000
D15 850
D16 11500
A16 November
C16 1100
D16 850
F16 11500
A17 December
C17 1200
D17 800
F17 11500
```

DEPARTMENTAL SHARE OF OVERHEAD COSTS

| | | | | | Dept. | | |
| Marketing Department: | Budget year 1984 | | | | Share | 23% | |
	Rent	Util.	Phone	Security	Salaries	Total	Monthly Share
January	7200	1200	650	1000	8400	18450	4244
February	7200	1200	650	1000	8400	18450	4244
March	7200	1100	750	1000	8400	18450	4244
April	7200	1000	750	1000	9700	19650	4520
May	7200	900	750	1000	9700	19550	4496
June	7200	900	800	1000	9700	19600	4508
July	7200	900	800	1000	10600	20500	4715
August	7200	900	750	1000	10600	20450	4704
September	7200	900	800	1000	10600	20500	4715
October	7200	1000	850	1000	11500	21550	4956
November	7200	1100	850	1000	11500	21650	4980
December	7200	1200	800	1000	11500	21700	4991

CALCULATING A MINIMUM PRICE

There are two basic schools of thought when it comes to determining the price for something: (1) go for whatever the market will bear, and (2) figure out your minimum price, based on costs, and then adjust upwards to a price that allows for fine tuning in response to market conditions. This model allows you to use the second approach.

To use it, you have to know what your company's fixed costs are, what a minimum acceptable gross margin is (gross margin is the difference between price, after subtracting sales costs, and what it cost to produce an item), the cost to produce each item, and the projected number of each item to be sold. You also need to decide what share of the fixed costs each product is to bear. This figure, as a decimal percentage, goes in column G.

The model calculates the total cost of producing each item, adds in the minimum gross margin, then computes the minimum price per item, given your assumptions.

This model lends itself easily to "What if?" analysis. You can change the fixed costs, or the minimum gross margin. You can change the relative weighting of the product shares. And of course, you can adjust the cost per item and the projected number sold. Each change will ripple through the model, changing the computed minimum price.

```
PRICING

A1   CALCULATING A MINIMUM PRICE
A3   Fixed Costs per yr
C3   117563
A4   Min. gross margin
C4   .18
F5   Cost plus
H5   " Minimum
C6   "      Cost
D6   Projected
E6   " Cost to
F6   "    Gross
G6   " Product
H6   "    Price
A7   Product
C7   per item
D7   " # Sold
E7   " Produce
F7   "    Margin
G7   "    Share
H7   " per Item
A8   "---------            Copy this to B8 through.H8.
A9   Power supplies
C9   25.64
```

```
D9   50000
E9   +C9*D9                          Copy this formula to E10 through E13,
                                     with both cell references relative.
F9   +E9+(C4*E9)                     Copy this formula to F10 through F13,
                                     with the references to E9 relative and
                                     the reference to C4 fixed.
G9   .11
H9   +((C3*G9)+F9)/D9                Copy this formula to H10 through H13,
                                     with the reference to C3 fixed and all
                                     other cell references relative.

A10  Switch A
C10  27.88
D10  35000
G10  .18
A11  Switch B
C11  95.33
D11  30000
G11  .16
A12  Controller
C12  5.63
D12  65000
G12  .08
A13  Terminal
C13  372.44
D13  20000
G13  .47
```

CALCULATING A MINIMUM PRICE

Fixed Costs per yr   117560
Min. gross margin   .18

Product	Cost per item	Projected # Sold	Cost to Produce	Cost plus Gross Margin	Product Share	Minimum Price per Item
Power supplies	25.64	50000	1282000	1512760	.11	30.51
Switch A	87.88	35000	3075800	3629444	.18	104.30
Switch B	95.33	30000	2859900	3374682	.16	113.12
Controller	5.63	65000	365950	431821	.08	6.79
Terminal	372.44	20000	7448800	8789584	.47	442.24

PRODUCTIVITY ANALYSIS

When you want to allocate bonuses among your staff, and you want to reward the most productive, you need some measure of productivity. While measuring the effectiveness of people-contact is always difficult, this model gives you some idea of how a retailer might approach such a task.

This model measures productivity for a given set of employees as the dollar volume of sales per day worked. Notice that some cameras in this model cost more than others, but that, except for the most expensive camera, approximately the same number of cameras was sold for each kind. There appear to be some specialties among the sale clerks, too: Collins sold 75% more of the most expensive camera than did Abrams, while Wood sold more than three times the number of the least expensive camera as Collins.

```
PRODUCTIVITY ANALYSIS

Use the Layout command to format columns G and H as value format,
fixed, with 2 decimal places.

C1   Keeler/Sherry Camera Equipment
C2   Productivity Analysis: September, 1984
A4   Camera A
B4   149.95
A5   Camera B
B5   105.49
A6   Camera C
B6   239.95
A7   Camera D
B7   178.67
B8   "     Days
C8   "    -------  Cameras Sold  -------
G8   "    Total
H8   "    $ Sold
A9   Clerk
B9   "  Worked
C9   "      A
D9   "      B
E9   "      C
F9   "      D
G9   "  Sales $
H9   "  Per Day
A10  "---------          Copy this to B10 through H10, and to A15
                         through H15.
A11  Abrams
B11  19
C11  15
D11  15
E11  8
F11  17
```

```
G11 +(B4*C11)+(B5*D11)+(B6*E11)+(B7*F11)        Copy this formula to
                                        G12 through G14, with fixed references
                                        to B4 through B7 and relative references
                                        to C11 through F11.
H11 +G11/B11                            Copy this formula to H12 through H14,
                                        with both cell references relative.
A12 Brown
B12 19
C12 14
D12 12
E12 12
F12 13
A13 Collins
B13 20
C13 17
D13 9
E13 14
F13 15
A14 Wood
B14 19
C14 20
D14 30
E14 9
F14 16
A16 Totals
C16 @SUM(C11..C14)        Copy this formula into D16 through H14,
                          with all cell references relative.

A18 Averages
C19 @AVG(B11..B14)        Copy this formula into C19 through H19,
                          with all cell references relative.
```

```
              Keeler/Sherry Camera Equipment
              Productivity Analysis: September, 1984

Camera A    149.95
Camera B    105.49
Camera C    239.95
Camera D    178.67
              Days   ------ Cameras Sold -------    Total   $ Sold
Clerk        Worked    A       B       C       D   Sales $  Per Day
-----------------------------------------------------------------------
Abrams         18      15      15       8      17  8431.25   468.40
Brown          19      14      12      12      13  6244.58   328.66
Collins        20      17       9      14      15  6857.86   342.89
Wood           19      20      30       9      16  8323.25   438.07
-----------------------------------------------------------------------
Totals                 66      66      43      61 29856.94  1578.02

Averages       19    16.5    16.5   10.75   15.25  7464.23   394.51
```

RANK CORRELATION

This model uses the Spearman Rank Correlation Test to find the closeness of assocation between two sets of rankings. Use this model and the formula in D18 to determine whether there is a positive or negative relationship, or no relationship, between two sets of data.

Here we have assumed that the person doing this exercise wants to know if there is any correlation between the number of times a store orders goods from a particular supplier, and what its annual sales are. In other words, the hypothesis is that if a store orders more frequently, it will have higher sales.

Column C shows the stores' relative ranking in terms of how often they order (the store that orders most frequently gets a 1; the store that orders least frequently gets an 8). Column D ranks the stores' annual sales.

The figure in D18 shows the correlation between the two rankings. If the number is 1.0, there is a perfect positive correlation; if − 1.0, there is a perfect negative correlation. Here, the number is very close to 1.0, so we can assume that there is a positive relationship and hence that the hypothesis is true.

RANK CORRELATION

C1	RANK CORRELATION	
C3	" Annual	
D3	" Diff.	
C4	" Order	
D4	" Sales	
E4	" between	
F4	" Diff.	
A5	Customer	
C5	" Rank	
D5	" Rank	
E5	" Ranks	
F5	" Squared	
A6	"---------	Copy this to B6 through F6, and to E15 and F15.
A7	A-1 Sporting Goods	
C7	6	
D7	5	
E7	+C7-D7	Copy this formula to E8 through E14, with both cell references relative.
F7	E7^2	Copy this formula to F8 through F14, with the cell reference relative.
A8	Western Suppliers	
C8	4	
D8	3	
A9	The Bike Shop	
C9	7	

```
D9   8
A10  Forsmans
C10  1
D10  1
A11  Big 5 Sports
C11  3
D11  4
A12  Wollman Bros.
C12  8
D12  7
A13  Sierra Sports
C13  5
D13  6
A14  Outdoor Shop
C14  2
D14  2
B16  "     N =
C16  @COUNT(C7..C14)
A18  Relationship between ranks:
D18  +1-((6*F16)/(C16*(C16^2-1)))
```

RANK CORRELATION

Customer	Order Rank	Annual Sales Rank	Diff. between Ranks	Diff. Squared
A-1 Sporting Goods	6	5	1	1
Western Suppliers	4	3	1	1
The Bike Shop	7	8	-1	1
Forsmans	1	1	0	0
Big 5 Sports	3	4	-1	1
Wollman Bros.	8	7	1	1
Sierra Sports	5	6	-1	1
Outdoor Shop	2	2	0	0
N =	8		0	6

Relationship between ranks: .9285714

REAL ESTATE MANAGEMENT

There are two models for this topic: the Income model, Real Estate Management—1, tracks the various forms of income for the 10-unit building that is the subject of these two models. The amount collected as damage deposit is shown for each apartment, along with a prepaid last month's rent.

Each month, as the rent is collected, it is shown in the appropriate cell. Where an apartment was rented for only part of the month, the amount collected is shown. When an apartment is vacant, as 104 was for the month of September, no damage deposit or last month's rent is shown.

For accounting purposes, the amounts held as damage deposits and last month's rent are not considered as income; they are classed as income only when they are actually used.

The second model, Real Estate Management—2, shows the monthly expenses of running such an apartment building. To keep track of which apartments need the most repair, repairs are shown by apartment number. (These could be such things as plumbing, painting, new carpets, etc.) Other expenses are shown below by category.

The second model shows only the first three months of expenses. If you wish, you can easily extend the model month by month, as you use it to keep track of your expenses.

```
REAL ESTATE MANAGMENT - 1:  Income

A1   REAL ESTATE MANAGEMENT - 1
A2   Income
E3   "  Damage
F3   "  Last Mo.
G3   "   Current
A4   Apt. No.
B4   "    Type
C4   Tenant
E4   "  Deposit
F4   "    Rent
G4   "    Rate
H4   "   January
I4   "  February
J4   "     March
K4   "     April
L4   "       May
M4   "      June
N4   "      July
O4   "    August
P4   September
Q4   "   October
```

```
R4    "  November
S4    "  December
A5    "=========          Copy this to B5 through S5.
A6    101
B6    "  Studio
C6    Robertson
E6    250
F6    300
G6    300
H6    275
I6    275
J6    275
K6    275
L6    300
O6    300
P6    300
A7    102
B7    "  Studio
C7    Kelly
E7    250
F7    300
G7    300
H7    275
I7    275
K7    275
L7    300
M7    300
N7    300
O7    300
P7    300
A8    103
B8    "1 Br
C8    Norris
E8    300
F8    350
G8    425
H8    375
I8    375
J8    375
K8    375
L8    425
M8    425
P8    425
A9    104
B9    "1 Br
G9    425
H9    400
I9    400
J9    400
K9    400
L9    425
M9    425
N9    425
O9    425
A10   105
B10   "2 Br
C10   Murphy
E10   400
F10   450
G10   550
I10   500
J10   500
K10   500
L10   550
M10   225
```

```
N10 550
O10 550
P10 550
A11 106
B11 "2 Br
C11 Nelson
E11 400
F11 500
G11 550
H11 500
I11 500
J11 500
K11 500
L11 550
M11 550
N11 550
O11 550
P11 550
A12 201
B12 1 Br
C12 Agretti
E12 300
F12 400
G12 400
H12 375
K12 400
L12 400
M12 400
N12 400
O12 400
P12 400
A13 202
B13 1 Br+
C13 Gioberti
E13 300
F13 375
G13 410
H13 375
I13 375
J13 375
K13 375
L13 410
M13 410
N13 410
O13 410
P13 410
A14 203
B14 2 Br
C14 Ewing
D14 350
F14 575
G14 575
H14 525
I14 525
J14 525
L14 575
M14 575
N14 575
O14 575
P14 575
A15 204
B15 2 Br
C15 Barnes
E15 350
F15 500
```

```
G15 575
H15 525
I15 525
J15 525
K15 525
L15 575
M15 575
N15 575
O15 575
P15 575
E16 "  --------         Copy this to F16 and H16 through S16.
A17 Totals
E17 @SUM(E6..E15)      Copy this formula to F17 and H17 through
                       S17, with both cell references relative.
```

REAL ESTATE MANAGEMENT - 1
Income

Apt. No	Type	Tenant	Damage Deposit	Last Mo. Rent	Current Rate	January
101	Studio	Robertson	250	300	300	275
102	Studio	Kelly	250	300	300	275
103	1Br	Norris	300	350	425	375
104	1Br				425	400
105	2Br	Murphy	400	450	550	
106	2Br	Nelson	400	500	550	500
201	1Br	Agretti	300	400	400	375
202	1Br+	Gioberti	300	375	410	375
203	2Br	Ewing	350	575	575	525
204	2Br	Barnes	350	500	575	525
Totals			2900	3750		3625

February	March	April	May	June	July	August	September
275	275	275	300			300	300
275	275	275	300	300	300	300	300
375	375	375	425	425			425
400	400	400	425	425	425	425	
500	500	500	550	225	550	550	550
500	500	500	550	550	550	550	550
		400	400	400	400	400	400
375	375	375	410	410	410	410	410
525	525		575	575	575	575	575
525	525	525	575	575	575	575	575
3750	3750	3625	4510	3885	3785	4085	4085

```
REAL ESTATE MANAGEMENT - 2

Expenses

A1   REAL ESTATE MANAGEMENT - 2
A2   Expenses
B3   "  January
C3   "  February
D3   "     March
A4   Repairs
A5   101
A6   102
A7   103
A8   104
A9   105
B9   117
A10  106
A11  201
C11  515
D11  94
A12  202
A13  203
A14  204
A15  Taxes
B14  115
C14  115
D14  115
A16  License
B16  220
A17  Insurance
C17  700
A18  Utilities
B18  157
C18  171
D18  149
A19  Advert.
B19  37
C19  44
D19  37
A20  Managemt.
B20  600
C20  600
D20  600
A21  Payrl tax
B21  90
C21  90
D21  90
A22  Gardening
B22  143
C22  145
D22  138
A23  Cleaning
B23  150
C23  150
D23  150
A24  Pest Ctrl
B24  35
D24  35
A25  Garbage
B25  27
C25  27
D25  27
A26  Dues
B26  28
D26  122
```

```
A27 Other
B27 43
C27 17
D27 25
B28 " --------          Copy this to C28 and D28.
A29 Total
B29 @SUM(B5..B27)        Copy this formula to C29 and D29 with
                         all cell references relative.
```

```
        REAL ESTATE MANAGEMENT - 2
        Expenses
                     January February    March
        Repairs
              101
              102
              103
              104
              105      117
              106
              201               515        94
              202
              203
              204
        Taxes        115       115        115
        License      200
        Insurance              700
        Utilities    157       171        149
        Advert.       37        44         37
        Managemt.    600       600        600
        Payrl tax     90        90         90
        Gandening    143       145        138
        Cleaning     150       150        150
        Pest Ctrl     35                   35
        Garbage       27        27         27
        Dues          28                  122
        Other         43        17         25
                   --------  --------   --------
        Total       1742      2574       1582
```

BUSINESS STARTUP ANALYSIS

This worksheet is a classic in terms of the items used as row headings for analyzing the costs of starting a service business. It shows only one kind of income, which here is assumed to be revenue derived from the sale of some service, such as consulting. (If you wish to start a business with more than one source of income, such as a service and the sale of some product, be sure to insert the proper rows and label them accordingly. If you are selling a product, you will also want to adjust the expense categories to show the cost of goods, and the cost of manufacturing or assembly labor, as well as the cost of selling the product.)

The key to the whole model is that it is a cash flow statement, with the profits or losses from last month's operations carried over into the next month.

This model has been constructed using numbers, rather than formulas, for each month's entries. The reason is to show different kinds of growth rates for each kind of entry. You can construct the model using formulas to show steady growth from month to month, but be careful if you do: seldom does income grow at a steady rate, such as 10% per month. And expenses have a nasty habit of changing at an irregular pace, too.

The value of setting up an analysis like this as a cash flow statement is that you can see, if your assumptions turn out to be true, just how bad things are going to get before you start making money on the venture. In this case, the person setting up this business is going to have to put up at least $5412 the first month, but that the business should start making money after that. In fact, by the end of the sixth month, he will have a tidy profit on his investment.

BUSINESS STARTUP ANALYSIS

Use the Layout command to format the block of columns C through H, rows 4 through 30 as value format, fixed, 0 decimal places.

```
A1   BUSINESS STARTUP ANALYSIS
C3   "   October
D3   " November
E3   " December
F3   "   January
G3   " February
H3   "     March
A4   Income
C4   5000
```

```
D4   12000
E4   10000
F4   14000
G4   13000
H4   17000
A6   Expenses
A7   " Prof. Salaries
C7   3000
D7   3000
E7   3000
F7   5000
G7   5000
H7   5000
A8   " Clerical Salaries
C8   1350
D8   1350
E8   1350
F8   1950
G8   1950
H8   1950
A9   " Taxes, Benefits
C8   .25*(C7+C8)            Copy this formula to D8 through H8, with
                           both cell references relative.
A11  " Legal
C11  250
D11  200
E11  50
F11  0
G11  0
H11  0
A12  " Accounting
C12  200
D12  100
E12  200
F12  50
G12  50
H12  100
A14  " Rent
C14  1000                  Copy this to D14 through H14.
A15  " Utilities
C15  200
D15  225
E15  250
F15  250
G15  250
H15  225
A16  " Phone
C16  150
D16  165
E16  190
F16  190
G16  210
H16  210
A18  " Equipment
C18  2000
D18  250
E18  100
F18  500
G18  100
H18  100
A19  " Supplies
C19  300
D19  100
E19  100
```

```
F19 100
G19 100
H19 I00
A20 " Mailing
C20 75
D20 75
E20 74
F20 100
G20 100
H20 100
A21 " Advertising
C21 500
D21 75
E21 0
F21 200
G21 0
H21 0
A22 " Printing
C22 200
D22 75
E22 0
F22 50
G22 0
H22 0
A23 " Misc.
C23 100
D23 100
E23 100
F23 100
G23 100
H23 100
C24 " --------          Copy this entry to D24 through H24.
                        Also copy it to C29 through G29.

A25 Total Expenses
C25 @SUM(C7..C23)       Copy this formula to D25 through H25,
                        with all cell references relative.

A27 Profit this month
C27 +C4-C25             Copy this formula to D27 through H27,
                        with both cell references relative.

A28 Prev. mo. profit
C28 0
D28 +C30               Copy this formula to E28 through H28,
                        with the cell reference relative.

A30 Net gain
C30 +C27+C28            Copy this formula to D30 through H30,
                        with both cell references relative.
```

	October	November	December	January	February	March
Income	5000	12000	10000	14000	13000	17000
Expenses						
Prof. Salaries	3000	3000	3000	5000	5000	5000
Clerical Salaries	1350	1350	1350	1950	1950	1950
Taxes, Benefits	1088	1088	1088	1738	1738	1738
Legal	250	200	50	0	0	0
Accounting	200	100	200	50	50	100

Rent	1000	1000	1000	1000	1000	1000
Utilities	200	225	250	250	250	225
Phone	150	165	190	190	210	210
Equipment	2000	250	100	500	100	100
Supplies	300	200	100	100	100	100
Mailing	75	75	75	100	100	100
Advertising	500	250	0	200	0	0
Printing	200	75	0	50	0	0
Misc.	100	100	100	100	100	100
	--------	--------	--------	--------	--------	--------
Total Expenses	10412	8078	7502	11228	10598	10622
Profit this month	-5412	3922	2498	2772	2402	6378
Prev. mo. profit	0	-5412	-1490	1008	3780	6182
	--------	--------	--------	--------	--------	--------
Net gain	-5412	-1490	1008	3780	6182	12560

STOCK REQUIREMENTS

This model makes use of AppleWorks' cut-and-paste abilities. For some of its source information, it uses part of the model developed for Inventory Valuation, shown earlier in this chapter. The listing section for this model shows only the data you need to enter after you have retrieved the data from the other model.

To construct this model, first be sure that the Inventory Valuation model is on the Desktop. Add it to the Desktop if it isn't already there.

Next, create this model as a spreadsheet file. Just so that you have some information in it, enter the information in A1 and A2.

Press Open-Apple-Q. This shows you the Desktop Index. Select the Inventory Valuation model and press Return. When the Inventory model appears on your screen, move the cursor to A2 and press Open-Apple-C. Copy the entire model, except for rows 1, 26, and 27, to the clipboard.

Press Open-Apple-Q to get the Desktop Index again, and select the Stock Requirements model. When it appears on your screen (it will only have information in two rows, remember), position the cursor at A3 and press Open-Apple-C; copy the information from the clipboard starting at this position. The Inventory model data appears now in your Stock Requirements model.

You don't want all of it, however, so you'll need to do a little selective blanking and deleting:

1. Blank the entry at A3 (you already have a date in row 2).

2. Delete Columns G and H.

3. So that the column headings make sense for this model, change them as follows:

   Column C should be headed August Inventory.
   Column D should be headed Used in Sept.
   Column E should be headed Added in Sept.

4. Create the data and formulas for column G, as shown in the listing.

Note that the Out-of-Stock calculation relies on the use of stock for this month. If the use-pattern for this month was not normal, the calculation should be adjusted to account for this.

The figure given for each item in Column G shows what portion of a month the current stock will last, given last month's usage. A number to the left of the decimal point reflects whole month's.

STOCK REQUIREMENTS

Use the Layout command to format column G as value format, fixed, with 2 decimal places.

A1   STOCK REQUIREMENTS
A2   October 1, 1984
G2   Months to
C3   "   August
D3   "   Used
E3   "   Added
G3   "   Out of
C4   Inventory
D4   " in Sept.
E4   " in Sept.
G4   "   Stock
G6   +F6/D6   Copy this formula into G7 through G9, G12 and
                         G13, G16 and G17, G20 and G21, and G24
                         through G26. All references are relative.

STOCK REQUIREMENTS
October 1, 1984   Months to
                   August   Used   Added   Current   Out of
                 Inventory in Sept. in Sept.   Number   Stock
PARTS
Base plates   120   115   20   25   .22
Stuffed pc boards   155   134   95   116   .87
Cases   244   105   30   169   1.61
Cords   46   115   120   51   .44

PACKAGES
Boxes   477   143   0   334   2.34
Labels   1033   144   0   889   6.17

SUPPLIES, MISC.
Solder, rolls   25   32   10   3   .09
Tape, rolls   34   14   6   26   1.86

WORK IN PROGRESS
Boards on base   23   110   100   13   .12
In case, no cord   44   109   98   33   .30

FINISHED GOODS
Assembled units   78   67   95   106   1.58
In boxes   155   166   112   101   .61
In shipping carton   120   288   240   72   .25

VALUE OF STOCKS

Here's one way you can keep track of the value of a portfolio of stocks. Once you have set up the model, on any given day you simply get the current prices for your stocks out of the newspaper and enter them under "Current Price." Add in any dividends you have received over the year. The model computes the current value and yield.

Though acquisition and sale dates are shown in this model, they are only for record-keeping. This model can't take the days-held into account in the formula for annual yield.

VALUE OF STOCKS

Use the Layout command to format Columns D, F, H, and L as value format, fixed, with 2 decimal places. You may have to repeat the command periodically as the formatting sometimes doesn't seem to apply to a given cell.

```
C1   Value of Stocks
A2   Today's date:
C2   "9/28/84
D3   " Purchase
E3   "  Date
F3   " Current
G3   " Current
H3   Dividends
A4   Name
C4   "# Shares
D4   "  Price
E4   Acquired
F4   "  Price
G4   Value
H4   per Share
A5   "=========        Copy this to B5 through L5.
A6   Stock 1
C6   2000
D6   15.50
E6   " 02/08/83
F6   22.75
G6   +C6*F6           Copy this formula to G7 through G15,
                      with both cell references relative.
I6   +G6+(C6*H6)      Copy this formula to I7 through I15,
                      with all cell references relative.
J6   +I6-(C6*D6)      Copy this formula to J7 through J15,
                      with all cell references relative.
K6   " 08/28/84
L6   +J6/(C6*D6)*100  Copy this formula to L7 through L15,
                      with all cell references relative.
A7   Stock 2
C7   500
D7   25.62
E7   " 02/20/83
F7   23.25
A8   Stock 3
C8   200
D8   40.25
```

```
E8   "  04/12/83
F8   49.00
H8   .50
A9   Stock 4
C9   200
D9   43.12
E9   "  06/06/83
F9   37.00
A10  Stock 5
C10  700
D10  10.50
E10  "  03/14/84
F10  12.25
K10  "  09/24/84
A11  Stock 6
C11  1000
D11  .75
E11  "  03/14/84
F11  5.37
A12  Stock 7
C12  100
D12  57.00
E12  "  "  06/13/84
F12  55.25
H12  1.27
K12  "  09/26/84
A13  Stock 8
C13  1500
D13  .25
E13  "  08/?8/84
F13  1.50
A14  Stock 9
C14  500
D14  12.74
E14  "  08/28/84
F14  11.75
A15  Stock 10
C15  100
D15  1.75
E15  "  09/24/84
F15  2.25
C16  "  --------          Copy this to I16 and J16.
A17  Totals
C17  @SUM(C5..C15)        Copy this formula to I17 and J17 with
                          both cell references relative.
```

Value of Stocks

Today's date: 9/28/84

Name	# Shares	Purchase Price	Date Acquired	Current Price
Stock 1	2000	15.50	02/08/83	22.75
Stock 2	500	25.62	02/20/83	23.25
Stock 3	200	40.25	04/12/83	49.00
Stock 4	200	43.12	06/06/83	37.00
Stock 5	700	10.50	03/14/84	12.25
Stock 6	1000	.75	03/14/84	5.37
Stock 7	100	57.00	06/13/84	56.25
Stock 8	1500	.25	08/28/84	1.50
Stock 9	500	12.75	08/28/84	11.75
Stock 10	1000	1.75	09/24/84	2.25
Totals	7700			

Current Value	Dividends per Share	Total Value	Net Change	Date Sold	Yield (as %)
45500		45500	14500	08/28/84	46.77
11625		11625	-1185		-9.25
9800	.50	9900	1850		22.98
7400		7400	-1224		-14.19
8575		8575	1225	09/04/84	16.67
5370		5370	4620		616.00
5625	1.27	5752	52	09/26/84	.91
2250		2250	1875		500.00
5875		5875	-500		-7.84
2250		2250	500		28.57
		104497	21713		

SUPPLIER COMPARISON

This little model helps you to compare the failure rates among the parts you receive from various suppliers. In this case, the model is looking at the comparative failure rate of a speaker as obtained from three different manufacturers. It looks at three types of failure: in an initial test, in a test as installed, and as a customer return.

The failure rates computed in rows 10 and 14 are simply percentages. However simple the formula may be, it does indicate which supplier seems to be providing the greatest reliability: though Carr Electronics hasn't delivered as many speakers as the other two suppliers, theirs seem to be of higher quality since they fail less.

```
SUPPLIER COMPARISON

C1    SUPPLIER COMPARISON
A3    Item being compared: 4" speakers
A5    Supplier
C5    Adams Supply
E5    Barnes Hardware
G5    Carr Electronics
A7    No. delivered
C7    110000
E7    255750
G7    50000
A8    No. tested
C8    450
E8    450
G8    200
A9    Failures
C9    29
E9    16
G9    4
A10   "%Failed
C10   +C9/C8*100          Copy this formula to E10, G10, C14, E14,
                          and G14 with both cell references
                          relative.

A12   Items installed
C12   95422
E12   205314
G12   41225
A13   Failed inst. test
C13   126
E13   327
G13   6
A14   "% Failed
A16   Customer returns
C16   13
E16   4
G16   0
```

```
                    SUPPLIER COMPARISON

Item being compared: 4" speakers

Supplier:          Adams Supply     Barnes Hardware   Carr Electronics

No. delivered        110000            255750            50000
No. tested             450               450              200
Failures                29                16                4
% Failed              6.44              3.56             2.00

Items installed      95422            205314            41225
Failed inst. test      126               327                6
% Failed               .13               .16              .01

Customer returns        13                 4                0
```

Selections from The SYBEX Library

Introduction to Computers

OVERCOMING COMPUTER FEAR
by Jeff Berner
112 pp., illustr., Ref. 0-145
This easy-going introduction to computers helps you separate the facts from the myths.

INTRODUCTION TO WORD PROCESSING
by Hal Glatzer
205 pp., 140 illustr., Ref. 0-076
Explains in plain language what a word processor can do, how it improves productivity, how to use a word processor and how to buy one wisely.

PARENTS, KIDS, AND COMPUTERS
by Lynne Alper and Meg Holmberg
145 pp., illustr., Ref. 0-151
This book answers your questions about the educational possibilities of home computers.

PROTECTING YOUR COMPUTER
by Rodnay Zaks
214 pp., 100 illustr., Ref. 0-239
The correct way to handle and care for all elements of a computer system, including what to do when something doesn't work.

YOUR FIRST COMPUTER
by Rodnay Zaks
258 pp., 150 illustr., Ref. 0-142
The most popular introduction to small computers and their peripherals: what they do and how to buy one.

THE SYBEX PERSONAL COMPUTER DICTIONARY
120 pp., Ref. 0-199
All the definitions and acronyms of micro-computer jargon defined in a handy pocket-sized edition. Includes translations of the most popular terms into ten languages.

Computer Books for Kids

MONICA THE COMPUTER MOUSE
by Donna Bearden, illustrated by Brad W. Foster
64 pp., illustr., Hardcover, Ref. 0-214
Lavishly illustrated in color, this book tells the story of Monica the mouse, as she travels around to learn about several different kinds of computers and the jobs they can do. For ages 5–8.

POWER UP! KIDS' GUIDE TO THE APPLE IIe® /IIc™
by Marty DeJonghe and Caroline Earhart
200 pp., illustr., Ref. 0-212
Colorful illustrations and a friendly robot highlight this guide to the Apple IIe/IIc for kids 8–11.

BANK STREET WRITING WITH YOUR APPLE®
by Stanley Schatt, Ph.D. and Jane Abrams Schatt, M.A.
150 pp., illustr., Ref. 0-189
These engaging exercises show children aged 10–13 how to use Bank Street Writer for fun, profit, and school work.

POWER UP! KIDS' GUIDE TO THE COMMODORE 64™

by Marty DeJonghe and Caroline Earhart

192 pp., illustr., Ref. 0-188

Colorful illustrations and a friendly robot highlight this guide to the Commodore 64 for kids 8–11.

Humor

COMPUTER CRAZY

by Daniel Le Noury

100 pp., illustr., Ref. 0-173

No matter how you feel about computers, these cartoons will have you laughing about them.

MOTHER GOOSE YOUR COMPUTER: A GROWNUP'S GARDEN OF SILICON SATIRE

by Paul Panish and Anna Belle Panish, illustrated by Terry Small

96 pp., illustr., Ref. 0-198

This richly illustrated hardcover book uses parodies of familiar Mother Goose rhymes to satirize the world of high technology.

CONFESSIONS OF AN INFOMANIAC

by Elizabeth M. Ferrarini

215 pp., Ref. 0-186

This is one woman's tongue-in-cheek revelations of her pursuit of men, money, and machines. Learn about the many shopping services, information banks, and electronic dating bulletin boards available by computer.

Special Interest

COMPUTER POWER FOR YOUR LAW OFFICE

by Daniel Remer

142 pp., Ref. 0-109

How to use computers to reach peak productivity in your law office, simply and inexpensively.

THE COLLEGE STUDENT'S PERSONAL COMPUTER HANDBOOK

by Bryan Pfaffenberger

210 pp., illustr., Ref. 0-170

This friendly guide will aid students in selecting a computer system for college study, managing information in a college course, and writing research papers.

CELESTIAL BASIC

by Eric Burgess

300 pp., 65 illustr., Ref. 0-087

A collection of BASIC programs that rapidly complete the chores of typical astronomical computations. It's like having a planetarium in your own home! Displays apparent movement of stars, planets and meteor showers.

COMPUTER POWER FOR YOUR ACCOUNTING FIRM

by James Morgan, C.P.A.

250 pp., illustr., Ref. 0-164

This book is a convenient source of information about computerizing your accounting office, with an emphasis on hardware and software options.

PERSONAL COMPUTERS AND SPECIAL NEEDS

by Frank G. Bowe

175 pp., illustr., Ref. 0-193

Learn how people are overcoming problems with hearing, vision, mobility, and learning, through the use of computer technology.

ESPIONAGE IN THE SILICON VALLEY

by John D. Halamka

200 pp., illustr., Ref. 0-225

Discover the behind-the-scenes stories of famous high-tech spy cases you've seen in the headlines.

ASTROLOGY ON YOUR PERSONAL COMPUTER

by Hank Friedman

225 pp., illustr., Ref. 0-226

An invaluable aid for astrologers who want to streamline their calculation and data management chores with the right combination of hardware and software.

Computer Specific

Apple II—Macintosh

THE EASY GUIDE TO YOUR APPLE II®
by Joseph Kascmer
147 pp., illustr., Ref. 0-122
A friendly introduction to the Apple II, II plus and the IIe.

BASIC EXERCISES FOR THE APPLE®
by J.P. Lamoitier
250 pp., 90 illustr., Ref. 0-084
Teaches Applesoft BASIC through actual practice, using graduated exercises drawn from everyday applications.

THE APPLE II® BASIC HANDBOOK
by Douglas Hergert
250 pp., illustr., Ref. 0-115
A complete listing with descriptions and instructive examples of each of the Apple II BASIC keywords and functions. A handy reference guide, organized like a dictionary.

APPLE II® BASIC PROGRAMS IN MINUTES
by Stanley R. Trost
150 pp., illustr., Ref. 0-121
A collection of ready-to-run programs for financial calculations, investment analysis, record keeping, and many more home and office applications. These programs can be entered on your Apple II plus or IIe in minutes!

YOUR FIRST APPLE II® PROGRAM
by Rodnay Zaks
182 pp., illustr., Ref. 0-136
This fully illustrated, easy-to-use introduction to Applesoft BASIC programming will have the reader programming in a matter of hours.

THE APPLE® CONNECTION
by James W. Coffron
264 pp., 120 illustr., Ref. 0-085
Teaches elementary interfacing and BASIC programming of the Apple for connection to external devices and household appliances.

THE APPLE IIc™: A PRACTICAL GUIDE
by Thomas Blackadar
175 pp., illustr., Ref. 0-241
Learn all you need to know about the Apple IIc! This jargon-free companion gives you a guided tour of Apple's new machine.

THE BEST OF EDUCATIONAL SOFTWARE FOR APPLE II® COMPUTERS
by Gary G. Bitter, Ph.D. and Kay Gore
300 pp., Ref. 0-206
Here is a handy guide for parents and an invaluable reference for educators who must make decisions about software purchases.

YOUR SECOND APPLE II® PROGRAM
by Gary Lippman
250 pp., illustr., Ref. 0-208
The many colorful illustrations in this book make it a delight for children and fun for adults who are mastering programming on any of the Apple II line of computers, including the new IIc.

THE PRO-DOS HANDBOOK
by Timothy Rice/Karen Rice
225 pp., illustr, Ref. 0-230
All Pro-DOS users, from beginning to advanced, will find this book packed with vital information. The book covers the basics, and then addresses itself to the Apple II user who needs to interface with Pro-DOS when programming in BASIC. Learn how Pro-DOS uses memory, and how it handles text files, binary files, graphics, and sound. Includes a chapter on machine language programming.

MACINTOSH™ FOR COLLEGE STUDENTS
by Bryan Pfaffenberger
250 pp., illustr., Ref. 0-227
Find out how to give yourself an edge in the race to get papers in on time and prepare for exams. This book covers everything you need to know about how to use the Macintosh for college study.

CP/M Systems

THE CP/M® HANDBOOK
by Rodnay Zaks
320 pp., 100 illustr., Ref 0-048
An indispensable reference and guide to CP/M—the most widely-used operating system for small computers.

MASTERING CP/M®
by Alan R. Miller
398 pp., illustr., Ref. 0-068
For advanced CP/M users or systems programmers who want maximum use of the CP/M operating system . . . takes up where our *CP/M Handbook* leaves off.

THE BEST OF CP/M® SOFTWARE
by John D. Halamka
250 pp., Ref. 0-100
This book reviews tried-and-tested, commercially available software for your CP/M system.

THE CP/M PLUS™ HANDBOOK
by Alan R. Miller
250 pp., illustr., Ref. 0-158
This guide is easy for beginners to understand, yet contains valuable information for advanced users of CP/M Plus (Version 3).

INSTANT CP/M:® A KEYSTROKE GUIDE
by Robert Levine
250 pp., illustr., Ref. 0-132
This novice's guide includes a complete explanation of terms and commands, showing how they appear on the screen and what they do—a quick, foolproof way to gain proficiency with CP/M.

Software Specific

Spreadsheets

VISICALC® FOR SCIENCE AND ENGINEERING
by Stanley R. Trost and Charles Pomernacki
203 pp., illustr., Ref. 0-096
More than 50 programs for solving technical problems in science and engineering. Applications range from math and statistics to electrical and electronic engineering.

DOING BUSINESS WITH MULTIPLAN™
by Richard Allen King and Stanley R. Trost
250 pp., illustr., Ref. 0-148
This book will show you how using Multiplan can be nearly as easy as learning to use a pocket calculator. It presents a collection of templates for business applications.

MASTERING VISICALC®
by Douglas Hergert
217 pp., 140 illustr., Ref. 0-090
Explains how to use the VisiCalc "electronic spreadsheet" functions and provides examples of each. Makes using this powerful program simple.

DOING BUSINESS WITH VISICALC®
by Stanley R. Trost
260 pp., illustr., Ref. 0-086
Presents accounting and management planning applications—from financial statements to master budgets; from pricing models to investment strategies.

DOING BUSINESS WITH SUPERCALC™
by Stanley R. Trost
248 pp., illustr., Ref. 0-095
Presents accounting and management planning applications—from financial statements to master budgets; from pricing models to investment strategies.

Word Processing

INTRODUCTION TO WORDSTAR®
by Arthur Naiman
202 pp., 30 illustr., Ref. 0-134
Makes it easy to learn WordStar, a powerful word processing program for personal computers.

PRACTICAL WORDSTAR® USES
by Julie Anne Arca
303 pp., illustr., Ref. 0-107
Pick your most time-consuming office tasks and this book will show you how to streamline them with WordStar.

THE FOOLPROOF GUIDE TO SCRIPSIT™ WORD PROCESSING
by Jeff Berner
179 pp., illustr., Ref. 0-098
Everything you need to know about SCRIPSIT—from starting out, to mastering document editing. This user-friendly guide is written in plain English, with a touch of wit.

THE COMPLETE GUIDE TO MULTIMATE™
by Carol Holcomb Dreger
250 pp., illustr., Ref. 0-229
A concise introduction to the many practical applications of this powerful word processing program.

THE THINKTANK™ BOOK
by Jonathan Kamin
200 pp., illustr., Ref. 0-224
Learn how the ThinkTank program can help you organize your thoughts, plans, and activities.

Data Base Management Systems

UNDERSTANDING dBASE II™
by Alan Simpson
260 pp., illustr., Ref. 0-147
Learn programming techniques for mailing label systems, bookkeeping, and data management, as well as ways to interface dBASE II with other software systems.

Integrated Software

MASTERING SYMPHONY™
by Douglas Cobb
763 pp., illustr., Ref. 0-244
This bestselling book provides all the information you will need to put Symphony to work for you right away. Packed with practical models for the business user.

SYMPHONY™ ENCORE: PROGRAM NOTES
by Dick Andersen
325 pp., illustr., Ref. 0-247
Organized as a reference tool, this book gives shortcuts for using Symphony commands and functions, with troubleshooting advice.

JAZZ ON THE MACINTOSH™
by Joseph Caggiano
400 pp., illustr., Ref. 0-265
The complete tutorial on the ins and outs of the season's hottest software, with tips on integrating its functions into efficient business projects.

Languages

BASIC

YOUR FIRST BASIC PROGRAM
by Rodnay Zaks
182 pp., illustr. in color, Ref. 0-092
A "how-to-program" book for the first time computer user, aged 8 to 88.

FIFTY BASIC EXERCISES
by J. P. Lamoitier
232 pp., 90 illustr., Ref. 0-056
Teaches BASIC through actual practice, using graduated exercises drawn from everyday applications. Programs written in Microsoft BASIC.

EXECUTIVE PLANNING WITH BASIC
by X. T. Bui
196 pp., 19 illustr., Ref. 0-083
An important collection of business management decision models in BASIC, including inventory management (EOQ), critical path analysis and PERT, financial ratio analysis, portfolio management, and much more.

BASIC PROGRAMS FOR SCIENTISTS AND ENGINEERS
by Alan R. Miller
318 pp., 120 illustr., Ref. 0-073
This book from the "Programs for Scientists and Engineers" series provides a library of problem-solving programs while developing the reader's proficiency in BASIC.

BASIC FOR BUSINESS
by Douglas Hergert
224 pp., 15 illustr., Ref. 0-080
A logically organized, no-nonsense introduction to BASIC programming for business applications. Includes many fully-explained accounting programs, and shows you how to write your own.

Pascal

INTRODUCTION TO PASCAL (Including UCSD Pascal™)
by Rodnay Zaks
420 pp., 130 illustr., Ref. 0-066
A step-by-step introduction for anyone who wants to learn the Pascal language. Describes UCSD and Standard Pascals. No technical background is assumed.

THE PASCAL HANDBOOK
by Jacques Tiberghien
486 pp., 270 illustr., Ref. 0-053
A dictionary of the Pascal language, defining every reserved word, operator, procedure, and function found in all major versions of Pascal.

APPLE® PASCAL GAMES
by Douglas Hergert and Joseph T. Kalash
372 pp., 40 illustr., Ref. 0-074
A collection of the most popular computer games in Pascal, challenging the reader not only to play but to investigate how games are implemented on the computer.

PASCAL PROGRAMS FOR SCIENTISTS AND ENGINEERS
by Alan R. Miller
374 pp., 120 illustr., Ref. 0-058
A comprehensive collection of frequently used algorithms for scientific and technical applications, programmed in Pascal. Includes programs for curve-fitting, integrals, statistical techniques, and more.

DOING BUSINESS WITH PASCAL
by Richard Hergert and Douglas Hergert
371 pp., illustr., Ref. 0-091
Practical tips for using Pascal programming in business. Covers design considerations, language extensions, and applications examples.

Other Languages

FORTRAN PROGRAMS FOR SCIENTISTS AND ENGINEERS
by Alan R. Miller
280 pp., 120 illustr., Ref. 0-082
This book from the "Programs for Scientists and Engineers" series provides a library of problem-solving programs while developing the reader's proficiency in FORTRAN.

A MICROPROGRAMMED APL IMPLEMENTATION
by Rodnay Zaks
350 pp., Ref. 0-005
An expert-level text presenting the complete conceptual analysis and design of an APL interpreter, and actual listing of the microcode.

UNDERSTANDING C
by Bruce H. Hunter
320 pp., Ref 0-123
Explains how to program in powerful C language for a variety of applications. Some programming experience assumed.

FIFTY PASCAL PROGRAMS

by Bruce H. Hunter

338 pp., illustr., Ref. 0-110

More than just a collection of useful programs! Structured programming techniques are emphasized and concepts such as data type creation and array manipulation are clearly illustrated.

Technical

Assembly Language

PROGRAMMING THE 6502

by Rodnay Zaks

386 pp., 160 illustr., Ref. 0-135

Assembly language programming for the 6502, from basic concepts to advanced data structures.

6502 APPLICATIONS

by Rodnay Zaks

278 pp., 200 illustr., Ref. 0-015

Real-life application techniques: the input/output book for the 6502.

ADVANCED 6502 PROGRAMMING

by Rodnay Zaks

292 pp., 140 illustr., Ref. 0-089

Third in the 6502 series. Teaches more advanced programming techniques, using games as a framework for learning.

PROGRAMMING THE Z80®

by Rodnay Zaks

624 pp., 200 illustr., Ref. 0-069

A complete course in programming the Z80 microprocessor and a thorough introduction to assembly language.

Z80® APPLICATIONS

by James W. Coffron

288 pp., illustr., Ref. 0-094

Covers techniques and applications for using peripheral devices with a Z80 based system.

PROGRAMMING THE 6809

by Rodnay Zaks and William Labiak

362 pp., 150 illustr., Ref. 0-078

This book explains how to program the 6809 microprocessor in assembly language. No prior programming knowledge required.

PROGRAMMING THE 8086™/8088™

by James W. Coffron

300 pp., illustr., Ref. 0-120

This book explains how to program the 8086 and 8088 microprocessors in assembly language. No prior programming knowledge required.

PROGRAMMING THE 68000™

by Steve Williams

250 pp., illustr., Ref. 0-133

This book introduces you to microprocessor operation, writing application programs, and the basics of I/O programming. Especially helpful for owners of the Apple Macintosh or Lisa.

Hardware

FROM CHIPS TO SYSTEMS: AN INTRODUCTION TO MICROPROCESSORS

by Rodnay Zaks

552 pp., 400 illustr., Ref. 0-063

A simple and comprehensive introduction to microprocessors from both a hardware and software standpoint: what they are, how they operate, how to assemble them into a complete system.

MICROPROCESSOR INTERFACING TECHNIQUES

by Rodnay Zaks and Austin Lesea

456 pp., 400 illustr., Ref. 0-029

Complete hardware and software interfacing techniques, including D to A conversion, peripherals, bus standards and troubleshooting.

THE RS-232 SOLUTION

by Joe Campbell

194 pp., illustr., Ref. 0-140

Finally, a book that will show you how to

correctly interface your computer to any RS-232-C peripheral.

Operating Systems

REAL WORLD UNIX™
by John D. Halamka
209 pp., Ref. 0-093
This book is written for the beginning and intermediate UNIX user in a practical, straightforward manner, with specific instructions given for many business applications.

INTRODUCTION TO THE UCSD p-SYSTEM™
by Charles W. Grant and Jon Butah
300 pp., 10 illustr., Ref. 0-061
A simple, clear introduction to the UCSD Pascal Operating System for beginners through experienced programmers.

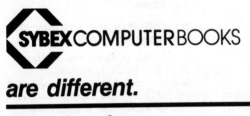